School
Social Work

Practice, Policy, and Research

Related books of interest

Child and Family Practice: A Relational Perspective
Shelley Cohen Konrad

Youth and Substance Use: Prevention, Intervention, and Recovery
Lori Holleran Steiker

Therapeutic Games and Guided Imagery, Volumes I and II
Monit Cheung

Character Formation and Identity in Adolescence
Randolph L. Lucente

Children and Loss: A Practical Handbook for Professionals
Elizabeth C. Pomeroy and Renée Bradford Garcia

**Evidence-Based Practices for Social Workers:
An Interdisciplinary Approach, Second Edition**
Thomas O'Hare

Advocacy Practice for Social Justice, Third Edition
Richard Hoefer

**Clinical Assessment for Social Workers:
Quantitative and Qualitative Methods, Fourth Edition**
Catheleen Jordan and Cynthia Franklin

**Disability: A Diversity Model Approach in Human Service Practice,
Third Edition**
Romel W. Mackelprang and Richard O. Salsgiver

EIGHTH EDITION

School
Social Work

Practice, Policy, and Research

CAROL RIPPEY MASSAT
Indiana University

MICHAEL S. KELLY
Loyola University Chicago

ROBERT CONSTABLE
Loyola University Chicago

OXFORD
UNIVERSITY PRESS

OXFORD
UNIVERSITY PRESS

Oxford University Press is a department of the University of Oxford.
It furthers the University's objective of excellence in research, scholarship,
and education by publishing worldwide. Oxford is a registered trade mark of
Oxford University Press in the UK and certain other countries.

Published in the United States of America by Oxford University Press
198 Madison Avenue, New York, NY 10016, United States of America.

© Oxford University Press 2016

Library of Congress Cataloging-in-Publication Data

School social work : practice, policy, and research / [compiled by]
Carol Rippey Massat, Indiana University, Michael S. Kelly, Loyola University Chicago,
Robert Constable, Loyola University Chicago. — Eighth edition.
    pages cm
  ISBN 978-0-190615-62-8 (pbk.)
  1. School social work—United States. I. Massat, Carol Rippey. II. Kelly, Michael S.
(Michael Stokely), 1968– III. Constable, Robert T. IV. Title.
  LB3013.4.S365   2016
  371.4'6—dc23

                                                        2015015522

ISBN 978-0-190615-62-8

5 7 9 8 6

Printed in Canada.

Cover photographs used with the permission of

© Aaron Belford | Dreamstime.com—School Yard Walk Photo

© Sonyae | Dreamstime.com—Kids Getting On School Bus Photo

© Dolgachov | Dreamstime.com—Group Of School Kids With Tablet Pc In
Classroom Photo

© Stylephotographs | Dreamstime.com—Children In Kindergarten Playing Photo

Contents

List of Figures

List of Tables

Preface

The eighth edition of *School Social Work: Practice, Policy, and Research* marks the further development of school social work as a social work specialization, as well as the development of this venerable textbook itself. American school social work is solidly in its second century now, and, despite ever-present concerns about limited resources, budgets, and school social worker to student ratios, school social work continues to grow, both in the United States and internationally. Throughout the United States and around the world, school social work is becoming increasingly essential to the educational process as families and communities strive to make schools safe and inclusive places for all children to learn, to grow, and to flourish. This eighth edition strives to reflect how school social work practice at the start of the twenty-first century effectively affects academic, behavioral, and social outcomes for youths and the school communities they serve.

Students growing up today face increasing risks toward their mental health, physical safety, and overall future as adults. Parents and schools are equally concerned about these challenges, and schools themselves are under increasing pressure to show that they are making progress on key academic and social-emotional learning (SEL) outcomes for all their students. School social workers, from their unique vantage point in the school, and also drawing on over a century of collective practice wisdom, have often been catalysts behind creative responses to meeting these challenges. Additionally, school social workers have increasingly become involved in bringing an evidence-informed practice (EIP) lens to their work, using the best available evidence and practice-based evidence to inform what they do to make their schools better. This eighth edition deepens our knowledge about these issues and updates many sections of the book to reflect these macro-practice and EIP realities. We have significantly revised all the returning chapters for this volume, and we are excited to welcome twenty-two new authors who have contributed twelve new chapters to this eighth edition.

The eighth edition of this book addresses many other key issues facing schools and school social workers today and reflects how the practice, policy, and research landscapes have changed since the last edition was published in 2009. For example, we feature new chapters on cultural competence (chapter 20), school social work and EIP (chapter 4), and the impact of the Common Core standards on school social work policy-practice (chapter 10). Building on efforts that started with the seventh edition, this edition locates many of the cutting-edge practice and policy issues of school social work today within the prevailing three-tiered model of intervention (often referred to under various acronyms such as RTI [response to intervention], PBIS [positive behavioral interventions and supports], and MTSS [multitiered systems of support]). We now have added updated content (as well as new chapters in the eighth edition) that explicitly locate school social work practice interventions within the three-tiered model and offer evidence-informed programs and strategies to maximize school social workers' effectiveness across all three tiers.

But not all things are new in this book: we have also sought to preserve and amplify some of the important components of the book through its first seven editions. As in previous editions, this edition provides a model of social work role development in the complex and diverse world of services within the school community. The model used in this book builds on the tasks that school social workers have always done well: assessment; consultation; planning; coordination; and individual, group, and family intervention. As education continues to move toward outcome-based, data-driven curriculum and policy mandates, school social work policy practice is also inherent to this role. This involves work with the whole school, the school community, and local, state, and federal policy development. A policy practice model seeks to reconstruct the meaning of schools as safe places where families and schools can work together and manage risks to their children's best development. Infused throughout each chapter of the book are case examples and content that exemplify the practice of school social work in all its diversity with bilingual students, immigrant children, members of minority and oppressed groups, and female students, among others. There is an ongoing focus on diversity, with a number of chapters that focus directly on how school social workers can better understand the roots of oppression for marginalized groups in the United States, and what culturally competent practice can look like in the twenty-first century.

The field of school social work, its practice, policy, and research, is being constructed by many different social workers interacting with their dynamic environments. Needs change and situations evolve, so that neither the future world of the school nor its students' needs can be typified or frozen in time. As stated earlier, one of these changes has been the movement toward EIP. This edition describes and critiques current applications of EIP in school social work. Principles of using EIP are described in chapter 4, and an evidence base for intervention is included throughout the book. The eighth edition reflects all of these changes while retaining the best parts of its theoretical perspective from previous editions. We hope that this book will be useful for both beginners in the field and veterans alike, and welcome your feedback on our new edition's changes.

This edition is a product of the work of forty-six authors who collectively provide ways to get a theoretical and methodological handle on the school social worker's role. With all of the diversity in roles, a remarkable unity in the material has always become apparent. Each author addresses different aspects of an emergent role. The authors also provide updated references to facilitate students' location of key source materials, Web sites, and online resources to obtain materials and information not yet in print.

ACKNOWLEDGMENTS

As the field of school social work continues to be constructed, we give special recognition to those whose vision has played a major part in this construction. Fondly missed, they remain with us in their writing and thought. Florence Poole envisioned a field of practice with practitioners guided by theory assisting the school to become a resource for children, and for children to use these school resources for their own growth. Carel Germain took a biological, ecological metaphor, a life model for social work practice, and used it to explain what social workers were doing. Marjorie McQueen Monkman, student of William E. Gordon, took Gordon's theories about building social work practice in new directions as she constructed ecological theory for school social work as a field of practice. Since the last edition, we have lost and warmly remember other contributors to earlier editions: John P. Flynn, Marguerite Tiefenthal, and Brooke Whitted. All of these individuals live on in the theories they have woven, and they assist all of us in understanding the potential in the school social worker's role.

Each of us acknowledges the patience and forbearance of our spouses, children, friends, and colleagues, who made the endeavor possible. We wish to express warm thanks to David Follmer, our friend and publisher of all eight editions. We give thanks also to all of the helpful staff at Lyceum Books, most notably our copy editor. Our students' struggles with learning such a complex role continue to inspire us. They will take the field forward. Finally, to this we add the readers of the first seven editions, now spanning three decades, who supported us in the belief that the content is worthwhile and usable, and who urged us to further refine and develop these ideas into this new edition.

Carol Rippey Massat
Michael S. Kelly
Robert Constable

Section I

History and General Perspectives in School Social Work

This introductory section draws on the rich heritage of *School Social Work: Practice, Policy, and Research,* and updates key components related to contemporary school social work practice. The first chapter, "The Role of the School Social Worker" by Robert Constable, gives a historical overview of school social work practice, bringing it from its early beginnings in the urban north of the United States to its current status as a mature subspecialty in social work engaged in multitiered levels of intervention and evidence-informed practice. A reprint of a classic from previous editions by the late school social work scholar Marjorie McQueen Monkman, "The Characteristic Focus of the School Social Worker in the Public Schools," lays out the ways that school social workers use the ecological perspective to design and deliver interventions in schools. Chapter 3, a new chapter by Kate Phillippo titled "'Moving Through a Land of Wonders Wild and New': Grounding School Social Work Practice in an Organizational, Ecosystemic Understanding of the School," situates contemporary school social work practice in current organizational theory.

Moving to the current context for school social work practice, Michael S. Kelly offers two new chapters for this edition: chapter 4, "Evidence-Informed Practice in the Real World of School Social Work Practice" and chapter 5, "School Social Work Supervision," a joint chapter collaboration with colleagues at Loyola Chicago's Family and School Partnership Program. Finally, three returning chapters on ethics, confidentiality, and consultation (chapter 6, "The Process of Ethical Decision Making in School Social Work," by James C. Raines; chapter 7, "Ethical and Legal Complexities of Confidentiality for School Social Workers," by Sandra Kopels; and chapter 8, "School Social Workers: School-Based Consultants Supporting a Multitiered System of Indirect Service," by Christine Anlauf Sabatino) return in updated form to help new practitioners begin to map out what effective and ethical school social work practice looks like in the early twenty-first century.

1

The Role of the School Social Worker

Robert Constable
Loyola University, Chicago

♦ Defining Concepts for the Social Worker's Role
♦ A Historical Analysis of the School Social Worker's Role
♦ Developing and Defining the Role

DEFINING CONCEPTS FOR THE SCHOOL SOCIAL WORKER'S ROLE

A beginning school social worker may feel like Alice (or Alex) in Wonderland as she tumbled into the Rabbit Hole, and landed in a long corridor, lined with locked doors (Goren, 1981). When school is in session, the doors are open, but there is confusion in the corridor, together with some undefined, imperceptible, underlying order (for more on the *Alice in Wonderland* metaphor, see appendix B and chapter 3). "What is this order? There must be some place for me, but I don't know it yet. The client-centered/systems change model I learned in school seems too general to fit. How can I be a mini agency, wedded to an educational process? I am expected to be competent in something, but where do I start?" We need to sort through a few basic concepts. These concepts need to be tested through actual, ongoing practice experience. They will not be completely clear until an "aha" moment, when things begin to come together.

Where Do School Social Workers Practice?

School social workers practice in the space where children, families, schools, and communities encounter one another, in the school community, where hopes can fail, where gaps exist, and where education can break down. The school community is not simply bound by geography, it comprises all those who engage in the educational process. Schooling is neither a building nor a collection of classrooms where teachers and pupils work together. Schooling encompasses a community of teachers, parents, students, and others, working in partnership with one another in the educational process. Parents and families have membership in the school community through their children. Teachers and other school personnel have accountability to parents, children, and the broader community. The social worker often helps the school community function more successfully, so that personal, familial, and community resources can be discovered and used to meet children's developmental needs.

What Is the Connection among Educational Policy, Programs, and School Social Work?

Across the United States, it is a top public priority that children develop well and that schools support that development. Educational policies and programs are developed to meet these priorities. As programs are developed, school social workers often help develop them, working with administrators and teachers on implementation, particularly where children are vulnerable and families unavailable. Administration, program development, implementation, and even policy development are as important as direct practice. Aspirations are often unfulfilled: policies can fail, and otherwise effective programs can fail with certain students. Nothing ever fits perfectly. Social workers have to work skillfully with individual and group situations to develop a better fit between programs and personal aspirations.

What Is the Purpose of School Social Work?

School social workers help make the educational process effective for students whose full participation in education is threatened or marginalized. School social workers work one on one with teachers, families, and children to address individual situations and needs. School social workers work with the whole school on positive policies and educational programs such as efforts to make schools safe for everyone. Their role is as complex as the worlds in which these students live. Intervening in the interactive relations of students and schools, school social work practice requires a wide range of skills.

The focus of the school social worker rests on the constellation of school, community, teacher, parent, and child. The school social worker must be able to relate to and work with all aspects of the child's situation. A basic skill underlying this is assessment, a systematic way of understanding and communicating what is happening and what is possible. Building on assessment, the social worker develops a plan to assist the total constellation—teacher and students in the classroom, parents in the family, and others—to work together to support the child in the successful completion of developmental steps. The basic questions are, (1) What should the role of the school social worker be in a particular school community? and (2) Where are the best places to intervene—the units of attention—in a particular situation?

How Is the Role of the Social Worker Developed?

There are some common understandings of the school social worker's role, which develop from district, state, and national policies. At the same time, some aspects of the role of the social worker can be different across state and school district lines and even in different school buildings in the same district. These differences are worked out with district staff, with others on the team, and with the principal. And so school social workers need to have an understanding of policies, as they have developed, and a vision of what is possible. They need to possess tools of analysis, be comfortable with the processes of negotiation, and be able to coordinate their interventions with the life of the school.

A HISTORICAL ANALYSIS OF THE SCHOOL SOCIAL WORKER'S ROLE

The focus of school social work has always followed the historic concerns of education and education policy. The first social workers in schools were hired in recognition of the fact that their legitimate focus was on the conditions, whether in the family, neighborhood, or the school itself, that prevented children from learning and the school from carrying out its mandate (Allen-Meares, Washington, & Welsh, 2000; Costin, 1978). School social work drew its legitimacy and function from its capability to make education work for groups of children who could not otherwise participate. It has reflected in its history the evolving awareness in education, and in society, of groups of children for whom education has not been effective—the children of immigrants, the impoverished, the economically and socially oppressed, the delinquent, and those with disabilities. It drew its function from the needs and eventually the rights of these groups as they became involved with the institution of education and confronted the expectation that they should achieve to their fullest potential. As school social workers defined their roles, they emerged from a match of the social work perspective, knowledge, values, and skills, with the missions and mandates of schools.

As education became modernized, a prescribed curriculum, standardized testing, and the grade system organized the school. In the United States the passage of compulsory school attendance laws, roughly from 1895 through 1918, marked a major shift in philosophies and policies governing education. Education, no longer for the elite, was a necessary part of preparation for modern life. It had to be for everyone. This belief became the basis for an ever-growing extension of education to all children at risk, whether populations of children with special needs, special histories, or disabilities.

A half-century later the U.S. Supreme Court articulated the belief that education for each child is a constitutional right, which, if available to any, must be available to all on an equal basis. The profundity of the change to education in society is succinctly and powerfully expressed in the landmark case of *Brown v. Board of Education of Topeka* (1954): "Today [education] is a principal instrument in . . . helping him [the child] to adjust normally to his environment. In these days, it is doubtful that any child may reasonably be expected to succeed in life if he is denied the opportunity of an education. Such an opportunity, where the state has undertaken to provide it, is a right which must be made available to all on equal terms."

Toward Respect for Individual Differences

The movement to individualize education for all children in the context of standards of achievement continues to be one of the central issues in education. Learners are different. For students to learn, the implications of these differences demand recognition. Learning within the norms of the grade system is now becoming somewhat more individualized. If education would be truly available to all, schools had a responsibility to adapt curricula to these individual differences. The passage of the Education for all Handicapped Children Act (1975) meant that all schools were required to educate every child regardless of disability and any accompanying special needs. Children with disabilities could receive individualized instruction with goals and educational resources tailored to their needs.

Philosophies of inclusiveness and respect for individual differences continue to shape the practice of education and provide the basis for the role of the school social worker. The correspondence between social work values, the emergent mission of education, and the role of the school social worker is illustrated by Allen-Meares (1999) in table 1.1. The mission of education, implicit in these values, becomes the basis for school social work as it emerged through the twentieth century. We can review this emergence.

The Beginnings of School Social Work

School social work began during the school year 1906–7 simultaneously in New York, Boston, Hartford (Costin, 1969a), and Chicago (McCullagh, 2000). These workers were not hired by the school systems, but rather worked in the school under the sponsorship of other agencies or civic groups. In New York it was a settlement house that sponsored the workers. Their purpose was to work between the school and communities of new

TABLE 1.1   Social Work Values

Social Work Values	Applications to Social Work in Schools
1. Recognition of the worth and dignity of each human being.	1. Each pupil is valued as an individual regardless of any unique characteristic.
2. The right to self-determination or self-realization.	2. Each pupil should be allowed to share in the learning process.
3. Respect for individual potential and support for an individual's aspirations to attain it.	3. Individual differences (including differences in rate of learning) should be recognized; intervention should be aimed at supporting pupils' education goals.
4. The right of each individual to be different from every other and to be accorded respect for those differences.	4. Each child, regardless of race and socioeconomic characteristics, has a right to equal treatment in the school.

immigrants, promoting understanding and communication (Lide, 1959). In Boston the Women's Education Association sponsored so-called visiting teachers who would work between the home and the school. In Hartford a psychology clinic developed a program of visiting teachers to assist the psychologist in securing histories of children and implementing the clinic's treatment plans and recommendations (Lide, 1959). In Chicago Louise Montgomery developed a social settlement type of program at the Hamline School, offering a wide range of services to its Stockyards District community (McCullagh, 2000). This unheralded experiment anticipated the much-later development of school-based services for the entire community. In many ways these diverse, early programs contained in both rough and seminal form all the elements of later school social work practice. Over the following century the diverse concerns of inclusiveness and recognition of individual differences, the concept of education as a relational process, and the developing mission for the schools would shape the role of the school social worker.

DEVELOPING AND DEFINING THE ROLE

The First Role Definition by a School System: The Rochester Schools

In 1913 the Rochester (New York) Board of Education hired visiting teachers for the first time. The commitment of the schools to hire visiting teachers was an acknowledgment of both the broadening mission of education and the possibility that social workers could be part of that mission. In justifying the appointments, the Rochester Board of Education noted that in the environment of the child outside the school there are forces that often thwart the school in its endeavors to educate. The school was now broadening and individualizing its mission, attempting to meet its responsibilities for the whole child (Lide, 1959).

Between School and Community: Jane Culbert

Only three years later in 1916 at the National Conference of Charities and Corrections a definition of school social work emerged in the presentation of Jane Culbert. The definition, full of the concepts of inclusion, respect for individual differences, and education as a relational process, focused on the environment of the child and the school, rather than on the child as an individual. The school social worker's role was "interpreting to the school the child's out-of-school life; supplementing the teacher's knowledge of the child . . . so that she may be able to teach the whole child . . . assisting the school to know the life of the neighborhood, in order that it may train the children to the life to which they look forward. Secondly the visiting teacher interprets to parents the demands of the school and explains the particular demands and needs of the child" (Culbert, 1916, p. 595).

This statement of role would be developed and typified by Julius Oppenheimer as the role of school–family–community liaison (Oppenheimer, as cited in Lide, 1959). From his study of 300 case reports made by school social workers or visiting teachers, he drew thirty-two core functions and considered this role to be primary. School social workers would aid in the reorganization of school administration and practices by supplying evidence of unfavorable conditions that underlie pupils' school difficulties and by pointing out needed changes (Allen-Meares, 2000, 2006).

From a Focus on the Environment to the "Maladjusted" Child: The Early Years

By 1920 the National Association of Visiting Teachers had been organized; it held its first meeting in New York City that year (McCullagh, 2000). Concern was expressed about the organization, administration, and role of visiting teachers (Allen-Meares, 2000). This organization, later the American Association of Visiting Teachers, would publish a journal, *The Bulletin,* until 1955. At that time it was merged into the newly established National Association of Social Workers (NASW). *The Bulletin* was the focus of the writing and the thinking of this emergent field of practice during these years. Influenced by the mental hygiene movement of its day, there was a gradual shift from a focus on the home and school environment toward a focus on the individual schoolchild and that child's needs. Eventually this focus would shift to casework as a vehicle for working with the individual child. The shift toward casework came from the Milford Conference in 1929 (American Association of Social Workers, 1929/1974); later development was crystallized by Edith Abbott's (1942) work on social work and professional education.

Fields of Practice with Casework in Common:
The Milford Conference

The basic issues and the possible future direction in the maturation of social work practice and theory were laid out in the Milford Conference report. By the end of the 1920s, a wide range of fields of practice had organized themselves around the different settings of school, hospital, court, settlement house, child welfare agency, family service agency, and so forth. Social work education followed an apprenticeship model, teaching what were perceived to be highly specialized and segmented fields of practice. The question of what all of these fields had in common became extremely important. In 1929, at the Milford Conference, the basic distinction between fields of practice, the specific practice that emerged from these fields, and the generic base for practice in these fields—that is, the knowledge, values, and skills of casework—was established. This distinction was extremely important for social work education and for the field of school social work in that it allowed each field of practice to flourish and develop on a common foundation of what was then the individualizing method: casework. The emergent profession of social work was indeed broad and diverse. Furthermore, no theory had emerged that could do more than offer a general orientation to helping. It still was up to the learner-practitioner and supervisor to find a way to relate theory to practice. This situation would continue in various permutations of the history of social work practice theory for more than a half-century. The casework theory identified as generic would not refer to a concrete practice separable from its manifestation in different fields. There was no generic practice, but generic knowledge, values, and skills would be a foundation for a further differentiation of practice.

The Distinction of Generic and Specific Knowledge for Practice:
Grace Marcus

The casework foundation of the 1920s and 1930s did not focus simply on a type of therapy with individuals, as some later versions did, but rather on working with persons and family units together. This was much more than a simple methodological base: it included knowledge and values. It had to be a conceptual foundation for practice that was always specific to a field. Practice differentiation took place in relation to specific, identified fields, such as school social work, medical social work, psychiatric social work, child welfare, family services, and so on. Grace Marcus clarified the distinction between the terms "generic" and "specific": "The term 'generic' does not apply to any actual, concrete practice of an agency or field but refers to an essential, common property of casework knowledge, ideas and skills which caseworkers of every field must command if they are to perform adequately their specific jobs. As for our other troublemaking word, 'specific,' it refers to the form casework takes within the particular administrative setting; it is the manifest use to which the generic store of knowledge has been put in meeting the particular purposes, problems, and conditions of the agency in dispensing its particular resources" (Marcus, 1938–39, n.p.).

Casework at the time was the most developed body of method theory, and it would be natural for Ruth Marcus to identify casework with a generic base. In a very short time group work, community organization, and other methods would develop in a parallel fashion. The distinction between generic and specific was important because it permitted professional differentiation on a common foundation and specified the relations of method theory, such as casework or group work, to their manifestations in fields of practice. Without a concept of practice in fields, methods such as casework or group work would be taught without much consideration of the contexts that define them and the purposes that make them different. At the same time, much of what was specific to a field of practice was taught through apprenticeship, and was not given a developed theoretical foundation in practice, policy, and research. This had to emerge later. As theory developed for fields of practice, such as school social work, the relations between method theories (casework, group work, administration, program development, policy development, etc.) and these fields would be reexamined and enriched.

The Rationale for School Social Work Practice: Florence Poole

In 1959 Florence Poole described a theoretical rationale for school social work practice derived from the right of every child to an education. Pupils who could not use what the school had to offer were "children who are being denied, obscure though the cause may be, nevertheless denied because they are unable to use fully their right to an education" (Poole, 1959, p. 357). It was the school's responsibility to offer them something that would help them to benefit from an education. Education would need to change to help children who were "having some particular difficulty in participating beneficially in a school experience" (Poole, 1959, p. 357). Her rationale eventually would mark a shift in the discussion of the school social work role. School social work would be essential to schools accomplishing their purpose: "At the present time we no longer see social work as a service appended to the schools. We see one of our most significant social institutions establishing social work as an integral part of its service, essential to the carrying out of its purpose. We recognize a clarity in the definition of the services as a social work service" (Poole, 1949, p. 454). She saw the clarity and uniqueness of social work service as coming from the societal function of the school. "[The worker] must be able to determine which needs within the school can be appropriately met through school social work service. She must be able to develop a method of offering the service which will fit in with the general organization and structure of the school, but which is identifiable as one requiring social work knowledge and skill. She must be able to define the service and her contribution in such a way that the school personnel can accept it as a service, which contributes to the major purpose of the school" (Poole, 1949, p. 455).

Florence Poole developed a functional approach to practice, built on the parameters of the mission of the school, the knowledge and skill of social work, and the worker's professional responsibility to determine what needs to be done and to develop an appropriate program for doing it. Her conception was simultaneously freer but also more focused on the potentially rich interaction of many possible social work methods and the mission of the school. The effect of this shift in emphasis from casework to school social work would be enormous. A variety of methods was now possible, governed by the complex mission and societal function of the school. The ensuing discussion of theory for school social work would become a question of the relation of methods to the needs of children and schools in the education process.

Poole shifted the focus from the problem pupil alone, who could not adjust and adapt to the school, to a focus on pupils and schools adapting to each other in the context of every child's right to an education. The conditions that interfere with the pupil's ability to connect with the educational system are diverse. Therefore, the functions of the school social worker would be flexible and wide ranging. They could be gradually developed within each school through concrete encounters with problems and needs.

A Period of Professional Centralization

Considerable development of school social work as a field of practice had already taken place from the mid-1920s through 1955; this development was the basis for the classic definitional work of Florence Poole. This growth in conceptualizing inherent differences in practice by fields trailed off by 1955 with the consolidation of the NASW. National organizations of social workers, representing different fields of practice, were merged into one single professional association. These national organizations were the American Association of Group Workers, the American Association of Medical Social Workers, the American Association of Psychiatric Social Workers, the American Association of Social Workers, and the National Association of School Social Workers. *The Bulletin* of the American Association of Visiting Teachers was merged into the new journal of the united social work profession, *Social Work.* With the loss of *The Bulletin,* school social work literature dropped off for a time. During the 1950s and the 1960s the major concern in the professional literature, in the profession, and in social work education had to do with what social workers had in common across different sectors of the profession.

The Transaction between Persons and Environments: Harriett Bartlett and William E. Gordon

During the late 1950s and through the 1960s, important work was done to clarify the common base of social work practice (Bartlett, 1971). Harriett Bartlett's and other's work built the foundation for a reorientation of methods and skills to a clarified professional perspective of the social worker. Bartlett (1959, 1971) worked with William E. Gordon (1969) to elaborate the concept of the transaction between individuals and their social environments into a common base and a fundamental beginning point for social work, something that Poole's work in school social work specifically foreshadowed. As the person-in-environment transaction became a unifying focus, it was no longer assumed that the individual was the primary object of help. The development and diffusion of group and environmental interventions and the use of a range of helping modalities in richly differentiated areas of practice would make Gordon's and Bartlett's work useful. The best summary of this work can be found in the 1979 report of the Joint NASW–CSWE (Council on Social Work Education) Task Force on Specialization (hereafter Joint Task Force), of which Gordon was a member (Joint Task Force, 1979).

> The fundamental zone of social work is where people and their environment are in exchange with each other. Social work historically has focused on the transaction zone where the exchange between people and the environment which impinges on them results in changes in both. Social work intervention aims at the coping capabilities of people and the demands and resources of their environment so that the transactions between them are helpful to both. Social work's concern extends to both the dysfunctional and deficient conditions at the juncture between people and their environment, and to the opportunities there for producing growth and improving the environment. It is the duality of focus on people and their environments that distinguishes social work from other professions. (Joint Task Force, 1979)

The Beginnings of Specialization

During the late 1960s and following years there arose a renewed interest in developing theory and practice in areas such as school social work. Generic approaches to practice were never an adequate theory or practice base for the complex practice that was emerging in each field. Differing fields, such as education and health, were demanding accountability to their own functions and goals. The survival of social work in different fields would demand an accountability to the purposes of the field of practice. There was a gradual redevelopment of literature, journals, and regional associations of social workers in different fields of practice.

The interest in specialization led to a profession-wide discussion of this issue and the report of the Joint Task Force in 1979. The Joint Task Force developed a classic formulation. Fields of practice in social work grew from the need for mediation between persons and social institutions to the need to meet common human needs (Bartlett, 1961). Practice within each field is defined by a clientele, a point of entry, a social institution with its institutional purposes, and the contribution of social work practice, its knowledge, values, and appropriateness to the institutional purpose and to common human needs. According to the Joint Task Force (1979), these needs and their institutions would include the following:

♦ The need for physical and mental well-being: Health system
♦ The need to know and to learn: Education system
♦ The need for justice: Justice system
♦ The need for economic security: Work/public assistance systems
♦ The need for self-realization, intimacy, and relationships: Family and child welfare systems (Joint Task Force, 1979)

In each area, the social worker works as a professional and mediates a relationship between persons and institutions. Specialization opened whole fields of knowledge and professional development, previously limited by the concentration on what methods were common among all areas of practice.

At this time, school social work was developing its own distinct identity, methodology, theory, and organization. It had large numbers of experienced practitioners, who were encouraged to remain in direct practice by the structure and incentives of the school field. These were some of the first and strongest advocates of a movement in the mid- to late-1970s to develop practice and theory. With the development of state school social work associations, and then school social work journals, the search for some balance between what was common to all fields and what was specific to school social work began again. The issues were not always clear. Students would struggle with this balance in their attempts to match classroom theory with an emerging practice field. Until the development of university preparation for specialized practice there was not always a good match.

Rethinking Casework in the Schools

During the 1960s the school social work literature reflected a broadened use of helping methods in schools and a developing interest in broader concerns affecting particular populations of students in schools. At the same time the social work profession experienced a renewed focus on social reform. The education literature, critical of the current organization of schools and the effectiveness of education, was preparing the way for school reform. Lela Costin (1969b) published a study of the importance school social workers attached to specific tasks, using a sample mainly derived from NASW members. Her findings showed a group of social workers whose description of social work reflected the clinical orientation of the social work literature of the 1940s and the 1950s. Reflecting on these findings, Costin (1972) showed disappointment at what she believed was an excessively narrow conception of role, given the changing mission of the school and the potentials of practice to assist that mission. Her next step would be to develop a picture of what the school social worker's role should be.

Four Models for Practice: John Alderson

Following Costin's research John Alderson used a similar instrument to study school social workers in Florida with a variety of levels of professional training. In his Florida sample, he found a much broader orientation. The workers ranked leadership and policy making either first or second in importance. Subsequently, he attempted a theoretical reconciliation of these findings with Costin's findings, and with the apparent clinical emphasis of many established school social work programs. He described four different models of school social work practice (Alderson, 1974). His first three models were governed by particular intervention methods, whether by clinical theory, social change theory, or school community organization. One method would then tend to exclude the others. The clinical model focused mainly on changing pupils identified as having social or emotional difficulties. The school change model focused on changing the environment and conditions of the school. The school community model focused on the relation of school to its community, particularly to deprived and disadvantaged communities.

His fourth model, the social interaction model, was of a very different order. The move was from static conceptions to a dynamic, flexible, and changing concept of role. Drawing on systems theory, the focus for practice would be on persons and environments, pupils (in families), and schools in reciprocal interaction. Social workers would adapt their roles to this interaction. Alderson's social interaction model had followed two decades of work of William E. Gordon, Harriett Bartlett, and the Committee on Social Work Practice, and the functional definition of a transactional, systems perspective in social work.

Seven Clusters of School Social Work Functions: Lela Costin

At about the same time, Lela Costin (1973) was also seeking to broaden conceptions of the school social work role. She developed the school community pupil relations model, which focused on "school and community defi-

ciencies and specific system characteristics as these interact with characteristics of pupils at various stress points in their life cycles" (Costin, 1973,
p. 137). She outlined seven broad groups of functions in the school social
worker's role. School social workers do (1) direct counseling with individuals, groups, and families, (2) advocacy, (3) consultation, (4) community linkage, (5) interdisciplinary team coordination, (6) needs assessment, and (7)
program and policy development (Costin, 1973). With its constant relation
of a diverse professional methodology to a developing school purpose, the
model hearkened back to the beginnings of school social work.

Broadening Approaches to Practice

Later research in school social work (Allen-Meares, 1977, 1994) showed that
school social workers in general were moving toward a practice model
emphasizing home–school–community relations with a major focus still on
problems faced by individual students. Other studies showed some general
broadening of roles taking place (Anlauf-Sabatino, 1982; Chavkin, 1993;
Constable, Kuzmickaite, Harrison, & Volkmann, 1999; Constable & Montgomery, 1985; Dennison, 1998; Lambert & Mullally, 1982; Timberlake,
Sabatino, & Hooper, 1982). Nevertheless there appeared to be considerable
diversity, with strong regional, state, local, urban, suburban, and rural differences. These findings from practice can be characterized by Lambert and
Mullally's (1982) pithy comment, "School social workers, at least in Ontario,
do not place importance on one focus—individual change or systems
change—to the exclusion of the other, but recognize the importance of
both" (p. 81). The conceptual problem was not a question of either individual change or systems change, but of how to organize the inevitable
methodological diversity inherent in the role and the function. When
method theories were taught outside of the dynamic context of a field of
practice, they tended to focus either on individual change or on systems
change as if the two were exclusive.

How to Describe Interrelation of Methods in Practice

The Clinical Quadrant. Frey and Dupper (2005, p. 36) developed
the clinical quadrant (figure 1.1) to bring together clinical and environmental interventions in school social work. The quadrant is a basis to describe
with some accuracy the method content of practice. As such, it also enables
the evaluation of existing research and moves toward evidence-informed
practice (EIP). The most recent of a number of integrational methods
approaches, the quadrant does encompass the method content of school
social work practice.

Ecological Systems Models. Ecological systems models emerged during this time as useful theoretical models to understand the school social

FIGURE 1.1   Clinical Quadrant

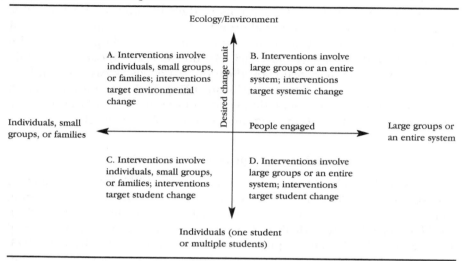

Ecology/Environment

A. Interventions involve individuals, small groups, or families; interventions target environmental change

B. Interventions involve large groups or an entire system; interventions target systemic change

Desired change unit

Individuals, small groups, or families

People engaged

Large groups or an entire system

C. Interventions involve individuals, small groups, or families; interventions target student change

D. Interventions involve large groups or an entire system; interventions target student change

Individuals (one student or multiple students)

worker's role and move beyond a focus on method alone. A system is an organized holistic unit of interdependent, transacting, and mutually influencing parts (individuals or collectivities and their subunits) within an identifiable (social-ecological) environment (Siporin, 1975). Ecology is the science of organism–environment interaction. The model leads to a view of person and environment as a unitary interacting system in which each constantly affects and shapes the other. It allows for an understanding of the relation of different methods of intervention and their theoretical bases. Behavior in the classroom may be understood better by understanding its context, its relations to other settings, and the relation of these settings to each other. As one learns to analyze the relations between systems, practice may build on this understanding. The model leads to clearer choices of where to intervene in the complexity of a system and when an intervention may be most effective. Germain (2006) uses ecological systems theory to clarify the dual function of social work, to "attend to the complexities of the environment, just as we attend to the complexities of the person" (p. 30). She moves to a health orientation from a medical-disease metaphor and to "engaging the progressive forces in people and situational assets, and effecting the removal or environmental obstacles to growth and adaptive functioning" (p. 30).

Monkman in chapter 2 draws a parsimonious analysis of school social work practice from the nature of schooling itself. Reflecting William E. Gordon, she defines a transaction as a relation between a person's coping behavior and the impinging environment. The social worker assists persons and environments to cope with and become resources for each other. When this transaction is in danger of breakdown, the social worker intervenes with a wide range of methods appropriate to the situation for a better match. She defines this transaction, making it more operational, more specific for the purpose of practice, and more specific for the purpose of future research.

These conceptual models provided a conceptual base to understand and analyze practice without allowing a narrowly preconceived method to dictate intervention. They allow for a set of dynamic relations in the school, with a clientele coping with maturational and educational goals and the integration of all of these. With a deeper focus on the interaction of social work and the education process, practice, policy, and research methodologies are related to each other. They become more focused when they are applied to dynamic and complex transactions within the school community.

Research on the Tasks of School Social Workers

During this period there was a growing interest in studying the actual tasks of practicing school social workers with a high degree of specificity. In 1989 a group of nineteen nationally recognized experts in school social work was asked to develop and list the tasks that entry-level school social workers would perform in their day-to-day professional roles. The result was a list of 104 tasks, evidence of the complexity of school social work. These tasks, when they were defined, fell along five job dimensions:

1. Relationships with and services to children and families
2. Relationships with and services to teachers and school staff
3. Services to other school personnel
4. Community services
5. Administrative and professional (Nelson, 1990)

Further research on these roles, tasks, and skills in one state found four areas of school social work to be both very important and frequently performed. In the order of their assumed importance these areas were

1. Consultation with others in the school system and the teamwork relationships that make consultation possible;
2. Assessment applied to a variety of different roles in direct service, in consultation, and in program development;
3. Direct work with children and parents in individual, group, and family modalities; and
4. Assistance with program development in schools (Constable et al., 1999).

Findings from a later national study of the school social worker's role concluded that "the characteristics of school social workers, the context in which they practice, and their practice choices remain largely unchanged over the past ten years" (Kelly et al., 2010, p. 132). These authors were very concerned about this finding. Perhaps school social workers had grown comfortable and were missing the boat in light of concurrent, dynamic changes in education. In education there was a new emphasis on prevention in the development of tiered prevention programs, whole-school intervention, and whole-classroom intervention programs. The old divisions between regular education and special education were being reworked with whole-school prevention programs. At the same time, similar to the earlier findings, most school social work time was spent responding to referrals through direct work with children and parents in individual, group, and family modalities. On the other hand, school social workers considered the time spent in consultation and joint assessment—shared teamwork activities where the school social worker works through and with others—more important than the individual work that still dominated the social worker's time, most likely because those activities affected more children.

Changes in the Field of Education

What were the changes taking place in the field of education in the first decades of the twenty-first century, that school social workers seemed to be missing? Since the early 1970s there were various waves of movements toward school reform at the national level, among the various state education agencies (SEAs) and in local education agencies (LEAs). The mission of schools had been expanding in response to the explication of a right to a free appropriate public education (FAPE) for children with disabilities, and recent concerns around violence, peer sexual harassment, and bullying in schools. The school social worker remained a primary provider of mental health services (Kelly et al., 2010)—an absorbing, but still unfulfilled, role. At the same time, education had become outcome and evidence informed (Kratochwill & Shernoff, 2003). There has been an emphasis on high professional qualifications to develop individualized interventions. In states with some investment in school social work, this emphasis on qualifications is meshing with movements toward specialization in school social work and within the broader profession. In accordance with national legislation, states have been setting standards for highly qualified school social workers, even introducing post–master's degree mentorships for more permanent certification on that level (Constable & Alvarez, 2006). On the other hand, demanding quality is costly at a time when state budgets are strained. For school social workers, the outcomes of all of this are uncertain. They depend on leadership and practice development among school social workers and academicians at the national level, and at the respective SEA and LEA levels.

Multitiered Prevention and Intervention: Positive Behavioral Interventions and Supports and Multitiered System Support

Two nationally recognized education practice models emphasize a whole-school, multitiered approach to intervention and support. Students at risk could be served on three levels. They could be served according to their needs in tier 1 in general education (prevention), in tier 2 through early intervention, and in tier 3 through more-intensive and more-individualized interventions. Positive behavioral interventions and supports (PBIS) (Sugai & Horner, 2008) is focused on classroom-wide intervention (see chapter 26). Multitiered systems of support (MTSS) is a classroom and team-based approach in general education for identification, assessment, planning, and intervention with students who are at risk for academic failure. Concerned with early identification and prevention, MTSS refines and individualizes classroom intervention for students in a manner similar to PBIS. In both PBIS and MTSS there is a more fluid exchange between special education and regular education. MTSS models generally organize educational approaches to students at risk of failure at the three levels of intervention discussed above. Assessments are performance based, rather than based on more-static test criteria. The choice of practical, evidence-informed interventions would depend on the assessment. The student's lack of response to less-targeted, group-oriented intervention would trigger a decision to develop more-individualized interventions. Working within an MTSS framework in a heightened collaborative process, school social workers, as team members, would provide consultation to teachers and work in focused ways at all levels with pupils, parents, and other resource persons and systems.

Teamwork

The concern has always existed that mildly challenged pupils were too swiftly categorized and shifted out of regular education, that referral for special services was the equivalent of placement, and that regular educators, for whatever reasons, were less willing to deal with a special needs pupil, when referral and removal was a possibility. With the 2001 development of standards-driven general education reform (No Child Left Behind Act), some blurring of special education and regular education has begun to occur. High-incidence disabilities—learning disabilities, emotional disturbance, mild mental retardation, and attention deficit disorders—would be serviced largely within general education by better, evidence-based teaching and teamwork (Fuchs, Fuchs, & Stecker, 2010). More recently a third alternative, Smart MTSS, envisages a high degree of specialization and teamwork with different children at different levels of the prevention framework, and better linkages between special education and regular education that would facilitate flexible entering and exiting from tier 3 intensive and individualized programs. Students would move across prevention levels according to their needs. A first grader with reading problems who is not helped at tier 2 (secondary prevention) would move to tier 3, hopefully respond well, and, within six months, achieve a level of performance indicating a need for access to first-grade material (Fuchs, Fuchs, & Compton, 2012).

Will School Social Workers Retain a Distinct Role?

Will the blurring of special education and general education and the emphasis on teamwork affect how school social workers or others on the team define their roles? Will their functions become blurred as well? Would a school social worker become simply one of a group of specialized instructional support personnel (SiSP) (Kelly, Frey, & Anderson-Butcher, 2011)? (SiSP is a current multidisciplinary certification endorsed by the U.S. Department of Education [USDOE] for certain circumstances.) Certainly this can and does happen without a clear, collaborative understanding of role, without professional leadership, and without a general ability of the profession itself to adapt and find ways its uniqueness can contribute to changing conditions. Good teamwork means learning each other's roles so that people can work together. Good teamwork allows for and encourages specialization, so that the truly skilled school social work practitioner is able to see ways that she or he can contribute to the complex arrangements needed to assist students to get intensive help at one level and then move with support to a higher level. If the school social worker has nothing distinct to offer, her membership in the team is at risk. Effective teamwork demands both distinctive roles and shared common responsibility for problem definition and intervention. The paradox is that the more the blurring of role, the less teamwork becomes possible, or the less teamwork is possible when roles are rigidly defined.

Evidence-Informed Practice

In a major policy development at the beginning of the millennium the Elementary and Secondary Education Act of 2001 (known as the No Child Left Behind Act) had mentioned more than one hundred times that educational service providers must use scientifically based research to support their decision making and interventions (Raines, 2004). EIP, described more fully in chapter 4, may mean different things to different people. To think about EIP, we must first think about evidence—where it can be found, how it can be used, and what the limits of a certain type of evidence may be. There are many types of evidence, some more general, some more specific to case situations, some involving numbers, some involving less-tangible qualities of a person, or a relationship, or an outcome. Much work has been done to make reviews of this developing evidence accessible to school social workers, including a large, systematic collection (Franklin, Harris, & Allen-Meares, 2006), and numerous Internet-based resources (see chapter 4).

Policy Practice

If school social workers are to survive in education, they need to continue to develop policy practice at three levels in response to emergent education policies. Most of the discussion of new developments in education and school social work in this chapter stems from national policy developments of long duration and predictability. These policy decisions take place at three different, but interrelated, levels: at the national level, at the state level (SEA), and finally at the local level (LEA). In the 1970s, when national laws and policies were developed formulating regulations for the development of services to children with disabilities, school social workers did respond at all these levels. They worked out ways for school social workers to take part in the individualized education program (IEP), for example. For school social work there have been loosely organized networks at the national level that have responded to national education policy developments, finding allies among different professional groups and different political persuasions. At SEA levels the process is similar, but the extent and quality of leadership has varied by state. Finally, at the LEA level there has been similar variability. Where leadership, which would respond to and interpret these developments, has been available, school social work seems to have done reasonably well. Where school social workers have been able and willing to respond to and interpret policy developments, practice has often reflected these developments. At the district level this means working with a district committee, installing and refining programs such as MTSS. At the state level it means working with the state department of education on professional standards. There are few specialists in policy practice as such. However, those who are invited to work on a committee seem to be people with four sets of qualifications: (1) They are known to be professionally competent at what they do. (2) They are committed to attend and contribute to committee processes. (3) They have some knowledge of the political process, including the ability to work constructively with persons where differences exist. (4) And they have sufficient longevity in their positions to become part of an effective network. Policy practice in schools is discussed in greater detail in chapter 19.

CONCLUSION

Bringing all of this together over recent history, the social worker's role continues to develop in response to developing education policy and changing conditions in schools. Teamwork and assessment are particularly important, as social workers move back and forth between general education and regular education, finding flexible and creative ways to respond to different situations. Policy practice has been and will be particularly important as social workers respond to and have an impact on developments at different levels where programs and policies are developed. In the future the predictable resource scarcity in local school districts and SEAs will demand the highest level of creativity, resiliency, and teamwork at the state and local levels to preserve some level of effective service to children and families. It will demand new partnerships of families and schools, and where school social work survives and flourishes it will of necessity come as the result of the state–local school alliance in education policy development. When policy builds on existing structures and resources, when it includes the family as the most important resource, it can lead to sustainable development.

To this date the school social work role has been resilient. It has shown an ability to change and develop in relation to changing conditions. School social work practice has reflected some of these changes in its increased involvement in consultation and teamwork with the broader school environment. At the same time, every study of the school social work role has pointed out that the largest proportion of school social worker time is spent on work at the individual, family, or classroom level to remove barriers to learning for specific students who have been referred for school social work services and to reduce the severity of these problems at school (Kelly et al., 2010).

References

Abbott, E. (1942). *Social welfare and professional education.* Chicago: University of Chicago Press.

Alderson, J. (1974). Models of school social work practice. In R. Sarri & F. Maple (Eds.), *The school in the community* (pp. 57–74). Washington, DC: National Association of Social Workers.

Allen-Meares, P. (1977). Analysis of tasks in school social work. *Social Work, 22,* 196–201.

Allen-Meares, P. (1994). Social work services in schools: A national study. *Social Work, 39*(4), 560–567.

Allen-Meares, P. (1999). The contributions of social workers to schooling—revisited. In R. Constable, S. McDonald, & J. Flynn (Eds.), *School social work: Practice, policy, and research perspectives* (4th ed., pp. 24–31). Chicago: Lyceum Books.

Allen-Meares, P. (2000). From the editor: Our professional values and the changing environment. *Journal of Social Work Education, 36*(2), 179–182.

Allen-Meares, P. (2006, Summer). One hundred years: A historical analysis of social work services in the schools. In C. R. Massat (Ed.), *100 years of school social work practice* (pp. 24–43). Special edition of *School Social Work Journal.* Chicago: Lyceum Books.

Allen-Meares, P., Washington, R. O., & Welsh, B. L. (2000). *Social work services in schools.* Boston: Allyn & Bacon.

American Association of Social Workers. (1974). *Social casework: Generic and specific: A report on the Milford conference.* Washington, DC: National Association of Social Workers. (Original work published 1929)

Anlauf-Sabatino, C. (1982). Consultation and school social work practice. In R. Constable & J. Flynn (Eds.), *School social work: Practice and research perspectives* (pp. 271–281). Homewood, IL: Dorsey Press.

Bartlett, H. (1959). The generic-specific concept in social work education and practice. In A. E. Kahn (Ed.), *Issues in American social work* (pp. 159–189). New York: Columbia University Press.

Bartlett, H. (1961). *Analyzing social work by fields.* New York: National Association of Social Workers.

Bartlett, H. (1971). *The common base of social work practice.* New York: National Association of Social Workers.

Brown v. Board of Education of Topeka (Kansas). 347 U.S. 483 (1954).

Chavkin, N. (1993). *The use of research in social work practice.* Westport, CT: Praeger.

Constable, R., & Alvarez, M. (2006). Moving into specialization in school social work. *School Social Work Journal, 30*(3), 116–131.

Constable, R., & Montgomery, E. (1985). A study of role conceptions of the school social worker. *Social Work in Education, 7*(4), 244–257.

Constable, R., Kuzmickaite, D., Harrison, W. D., & Volkmann, L. (1999). The emergent role of the school social worker in Indiana. *School Social Work Journal, 24*(1), 1–14.

Costin, L. (1969a). A historical review of school social work. *Social Casework, 50,* 439–453.

Costin, L. (1969b). An analysis of the tasks in school social work. *Social Service Review, 43,* 274–285.

Costin, L. (1972). Adaptations in the delivery of school social work services. *Social Casework, 53,* 350.

Costin, L. (1973). School social work practice: A new model. *Social Work, 20*(2), 135–139.

Costin, L. (1978). *Social work services in schools: Historical perspectives and current directions.* (Continuing Education Series # 8). Washington, DC: National Association of Social Workers.

Culbert, J. (1916). Visiting teachers and their activities. In *Proceedings of the National Conference on Charities and Corrections* (p. 595). Chicago: Heldman.

Dennison, S. (1998). School social work roles and working conditions in a southern state. *School Social Work Journal, 23*(1), 44–54.

Education for All Handicapped Children Act of 1975, Pub. L. 94-142 (1975).

Franklin, C., Harris, M. B., & Allen-Meares, P. (Eds.). (2006). *The school services sourcebook: A guide for school-based professionals.* New York: Oxford University Press.

Frey, A. J., & Dupper, D. J. (2005). A broader conceptual approach to clinical practice for the 21st century. *Children & Schools, 27*(1), 33–44.

Fuchs, D., Fuchs, L. S., & Compton, D. L. (2012). Smart RTI: A next-generation approach to multilevel prevention. *Exceptional Children, 78*(3), 263–279.

Fuchs, D., Fuchs, L. S., & Stecker, P. M. (2010). The "blurring" of special education in a new continuum of general education placements and services. *Exceptional Children, 76*(3), 301–324.

Germain, C. (2006). An ecological perspective on social work in the schools. In R. Constable, C. Massat, S. McDonald, & J. Flynn (Eds.), *School social work: Practice, policy and research* (pp. 28–39). Chicago: Lyceum Books.

Gordon, W. E. (1969). Basic constructs for an integrative and generative conception of social work. In G. Hearn (Ed.), *The general systems approach: Contributions towards an holistic conception of social work* (n.p.). New York: Council on Social Work Education.

Goren, S. G. (1981). The wonderland of social work in the schools, or how Alice learned to cope. *School Social Work Journal, 6*(1), 19–26.

Joint NASW-CSWE Task Force on Specialization (Joint Task Force). (1979). *Specialization in the social work profession.* NASW Document No. 79-310-08. Washington, DC: National Association of Social Workers.

Kelly, M. S., Berzin, S. C., Frey, A., Alvarez, M., Shaffer, G., & O'Brien, K. (2010). The state of school social work: Findings from the national school social work survey. *School Mental Health, 2,* 132–141. doi:10.1007/s12310-010-9034-5

Kelly, M. S., Frey, A. J., & Anderson-Butcher, D. (2011). Writing the job description for school social workers in 2031. *Children & Schools, 33*(2), 67–69.

Kratochwill, T. R., & Shernoff, E. S. (2003). Evidence-based practice: Promoting evidence-based interventions in school psychology. *School Psychology Quarterly, 18*(4), 389–408. http://dx.doi.org/10.1521/scpq.18.4.389.27000

Lambert, C., & Mullally, R. (1982). School social work: The congruence of task importance and level of effort. In R. Constable & J. Flynn (Eds.), *School social work: Practice and research perspectives* (pp. 72–99). Homewood, IL: Dorsey Press.

Lide, P. (1959). A study of historical influences of major importance in determining the present function of the school social worker. In G. Lee (Ed.), *Helping the troubled school child* (n.p.). New York: National Association of Social Workers.

Marcus, G. (1938–39). The generic and specific in social work: Recent developments in our thinking. *American Association of Psychiatric Social Workers, 3/4.*

McCullagh, J. (2000). School social work in Chicago: An unrecognized pioneer program. *School Social Work Journal, 25*(1), 1–14.

Nelson, C. (1990). *A job analysis of school social workers.* Princeton, NJ: Educational Testing Service.

No Child Left Behind Act of 2001, Pub. L. 107-110 (2002).

Poole, F. (1949, December). An analysis of the characteristics of the school social worker. *Social Service Review, 23,* 454–459.

Poole, F. (1959). The school social worker's contribution to the classroom teacher. In G. Lee (Ed.), *Helping the troubled school child.* New York: National Association of Social Workers.

Raines, J. C. (2004). Evidence-based practice in school social work: A process in perspective. *Children & Schools, 26*(2).

Siporin, M. (1975). *Introduction to social work practice.* New York: Macmillan.

Sugai, G., & Horner, R. H. (2008). What we know and need to know about preventing problem behavior in schools. *Exceptionality, 16*(2), 67–77.

Timberlake, E., Sabatino, C., & Hooper, S. (1982). School social work practice and PL 94–142. In R. Constable & J. Flynn (Eds.), *School social work: Practice and research perspectives* (pp. 49–72). Homewood, IL: Dorsey Press.

2

The Characteristic Focus of the Social Worker in the Public Schools

Marjorie McQueen Monkman

- ◆ The Characteristic Focus of Social Work
- ◆ Ecological Perspective
- ◆ Social Work Knowledge
- ◆ Transactions Individuals Environment Framework: Outcome Categories
- ◆ Concepts for Analyzing Resources
- ◆ Values
- ◆ Social Work Activities
- ◆ The Worker

PREFACE TO MARJORIE MONKMAN CHAPTER

The eighth edition of *School Social Work: Practice, Policy, and Research* begins with the history of the field. School social work has been in place for more than a hundred years. It has evolved and changed, but certain things endure. A component that has stood the test of time is the systemic, multi-layered perspective on school social work practice. One significant contributor to this focus was Marjorie Monkman who influenced the field and the perspective of this book throughout all eight editions. Marjorie Monkman influenced the major thinkers in the field of school social work, including generations who have read different editions of this book, as it has developed since 1983. Both Robert Constable and Carol Rippey Massat, two of the editors of this volume, worked with Marjorie Monkman and knew and respected her work from its beginning. This chapter is foundational to the development of school social work as a field. Marjorie Monkman, at the University of Illinois, worked in the tradition of William Gordon to develop the Transactions Individuals Environment (T.I.E.) framework in the 1970s that frames the practice of school social work in the context of practice at multiple levels of the environment, in which intervention occurs at the place where individuals interact with their environment. Professor Monkman helped the field to move beyond one-on-one clinical practice to school social work practice that includes change of the school environment. This places the concerns of the child in the transaction between student and environment rather than within individual children and their families, or in dysfunctional educators. This perspective assists school social workers to move beyond a singular focus to one that moves flexibly across systems to find the places in that transaction where change can occur. This perspective remains a critical one for school social workers. The movement of evidence-informed practice tends to focus specifically on the intervention itself. However, the T.I.E. framework is a perspective that permits us to step back and look at a situation as a transactional one, in which evidence-informed interventions could be selected to intervene both with children and families, and with aspects of the school and community environment. Welcome to the broader vision articulated for school social work practice by Marjorie Monkman.

Carol Rippey Massat, April 2015

Federal and state legislation and major legal decisions have given recognition to school social work services and provided an opportunity to broaden these services from the traditional roles. The recognition of school social work services in these laws and policies creates greater expectations for the worker and challenges the profession. The purpose of this chapter is to conceptualize the focus of school social work and the role of the individual worker in utilizing this focus, in developing new techniques in practice, and in demonstrating desired change.

It is hard to overestimate the importance of the individual worker's contribution to change in the practice situation. Workers carry a heavy responsibility for what they bring to the practice situation. They bring a characteristic professional focus that is both broad and unique. The worker's focus makes it possible for him or her to identify knowledge needed for intervention. The worker brings activities and skills for bringing about desired changes. The worker brings values that lead to the selection of perspective, knowledge, and action. The worker brings the contribution of charisma and personal style. It is through the social worker that the professional focus, knowledge, values, and activities impinge on the practice situation. The role of the worker is formed from these attributes as they interact with the particular structure and expectations of the setting (see figure 2.1).

FIGURE 2.1   Contributions of the Worker

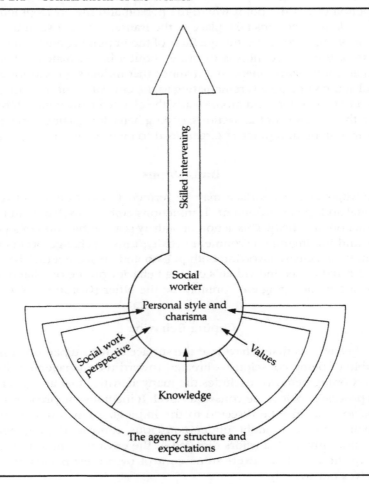

THE CHARACTERISTIC FOCUS OF SOCIAL WORK

From the beginning, the social work focus has been identified as resting on the person in the situation, a dual focus. As a result of this focus, social workers work with persons in diverse aspects of life, perhaps more than any other helping discipline. The conceptualization of the person in the situation has been enhanced for social work by the work of Harriett Bartlett (1970), William E. Gordon (1969), and others (Germain & Gitterman, 1980; Gitterman & Germain, 1976; Monkman, 1976, 1978, 1981, 1983; Monkman & Meares, 1984; Pincus & Minahan, 1972; Schwartz, 1969). These theorists have conceptualized the traditional focus in a manner that more accurately reflects the roots and multiple avenues of practice. Their

approach to defining the point of intervention in social work is to emphasize phenomena at the point where the person and the environment meet.
Social work interventions take place in the transactions between the coping
behavior of the person and the qualities of the impinging environment. The
purpose of the intervention is to bring about a better match between the
person and the environment in a manner that induces growth for the person and at the same time is remediating to the environment (Gordon, 1969).

In order to understand more clearly the characteristic focus of the social
worker, the concepts of transactions, coping behavior, quality of the impinging environment, and practice target need to be more clearly explicated.

Transactions

The activities at the interface may be termed transaction(s) between the
individual and the environment. Transactions embody exchange in the context of action or activity. This action or activity is a combination of a person's
activity and impinging environment activity; thus, exchange occurs only in
the context of activity involving both person and environment. The transaction is created by the individual's coping behavior on the one hand and the
activity of the impinging environment on the other (Gordon, 1969).

Coping Behavior

Coping behavior is that behavior at the surface of the human organism that
is capable of being consciously directed toward the management of transactions. Coping behavior excludes the many activities that are governed by
neural processes below the conscious level. It includes the broad repertoire
of behavior that may be directed to the impinging environment and that
potentially can be brought under conscious control. Coping behaviors
include not only the behaviors directed to the environment, but also those
efforts of individuals to exert some control over their behaviors—to use
themselves purposively.

Coping behaviors are learned behaviors, and once learned they become
established as coping patterns. Significant repetitions in coping behavior by
individuals or groups of individuals suggest coping patterns that may at
times become the focus of the interventive action. Looking for these patterns in what people are experiencing and how they are responding to a set
of environmental conditions takes us beyond our traditional concern for the
uniqueness and integrity of each individual. If we know something about
the conditions and about human coping, we can say something in some
detail and substance about the response of a clientele to a social institution
such as education, and from this we can develop the appropriate response
of school social work. In a relationship with any one individual, we respond
to that person as a unique human being and as a part of a larger collectivity.

We respect and encourage the effort of an individual with disabilities to overcome adversity and/or social discrimination, but we know that some of the adversity and discrimination is shared with other persons with disabilities. This knowledge is as much a base for action as is our knowledge of his or her unique response to adversity and discrimination.

People cope with themselves as well as with the environment, and this is also learned behavior. These behaviors, as they are developed over time, incorporate expectations and feedback from the environment. The ways individuals and groups cope are related to the information they have about themselves or their environment—how they perceive self and environment. This information is patterned into a cognitive structure that directs the coping behaviors and could even direct the perception of the environment in a manner that will make it difficult to receive further information as feedback from the environment. There is a circular relation between what we usually do to cope with the environment and how we perceive things. An understanding of this relation is the crucial assessment tool. If coping behaviors and patterns are not in keeping with the environment as we perceive it, we may then examine the information and the perceptions of the coping persons. This assessment is directed toward patterns of perception and action rather than seeking some type of single cause within the individual.

Coping is an active, creative behavior that continually breaks the boundaries of the given. Adapting is seen as a passive concept that implies that the person simply takes in the output from the environment. Some writers connect coping with stress in adapting and refer to coping as those behaviors emitted when there is stress in adapting. We would say that stress is inherent in any growing process, but that it is important to assess the degree of stress to understand the coping patterns adopted. The person is considered able to cope when he or she is dealing with the stress (Gordon, 1969).

Quality of the Impinging Environment

The other side of the transaction field is the environment. Social work practice has not confined its concern to the person in any particular situation— that is, at home, in the hospital, in school, or in any other situation. No other profession seems to follow people so extensively into their daily habitats. We have been interested in how the qualities of any of these situations interact with the coping behaviors. As in the case of the coping behaviors, Gordon (1969) gave a way of partializing the qualities of a situation. He defined the qualities of the impinging environment as those qualities at the surface of the environmental system that the person is actually in contact with, rather than below-the-surface structures, which are inferred to be responsible for the nature of what the human organism actually confronts.

Although emphasis on the environmental side is on the impingements, it is recognized that it is through one's knowledge of what is behind the impingements that enables the person to arrange for changes in those impingements in desired directions. It is often necessary to work for change on several levels. For example, a worker may be working with a truant child in an effort to get the child to return to school. At the same time, the worker may find that the teacher is happier with the child truant and that the administration is indifferent. Intervention may be needed at all three levels if the child is to return and remain in school (figure 2.2).

Practice Target

Transaction has been defined as activity that combines coping behaviors and the quality of the impinging environment. Through these transactions there is an exchange between the components of each side. The goal of social work practice is matching—that is, bringing about a fit that makes for positive outcomes both for the person and for the environment. Professional intervention for bringing about a match may include efforts to change the coping behavior, the quality of the impinging environment, or both (Gordon, 1969).

Social work is concerned with what will happen to the coping behaviors and the quality of the impinging environment as a result of the exchanges between them. The relation of coping and environment is reciprocal. Thus coping behavior and/or quality of the impinging environment could become what we are seeking to change and thus our measures of outcome or depen-

FIGURE 2.2   T.I.E. Framework: Transactions between Individuals and Environments

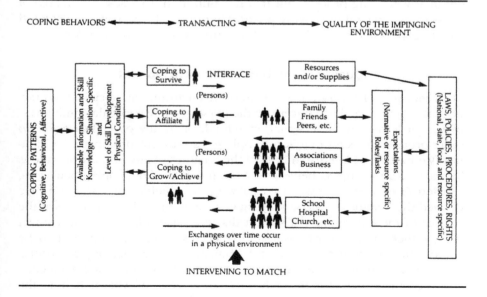

dent variables. To the degree that activity in the transaction changes, we may predict consequent changes in either or both the coping behavior and the environmental side.

ECOLOGICAL PERSPECTIVE

We are essentially operating from an ecological perspective. Ecology seeks to understand the reciprocal relation between organisms and environment: how organisms shape the environment to its needs and how this shaping enhances the life-supporting properties of the environment (Germain & Gitterman, 1980). For social work, the ecological perspective appears to fit our historical view much better than the medical or disease perspective that we seem to have adopted in past decades. The ecological perspective is essentially a perspective, a point of view, for relationships that take place in reality; it is a way of perceiving these relationships more clearly.

One of the reasons for the better fit of the ecological perspective to social work is that it is a multicausal rather than a linear causal perspective; that is, it makes possible a view of multifaceted relationships. From this perspective, our attention is called to the consequences of transactions between people and environment, but the metaphors, models, and/or theories we have previously borrowed, have focused more on cause of action and have tended to be one-sided and unidirectional.

SOCIAL WORK KNOWLEDGE

A basic area of knowledge for social work is knowledge of the needs of people and how these needs are met. People individually and collectively have needs for physical well-being. These needs consist of food, shelter, and so on, which may be identified as needs for surviving. People have a need for relationships, including intimacy and other forms of affiliating. People have a need for growth, which may include their need to know, to learn, to develop their talents, and to experience mental and emotional well-being.

A second major area of knowledge for social work is knowledge of the institutions or societal resources that have been established to meet these needs. We need knowledge of the major structures and processes involved in resource provision and development. This area is quite complex and includes expectations, policies, procedures, and so on.

The third major area of knowledge is knowledge of the match between these institutions and the needs of the people. From the perspective of social work, this is knowledge of the transactions and the result of these transactions for people and their environments. For example, the Education for All Handicapped Children Act of 1975 and subsequently the Individuals with Disabilities Education Act (IDEA) of 1990 represent environmental policy change that alters societal expectations and resources for exceptional children and, in turn, affects all children. The environmental impingements that individual children experience will change as these policies change. The differences in the transactions between pupils and their teachers, peers, and even the physical structure of the school have become a part of the general experience of children. However, these children continue struggling to cope with change and new events brought on by these policies. These transactions are particularized and occur in time and space (at a particular time and in a particular place), as do all living transactions.

The purpose of social work activity is to improve the match between coping behaviors and the quality of the impinging environment so that the stress in these transactions is not so great that it is destructive to the coping abilities of the individual or the environment. Changes are always occurring, and people are always coping or striving to manage change. Our purpose is not only to bring a match that is not destructive, but also, if possible, to bring a match that makes the person better able to cope with further change and that makes the environment less stressful to others.

As our focus becomes clearer, we could make the knowledge we have of transactions more explicit for social workers and other disciplines. To do this we need to develop our focus in a way that makes what we aim to change, coping behavior, and the impinging environment, more explicit. Figure 2.2 illustrates the concepts we will be discussing.

TRANSACTIONS INDIVIDUALS ENVIRONMENT FRAMEWORK: OUTCOME CATEGORIES

Coping Behaviors

Social workers basically deal with at least three categories of coping behaviors and three categories of the impinging environment (Monkman, 1978). This framework for dealing with the transactions between individuals and environments is called the T.I.E. framework. Surviving, affiliating, growing, and achieving together form a continuum of coping. There are then three categories of coping behaviors: (1) coping behaviors for surviving, (2) coping behaviors for affiliation, and (3) coping behaviors for growing and achieving. These categories help us set priorities for practice intervention. Coping behaviors at any time are affected by information from past coping experience and build themselves over time. Our first consideration is whether the client has the capacity to obtain and use the necessities for surviving, and the second, for affiliating. Both surviving and affiliating skills seem to be prerequisites to growing and achieving.

Coping behaviors for surviving are those behaviors that enable the person to obtain and use resources that make it possible to continue life or activity. To survive we need to have the capacity to obtain food, shelter, clothing, and medical treatment, and to have access to these through locomotion.

Coping behaviors for affiliating are those behaviors that enable the person to unite in a close connection to others in the environment. Subcategories of affiliating behaviors are (1) the capacity to obtain and use personal relationships, and (2) the ability to use organizations and organizational structure. Social workers would have great difficulty conceiving of a person apart from his or her social relations. Each individual experiences social relations through organizations and groups, families, schools, clubs, church, and such.

Coping behaviors for growing and achieving are those behaviors that enable the person to perform for, and to contribute to, him- or herself and others. Subcategories of coping behaviors for growing are developing and using (1) cognitive capacities, (2) physical capacities, (3) economic capacities, and (4) emotional capacities.

Quality of the Impinging Environment

The environment can be seen as comprising (1) resources, (2) expectations, and (3) laws and policies. The categories of the environment do not have a priority of their own. Rather, because our major value is the person, the priority of the categories is established in the match with coping behaviors.

Resources. Resources are supplies that can be drawn on when needed or can be turned to for support. Pincus and Minahan (1972) characterized resource systems as informal, formal, and societal. Informal resource systems consist of family, neighbors, coworkers, and the like. Formal resource systems could be membership organizations or formal associations that promote the interest of the member, such as Alcoholics Anonymous, the Association for Retarded Citizens, and so on. Societal resource systems are structured services and service institutions, such as schools, hospitals, social security programs, courts, police agencies, and so on. Resource systems may be adequate or inadequate and provide opportunities, incentives, or limitations. In many situations there are no resources to match the coping behaviors for surviving, affiliating, and growing.

Expectations. Expectations are the patterned performances and normative obligations that are grounded in established societal structures. Expectations can involve roles and tasks. Social workers recognize these structures and recognize that a positive role complementarity usually leads to greater mutual satisfaction and growth. However, it is not our purpose as social workers simply to help people adapt to societal roles or to perform all expected tasks. Roles are the patterned, functional behaviors that are performed by the collection of persons. Examples of roles are mother, father, social worker, physician, and so on. Although these are normative patterns in our society, individuals do not always agree on the specific behaviors of a role. Roles do change, because they are socially defined and functionally oriented. Sometimes this societal change is not acceptable to the individual and creates a mismatch between coping behaviors and the environment.

The concept of task is a way of describing the pressures placed on people by various life situations. These tasks "have to do with daily living, such as growing up in the family, and also with the common traumatic situations such as bereavement, separation, illness, or financial difficulties" (Bartlett, 1970, n.p.). These tasks call for coping responses from the people involved in the situation.

Laws and Policies. Laws and policies are those binding customs or rules of conduct created by a controlling authority, such as legislation, legal decisions, and majority pressures. Subcategories of laws and policies are rights and responsibilities, procedures, sanctions, and inhibiting or restricting factors. As a category, laws and policies are seen as necessary and positive components of the environment. Yet, it is also recognized that many single laws or policies have negative effects for groups of people. Some of our policies make survival more difficult. In some cases, particularly for welfare clients, the act of receiving assistance from welfare agencies may make affiliation almost impossible.

Expectations, laws, policies, and procedures are communicated through resources. The quality of output from a resource, such as a school, is very much affected by the state and national policies that have been adopted. The ultimate test of these policies is the match they make with coping behaviors of those persons with whom the school transacts, namely children. Thus, if these transactions are destructive to the coping behaviors of children, the procedure for implementing or the policy itself is in need of change. This is another way of saying that policy is a legitimate target for change. Social workers are often in the best position for evaluating the match between policy and coping. The classroom is an example that may make the interrelationship of the environmental categories clearer. The expectations for tasks to be accomplished in the classroom come to the child through the teacher (and others). The teacher is a resource to the child, but unless he or she is able to bring the expectations in line with the coping behaviors of the child, there is no match. In some cases, the coping behaviors are so different from the expectations that other resources are necessary. Social workers might intervene in the environment and/or in coping behaviors of schoolchildren—that is, in the resources, expectations, policies, procedures, and/or in the coping. In some situations, however, change might be indicated in all six outcome categories.

Research Evidence

An exploratory study (Monkman & Meares, 1984) using a random sample of Illinois school social workers and utilizing the focus described in this chapter (the T.I.E. framework) lends evidence to the fit of this framework to practice. The data show that coping behavior and environment outcome categories were selected in approximately equal amounts. A national study using a random sample of direct-practice master of social work degrees (MSWs) from a variety of practice settings (Monkman, 1989) gave additional evidence that social workers' outcomes are located in the categories described in this framework.

Matching Person and Environment

The discussion to follow will be an oversimplification of the interrelation between transaction and the matching process, but it is a first step in utilizing the framework developed thus far. Two populations will be used as examples (figure 2.3).

The first population to be considered comprises unmarried teenage parents. To be of help to this group it is important to consider the match between behaviors for surviving, affiliating, and growing and each of the categories on the environmental side. To give a few specific examples: placing the teenage mother on homebound instruction may enhance cognitive

FIGURE 2.3   The Characteristic Focus of School Social Work

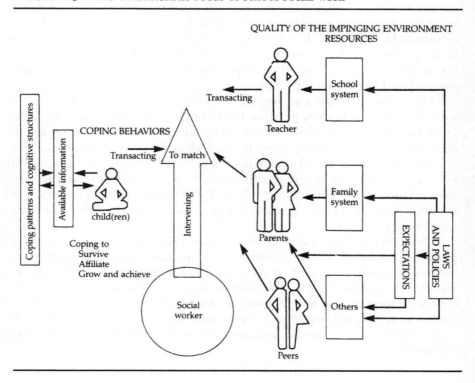

achievement but may be destructive to affiliation in interpersonal relationships and affiliation with society and/or organizations. The student may not be aware of laws and policies that can affect her decision to have her baby and keep her baby. Knowledge of the task of being a mother is important for both the mother and the child.

Another population would be developmentally delayed children. Again, we are concerned with matching in all six categories. Many of the programs presently developed for developmentally delayed children are geared to maximizing cognitive development—or more specifically, academic achievement. Most of these programs do not develop affiliating or surviving skills. Very little energy is put into making a better match between the coping behaviors of the developmentally delayed child and the wide range of tasks for daily living.

It is important to remember that our outcome variables are both coping behaviors and the quality of the impinging environment. We may affect either or both. In the case of the teenage parent, the social worker may have helped to change her behavior in all three categories, as well as increasing resources. The worker may have made information about expectations, laws, and policies more available to her and may have changed some of the expectations emanating from her impinging environment; for example, the worker may have changed the demands to give up her baby or to keep her baby. For the developmentally delayed child, he or she may have developed resources for increasing his or her affiliating behavior. He or she may even have measures of change in these behaviors. The worker may have helped his or her parents change their expectations so that they do not make impossible demands on the child.

Often, social work interventions include teaming with other social workers and other helping persons. For example, many growing and achieving behaviors for schoolchildren require teaming with teachers of these children. Teachers spend many more hours with children than social workers do. They have more direct opportunities to develop coping behaviors and skills in children. By teaming with teachers, social workers can increase their change possibilities for children. By bringing these two resources together, they can make a greater change in some aspect of the children's environment.

The point of these examples is to show that this framework makes it possible for us to partialize, generalize, and measure change in practice situations. It is possible to make each of these examples more explicit depending on the conditions of your practice situation. To bring about these changes a worker may, for instance, use knowledge of organizations, skills for working with groups, skills for data collecting, and skills for communicating. The worker must also determine the major critical exchanges in the transaction.

CONCEPTS FOR ANALYZING RESOURCES

Resources have been identified as a major component of the environment. Resources such as family, school, hospitals, and so on, may be viewed as systems. Concepts from the general systems model are useful for conceptualizing and organizing data in the various resource systems. These concepts may be used to call our attention to the skills necessary for the worker to get in and out of a resource system. This model calls to our attention such questions as these: (1) For what is the major energy in the system being used? (2) Is tension in the system a productive or a destructive force? (3) What effect will change in one part of the system have on the other parts? Social workers, such as those employed in schools, become parts of systems. However, although the worker is a part of the system, the worker also intervenes in the system itself as a resource for children (Monkman, 1981).

Understanding Organizations

Workers need to understand what makes organizations operate if they will be able to use the school or other social agencies as a resource. For example, organizations have a managerial structure that is generally hierarchical. Organizational structure can be best understood in relation to organizational process. Workers need to understand the informal power that can be gained either from interpersonal relationships or from assuming responsibilities, as well as power that comes from the formal structural arrangements.

A second, but no less important, process variable is communication. Communication serves a linkage function. It links various parts of the organization by information flow. This may be individual to individual, individual to group, unit to unit, unit to superstructure, and so on. Communication has been called the lifeblood of organizations or systems. Social workers have a particular responsibility for developing and maintaining channels of communication if they are to accomplish their own missions.

The climate of an organization has a major effect on its productivity. Climate describes expectancies and incentives and represents a property that is perceived directly or indirectly by individuals in the organization. Climate is made up of such phenomena as warmth, support, conflict, identity, reward, and risk. For social workers, climate is seen as a major quality of resources and is often a target for change.

The earlier discussion makes clear that resources are dependent variables or targets for change for social workers. Resources for clients may take a variety of meanings and may in particular be the setting or places of employment for social workers. Thus, it is imperative for social workers to understand the systems or organizations of which they may be a part and to know and ask the essential questions for assessing resources.

In addition, organizational systems have external environments. The exchange between an organization and its environment is essential to the growth of the organization. Organizational environment may be thought of in two categories: (1) general environment, and (2) specific environment.

The general environment consists of conditions that must be of concern to all organizations. Examples of these would include political, economic, demographic, cultural, technological, and legal conditions. The specific environment includes other organizations with which the organization interacts frequently or particular individuals who are crucial to the organization. Examples of the specific environment of a school system are the parents of the children enrolled in the school, the local mental health center, the local child welfare services, the juvenile court, and so forth.

Social Networks

Environments are made up of networks of resources. An important, but sometimes neglected, network is the informal social network for the client: that is, peers, neighbors, friends, relatives, and so on. Each of the persons individually is an important resource for the client, but the linkage and relationship between these persons in the network are also important. Professionals are aware of the negative potential of peer influence on children. However, the positive aspects of these relationships are also useful to practice. Within these networks can be found members who serve as effective informal helpers. Knowledge of social networks and the ability to assess these in practice situations is becoming increasingly important as people become more mobile and lose continuing contact with their own roots. Mobility weakens these linkages, increases isolation and loss, and simultaneously makes network relationships more important.

Networks of Service Organizations

Social workers are often in the position of developing networks of service organizations for clients. Many of our practice situations involve a service network such as the school, family, state child welfare agency, and the courts or judicial system. Social workers are particularly concerned about the relations between these resource systems. This is a domain of social work practice. Social workers may develop and use these inter-resource linkages, establish channels of communication between these resources, and develop new resources. Thus, the school social workers are in the middle of a system, within an organizational structure, in an environment of social and environmental networks. In order to enhance the development of linkages between various human service organizations, they need to have knowledge of systems variables and organizational variables. Knowledge of the relations of change taking place in differing parts of the system, of the tendency of systems to maintain themselves and to tighten their boundaries when threatened, can make the worker much more sensitive to the necessary steps in developing linkages between agencies.

We have reviewed concepts and knowledge applicable to the environmental aspects of school social work practice. Other areas of knowledge are equally applicable. These might be (1) knowledge of normal growth and development of children and the stress in coping that accompanies different growth stages, (2) knowledge of exceptional children, (3) knowledge of various learning processes, (4) knowledge of specific resources, (5) knowledge of major policy and policy issues affecting practices in the school setting, and (6) knowledge of positive and negative transaction patterns. Certainly, the earlier discussion gives evidence of the breadth of knowledge that social workers need to bring to practice in the school setting. Although we borrow knowledge from psychology, sociology, economics, political science, education, and so on, we borrow from them in relation to our perspectives and to accomplish the purposes of social work.

VALUES

Values guide the action of social work from the preferred perspective to the preferred action. A clarification of types of values is helpful in determining the role of a specific value in practice. Siporin (1975) has defined ten different types of values; five of these are particularly useful to social work:

1. Ultimate (conceived, or absolute) value is a general, abstract formulation, such as liberty, justice, progress, self-realization, or the worth of the individual.
2. Instrumental value is more specific and immediately applicable, such as acceptance of others, equality of opportunity for education, or safeguarding the confidentiality of client information. This is also termed a "utility value," in referring specifically to the property of things as good or beneficial because of their usefulness to an end.
3. Personal value refers to what an individual considers good and right, or what is generally so considered as right or beneficial for an individual, such as individuality, self-respect, self-reliance, privacy, and self-realization.
4. Scientific value is one to which scientists commit themselves and that they believe should govern scientific behavior: rationality, objectivity, progress, and critical inquiry. Society is increasingly accepting these as general social values.
5. Professional value is one to which professional people commit themselves and accept as a basis for professional behavior, such as competence, impartiality, or placing a client's interest first.

The primary and ultimate value in social work seems to be, "It is good and desirable for man(kind) to fulfill his/her potential, to realize himself/herself, and to balance this with essentially equal efforts to help others fulfill their capacities and realize themselves" (Gordon, 1962, n.p.). This value represents our dual focus on people and their environment, which has characterized social work practice from its beginning. From our ultimate values follow instrumental values that guide actions in practice. An example of an instrumental value is the right to self-determination. This instrumental value guides our practice, unless it is in conflict with our ultimate value—that is, the individual's self-determination is destructive to him- or herself or others. Knowledge is usually required to make this determination. Thus, values and knowledge are different, but interrelated, in their application to practice. Values, however, give us purpose and ethical structure in social work.

We are careful not to inflict our personal values on others, while we accept professional values as a basis for our professional behavior. Hopefully, our personal values are not in conflict with the professional and ultimate values. Yet the professional values may not encompass all of our personal values. An example of this difference may be seen in relation to divorce. An individual worker may believe that divorce would be personally wrong, but his or her professional values would enable the worker to help clients make the decision for themselves whether to divorce.

It is important to remember that social work has a philosophical base and continues to require judgment as to means and ends. The judgment, however, can be made with more-explicit awareness of the knowledge and value implications.

Social workers must be able to understand the differences between knowledge and values and the relationship of the two. "Value" refers to what persons prefer or would want to be. This preference may involve all the devotion or sacrifice of which one is capable. "Knowledge" denotes the picture we have built up of the world and ourselves as it is, not necessarily as we would prefer it to be. It is a picture derived from the most rigorous interpretation we are capable of giving to the most objective sense data we are able to obtain (Gordon, 1962). The future of social work may be dependent on this discrimination. That is, if a value is used as a guide in professional action when knowledge is called for, the resulting action is likely to be ineffective. If knowledge is called on when a value is needed as a guide to action, the resulting action may be destructive. Thus, "Both outcomes greatly reduce the potential for human welfare residing in the profession's heritage of both knowledge and values. Man's ability over time to bring some aspect of the world into conformity with his preferences (realize his values) seems to be directly proportional to his ability to bring his statements and perceptions into conformity with the world as it now is (develop the relevant science)" (Gordon, 1962, n.p.).

SOCIAL WORK ACTIVITIES

Social work activities involve assessing, relating, communicating, planning, implementing, and evaluating. Assessing is the bridging concept between action and knowledge and values. This does not mean to imply that assessing is a first step that occurs before any other activity. It is rather a continuous process as other data continue to be gathered. The social work perspective makes explicit the view of the phenomena into which we intervene. Knowledge gives us the most accurate picture of these phenomena that we are able to obtain at any one time. Values lead in the choice of perspectives, in the desire to obtain knowledge, and in the choice of action approaches. The first step in any practice situation is to assess that situation from our perspective, with our knowledge, and in relationship to our values. This step leads to change action.

In most practice situations, assessing occurs simultaneously with relating. The idea of establishing a relationship has been common in social work literature from the beginning. In more recent years, it has been discussed as a process activity that leads to an end change, resulting in the phenomena into which we intervene. At times in the past it has been confused with an end in itself or an outcome variable. Certainly, to establish a relationship may be seen as an interim goal, but not as an outcome in the practice situation. Social work places considerable importance on the skill required to relate to the major factors involved in any practice situation, whether client or resource.

Communicating is an essential activity in practice. Most of our data are collected through communicating. To a large extent the accuracy of our data is dependent on our ability to ask questions and clarify answers. It is through communicating that we express our desire and ability to relate and to help.

Planning activities lead to change goals and tasks for each party involved in a practice situation. Plans need to be based on the assessment of the practice situation, including the resources available to carry out these plans. Some plans include developing other resources, as well as bringing about a match between person(s), coping behaviors, and existing resources. Planning includes time lines and criteria for assessing change, and contracts are the tools used to bridge planning and implementation.

Implementing a change plan is the activity involved in accomplishing these various tasks and goals. Implementing may involve linking people with resources, changing expectations of the client or of the resource(s), developing or changing policy, changing the procedures in a resource system, or developing new or more-effective coping behaviors in person(s), and so on.

Evaluating is part of the assessing process. In the beginning, we assess where the various parts of the practice situation are and, in the end, we evaluate or assess the changes in the various parts. We also evaluate activities that the change processes have accomplished. Evaluation is an assessment of both the outcome and the process. Assessment of outcome is not possible without a perspective that makes our outcome measures clear. It is because in the past this focus has not been explicit that we have been vague and inaccurate and/or confused the relating process with an outcome measure. Assessing and evaluating are continuous processes that should be linked to our characteristic focus, knowledge, and values. Our assessing and planning processes need to be done in a manner that makes evaluation possible.

Each of these process activities involves and includes many skills. They simply serve as a way of organizing our various skill areas. While there is a beginning and an ending to the change process, the steps in this process are not mutually exclusive or linear steps. They are rather interrelated and purposeful activities that together accomplish a result.

THE WORKER

While workers may bring the characteristic focus, knowledge, values, and actions of the profession, they also bring themselves as resources to the change process. Workers, like clients, have past experiences, information, cognitive structures or preferred views of transactions, and predictions about consequences of certain kinds of transactions. Each worker brings his or her own style of transacting. It is the responsibility of the worker to constantly change his or her perceptions in the light of new knowledge, more-accurate facts from the situation, new resources, and so on.

Workers often tend to prefer particular practice activities. However, the workers' preferred skills should not blunt the awareness of what is needed in any particular situation. For example, some workers have knowledge of interventions to change coping behaviors of individuals. The specific knowledge, plus workers' preference for their individual activities, may lead to a limited practice. Various combinations of selected knowledge and individual preference may lead to a limited perspective for assessing and may lead workers to ignore the important aspects of the practice situation. Workers may fail to develop skills for working with groups, the school system, or other community resources.

Many school social workers were trained at a time when methods of practice were the major divisions of training. Workers were trained to do either casework, group work, community organization, and/or intervention at the policy or administrative level. The major method for a school social worker was casework. In more recent years, it has been recognized that there are many common activities in practice. It has also been recognized that change may be enhanced through collaboration and exchange with others who share common change goals. It is the responsibility of practitioners to keep up with changes in knowledge and to develop their skill level to incorporate new practice activities as they develop and are tested.

There is nothing, however, in the professional methodology or activities that can subordinate the unique, personal artistic contributions that each worker brings to the helping process. Certainly, the individual's sensitive capacity to experience and express empathy and caring are valued among social workers. It is, however, the responsibility of individual workers to evaluate the effects of their individual style on any change process. It is the worker's responsibility to recognize strengths and limitations. Unique qualities and personal style must be self-conscious and disciplined, just as discipline is inherent in the definition of art itself.

CONCLUSION

We have analyzed and specified the components, characteristic focus, the knowledge, the values, and the skills that social workers contribute to the public schools. This contribution is significant and provides a response that can be uniquely useful to education in meeting the challenges of its changing mandate. In specifying the components of practice, we see the model developed as useful, both for clarification of the contribution of the social worker and as a tool for building social work knowledge, and for research testing of theory. Because the construction of a model is the first step toward measurement and testing, we would see the elements of the model as a first step toward the measurement and testing of components of social work practice, and we have developed them with that intention. For each social worker, the task of participating in the development of new knowledge is just as important as application of the characteristic focus of the profession and its knowledge, values, and skills. There is much creative work to be done. The responsibility may seem heavy, but the challenge is exciting.

References

Bartlett, H. (1970). *The common base of social work practice*. New York: National Association of Social Workers.

Education for All Handicapped Children Act of 1975, Pub. L. 94-142 (1975).

Germain, C. B., & Gitterman, A. (1980). *The life model of social work practice*. New York: Columbia University Press.

Gitterman, A., & Germain, C. (1976). Social work practice: A life model. *Social Service Review, 50*, 601–610.

Gordon, W. E. (1962, October). A critique of the working definition. *Social Work, 9*, 3–13.

Gordon, W. E. (1969). Basic constructs for an integrative and generative conception of social work. In G. Hearn (Ed.), *The general systems approach: Contributions toward an holistic conception of social work* (pp. 5–11). New York: Council on Social Work Education.

Individuals with Disabilities Education Act (IDEA) of 1990, Pub. L. 105-17, U.S.C. 11401 et seq. (1990).

Monkman, M. M. (1976). A framework for effective social work intervention in the public schools. *School Social Work Journal, 1*(1), 7–16.

Monkman, M. M. (1978). A broader, more comprehensive view of school social work practice. *School Social Work Journal, 2*(2), 89–96.

Monkman, M. M. (1981). An outcome focus for differential levels of school social work practice. In *Professional issues for social workers in schools* (pp. 138–150). Conference Proceedings. Silver Spring, MD: National Association of Social Workers.

Monkman, M. M. (1983). The specialization of school social work and a model for differential levels of practice. In D. G. Miller (Ed.), *Differential levels of students support services: Including crisis remediation and prevention/developmental approaches* (n.p.). Minneapolis, MN: Department of Education.

Monkman, M. M. (1989). *A national study of outcome objectives in social work practice: Person and environment*. Unpublished.

Monkman, M. M., & Meares, P. A. (1984). An exploratory study of school social work and its fit to the T.I.E. framework. *School Social Work, 19*(1), 9–22.

Pincus, A., & Minahan, A. (1972). *Social work practice, model and method*. Itasca, IL: F. E. Peacock.

Schwartz, W. (1969). Private troubles and public issues: One social work job or two? In *Social welfare forum* (pp. 22–43). New York: Columbia University Press.

Siporin, M. (1975). *Introduction to social work practice*. New York: Macmillan.

3

"Moving through a Land of Wonders Wild and New": Grounding School Social Work Practice in an Organizational, Ecosystemic Understanding of the School

Kate Phillippo

Loyola University Chicago School of Education

- ◆ Recognize the Immediate and Broader Environment
- ◆ The School as Part of Nested Ecological Systems
- ◆ Organizational Characteristics of Schools
- ◆ Respond Thoughtfully with Attuned Intervention
- ◆ Cultivate Relevance to the School Community

Lewis Carroll began his classic tale, *Alice's Adventures in Wonderland,* with a poem that built readers' anticipation of Alice's adventures "moving through a land of wonders wild and new" (Carroll, 1865/1948, p. 7). As the tale began, Alice fell down a rabbit hole, unsure of where she was or where she was headed. "Please, ma'am, is this New Zealand? Or Australia?" she wondered (Carroll, 1865/1948, p. 12). Once she landed, her uncertainty and confusion flourished as she found herself shrinking, growing, and coming face to face with creatures that ranged from kind, to curious, to menacing (or all three at once). Alice found herself on her own, making her way through an unfamiliar land, where the things she knew before did not seem to help her. Yet she thoughtfully made her way through, learning as she went by asking a multitude of questions, taking in new information, and making use of the alliances she forged and the tools she acquired on her way.

Alice's experiences were only a dream, yet her story may ring true for many new school social workers. Finding themselves seemingly alone in schools that look like ordinary places where teachers teach and students learn, new school social workers (and, often more-seasoned school social workers as well!) find schools to be perplexing, unpredictable workplaces with an evolving cast of characters and a constant churn of written and unwritten rules. It is this analogy that Sally Goren (1981) developed in "The Wonderland of Social Work in the Schools, or How Alice Learned to Cope" (see appendix B). Goren built on her Alice in Wonderland analogy, arguing that school social workers need to make themselves visible, viable, and valuable. This analogy has resonated through the years with school social workers, appearing in 2013 as the Illinois Association for School Social Workers' chosen theme for national school social work week. With this chapter, I revisit and develop this apt analogy.

School social work can be bewildering and overwhelming to school social work interns and beginning school social workers, making them feel at times as though they have fallen into another world in which their knowledge and skills seem inadequate, or even problematic. But their efforts to learn about, to understand, and to work with schools will not only empower them, but also, and more importantly, will benefit those whom they serve. In this chapter I argue that school social workers need to recognize their immediate and broader environments, as represented by schools' ecosystemic and organizational characteristics, and then respond to the knowledge about their schools that they gather. In this way, school social workers can make their work relevant to those around them, providing attuned, relevant, and therefore effective school social work services.

RECOGNIZE THE IMMEDIATE AND BROADER ENVIRONMENT

At first, Alice found Wonderland a strange, incomprehensible, and at times threatening place. She encountered disappearing highways, accusatory pigeons, pebbles that turned into cakes, and a theft trial in which nonsensical poems served as evidence. Similarly, beginning school social workers may find themselves bewildered by the schools in which they work. Student needs may be trumped by faculty grudges. The school nurse may hold more power than the superintendent. The Halloween parade may take on the tension and political charge of a made-for-TV drama. The school social worker who can recognize her school's immediate and broader environments—particularly the characteristics that make her school seem like such a strange place—will be in a position to understand and in turn respond effectively to her professional Wonderland.

THE SCHOOL AS PART OF NESTED ECOLOGICAL SYSTEMS

This orientation is familiar to school social workers. It reflects the person-in-environment orientation that school social work candidates encounter from the earliest days of training, and that our profession's leaders have stressed throughout the history of our profession (Gibelman, 1999). When school social workers apply this familiar, essential perspective to their work in schools, they see themselves as professionals-in-organizations. Likewise, this perspective extends to students, parents, and educators whom school social workers encounter within schools. Schools have distinct systemic and organizational characteristics and are embedded in their communities and in our larger society.

This perspective, also suggested by Goren (1981), draws heavily from Bronfenbrenner's ecological systems theory (1979) as well as his later bio-ecological model of human development (Bronfenbrenner, 2005; Bronfenbrenner & Morris, 2006), which depicts the individual as a person who interacts with a set of nested, interrelated, reciprocally interacting systems. Allen-Meares (2010), Frey and Dupper (2005), Germain (2006), and Monkman (2009) all make this connection when discussing school social work. These systems expand outward from microsystems (smaller interactive systems such as family, peer groups, and school, in which the individual participates regularly) to mesosystems (the relationships that develop between two or more microsystems) to exosystems (contexts in which the individual does not necessarily participate directly, such as community organizations and school boards) to macrosystems (broad cultural systems that involve beliefs, customs, and patterns of behavior). Two aspects of ecological systems theory are key to understanding it and its relevance to work in schools: (1) these systems' interrelation to one another, and (2) the individual's capacity to coconstruct and shape (rather than just be shaped by) the systems in which he participates (Kondrat, 2002).

Schools are microsystems situated in nested environmental contexts. When the school social worker takes a professional-in-organization approach to her work, she sees the school as a microsystem that is, itself, made up of an array of smaller, interrelated microsystems (e.g., student peer groups, classrooms, teams, parent groups, and formal and informal faculty member groupings), interacting with one another as well as with exosystems (e.g., local and more distant governmental and nonprofit organizations) and broader macrosystems (e.g., a national culture that values individual rather than collective rights and responsibilities). Schools have the potential to shape, and are also subject to the influence of, the systems of which they are part. This perspective represents a critical first step of grasping how schools work, in that evolving, multiple, interlocking systems together shape day-to-day life in schools. When addressing ongoing conflict among high school students from different racial groups, for example, a school social worker would need to learn about a number of systems within and beyond the school. This might include peer groups, academic tracks and extracurricular opportunities within the school, student-educator relationships, youth development and civic resources within the community, and predominant cultural views of the different groups involved. Furthermore, a school social worker would consider from an ecosystemic perspective whether race factored into these different systems' qualities. For example, she might explore whether one group of students encountered differing levels of youth development resources in the community, or whether one group was disproportionately represented in a particular academic track within the school.

To better understand the systems of which the school is part, there are a number of steps that new school social workers can take. Periodic school-based needs assessments are an important start, and should involve, to begin with, an assessment of the school's needs and current uses of social work services. (See Bleyer and Joiner's chapter in this volume for information on conducting needs assessments in schools; see also Dudley [2014] for models of organization-level needs assessments.) Among the information that a school social worker gathers in a thorough needs assessment, it is important to include the following: how school social work services have been used to date, which groups and individuals have determined school social work priorities, strengths and needs among faculty and students, and recent events or trends that have affected the school (e.g., leadership turnover or changes in the school's enrollment). Needs assessments are enhanced by surveys or other tools that systematically provide data for school social workers and their colleagues to review and analyze.

Beginning school social workers will also benefit greatly from learning directly about the community in which their school sits. This work can begin with a walking, driving, or public transportation tour of the community in which they work, ideally with a colleague or community resident with extensive local knowledge. This information gathering can include efforts to learn about current and past local issues and politics, as well as the people living in the community, patterns of migration into or out of the community, and changes in the distribution of populations across a community (e.g., gentrification or recent growth of a population within the community). Census or other demographic information can be another helpful source of information on population growth, change, and distribution. Knowledge about one's school community should also incorporate an understanding of how factors such as race, ethnicity, and socioeconomic status have shaped the community over time. Cuban (2010) asserts that cities do not simply exist in the present, but rather evolve and adapt over time, bringing along layers of historical events that "are compressed into social, political and organizational patterns that inescapably influence current actions" (p. 2). It is these patterns—which shape people's opportunities, expectations, and interactions—that school social workers will benefit from understanding as they attempt to engage with community members (e.g., educators, school board members, students, parents, and service providers).

Furthermore, school social workers' knowledge of local, state, and national issues in education will help them to grasp the classroom experiences of educators, parents, and students. For example, contemporary shifts to Common Core curriculum, and the spread of charter schools as school reform models, and increasing emphasis on teacher performance evaluation all shape individuals' day-to-day experience of school. Gathering information about contemporary issues in education—at local, state, and national levels—is an activity that demands ongoing, deliberate effort. Had Alice assessed the situation around her only one time while she was in Wonderland, she might have ended up lost or trampled underfoot, as her circumstances and others' expectations of her changed in often unpredictable ways. To keep up with evolving issues in education, school social workers can consult national and local media (print, electronic, and broadcast) and education blogs. The social worker must read these sources with a critical eye, however, since they can at times reflect the biases of the individuals or organizations producing the work. Teachers and administrators can also share information about local, state, and national policies that affect their work.

ORGANIZATIONAL CHARACTERISTICS OF SCHOOLS

School social workers can also recognize and understand different organizational characteristics of their schools; this will help them make sense of how individuals in schools make decisions, prioritize, communicate, and address conflict. Three key organizational characteristics concern (1) the school's organizational culture, (2) structuring of power, and (3) openness toward its environment.

All organizations, including schools, have their own distinctive organizational culture, which Schein (1992) describes as "a pattern of shared basic assumptions that the group learned as it solved its problems of external adaptation and internal integration, that has worked well enough to be considered valid and, therefore to be taught to new members as the correct way to perceive, think, and feel in relation to those problems" (p. 12). In other words, organizations have determined the ways in which members approach, understand, and solve (or try to solve) the problems and challenges that come along with their line of work. While some scholars look at organizational culture as made up of meanings that are shared among members, others note that there can be disagreement about the nature of work in an organization and about the "correct" way to approach one's work (Martin, 1992). Similarly, we can recognize school cultures, from schools where children and adults contentedly follow time-honored traditions, to schools that prioritize innovation and see challenges to conventions as normal and expected, to schools where conflict seems like a permanent fixture. While some schools may embed their culture in highly codified and identifiable procedures and codes, other schools can have unspoken expectations that newcomers may find difficult to identify until they violate them. Culture varies from school to school, and can often vary across classrooms or academic departments (McLaughlin & Talbert, 2006). When the school social worker encounters something that is taken for granted as "the way this school works," she has found school culture.

The ways in which power is structured into schools can also help the beginning school social worker understand how her school functions. Power can be highly centralized, organized around a central office or leader; or it can be more diffuse, spread out among different groups or individuals. U.S. schools are known as decentralized—largely controlled at the local level—compared to schools in other nations where teaching and learning are tightly coordinated and overseen by national departments of education (e.g., in France, Singapore, and Cuba). Americans' preference for local control of schools is reflected in states' (not the U.S. Constitution's) legal responsibility to provide public education, the high proportion of school funds that come from state and local funding sources, and local school boards' right to choose their schools' curricula. Within this tradition, however, some schools and school systems are highly centralized (with substantial input from leaders over activities such as curriculum selection and hiring) while others operate with more substantial leeway. Some schools, for example, demonstrate distributed leadership across a number of individuals—specialists, teachers, parents, and external partners—rather than leaving leadership concentrated in the principal's or superintendent's role (Spillane, 2006). Power can be assigned formally, with authority and responsibility given to a particular position with a designated chain of command and span of authority, or can be informally claimed by individuals with schools (e.g., a charismatic or veteran teacher) or outside of them (e.g., civic leaders or donors). Varying ways in which power is designated, as well as the scope of individuals' and groups' powers, have different implications for the school social worker, who must understand and navigate existing power arrangements as she advocates for students, introduces change into the school system, and determines priorities for her work.

A third organizational characteristic of schools that is critical to understanding and working effectively within them is the school's degree of openness to its environment. Since ecological systems theory holds that different systems influence one another, it is unavoidable that schools will (and can) influence and be influenced by their surrounding environment—the community in which the school is located, cultural values and practices, policies at the local, state, and national levels, and events and trends in broader society (e.g., an increase in unemployment, or changes in migration patterns). Still, schools vary with regard to how much they engage with their surrounding environments. Efforts to develop and sustain school–community partnerships and initiatives that engage parents in schools reflect a school's openness to the environment. Such an approach can bring in resources such as services, knowledge, and local leadership that can benefit students and teachers. Some school administrators may fail to connect with external constituencies, for a variety of reasons. School leadership may try to buffer educators and students from distracting outside interferences (Bidwell, 2001) or may see the surrounding environment as one that holds little (or negative) value with regard to teaching and learning (Astor, Benbenishty, & Estrada, 2009; Bryk, Sebring, Allensworth, Luppescu, & Easton, 2010). Such isolation, however, runs the risk of cutting schools off from valuable human and nonhuman resources, and may also weaken educators' attunement to student and community strengths and needs. School social work practice in a closed school system could be difficult due to limitations of resources and school personnel's lack of familiarity with (or distrust of) outside resources. At the same time, practice in more-open systems offers needed resources but also requires mindful management of school-environment connections in order to ensure that they are coherent with the school's existing goals and initiatives (Newmann, Smith, Allensworth, & Bryk, 2001).

As a school social worker takes in organizational and ecological information on her school, she stands to gain important knowledge about who and what she will encounter in her work, as well as explanations for that which she encounters. This critical knowledge provides the basis for her actions in practice.

RESPOND THOUGHTFULLY WITH ATTUNED INTERVENTION

Alice did not just learn about the personalities and terrain of Wonderland because she was curious about them (which, to be fair, she was). New knowledge was critical in helping Alice understand her surroundings so that she could navigate the "wonders wild and new" that kept coming her way, and that grounded her responses to her surroundings and experiences. In the story, we see an increasingly informed Alice who was thoughtful about what she had at her disposal and how she used it. Alice was first alarmed as she drank a potion that shrunk her to a height of ten inches and then ate a cake that made her grow so tall that her head hit the room's ceiling. With time, though, Alice became more strategic about changing her size (intentionally rather than by accident), and less intimidated by the creatures she encountered. As this occurred, her responses to a seemingly endless march of surprises and challenges became calmer, more confident, and more effective. Similarly, ecological and organizational knowledge can ground new school social workers' choices of interventions that respond to situations, demands, and need. The use of such knowledge in choosing interventions can make them more attuned and, therefore, more effective and well received. The recognition that a school system is highly formalized, for example, would require a school social worker to work with formal channels as she advocates for students and brings innovative practices in to address existing needs. In this section I focus on three things that I suggest school social workers keep in mind as they strive to intervene in their schools in a responsive manner: (1) a strengths orientation toward the school system and its members, (2) thoughtful selection of intervention models and practices, and (3) responsiveness through role definition.

A Strengths Orientation

Social workers know that a strengths-based focus on individuals and families is critical to their work. A respect for clients' dignity and worth, as well as the diversity of life experiences, assets, and values that inform individuals' perspectives, is core to our profession, as is reflected in the National Association of Social Workers (NASW) Code of Ethics (2008). Rather than a deficit-based view of the challenges and problems that bring individuals into contact with the helping professions, social workers challenge themselves to identify client strengths and capacities that can be used to address any current difficulties. Theory and practice that explicitly take this perspective includes strengths-based assessment (e.g., Epstein, 1999), solution-focused brief therapy (e.g., Kelly, Kim, & Franklin, 2008; Lipchik, Derks, LaCourt, & Nunnally, 2012), positive psychology (e.g., Park, Peterson, & Seligman, 2004), the developmental assets model (e.g., Edwards, Mumford, Shillingford, & Serra-Roldan, 2007), and resilience theory (e.g., Werner & Smith, 2001).

The school and its community members should likewise be viewed from a strengths perspective. As in Wonderland, people, structures, and norms in schools can appear unusual, bizarre, nonproductive, or even damaging. School social workers are clearly responsible for acting on unsafe or unethical behavior they learn about. Beyond these duties, new school social workers can work with their colleagues to identify capacities within schools that have the potential to address individual, interpersonal, or more-systemic difficulties. Knowledge of a school's ecosystemic and organizational character-istics can serve a school social worker well. A base of committed parents and community members, for example, can make substantial changes in school climate and achievement where more-conventional school reform efforts have not gained traction (Warren & Mapp, 2011). Schools in communities that struggle with violence or socioeconomic isolation may have skilled, loyal teachers and leaders who are willing to innovate on behalf of their stu-dents (Astor et al., 2009; Bryk et al., 2010). Student populations judged as low-performing according to standardized test scores often possess diverse funds of knowledge drawing from household and community experiences that can contribute to their own and the school's growth (Gonzalez, Moll, & Amanti, 2013). Ask yourself: What resources exist in your school or its sur-rounding community that can extend the school's reach or your own pro-fessional reach?

Students, educators, school leaders, community members, and organi-zations possess strengths that can potentially benefit schools. When I was charged by a suburban school principal with the task of promoting Latino parent involvement, I found that parents in that particular school commu-nity could not attend traditional school events due to a lack of public trans-portation in that community, residing far from the school (in part due to dis-trict policies intended to promote racial and ethnic diversity in school enrollment by expanding the attendance area), and having work schedules that conflicted with the school schedule. After consulting with parents, teachers, and local organizations, I learned that a community organization that already served many of the parents I sought to engage was located near their homes and had evening hours. That organization's leader opened her doors to me, my school's teachers, and parents, and we had a series of par-ent-focused events there that were standing-room-only. Those events forged needed connections between parents and teachers. The process of looking at a school's resources and strengths, even when there are challenges or outright problems that demand attention, reframes school social work prac-tice from the remedy of deficits to the identification and channeling of a school's and community's unique strengths.

Thoughtful Selection of Intervention Models and Practices

Knowledge of a school's strengths and needs, along with its organizational and ecosystemic characteristics, can guide school social workers' selection of interventions when they are needed. This knowledge can help the school social worker identify the suitable focus (or foci) for intervention. Frey and Dupper (2005) claim that individual and small-group therapy is often over-subscribed in schools when broader, more-systemic interventions may stand a better chance at addressing the difficulties that students, families, and edu-cators face. Individual treatment to reduce student bullying behavior, for example, may be less effective at reducing a school's incidence of peer aggression than an approach that includes classroom and school-wide intervention (Howe, Marini, Haymes, & Tenor, 2013). Along these lines, intervention that engages teachers has been shown to positively affect student outcomes (Franklin, Kim, Ryan, Kelly, & Montgomery, 2012). Intervention methods such as response to intervention—RTI, and now referred to as multitiered system of supports, or MTSS (Clark & Alvarez, 2010)—and positive behavioral interventions and supports (PBIS) (Horner et al., 2009) take this approach, differentiating between universal, targeted (toward students identified as being at risk for academic or social difficulties) and more-intensive interventions (for smaller groups of students experiencing persistent difficulties). These models themselves are ecosystemically oriented. They acknowledge the presence of different systemic locations for intervention, and also suggest that macrosystemic community intervention may be more effective at addressing issues beyond the scope of what schools themselves can address.

Also important is the selection of interventions that are known to be effective in the school setting and with that school's particular population. Fortunately, today's school social workers work in an era where the base of evidence-based interventions continues to expand. Sources for such interventions include *The School Services Sourcebook* (Franklin, Harris, & Allen-Meares, 2013) and the list of federally and privately rated programs that promote healthy development and reduce violence from the Center for the Study and Prevention of Violence (2014). The importance of attuned intervention connects back to the school social worker's knowledge of the school, the microsystems it contains, and the systems in which it is embedded. How does this particular intervention fit with a school community's characteristics, strengths, and needs? Has that intervention been used effectively in school settings? Kelly, Raines, Stone, and Frey (2010) raise this question when discussing school social workers' adaptation of evidence-informed practices. They stress the importance of considering interventions' suitability for the school context, as well as their match with students' developmental level and cultural background.

Culturally competent practice is also essential to school social workers' responses to the support needs present at her school. Interventions may be proven for specific populations other than the population a school social worker is striving to serve. For example, Merrell, Gueldner, Ross, and Isava (2008) found that 44 percent of the students in their meta-analysis of bullying interventions were from the United Kingdom, which surfaced questions about those interventions' suitability for students with other sociocultural backgrounds. In addition to the matter of interventions' cultural suitability, it is important that school social workers consider how their actions will be perceived within a school community. The dramatic overrepresentation of African American parents among those reported for suspected abuse and neglect (Drake et al., 2011), for example, may contribute to suspicion of a school social worker's involvement in such reports in a predominantly African American school. Work in this area would need to address issues of cultural differences in childrearing practices and to maximize parent agency in dealing with child welfare organizations, in order to not engender mistrust of school social workers. Another matter relevant to culturally competent school social work practice is that involving educators' practice. Since the United States' teacher workforce remains predominantly white as our nation's population grows more racially and ethnically diverse, teachers' understanding of culturally relevant pedagogical and relational practices is essential. School social workers stand in a position to promote such efforts at classroom and school-wide levels by recognizing school-wide trends in student–teacher interactions and helping to arrange or provide professional learning experiences that address tensions or knowledge gaps in this area.

Responsiveness through Role Definition

A final aspect of responsiveness to the school community involves how the school social worker defines her role and sets priorities. While social work principles and values must guide these efforts, so must the matter of the particular school's strengths, needs, and priorities. If a school does not want or need small group treatment of students, parent involvement programs, or teacher professional development from its school social worker, for example, these services should not be a major thrust of the school social worker's defined role, even if that practitioner possesses a passion or particular skill in that area. School social workers in dynamic, complex school environments are best off defining their professional roles and responsibilities in collaboration with those whom they serve. Roles and responsibilities will likely evolve over time (sometimes in the period of a week or even a day). This reality may cause feelings of instability or even Wonderland-like disorientation, but a school social worker's ability to define her work as demands arise and shift reflects the responsiveness that school communities need and value.

CULTIVATE RELEVANCE TO THE SCHOOL COMMUNITY

By virtue of their recognition of and responsiveness to the broader school community, school social workers stand in a position to make themselves and their work relevant to their schools. Goren (1981) speaks of visibility, viability, and value as necessary characteristics that the school social worker must establish and promote in order to continue in her employment with a school (by making herself indispensable, receiving positive evaluations, and being allowed to control how she sets priorities for her work). I contend that continuation of employment as a school social worker is not a matter of strategy (nor, ethically, an end in itself), but instead is a matter of the school social worker's relevance. Educators want and fight to keep social workers who help them accomplish their goals, extend their reach, and give them valuable perspective on serving their shared students.

A school social worker's visibility and viability, as Goren suggests, are important. It is indeed important to be "seen in action" (Goren, 2006, p. 61) to be making meaningful contributions to a school community. A school social worker can make such contributions by figuratively rolling up her sleeves to help make a school work, whether by assisting with playground supervision, taking a leadership role in a crisis that affects the school, or volunteering for a school-wide, multidisciplinary committee. (All of these activities also present powerful opportunities to learn about the school and the individuals within it.) However, that visibility has the potential to reflect much more than professional self-interest or self-preservation. Visibility at the right places at the right times should reflect the school social worker's attunement to the school as an organization and as a unique, dynamic system. In other words, a school social worker's visibility is a signal that she is working in places and on issues that are important to those around her. A school social worker's visibility, viability, and value, then, are best integrated with the results of her assessment of the school. If a school is struggling under accountability mandates and has strong informal leadership, a school social worker can collaboratively identify areas of priority for the school's (and her) actions, as well as individuals with whom she can work to contribute to the school's response to these external pressures. If student mental health needs are shaped by pervasive community violence, the school social worker can make herself authentically visible, viable, and valuable by addressing student reactions to violence through three-tiered interventions and through collaboration with local organizations with expertise not only on treating the effects of violence, but also with expertise on the local community itself.

If a school social worker strives to become "important and significant to everyone and in every way" (Goren, 2006, p. 59), I suggest that she can most powerfully do this by gathering and responding to knowledge of how her school works and what strengths and needs it has.

CONCLUSION

After Alice awoke at the end of her adventure (and Carroll's story), she concluded "what a wonderful dream it had been" (Carroll, 1865/1948, p. 59). Given the frightening, confusing, and dumbfounding experiences she had in Wonderland, this conclusion is striking. By "wonderful," Alice seemed to refer to her experiences of newness, of solving problems, and of finding wisdom and courage. School social workers may find themselves working in a place of curious adventures where they will face unexpected challenges.

Under those circumstances, they can learn, take action, and influence school systems and practices. Some days, the school social worker may find herself feeling as if she is trying to hit a live hedgehog with an ornery flamingo in the middle of a croquet game that has no rules. Other days, the school social worker may feel like Alice when she successfully navigated playing cards that spoke menacingly to her, confident of what did and did not constitute a real threat.

This perspective on school social work is valuable. It stands as a reminder to school social workers to view the school as a dynamic organization embedded in a rich, complex, evolving ecology. In this way, each school represents an evolving reality. Schools should look somewhat unfamiliar and worthy of curiosity, like something that requires reflection, recognition, understanding, and attuned responsiveness.

References

Allen-Meares, P. (2010). *Social work services in schools* (6th ed.). New York: Pearson.

Astor, R. A., Benbenishty, R., & Estrada, J. (2009). School violence and theoretically atypical schools: The principal's centrality in orchestrating safe schools. *American Educational Research Journal, 46*(2), 423–461.

Bidwell, C. E. (2001). Analyzing schools as organizations: Long-term permanence and short-term change. *Sociology of Education, 74,* 100–114.

Bronfenbrenner, U. (1979). *The ecology of human development: Experiments in nature and design.* Cambridge, MA: Harvard University Press.

Bronfenbrenner, U. (2005). The bioecological theory of human development. In U. Bronfenbrenner (Ed.), *Making human beings human: Bioecological perspectives on human development* (pp. 3–15). Thousand Oaks, CA: Sage.

Bronfenbrenner, U., & Morris, P. A. (2006). The bioecological model of human development. In W. Damon & R. M. Lerner (Eds.), *Handbook of child psychology,* Vol. 1: *Theoretical models of human development* (6th ed., pp. 793–828). New York: John Wiley & Sons.

Bryk, A. S., Sebring, P. B., Allensworth, E., Luppescu, S., & Easton, J. Q. (2010). *Organizing schools for improvement: Lessons from Chicago.* Chicago: University of Chicago Press.

Carroll, L. (1948). *Alice's adventures in wonderland.* Retrieved from https://www.gutenberg.org/files/11/11-h/11-h.htm (Original work published 1865)

Center for the Study and Prevention of Violence. (2014). *Blueprints programs.* http://www.blueprintsprograms.com/allPrograms.php

Clark, J. P., & Alvarez, M. (2010). *Response to intervention: A guide for school social workers.* New York: Oxford University Press.

Cuban, L. (2010). *As good as it gets: What school reform brought to Austin.* Cambridge, MA: Harvard University Press.

Drake, B., Jolley, J. M., Lanier, P., Fluke, J., Barth, R. P., & Jonson-Reid, M. (2011). Racial bias in child protection? A comparison of competing explanations using national data. *Pediatrics, 127*(3), 471–478.

Dudley, J. (2014). *Social work evaluation: Enhancing what we do* (2nd ed.). Chicago: Lyceum Books.

Edwards, O. W., Mumford, V. E., Shillingford, M. A., & Serra-Roldan, R. (2007). Developmental assets: A prevention framework for students considered at risk. *Children & Schools, 29,* 145–153.

Epstein, M. H. (1999). The development and validation of a scale to assess the emotional and behavioral strengths of children and adolescents. *Remedial and Special Education, 20,* 258–262.

Franklin, C. G., Kim, J. S., Ryan, T. N., Kelly, M. S., & Montgomery, K. L. (2012). Teacher involvement in school mental health interventions: A systematic review. *Children and Youth Services Review, 34*(5), 973–982.

Franklin, C., Harris, M. B., & Allen-Meares, P. (2013). *The school services sourcebook: A guide for practitioners* (2nd ed.). New York: Oxford University Press.

Frey, A. J., & Dupper, D. R. (2005). A broader conceptual approach to clinical practice for the 21st century. *Children and Schools, 27*(1), 33–44.

Germain, C. (2006). An ecological perspective on social work in the schools. In R. Constable, C. R. Massat, S. McDonald, & J. P. Flynn (Eds.), *School social work: Practice, policy and research* (6th ed., pp. 28–39). Chicago: Lyceum Books.

Gibelman, M. (1999). The search for identity: Defining social work—past, present and future. *Social Work, 44,* 298–310.

Gonzalez, N., Moll, L., & Amanti, C. (2013). *Funds of knowledge: Theorizing practices in households, communities, and classrooms.* New York: Routledge.

Goren, S. G. (1981). The wonderland of social work in the schools, or how Alice learned to cope. *School Social Work Journal, 6*(1), 19–26.

Goren, S. (2006). The wonderland of social work in the schools, or How Alice learned to cope. In R. Constable, C. R. Massat, S. McDonald, & J. Flynn (Eds.), *School social work: Practice, policy, and research* (5th ed., 53–60). Chicago: Lyceum Books.

Horner, R. H., Sugai, G., Smolkowski, K., Eber, L., Nakasato, J., Todd, A. W., & Esperanza, J. (2009). A randomized, wait-list controlled effectiveness trial assessing school-wide positive behavior support in elementary schools. *Journal of Positive Behavior Interventions, 11*(3), 133–144.

Howe, E., Marini, J. W., Haymes, E., & Tenor, T. (2013). Bullying: Best practices for prevention and intervention in schools. In C. Franklin, M. B. Harris, & P. Allen-Meares (Eds.), *The school services sourcebook: A guide for school-based professionals* (2nd ed., pp. 473–480). New York: Oxford University Press.

Kelly, M. S., Kim, J. S., & Franklin, C. (2008). *Solution-focused brief therapy in schools: A 360-degree view of research and practice.* New York: Oxford University Press.

Kelly, M. S., Raines, J. C., Stone, S. I., & Frey, A. J. (2010). *School social work: An evidence-informed framework for practice.* New York: Oxford University Press.

Kondrat, M. E. (2002). Actor-centered social work: Re-visioning "person-in-environment" through a critical theory lens. *Social Work, 47*(4), 435–448.

Lipchik, E., Derks, J., LaCourt, M., & Nunnally, E. (2012). The evolution of solution-focused brief therapy. In C. Franklin, T. S. Trepper, W. J. Gingerich, & E. E. McCollum (Eds.), *Solution-focused brief therapy: A handbook of evidence-based practice* (pp. 3–19). New York: Oxford University Press.

Martin, J. (1992). *Cultures in organizations: Three perspectives.* New York: Oxford University Press.

McLaughlin, M. W., & Talbert, J. E. (2006). *Building school-based teacher learning communities: Professional strategies to improve student achievement*. New York: Teachers College Press.

Merrell, K. W., Gueldner, B. A., Ross, S. W., & Isava, D. M. (2008). How effective are school bullying intervention programs? A meta-analysis of intervention research. *School Psychology Quarterly, 23*(1), 26–42.

Monkman, M. (2009). The characteristic focus of social workers in schools. In C. R. Massat, R. Constable, S. McDonald, & J. P. Flynn (Eds.), *School social work: Practice, policy and research* (7th ed., pp. 30–48). Chicago: Lyceum Books.

National Association of Social Workers (NASW). (2008). *Code of ethics*. Retrieved from https://www.socialworkers.org/pubs/code/code.asp

Newmann, F. M., Smith, B., Allensworth, E., & Bryk, A. S. (2001). *School instructional program coherence: Benefits and challenges*. Chicago: Chicago Consortium on School Research.

Park, N., Peterson, C., & Seligman, M. E. P. (2004). Strengths of character and well-being. *Journal of Social and Clinical Psychology, 23*, 603–619.

Schein, E. H. (1992). *Organizational culture and leadership* (2nd ed.). San Francisco: Jossey-Bass.

Spillane, J. (2006). *Distributed leadership*. San Francisco: Jossey-Bass.

Warren, M. R., & Mapp, K. L. (2011). *A match on dry grass: Community organizing as a catalyst for school reform*. New York: Oxford University Press.

Werner, E. E., & Smith, R. S. (2001). *Journeys from childhood to midlife: Risk, resilience and recovery*. Ithaca, NY: Cornell University Press.

4

Evidence-Informed Practice in the Real World of School Social Work

Michael S. Kelly
Loyola University Chicago

SCHOOL SOCIAL WORKERS' USE OF EVIDENCE IN THEIR PRACTICE

In some ways, a chapter on evidence and school social work should be a nonstarter. Some could argue that this chapter should not need to be written for a book like this one. After all, if there is evidence for what works in school social work practice (and as we shall see in many chapters across this book, there is), isn't everybody already using that evidence? If evidence exists for specific interventions to address the common problems that students, families, teachers, and schools face everyday, wouldn't it be reasonable to assume that that evidence is already readily available for school social workers in the United States and around the world to access and use in their practices?

In fact, there are many reasons for a chapter like this one, especially in this eighth edition of this text. Despite a growing literature on the effectiveness of school social work practice across all three tiers (Allen-Meares, Montgomery, & Kim, 2013; Franklin, Kim, & Tripodi, 2009; Kelly, Raines, Stone, & Frey, 2010), this literature is often perceived by practitioners as hard to find and difficult to interpret (Raines, 2008). Even when they can find the work, it may not be in the form of empirical studies that fit specific school populations (Kelly, Raines, et al., 2010). Finally, a host of professional and structural barriers exist that make it challenging for contemporary school social work practitioners to find, appraise, and apply evidence (Powers, Bowen, & Bowen, 2011; Raines, 2004, 2008).

This chapter will include a clear definition of evidence-informed practice (EIP) in schools, and a rationale for why EIP matters. The processes of carrying out evidence-informed practice in schools will be detailed, as will be an exploration of the real-world obstacles to doing EIP in schools. Because evidence is not always available to address every problem school social workers deal with, this chapter will grapple with the limitations of EIP and what school social workers might do to utilize EIP when there is little or no relevant evidence for the problem they are working on. Finally, this chapter will discuss implications of EIP for diverse school settings and international school social work.

DEFINING EVIDENCE-INFORMED PRACTICE

EIP is defined for this chapter as a process of transparent, culturally sensitive, and pragmatic practice choices with a client that draws on the best available empirical evidence to help clients solve their problems. In a school context, this EIP approach is particularly useful in helping parents, teachers, and students understand the myriad problems that present in schools (Franklin & Kelly, 2009; Kelly, Raines, et al., 2010; Raines, 2008). EIP is often caricatured as being rigid or dependent solely on manualized treatments (Gibbs & Gambrill, 2002; Kelly, 2008). The EIP approach described in this chapter, based on the work of social work scholars like Gambrill (2001) and Gibbs (2003), is characterized by the use of evidence to inform practice choices that ultimately are implemented by a collaboration between the social work practitioner and his or her client, based on cultural, developmental, and ethical factors. This section describes the basic tenets of this EIP approach and describes the advantages of using it in school social work practice. Additionally, in the following section EIP resources and research findings will be shared to help readers quickly access the best available research evidence to enhance their service to children in schools.

Evidence-based practice (EBP) is a movement that began in medicine (Gambrill, 1999; Sackett, Rosenberg, Gray, Haynes, & Richardson, 1996) and quickly spread into mental health disciplines, including social work (Gibbs, 2003). The EIP movement in medicine and mental health has sought to equip health-care providers and mental health practitioners with the best and most current empirical evidence to help them assist their patients/clients (Gambrill, 2001; Gibbs, 2003). In addition to using practitioners' experience and practice wisdom, EIP challenges school social workers to collaborate with clients on solving client problems using interventions that emphasize client preferences and empirical evidence, rather than using interventions that solely emanate from the so-called expert status of the practitioner.

The EIP process being advanced in this chapter acknowledges the importance of the practitioner–client relationship in making EIP work. This chapter's approach to EIP preserves the all-important clinical relationship that school social workers create with their clients while still incorporating the best available empirical evidence to inform the choice of how best to intervene in the presenting problem of the school client. This crucial client–practitioner piece is at times absent from some of the discussions in educational settings of EIP. Indeed, the field has seen calls for empirically validated treatments (referred to as EVTs or ESTs) in numerous social work, psychological, education, and special education regulations and policy statements. These policy statements and laws have called for practitioners to use research-based, scientifically based, or empirically validated interventions in their work with children (Hoagwood & Johnson, 2003).

THE PROCESS OF BECOMING EVIDENCE INFORMED

The EIP process discussed in this chapter allows for the use of empirically validated treatments or empirically supported treatments, but not at the expense of failing to establish the school social worker–client rapport that is central to successful work in schools. It also values the practice wisdom of school social workers and client values, but not at the expense of privileging a school's social workers adherence to "what we've always done," which is really a form of authority-based practice that disempowers clients (Gambrill, 2001; Raines, 2008). Applications of an EIP process to practice can differ in small but significant ways for each client and problem context. An overall EIP process that we feature here tends to follow similar steps based on Gibbs's (2003) conceptual framework and includes the following:

1. Identification of a problem that the client (and often, in the case of children, the client system) wants to resolve.

2. Creation of an answerable question related to the problem. This answerable question should engage the interest of the client, speak to the client's particular context (culturally, developmentally, and socioeconomically), and assist either in understanding the problem more clearly or in selecting an appropriate and effective intervention.
3. Consultation of the evidence base by the school social worker (usually through online research databases) to identify the best available evidence to address the problem.
4. Presentation of that evidence in the next session to the client in concise and developmentally appropriate language to help the school social worker and client make decisions about next steps to take, including interventions to implement to address the problem.
5. Evaluation of the intervention plan undertaken with consideration either of termination or a repeat of this five-step process to address another problem that has arisen in treatment.

This process (Gibbs, 2003) can be seen in figure 4.1, and is elaborated in a case example at the end of the chapter.

This EIP process differs sharply from the typical way that EBP is understood in the field, where EBP is viewed as a set of empirically validated treatments or empirically supported treatments that have already been rigorously tested and essentially "approved" by an expert authority, often a governmental body or evidence-based clearinghouse (Kelly, Raines, et al., 2010). Where EIP is a verb (the process), this other version of EBP is reduced to a collection of nouns (the specific interventions) that though rigorously evaluated, may not relate well to the specific client context and concerns that school social workers see in actual practice (Raines, 2008; Thyer & Myers, 2011).

An additional way of looking at EIP is to consider what school social workers can do to address situations where the search for empirical evidence for their answerable EIP question comes up short. In this case, the tools often used in data-driven decision making in schools (most often seen in the response to intervention [RTI]/positive behavioral interventions and supports [PBIS] three-tiered frameworks that we detail in other chapters in

FIGURE 4.1   Evidence-based Practice Process for School Social Workers

Step 1: Identification of problem by client and school social worker
Step 2: Creating an answerable EIP question to address client's problem
Step 3: Consulting online databases to find the best available evidence for the EIP question
Step 4: Sharing the evidence with clients in accessible language and devising further interventions based on the evidence
Step 5: Evaluating the interventions generated by the EIP process and repeating the process as needed

this book) can be helpful in generating practice-based evidence (Kelly, 2014; Paternite, 2005; Raines, 2008). To do this, school social workers would first need to examine what is known about the specific answerable question, and if finding little or nothing, then design an intervention in collaboration with their school clients, with the understanding that they would collect EBP data on the impact of their intervention (usually through a pre-/posttest or single-subject design framework). While not evidence that would rise to the level of generalizability expected in peer-reviewed research studies, these data can nonetheless be invaluable in assisting school social workers to evaluate the impact of their interventions (Kelly, 2011).

WHY EVIDENCE-INFORMED PRACTICE?

All of that said, it is understandable that many school social workers reading this text might hear these calls for them to be more research-based and evidence-informed in their work as just more platitudes from out-of-touch academics. And while EIP can sound like yet another example of ivory tower scholars scolding practitioners, there are some compelling real-world reasons for school social workers to become more evidence informed in their work:

1. Our Outcomes Increasingly Matter. School social workers, like all educators today, are expected to demonstrate that the work they do with students makes a difference (Kelly, Raines, et al., 2010). Becoming comfortable with the tools involved in EIP increases the likelihood that school social workers will be employing interventions and strategies that will lead to positive social, behavioral, emotional, and academic outcomes for their schools (Franklin & Kelly, 2009).

2. Evidence-Informed Practice Is Embedded throughout Social Work's Code of Ethics. The NASW Code of Ethics (2008) has several places that directly address the need for social workers to integrate EIP into their work. In 5.02 (c) "Evaluation and Research" the Code of Ethics states, "(c) Social workers should critically examine and keep current with emerging knowledge relevant to social work and fully use evaluation and research evidence in their professional practice" (NASW, 2008). This fairly explicit exhortation to do EIP is supported by an earlier section on what constitutes competent social work practice. In 1.04 "Competence," the Code of Ethics states,

> (b) Social workers should provide services in substantive areas or use intervention techniques or approaches that are new to them *only after engaging in appropriate study, training, consultation, and supervision* from people who are competent in those interventions or techniques.

> (c) When generally recognized standards do not exist with respect to an emerging area of practice, social workers should exercise careful judgment

and take responsible steps (*including appropriate education, research, training, consultation, and supervision*) to ensure the competence of their work and to protect clients from harm. (NASW, 2008, emphasis added)

THE EVIDENCE-INFORMED PRACTICE

School social workers need to have an EIP lens to be able to do this work competently and ethically.

1. Our School Clients Want to Know "What Works," too. The interest in showing that we can provide effective services is not limited to principals and superintendents. The students, parents, and teachers that I served had their own ideas about evidence (often things that they saw on the Internet after a quick Google search or things they heard on the radio), and they would bring that information in and ask me what I thought "worked" for their specific problem.

While they were asking me this in part for whatever practice wisdom I could offer, they also had specific concerns that they wanted me to address based on "evidence" that they had picked up. To be able to bring EIP to bear on those conversations was invaluable, as it created a third party in the room (the evidence I was able to bring to the table) that allowed us to more openly discuss their concerns.

2. Most Importantly, We Want to Know What Works to Better Serve Our Clients. No school social workers I have ever met try to be ineffective or harmful to their clients. None of the school social workers I have trained over the years have told me that they want to conduct interventions or share information with clients that they believe will produce a neutral or poor outcome. The best of our field wants to be constantly learning and doing new things to help our clients, and EIP is a tool to ensure that we are following our ethical mandates to stay current with current research on key problems that our school clients face (Raines, 2008).

WHAT WE KNOW ABOUT THE STATE OF SCHOOL SOCIAL WORK RE: EVIDENCE-INFORMED PRACTICE

Since 1980 there have been more than forty rigorous empirical studies on school social work interventions (Allen-Meares et al., 2013; Franklin et al., 2009). The Franklin et al. (2009) meta-analysis for studies from 1980 to 2007 showed that school social work interventions had a weighted overall effect size of .23 for student externalizing problems (small effect size) and .40 for internalizing problems (medium effect size), indicating that school social work interventions can and do make meaningful differences for schools, though these effect sizes are often under-reported by researchers and governmental agencies when they tout "effective" programs, making it hard for practitioners to know how effective these programs really are (Powers et al., 2011). These findings compare to samples of studies conducted by other school mental health professionals and academic disciplines that show that a small but growing body of research exists that shows that school-based interventions work to increase social-emotional learning (SEL), decrease behavior problems, and improve overall school academic outcomes (Alvarez, Bye, Bryant, & Mumm, 2013; Baskin, Slaten, Sorenson, Glover-Russell, & Merson, 2010; Durlak, Weissberg, Dymnicki, Taylor, & Schellinger, 2011; Franklin, Kim, Ryan, Kelly, & Montgomery, 2012; Stone, Shields, Hilinski, & Sanford, 2013). This interest in EIP is reflected in a variety of recent published scholarly work in school social work (Franklin et al., 2012; Kelly, Raines, et al., 2010; Powers et al., 2011; Raines, 2008; Sabatino, Kelly, Moriarity, & Lean, 2013) and is an essential component of the School Social Work Association of America's new School Social Work National Practice Model (Frey et al., 2012).

Despite the growth in EIP resources and some clear evidence about what works in school social work, school social workers (and school mental health practitioners more broadly) report that they are not utilizing EIP regularly in their work (Evans, Koch, Brady, Meszaros, & Sadler, 2013; Kelly, Berzin, et al., 2010; Kelly & Lueck, 2011; Langley, Nadeem, Kataoka, Stein, & Jaycox, 2010). Practitioners report a myriad of barriers to doing EIP: high caseloads, multiple school assignments, crisis intervention needs, and overwhelming paperwork demands affect their ability to do EIP (Dupper, Rocha, Jackson, & Lodato, 2014; Kelly, Berzin, et al., 2010; Teasley, Canifield, Archuleta, Crutchfield, & Chavis, 2012). In a later section I will offer some further thoughts on the barriers to EIP in school social work based on our survey research and years of training school social workers and what might be done to overcome these barriers to EIP. First, let's take a look at a complex case and how EIP might be applied to it: the case of Marty.

EVIDENCE-INFORMED PRACTICE IN ACTION: THE CASE OF MARTY

Marty, a sixteen-year-old high schooler with Asperger's syndrome, an autism spectrum disorder (ASD), has great difficulty understanding the complexity of social relationships around him. He feels anxiety and depression as he struggles with the contrast of his expectations of himself and the actuality of his situation. Some classmates, noticing his awkwardness, tease him unmercifully; others are sympathetic, but reserved. His unusual behavior and growing stance of victimhood reinforces the teasing. With almost a phobia about numbers, structure, and time, he has a mathematics learning disability. His intelligence is fairly high, and his verbal skills are excellent. With his energy taken up with his situation, he does poorly academically. His teachers either come down hard on him or sympathize with him and modify expectations below his actual ability. At home his verbal abuse of his high-achieving younger sister is extreme. His mother feels caught in a protective relationship with him. She constantly modifies expectations in his favor. His father, a busy and successful engineer, withdraws from Marty into his work. Marty mainly sees himself as a victim, has very little awareness of his difficulty in social skills, and has little motivation to change. Although he is generally related to his situation, Colin, his school social worker, has worked with Marty for the past several years, but is wondering how best to help him now.

Marty's situation involves multiple transactions—with schoolmates, teachers, parents, and his sister. The school social worker must work with this constellation of issues and attempt to identify answerable questions with the EIP process to decide where first to intervene. Because Marty's situation could present itself with many options for doing EIP, I offer a range of questions that Colin might pursue with him, based on his interests:

- ◆ What school-based interventions are most effective for increasing the social skills of teenagers with ASD?
- ◆ What are the most important risk factors for adolescents with ASD for teachers and parents to be aware of, particularly in the areas of bullying and victimization?
- ◆ What are the key classroom modifications and accommodations that are needed for teenagers with ASD? What does not work in supporting students this age with ASD?

Colin would engage with the free evidence-informed resources noted at the back of this chapter (Step 3), likely going to ones that could describe ASD and related learning disability issues specifically (e.g., The Interactive Autism Network, National Center for Learning Disabilities), resources that give information about interventions for youths (e.g., tripdatabase.com, and the Substance Abuse and Mental Health Services Administration's [SAMHSA] National Registry of Evidence-based Programs and Practices [NRREP] Web site), and resources that suggest ways to modify the educational environment (de Bruin, Deppeler, Moore, & Diamond, 2013; Fleury et al., 2014). For example, there is a sizeable evidence base related to bullying issues in schools (Kelly, Raines, et al., 2010), and Colin may begin with Marty's concern about being a bullied victim, using the social work maxim, "Start where the client is." Colin is likely to work with the school environment around the bullying problem, to identify adults that Marty can turn to if he is being bullied, and to connect him with the school's peer mediation program when indicated. He will also likely help him explore these issues further (including how he acts in social situations) via the social skills group Colin would likely invite him to join, since he believes that meeting solely with him one on one is no longer productive, given his social issues.

Colin would also try to help Marty to refine his concerns and his question to include himself as well as the others in school (Steps 1 and 2). He will help Marty to discover that he can affect his situation. He will also work with teachers around Marty's identified academic concerns, and will likely work with the family around their concerns as part of his plan with Marty. He will use his collaborative relationship with the mental health clinic to get consultation, make an appointment for Marty, and do some possible planning in case his situation deteriorates.

Colin is also likely to use their long-term working relationship to help Marty and to plan together around social skill development. Once again, there is a literature on which to draw to find a range of social skills interventions, including participation in social skills groups, such as those described by LeCroy in chapter 27, tier 2 strategies discussed by Lindsey in chapter 26, and mental health interventions referred to by Kelly in chapter 32. For a good review of ASD-related interventions and various EBP resources, see Missouri Autism Guidelines Initiative (2012), and Bellini, Peters, Benner, and Hopf (2007).

There is available research evidence, mainly reflecting individual and family clinical interventions, for helping Marty with his social skills (Bellini et al., 2007; Gantman, Kapp, Orenski, & Laugeson, 2012; Laugeson, Frankel, Gantman, Dillon, & Mogil, 2012) and in better understanding his risk profile (Cappadocia, Weiss, & Pepler, 2012; Duerden et al., 2012; Simonoff et al., 2013). Another source of knowledge could be Colin's three years of experience in a high school as a source of practice-based evidence, especially if Colin has data on how kids like Marty have fared in their school.

This case illustrates the ways in which each relational situation is different, and the ways in which complex and multisystemic interventions are often needed to address mental health issues. The school social worker is not the only person working with Marty and his family. Colin brings together work done by the assistant principal (school bullying policy), Marty's teachers (classroom modifications and accommodations), his parents (learning about the risk factors for Marty to possibly do some psychoeducation with them), and a psychiatrist and psychologist from the mental health center (to discuss possible mental health/pharmacological treatments evaluated in the EIP process). The school social worker does not work toward a cure, but rather toward a better adjustment. His overall purpose is to help Marty to become more productively engaged in school, in the community, with his family, and with some friends.

Gibbs's basic five-step process differentiates itself in a number of ways as a social worker deals with the complexity of any problem, the developing evidence base, the actuality of a school and family situation, and the uniqueness of every relationship. Right now, Marty may not be ready for much of

Step 4. It may take quite a bit of work to assist him to come to a point where he feels he could do anything constructive about his problems. That said, the importance of putting clients in the position of interacting with evidence about their life is crucial: Marty will need to figure out how to get along better with his peers and his family and to seek help if he is being bullied, and possibly also to further learn more about the specific issues related to his disability. An EIP process can help him begin to see himself as not alone, and offer him hope that others with his struggles have found help.

However, that does not mean that other key members of Marty's client system cannot be helped by an EIP process, specifically Steps 4 and 5. Colin may need to work to create a lot of environmental modifications to create safety before Marty can begin to form a stable and productive relationship with any part of it. Moreover, each practitioner has a personal style. Colin knows what he thinks will be effective, based on his practice wisdom and previous work with Marty. He also has to adapt the possible interventions to the school context. EIP provides general principles of effective practice, now in balance with personal style and uniqueness, which arises from any real relationship of two persons. EIP can inform a general helping process, but the process is ultimately unique to the persons involved and to their relationship with each other.

FURTHER THOUGHTS ON EVIDENCE-INFORMED PRACTICE

As stated earlier, the approach to EIP described here should not be conflated with an EIP approach that emphasizes specific interventions over others because those interventions are considered empirically validated treatments that have been rigorously evaluated by intervention researchers using large sample sizes, control groups, and random assignment to treatment conditions (Kelly, Berzin, et al., 2010; Stone & Gambrill, 2007). While evidence from such studies (usually referred to as randomized controlled trials) are useful and often show strong evidence of intervention effectiveness, such evidence is ultimately unlikely to have a significant impact if the critical components of client preference and school social worker practice wisdom are removed from the process and made subservient to the intervention itself. The EIP process advocated in this chapter provides for numerous advantages for school social workers wishing to become more evidence-based and to increase their engagement with their clients. Advantages of using this EIP process approach include (1) the ability for school social workers to feel confident that they are using the best available evidence to help clients with their problems; (2) an increase in engagement between client and school social workers as they work together collaboratively on client problems (many clients come to an EIP session eager to hear "what the evidence says"); and (3) enhancement of cultural competency skills for school social workers, as the EIP process discussed here challenges practitioners to adapt empirical evidence to a client's cultural contexts.

Additionally, a robust finding in the psychotherapy literature indicates that the therapist–client alliance and client strengths are more important for psychotherapy treatment effectiveness than are specific techniques (Duncan, Miller, Wampold, & Hubble, 2010; Wampold, 2001). Practitioners will need to cultivate a degree of skepticism and critical thinking skills when presented with interventions that are called "best practices" for treating childhood mental health disorders, pending further evidence that specific ingredients of therapeutic interventions with children make the most difference for most students. While it is certainly possible that programs and interventions may someday become universal best practices for students with specific mental health disorders, the evidence base is still too thin to state categorically that specific school-based interventions for childhood mental health disorders are effective for most children most of the time, without also considering client preferences, client comorbidity factors (e.g., children who are diagnosed with both attention deficit hyperactivity disorder and anxiety), the skills of the practitioners delivering the intervention, and other socioeconomic/cultural/developmental variables that are often screened out of the intervention research process (Gibbs, 2003; Mullen, Bellamy, Bledsoe, & Francois, 2007).

BARRIERS TO EVIDENCE-INFORMED PRACTICE IN SCHOOLS

Earlier in the chapter we discussed some research findings that indicate that there are significant barriers that affect why so many school social workers report not consistently using EIP in their work. In addition to the empirical literature cited earlier, I also want to offer some of my own practice wisdom here based on my fourteen years as a school social worker as well as ten years as a leader of Loyola's Family and School Partnership Program (Kelly, Bluestone-Miller, Mervis, & Fuerst, 2012), a program of training and consultation groups that has brought EIP tools and technical assistance to hundreds of school-based mental health practitioners in the past decade. Here they are, in no particular order:

1. Access to Evidence-Informed Practice Resources. One of the most perplexing aspects of trying to be an EIP school social worker in the United States is the restricted access most practitioners experience when they try to search for evidence-based resources. Many of these resources are free, but for most school social workers, their access to up-to-date journals and academic books ends when they graduate from their master's program, due to the subscription paywall that is imposed on graduates who no longer have active student accounts at their university (Raines, 2008). This disconnect is not true of other countries who have more fully embraced open-source publishing and EIP in general, but is unfortunately a real and persistent barrier here (Gambrill, 2006; Thyer & Myers, 2011).

2. What to Do When You Find Something (How Do You Appraise the Evidence?). This is a serious issue that cuts across multiple fronts: the preservice training school social workers got in reading and appraising empirical research (Berzin & O'Connor, 2010; Kelly, Berzin, et al., 2010), the persistent push to view EIP as solely a collection of interventions on some EBP list that practitioners should just do without questioning, and the general unease some school social workers have with the idea of evidence as something that trumps other qualities of effective interventions (e.g., the school social worker–student relationship). What could be a relatively straightforward set of appraisal skills (outlined in figure 4.1) can feel unnecessarily cumbersome and challenging to practitioners who are not themselves ready to do this appraisal.

3. Time, Time, Time. There is a strong perception among practitioners that this approach simply takes too much time. Given how hard it still is to do EIP due to the limited access issues noted above, this is a fair critique, especially because of what is known about the many tasks that affect school social workers' time (Allen-Meares, 1994; Kelly, 2008; Kelly, Berzin, et al., 2010). This is also not new to school social workers trying to do EIP: one of the founders of EBM (Sackett) wrote about the need to adapt the EIP steps to specific contexts (Gambrill, 2006). In my own consultation with practitioners, I recommend that they start small, selecting no more than five students on their regular caseload to do EIP in the first year, and using those findings in collaboration with their school social work department to develop a living library of resources that the entire department can begin to access over time.

4. Motivation: The Comforts of Authority-based Practice. One of the toughest barriers to get over with EIP is the one that is hardest to admit to ourselves as practitioners: EIP is hard to do, and it can at times threaten our desire to feel confident in what we know as school-based experts when our EIP searches reveal little or no evidence for the questions we have cocreated with clients (Kelly, 2008). In many ways, it can be easier to stay set in our ways in our own authority-based practice and to not look for new evidence that might change how we view our work with our school clients. However, at the risk of being authority-based myself in writing this, in fourteen years of doing this work and now almost a decade of teaching it, I can say that EIP is actually not just good for our clients—it is good for us. It allows us to step out of the expert role and instead join with our clients in a way that makes the hierarchical relationship inherent in a client–worker relationship more flat and more collaborative (Gambrill, 1999; Kelly, 2008; Raines, 2008).

CONCLUSION

EIP enters its third decade as a vital but still underutilized set of tools in school social work practice. The push for school social workers to be more data-driven and to use EBPs in their day-to-day work appears to be here to stay (Kelly, Frey, & Anderson-Butcher, 2011). The challenges of increasing access to EIP resources for practitioners will continue to be a keen concern of school social work researchers (Powers et al., 2011; Sabatino et al., 2013). Through the various chapters that follow in this book, I hope that the ninth edition of this volume will find EIP becoming even more a standard of practice in our field.

References

Allen-Meares, P. (1994). Social work services in schools: A national study of entry-level tasks. *Social Work, 39*(5), 560–565.

Allen-Meares, P., Montgomery, K. L., & Kim, J. S. (2013). School-based social work interventions: A cross-national systematic review. *Social Work, 58*(3), 253–262.

Alvarez, M. E., Bye, L., Bryant, R., & Mumm, A. M. (2013). School social workers and educational outcomes. *Children & Schools, 35*(4), 235–243.

Baskin, T. W., Slaten, C. D., Sorenson, C., Glover-Russell, J., & Merson, D. N. (2010). Does youth psychotherapy improve academically related outcomes? A meta-analysis. *Journal of Counseling Psychology, 57*, 290–296.

Bellini, S., Peters, J. K., Benner, L., & Hopf, A. (2007). A meta-analysis of school-based social skills interventions for children with autism spectrum disorders. *Remedial and Special Education, 28*(3), 153–162.

Berzin, S. C., & O'Connor, S. (2010). Educating today's school social workers: Are school social work courses responding to the changing context? *Children & Schools, 32*(4), 237–249.

Cappadocia, M. C., Weiss, J. A., & Pepler, D. (2012). Bullying experiences among children and youth with autism spectrum disorders. *Journal of Autism and Developmental Disorders, 42*(2), 266–277.

de Bruin, C. L., Deppeler, J. M., Moore, D. W., & Diamond, N. T. (2013). Public school–based interventions for adolescents and young adults with an autism spectrum disorder: A meta-analysis. *Review of Educational Research, 83*(4), 521–550.

Duerden, E. G., Oatley, H. K., Mak-Fan, K. M., McGrath, P. A., Taylor, M. J., Szatmari, P., & Roberts, S. W. (2012). Risk factors associated with self-injurious behaviors in children and adolescents with autism spectrum disorders. *Journal of Autism and Developmental Disorders, 42*(11), 2460–2470.

Duncan, B. L., Miller, S. D., Wampold, B. E., & Hubble, M. A. (2010). *The heart and soul of change: Delivering what works in therapy*. Washington, DC: American Psychological Association Press.

Dupper, D. R., Rocha, C., Jackson, R. F., & Lodato, G. A. (2014). Broadly trained but narrowly used? Factors that predict the performance of environmental versus individual tasks by school social workers. *Children & Schools, 36*(2), 71–77.

Durlak, J. A., Weissberg, R. P., Dymnicki, A. B., Taylor, R. D., & Schellinger, K. (2011). The impact of enhancing students' social and emotional learning: A meta-analysis of school-based universal interventions. *Child Development, 82*, 474–501.

Evans, S. W., Koch, J. R., Brady, C., Meszaros, P., & Sadler, J. (2013). Community and school mental health professionals' knowledge and use of evidence based substance use prevention programs. *Administration and Policy in Mental Health and Mental Health Services Research, 40*(4), 319–330.

Fleury, V. P., Hedges, S., Hume, K., Browder, D. M., Thompson, J. L., Fallin, K., . . . & Vaughn, S. (2014). Addressing the academic needs of adolescents with autism spectrum disorder in secondary education. *Remedial and Special Education, 35*(2), 68–79.

Franklin, C., & Kelly, M. S. (2009). Becoming evidence-informed in the real world of school social work practice. *Children & Schools, 31*(1), 46–56.

Franklin, C. G., Kim, J. S., Ryan, T. N., Kelly, M. S., & Montgomery, K. L. (2012). Teacher involvement in school mental health interventions: A systematic review. *Children and Youth Services Review, 34*(5), 973–982.

Franklin, C., Kim, J. S., & Tripodi, S. J. (2009). A meta-analysis of published school social work practice studies 1980–2007. *Research on Social Work Practice, 19*(6), 667–677.

Frey, A. J., Alvarez, M. E., Sabatino, C. A., Lindsey, B. C., Dupper, D. R., Raines, J. C., . . . & Norris, M. P. (2012). The Development of a National School Social Work Practice Model. *Children & Schools, 34*(3), 131–134.

Gambrill, E. (1999). Evidence-based practice: An alternative to authority-based practice. *Families in Society: The Journal of Contemporary Social Services, 80*(4), 341–350.

Gambrill, E. (2001). Social work: An authority-based profession. *Research on Social Work Practice, 11*(2), 166–175.

Gambrill, E. (2006). Evidence-based practice and policy: Choices ahead. *Research on Social Work Practice, 16*(3), 338–357.

Gantman, A., Kapp, S. K., Orenski, K., & Laugeson, E. A. (2012). Social skills training for young adults with high-functioning autism spectrum disorders: A randomized controlled pilot study. *Journal of Autism and Developmental Disorders, 42*(6), 1094–1103.

Gibbs, L. E. (2003). *Evidence-based practice for the helping professions: A practical guide with integrated multimedia,* Vol. 1. Independence, KY: Cengage Learning.

Gibbs, L., & Gambrill, E. (2002). Evidence-based practice: Counterarguments to objections. *Research on Social Work Practice, 12*(3), 452–476.

Hoagwood, K., & Johnson, J. (2003). School psychology: A public health framework. *Journal of School Psychology, 41*(1), 3–21.

Kelly, M. S. (2008). *The domains and demands of school social work practice: A guide to working effectively with students, families and schools.* New York: Oxford University Press.

Kelly, M. S. (2011). Data-driven decision making in school-based mental health: How is it possible? *Advances in School Mental Health Promotion, 4*(4), 2–4.

Kelly, M. S. (2014). Response to intervention in schools. In *Encylcopedia of Social Work.* Washington, DC: National Association of Social Workers. doi:10.1093/acrefore/ 9780199975839.013.1013

Kelly, M. S., Berzin, S. C., Frey, A., Alvarez, M., Shaffer, G., & O'Brien, K. (2010). The state of school social work: Findings from the national school social work survey. *School Mental Health, 2*(3), 132–141.

Kelly, M. S., Frey, A. J., & Anderson-Butcher, D. (2011). Writing the job description for school social workers in 2031. *Children & Schools, 33*(2), 67–69.

Kelly, M. S., & Lueck, C. (2011). Adopting a data-driven public health framework in schools: Results from a multi-disciplinary survey on school-based mental health practice. *Advances in School Mental Health Promotion, 4*(4), 5–12.

Kelly, M. S., Raines, J., Stone, S., & Frey, A. (2010). *School social work: An evidence-informed framework for practice.* New York: Oxford University Press.

Kelly, M. S., Bluestone-Miller, R., Mervis, B., & Fuerst, R. (2012). The Family and School Partnership Program: A framework for professional development. *Children & Schools, 34*(4), 249–252.

Langley, A. K., Nadeem, E., Kataoka, S. H., Stein, B. D., & Jaycox, L. H. (2010). Evidence-based mental health programs in schools: Barriers and facilitators of successful implementation. *School Mental Health, 2*(3), 105–113.

Laugeson, E. A., Frankel, F., Gantman, A., Dillon, A. R., & Mogil, C. (2012). Evidence-based social skills training for adolescents with autism spectrum disorders: The UCLA PEERS program. *Journal of Autism and Developmental Disorders, 42*(6), 1025–1036.

Missouri Autism Guidelines Initiative. (2012). *Autism spectrum disorders: Guide to evidence-based interventions.* Retrieved from http://autismguidelines.dmh.mo.gov/documents/Interventions.pdf

Mullen, E. J., Bellamy, J. L., Bledsoe, S. E., & Francois, J. J. (2007). Teaching evidence-based practice. *Research on Social Work Practice, 17*(5), 574–582.

National Association of Social Workers (NASW). (2008). *Code of ethics.* Retrieved from https://www.socialworkers.org/pubs/code/code.asp

Paternite, C. E. (2005). School-based mental health programs and services: Overview and introduction to the special issue. *Journal of Abnormal Child Psychology, 33*(6), 657–663.

Powers, J. D., Bowen, N. K., & Bowen, G. L. (2011). Evidence-based programs in school settings: Barriers and recent advances. *Journal of Evidence-based Social Work, 7*(4), 313–331.

Raines, J. C. (2004). Evidence-based practice in school social work: A process in perspective. *Children & Schools, 26*(2), 71–85.

Raines, J. C. (2008). *Evidence based practice in school mental health.* New York: Oxford University Press.

Sabatino, C. A., Kelly, E. C., Moriarity, J., & Lean, E. (2013). Response to intervention: A guide to scientifically based research for school social work services. *Children & Schools, 35*(4), 213–223.

Sackett, D. L., Rosenberg, W. M. C., Gray, J. A. M., Haynes, R. B., & Richardson, W. D. (1996). Evidence based medicine: What it is and what it isn't. *British Medical Journal, 31*(2), 71–72.

Simonoff, E., Jones, C. R., Baird, G., Pickles, A., Happé, F., & Charman, T. (2013). The persistence and stability of psychiatric problems in adolescents with autism spectrum disorders. *Journal of Child Psychology and Psychiatry, 54*(2), 186–194.

Stone, S., & Gambrill, E. (2007). Do school social work textbooks provide a sound guide for education and practice? *Children & Schools, 29*(2), 109–118.

Stone, S., Shields, J. P., Hilinski, A., & Sanford, V. (2013). Association between addition of learning support professionals and school performance: An exploratory study. *Research on Social Work Practice, 23*(1), 66–72.

Teasley, M., Canifield, J. P., Archuleta, A. J., Crutchfield, J., & Chavis, A. M. (2012). Perceived barriers and facilitators to school social work practice: A mixed-methods study. *Children & Schools, 34*(3), 145–153.

Thyer, B. A., & Myers, L. L. (2011). The quest for evidence-based practice: A view from the United States. *Journal of Social Work, 11*(1), 8–25.

Wampold, B. (2001). *The great psychotherapy debate: Models, methods, and findings.* Mahwah, NJ: Erlbaum.

5

School Social Work Supervision

Robin Bluestone-Miller
Amy Greenberg
Bonnie Mervis
Adjunct Faculty, Family and School Partnerships Program,
Loyola University Chicago

Michael S. Kelly
Loyola University Chicago

- ◆ School Social Work in the Context of Educational Reform
- ◆ Domains of Supervision
- ◆ The Danielson Framework and School Social Work Supervision
- ◆ Elements of Successful Supervisory Relationships in School Social Work
- ◆ Models of School Social Work Supervision
- ◆ A Model of School Social Work Consultation and Supervision: The Family and School Partnerships Program

School social work occupies a unique place within the field of social work, which creates a need for specialized supervision. In contrast to other areas of social work practice, many school social workers report no direct social work supervision in their school settings after their initial experience as field supervisees in their school social work internships (Kelly, Berzin, et al., 2010). Supervision or consultation is considered a necessary component in all areas of social work (National Association of Social Workers [NASW], 2012): it is important in helping practitioners develop increased knowledge and competence, it is necessary for state licensure, and it helps to protect social workers in instances where their competence or decisions come into question.

School social work is rooted within both the values and practices of social work and those of education, which creates special challenges for school social workers (Phillippo & Blosser, 2013). They are bound by educational mandates and must deliver many of their services within the framework of policies set by the federal government, their states, and their school districts. Some of these policies may be at odds with basic social work values (Garrett & Barretta-Herman, 1995). Two examples: School social workers may be expected to share information with teachers that the social worker believes to be confidential. Or a school policy that permits only heterosexual teen couples to attend school dances would work against the social justice imperative of the social work profession.

There are other aspects of school social work that also present challenges, particularly given that survey research on school social work practice has shown that school social workers are often the only mental health professional many students and families encounter regularly (Kelly, Berzin, et al., 2010). Students present with a wide range of issues, family situations, medical and neurological conditions, as well as significant economic and environmental challenges. The school social worker is often the only mental health professional in his or her building(s) and is expected to be knowledgeable about all of these areas. Many school social workers report feeling isolated, and report that they have a need to share ideas and gain input about what interventions are most appropriate. Supervision is one way to address these needs (Kelly, 2008; Kelly, Bluestone-Miller, Mervis, & Fuerst, 2012).

The context of schools tends to challenge school social work practitioners to intervene at both the individual and school-wide levels to address student problems. This presents both challenges and opportunities for intervention. School social workers often are involved in prevention programs within their schools regarding bullying, drug use, and violence; provide education about social/emotional issues to teachers and parents; and work with classrooms, groups of students, and faculty (Kelly, Raines, Stone, & Frey, 2010). While providing these services, school social workers are required to follow laws regarding education, special education, and all of the current trends in education such as least restrictive environment, multitiered system of support, and positive behavioral interventions and supports. They must be able to deliver their services within the guidelines of these initiatives, provide evidence-based interventions, write measurable goals, collect data, and chart progress (Alvarez et al., 2012; Peckover et al., 2012). Collaboration with teachers and administrators to advocate for children and to problem-solve is also a main component of the school social workers' jobs (Berzin et al., 2011). Supervision can help school social workers stay current with laws and education policy.

In providing this wide range of services in a secondary setting, school social workers need a firm grasp on the boundaries of confidentiality and other ethical issues. Helping school social workers navigate complicated situations concerning confidentiality and ethics is an important component of supervision. Supervisors can help the workers to clarify the ethical issues and determine what information should be shared or what action taken (Garrett, 2012; see also chapters 6 and 7, this volume, on ethics and confidentiality issues). Supervisors can also help school social workers develop practices that address these issues with families and help them deal with administrators and teachers who may be pressing for information they believe they cannot share. Teachers and administrators are bound by somewhat different confidentiality requirements than social workers are (Association of American Educators, 2013; National Education Association, 2014). Nonetheless, educators are responsible for the children they serve and need adequate and accurate information on which to base decisions. Knowledge about a student's social/emotional challenges may help a teacher understand a child's unusual behaviors and respond more empathically and effectively. The need to share information, however, can lead to ethical dilemmas for school social workers who feel caught between their obligation to maintain confidentiality and the demands of the professionals who control their employment. There is the further dilemma posed by the individualized education program process, where the information gathered is often expected to be shared with the team (Raines & Dibble, 2010; see also chapters 6 and 16, this volume, on ethical decision making and adaptive behavior).

All of these aspects of school social work practice create a strong need for supportive and knowledgeable supervision, which may not always be available. Based on the authors' collective years of practice in schools, many school social workers are supervised by people outside the field of social work, such as principals or special education coordinators. While such supervision can provide needed administrative and educational support/ knowledge, it does not provide adequate supervision for practitioners' clinical or ethical needs specific to the mental health role they play. Hensley (2003) conducted research on the value of clinical social workers providing supervision for social workers. She found that both students' and new clinicians' experiences with social work supervisors were highly influential in the formation of their professional competence and identity. Although there are still few empirical studies that show the benefit of supervision on these outcomes (Bogo & McKnight, 2006; Hair, 2013), the supervisors in Hensley's study helped lessen stress and burnout: "Obviously supervisors serve as role models to the young social workers they supervise and this gives added emphasis to the importance of those qualities in a supervisor that not only enhance teaching and training but also are associated with clients receiving good care" (Hensley, 2003, p. 101).

One state association, the Illinois Association of School Social Workers (IASSW; 1989), has incorporated these concerns and values into their supervision and evaluation position statement:

IASSW endorses the position that all school social workers have a right to appropriate supervision and evaluation by a qualified social worker. . . . The school setting is a secondary social work practice area where the majority of staff is not trained in social work practices and theory. Generally, school administrators are not trained to understand social work methodology. Therefore, different qualifications are necessary to provide meaningful supervision to the school social worker. For supervision to be effective, it must provide an opportunity for growth and exchange of ideas. It is ideal for school social workers to be supervised by qualified school social workers; however, if this is not possible, it is advised to provide a consulting technical supervisor and/or access to other school social workers for consultation. Therefore, IASSW advocates that all school social workers be supervised and evaluated by certified social work supervisors. (IASSW, 1989)

SCHOOL SOCIAL WORK IN THE CONTEXT OF EDUCATIONAL REFORM

When one of the authors was a social work graduate student during the 1970s, her supervisor at a suburban high school informed her that she was not to tell teachers any information about the students with whom she was working. He said, "Tell them it is confidential." Of course, that was before educational reform. There was no formal referral process for support services or individualized education programs or any kind of data gathering where one had to show that social work services were having a positive impact behaviorally or academically. At this suburban high school, parents requested social work services for their child because the child had no friends or the parents were going through a divorce. Teachers requested social work services because a student had behavioral problems. The social work department was seen as a mini–mental health clinic that operated in parallel with the educational system. Sometimes parents and school social workers collaborated about the child's issues or there was a referral to a community agency or private psychiatrist. It was a rare occasion when the teacher, social worker, and student met to discuss how to remove barriers to learning.

Fast forward to 2002 where the emphasis on educational outcomes and accountability started to take hold with the No Child Left Behind Act. There was concern about the different levels of academic performance of students from diverse racial, ethnic, and economic backgrounds (Barry, 2005). Increasing numbers of students were being diagnosed with attention deficit hyperactivity disorder, autism spectrum disorders, and issues caused by posttraumatic stress disorder related to community violence, and school bullying. All of these issues challenged educational systems to look for new intervention models in schools, as required by the Individuals with Disabilities Educational Improvement Act of 2004. This act supported the use of evidence-based interventions and required these services to demonstrate measureable student improvement (Kelly, Raines, et al., 2010).

Over the past decade, there has been a tremendous shift in the role of the school social worker from the focus on providing individual and small-group work to a capacity-building, multitiered approach (Dupper, Rocha, Jackson, & Lodato, 2014; Kelly, Frey, et al., 2010). An important role of the supervisor is to help school social workers become comfortable collecting data and using these data to inform the next step with students. Because graduate schools do not always teach students about data collection and evidence-informed interventions, most new school social workers need support in becoming adept at using a comprehensive approach that targets multiple intervention agents (teachers, parents, peers) and intervenes at multiple levels (school, home, community) (Kelly, Frey, et al., 2010). With such a challenging and complex role, support through supervision appears to be critical.

Since school social work practice requires this complex model that includes the use of systemic interventions, supervisors must be well versed in school-wide interventions, as well as individual, group, and classroom approaches. An article by Frey and Dupper (2005) about the broader role for the twenty-first century recommended a clinical quadrant model of school social work. By using an ecological approach, school social workers can design interventions that focus on the school environment and systemic change as well as interventions that are directed toward the individual, small groups, or families. Today when teachers want to talk about students, school social workers have many tools to offer and a lot to talk about with them!

DOMAINS OF SUPERVISION

Having an outstanding supervisor can set supervisees on a solid footing that will influence them for their entire careers. Historically, our field has identified three kinds of supervision: administrative/managerial, educational/supportive, and clinical (NASW, 1999). Recent scholarship has deepened this focus to address four main tasks for supervisors of social workers: (1) supervising direct practice, (2) assisting social workers with their professional impact on the systems they serve, (3) promoting continued learning on the part of the supervisee, and (4) addressing issues related to the specific social work job context (paperwork, billing, hours, etc.) (Shulman, 2013). Because there may be overlap in some school districts for the areas Shulman identifies and because, for many of us, there has never been a direct supervisor in our school social work career who was a school social worker after the initial field experience, we concentrate on three historical areas of supervision in this chapter.

Administrative/Managerial Supervision

Administrative supervision is necessary to maintain effective school social work practice and to ensure that staff adheres to best practice guidelines.

Administrative/managerial type supervision involves the day-to-day operations of the school social worker. It includes record-keeping, compliance with regulations, time management, and documentation. Staff that may provide administrative supervision could be the school principal, student services director, social work manager, and/or special education coordinator. This individual supervisor may be an appropriate person to provide day-to-day supervision, but cannot fully address social work practice issues.

Unlike many other areas of social work practice, school social work is a subspecialty where practitioners consistently report not having a direct supervisor who is a social worker (Kelly, 2008; Kelly, Berzin, et al., 2010). While the supervision provided by a principal or special education director is essential, it is problematic when it comes to providing direct clinical supervision and empowering school social workers to become more effective in their practice. It is often not relevant to the daily functions of the role of a school social worker, but is instead designed to address the overall needs of faculty and staff in a school.

Educational/Supportive Supervision

Educational supervision for school social workers mandates that the supervisor have a knowledge base and experience in the practice of school social work. Practice issues address a variety of areas, including appropriate clinical techniques, proper implementation of best practices, specific case consultation, building a therapeutic alliance, and skill-building. The supervisor should also be aware of resources and tools that clinicians need to further enhance their effectiveness. Supportive supervision has been evidenced to promote job satisfaction (Staudt, 1997) and to encourage self-care to minimize compassion fatigue and burnout (Garrett & Barretta-Herman, 1995). Supportive supervision may focus on clinicians' mission, values, and ethics, as well as on job satisfaction. This approach to supervision would ultimately help to provide a balance between personal boundaries and demands within the milieu. Field instruction experiences should have an educational and supportive supervision component. The participation of the supervisee in educational opportunities, professional developments, workshops, seminars, in-services, trainings, or school-based team building is critical to the clinicians' professional growth. It is the job of the supervisor to ensure that the supervisee has these types of opportunities.

Clinical Supervision

Clinical supervision looks very different from administrative/managerial supervision, but may overlap with educational/supportive supervision. This type of supervisor will have a professional degree and be experienced in the same discipline as the school social worker. Before starting any relationship, social workers know that setting and measuring goals is the first order of business. The same is true for the clinical supervisory relationship. By asking the supervisee questions about what he or she wishes to learn and accomplish in supervision, the supervisor is acting as a good role model and mirrors a good client–social worker partnership. Most supervisors have the supervisee assess his or her own strengths and weaknesses initially and at frequent intervals thereafter. Simultaneously, the supervisee should also be giving feedback to the supervisor about how things are going. Because many school social workers do not have a supervisor who has an MSW (master of social work degree), they are often required to seek this supervision from private practitioners, or from a program like Loyola University's Family and School Partnerships Program, detailed later in this chapter.

THE DANIELSON FRAMEWORK AND SCHOOL SOCIAL WORK SUPERVISION

Currently more school systems are using an evaluation tool that has a relevant rubric. For instance, the School Social Work Association of America (SSWAA) is recommending the Danielson framework as a way to evaluate school social workers (SSWAA, 2013). Charlotte Danielson has become a national expert in establishing frameworks in various forms of evaluations on teacher effectiveness (Danielson, 2007). Academics in the field have begun to find ways to adapt this model to help evaluate school social workers' effectiveness (Alvarez & Anderson-Ketchmark, 2011). In one example of this application and adaptation, managerial supervisors in Chicago Public Schools are being taught how to use the Danielson framework to evaluate their supervisees. The rating scale for each of the domains includes "distinguished," "proficient," "basic," and "unsatisfactory." Within each domain is an explanation of expectations for each of the four ratings so that the framework can specifically address areas for growth and improvement. We excerpt the Chicago Public Schools framework for school social work services here:

1. The domain of *planning and preparation* requires that School Social Workers demonstrate knowledge and skill; establish goals for services appropriate to the setting and students served; demonstrate knowledge of resources, both within and beyond the school and district and establish a plan that consists of a work plan using a needs assessment.
2. The *contexts for learning* states that school social workers will create an environment of respect and rapport; organize time effectively; establish and maintain clear procedures for referrals and to provide support within a culture of positive student behavior throughout the school.

3. The domain of *delivery of service and resources* states that school social workers will assess students' social and emotional needs; assist students and teachers in the formation and implementation of academic; personal/social and behavior plans, based on knowledge of student needs; communicate intervention plan and progress with students and families; collect information and write reports; and demonstrate flexibility and responsiveness.

4. The final area is *professional responsibilities* which requires reflecting on practice; maintaining effective documentation of student progress; communicating with families (as allowed by confidentiality laws and social work ethics); growing and developing professionally and demonstrating professionalism. (Personal communication with the author, A. Greenberg, from her work with CPS; used with permission from CPS and C. Danielson)

While it is definitely welcome to have a framework that national and local school social workers have adapted to address specific school social work job roles, the larger issue remains of who will do the evaluating based on this or any other framework. As we have seen from the past two decades of research on school social work practice (as well as from our own experience in the field), unlike most other social work practice areas, most school social workers are likely to have a non–social worker as their supervisor for most of their career after they finish their field placement. For the next few sections of this chapter, we share what is known about effective supervisory relationships in school social work, as well as possible models of delivering supportive/clinical supervision.

ELEMENTS OF SUCCESSFUL SUPERVISORY RELATIONSHIPS IN SCHOOL SOCIAL WORK

It is important for a good supervisory relationship to be collaborative, whether the supervisee is a field practice student or a veteran school social work practitioner. In order to enhance this collaboration, the supervisor can use the session rating scale (Duncan et al., 2003) to get the supervisee's perception of how the supervisory relationship is going. The scale has only a few questions that have a Likert rating scale on topics related to relationship, goals, approach, and overall feeling about the meeting (Duncan et al., 2003). This tool can also be used for school social workers to allow their clients/students to give feedback on how the social work relationship is going. Effective supervision should include ongoing dialogue about cases and situations so that the supervisee always has a chance to give ideas and make decisions about how to intervene. We expect the supervisor to act appropriately and to set boundaries, making the supervisees feel comfortable, but also letting them know that it is a professional and not a social relationship.

In addition to being knowledgeable about laws pertaining to special education, the supervisor should become familiar with the school district's forms and processes of evaluating students. This may differ widely from school to school. Supervisors may be managers as well as clinical supervisors. There are more areas for conflict when a supervisor wears both hats. A school social worker may be doing an excellent clinical job but not completing mandatory forms in a timely manner, or coming late to work. These areas need to be addressed because they are requirements of the job and need to be considered.

For post-MSW practitioners, many supervisors provide their service as part of the licensing for clinical hours to become a licensed social worker or licensed clinical social worker. This can involve different components that are different from a more standard employer–employee supervisory relationship, though to be sure many clinical social work agencies offer this type of supervision to new employees as a benefit. Because many school social workers do not have a licensed clinical social worker as a supervisor, they are required to find other ways to get their clinical hours supervised. Most states require that licensing supervision occur during full-time employment for a minimum of two years before the candidates are eligible for the higher credential. Supervisors should be knowledgeable about the state's requirements, but school districts do not necessarily require that the school social worker have a clinical license. Nonetheless, many do choose to get clinical licensure to show that they have an advanced credential. Some school districts do Medicaid billing for their students who qualify, and it is necessary to have the state license to complete those forms.

All of the authors of this chapter have provided this type of supervision within the context of Loyola University's Family and School Partnerships Program and their own private practices. Here is an example of the feedback that one of the authors has received about her supervision. "The consistency allows me to stay focused on learning and improving." The same school social worker continued, "In clinical supervision, the facilitator is licensed in your field, compared to day-to-day supervision, where that is not necessarily the case." Other supervisees have commented that they enjoy working with other professionals in a group supervision setting because it benefits them to help others problem-solve and to receive feedback on cases and other professional challenges.

According to NASW's "Best Practice Standards in Social Work Supervision," supervisors should ensure that the services provided to clients by supervisees meet or exceed standards of practice (NASW, 2013). According to the NASW Code of Ethics (1999), supervisees and school districts can be protected against malpractice when a competent supervisor has been consulted. Also mentioned in the NASW Code of Ethics is the following: "Social workers who provide supervision or consultation are responsible for setting clear, appropriate and culturally sensitive boundaries. . . . Therefore, one should document supervision meetings and discussions; monitor supervisee's professional work activities; identify actions that might pose a danger to health and/or welfare of the supervisee's clients and take prompt and appropriate remedial measures; and identify and address any condition that may impair a supervisee's ability to practice social work with reasonable skill, judgment and safety" (NASW, 1999, pp. 14–18).

Research on the field work supervisory relationship has revealed that students value supervisors who are supportive, open to differences, available, and able to develop positive relationships with the supervisee (Bennett, 2008). Bennett reported that by using the components of attachment theory in understanding their supervisees, supervisors can provide a safe space for critique and support that helps the supervisees develop a professional sense of self and become confident in their social work identity (Bennett, Brintzenhofe-Szoc, Mohr, & Saks, 2008).

Whether the supervisee is a student or practicing school social worker, it is important for the supervisor to require written material, such as process recordings or case presentations that include social developmental histories, treatment plans, and diagnostic assessments. The supervisee should be held accountable for not only interviewing techniques, but also for how well she or he conveys information in writing. Doing social developmental studies can be a large part of a school social worker's job description, so those studies should be included in the supervisory process.

Since all school personnel are mandated reporters, learning state guidelines and procedures for filing a child abuse report is another area that should be addressed in supervision. The laws for reporting child abuse for mandated reporters always supersede school policy. Sometimes administrators think they have a choice in this area, but school social workers need to be clear on their roles and legal responsibilities.

Safety in practice is always a priority, and it is incumbent on supervisors to help their supervisees assess their own safety in meeting with clients. Issues such as workplace conflict, protection of property, assaults, threats, or harassment need to be covered during the supervision process. It is critical for the supervisor to cover training and planning for emergency or crisis events. Several safety situations that were discussed in one of the authors' supervision sessions resulted in the following advice:

1. When meeting after 5:00 P.M. with a student's divorced father, who had a history of violent behavior toward his wife, ask the principal or another teacher to attend the meeting with you or to call the office to check on safety.
2. Do not drive any student alone in your car, or leave the school property with a solo student, even in an emergency. Call the parents or 911 and let the police, fire department, and so on, handle it. There are too many liability issues or misunderstandings that can occur to make this a wise action.

MODELS OF SCHOOL SOCIAL WORK SUPERVISION

There are a number of models of supervision and consultation in social work, and some fit better than others with the needs of school social workers. New graduates from MSW programs do not always have the tools to function independently in a school system where they are the only mental health workers. An analysis of fifty-eight MSW programs by Berzin and O'Connor (2010) found that "school social work syllabuses provided limited exposure to content on general education outcomes and goals . . . and are limited in content addressing the changing educational landscape" (Berzin & O'Connor, pp. 237–238). School social work supervisors are forced to fill in the blanks.

The more traditional model of clinical supervision involves having individual meetings or small group meetings with the supervisor. Individual supervision is often not feasible or cost-effective in larger districts, but can work well in schools when there is an experienced social worker in the same building or within a small district. Often districts will assign a mentor to new school social workers, some of whom can function as supervisors. Typically, one-to-one supervision is provided only for new staff, but is also the primary model for field instruction for MSW students.

Sometimes, one or more districts offer small group supervision for their new social workers, often with a head social worker leading the meetings. Small group supervision not only serves to meet the professional needs of the new social workers, but also can provide them with the necessary supervision hours needed to obtain licensure. These groups may also be available as consultation for all the workers in the district. This model has the advantage of providing ongoing support for school social workers throughout their employment with the district. Often the social workers involved are at different stages of their careers and can offer each other different perspectives. They also work within the same system and often share administrators, such as special services coordinators. This puts workers in a unique position to understand each other's experiences and to discuss systems and community as well as clinical issues. They can share their knowledge of resources within the community and can plan interventions on a district- or community-wide level. This model can greatly reduce the sense of isolation experienced by many school social workers who are the only ones in their buildings with the same position.

Some school districts do not offer any kind of formal supervision; many school social workers have addressed this problem by developing peer support/supervision groups on their own. They find ways to meet with one another, either at times when teachers are meeting on educational topics or on their own time, after school or at lunch. These groups function in the same way as group supervision provided by the district, with a few exceptions. One exception is that there is no formal supervisor, so often discussion can be more candid. A disadvantage is that these groups do not provide the formal supervision necessary for licensure.

Online supervision, as a group, chat room, or one to one, is another vehicle for those who do not have access to face-to-face supervision. It is a viable option for those who live in remote geographical areas or who are not able to leave their homes after working hours. The online method will need to consider confidentiality where the names of students and schools are disguised. This type of supervision can allow for the sharing of articles or cases that are shared in advance by e-mail. Stofle and Hamilton (1998) reported this type of supervision as being successful.

A MODEL OF SCHOOL SOCIAL WORK CONSULTATION AND SUPERVISION: THE FAMILY AND SCHOOL PARTNERSHIPS PROGRAM

In the Chicago area, the Loyola University School of Social Work provides a unique program, the Family and School Partnerships Program, that specifically addresses the often-unmet need for supervision and consultation among school social workers (Kelly et al., 2012). The program evolved from offering only consultation groups, to providing workshops and online classes that were focused on helping school-based mental health professionals gain the support and expertise they need to advance their competency. The consultation groups provide supervision hours for licensure, and both the groups and the academic portion of the program provide continuing education units or continuing professional development units for lane advancement in schools. The groups meet for two hours every other week throughout the academic year. They offer consultation on specific cases and systemic situations through discussion; this discussion provides the combined expertise of the group members and the leader, as well as a didactic component. The program has a systemic orientation and philosophy that reflects strength-based assessment and emphasizes evidence-based practice, resilience building, and a multitiered system of supports (or three-tiered approaches). The program also supports collaboration with educators on social-emotional learning goals and collaboration with home, school, and community agencies.

Each group differs slightly based on the style of the leader, but all include a period of time during which the group can address impromptu issues or problems (often referred to as check-in time), and a time for a formal, written presentation involving a client or systemic concern. Group members present at least two formal case presentations and are encouraged to intervene at all levels of the system and to plan or implement a systemic intervention in their school.

One of the cases presented in a suburban group was of a ten-year-old boy in fourth grade. The boy, whom we will call Jay, was receiving special education support for a specific learning disability and speech/language impairment for more than 50 percent of his day. Jay had lived for the past three years with a friend of the family, whom he referred to as Grandma. The mother reported using alcohol during her pregnancy and Jay had been diagnosed with attention deficit hyperactivity disorder. Jay had intermittent and limited contact with his mother. His father was unknown. Grandma was frustrated with his behavior and had been reported to the Department of Children and Family Services on several occasions for using corporal punishment.

The presenting problems that had increased in the past few months included Jay's off-task, avoidant, and defiant behavior during academic time, not following directions, lying, stealing, and vandalism. The school social worker sought consultation on the case to help her gain insight into the recent increase in Jay's problem behaviors and to explore possible avenues for further interventions and support in the school setting. She noted many strengths for Jay, including significant academic progress since he had entered the school as well as strong survival skills. He was friendly, with a good sense of humor, and was able to relate well with adults and his peers. He also had the ability to talk about his feelings. There were a number of supports in Jay's environment including Grandma's involvement and positive relationships with school personnel and neighborhood friends.

The group provided support to the school social worker for doing a good job on such a complicated case. There was discussion on the possible reasons for the increase in Jay's acting-out behaviors. As a result of the discussion and suggestions of the group, the school social worker implemented the following interventions:

- The social worker completed a new functional behavior analysis and behavior intervention plan.
- The social worker met with the guardian (Grandma) to discuss results and encourage positive relations between school and home.
- The school social worker and local school liaison police officer met to discuss the meaning and implications of Jay's stealing and vandalism.
- An intervention specialist worked with Jay to create an instructional video about proper ways to behave in the hallway. The specialist had watched the video several times and shared it with teachers and peers, and Jay had received positive feedback and attention.
- The school social worker increased her time with him. Jay created a series of stop-and-think cards that he could use as visual reminders. The school social worker also utilized various impulse control exercises to improve Jay's ability to stop himself when his teachers directed him to do so.

◆ Arrangements were made to provide a more structured environment for Jay. He started to take the special education transportation in lieu of the regular schoolbus, and ate lunch in the special education classroom.

◆ The social worker had Jay enroll in summer school to provide more structured and constructive use of his time.

As this case exemplifies, discussing cases and writing up case study evaluations for the group helps the school social worker feel less overwhelmed and clarify his or her thinking. It helps the worker to reframe and prioritize interventions to the school. Groups relieve some of the stress school social workers experience when they are the only mental health provider in a setting. By working closely together and sharing concerns, group members become close and develop into a support network for each other.

CONCLUSION

School social work supervisors will wear many hats by providing clinical consultation, supportive and administrative assistance, as well as pedagogical instruction at times. Supervision helps workers deal with isolation and stress, and helps to prevent burnout. It is imperative for supervisors to encourage their supervisees to follow a multitiered approach that focuses on systemic issues, prevention, and services to educators; and to encourage them to be up to date on evidence-based practices (Franklin & Kelly, 2009). An article by Professor Berzin in 2010 (Berzin & O'Connor, 2010) has suggested that even the most recent graduates may not have been taught the latest methods of collecting empirical data or aligning social work and educational goals. After looking at different models of supervision and how much the role of the school social worker has changed and will continue to change (Kelly, Frey, & Anderson-Butcher, 2011), it is clear that the school social work supervisor has a necessary and important job in helping to support and aid in the professional growth of the school social worker.

References
Alvarez, M. E., & Anderson-Ketchmark, C. (2011). Danielson's framework for teaching. *Children & Schools, 33*(1), 61–63.

Alvarez, M. E., Sabatino, C. A., Frey, A. J., Dupper, D. R., Lindsey, B., Raines, J. C., . . . & Norris, M. (2012). Implications of race to the top grants on evaluation of school social workers. *Children & Schools, 34*(4), 195–199.

Association of American Educators. (2013). *Code of ethics for educators*. Retrieved from www.aaeteachers.org

Barry, B. (2005). *NEA research brief on the achievement gap*. Retrieved from http://www.nea.org/home/AchievementGaps.html

Bennett, C. S. (2008). Attachment-informed supervision for social work field education. *Clinical Social Work Journal, 36,* 97–107.

Bennett, C. S., Brintzenhofe-Szoc, K., Mohr, J., & Saks, L. V. (2008). General and supervision-specific attachment styles: Relations to student perceptions of field supervisors. *Journal of Social Work Education, 44*(2), 75–94.

Berzin, S., & O'Connor, S. (2010). Educating today's school social worker: Are school social work courses responding to the changing context? *Children & Schools, 32*(4), 237–249.

Berzin, S. C., O'Brien, K. H. M., Frey, A., Kelly, M. S., Alvarez, M. E., & Shaffer, G. L. (2011). Meeting the social and behavioral health needs of students: Rethinking the relationship between teachers and school social workers. *Journal of School Health, 81*(8), 493–501.

Bogo, M., & McKnight, K. (2006). Clinical supervision in social work: A review of the research literature. *The Clinical Supervisor, 24*(1–2), 49–67.

Danielson, C. (2007). *Enhancing professional practice: A framework for teaching.* Alexandria, VA: Association for Supervision and Curriculum Development.

Duncan, B., Miller, S., Sparks, J., Reynolds, J., Claud, D., Brown, J., & Johnson, L. (2003). The session rating scale: Psychometric properties of "working" alliance scale. *Journal of Brief Therapy, 3*(1), 3–12.

Dupper, D. R., Rocha, C., Jackson, R. F., & Lodato, G. A. (2014). Broadly trained but narrowly used? Factors that predict the performance of environmental versus individual tasks by school social workers. *Children & Schools, 36*(2), 71–77.

Franklin, C., & Kelly, M. S. (2009). Becoming evidence-informed in the real world of school social work practice. *Children & Schools, 31,* 46–56.

Frey, A. J., & Dupper, D. R. (2005). A broader conceptual approach to clinical practice for the 21st century. *Children & Schools, 27,* 33–44.

Garrett, K. J. (2012). Managing school social work records. *Children & Schools, 34*(4), 239–248.

Garrett, K. J., & Barretta-Herman, A. (1995). Missing links: Professional development in school social work. *Social Work in Education, 17*(4), 235–243.

Hair, H. J. (2013). The purpose and duration of supervision, and the training and discipline of supervisors: What social workers say they need to provide effective services. *British Journal of Social Work, 43*(8), 1562–1588.

Hensley, P. H. (2003). The value of supervision. *The Clinical Supervisor, 21*(1), 97–110.

Illinois Association of School Social Workers (IASSW). (1989). *Supervision and evaluation.* Retrieved from http://iassw.org/supervision-and-evaluation/

Individuals with Disabilities Education Improvement Act of 2004 (IDEIA), Pub. L. 108-446, 118 Stat. 2647 (2004).

Kelly, M. S. (2008). *The domains and demands of school social work practice: A guide to working effectively with students, families and schools.* New York: Oxford University Press.

Kelly, M. S., Berzin, S., Frey, A., Alvarez, M., Shaffer, G., & O'Brien, K. (2010). The state of school social work: Findings from the national school social work survey. *School Mental Health, 2*(3), 132–141.

Kelly, M. S., Bluestone-Miller, R., Mervis, B., & Fuerst, R. (2012). The family and school partnerships program: A framework for professional development. *Children & Schools, 34,* 1–4.

Kelly, M. S., Frey, A. J., Alvarez, M., Berzin, S., Shaffer, G., & O'Brien, K. (2010). School social work practice and response to intervention, *Children & Schools, 32,* 201–209.

Kelly, M. S., Frey, A., & Anderson-Butcher, D. (2011). Writing the job description for school social workers in 2031. *Children & Schools, 33*(2), 67–69.

Kelly, M. S., Raines, J. C., Stone, S., & Frey, A. (2010). *School social work: An evidence-informed framework for practice.* New York: Oxford University Press.

National Association of Social Workers (NASW). (1999). 3.01 Supervision and Consultation. *NASW code of ethics.* Washington, DC: Author. Retrieved from http://www.socialworkers.org/pubs/code/code.asp

National Association of Social Workers (NASW). (2012). *Best practice standards for professional development.* Washington, DC: Author. Retrieved from http://www.social workers.org/practice/naswstandards/socialworksupervision/SUPERVISION%20 STANDARDS2%20Public%20Comment%20Draft%20August%2016.pdf

National Association of Social Workers (NASW). (2013). *Best practice standards in social work supervision.* Retrieved from www.naswdc.org/practice/naswstandards/ supervisionstandards2013.pdf

National Education Association (NEA). (2014). *Code of ethics.* Retrieved from http://www.nea.org/home/30442.htm

No Child Left Behind Act of 2001, Pub. L. 107-110 (2002).

Peckover, C. A., Vasquez, M. L., Van Housen, S. L., Saunders, J. A., & Allen, L. (2012). Preparing school social work for the future: An update of school social workers' tasks in Iowa. *Children & Schools, 35,* 9–17.

Phillippo, K., & Blosser, A. (2013). Specialty practice or interstitial practice? A reconsideration of school social work's past and present. *Children & Schools, 35,* 19–31.

Raines, J. C., & Dibble, N. T. (2010). *Ethical decision making in school mental health.* New York: Oxford University Press.

School Social Work Association of America (SSWAA). (2013). *National evaluation framework for school social work practice.* Retrieved from http://c.ymcdn.com/ sites/www.sswaa.org/resource/resmgr/Evaluation/SSWAANationalEvalFrameworkFI .pdf?hhSearchTerms=%22Danielson+and+Framework%22

Shulman, L. (2013). Supervision. *Encyclopedia of social work online.* Retrieved from http://socialwork.oxfordre.com/

Staudt, M. (1997). Correlates of job satisfaction in school social work. *Social Work in Education, 19,* 43–51.

Stofle, G., & Hamilton, S. (1998). Online supervision for social workers. *New Social Worker, 5,* 4. Retrieved from http://www.socialworker.com/feature-articles/field-placement/Online_Supervision_for_Social_Workers/

6

The Process of Ethical Decision Making in School Social Work

James C. Raines
California State University Monterey Bay

- ◆ Procedure and Principles
- ◆ Ethics and the Law
- ◆ Issues in Record Keeping

School social workers are constantly confronted with the conundrums of ethical decision making, particularly with regard to which student disclosures to keep confidential and which to divulge in the interest of school or student safety. Confidentiality issues permeate the school social worker's landscape. Consider the following scenarios:

A thirteen-year-old girl is sexually involved with a seventeen-year-old boy. Currently, they are "only" having oral sex, but he is pressuring her to "go all the way." She reports that she is the only virgin in her peer group and that the others make fun of her. She is scared to tell her very religious parents because she is afraid they will send her to a strict parochial school. State laws prohibit sexual contact with minors under age thirteen as well as where the age difference is five or more years, so there is no legal guidance in this case (Guttmacher Institute, 2015).

A fifteen-year-old boy reveals that he has been involved in cutting. The wounds are all superficial and uninfected. He denies any suicidal thoughts or intent— it is merely his way of coping with feelings of numbness and existential angst about his future. He does not want to tell his single mother because the last time she found out she sent him to an inpatient psychiatric program. The recent research clearly differentiates cutting from suicidal attempts, so the literature warns against overreacting in such cases.

A twelve-year-old boy who is angry about his poor grades and disciplinary record threatens to "blow up" the school. He does not have any specific plans, nor does he possess any of the skills or materials for bomb making. He does not want his foster parents to know because he is afraid they will send him back to the group home where he would be the youngest and most vulnerable kid. Unfortunately, all the necessary bomb-making information is readily available on the Internet so he could obtain it if he wanted to.

Each ethical dilemma is also a practice problem. The good school social worker has already clarified confidentiality and its limits in the youth's language. The social worker and client create a contract in order to help them deal with an unacceptable situation. The social worker and student are partners in managing the predicament. The social worker can help the student in this by a simultaneous focus on the person and the broader environment. That might involve helping the youth get in contact with persons who could be of help or opening some dialogue with parents. The social worker tells the youth that to continue meeting, the social worker needs to have some contact with parents. Before the social worker makes contact with others, she first discusses the issue with the student so that together they can come to a joint approach. This process becomes part of the first session in some way and continues through the relationship. In the context of practice, the question of whether to reveal, what to reveal, and to whom to reveal it remains central to the work of the school social worker. This chapter offers a procedure and principles for deciding some of the basic issues in school social work practice: whether to share information, how to share it, and how much to share. It also addresses the relationship between ethics and the law and provides a checklist to ensure confidentiality. All of the anecdotes in this chapter use pseudonyms; details have been changed to protect the identities of the participants.

PROCEDURE AND PRINCIPLES

There are seven steps that school social workers can use to work through the decision about whether to divulge confidential student material. Skipping or shortchanging any of these steps tends to reduce the quality of the decision.

Step 1: Know Yourself.

Social workers must differentiate between their personal values and their professional values (Abramson, 1996). Social workers are bound by the National Association of Social Workers (NASW) Code of Ethics (Jensen, 2002). There are six core social work values in the code that become ethical principles: (1) service, (2) social justice, (3) the dignity and worth of the person, (4) the importance of human relationships, (5) integrity, and (6) competence. These explicit values are normative for all professional social workers regardless of their practice settings or roles, but practitioners facing specific situations may also apply values that are implicit in the NASW Code. For example, Raines and Dibble (2011) argue that protection of life is an implicit value when the code allows social workers to violate confidentiality when the student is a danger to self or others. Other implicit values include equality, autonomy and freedom, least harm, quality of life, privacy and confidentiality, and truthfulness and full-disclosure (Loewenberg, Dolgoff, & Harrington, 2000).

Many ethical thinkers have tended to approach problems on the basis of unchangeable principles that are intrinsically right or wrong (deontologists). They may hold an absolute standard of truth telling with others. Others may gauge their actions through an analysis of the goodness of their consequences (consequentialists). The latter, as relativists, would ultimately hold that the end justifies the means (Reamer, 2006). For example, they may think it is permissible to deceive the welfare system in order to obtain a livable income for clients. The most common form of the relativist approach is the utilitarian model, according to which one must weigh the costs and benefits of every decision. For example, those using a utilitarian approach may hold that both honesty and deception have risks and rewards that vary according to the situation.

There is often a problem with the way the issue is framed: Ethical dilemmas by their very nature reduce options into simplistic either-or solutions, neither of which is very palatable. The wise social worker will recognize that most dilemmas are quick and simple solutions to longstanding and complex problems. For example, the question, "Should I tell?" leaves sole responsibility on the practitioner, when the best course of action may be that the worker helps the student to tell those with a need to know.

When deciding which ethical value(s) should take precedence, workers should be aware of four caveats. First, the explicit values may not be exhaustive. Social workers may decide that other values may need to be integrated with the values stated there. Second, the ranking of the values may change depending on the situation. For example, protection of life may take precedence over confidentiality when a student is suicidal, but it may take second place to quality of life when the same student is brain dead and on life support. Third, some of the principles imply that social workers will be able to predict accurately the outcomes of their decisions. In actuality, we seldom possess 20/20 foresight. Finally, practitioners may disagree about how a particular principle should be put into practice.

The final aspect of self-awareness relates to countertransference. Each of us probably has a proclivity to tell or not to tell. Those with the tendency to tell may have experienced a foreseeable harm that could have been averted if only someone had had the courage to speak out. Perhaps we were bullied, sexually harassed or assaulted, abused, or neglected. We may have suffered quietly because we lacked a champion to protect us. Social workers with a secret wish to rescue or shield others from harm will need to think twice before breaking a confidence. Those with a tendency not to tell may subconsciously equate telling with tattling. Social workers who have a strong need to be liked by students will need to develop thick skin before they feel comfortable violating student confidences.

Step 2: Analyze the Dilemma.

It is helpful to obtain the answers to several questions, some of which may be deceptively complex. There are four important issues within this step.

First, an important question is, "Who is the primary client?" The NASW Code of Ethics (2008) is particularly unhelpful at this point. It states only that the term "'clients' is used inclusively to refer to individuals, families, groups, organizations, and communities" (p. 1). There is no doubt that any of these *can* be a client, but this definition, unfortunately, does not answer the question of who actually *is* the client. Kopels and Lindsey (2006) rightly see this issue as the crux of many dilemmas about confidentiality: "A social worker's view of who the client is is another factor that complicates decision making about confidentiality. When social workers view students, school administrators, teachers, parents, and the community equally as clients, then it becomes almost impossible to sort out who is entitled to information about a student. When school social workers do not view the student as their *only client*, then the worker is forced to juggle the competing interests of all these other stakeholders" (p. 75, emphasis added).

Somewhere between the NASW's implied "everyone is a client" and Kopels and Lindsey's (2006) idea that only the student is the client is a middle ground that regards the student as the primary client (Raines & Dibble, 2011). This implies that a social worker's primary fiduciary responsibility is to the student, but that he or she may have secondary responsibilities to those who also have a responsibility to act in the student's best interests. Thus, parents and teachers (who often assume an in loco parentis role) may also be recipients of social work services and deserve some consideration in light of their special caretaking duties (Tan, Passerini, & Stewart, 2007).

Second, who are the stakeholders? Stakeholders are concerned parties with a vested interest in the outcome, not competing clients, as some have suggested (McWhinney, Haskins-Herkenham, & Hare, 1992; Prichard, 1999). Loewenberg et al. (2000) identify several participants in the social work process. Clients are people (or systems) who knowingly (not always voluntarily) enter into a formal, contractual, and goal-driven relationship with the social worker. Beyond the client system (individual, family, or group), there are three other important groups in school settings. First, there are colleagues (other social workers, psychologists, or teachers), who also provide professional services to students. Second, there are administrators (superintendents, special education coordinators, principals, or deans), who have responsibility for the educational community. Finally, there are family members (parents, stepparents, or foster parents), who have legal responsibility for the student. Any of these may arguably have a right to know about dangerous conduct. If any of these groups believe their rights have been disregarded, they have the potential to increase the cost of confidentiality to the practitioner. These costs may include professional ostracism from colleagues, loss of promotion or position by administrators, and litigation by family members. Thus, it would be naive to underestimate the importance of stakeholders in the process.

Third, which values are in conflict? In the introductory scenarios, one of the applicable NASW values is the importance placed on human relationships. Berman-Rossi and Rossi (1990) note that confidentiality provides the basis for client self-disclosure and the sharing of intimate details. On the other hand, another NASW value is social justice. The social worker has a duty to protect both the educational community and the student. One hopes that a commitment to a third value, integrity, will help balance the conflicting demands.

Another set of potentially competing values is self-determination versus paternalism. A superficial reading of the NASW Code of Ethics (2008) would suggest that social workers should always choose client self-determination. This assumption reveals a flaw in the code: it presumes an adult-to-adult relationship that is mutual and egalitarian (Prichard, 1999). In schools, our clients are usually legal minors who cannot give informed consent for themselves. Parents or legal guardians must sign both informed consent to treatment as well as release of information forms (Jonson-Reid, 2000). Paternalism has a negative reputation, which is sometimes undeserved (Staller & Kirk, 1997). A child is both emotionally and intellectually dependent on adults to make decisions in the child's best interests. What seems to be needed is a procedure for informed assent. This differs from informed consent in that it is not legally binding but serves the clinical function of providing for some self-determination in the social work process. It is especially helpful with those cases where the child is not self-referred and may not initially see the value of social work services. When the child is an involuntary client, the parents may be the ones giving informed consent to the ultimate goals of treatment, but the child should still have some voice in the instrumental means about how to achieve these goals (Cone & Dalenberg, 2004).

When I receive referrals for social work services, I explain what I will routinely share with others, including parents and teachers. Routine disclosures typically involve three points. First, I usually provide the percentage of sessions attended out of the number scheduled. Second, I often provide the topics, not details, of what we have discussed—this is done primarily to help parents or teachers empathize with the student and increase their support for the student. Finally, I typically provide an opinion about whether the student is making progress; this helps parents to know if school-based counseling is working or whether they should try something different. If these routine disclosures are acceptable, I ask students to give their assent to treatment. If these routine disclosures are unacceptable, I try to assess whether the child's problem may interfere with his or her capacity to assent to treatment. For example, students who are oppositional, anorexic, or addicted may be unable to admit they need help (Tan et al., 2007). When this is the case, parental consent must suffice.

Step 3: Seek Consultation.

The third step in the decision process is to obtain outside expertise. One of the dangers in social work licensing laws is that they certify professionals for independent practice. This tends to convey the notion that when practitioners have reached this level, they no longer need supervision or consultation from their colleagues—but nothing could be farther from the truth. The NASW Code of Ethics (2008) makes it very clear that "social workers should seek the advice and counsel of colleagues whenever such consultation is in the best interests of clients" (p. 16). This consultation should be sought from colleagues with adequate expertise. There are two kinds of expertise that are important when it comes to ethical issues. The first type of expertise is clinical consultation. Social workers do not need to breach confidentiality to obtain this advice. Counsel can be sought while keeping the client's identity anonymous by sharing only the most pertinent details of a case.

The clinical consultant should be intimately familiar with the NASW Code of Ethics (2008). Compared to psychologists and counselors, social workers have the highest hurdles to overcome before they can breach client confidentiality. The NASW Code of Ethics makes it very clear that four conditions must be met before disclosure can occur without prior consent: "Social workers should protect the confidentiality of all information in the course of professional service, except for compelling professional reasons. The general expectation that social workers will keep information confidential does not apply when disclosure is necessary to prevent *serious, foreseeable,* and *imminent* harm to a client or other *identifiable* person" (Sec. 1.07 [c], emphasis added).

The NASW Code of Ethics (2008) also clarifies that the amount to be shared should be construed as narrowly as possible: "In all instances, social workers should disclose the *least* amount of confidential information necessary to achieve the desired purpose . . . for which the disclosure is made should be revealed" (Sec. 1.07 [c], emphasis added). Prior to disclosing information, however, the Code requires that "social workers should inform clients, to the extent possible, about the disclosure of confidential information and the potential consequences, when feasible *before* the disclosure is made" (Sec. 1.07 [d], emphasis added). This latter requirement is one area where social workers are most vulnerable to a charge of acting unethically. Whether it is due to fear of the client's (or parent's) anger or sheer cowardice makes little difference. Treating others as we would prefer to be treated ourselves requires honestly telling clients that a disclosure is in the offing. In my experience, most clients are ultimately thankful for the forewarning.

The second type of expertise is legal advice. There are two main sources of legal guidance. First, social workers need to understand what laws apply to the case. Laws that address the social worker–student relationship include the Family Educational Rights and Privacy Act (FERPA) of 1974 and the Health Insurance Portability and Accountability Act (HIPAA) of 1996.

FERPA should be familiar to all public-school mental health professionals. This law allows for treatment records to be considered sole possession files that belong exclusively to mental health professionals or their substitutes (Raines & Ahlman, 2004). It also protects certain group records from inspection since revelation for one would entail a revelation for all. One particular sore spot in FERPA is the provision that allows for the nonconsensual release of information to a wide range of school personnel, such as "other school officials, including teachers within the educational institution or local educational agency, who have been determined by such agency or institution to have *legitimate educational interests*" (Sec. [b][1][A], emphasis added). The phrase "legitimate educational interests" has become a point of contention between school-based mental health professionals and other school personnel, especially teachers and principals. Raines and Dibble (2011) note that since FERPA leaves the discretion of what those interests are up to the local education agency, it may be wise for social workers to organize a task force made up of the vested constituency groups to establish district policy on this issue.

HIPAA, however, is probably less familiar to many school-based social workers. According to Overcamp-Martini (2006), HIPAA pertains to social work practice whenever practitioners make medical claims for third-party reimbursement, such as Medicaid. HIPAA protects psychotherapy notes from both parental and patient access. The federal definition of these records follows:

> Notes recorded (in any medium) by a health care provider who is a mental health professional documenting or analyzing the contents of a conversation during a private counseling session or a group, joint, or family counseling session and that are separated from the rest of the individual's medical record. Psychotherapy notes excludes medication prescription and monitoring, counseling session start and stop times, the modalities and frequencies of treatment furnished, results of clinical tests, and any summary of the following items: diagnosis, functional status, the treatment plan, symptoms, prognosis, and progress to date. (U.S. Department of Health and Human Services, 2003, p. 21, fn47)

Both FERPA and HIPAA are federal laws, but states may decide to go beyond these statutes in their own laws. Therefore, school social workers should seek legal advice from someone familiar with both state and federal legislation.

Second, social workers need to understand what case law applies to the issue. Case law refers to judicial decisions that clarify vague portions of a law. They often provide rules of interpretation or precedents that other courts may follow. All social workers should be familiar with the court case *Tarasoff v. Regents of the University of California* (1976). The California Supreme Court determined that mental health professionals had a duty to protect when they knew or should have known that a client posed an immediate danger to a specific person or persons. Social workers should also determine the extent to which their state courts have affirmed the *Tarasoff* precedent or their state legislatures have codified the *Tarasoff* principles (Kopels & Lindsey, 2006).

Step 4: Identify the Courses of Action.

For any ethical quandary, there are usually at least three different courses of action and sometimes more. Given the examples that began this chapter, a social worker could decide (1) to keep all the material confidential to maintain the primacy of the therapeutic relationship and try to help clients resolve conflicting feelings about hiding such important issues from those who care for them, (2) to divulge the confidential material to protect the student or school's well-being and try to help the client understand why such a disclosure was important, or (3) to share the ethical dilemma with the client and try to empower him or her to disclose the problem to those who need to know.

In general, the more mature the student, the more the social worker should share the ethical problem and empower the student to participate in managing the problem. This has two benefits. First, it models the conscientious consideration of moral dilemmas. Second, it helps students to avoid seeing solutions in an either-or fashion and to find middle ground. An example will illustrate:

Eric was a thirteen-year-old eighth grader with a serious marijuana problem that was affecting the completion of his schoolwork. He was the only son of two working parents who did not provide any supervision after school until they arrived home after 6:00 P.M. He was very afraid of disappointing his parents and what measures they might take to curb his freedom. I reflected that it sounded as if he could not overcome this on his own and that he needed his family's help. I suggested that there were three ways we could handle it: (1) I could call his parents and share this with them directly while he listened; (2) I could meet with both him and his parents together to mediate between them; or (3) I could help him practice self-disclosure to his parents through role-playing. Eric worried aloud that his mother would go "ballistic" and offered a fourth option, where he would tell his father alone first. I compromised on this point and Eric chose to go with his fourth option.

Sharing the steps of ethical decision making with middle school– and high school–age youths is one way to improve their capacity for good ethical decision making as young adults.

Step 5: Manage the Clinical Concerns.

There are three major clinical issues when considering whether to abridge client confidentiality. These include maintaining a standard of care, managing student reactions, and managing parental reactions.

First, when making decisions about confidentiality, it is essential that social workers demonstrate that they know and use the standard of care. A standard of care is simply what an ordinary, reasonable, and prudent professional with similar training would do under similar circumstances. For dangerous clients, it is imperative that practitioners never underestimate or minimize the potential danger. Cooper and Lesser (2002) recommend assessing (1) the frequency of the client's violent ideas (e.g., monthly, weekly, daily, obsessively), (2) the duration of those ideas (e.g., fleeting, episodic, or sustained), (3) the concreteness of the plan (i.e., its lethality, locality, imminence, and plausibility), and (4) the extent to which preparation has begun (i.e., gathering materials and knowledge/skill for its implementation). One might also add the client's degree of emotional dysregulation (Newhill, 2003). This includes clients' emotional sensitivity (how quickly they react), emotional intensity (on a scale from 1 to 10), and ability to calm themselves back to a normal state. These inquiries should be considered in the context of the client's history of violence, and immediate precipitating events (Center for Mental Health in Schools at UCLA, 2003).

Second, practitioners should know that every student reacts differently to confrontation about a possible violation of privileged disclosure. Regardless of how well students are oriented to treatment and how well they participate in giving informed assent, many will feel hurt, angry, and betrayed by the social worker. It is most important to protect the therapeutic relationship by remaining empathic and reflecting both the spoken and unspoken feelings of the client (Raines, 1990). This bond enables practitioners to engage students in introspection about why they revealed the information. Next, give the student as much choice as is developmentally appropriate. This does not mean, however, that social workers should shirk their ethical responsibilities. It does mean that students should be informed about what choices they have. This gives the student a sense of ownership and control over the circumstances.

Third, practitioners need to know that parents can react very strongly about the decision to remain secretive. Unlike their children, parents often have the ability to significantly increase the amount of pressure a social worker feels to disclose sensitive information by calling the principal, superintendent, and members of the school board. It helps to have a clear policy from the start because it allows the social worker to remind parents of the initial agreement. Mitchell, Disque, and Robertson (2002) recommend some additional clinical approaches: First, school social workers should listen empathically to the parents' concerns, validate their feelings, and join with them around wanting what is best for the student. Second, it can help for school social workers to coach the parents in how to listen nonreactively to their children's concerns. This can be accomplished by inquiring whether there have been some disclosures at home that have them worried and asking how they might facilitate parent-child discussion over the issues. Third, it may help for the workers to point out that an important part of adolescence is a growing independence that involves talking with trusted adults about private issues. This can be done by asking the parents if they had significant nonparental relationships when they were growing up and exploring what this relationship meant to them at the time. Finally, it may help to offer a family session to address the issues. This helps to take the social worker out of the middle and facilitate good family communication skills on the part of the parents and the student.

Step 6: Enact the Decision.

Once the dilemma has been analyzed, consultation obtained, courses of action identified, and clinical concerns managed, it would seem like the time to implement the resolution, but Raines and Dibble (2011) recommend that school social workers first ask themselves five final questions:

1. Golden rule: If I were the primary client, would I want a social worker to handle this situation with this same course of action?
2. Fiduciary responsibility: If I proceed with this course of action, will I have faithfully discharged my social work responsibilities to my client?
3. Generalizability: Would I treat another student the same way in the same situation? If the answer is no, are there legitimate reasons for different treatment?
4. Publicity: Would I feel comfortable if the details of my decision were somehow made public?
5. Universality: If another social worker sought me out for consultation on this ethical predicament, would I still recommend this course of action?

More often than not there are consequences that could not have been predicted (Robison & Reeser, 2000). Some stakeholders may be angry that they were not told about the problem sooner or may want to punish the student for a crime he or she has not (yet) committed. Some stakeholders may feel embarrassed or envious that the student trusted the social worker with intimacies when they have known the child longer. The school social workers should emphasize that the primary purpose is to protect people now, and applaud the student's courage for having told anyone. This will help to keep the discussion focused on protection, the present, and the positives.

Step 7: Reflect on the Process.

Mattison (2000) recommends that after the issue has been resolved, it is helpful to reexamine the process. Ask yourself the following questions:

1. To what degree did my personal values influence this decision?
2. To what extent did other participants influence my choices?
3. Were there courses of action that I failed to consider?
4. Should I have consulted other people?
5. Were there clinical concerns that I missed or underestimated?
6. In hindsight did I make the right decision?
7. What precautions (e.g., ethical orientation or informed assent) should I take to prevent potential problems in the future?

Social workers would be wise to consistently evaluate the outcomes of their ethical decision making in order to identify prejudicial patterns of disclosure or iatrogenic effects related to disclosure.

ETHICS AND THE LAW

Too often social workers have confused the boundary between their ethical and their legal obligations (Reamer, 2005). Lawsuits and subpoenas are insufficient reasons to breach confidentiality (Dickson, 1998). Another court case with which all practitioners should become familiar is *Jaffee v. Redmond* (1996). This case involved a social worker who refused to hand over records about her client's state of mind after her client killed someone in the line of duty (Nye, 1999). She was held in contempt of court and the case was appealed to the U.S. Supreme Court, where the high court established that client privilege extended to psychotherapists and that mental health was a public good that should be protected under the law (Lens, 2000). Social workers should not view themselves as agents of the state nor feel compelled to report a client's past crimes. The exception to this rule is when the crime is especially heinous because it involves vulnerable victims who are both defenseless and dependent on others (e.g., child abuse and elder abuse).

Most states where there is licensing of social workers recognize the protection of privileged communication. The social worker is obligated not to disclose them, except under certain narrowly defined circumstances. It is important to know the privileged communication statute that governs your practice. Even when social workers are obligated to respond to a subpoena, they can request that the court limit the order as narrowly as possible, ask for an *in camera* (in chambers) review, insist that the records remain under seal, and require that all records be returned at the end of the trial.

Moral conundrums, then, could be placed on a typology consisting of two dimensions: ethical issues and legal issues (figure 6.1). Such a schema results in four categories of quandaries. First, some questions concern neither ethical nor legal issues. An example is the decision about whether social workers should disclose their feelings to clients. In general, practitioners are on safer ground when disclosing present feelings about the therapeutic process than they are disclosing details on their personal lives (Raines, 1996), but this is primarily a clinical issue, rather than a moral one. Second, some quandaries, such as the ethical orientation of clients, are only ethical issues, not legal ones. It is wise to inform all clients (even those transferred from other workers) about one's own approach to confidentiality, but this is not a legal mandate. Third, other controversies, such as a duty to warn others of a client's potential for violence, are both ethical and legal issues (Kopels & Kagle, 1993). When we accept a student as one of our clients, we embark on a fiduciary relationship (Kutchins, 1991). We can violate a client's privilege only for compelling reasons. Finally, some questions, such as whether school social workers should obtain clinical licensure, are mainly legal issues.

ISSUES IN RECORD KEEPING

All social workers should be familiar with the requirements of the FERPA, which guarantees parents both access and control over the dissemination of school records (Jonson-Reid, 2000). This legislation requires knowing the difference between which files are official education records and which are not. Social workers' private notes are not part of the school record, nor are sole possession files stored on a computer (School Social Work Association

FIGURE 6.1   Ethical-Legal Typology

Ethical but not legal issue	Both an ethical and a legal issue
Neither an ethical nor a legal issue	Legal but not ethical issue

of America, 2001). These documents should be stored under lock and key or protected by passwords if they are on a computer. Social developmental studies (SDSs), case progress notes, functional behavioral assessments (FBAs), behavior intervention plans (BIPs), and individualized education program (IEP) documents, however, are official school records. Case progress notes should contain dates of meetings, general topics discussed, and interventions employed. They should not contain intimate details, process recordings, or clinical impressions. Thus, social workers would be wise to write these documents in a way that does not offend clients or their parents.

The question of what information should be shared with teachers and other members of the team is an important one. The sharing of information, often necessary for team functioning, is first of all limited to what the individual team member needs to know to carry out his or her function. A teacher, concerned about a particular child who is sleeping in class, may simply need to know that the child is very upset about things happening in the home without having to know the details. The consultation with the teacher can be geared to suggesting strategies to help her enable the child to become a part of the class learning process, with the social worker working individually with the child, the family situation, and possibly other agencies. School social workers should inform students and parents that information gathered under the IEP process is generally shared with all members of the IEP team. It is, however, at the social worker's discretion in collaboration with parents and student to reveal only what is necessary for the team's functioning.

CONCLUSION

The ethics of social work have evolved considerably over the past one hundred years (Reamer, 1998). Hopefully, in its next incarnation the NASW Code of Ethics (2008) will pay more attention to ethical dilemmas involving minors working with social workers in host settings, such as schools. This process is one practitioner's viewpoint based on a review of the literature and accumulated practice wisdom. Good social workers can disagree and still be good social workers (e.g., Kopels [1992] vs. Kardon [1993]). Legally we may have a duty to warn about imminent crimes, but we do not have a duty to report past crimes, unless it involves a mandated report, such as child abuse and neglect. Reamer (2000) suggests that one of the ways that social workers can protect themselves is to diligently document their decision-making process. The process of the decision may ultimately be more important than the product of the decision because it demonstrates the decision was made carefully and with great deliberation (Reamer, 2005). For this reason, I have not provided any solutions to the dilemmas that began this paper, but I offer a confidentiality checklist (figure 6.2) as discussion fodder to which this process can be applied.

FIGURE 6.2   Confidentiality Checklist

- ◆ I have clarified my own personal and professional values.
- ◆ I have identified the primary client and stakeholders in ethical issues.
- ◆ I have identified the primary competing values.
- ◆ I regularly provide an ethical orientation to new clients.
- ◆ I obtain informed consent (and informed assent) to treatment.
- ◆ I obtain clinical consultation about difficult issues.
- ◆ I obtain legal advice about difficult issues.
- ◆ I am familiar with the laws regarding the treatment and rights of minors.
- ◆ I have identified at least three courses of action.
- ◆ I carefully consider the clinical implications.
- ◆ I make sure the decision is sensitive, fiduciary, impartial, justifiable, and generalizable.
- ◆ I review and document the process of decision making.
- ◆ I always keep my personal written notes in a locked file cabinet.
- ◆ I always use a computer password to protect private electronic files.
- ◆ I always write public documents in clear, unoffensive language.

References

Abramson, M. (1996). Reflections on knowing oneself ethically: Toward a working framework for social work practice. *Families in Society, 77*(4), 195–202.

Berman-Rossi, T., & Rossi, P. (1990). Confidentiality and informed consent in school social work. *Social Work in Education, 12*(3), 195–207.

Center for Mental Health in Schools at UCLA. (2003). *A technical assistance sampler on school interventions to prevent youth suicide.* Los Angeles: Author. Retrieved from http://www.pdffiller.com/22103259-SchoolInterventions_UCLApdf-Center-for-Mental-Health-in-Schools-at-UCLA—American—Various-Fillable-Forms

Cone, J. D., & Dalenberg, C. J. (2004). Ethics concerns in outcome assessment. In M. E. Maruish (Ed.), *The use of psychological testing for treatment planning and outcomes assessment,* Vol. 1: *General considerations* (3rd ed., pp. 335–365). Mahwah, NJ: Lawrence Erlbaum.

Cooper, M. G., & Lesser, J. G. (2002). *Clinical social work practice: An integrated approach.* Boston: Allyn & Bacon.

Dickson, D. T. (1998). *Confidentiality and privacy in social work.* New York: Free Press.

Family Educational Rights and Privacy Act of 1974 (FERPA), Pub. L. 93-380, 88 Stat. 571 (1974).

Guttmacher Institute (2015, June 1). *State policies in brief: An overview of minors' consent law.* Retrieved from http://www.guttmacher.org/statecenter/spibs/spib_OMCL.pdf

Health Insurance Portability and Accountability Act of 1996 (HIPAA), Pub. L. 104-191, 110 Stat. (1996).

Jaffee v. Redmond, 116 S. Ct. 1923 (1996).

Jensen, G. (2002, November 15). *Ethically and practically speaking: Managing your malpractice liability.* Workshop presented at Illinois State University, Normal, IL.

Jonson-Reid, M. (2000). Understanding confidentiality in school-based interagency projects. *Social Work in Education, 22*(1), 33–45.

Kardon, S. (1993). Confidentiality: A different perspective. *Social Work in Education,* *15*(4), 247–249.

Kopels, S. (1992). Confidentiality and the school social worker. *Social Work in Education,* *14*(4), 203–204.

Kopels, S., & Kagle, J. D. (1993). Do social workers have a duty to warn? *Social Service Review,* *67*(1), 10–26.

Kopels, S., & Lindsey, B. (2006). The complexity of confidentiality in schools today: The school social worker context. *School Social Work Journal* (special 100th anniversary issue), 61–78.

Kutchins, H. (1991). The fiduciary relationship: The legal basis for social work responsibility to clients. *Social Work, 36*(2), 106–113.

Lens, V. (2000). Protecting the confidentiality of the therapeutic relationship: Jaffee v. Redmond. *Social Work, 45*(3), 273–276.

Loewenberg, F., Dolgoff, R., & Harrington, D. (2000). *Ethical decisions for social work practice* (6th ed.). Itasca, IL: F. E. Peacock.

Mattison, M. (2000). Ethical decision making: The person in the process. *Social Work, 45*(3), 201–212.

McWhinney, M., Haskins-Herkenham, D., & Hare, I. (1992). NASW Commission on Education position statement: The school social worker and confidentiality. *School Social Work Journal, 17*(1), 38–46.

Mitchell, C. W., Disque, J. G., & Robertson, P. (2002). When parents want to know: Responding to parental demands for confidential information. *Professional School Counseling, 6*(2), 156–161.

National Association of Social Workers (NASW). (2008). *Code of ethics.* Retrieved from https://www.socialworkers.org/pubs/code/code.asp

Newhill, C. E. (2003).*Client violence in social work practice: Prevention, intervention, and research.* New York: Guilford Press.

Nye, S. G. (1999).Confidentiality and privilege of mental health records in ADA and Rehabilitation Act cases. *Social Work Networker, 38*(5), 8–9.

Overcamp-Martini, M. A. (2006). HIPAA and the electronic transfer of student information. In C. Franklin, M. B. Harris, & P. Allen-Meares (Eds.), *School social work and mental health worker's training and resource manual* (pp. 905–912). New York: Oxford University Press.

Prichard, D. C. (1999). Breaking confidence: When silence kills. *Reflections, 5*(2), 43–51.

Raines, J. C. (1990). Empathy in clinical social work. *Clinical Social Work Journal, 18*(1), 57–72.

Raines, J. C. (1996). Self-disclosure in clinical social work. *Clinical Social Work Journal, 24*(4), 357–375.

Raines, J. C., & Ahlman, C. (2004). No substitute for competence: How to survive and thrive as a substitute school social worker. *School Social Work Journal, 28*(2), 37–52.

Raines, J. C., & Dibble, N. T. (2011). *Ethical decision making in school mental health.* New York: Oxford University Press.

Reamer, F. G. (1998). The evolution of social work ethics. *Social Work, 43*(6), 488–500.

Reamer, F. G. (2000). The social work ethics audit: A risk-management strategy. *Social Work, 45*(4), 355–366.

Reamer, F. G. (2005). Ethical and legal standards in social work: Consistency and conflict. *Families in Society, 86*(2), 163–169.

Reamer, F. G. (2006). *Social work values and ethics* (3rd ed.). New York: Columbia University Press.

Robison, W., & Reeser, L. C. (2000). *Ethical decision making in social work*. Boston: Allyn & Bacon.

School Social Work Association of America (SSWAA). (2001). *Resolution statement: School social workers and confidentiality*. Northlake, IL: Author. Retrieved from http://c.ymcdn.com/sites/www.sswaa.org/resource/resmgr/imported/School%20Social%20Workers%20and%20Confidentiality.pdf

Staller, K. M., & Kirk, S. A. (1997). Unjust freedom: The ethics of client self-determination in runaway youth shelters. *Child and Adolescent Social Work Journal, 14*(3), 223–242.

Tan, J. O. A., Passerini, G. E., & Stewart, A. (2007). Consent and confidentiality in clinical work with young people. *Clinical Child Psychology & Psychiatry, 12*(2), 191–210.

Tarasoff v. Regents of the University of California, 551 P. 2d 334 (1976).

U.S. Department of Health and Human Services (DHHS). (2003, May). *OCR privacy brief: Summary of the HIPAA privacy rule*. Washington, DC: Author. Retrieved from http://www.hhs.gov/ocr/privacy/hipaa/understanding/summary/privacysummary.pdf

7

Ethical and Legal Complexities of Confidentiality for School Social Workers

Sandra Kopels

University of Illinois at Urbana-Champaign

♦ Ethical Issues Related to Confidentiality in School Social Work Practice
♦ Legal Issues Related to Confidentiality in School Social Work Practice
♦ Other Factors that Influence Confidentiality

Ethical issues, particularly confidentiality, are among the most deeply felt struggles for school social workers. James C. Raines (chapter 6) uses confidentiality scenarios to outline the process of ethical decision making in schools. These ethical decision-making processes are critical to school social workers' abilities to assist students to be successful in the school environment. The processes are complicated by the broad role of the school social worker, and the multiple points of intervention involved in school social work practice. School social workers assist students by providing or arranging for services to meet the needs of children. In addition to providing individual, group, and other services directly to children and their parents, school social workers frequently team with other members of the school environment. School social workers also work with a wide variety of individuals and organizations based outside the school, such as mental health agencies, child welfare services, probation officers, and health-care providers. Because of this complex role, school social workers need to clarify confidentiality issues in their practice.

This chapter focuses in what circumstances, with whom, and how much information can be revealed to persons within and outside the school. Whether school social workers work individually with children and their families, are part of a school-based team, or work with providers outside the school environment, the sharing of information with others is a concern common to all school social work roles and functions. In the course of providing services to children and families, school social workers are asked to discuss children and their needs with people both within and outside the school environment. School social workers face dilemmas when they are asked to disclose to others the confidential information they learned in the course of providing services to children and families. Consider these examples:

A high school English teacher refers a student to the school social worker because of her concerns that the student may be depressed. The school social worker meets with the student to assess for objective symptoms of depression and determines that the student is depressed and would benefit from individual counseling. A short time later, the student gets into a fight at school, and a teacher refers him to the principal for disciplinary action. The student tells the principal that he has been receiving counseling from the school social worker. The principal is considering expelling the student from school and wants to know why the student is seeing the social worker and what information the social worker may have that explains the student's behavior. Should the social worker give the principal details regarding the student's depression? How much information and what type of information should the social worker provide to persuade the principal not to expel the student?

The mother of a student contacts the school social worker because she and her husband have decided to divorce after years of constant fighting. She asks the social worker to meet with her child to help her adjust to the divorce and to the fact that her father has moved out of their home. The school social worker meets with the student and invites her to join a school-based group for children of divorce. The student agrees and attends regularly for one semester, sharing her feelings about her parents, their conflict, and their divorce. The school social worker later receives a phone call from the student's father, who inquires about his child's progress and wants to know what his daughter has said about him and her mother. If the father has the right to know about his child's progress, does he also have the right to learn the details of the sessions so he can use them as evidence in the upcoming divorce? Does the school social worker have to share information with the father because he is a parent? What about sharing with the mother who arranged for the services? What if the child does not want her parents to know what they have discussed in their sessions? Can the school social worker be subpoenaed to court and be required to disclose what the student told him or her?

A school social worker learns that a family in the school district has become homeless. The social worker wants to refer the family to a local shelter. When the social worker calls the shelter, he learns that the shelter has space for only one additional family; the shelter has received inquiries from other agencies about other homeless families, and the shelter will make its own determination about who gets the vacancy based on the severity of the needs. The shelter wants to know what the relevant family issues are and what is so urgent about their situation. Can the school social worker disclose the family's situation to the shelter and share personal details about the family so that the shelter will take them in?

A school social worker attends a discharge-planning meeting at a psychiatric hospital for a high school student with whom the social worker worked during the previous academic year. The student has been hospitalized in this psychiatric facility because of a suicide attempt she made over the summer. The psychiatrist stresses to the social worker that the student is extremely embarrassed about her hospitalization and does not want anyone to know what happened. The hospital's therapeutic team expresses concern that if others learn about the suicide attempt the student may try again. The psychiatrist and the other team members want to know the school social worker's perceptions of the student's needs and whether anyone in the school needs to know of the student's hospitalization and suicide attempt. Should the social worker share her views of the student's needs? Should she honor the therapeutic team's concerns and keep the information confidential? If she tells others in the school about the student's hospitalization, with whom can she share the information, and how much information can she disclose? Can the school social worker be sure that whomever she tells about the student's needs will not reveal this information?

ETHICAL ISSUES RELATED TO CONFIDENTIALITY IN SCHOOL SOCIAL WORK PRACTICE

Unfortunately, there are no easy answers to any of the above questions. Each question involves many factors that require judgment on the part of the school social worker. School social workers must learn to balance other individuals' desires for information about children and families against their ethical obligations to maintain the confidentiality of their clients' communications to them.

National Association of Social Workers Code of Ethics

The starting point for all social workers in understanding their ethical obligations to their clients is the National Association of Social Workers (NASW) Code of Ethics (2008). Whether or not a social worker belongs to NASW, the NASW Code of Ethics serves as the basis for the social work profession's ethical duties to clients and others. The NASW Code of Ethics discusses social workers' ethical duties to maintain the confidentiality of client information. The NASW Code of Ethics is also the standard by which social workers will be judged if they are alleged to have violated their clients' confidentiality.

The current NASW Code of Ethics, approved in 1996 and updated in 2008, contains eighteen specific provisions pertaining to privacy and confidentiality. The confidentiality provisions include topics such as limitations on confidentiality, securing client consent, the handling and disposal of written and electronic records, management of records after a client's death, and so on. The most pertinent provision related to maintaining and revealing client confidentiality is found in section 1.07(c): "Social workers should protect the confidentiality of all information obtained in the course of professional service, except for compelling professional reasons. The general expectation that social workers will keep information confidential does not apply when disclosure is necessary to prevent serious, foreseeable, and imminent harm to a client or other identifiable person. In all instances, social workers should disclose the least amount of confidential information necessary to achieve the desired purpose; only information that is directly relevant to the purpose for which the disclosure is made should be revealed" (NASW, 2008, 1.07 [c]). To distill this ethical provision to its most basic form, the Code states that social workers should keep all client information confidential, except when there are compelling professional reasons to disclose such information. The Code requires social workers to maintain confidentiality except when the disclosure is necessary to prevent serious harm or injury to a client or another person. Additionally, when the social worker decides to disclose client information, the social worker should reveal the minimum amount of information that is necessary under the circumstances.

While seemingly simple, applying the confidentiality provisions of the NASW Code of Ethics in the school setting is quite complex. This complexity arises partly because the situations that comprise "compelling professional reasons" are not defined in the Code and because "compelling professional reasons" vary in the eye of the beholders. Moreover, social workers who work in the school environment play a role in the lives of children that is different from the role of most other school personnel, whose professions may not require or value the maintenance of confidentiality. Additionally, the Code of Ethics does not differentiate between working with adult clients and working with minor clients. The fact that children do not have the same legal status as adults adds more difficulty to decision making about maintaining or disclosing information. Some of the complexities of maintaining confidentiality in the school environment are addressed in this chapter. First, however, we must address the question of to whom school social workers owe their ethical obligation of confidentiality.

Position Statements on Confidentiality and the School Social Worker

The NASW Commission on Education, the School Social Work Association of America (SSWAA), and other professional organizations specializing in the interests of school social workers have issued position statements to assist school social workers in handling the difficult confidentiality issues that arise for social workers in the school setting. These statements do not attempt to provide to school social workers the specific instances regarding when confidentiality should be maintained and when information should be disclosed. Instead, the statements offer general principles to guide conduct in situations involving school social workers and confidentiality.

In 1991 the NASW Commission on Education issued a position statement entitled "The School Social Worker and Confidentiality" (NASW Commission on Education, 1991). The position statement begins by recognizing the interplay between law and ethics: "This position statement offers general principles to guide conduct and the judicious appraisal of conduct in situations involving the school social worker and confidentiality" (p. 1). It provides confidentiality guidelines for specific topics such as informed consent, interviewing children, child abuse and neglect, substance abuse, and intended harm to self and others. It concludes by noting that school social workers must be thoroughly familiar with applicable legal regulations and employ ethical decision making when making difficult and sensitive judgments relating to confidentiality.

The SSWAA also adopted its own position statement on confidentiality in the schools entitled "School Social Workers and Confidentiality" in 1991. The SSWAA statement expresses the belief that confidentiality is an underlying principle of school social work and that it is essential to establishing an atmosphere of confidence and trust between school social workers and the individuals they serve. It notes that a careful balance between ethical and legal responsibilities is a requirement of the provision of services to students in the school setting and that school social workers must weigh the consequences of sharing information and assume responsibility for their decisions. The SSWAA statement concludes that the best interests of students should serve as a guide in decisions regarding confidential information.

The position statements share a number of common themes. Each notes that ethics and law play a part in the decision making surrounding the release of client information. Each statement recognizes that the laws governing information disclosure are complicated and that they often conflict. Each statement makes clear that social workers should be familiar with federal, state, and local laws that govern responsibilities related to confidentiality in specific situations. However, the position statements differ regarding whom school social workers are responsible to and how they should balance these duties.

Who Is the Client?

The NASW Commission on Education's position statement (1991) asserts that the school social worker has ethical obligations to more than one client in any given situation and views the student, parents, school personnel, and community as clients of the school social worker. The NASW position statement acknowledges that "the multiplicity" of clients contributes to the complexities of decision making for school social workers about confidentiality. The NASW position statement also explains that the responsibility of the school social worker to maintain student confidentiality needs to be balanced with the social worker's responsibility to parents and school administrators.

The SSWAA position statement (1991) differs in that it observes that information is communicated to school social workers by students and families with the expectation that the information will remain confidential. The statement acknowledges that school social workers may be members of teams and may be confronted by situations where the disclosure of information is critical to providing assistance to students and families. Thus the SSWAA position statement reasons that information should be shared with other school personnel only on a need-to-know basis and only for professional reasons. The statement further points out that the school social worker's responsibility to maintain confidentiality must be weighed against his or her responsibility to the family and school community. The statement concludes by recognizing that the school social worker's focus must always remain on what is in the best interests of students.

Kopels (1992) challenged the stance of the NASW Commission on Education position's statement that school social workers have a multiplicity of clients to whom they have an ethical obligation. She argued that viewing parents, school personnel, and the community as clients of the school social worker elevates them to an equal status with students as the social workers' clients. Instead, Kopels considered these other parties to be stakeholders who may have genuine concerns and legitimate reasons to want information about children, yet their interests do not give them the status of clients. Kopels believed that if these others were considered to be clients, there would be no logical or systematic way to resolve confidentiality conflicts. Kardon (1993) objected to Kopels' position. Kardon agreed that labeling all school personnel and the community as the school social worker's clients was overly expansive, but he disagreed with the view that students were the social worker's clients. Kardon wrote that adhering to the standard of confidentiality interferes with school social workers' ability to work successfully in schools. Kopels (1993) countered that the ethical obligation to safeguard client confidentiality is owed to the student as client, and that decisions regarding information disclosure must be balanced against the primacy of the school social worker's obligation to the student.

Other authors have written about ethical issues that school social workers face in schools (e.g., Garrett, 1994; Jonson-Reid, 2000). Still others have created ethical decision-making models to assist social workers in their decisions regarding which student disclosures to keep confidential and which to reveal for the best interest of the student or the school (e.g., Dibble, 2006;

Raines, 2004; Raines & Dibble, 2010; Reamer, 2005; Strom-Gottfried, 2008). However, while acknowledging that school social workers need to consider certain ethical and legal issues and their own personal values when deciding to maintain or release confidential information, these authors do not directly answer the question of who is the client of the school social worker.

The host setting of the school makes it more difficult for school social workers to determine who their client is, compared to social workers who practice in nonhost settings (SSWAA, 2008). When school social workers believe that they owe duties to more than one client, their decision making about confidentiality becomes confused and more complicated than it needs to be. When school social workers view students, school administrators, teachers, parents, and the community as clients, it becomes almost impossible to sort out who is entitled to information about a student. Having a multiplicity of clients creates ethical conflicts where none really exists. When school social workers raise all interested individuals to the status of clients and then attempt to balance the interests of these multiple "clients," they introduce unnecessary complications.

Parents, teachers, school administrators, and the broader community are interested in the lives and functioning of the children with whom they interact. They need and want information about these children to fulfill their own responsibilities to them. Parents have legal responsibility for their children and usually have deep love for them and the desire that they develop into healthy, functioning individuals. Teachers and other professionals in the school are colleagues of the social worker and typically share the social workers' responsibility and concern for children's educational development. School principals and other administrators have supervisory authority over the social worker and are concerned for the overall educational condition and safety for all students. They care about how a particular child may help or hinder their responsibilities. The broader community has more-expansive interests: community members may be concerned about the safety of their neighborhoods as well as the overall performance of their school systems or how their tax dollars are being spent. All of these groups with vested interests—parents, teachers, school administrators, the community—become stakeholders who may request or demand information about students. However, their concern or interest about a child is different from their right to know such information.

School social workers should maintain the confidentiality of the student unless there are compelling professional reasons to disclose the information to stakeholders. When social workers provide services to family members in addition to the student, the family members may also be considered school social work clients. School social workers incur a similar obligation to protect the confidentiality of family members' information absent compelling reasons for disclosure.

Compelling Professional Reasons

The 1979 version of the NASW Code of Ethics contained language that instructed social workers to keep clients' confidences unless they had compelling professional reasons to disclose information. Provision H(1) stated that "The social worker should share with others confidences revealed by clients, without their consent, only for compelling professional reasons" (NASW, 1979). Provision 1.07 (c) of the current NASW Code of Ethics states, "Social workers should protect the confidentiality of all information obtained in the course of professional service, except for compelling professional reasons. The general expectation that social workers will keep information confidential does not apply when disclosure is necessary to prevent serious, foreseeable, and imminent harm to a client or other identifiable person" (NASW, 2008, 1.07 [c]). Each of these versions of the Code requires social workers to protect confidentiality unless there are compelling professional reasons for not doing so. However, neither version of the Code defines the phrase "compelling professional reasons."

The current Code contains a statement that releases social workers from the expectation of maintaining confidentiality in certain situations, namely when "disclosure is necessary to prevent serious, foreseeable, and imminent harm to a client or other identifiable person" (NASW, 2008, 1.07 [c]). This statement was added to allow social workers to disclose confidential information in situations involving client violence to themselves or others, consistent with the duties imposed by case law (discussed later in this chapter).

Social workers who have compelling professional reasons for disclosing client information are allowed to do so as an exception to the general rule of protecting client confidences. The phrase "compelling professional reasons," although not defined, is generally understood to cover situations where the law requires social workers to disclose information (e.g., child abuse or elder abuse) or situations where the social worker believes disclosure may prevent serious physical harm. Social workers retain discretion and can rely on their professional judgment to disclose information in these limited circumstances. When school social workers learn something that causes them serious concern about the physical safety for students or staff in their schools, they have compelling professional reasons to disclose the information.

Some school social workers use "compelling professional reasons" as their justification for disclosing information to parents, school personnel, or others. They may believe that when they learn about something that they view as harmful to a child, they have compelling professional reasons to disclose it, as appropriate, to parents, colleagues, administrators, or others. For example, if a school social worker learns that a student is shoplifting, he or she may believe it is important to tell the student's parents so they can correct the child's actions and so the student does not get caught and face legal troubles. Arguably, social workers who act to protect a child may be able to ethically justify their decision to disclose, especially if they rely on an ethical decision-making model. Other social workers may consider that telling parents about a child's shoplifting is not a compelling enough reason to violate the student's confidentiality.

Some school social workers use "compelling professional reasons" as a justification to disclose to others almost any information they learn about a child. For example, a school social worker tells the classroom teacher that the affair a child's mother is having with a neighbor is the source of discord in the home and the child's difficulties in school. In this situation, while the social worker may believe that she has compelling professional reasons (the child's school success) to reveal the information to the teacher, most professionals would not consider disclosing the information about the mother's affair to be a compelling professional reason. Instead, some school social workers may simply tell the teacher that the child's home life may be affecting the child's school performance while other school social workers would say nothing to the teacher. Unfortunately, the Code of Ethics does not provide more direction to social workers on which reasons should be considered compelling.

Professionalism vs. Confidentiality

The preceding discussion may leave the reader with the mistaken impression that school social workers have no obligation to maintain the confidentiality of anyone other than students or their family members. That is not the case. Rather, the preceding sections discuss who should be considered the client of the school social worker to whom the duty of confidentiality is owed.

School social workers have responsibilities pertaining to multiple entities, including their colleagues, administrators, and the broader community. School social workers have the obligation to act professionally in their jobs. As professionals, school social workers should operate in ways that demonstrate respect for their colleagues and their employers. In some situations, colleagues may share personal information about themselves with the school social worker in the course of their professional relationships. For example, a teacher may tell the social worker about her own drinking or drug use. The social worker should keep that information to him- or herself unless the teacher's drinking interferes with her classroom performance. In other situations, administrators may seek out the social worker's advice about sensitive matters. For example, a principal may ask the school social worker how to handle talking to an employee who is suspected of using the school's computers to view pornography. In both of these situations, the school social worker would maintain the confidentiality of the communication—not because the teacher or the principal is the client of the social worker, but rather because the social worker has a professional and ethical responsibility to act in ways that show respect for the dignity of others. Similarly, school social workers should not gossip about the daily happenings at their schools or about their colleagues or the parents of schoolchildren. The school social worker should not share school gossip—not because these individuals are their clients, but instead because the social worker should always act in a professional manner.

LEGAL ISSUES RELATED TO CONFIDENTIALITY IN SCHOOL SOCIAL WORK PRACTICE

School social workers can consult the NASW Code of Ethics, professional position statements, and scholarly literature on confidentiality to determine best practice principles regarding how to handle situations that concern disclosure of information regarding children or their families. These sources all share the recognition of the complexities pertaining to maintaining confidentiality in schools. These sources also share an emphasis on the role ethics play in professional practice, and provide school social workers with possible ways to think about resolving their ethical conflicts. However, the NASW Code of Ethics, position statements, and the literature on confidentiality do not provide school social workers with sufficient guidance on the legal issues that complicate confidentiality. The information that follows may assist school social workers in recognizing the impact of certain legal issues on ethical school social work practice and confidentiality.

Child Abuse and Neglect Reporting

One of the most problematic issues for school social workers is deciding when information should be disclosed for the protection of the student and others. The lack of understanding of the duty to report, the duty to warn, and the duty to protect leads to confusion about social workers' duties to disclose client confidences to protect clients and others (Kopels & Kagle, 1993). Social workers confuse their requirements as mandated reporters to disclose information related to child abuse and neglect with their discretionary ability to disclose certain information in situations when they think the students or others may be at risk of harm.

Until the early 1970s, social workers had no duty to intervene when children with whom they worked experienced child abuse or neglect. In 1974 Congress enacted the Child Abuse Prevention and Treatment Act (CAPTA). CAPTA provides federal funding to states in support of prevention, assessment, investigation, prosecution, and treatment activities related to child abuse and neglect. To receive CAPTA funding, states must have a system in place for the reporting of child abuse and neglect. Laws in all states set out what actions constitute abuse and neglect, which persons are considered to be perpetrators of child abuse and neglect, which professionals have to report child abuse and neglect, how quickly the abuse and neglect must be reported, and where those professionals should report suspected abuse and neglect.

In other words, the law mandates how and when child abuse and neglect must be reported. In all fifty states, Guam, Puerto Rico, and other U.S. territories, social workers are mandated reporters (Kopels, 2006). Therefore, when social workers suspect that a child with whom they are working may be abused or neglected, they must report their suspicions.

Since the enactment of mandatory reporting, school social workers who learn of or suspect child abuse or neglect must make a report, regardless of whether the source of the knowledge is the student, the parent, other school personnel, or outside sources. At first glance, it may seem that mandated reporting is in conflict with the idea of maintaining client confidentiality. However, the protection of children through reporting of child abuse and neglect is considered to be a compelling professional reason sufficient to justify the disclosure of confidential information. Additionally, in settings where strict confidentiality laws exist (e.g., substance abuse treatment settings or mental health facilities), most states have exceptions written into their confidentiality laws that allow for child abuse and neglect reporting. In these situations, the mandated reporter can disclose such information without fear of being sued for the breach of his or her duty to maintain confidentiality. Because child abuse and neglect reporting is mandatory, social workers routinely act to protect children when they suspect a child is being harmed by their caregivers. In effect, there is almost no discretion necessary on the part of school social workers in reporting child abuse and neglect if they have a reasonable belief that it has occurred. However, because social workers know they must report child abuse and neglect, they often believe that they are responsible for reporting any situation in which they believe a child is endangered by anyone who might harm a child. They mistakenly expand their duty to report child abuse or neglect to any situation in which a child may be at risk.

Harm to Self or Others and the Duty to Warn

As mentioned above, the mandated reporting of child abuse and neglect derives from legislation enacted in all states and territories to ensure the protection of children. There are other situations in which social workers may be expected to protect their clients and third parties from the actions of their clients if they threaten harm to themselves or others. The issue of client actions that trigger the social worker's duty to warn or protect others is very misunderstood. Much of the confusion about the duty to warn or protect stems from the fact that there is no uniform understanding of these duties and that even referring to them as duties is misleading. Rothstein (2014) urges a unitary standard for dealing with these duties, rather than the fifty-one jurisdiction-specific ways that currently exist.

The disclosure of client information for the protection of the client and others stems from the landmark court case of *Tarasoff v. Regents of the University of California* (1974). The case involved a graduate student, Prosenjit Poddar, who told his psychologist that he intended to kill an unnamed but identifiable woman, Tatiana Tarasoff. Although the psychologist took steps to have the campus police detain him, Poddar later killed Tarasoff. Tarasoff's parents sued the psychologist and others for their failure to warn them of the harm Poddar posed to Tarasoff.

The California Supreme Court issued a ruling that established "when a doctor or a psychotherapist, in the exercise of his professional skill and knowledge, determines, or should determine, that a warning is essential to avert danger arising from the medical or psychological condition of his patient, he incurs a legal obligation to give that warning" (*Tarasoff v. Regents of the University of California,* 1974). This Tarasoff case created a duty of professionals to warn others to avert danger. Two years later, on its own, the California Supreme Court amended its previous ruling and changed the duty to warn to a duty to protect (*Tarasoff v. Regents of the University of California,* 1976). The court in that second decision stated that the "discharge of the duty to protect can occur in a variety of ways, including warning the intended victim or others likely to apprise the victim of the danger, to notify the police, or to take whatever other steps are reasonably necessary under the circumstances." The ruling by the California Supreme Court in the Tarasoff decision (1976) created the precedent that psychotherapists need to warn or protect third parties when their clients may be violent to others. Social workers and other psychotherapists tend to believe that the Tarasoff case requires them to disclose information about their clients to avoid harm to the clients or others.

Due to a general misunderstanding of what the Tarasoff case actually requires, however, many social workers mistakenly believe that they have a duty to warn of any potentially dangerous situation, and therefore routinely disclose information that they should withhold (Kopels & Kagle, 1993). Because the Tarasoff case occurred in California, any obligations that the court imposed on psychotherapists apply to California practitioners only. In other states, courts have reached different results (Kagle & Kopels, 1994). For example, in 1999 the Texas Supreme Court (*Thapar v. Zezulka,* 1999) and in 2009 the Illinois Supreme Court (*Tedrick v. Community Resource Center, Inc.,* 2009) each ruled that their respective states do not follow the reasoning in the Tarasoff case. Additionally, in response to the Tarasoff case many state legislatures passed laws that lay out practitioners' duties in situations involving harm. These laws also limit practitioners' liability for disclosing or failing to disclose information when they act in accordance with what their states' legislation requires (Kopels & Kagle, 1993; Rothstein, 2014). Other states impose the obligation to protect third parties only on certain, designated professionals. For example, some states may require clinical social workers to protect third parties whereas other states may not place the same requirement on social workers. Additionally, most states have amended their laws on confidentiality of health and mental health information to allow for an exception to maintaining confidentiality when disclosure of client information is necessary to warn or protect third parties.

In spite of the conventional wisdom, there is no consistent, nationwide approach to handling situations where clients are dangerous to themselves or others. In the schools, social workers encounter situations where students disclose that they are depressed and suicidal, angry and homicidal, and everything in between. Social workers will learn that the students with whom they work are pregnant, self-mutilating, being bullied, using alcohol or drugs, members of gangs, struggling with their sexual identities, having unprotected sex, and so on. School social workers must use their professional discretion to decide when their clients pose actual physical danger to themselves or others. Unlike situations involving child abuse and neglect, in which social workers are required to act and report their suspicions of abuse or neglect, the duty to warn or protect involves the social workers' use of clinical judgment to assess the degree of danger or harm to the student or others and to take action, if warranted.

Physical Violence vs. Harmful Acts

Another misunderstanding among practitioners that arose as a result of the Tarasoff case concerns the fact that the duty to warn or the duty to protect applies only to situations where actual violence has been threatened. Under Tarasoff, when a therapist determines or should have determined that the client poses danger to another person, that therapist is obligated to take action to protect others. The Tarasoff case, cases from other states, and most of the legislation created to balance when therapists should be responsible for taking action to protect others only create the responsibility to act when clients threaten serious physical harm or violence to themselves or others. For the school social worker, the potential for physical harm to a student or others in the school environment (e.g., classmates, teachers, administrators, or other personnel) is readily apparent in situations involving threats of suicide, self-mutilation, bullying, weapons in schools, gang behavior, and other violence directed toward others.

However, most of the time students disclose information that does not involve the threat of physical violence. Instead, they disclose information about actions that may be considered serious and troublesome, and that the social worker is alarmed to hear about, but physical violence is not involved. The question that the social worker is left with is whether he or she needs to maintain the confidentiality of the student's disclosure.

Social workers often incorrectly believe that the Tarasoff case expands their perceived responsibilities to many situations other than those involving physical violence. School social workers often believe that they have a duty to warn or protect when they learn that students are engaging in behaviors that are illegal for children to do (e.g., drinking alcohol) and/or that may be harmful to them (e.g., having unprotected sex). A school social worker who learns that a student is engaging in unprotected sexual intercourse, is pregnant, or is using alcohol or drugs may view the situation as potentially dangerous to the student. The social worker may feel the need to disclose the information to the student's parents to protect the student from the danger caused by the student's condition. From a legal perspective, however, the fact that no physical violence is involved may not create any obligation to act.

While the school social worker may have no legal obligation to take action in situations that do not involve violence, the social worker may still have an ethical obligation to do something on behalf of a child. For example, a student's disclosure that he is smoking marijuana (an illegal activity in most states) clearly creates a dilemma for the school social worker who wants to protect the student from himself. Some school social workers would talk to the student, assess the situation, discourage drug use, and make a referral for treatment, but would maintain the confidentiality of the student's disclosure. Other school social workers may feel the need to disclose the information to the parents so that they can deal with the situation or to teachers so that they may understand the student. If so, the social worker should consider the level of the student's impairment in functioning (if any), how often the student smokes marijuana (e.g., daily or only at parties), how old the student is (e.g., twelve years old or seventeen years old), whether the student's grades have been stable or have dropped, whether the student drives while under the influence, the positive and negative consequences to the student as a result of making the disclosure, to whom the disclosure should be made (parent, teacher, administrator), and the likely benefit to the student before making a decision about whether to reveal the information.

Another example of a condition that may be harmful to a child but does not involve violence is when a student discloses to the social worker that she is pregnant. Some school social workers would talk to the student, find out whether she has told her parents, advise her to do so if she has not, help her seek prenatal care, and refer her to services for pregnant teens, all while keeping the information confidential. Other school social workers may feel the need to tell the parents or the teacher so that they understand the student's situation. If the social worker wants to disclose the information, the social worker must assess how far along the student is in her pregnancy (e.g., two months compared with seven months), the dangers to the student and the fetus that stem from the lack of health care, and the consequences of the disclosure for the student. While there may be no duty to warn because the student is not threatening physical violence, the social worker may be able to discretionarily disclose the information to protect the student from harm. Unfortunately, there is no formula for deciding at what point the potential for harm to self or others triggers a responsibility to act.

Imminence of Physical Violence

Related to social workers' misunderstanding of the duty to warn of physical violence is the concept of the imminence of the potential violence. Under the Tarasoff ruling and most legislation created in response to the duty to warn, any duty a professional may have typically occurs only when actual physical danger is imminent. In other words, when a social worker discloses information about a client's harmful actions or threats, she might make the disclosure to prevent the furtherance of immediate physical harm to the client or others. If a student tells the social worker that he brought a gun to school today and is going to "get" the student who stole his backpack, the social worker should immediately disclose this information to the administration and follow the school's protocol for dealing with critical incidents. Not only does a gun present a serious threat of physical violence to other students, but in addition the harm is imminent. Similarly, if a student threatens that she is going to blow up the school tomorrow, the social worker should take action.

However, it is often the case that students disclose information to the social worker about former but not current behaviors. Learning about this information may prove problematic for the social worker because the concerning behaviors are in the past and not imminent. For example, if students disclose that they formerly used drugs but no longer do, or that they used to cut themselves but no longer do, any harm resulting from these activities is in the past. The students' disclosures do not suggest physical harm to others, nor is there any imminent harm to the students. The social worker would not have to disclose this information to others, although parents, teachers, and administrators may be interested in these facts.

The contours of the duty to warn does not always coincide with the ethical notion of social workers maintaining confidentiality unless there is a compelling reason for disclosure. Students often disclose activities they engage in that neither relate to physical harm to themselves or others nor involve behaviors in which they are currently engaging. If a school social worker chooses to disclose to parents information about students' former drug use or cutting behaviors that the student no longer engages in, the social worker should do so only if he or she believes the student will reengage in this behavior soon (e.g., due to a relapse in drug use or because the student is not handling new stresses). In other words, there should be a compelling professional reason for the social worker to disclose this information. Otherwise, confidentiality should be maintained.

This discussion should not leave the reader with the idea that school social workers should take no action unless they learn from students or others that physical violence is imminent. Instead, this discussion is meant to demonstrate the complexities of the school social worker's role in maintaining confidentiality. State and federal law as well as court decisions around the country also contribute to the complexities of deciding whether to share information with others.

Age of the Child

The fact that children are minors complicates legal decision making related to the imminence of harm. School social workers may be more concerned about a young child who engages in the same activities as an older child, and might view the same activity as more harmful for the younger child. For example, a student may disclose to the school social worker that she is having sexual intercourse with her eighteen-year-old boyfriend. While it may not be advisable for adolescents of any age to have sexual relationships, the social worker may view the behavior as more imminently harmful if the student is twelve years old rather than seventeen. If the student is twelve years of age, the social worker may view the student as less mature and may assess the sexual relationship as more exploitative and more dangerous for the student, and thus choose to disclose the information to the parents. If the student is seventeen years old, the social worker may decide that the sexual activity, while unwise, is consensual and keep the information confidential.

Similarly, when a twelve-year-old student discloses that she is pregnant, the age of the child may influence the social worker's decision to maintain or disclose the student's confidence. If a pregnant twelve-year-old girl has not told her parents about her pregnancy, the social worker may be more concerned that this younger child lacks the maturity to appreciate the consequences of the pregnancy to her body and the fetus. The school social worker may believe that by telling the parents, he or she is helping the student and the baby. On the other hand, an older student who does not want to tell her parents about her pregnancy may have a more realistic view of her situation. The student may know from experience that her parents may beat her or kick her out of the home if they learn she is pregnant. The older student has more ability to get the prenatal care that the fetus requires if she decides to maintain her pregnancy, and is more likely to be mature enough to weigh the consequences of her decisions. The social worker may honor the student's confidences. Before a social worker reveals information to the parents, the social worker should work with the student to encourage her to tell her parents about the pregnancy, so that the social worker does not have to be the one to reveal the information.

Ironically, in some situations student behaviors are problematic for the school social worker who learns of them solely because the student is a minor. Students who drink alcohol are engaging in behavior that would be considered legal if they were adults. It is their status as children that makes the drinking unlawful and creates a possible responsibility to disclose the behavior to parents. Social workers who work with adults have no similar legal responsibility to report their clients' drinking to anyone. As another example, curfew laws apply only to minors. Adults are free to come and go at any hour, as they choose. If a student tells her school social worker that she is babysitting for the neighbors and comes home after curfew, the student is violating curfew laws. However, if the student were eighteen or older, the student's behavior would be considered legal and would not violate any laws because the student would be considered an adult.

Age, State Law, and the Health Insurance Portability and Accountability Act

As a general rule, children are viewed as incompetent to make decisions until they reach the age of majority (as defined by each state). Exceptions to this general rule include situations where children are legally emancipated before they reach majority age. Many states have provisions in their laws that allow children, usually over age sixteen, to become legally emancipated so that they are considered to be adults. Additionally, certain laws specify situations in which the legislature has recognized that the child is mature enough to make his or her own decisions regarding particular topics. For example, in some states, children above a certain age (e.g., twelve or fourteen) can make treatment and health decisions concerning alcohol or drug use, mental health, and the use of birth control or abortion services. There is little consistency among states regarding special treatment of minors in various situations under the law.

The Health Insurance Portability and Accountability Act of 1996 (HIPAA) is a federal law that applies to protected health information. Protected health information is individually identifiable health information about a person's health care, mental health, or behavioral health. HIPAA creates a set of minimum, national standards for protecting individuals' health information. HIPAA preempts state law if a state's laws offer less privacy protections than HIPAA. If a state's laws are considered more stringent (i.e., the state's laws offer more privacy protection than the minimum created under HIPAA), then the state law must be followed.

HIPAA is consistent with the law's general treatment of minors. As is true in most laws, regulations, and court decisions relating to children and families, HIPAA treats parents and guardians as the authorized representatives of their minors. Personnel who work with minors must look to their parents and guardians as those entitled to make health-care decisions, and must release their children's protected health information to them.

When state law gives certain rights to minors, however, the parent or guardian no longer has those rights. HIPAA defers to any state laws that confer greater rights to minors. When laws in a state provide certain rights to minors rather than to their parents (e.g., the right to consent to and receive alcohol counseling), then social workers should look to the minors for the authorization to disclose the minors' information. Under these state laws, the minor is the person from whom social workers need to secure consent for treatment or the release of information.

The Family Educational Rights and Privacy Act

Under HIPAA, personal health information does not include education records. While a student's school records are filled with personal and private information about the student, an earlier law governs access to and disclosure of student records. The Family Educational Rights and Privacy Act of 1974 (FERPA) is a federal law that pertains specifically to education records. Under FERPA, parents have the right to consent to disclosure of their children's information until the child reaches the age of eighteen. At age eighteen, all rights transfer to the student (who is then an eligible student under the language of FERPA).

FERPA gives parents and eligible students the right to inspect and review education records and to request that schools correct the records if they are inaccurate, misleading, or improper. Parents and eligible students have the right to insert into the record a statement that provides for their perspective about any disputed portions of the record.

FERPA distinguishes between different types of information in students' education record. Directory information includes factual information about children including their age, address, grades, dates of attendance, and so on. Parental consent is not required for the release of directory information, as long as parents are provided with notice of the school's policy regarding disclosure of directory information.

In contrast, written permission from parents or the eligible child is required to release any personally identifiable information in the education records. In cases where a school social worker needs to disclose information about a student to individuals and agencies outside the school environment, the school social worker should ask the child's parents for consent to communicate about the child. Under FERPA, consent is not needed to disclose information from the school record in emergency situations, to lawful authorities, and to individuals within the school environment who have legitimate educational interests in having the information.

FERPA applies to the education records of students, which includes information that is in written or recorded form. Many of the records created by school social workers are subject to the provisions of FERPA. For example, school social workers generate social developmental studies, conduct and record functional behavioral analyses, provide and document social work minutes in individualized education programs (IEPs), engage in and record notes of individual and group counseling sessions, and so on. These records are subject to the provisions of FERPA (Kagle & Kopels, 2008). In contrast, FERPA does not apply to the personal notes of school social workers, nor does it apply to written records that are not educational in nature. School records contain many sources of information, such as mental health, alcohol/drug, and medical records generated by outside agencies. While these latter sources of records may not be education records under FERPA, they may be considered personal health information under HIPAA.

Clearly, social workers must be familiar with the laws of their own state that pertain to different aspects of school social work practice. School social workers should also have a working knowledge of federal and state laws that govern issues related to consent for treatment, access to and disclosure of records, and how the age of the child may affect these issues. State and federal laws may differentially affect how workers outside the school setting handle confidentiality concerns (e.g., alcohol treatment centers, mental health facilities) and the responsibilities of different professionals (e.g., social workers vs. teachers). In addition, the type of presenting problem (e.g., sexual disease transmission, child abuse) may have some bearing on confidentiality concerns.

OTHER FACTORS THAT INFLUENCE CONFIDENTIALITY

There are additional factors that school social workers should keep in mind when considering whether to disclose client information. These include release of information forms, subpoenas from court, necessary disclosures and the minimum possible information, and the consequences of disclosure without consent.

Release of Information Forms

It may seem obvious, but decisions about disclosing information are greatly simplified when social workers obtain signed releases of information or other consent forms from the students they work with or their parents, if the parents are the persons authorized under the law to disclose information about the students. A release of information form is a document that allows an approved individual to consent to the disclosure of information to a person or agency. The content of a release of information form may be delineated under the law and usually involves information such as the types of information to be released, to whom it should be released, how long the release is valid, and the consequences of refusing to authorize consent. Releases of information should be in writing. Unless there is an emergency, a school social worker should not rely on an oral consent to release of information from the student, the parent, or the guardian.

When a school social worker needs to disclose information about a student to individuals and agencies outside the school environment, he or she should ask the child or the parents to sign release of information forms that allow the school social worker to lawfully share information about a student. The social worker can discuss with the parents the type of information that he or she needs to disclose, the purpose of the disclosure, and what might happen to the child or the family if the information is shared with others.

Subpoenas from Court

Subpoenas are orders issued by a court for testimony or for records. Subpoenas are especially problematic for social workers and other mental health professionals because subpoenas often seek information about which the professionals have a duty to maintain confidentiality (Kagle & Kopels, 2008). For example, a school social worker provides services to a fourteen-year-old student who discloses that her mother is having an affair with a neighbor. The student says that her parents are constantly arguing and that her father is extremely belittling to her mother. The father decides to file for divorce from the mother and seeks custody of the daughter. The father may subpoena the records of the social worker that contain documentation of the daughter's statements about the affair or subpoena the testimony of the social worker about the statements the daughter made. The student tells the social worker that she does not want the social worker to disclose the information because she does not want to be caught in the middle of her parents' discord. However, the subpoena requires the social worker to respond to the order. The social worker is caught in the middle of a conflict between the need to maintain confidentiality and the requirement to disclose the information in accordance with the subpoena.

Social workers must respond to the receipt of the subpoena although the response may not necessarily be to testify in court or to turn over the records. There are numerous factors that may make the issuance of a subpoena invalid (Kagle & Kopels, 2008). Social workers need to take actions such as asking the client to sign a release of information that allows the social worker to disclose the records and consulting with an attorney about complying with the subpoena. When a client refuses to sign a release of information, social workers are ethically required to act to protect the client's confidentiality.

Necessary Disclosures and the Minimum Possible Information

To do their jobs effectively, school social workers often team with other service providers both within and outside the school to ensure that students receive the services that are most appropriate to their needs. Working as a team member often requires the sharing of information. However, there are a number of ways that sharing information with team members can be handled to reduce concerns about confidentiality. Social workers should always share the least amount of information necessary under the situation.

In some types of school teams, the school social worker does not have any clinical responsibility for a student but is simply a member of a team that convenes to address a specific mission. For example, if a social worker is a member of a positive behavioral interventions and supports team, the social worker, like all other members of the team, looks at ways that consistent behavioral rules will increase positive behaviors throughout the school.

The positive behavioral interventions and supports team discussions often concern general behavioral expectations for all students and do not address the behaviors of individual students. When the social worker contributes his or her knowledge of behavioral techniques or the developmental stages of children, the social worker is talking generally about students' needs and not about the therapeutic requirements of any specific child. Confidentiality would not be a concern here because confidential communications are not involved.

A multitiered system of supports requires different types of interventions at different levels of intensity, based on the needs of students. Social workers may have brief, informal interactions with students as part of tier 1 interventions or they may provide more-formal and more-intensive tier 2 or tier 3 services.

At later team meetings about the student, the social worker might be asked to disclose information about the child. The social worker should contribute as little specific information as is necessary for the goal of service. The social worker may disclose general information about the child's progress without disclosing any other aspects of the student's issues that the social worker learns of through more-intensive interventions.

School social workers often are members of teams that create IEPs for children with disabilities who have special education needs. The development of an IEP requires the team to have detailed knowledge of a child's specific needs and functioning. For example, the team must understand the child's present levels of academic achievement and functional performance and how the disability affects the child's involvement and progress in the curriculum. The team must obtain this knowledge so that it can fashion goals that meet the child's needs. In generating an IEP that meets a specific child's individual needs, the school social worker, like all other team members, must share information about the child with other team members. In cases where the need for or continuation of school social work services are being contemplated, the social worker may have to reveal information about the child and his or her needs to explain why the child requires the initiation or continuation of such services. In the special education context, sharing information with other team members is not a confidentiality concern. Under federal special education regulations, IEP team members are explicitly allowed to share information to produce a plan for the child. Despite this legal sanctioning of sharing information, the school social worker still should disclose the minimum amount of information that will accomplish the purpose of obtaining services for the child.

Under all circumstances, school social workers must continually assess whether it is truly necessary to disclose confidential information about a student to someone else. If, after careful consideration, the social worker decides that compelling professional or legal reasons support disclosure, the next step is to ensure that he or she discloses the least amount of information necessary. In order to protect the privacy of the student, the social worker should release the minimum information necessary for the purpose. For example, if the social worker believes it is necessary to tell the teacher about marital discord in the home that is negatively affecting the child's behavior, it is not necessary to tell the teacher that the student's father gets drunk all the time, which angers the mother, who then goes out and has affairs. Instead, the social worker should simply state that the child is reacting to strife in his home. School social workers should always release the least amount of information they can even when they have client consent or determine that the disclosure is consistent with ethical or legal considerations.

The Consequences of Disclosure without Consent

School social workers may encounter practice situations where they are tempted to disclose confidential information because they believe it is in the best interest of their clients or third parties to do so. At other times the discomfort of learning delicate information leads social workers to want to share the information with someone else, a colleague, supervisor, intimate partner, or friend, so that they have a sounding board for their own feelings. In those cases, the social worker is placing his or her own needs above the interest of the client. In still other situations, social workers know that they should not disclose information but do so anyway, just because the information is really interesting. Before disclosing information without legal or ethical justification, practitioners must ask themselves whether such disclosure is truly worth the risk.

From a practical perspective, disclosure of students' information against the wishes of students can greatly reduce a social worker's effectiveness. When a student tells a social worker something that the student considers a confidence, yet the social worker discloses it to the parents or others, the student will be angry and upset. In some situations, the seriousness of the information outweighs the fact that the student will be angry. For example, a sixteen-year-old tells the social worker that he recently got his driver's license and drove his friends to a party, where they all got "really wasted." If the social worker discloses this to the parents, there may be consequences for the student; for example, the parents may watch the student's actions more closely, require the student to go for drug counseling, or revoke his driving privileges. While the student may be upset, the social worker can defend his or her actions ethically and legally because of the student's dangerous behavior.

In other situations, the student's anger may be justified. For example, if a sixteen-year-old student tells the social worker that he believes he is gay, and the social worker informs the parents that their son is gay, the student will be upset. The social worker cannot justify his or her actions ethically or legally because there are no compelling reasons to permit the disclosure. The social worker would find it difficult to explain to the student why he or she chose to disclose the sexual orientation and what would be gained by the disclosure. Additionally, the student will undoubtedly talk to his friends and caution them not to talk to the social worker because he or she cannot be trusted. The distrust will spread throughout the student body and have long-term consequences on the social worker's effectiveness with students.

In addition to practical concerns, social workers who fail to uphold confidentiality consistent with their professional ethics or legal obligations may face other consequences. When social workers violate the law or professional ethics, they may be subject to lawsuits for breach of confidentiality or malpractice. They may also find themselves sanctioned by social work regulatory boards or professional associations. In all situations, before disclosing information the social worker should analyze the issues, including the personal and professional costs and benefits to them and their clients. Social workers can also seek professional guidance from and consult with supervisors or other colleagues.

CONCLUSION

The profession of school social work has evolved significantly from the early days, when social workers served as liaisons between immigrant children in settlement houses and schools. The issue of school social workers maintaining confidentiality has evolved as well, becoming increasingly complicated and reflecting the problems facing school social workers today. Social workers can seek guidance regarding confidentiality from the NASW Code of Ethics, the position statements of school social work professional organizations, and the professional literature. School social workers should act in accordance with their ethical codes, use an ethical decision-making model (Raines & Dibble, 2010; Strom-Gottfried, 2008), and strive to maintain the confidentiality of information shared with them. If they release confidential information, they should do so only with written releases of information or if they have compelling professional reasons for disclosure. Additionally, school social workers must be cognizant of legal issues that affect confidentiality generally, as well as specific legal issues that arise in practice in their states. These factors only increase the ethical and legal complexities of dealing with confidentiality in schools.

References

Child Abuse Prevention and Treatment Act (CAPTA), Pub. L. 93-247; 42 U.S.C. § 5101 et seq. (1974).

Dibble, N. (2006). *Ethical issues and professional boundaries for school social workers*. Paper presented at the Midwest School Social Work Conference, Arlington Heights, IL.

Family Educational Rights and Privacy Act of 1974 (FERPA), Pub. L. 93-380, 88 Stat. 571 (1974).

Garrett, K. R. (1994). Caught in a bind: Ethical decision making in schools. *Social Work in Education, 16*(2), 97–105.

Health Insurance Portability and Accountability Act of 1996 (HIPAA), Pub. L. 104-191, 110 Stat. (1996).

Jonson-Reid, M. (2000). Understanding confidentiality in school-based interagency projects. *Social Work in Education, 22*(1), 33–45.

Kagle, J. D., & Kopels, S. (1994). Confidentiality after Tarasoff. *Health and Social Work, 19*(3), 217–222.

Kagle, J. D., & Kopels, S. (2008). *Social work records* (3rd ed.). Long Grove, IL: Waveland Press.

Kardon, S. (1993). Confidentiality: A different perspective. *Social Work in Education, 15*(4), 247–250.

Kopels, S. (1992). Confidentiality and the school social worker. *Social Work in Education, 14*(4), 203–205.

Kopels, S. (1993). Response to "Confidentiality: A Different Perspective." *Social Work in Education, 15*(4), 250–252.

Kopels, S. (2006). Laws and procedures for reporting child abuse: An overview. In C. Franklin, M. B. Harris, & P. Allen-Meares (Eds.), *The school services sourcebook* (pp. 369–375). New York: Oxford University Press.

Kopels, S., & Kagle, J. D. (1993). Do social workers have a duty to warn? *Social Service Review, 67*(1), 101–126.

NASW Commission on Education. (1991). The school social worker and confidentiality. *School Social Work Journal, 17*(2), 38–46.

National Association of Social Workers (NASW). (1979). *Code of ethics.* Retrieved from https://www.socialworkers.org/nasw/ethics/ethicshistory.asp

National Association of Social Workers (NASW). (2008). *Code of ethics.* Retrieved from https://www.socialworkers.org/pubs/code/code.asp

Raines, J. C. (2004). To tell or not to tell: Ethical issues regarding confidentiality. *School Social Work Journal, 28*(2), 62–78.

Raines, J. C., & Dibble, N. T. (2010). *Ethical decision making in school mental health*. New York: Oxford University Press.

Reamer, F. G. (2005). Update on confidentiality issues in practice with children: Ethics risk management. *Children & Schools, 27*(2), 117–120.

Rothstein, M. A. (2014). Tarasoff duties after Newtown. *Journal of Law, Medicine and Ethics, 42*(1), 104–109.

School Social Work Association of America (SSWAA). (1991). *School social workers and confidentiality.* Retrieved from http://sswaa.affiniscape.com/associations/13190/files/School%20Social%20Workers%20and%20Confidentiality.pdf

School Social Work Association of America (SSWAA). (2008). *School social work in a host setting.* Retrieved from http://sswaa.affiniscape.com/associations/13190/files/School%20Social%20Work%20in%20a%20Host%20Setting.pdf

Strom-Gottfried, K. J. (2008). *The ethics of practice with minors: High stakes, hard choices.* Chicago: Lyceum Books.

Tarasoff v. Regents of the University of California, 13 Cal. 3d 177; 529 P.2d 553 (1974).

Tarasoff v. Regents of the University of California, 17 Cal. 3d 425, 551 P.2d 334 (1976).

Tedrick v. Community Resource Center, Inc., 235 Ill. 2d. 155 (2009).

Thapar v. Zezulka, 994 S. W. 2d. 635 (Texas, 1999).

8

School Social Workers: School-Based Consultants Supporting a Multitiered System of Indirect Service

Christine Anlauf Sabatino

The Catholic University of America

◆ Consultation Theory and Practice
◆ Organizational Consultation
◆ Program Consultation
◆ Education and Training Consultation
◆ Mental Health Consultation
◆ Behavioral Consultation
◆ Clinical Consultation

CONSULTATION THEORY AND PRACTICE

Consultation is defined as an indirect method of practice that assists others to become more effective in their professional work. It is a specialized inter-action between professionals who hold the roles of consultant and consul-tee (Caplan, 1970). The consultant is someone who has unique expertise that the consultee believes will help resolve a particular work-related diffi-culty. The consultant assists the consultee by using a strengths-based prob-lem-solving process that "emphasizes the client's resources, capabilities, support systems, and motivation to meet challenges and overcome adversity" (Barker, 2003, p. 420). Social work consultation is able to address multiple school challenges that create barriers to academic and behavioral performance and interfere with the ability of people, groups, programs, organizations, and communities to attain school success, human dignity, and social justice.

This definition of consultation is in contrast to its general meaning that connotes a broad discussion between professionals about a problematic setting, population, problem, or practice, or connotes common advice-seeking and advice-giving (Caplan & Caplan, 1999; Gallessich, 1982). Furthermore, social work intervention methods most often focus on providing direct service to clients. Consultation is different because the consultant rarely has direct contact with the target client-system. Rather, assessment and intervention are undertaken in partnership with the consultee, who is ultimately responsible for providing the direct service.

Caplan and Caplan (1999) refer to this interaction as the coordinate relationship that views consultees as fully competent professionals who retain full authority for school situations. Thus, consultants leave control of service delivery to consultees who have primary responsibility for the work-related issues. In other words, consultants step back and allow another professional to be in charge of the strengths-based problem-solving processes. In fact, this type of professional interaction is far more complicated than working directly with clients (Caplan, 1970). In addition, the consultation relationship is unique because it is entirely voluntary (Caplan, 1970). Consultees are free to accept or reject the consultants' assessments and recommendations. They are under no obligation to accept consultants' suggestions. This stance is one of the defining characteristics of consultation. Again, it challenges consultants to let go of managing the problem situation and transfers authority and responsibility for the change process to another professional.

Consultation is not tied exclusively to any one profession. Its scholarship and research is found in social work, psychology, education, nursing, counseling, and business. Across all disciplines, however, core characteristics are found. Parsons (1996) identified them as follows:

1. Consultation is a strengths-based problem-solving process.
2. It takes place between a consultant and a consultee who has responsibility for providing direct service to the client system, which may be persons, groups, programs, organizations, or communities.
3. Consultation is based on a voluntary professional relationship.
4. It aims to resolve work-related problems of the consultee.
5. Consultation requires the consultant and consultee to share equally in resolving the work-related difficulty.
6. Consultation prepares the consultee to deal with similar issues in the future.

Several practice principles help both the consultant and the consultee shift their focus from direct practice work to indirect practice work, and engage in a voluntary, collaborative relationship. These principles are time, change, relationship, atmosphere, and language (Caplan, 1970).

Time. Understanding school social work consultation is confusing for some faculty and staff (Caplan, 1970). In fact, there may be an unspoken wish for the school social worker to take the lead and carry direct responsibility for work-related problems. This is understandable given our historic role in working with individual children to overcome academic and behavioral health challenges to school performance (Costin, 1969). Therefore, school personnel need time to understand intellectually and practically how consultation actually works.

Consultees need help understanding what their role is in the process, what information they are expected to provide, what tasks they will undertake, and what outcomes they can expect. They also need to understand the role of a consultant, what expertise the consultant will provide, and what kind of help to expect. Quite often some part of this framework is revisited during each consultation session, helping everyone stay focused on the differences between direct and indirect services. Helping school personnel understand what the consultation process is and is not is well worth the time expended.

Change. Often consultees are in a hurry to resolve problem situations as quickly as possible, yet few major school problems can be corrected rapidly (Caplan, 1970). Consultees need to understand that the change process may need the input and coordination of many people to address the identified challenges. Therefore, it is import to ask consultees what change they wish to see and to clarify the type of change possible under the current circumstances so the process is not a disappointment or viewed as a failure. Here, again, it is important to remind consultees that it takes time to create changes in home–school–community circumstances.

Relationship. The consultation relationship, like all school social work relationships, is the primary medium through which change occurs (Caplan, 1970). Each consultation relationship is unique, reflecting distinctive interactional characteristics and situational needs. To strengthen the relationship, the consultant establishes a belief bond (Bisman, 1994) with the consultee. This bond is characterized by a shared belief that the consultant has expertise, new information, and original perspectives for addressing the situation, and that, by working together, progress will be made toward overcoming the consultee's work-related difficulties.

Atmosphere. Consultees reveal their mistakes and failures during the consultation process (Caplan, 1970). They may feel embarrassed when exposing their work difficulties to another professional, especially one they see on a regular basis. Therefore, an atmosphere of trust and respect is essential. The consultee must feel accepted and respected. The consultation process will truly thrive when the consultant maintains a nonjudgmental attitude and creates an atmosphere that conveys, "We've all done goofy things and fallen on our faces."

Language. It is important to use language that demonstrates an understanding of the school organization, and its purpose, culture, and values (Caplan, 1970). Using the consultees' professional language enhances the consultation processes as well as the power and authority implicit in the consultative role. Using professional social work jargon does not demonstrate competence. Rather, using educational language advances the school social work consultation process. It demonstrates an understanding of the broader contextual issues that interfere with academic and behavioral success.

Gallessich (1982) suggests that there are six different consultation models with each having a clear application to school social work practice. These models are (1) organizational, (2) program, (3) education and training, (4) mental health, (5) behavioral, and (6) clinical consultation. Furthermore, she proposes that the models are differentiated by certain factors, among them problem formulation, goals, and methods.

ORGANIZATIONAL CONSULTATION

School social work consultation at the organizational level is the art of assisting school personnel to become more effective in dealing with complex structural and process issues (Constable & Thomas, 2009). Research has found that macro-oriented tasks and organizational services are underutilized aspects of school social work practice models (Frey & Walker, 2007). Blome (2014), however, notes that most social work is practiced within an organization; there is ample evidence that organizational culture and structure affect client outcomes (Glisson & Hemmelgarn, 1998; Yoo & Brooks, 2005). Given the historical person-in-environment paradigm of the profession and the current multitiered system of supports (MTSS) approach in education, it is ironic that school social workers often do not begin analysis of school issues by examining the interconnectedness between the organizational setting and the problem situation.

Organizational consultation considers a consultee to be an entire school district, school building, or group within a school. Problem formulation revolves around school structures and processes, and how these factors affect successful organizational operations. The overarching goal is to support and enhance the leadership, administration, and staff; and to foster and upgrade information exchange, coordination of activities, and decision-making processes.

Organizational consultation alters the ways an organization approaches a structural or procedural issue so that change occurs on the systemic level, thereby producing a positive impact for many subsystems (Blome, 2014; Constable & Thomas, 2009). The primary method of organizational consultation is to facilitate new ways of problem solving. The consultation supports and encourages the organization's growth and development, while also holding it responsible for making a plan and taking action.

Hazel (2007) identifies seven steps in problem solving:

1. Identify stakeholders and establish a work group.
2. Identify the issue or desired outcome.
3. Determine the incidence or prevalence of the issue.
4. Formulate potential causes of the issue.
5. Explore possible interventions at multiple points.
6. Outline the expected results.
7. Monitor implementation and change outcomes.

As Blome (2014) states, "The ability to assess a situation, to collect data, to engage others in problem solving, to plan an intervention, to monitor the implementation, and to evaluate the results of an intervention are primary strengths of social workers. Using these skills at the organizational level may be a new approach for clinically trained school social work practitioners, but the knowledge, skills, and behaviors already exist and can be expanded to the broader system level" (p. 29).

Multitiered System of Supports

Organizational consultation is consistent with tier 1 or school-wide interventions (Sabatino, 2009). It is intended to support the mission of education, create a culture of prevention, and address psychosocial issues that negatively affect student learning. As such, organizational consultation actively enlists the community, school, parents, and students in collaborating on issues that negatively affect student performance and school success.

Case Illustrations

School social workers are mandated reporters for suspected child maltreatment. In the real world child maltreatment incidents are complex, confusing, and stressful for school personnel. Consequently, the issues surrounding the reporting of suspected child maltreatment will be used as the case example for all six models of consultation.

Reporting Suspected Child Abuse and Organizational Consultation

Some schools develop a climate and culture that equates child protective services (CPS) referrals with breaking up a family. This perception may create reluctance to make CPS referrals, but consultation can address this reluctance from many different directions. We begin with illustrating how organizational consultation can take up this topic.

Organizational consultants refrain from legalistic or judgmental approaches; instead, they explore structural and process issues that create this viewpoint. They explore questions such as these: (1) Does school leadership foster or impede adherence to mandated reporting laws? (2) Do administrative and management arrangements foster or impede referrals to CPS? (3) Are staff policy and procedures in place for suspected CPS cases? (4) Are there formal or informal processes that foster or impede exchanging information about suspected abuse cases? (5) Are there processes to coordinate CPS referrals? (6) Is there a top-down or a collaborative decision-making process for CPS referral? The answers to these questions help focus on specific factors to concentrate on using Hazel's (2007) action steps. This approach helps to explain whether the idea that CPS referrals break up families is related to school climate (the individual's way of perceiving) or to culture (the organization's ways of doing) (Glisson & James, 2002).

For more information on organizational consultation, see Blake and Mouton (1987); Bowman and Deal (2008); and Cawsey, Deszca, and Ingols (2012).

PROGRAM CONSULTATION

A program is defined as "an organized collection of activities designed to reach certain objectives" (Royce & Thyer, 2010, p. 5). Within the school system there are different groups of students whose learning needs and developmental problems interfere with their ability to reap the benefit of their education. For them, special programs are necessary for achieving school success. Program consultation helps schools expand their services to address these school needs, close gaps in service, and adopt promising new interventions supported by scientifically supported best practices (W. K. Kellogg Foundation, 2006).

Scholarship and research call on school social workers to undertake a broader range of macro tasks in a richer and fuller way to demonstrate their professional capabilities, or risk becoming undervalued by school systems (Dupper, 2003; Garrett, 2006). In view of this perspective, a program consultation model that positions school social workers to address the special needs of groups of students is a very important practice tool.

Program consultation defines problems as the failure of policies and services to bring about changes that are intended to meet the special needs of an identified school group or population. There is an unexpected outcome related to the development, operation, or evaluation of the program, or there is a lack of mainstream institutional support for the program.

The goal of program consultation is to meet the needs of school populations unable to participate or succeed in academic and school life using traditional services and pathways. It creates policies, and it develops and implements highly specialized services that support a specific population or fulfill an unmet need.

The W. K. Kellogg Foundation (2006) suggests the following questions be asked as the primary method for program consultation.

♦ Is there agreement among stakeholders, and is there a clear and specific problem statement that is easy to understand and to evaluate?

♦ Does the infrastructure support the program, including investments in social, financial, political, and stakeholder capital?

♦ Are current specific programs and activities the appropriate strategies for achieving goals and objectives, including clarity about who is responsible for them?

♦ Are program processes acceptable and cost-effective to the school? Do they include developing time frames, setting targets, documenting practices, and monitoring implementation and outcomes?

♦ What is the expected change in attitude, behavior, knowledge, skill, situation, or level of functioning?

♦ How does the program have a positive effect on those indirectly affected by the identified problem?

Programs often begin with broad ideas and only after implementation, analysis, and revision do they successfully narrow and refine their approach to a school problem. By examining the elements of a logic model—program infrastructure, interventions, processes, outcomes, and impact—school social workers ensure that program consultation is systematic and comprehensive. It helps answer the question of whether there are alternative or more-effective ways to equip schools to serve at-risk student populations. School success is dependent on creative programs, inventive planning, and improved service delivery systems.

Program Consultation and Reporting Suspected Child Abuse

The mission of CPS is to protect children from physical abuse, emotional neglect, and inadequate supervision. Schools play a key role in maintaining the well-being of students at risk for physical and emotional harm. Yet, the relationship between school districts and local child welfare programs is often tenuous and, in some cases, fraught with issues.

Program consultation offers an important approach to help schools clarify ambiguity and establish well-functioning referral programs. To achieve this outcome, consultants work to engage stakeholders, create investment, examine current practices and processes, identify expected changes, and recognize unintended consequences.

Multitiered System of Supports

Program consultation is consistent with MTSS tier 2 services. Consultants focus on the successful development, implementation, and evaluation of highly specialized programs for groups or classes of students with special needs. These programs may be in general education, special education, early intervention, alternative education, or in an area often overlooked in school social work program consultation—the after-school program.

For more information, see Fraser, Richman, Galinsky, and Day (2009); Kettner, Moroney, and Martin (2008); and W. K. Kellogg Foundation (2006).

EDUCATION AND TRAINING CONSULTATION

Students, faculty, family, and community stakeholders encounter challenges to school success that fall outside of their professional training, experience, and resources. Education and training consultation is the model that addresses these issues from different directions. The model incorporates three different approaches to resolving work-related problems: (1) information and referral services, (2) interdisciplinary coordination and interagency collaboration, and (3) staff development and in-service training.

Problem formulation centers on the need for familiarity with school and community resources; coordination of school-based services and collaboration with community-based programs and services; and expanding school personnel's information and technology on salient school issues. Therefore, the goals are professional networking and resource development, synchronizing school teamwork and community agency collaboration, and transmission of needed information and technology.

Information and Referral Services

Information and referral services require consultants to find and organize information about multiple school and community services in order to facilitate access by consultees. Methods include (1) simply providing information about community service, (2) directing the consultee to an appropriate resource, or (3) facilitating a referral by direct contact with a service provider on behalf of consultees (Poe, 2006).

School social workers do not always perceive and sometimes are ambivalent about their information and referral activities, seeing them more as concrete services and less as professional social work. This model, however, provides an entry point to the school system for many who might otherwise be underserved and brings attention to consultation services that increase the visibility and impact of school social work services.

Interdisciplinary Coordination and Interagency Collaboration

Multidisciplinary team coordination is an interactional process wherein professionals who possess different professional tasks and organizational perspectives work together toward improving school outcomes. The student assistance team is the classic school example of a multidisciplinary team comprising various professionals who work together as student instructional support personnel.

Interagency collaboration is the creation of a comprehensive system of care for a shared problem. In some instances this might mean establishing clear patterns of communication among various professionals associated with a situation. In other cases it might mean the creation of an entirely new entity with a specific, shared mission for all organizations, such as an early intervention collaborative council.

Foster-Fishman, Berkowitz, Lounsbury, Jacobson, and Allen (2001) identified four elements key to successful work coordination and collaboration: (1) professional motivation, (2) interactional processes, (3) clear objectives, and (4) effective organizational leadership. For school social work consultants, this translates into being knowledgeable about the norms and perspectives of colleagues' professions and settings, developing a respectful and positive work climate, identifying a clear overarching goal as well as long- and short-term objectives, and establishing formal procedures for resolving disputes.

Without processing different perspectives of the involved disciplines and agencies, successful coordination and collaboration cannot be achieved. This is because each profession and each agency acculturates its members to their roles, values, ethics, and practices (Bronstein, 2003). This socialization process creates self-directed practitioners as well as professional and organizational allegiances. Successful coordination and collaboration is characterized by respect for the assets of each profession regardless of the setting or the profession's status in the hierarchy of an organization. Methods to be used include creating a shared vision, valuing coworkers' diverse competencies, and establishing inclusive decision-making processes (Foster-Fishman et al., 2001).

Structural characteristics (Bronstein, 2003) have a strong influence on consultation as well. Problems occur when participants are unclear about the aims of their work, already carry large and stressful workloads, lack administrative support for their additional efforts, and need resources to accomplish tasks. Developing a common understanding of issues, establishing open communication, processing conflicts, and securing necessary resources help establish a framework that supports the efforts of all involved.

Interpersonal characteristics (Bronstein, 2003) cannot be underestimated in terms of their influence on team coordination and agency collaboration. Relational skills consisting of trust, respect, and empathy affect the dynamics of every meeting and every situation (Foster-Fishman et al., 2001). These prosocial characteristics increase the bonds and connections between professionals.

Some professionals and organizations prefer to operate within their own silos. They need assistance in changing tendencies to operate in isolation. School social work coordination and collaboration help remind colleagues that schools and communities are bound by a shared commitment to support the academic, physical, social, and emotional well-being of students and their families.

Staff Development and In-Service Training

Staff development and in-service training are the third track in education and training consultation. In contrast to traditional methods, this consultation model empowers consultees to determine where they need to close gaps in information, skill, and technology (Friedman, 2013). In other words, consultation is a two-way street where the consultant and the consultee plan together the purpose and content of the information exchange.

This stance is rooted in adult learning theories that assume a consultee is someone "who (1) has an independent self-concept and can direct his or her own learning; (2) has accumulated a reservoir of life experiences that serve as a rich resource for learning; (3) has learning needs closely related to changing social roles; (4) is problem-centered and interested in immediate application of knowledge; and (5) is motivated to learn by internal rather than external factors" (Merriam, 2001, p. 5).

Education and training methods may include workshops, media and materials, structured learning experiences, role modeling, technology training, discussion groups, pairing up with a learning partner, panels, game shows, and case studies (Friedman, 2013). The selected method, however, should be consistent with the goals designed by the school, consultees, and consultant (Gallessich, 1982).

Together, these three approaches demonstrate the breadth and depth of backstage work by school social workers that is critical to carrying out onstage activities that resolve school issues and promote school success. The checklists currently used by school systems to track pupil services provide a limited list of practice tasks that do not capture the scope of work undertaken each month. Reframing information and referral work, multidisciplinary coordination and community collaboration, and staff development and in-service workshops could go a long way toward identifying a large percentage of school social work services that go unreported or unrecognized by the school system.

Education and Training Consultation and Reporting Suspected Child Abuse

Education and training consultation addresses this issue in multiple ways. School social workers use information and referral services when they develop strong professional connections with local CPS staff with whom the school social worker can confer about a child's situation. Coordination and collaboration occur when the child study team helps coordinate a wraparound service plan for a maltreated child and participates in multiagency collaboration to address multiple family needs. Professional development and in-service trainings serve as perfect venues for increasing knowledge and confidence in addressing suspected child maltreatment.

Multitiered System of Supports

Education and training consultation are used as both tier 1 and tier 2 services. Presentations to public sector and private sector partners, Parent-Teacher Association workshops, and staff development seminars are universal (tier 1) ways to expand the capacities of school personnel and community partners to enhance school communities. Working with student groups and school departments to provide new information, teach new skills, and demonstrate educational technology are targeted methods of delivering education and training consultation. For more information, see the following sources.

Information and Referral Services. Alliance for Information and Referral Services, at http://www.airs.org/

United Way World Wide, at http://www.211us.org/

Interdisciplinary Collaboration and Interagency Coordination. Promise Neighborhood, at http://www2.ed.gov/programs/promiseneighborhoods/index.html

The Campaign for Grade Level Reading, at http://gradelevelreading.net/

Staff Development and Continuing Education. 360 Education Solution, at http://www.360-edu.com/professional_development.php

PBS Teacher Line, at http://www.pbs.org/teacherline/

Professional Development, at http://www2.ed.gov/teachers

MENTAL HEALTH CONSULTATION

Reports by the U.S. Surgeon General (U.S. Public Health Service, 2000) and Institute of Medicine (2009) indicate that mental health promotion efforts are key to successful child development. Furthermore, research finds that school-based universal interventions that foster social and emotional student competencies are positively connected to academic performance (Durlak, Weissberg, Dymnicki, Taylor, & Schellinger, 2011).

Mental health consultation promotes awareness of the social and emotional core competencies associated with school-wide, classroom, and individual academic and behavioral success. Among these competencies are self-awareness, self-management, social awareness, relationship skills, and responsible decision making (CASEL, 2013). It expands school social workers' understanding of interpersonal dynamics interfering with school success and addresses barriers to the teaching-learning process.

The mental health consultation model views the origin and nature of work-related problems as maladaptive responses to the socioemotional components of difficult work situations. Therefore, the goal of mental health consultation is the dissemination of mental health principles and processes (Caplan & Caplan, 1999). Using their mental health expertise, consultants help consultees develop cognitive awareness and emotional mastery of problem situations. The aim is to promote, prevent, and remediate mental health concerns and improve problem-solving skills directed at these efforts.

When the school culture, classroom group, or student conduct do not foster well-being, consultation centers on an exploration of potential connections between observable symptoms, underlying dynamics, sociocultural factors, and school outcomes. In other words, consultants educate consultees to view the problem from a new perspective, while using emotional support to encourage them to experiment with innovative techniques to resolve the school problem.

Four concepts guide a school social work consultant's understanding of the problem situation and intervention methods (Caplan & Caplan, 1993). The concepts are (1) knowledge, (2) skill, (3) confidence, and/or (4) objectivity. Each concept has a methodology to guide the change processes.

Knowledge. Knowledge about mental disorders, psychotropic medications, death, violence, and trauma is not ordinarily included in early professional education or teacher training programs. Using an ecological-developmental framework, consultants provide information on internalizing and externalizing mental health disorders, psychotropic medications, family dynamics, systems stressors, and cultural norms as well as strengths, resilience, and protective factors. Assisting school personnel to cognitively grasp what is happening by providing information and supplying context helps such personnel to come to terms with and understand stressful work situations.

Skill. In other instances consultees understand a problematic work situation but lack the ability to successfully respond to the situation. Ideas about best practices are limited or outside the range of the consultee's toolkit. The consultant's task is to intervene by jointly brainstorming alternative courses of action that might not have been considered or tried. The consultant does not take the lead in suggesting specific intervention techniques or practice skills because this might tip the interactions toward an administrative or supervisory role. Another approach is to suggest that the consultee seek out suggestions from a master teacher or administrator who is properly positioned to give direct advice and likely to have many ideas about alternative educational methods.

Confidence. Sometimes the problem is that consultees lose confidence in their abilities to manage stressful work situations. They question their self-efficacy and lose their belief in their professional selves (Hepworth, Rooney, Dewberrey Rooney, Strom-Gottfried, & Larsen, 2010). They doubt their capacity to successfully problem-solve, accomplish certain tasks, or perform new behaviors.

In these instances, consultants acknowledge self-doubts, help consultees become aware of their strengths, and convey a sense of hope in regard to the situation. They provide emotional support by taking the position that a consultee has the capacity to grow and change in many ways. Consultants work with consultees to explore successes, recognize coping capacities, and build on current skills and resources.

Objectivity. In some instances, consultees become emotionally caught up in a work situation, lose emotional equilibrium, and are unable to use their knowledge, skill, and confidence to resolve the current problem situation. This may be because they experience a lack of objectivity about the work-related problem. Among reasons for lack of objectivity are (1) becoming personally involved, (2) over-identifying with the client, (3) transference reactions, (4) distorted perceptions, and (5) personal theme interference (Caplan & Caplan, 1993). These types of problems in objectivity are generally outside the conscious awareness of the consultee. Thus, consultees' work performance is challenged by ideas, thoughts, feelings, memories, and experiences that are unconscious and pushed to the back of the mind.

The consultative role, boundary definitions, and collaborative relationship prevent examination of consultees' private lives to discern the source of underlying conflicts. In fact, consultants need not know the etiology of a lack of objectivity because relevant material will be presented under the guise of describing the client's issues. Instead, consultants support defense structures by accepting the proxy scenario, empathizing with consultees, and using the projected issues and metaphors as the content and vehicle for regaining professional composure and psychological neutrality (Caplan & Caplan, 1993). Even when consultees give permission, overtly or covertly, to discuss their personal history as part of the consultant process, consultants are bound to decline the invitation. This refusal may create awkwardness, but it reinforces the very nature of consultation—to focus exclusively on work-related problems.

Mental Health Consultation and Reporting Suspected Child Abuse

Mental health consultation focuses on increasing knowledge, skill, confidence, and objectivity of the consultee to resolve school issues. Determining which of these concepts is associated with the questions and concerns about reporting a suspected case of child maltreatment goes a long way toward increasing the professionalism of school personnel.

Multitiered System of Supports

Mental health consultation is applicable to all three levels of the MTSS. The dissemination of mental health principles and processes is possible on a school-wide, group-wide, and targeted level. This is often seen in a school's code of conduct, classroom rules, and interpersonal dynamics that foster a positive school culture, group interactions, and personal communication. In this way, mental health consultation offers a rich approach to supporting school personnel as they face today's educational pressures that are intended to increase staff retention and decrease burnout.

For more information, see Caplan (1970); Caplan and Caplan (1999); and Mannino, Trickett, Shore, Kidder, and Levin (1986).

BEHAVIORAL CONSULTATION

Behavioral consultation focuses on shaping prosocial conduct. The aim of behavioral consultation is to increase desired behaviors and decrease undesired behaviors throughout the school, within the classroom, and by individual students (Spiegler & Guevremont, 2010). It seeks to prevent undesired behaviors and replace them with desired behaviors. To accomplish this outcome, the model employs behavior theory to evaluate what is causing and maintaining adaptive and maladaptive behavioral performance. It is vital that school social workers know behavioral consultation theory and practice because unacceptable pupil behaviors affect not only the students involved, but also all those coming in contact with those students (Early, 2014).

For behavioral consultants, maladaptive behaviors, ineffective classroom environments, and negative school climate or culture are "either being cued by some environmental antecedents, being reinforced by some environmental consequence, or both" (Early, 2014, p. 81). In prosocial terms, positive behaviors are learned through "establishing a system of stimulating and reinforcing expected behaviors and by setting up an ongoing system of maintenance" (Early, 2014, p. 81). Hence, consultation practice methods focus on contingencies that support the unwanted behaviors.

The focus of change must be expressed in clear, simple, observable, and measurable behavioral terms, rather than attitudes, characteristics, or diagnostic categories. The target of change is behavior that someone within the school system desires to change, either increasing an adaptive behavior or decreasing a maladaptive behavior. The agent of change in a school system is the school staff, not the consultant. The consultant is the facilitator of change who strengthens the capacity of the agent of change to make targeted changes happen.

The practice method involves assessing, preventing, and replacing unwanted behaviors. Assessment begins with an exploration and identification of the problem. Data collection questions are the following:

- ◆ What are the target behaviors that are of concern? (target behaviors)
- ◆ Where, when, how often do they occur? (setting conditions)
- ◆ What triggers the behavior? (antecedent events)
- ◆ What increases the likelihood of the behavior occurring? (reinforcing consequences)

♦ What is done by others to stop the behavior? (suppressing consequences)

♦ What is gained (in the suppression) by the person attempting to stop the behavior?

The answers to these questions lead to a hypothesized function for the behavior. In other words, what function does the behavior serve to help the student avoid something, get something, or escape from something?

This approach is commonly known as a functional behavioral assessment that focuses on undesired behaviors. And as Weiss and Knoster (2008) state, "A person with seriously difficult behavior is unlikely to be acting out of a desire to be troublesome but rather acts as he or she does because some need (i.e., function) is not met and/or the person feels as if others are not listening to him or her" (p. 74).

Consistent with a professional social work strengths perspective, Early (2014) offers an adaptive behavior assessment approach that includes the following components:

♦ Adaptive target behaviors (establishment of a baseline for its occurrence).

♦ Inhibiting conditions (general conditions or environmental situations that reduce the likelihood that a desired behavior will occur).

♦ Attempted or potential antecedent events (specific immediate events that have been tried unsuccessfully to trigger the desired behavior, or potential cues that have yet to be tried). A cue or prompt can serve to intentionally promote a positive behavior that replaces a negative behavior.

♦ Attempted or potential reinforcing consequences (natural or imposed consequences that have the potential to strengthen the behavior but have not been attempted or used consistently).

♦ Hypothesized reason for the behavior being too weak (the consultant's and the consultee's best guess regarding the attempted maintaining conditions, and ideas about more-effective antecedent and reinforcing consequences).

Functional behavioral assessments and adaptive behavior assessments are consistent with behavior theory, specifically operant conditioning. Both frameworks provide an empirically supported theoretical foundation for school social work consultation as well as a scientifically supported practice model to resolving behavioral challenges.

Behavioral Consultation and Reporting Suspected Child Abuse

One of the first places an abused child displays negative behaviors indicative of his or her situation is often in the school. By working with teachers to identify maladaptive behaviors and to replace them with adaptive behaviors, by charting successes and failures of these efforts, and by recording family engagement with the school on behavior issues, schools provide critical information for CPS, mental health systems, and courts that can only be gained using the methods and change processes found in behavioral consultation.

Multitiered System of Supports

Behavioral consultation is used as a tier 1, 2, and 3 service. Behavior changes are achieved through school-wide consultation services that improve the quality of school life for all members (tier 1). Classroom services modify or amplify behaviors for the entire class, thus enhancing the classroom learning environment (tier 2). And behavioral consultation is used with individual students to increase their academic, social, and behavioral competencies (tier 3).

For additional information, see Early (2014).

CLINICAL CONSULTATION

Clinical consultation uses three approaches to resolving school-related work problems: (1) Expertise is provided to the student assistance team in the form of the social case history for special education evaluations. (2) Expertise is provided to home-based or class-based early intervention teams about a family's priorities, resources, and concerns regarding its members' ability to address developmental delays. (3) Expertise is provided on the impact of crises or traumas on students, faculty, families, or school life (Mayer, 2014).

In this consultation model the problem is formulated as the school's inability to support academic and developmental growth, leading to the need for an expert evaluation to determine barriers to learning and recommendations. The goal is development of specialized educational plans, known as the individualized education program (IEP) for children ages five to twenty-one, and the individualized family service plan (IFSP) for children birth to five years of age.

Successful clinical consultation is contingent on the social work consultant's expertise related to the person-in-environment perspective as well as human development throughout the life cycle. This knowledge is critical to the differential diagnosis of normative and appropriate situations versus those that are uncommon or unexpected.

A comprehensive assessment requires considerable time to gather the data necessary to formulate an informed professional conclusion. Hepworth et al. (2010) suggest using a wide variety of data sources, including direct observation of behavior in the classroom or home and other related settings, direct observation of interactions, information provided by others, tests/assessment instruments, and social worker experiences with the child and family. Thomas, Tiefenthal, Constable, and Leyba (2009) indicate that social workers should also gather data via parent interviews, social and health histories, assessment of the learning and family environment, consultation with teachers, review of the student's academic file, and consultation with other agencies. Studying the student's and family's reaction to the situation, coping efforts, and factors such as class, society, and culture add richness and depth to the assessment (Hepworth et al., 2010). Furthermore, assessments for students from diverse backgrounds need to include English language proficiency, experience of discrimination, and immigration status (Clarke, Kim, & Spencer, 2012).

It is not sufficient to gather data and form conclusions. Consultants must be able to demonstrate their ability to clearly articulate ideas in a report that can be easily understood by the other members of the multidisciplinary team involved in the decision-making and planning processes. The report must be well-organized and based on facts; where conclusions are offered, they need to be supported by objective analysis of the data included in the report (Sidell, 2011). Thomas et al. (2009) indicate that the assessment should include the following nine categories:

1. Identifying information
2. Reason child was referred
3. Information sources
4. Child developmental history
5. Child school history
6. Culture, family history, current issues
7. Current functioning
8. Conclusions and recommendations
9. Signature of the school social worker

Unfortunately, schools need to respond to highly traumatic crisis situations, including natural disasters; deaths due to suicide, illness, accident, or violent attack; and students who go missing. These examples call for the third approach to clinical consultation where the consultant helps develop prevention and intervention plans that assist the individual, class, grade, or school to navigate crises and trauma. They also can provide, coordinate, and organize longer-term counseling and additional help if needed.

Clinical consultation related to trauma in a school is likely to begin with an assessment. Trauma assessment begins with differentiating Type I trauma, which consists of a one-time event, from Type II trauma, which is characterized by the experience of multiple or continuous traumas (Callahan, 2009). This distinction is critical because Type I trauma can use clinical case consultation, but Type II consultation requires mental health consultation or referral to community-based resources, as it necessitates a longer intervention process (Callahan, 2009). The assessment process should not just focus on the problems in psychosocial functioning after the crisis: it is imperative that resources and assets also be included in the assessment (Bragin, 2011).

Callahan (2009) stresses the importance of remembering that, during the crisis event, the focus is on safety, not treatment. After the crisis, members of the school community may be able to begin treatment. A sense of safety, security, and comfort is critical for the therapeutic process (Graziano, 2011). Without these steps and a focus on ensuring safety, academic learning and behavioral conduct will suffer.

School social work consultants contribute a unique element to the prevention, intervention, and remediation of a school crisis through their knowledge and appreciation of cultural differences, recognizing that these differences can influence how someone experiences a crisis event and how that person responds after the event. School social workers engaged in clinical consultation in the schools are in a position to ensure that everyone in the school is assessed and trained to pay particular attention to the most vulnerable and oppressed (Mayer, 2014).

Clinical Consultation and Reporting Suspected Child Abuse

Besides expertise in child assessment and family work, school social workers bring their knowledge of current federal, state, and local laws as well as district policies and procedures on the topic of reporting suspected child abuse. They are able to examine how the historical and current political, social, economic, and cultural climates affect the context for referrals in a culturally sensitive way, recognizing diversity issues, and challenging barriers as a result of collaborative team relationships.

Trained school social workers are in an ideal position to use IEP and IFSP assessments to rule in or rule out suspected child abuse. Their access to students, families, school personnel, and community agencies to complete data collection provides many opportunities to identify risk factors as well as supporting documents that may solidify initial impressions of abuse and neglect. In the horrific event that a student suffers or dies as a result of child abuse, clinical consultants are equipped to step forward to restore equilibrium after such a traumatic event to "reduce stress, relieve symptoms, restore functioning, and prevent further deterioration" (Hepworth et al., 2010, p. 379).

Multitiered System of Supports

The IEP social case history and the IFSP family priorities, resources, and concerns are a tier 3 service directed toward a single student. Responses to crisis and trauma are tier 1, 2, and 3 services (Knox, Powell, & Roberts, 2012). Tier 1 services include the school-wide effort to prepare and respond to crises. Tier 2 services include group screening efforts to identify maladaptive reactions to crisis or trauma by student groups or classroom groups. Tier 3 services include individual student or family referrals for more-intensive services when needed.

For additional information, see the following Web sites:

◆ Disaster assistance, at www.disasterassistance.gov
◆ Early Childhood Technical Assistance Center, at http://www.ecta center.org
◆ International Society for Traumatic Stress Studies, at http://www.istss .org/home.htm
◆ Keep Schools Safe, at www.keepschoolssafe.org
◆ National Dissemination Center for Children with Disabilities, at http://nichcy.org
◆ Research and Training Center on Early Childhood Development, at http://www.researchtopractice.info/productCenterscope.php
◆ The National Child Traumatic Stress Network, at http://www.nctsnet .org/

CONCLUSION

School social work consultation helps school systems fulfill their educational mission by helping school personnel to be more effective in their work. In reality, school social workers engage in consultation work on a daily basis, but they rarely connect disparate practice tasks with specific consultation models (Sabatino, 2014). The aim of this chapter is to help school social workers begin to recognize how much of their daily routine is highly consistent with key concepts of various consultation practice models that are a powerful, cost-effective way to realize the promise of the whole-school approach (Blaber & Bershad, 2011) for achieving school success and student well-being.

References

Barker, R. L. (2003). *The social work dictionary* (5th ed.). Washington, DC: National Association of Social Workers.

Bisman, C. (1994). *Social work practice: Cases and principles*. Pacific Grove, CA: Brooks/ Cole.

Blaber, C., & Bershad, C. (2011). *Realizing the promise of the whole-child school approach to children's mental health: A practical guide for schools*. Waltham, MA: Education Development Center.

Blake, R., & Mouton, J. S. (1987). *Consultation: A handbook for individual and organization development* (2nd ed.). Reading, MA: Addison-Wesley.

Blome, W. W. (2014). Organizational consultation. In C. A. Sabatino (Ed.), *Consultation theory and practice: A handbook for school social workers* (pp. 29–42). New York: Oxford University Press.

Bowman, L. G., & Deal, T. E. (2008). *Reframing organizations: Artistry, choice, and leadership* (4th ed.). San Francisco: Jossey-Bass.

Bragin, M. (2011). Clinical social work in situations of disaster and terrorism. In J. R. Brandell (Ed.), *Theory and practice in clinical social work* (2nd ed., pp. 373–406). Thousand Oaks, CA: Sage.

Bronstein, L. (2003). A model for interdisciplinary collaboration. *Social Work, 48*(3), 297–306.

Callahan, J. (2009). School-based crisis intervention for traumatic events. In C. R. Massat, R. Constable, S. McDonald, & J. P. Flynn (Eds.), *School social work: Practice, policy and research* (7th ed., pp. 638–661). Chicago: Lyceum Books.

Caplan, G. (1970). *The theory and practice of mental health consultation*. New York: Basic Books.

Caplan, G., & Caplan, R. B. (1993). *Mental health consultation and collaboration*. New York: Jossey-Bass.

Caplan, G., & Caplan, R. B. (1999). *Mental health consultation and collaboration*. New York: Jossey-Bass. Paperback: Long Grove, IL: Waveland Press.

CASEL. (2013). *Social and emotional learning competencies*. Retrieved from http://www.casel.org/guide

Cawsey, T., Deszca, G., & Ingols, C. (2012). *Organizational change: An action-oriented toolkit* (2nd ed.). Los Angeles: Sage.

Clarke, J. S., Kim, I., & Spencer, M. S. (2012). Engaging with culturally and racially diverse families. In C. Franklin, M. B. Harris, & P. Allen-Meares (Eds.), *The school services sourcebook* (2nd ed., pp. 765–774). New York: Oxford University Press.

Constable, R., & Thomas, G. (2009). Assessment, multidisciplinary teamwork, and consultation: Foundations for role development. In C. R. Massat, R. Constable, S. McDonald, & J. P. Flynn (Eds.), *School social work: Practice, policy and research* (7th ed., pp. 321–338). Chicago: Lyceum Books.

Costin, L. B. (1969). An analysis of the tasks in school social work. *Social Service Review, 43*, 247–285.

Dupper, D. (2003). *School social work: Skills and interventions for effective practice*. Hoboken, NJ: John Wiley & Sons.

Durlak, J. A., Weissberg, R. P., Dymnicki, A. B., Taylor, R. D., & Schellinger, K. (2011). The impact of enhancing students' social and emotional learning: A meta-analysis of school-based universal interventions. *Child Development, 82*, 405–432. Retrieved from http://onlinelibrary.wiley.com/doi/10.1111/j.1467-8624.2010.01564.x/pdf

Early, B. P. (2014). Behavioral consultation. In C. A. Sabatino (Ed.), *Consultation theory and practice: A handbook for school social workers* (pp. 77–99). New York: Oxford University Press.

Foster-Fishman, P., Berkowitz, S., Lounsbury, D., Jacobson, S., & Allen, N. (2001). Building collaborative capacity in community coalitions: A review and integrative framework. *American Journal of Community Psychology, 29*(2), 241–261.

Fraser, M. W., Richman, J. M., Galinsky, M. J., & Day, S. H. (2009). *Intervention research: Developing social programs*. New York: Oxford University Press.

Frey, A. J., & Walker, H. (2007). School social work at the school organization level. In M. Bye & M. Alvarez (Eds.), *School social work: From theory to practice*. Belmont, CA: Thomson Brooks/Cole.

Friedman, B. D. (2013). *How to teach effectively: A brief guide*. Chicago: Lyceum Books.

Gallessich, J. (1982). *The profession and practice of consultation*. San Francisco: Jossey-Bass.

Garrett, K. J. (2006). Making the case for school social work. *Children & Schools, 28*(2), 115–121.

Glisson, C., & Hemmelgarn, A. (1998). The effects of organizational climate and inter-organizational coordination on the quality and outcomes of children's service systems. *Child Abuse & Neglect, 22*(5), 401–421.

Glisson, C., & James, L. R. (2002). The cross-level effects of culture and climate in human service teams. *Journal of Organizational Behavior, 23,* 767–794. doi:10.1002/job.162

Graziano, R. (2011). The challenge of clinical work with survivors of trauma. In J. R. Brandell (Ed.), *Theory and practice in clinical social work* (2nd ed., pp. 347–371). Thousand Oaks, CA: Sage.

Hazel, C. (2007). Timeless and timely advice: A commentary on "Consultation to facilitate planned organizational change in schools." *Journal of Educational & Psychological Consultation, 17*(2/3), 125–132.

Hepworth, D., Rooney, R., Dewberrey Rooney, G., Strom-Gottfried, K., & Larsen, J. A. (2010). *Direct social work practice* (8th ed.). Belmont, CA: Brooks/Cole, Cengage Learning.

Institute of Medicine. (2009). *Preventing mental, emotional, and behavioral disorders among young people: Progress and possibilities.* Washington, DC: National Academies Press.

Kettner, P. M., Moroney, R. M., & Martin, L. L. (2008). *Designing and managing programs: An effectiveness-based approach.* Thousand Oaks, CA: Sage.

Knox, K. S., Powell, T., & Roberts, A. R. (2012). Developing school-wide and district-wide prevention/intervention protocols for natural disasters. In C. Franklin, M. B. Harris, & P. Allen-Meares (Eds.), *The school services sourcebook* (2nd ed., pp. 569–578). New York: Oxford University Press.

Mannino, F. V., Trickett, E., Shore, M., Kidder, M. G., & Levin, G. (1986). *Handbook of mental health consultation.* Baltimore: NIMH, DHHS Publication No. ADM 86-1446.

Mayer, L. M. (2014). Clinical consultation. In C. A. Sabatino (Ed.), *Consultation theory and practice: A handbook for school social workers* (pp. 100–118). New York: Oxford University Press.

Merriam, S. B. (2001). Andragogy and self-directed learning: Pillars of adult learning theory. *New Update on Adult Learning Theory, 89*(Spring), 3–15.

Parsons, R. P. (1996). *The skilled consultant: A systemic approach to the theory and practice of consultation.* Boston: Allyn & Bacon.

Poe, J. (2006). Information and referral services: A brief history. *The Southeastern Librarian, 54*(1), 36–41.

Royce, D., & Thyer, B. A. (2010). *Program evaluation: An introduction.* Belmont, CA: Wadsworth Cengage Learning.

Sabatino, C. A. (2009). School social work consultation models and response to intervention: A perfect match. *Children & Schools, 31*(4), 197–206.

Sabatino, C. A. (2014). *Consultation theory and practice: A handbook for school social workers.* New York: Oxford University Press.

Sidell, N. L. (2011). *Social work documentation: A guide to strengthening your case recording.* Washington, DC: National Association of Social Workers.

Spiegler, M., & Guevremont, D. (2010). *Contemporary behavioral therapy* (5th ed.). Belmont, CA: Wadsworth, Cengage Learning.

Thomas, G., Tiefenthal, M., Constable, R., & Leyba, E. G. (2009). Assessment of the learning environment, case study assessment, and functional behavioral analyses. In C. R. Massat, R. Constable, S. McDonald, & J. P. Flynn (Eds.), *School social work: Practice, policy and research* (7th ed., pp. 408–430). Chicago: Lyceum Books.

U.S. Public Health Service. (2000). *Report of the Surgeon General's Conference on children's mental health: A national action agenda.* Washington, DC: Department of Health and Human Services.

W. K. Kellogg Foundation. (2006). *Logic model development guide.* Retrieved from http://www.wkkf.org/knowledge-center/resources/2006/02/WK-Kellogg-Foundation-Logic-Model-Development-Guide.aspx

Weiss, N., & Knoster, T. (2008). It may be nonaversive, but is it a positive approach? Relevant questions to ask throughout the process of behavioral assessment and intervention. *Journal of Positive Behavioral Interventions, 10*(1), 72–78.

Yoo, J., & Brooks, D. (2005). The role of organizational variables in predicting service effectiveness: An analysis of a multilevel model. *Research on Social Work Practice, 15*(4), 267–277.

Section II

The Policy Context for School Social Work Practice

School social work practice takes place within a complex set of public policies that govern schools. At the federal, state, and local levels, these policies regulate, drive, and influence the actions of schools and school social workers. In this section, some key policies and their histories are described. Special education law is central to school social work practice, and those policies are described in chapter 9, "Educational Mandates for Children with Disabilities: School Policies, Case Law, and the School Social Worker," by Sandra Kopels, Malcolm Rich, and Carol Rippey Massat. The issue of emerging common standards for academic and social emotional learning is a critical new development in education in the United States, and is addressed in section II. While special education law addresses access to education for persons with disabilities, public policies in the United States have also limited education for oppressed populations. At this point in history, we have been forcefully reminded of the legacies of racism and oppression in U.S. history. We focus on policies affecting African American children in this section of the book, and move on to a focus on educational policies and their effect on more broadly defined historically oppressed populations. In chapter 10, "The School Social Work Contribution to Meeting National Standards for Social Emotional Learning," Brenda Lindsey, Kari Smith, Tory Cox, and Michelle Alvarez describe the emerging focus on policies to support national standards for social emotional learning. Throughout history, local, state, and federal policies have moved toward education for all citizens as a common good. However, forces within our society continue to challenge equity in education for persons with disabilities, members of minority racial and ethnic groups, sexual minorities, women, and other oppressed groups. As school social workers, our code of ethics calls for us to advocate for social justice, but that advocacy begins with a foundation of knowledge about history and provisions of existing policies that affect children and schools every day. In this section of the book, we focus on these policies and their history. Chapter 11 by Cassandra McKay-Jackson and Carol Rippey Massat focuses on "A History of the Education of African American Children." McKay-Jackson and Massat in chapter 12, "Policy and Law Affecting School Social Work with Vulnerable Populations," continue this focus on educational policies that affect members of oppressed groups. Finally, in chapter 13, "Bullying and Sexual Harassment in Schools," Susan Fineran discusses policies related to bullying and sexual harassment in school settings. Section II develops the history and context affecting students with disabilities, and education of students from oppressed populations in the United States, laying the groundwork for understanding of this history and related policies, and preparing school social workers for policy practice.

9

Educational Mandates for Children with Disabilities: School Policies, Case Law, and the School Social Worker

Sandra Kopels
University of Illinois at Urbana Champaign

Malcolm Rich
Whitted and Cleary LLC

Carol Rippey Massat
Indiana University School of Social Work, South Bend

◆ What Are the Educational Rights of Children with Disabilities?
◆ How Does the Special Education System Work?
◆ What Is the Role of the Local School System?
◆ Who Is the Child with Disabilities?
◆ What Are Social Work Services in the Schools?
◆ What Is Special Education?
◆ What Are Related Services?
◆ What Is an Individualized Education Program?
◆ What Services Must the School Provide?
◆ What Is Placement in the Least Restrictive Environment?
◆ What Are Placement Procedures?

◆ Can Students with Disabilities Be Suspended or Expelled?
◆ What Are Provisions for a Resolution Session, for Mediation, and for an Impartial Due Process Hearing?
◆ What Are Due Process and Judicial Review?

This chapter is one of several in the book that focus on the implementation for school social workers of the mandate to provide a free appropriate public education (FAPE) to children with disabilities.[1] Here we provide an overview of the current law and its interpretation in court decisions. Later chapters discuss the process of assessing eligibility for special education services.

The basis of special education policy in the United States is a succession of court cases, federal laws, and amendments, together with their accompanying regulations and interpretations, beginning in 1975 and continuing through the present. This succession of laws, beginning with the Education for All Handicapped Children Act of 1975 and culminating in the Individuals with Disabilities Education Act of 1990 (IDEA) and its amended versions, require that every state and the District of Columbia ensure FAPE is available to all children with disabilities. The education of unserved or underserved children with disabilities is as much of a priority as is providing education to all children. Special education services must be provided to all qualifying children with disabilities. Generally, a student must meet a definition of disability and require special education and appropriate related services. There is no financial needs test. The law is heavily parent/guardian oriented and requires states to maximize parental involvement in educational decision making every step of the way. Parents of pupils with disabilities or the schools may invoke a formal administrative system for the resolution of disputes with due process procedural safeguards. Throughout this system, detailed steps of identification, evaluation, determination of eligibility, planning, service, and administrative appeals are set forth. The school social worker, as a school staff member, is an important figure throughout the process. School social workers, who inevitably work with children with disabilities and the special education system, need a working knowledge of the requirements of the succession of special education laws, beginning with the Education for All Handicapped Children Act of 1975, that define the rights of students and disabilities, and the responsibilities of schools to educate these children.

---

1. *Editor's note:* Brooke Whitted, author of the earlier versions of this chapter, passed away in July 2014.

WHAT ARE THE EDUCATIONAL RIGHTS OF CHILDREN WITH DISABILITIES?

Over a period of forty years, a cumulative body of law, court decisions, and policies has developed in relation to the educational rights of children with disabilities to receive a FAPE. These rights became incorporated into IDEA (1990) and its amendments, most recently the Individuals with Disabilities Education Improvement Act of 2004 (IDEIA). When we refer to this cumulative body of law, we are referring to legal principles, codified in 20 United States Code, sections 1401–1482 (cited as 20 U.S.C. 1401–1482). When we refer to federal regulations, we are referring to 34 Code of Federal Regulations parts 300 and following (here cited as 34 C.F.R. 300.xx). These provisions are frequently updated as the law and its regulations develop and can be found in any law library or on the Internet. Each state education agency (SEA) develops its own regulations following the federal regulations; these can generally be accessed from your SEA's Web site. For the school social worker in the United States, the contents of this chapter provide a general update on the most recent provisions of the law including the IDEIA (2004). It is important for social workers in the United States to be familiar with this evolving body of law and its updates in order to design school social work roles that help the school respond to these mandates.

For the international reader, practicing in a different legal orbit, it is important to see the relation of law to school policy and from this policy to the school social worker's role. The difference in the U.S. legal tradition from that of other nations is the absence of a national education ministry that would actively manage local schools. While the federal government creates certain laws, policies, standards, and guidance to be incorporated into schools, the management of schools has historically been a state and local responsibility.

In the face of educational neglect of children with disabilities prior to 1968, the rights of children to a FAPE have had considerable development in the United States. Turnbull and Turnbull (1998) classically summarize this tradition in the form of six rights:

1. The right to attend school, or the principle of zero reject. Each school-age person with or without a disability has the right to be educated in a system of FAPE. Agencies and professionals may not expel or suspend students for certain behaviors or without following certain procedures, they may not exclude students on the basis that they are incapable of learning, and they may not limit the access of students to school on the basis of their having contagious diseases.
2. The right to a fair appraisal of their strengths and needs, or the principle of nondiscriminatory evaluation. Schools must consider socioeconomic status, language, and other factors in assessment and

evaluation of a child and must not allow such factors to bias the student's evaluation; agencies and professionals must obtain an accurate, nonbiased portrait of each student that considers their native language, communication styles in the homes, and so on. Placement and service decisions must be based on facts, and not simply on categories; decisions must be based on what students are doing and are capable of doing, in relation to behavioral outcomes individualized for the student. The resulting education would remedy the student's impairments and build on strengths.

3. The right to a beneficial experience in school, or the principle of FAPE, means that schools must individualize each student's education, provide needed related services, engage in a fair process for determining what is appropriate for each student, and ensure that the student's education indeed confers a benefit. Education should have a positive outcome for each student. The emphasis of this discussion is not simply on provision of access to education, but also on adapting the system and on building capacities in the person with a disability so that he or she attains certain results. Educational services need to be provided at no cost to the parents and meet the standards determined appropriate by the SEA.

4. The right to be included in the general education curriculum and other activities. This principle means that the schools must include the student in the general education program and may not remove a student from it unless the student cannot benefit from being in that program, even after the provision of supplementary aids and services and necessary related services.

5. The right to be treated fairly. The principle of procedural due process means that the school must provide certain kinds of information (notice and access to records) to the parents of students, special protection when their parents are unavailable (and the school instead is dealing with surrogate parents), and access to a fair hearing process.

6. The right to be included in the decision-making process. The principle of parent and student participation means the schools must structure decision-making processes (including policy decisions on a statewide level) in such a way that parents and students have opportunities to affect meaningfully the education the students are receiving. A related principle of enhanced accountability to pupils and parents is moving in the direction of report cards related to individualized goals and educational programs.

HOW DOES THE SPECIAL EDUCATION SYSTEM WORK?

It is important to understand the impact of laws, court decisions, and policies on state and local educational systems. To respect the rights of children with disabilities to a FAPE and to qualify for federal financial assistance under IDEIA, a state must demonstrate that it has in effect a policy that ensures that all children with disabilities between the ages of three and twenty-one have the right to a FAPE (20 U.S.C. 1412). That policy must be written in the form of a state plan, and is subject to reapproval every three years by the U.S. Department of Education. Children with disabilities must be educated to the maximum extent appropriate with children who are not disabled. This is called the least restrictive environment (LRE) mandate (20 U.S.C. 1412[5]). The FAPE required by IDEA must be tailored to the unique needs of each child through a document called an individualized education program (IEP), prepared at a formal meeting between a qualified representative of the local education agency (LEA), the child's teacher, the child's parents or guardian, and, where appropriate, the child. Parental involvement and consultation in this process must be maximized. IDEIA also imposes on the states detailed procedural requirements—that is, a set of rules outlining exactly how the educational rights of children with disabilities are to be protected. The rights of parents to consent to the provision or termination of special education services, to question the decisions of educational personnel, and to invoke a highly specific administrative hearing process are all outlined in IDEIA (20 U.S.C. 1415 et seq.). Parents or schools may request mediation or an impartial due process hearing to appeal virtually any educational decision. Any party dissatisfied with the results of the initial due process hearing may request and receive an impartial review according to procedures established by the SEA and, if not satisfied with that review, may then appeal to the courts.

Special education law has long placed an affirmative duty on school systems to seek out all children in need of special education, from birth to age twenty-one. This system, called Child Find, must be a part of every state plan. IDEIA (2004) expanded the role of Child Find to require that school districts provide services for homeless children, wards of the state, and students in private schools (20 U.S.C. 1400, Section 612[a][3]).

Although IDEIA (2004) leaves to the states many details concerning development and implementation of particular programs, it imposes substantial requirements to be followed in the discharge of the states' responsibilities. Noncompliance with federal procedural requirements may be sanctioned by withholding federal dollars flowing to the offending agency. For example, the U.S. Department of Education may investigate an SEA for failing to educate children in the LRE. Such a failure would be evidenced by a pattern of educating children with physical disabilities in separate facilities even though the children in question may have no problems in learning other than the physical ones that challenge them. The federal law requires that education of children with disabilities be, to the maximum extent appropriate, with children without disabilities. The failure of a particular state to meet this requirement raises a risk of sanctions.

WHAT IS THE ROLE OF THE LOCAL SCHOOL SYSTEM?

The law ultimately obligates the LEA to provide a FAPE with related services to all children with disabilities. The federal legal mandate requires the local school district to be the agency of last resort for the provision of specialized services to this population of children. Other child-serving agencies might engage in interagency squabbles concerning who should pay for or provide services. LEAs and the respective SEAs are not able to engage in such finger pointing. Thus the educational sector—even in a time of shrinking resources—is and has been a consistent source of dollars for children's services.

WHO IS THE CHILD WITH DISABILITIES?

IDEIA (2004) regulations define a child with a disability as "a child evaluated . . . as having mental retardation, a hearing impairment (including deafness), a speech or language impairment, a visual impairment (including blindness), a serious emotional disturbance, . . . an orthopedic impairment, autism, traumatic brain injury, another health impairment, a specific learning disability, deaf-blindness, or multiple disabilities, and who, by reason thereof, needs special education and related services" (34 C.F.R. 300.8).

Eligibility runs from birth to age twenty-one. The key to eligibility is having a listed disability; because of the disability, the child needs special education and related services. Having a disability implies difficulty in dealing with one's environment and indeed with the very programs and supports intended to help. The purpose of IDEIA (2004) cannot be achieved without a profession, such as school social work, that focuses on the child, family, and learning environment, each in relation to the other, and that views the child as a whole.

WHAT ARE SOCIAL WORK SERVICES IN THE SCHOOLS?

Social work services in schools include

1. Preparing a social or developmental history on a child with a disability;
2. Group and individual counseling with the child and family;
3. Working in partnership with parents and others on those problems in a child's living situation (home, school, and community) that affect the child's adjustment in school;
4. Mobilizing school and community resources to enable the child to learn as effectively as possible in his or her educational program; and
5. Assisting in developing positive behavioral intervention strategies. (34 C.F.R. 300.34 [14]).

Social work addresses the fit between schooling and the needs of children with disabilities and their parents. A particular group of children who experience difficulties in school and usually need social work assistance are those who are emotionally disturbed. Emotional disturbance is a condition exhibiting one or more of the following characteristics over a long period of time and to a marked degree that adversely affects educational performance:

- An inability to learn that cannot be explained by intellectual, sensory, or health factors.
- An inability to build or maintain satisfactory interpersonal relationships with peers and teachers.
- Inappropriate types of behavior or feelings under normal circumstances.
- A general pervasive mood of unhappiness or depression.
- A tendency to develop physical symptoms or fears associated with personal or school problems. (34 C.F.R. 300.8 [c][4]).

WHAT IS SPECIAL EDUCATION?

Special education and related services are defined individually for each pupil by a multidisciplinary team—that is, in each particular situation and for each child. The team, which must include the parents or guardians, prepares the IEP. The need for special education and related services is a key to the definition of the child with a disability. A child who has a health condition is not necessarily considered a child with a disability unless that child's condition also requires special education and related services. Thus, because of that disability and based on a complete, multifaceted, nondiscriminatory assessment (hereafter assessment), there is a need for special education and related services. According to IDEIA (2004), special education means specially designed instruction, at no cost to the parent, to meet the unique needs of a child with a disability. This includes classroom instruction, instruction in physical education, home instruction, and instruction in hospitals and institutions (34 C.F.R. 300.39). IDEIA (2004) mandated that all special education teachers must be highly qualified and meet the same standards as those outlined in the No Child Left Behind Act of 2001.

Schools offer special education once a child has been found eligible for services through a formal case study evaluation. An initial case study evaluation must take place within sixty calendar days of the request for the evaluation, unless the state utilizes its own timeline. Similarly, reevaluations for continuing eligibility for special education services must also take place within sixty calendar days.

WHAT ARE RELATED SERVICES?

Related services means developmental, corrective, and other supportive services as are required to assist a child with a disability to benefit from special education. The term "related services" includes such services as transportation, speech pathology and audiology, psychological services, physical and occupational therapy, recreation, early identification and assessment of disabilities in children, counseling services, and medical services for diagnostic or evaluation purposes. It also includes school nurse services, interpreting services, social work services in schools, and parent counseling and training (34 C.F.R. 300.34).

WHAT IS AN INDIVIDUALIZED EDUCATION PROGRAM?

The IEP is the blueprint for all that happens in the education of a child with disabilities. It is a series of guidelines for educators to follow in conferring educational benefit and a useful document for parents to follow in determining whether those benefits are being made available. School districts must write an IEP before they can provide services; IDEIA (2004) is quite detailed in its specification of the contents of this document. For example, the IEP must include a "statement of measurable annual goals, including academic and functional goals" (20 U.S.C. 1400, Section 614[d][1][A]). Transition planning must be documented for students not later than the first IEP in effect when a child turns age sixteen, and such planning must include appropriate, measurable postsecondary goals and a listing of transition services needed to help students reach these goals.

Parental participation is key to IEP development. IDEIA (2004) broadens the definition of "parent" to include natural or adoptive parents, guardians, a person acting in place of a parent such as a grandparent or stepparent, or duly appointed surrogate parents. Foster parents may serve as surrogate parents if the natural parents do not have the authority to make educational decisions, according to state law, and the foster parents have a parental relationship with the child, are willing, and have no conflict of interest (20 U.S.C. 1402 [23]).

The role of the regular education teacher at IEP meetings was strengthened in IDEIA (2004). Regular education teachers must help "determine the appropriate behavior interventions and strategies, and supplemental aids and services that are necessary for their classrooms (20 U.S.C. 1414 [d][3][C]).

All IEPs must be reviewed at least every year. A new IEP needs to be written at least every three years. Parents or guardians are always entitled to question IEPs through due process procedures (20 U.S.C. 1414 [a][5]). Many SEAs publish manuals on how to write an IEP, and all states have organizations and resource centers to assist parents and guardians in understanding the process of writing an IEP. The input of the school social worker during the drafting of the IEP often has a substantial effect on the recommendations made, and social work services are often among the crucial related services in the IEP. School districts sometimes list their recommendations for the pupil prior to drafting an IEP, but this is a significant procedural error. IDEIA (2004) requires the assessment to be done first and then the IEP to be completed, on the logical assumption that recommendations for a particular educational setting and specific services cannot possibly be made until the needs of the child are determined. When recommendations are made before the IEP is drafted, this may indicate that school authorities are simply offering the program they have available, rather than creating a customized program to meet all of the needs of the child. It is legally improper and a violation of IDEIA (2004) for recommendations to be based on administrative convenience, costs, waiting lists, or any factors other than the needs of the particular child with a disability in question.

The parent or guardian of a child covered by IDEIA (2004) must be given prior notice whenever the school district proposes a change in the educational placement of a child, or a change in its provision of a FAPE for the child (20 U.S.C. 1415 [b][3]). This notice must contain an official explanation for the change being proposed, and the reasons why other less restrictive options were rejected (20 U.S.C. 1415 [c][1][E]). The consent of a parent or guardian is required for the initiation or termination of educational benefits (34 C.F.R. 300.300). It is good practice to secure this consent for a reevaluation and/or change of the program. The parent has the right to ask for revisions in the child's IEP (34 C.F.R. 300.324). Notification of proposed changes, regardless of their magnitude, is required in all instances under IDEIA (2004) because the right to demand a hearing is always vested in the parent or guardian who disagrees with the changes. Once a year, at the minimum, the parent should be given a complete description of available procedural safeguards (34 C.F.R. 300.504). Changes to an IEP may be made by amendment without redrafting the entire IEP. A school district and a parent may agree not to convene an IEP team meeting for the purposes of modifying an IEP, and instead "may develop a written document to amend or modify the child's current IEP" (34 CFR 300.324[a][4][i]). The child's IEP team needs to be informed of any changes, and the parents need to receive a revised copy of the IEP with the amendments incorporated. The failure to implement an IEP has been held to constitute a change in the child's educational placement, as well as a failure to provide a FAPE. An IEP is not, however, a contract, nor is it a guarantee that the child will achieve the results contemplated.

WHAT SERVICES MUST THE SCHOOL PROVIDE?

The LEA is obligated to provide the special education and related services (or for certain other children supplementary aids and services) required so that the pupil can attain the objectives stated in the IEP. The components of an IEP are special education, related services, supplementary aids and services, program modifications, and personal support. These components are to benefit the student so that he or she may

1. Advance appropriately toward attaining the annual goals,
2. Be involved and progress in the general curriculum and participate in extracurricular activities and other nonacademic activities, and

3. Be educated and participate with other children with disabilities and children without disabilities in those extracurricular and nonacademic activities.

The mandate for use of related services is broad, going beyond special education to include what is necessary for the child to participate in general education and extracurricular activities.

Social Work Services

Under IDEIA (2004), the educational sector is required to pay for related services, which would include any services required to assist a child to benefit from special education. A key issue has been what level of related services is necessary for a child to benefit from special education. The *Rowley* case involved a hearing-impaired girl who understood only about half of what was occurring in class. Nevertheless, Amy Rowley received A's and B's because of her high intelligence (*Board of Education of Hendrick Hudson Central School District, Westchester County v. Rowley*, 1982). Her parents wanted the school to provide a full-time sign language interpreter to attend class with her, but the Supreme Court held that the student was not so entitled, as she was already receiving an educational benefit without the interpreter.

Rowley generally is used by schools to argue that they are not required to provide the best education—only an education that is minimally appropriate and available. Social workers should likewise be aware that the recommendations contained in their reports should address services necessary to minimally enable the child to benefit from educational programming. For instance, some students with depression may need nonmedical psychotherapy to attend to instructional tasks. In some cases, such psychotherapy has been held to be a related service that the schools must provide. The distinction between a fundable service and a nonfundable service turns on whether mental health services, psychotherapy, or social work services (as they are defined earlier) would assist a particular student to benefit from special education. In a number of decisions, the courts further defined a service-benefit standard. The standard involves evaluating two criteria: (1) whether the program is designed to improve the student's educational performance, and (2) whether the program is based on the student's classification (e.g., a child challenged with emotional disturbance).

Psychotherapy

On the other hand, in another decision a court held that the service-benefit standard for determining whether psychotherapy is a related service is overly broad and inordinately encompassing. When the justification of the services is only psychological improvement, the LEA is not responsible for providing mental health services to the student. For mental health services to be a required service, the LEA must clearly demonstrate that social work services would assist students to benefit from special education. In school social work, the general language for demonstrating this is found in the previous definition of school social work services. For many years, school social workers have defined their practice in relation to education, as the present book will attest. The use of the term "social work services" should be inserted into a child's IEP to differentiate services provided by school social workers from services provided by school psychologists, counselors, or other school personnel.

Children Unable to Benefit from Education

There are several thousand children in the United States so lacking in brain capacity that they are unable to benefit from any educational services. The U.S. Supreme Court declined to review a hotly contested case in which a child lacking any cortex was held to be entitled to related services, even though he was unlikely to benefit from services. The *Timothy W.* case originated in Rochester, New Hampshire, where the school district argued that providing any services to such child who was so hopelessly disabled would be a waste of tax dollars better spent on children with less disability (*Timothy W. v. Rochester, New Hampshire School District,* 1989). The appellate court, however, relied on the statutory language of IDEIA (2004), the legislative history behind it, and case law interpreting it, and ruled that all children with disabilities are entitled to a public education, regardless of the severity of their disability.

If a child needs a residential setting in order to benefit from education, the schools must pay for such a setting, and there can be no charges to the parents or guardian. If other agencies are active and are able to pay part of the cost, such payments are allowed as long as such agencies do not charge the parent. When a school district writes an IEP stating that another agency is to provide some of the services, the school district is still the agency of last resort, and parents may rightfully turn to the schools for recompense.

A well-known U.S. Supreme Court case has held that clean intermittent catheterization (CIC) is a related service (*Irving Independent School District v. Tatro,* 1984). Amber Tatro needed CIC several times daily in order to stay in class and to benefit from educational services. In *Tatro,* the schools argued that CIC was a medical service and therefore not a related service. The U.S. Supreme Court did not agree, noting that CIC was not exclusively within the province of physicians and could be administered easily by the school nurse. The school district was required to provide this service.

WHAT IS PLACEMENT IN THE LEAST RESTRICTIVE ENVIRONMENT?

One additional principle, that of the LRE, governs the all-important placement process. This principle is defined in the law as follows: "To the maximum extent appropriate, children with disabilities . . . are educated with children who are nondisabled, and special classes, separate schooling, or other removal of children with disabilities from the regular education environment occurs only if the nature or severity of the disability of a child is such that education in regular classes with the use of supplementary aids and services cannot be achieved satisfactorily" (20 U.S.C. 1412 [a][5][A]).

This principle is extremely important in achieving the general purposes of IDEIA (2004). Related services in the IEP, including the school social worker's contribution, are intended to assist the pupil to advance appropriately toward attaining his or her annual goals, to be involved with and to progress in the general curriculum, to participate in extracurricular and other nonacademic activities, and to be educated and to participate with other children with disabilities and children without disabilities in the general curriculum. The principle of inclusion presumes that the child with disabilities should participate in the general curriculum. It requires the IEP to describe the extent, if any, to which the child will not participate with children without disabilities in regular classes and in extracurricular and other nonacademic activities.

However, the term "inclusion" is not to be found anywhere in the IDEIA (2004) legal mandate. In recent years some advocates have said that the special education system is not working, and that to benefit from educational services, students must be fully included in the mainstream school environment. Many have gone so far as to present this concept as a part of the law, and to tell parents this new "law" says they must cooperate in the full mainstreaming of their children. Nothing could be farther from the truth. The law governing the LRE has not changed; it merely requires that, to the maximum extent appropriate, children with disabilities should be educated with children without disabilities. Although there is a presumption that the child with disabilities should participate in the general curriculum when appropriate, no federal law has ever mandated full inclusion without consideration of educational needs. Federal law requires all school districts to make available a full continuum of alternatives from the least restrictive (e.g., complete mainstreaming with one resource period per day) to the most restrictive (private residential placement). Part of the school social worker's role in these cases is to work with pupil, parents, and the school to construct this environment.

WHAT ARE PLACEMENT PROCEDURES?

Placement procedures make the connection between the assessment and the IEP. Disabilities are inevitably connected with social functioning in one way or another. If assessments are to be complete, multifaceted, and nondiscriminatory, as the law prescribes, the school social worker should participate in most assessments. In some school districts, the social worker is the person responsible for the social developmental study of the child. The social worker's understanding of the child's current adaptation to home and school environments, the child's previous developmental steps, and the culture and functioning of the family is essential to any assessment. In the same vein, the annual goals for the child, the corresponding education program, and related services, as developed in the IEP, often explicitly involve tasks for the social worker with the child, with the family, and with education professionals. In the process of interpreting evaluation data and planning an IEP, the multidisciplinary team needs to

(i). Draw upon information from a variety of sources, including adaptive and achievement tests, parent input, and teacher recommendations, as well as information about the child's physical condition, social or cultural background, and adaptive behavior; and

(ii). Ensure that information obtained from all of these sources is documented and carefully considered. (34 C.F.R. 300.306)

CAN STUDENTS WITH DISABILITIES BE SUSPENDED OR EXPELLED?

In *Honig v. Doe* (1988), the U.S. Supreme Court set forth guidelines that educators have actively and hotly debated ever since. Two California cases related to *Honig* involved violent, acting-out pupils who were suspended indefinitely under the California statute that allowed indefinite suspensions; both were later expelled. The school district's attorneys argued that Congress could not possibly have intended that the schools be required to keep serving dangerous, emotionally disturbed pupils, when staff members and other students were in peril. The Supreme Court held that Congress "very much meant to strip schools of the unilateral authority they had traditionally employed to exclude disabled students, particularly emotionally disturbed students, from schools" (*Honig v. Doe*, 1988, p. 321). In this case, the U.S. Supreme Court demonstrated its reluctance to read into IDEA meanings that Congress had never expressed.

The net effect of this case is that a school may not remove a pupil with a disability from school for behavior that is a manifestation of the disabling condition without the consent of the parents. To determine whether the behavior was or was not a manifestation of the disability, the IEP team must consider whether (1) the conduct in question was caused by or had a direct and substantial relationship to the child's disability, and (2) whether the conduct in question was a direct result of the school district's failure to implement the IEP (20 U.S.C. 1415[k][1][E]). If a district does find a child's behavior to be related to his or her disability, then it is required to (1) create a functional behavioral assessment (FBA) and a behavior intervention plan (BIP) for the child (see section III of this book) or revise a child's FBA and BIP if one was already completed, and (2) return the child to his or her previous educational placement. The Supreme Court has clearly expressed its view that allowing schools to suspend pupils who are dangerous to themselves and others for up to ten days cumulatively per school year gives educational authorities sufficient time to seek parental consent, negotiate alternatives, or go to court to obtain permission of a judge for the removal. Additionally, IDEIA (2004) law has created certain circumstances (students bringing guns to school; knowingly possessing, using, or selling dangerous drugs; or inflicting serious bodily injury on another person in school) where the school may go beyond the ten-day limit, possibly up to forty-five school (not calendar) days (20 U.S.C. 1415[k][1][G]). If a student with a disability brings guns to school; knowingly possesses, uses, or sells dangerous drugs; or inflicts serious bodily injury on another person in school, the school can place the student in an alternative education setting for up to forty-five days. In these cases, during a parental or school-initiated appeals process, the child would remain at the alternative placement during the pendency of the dispute (20 U.S.C. 1415[k][1][G]). In any case, a change of placement occurs if removal is more than ten consecutive school days, or if there is a series of removals totaling more than ten days in one academic year. The school must provide the child with a FAPE, and an FBA and a BIP; the school also might need to provide modifications of the original program needed (20 U.S.C. 1415[k][1][D]).

IDEIA (2004) also provides some protections for children not yet determined eligible for special education if a school district has knowledge that a child has a disability. The school district is considered to have knowledge of the disability if the parent expressed concern about a possible disability to the school in writing, if the parent requested a case study evaluation, or if a teacher or other school district employee expressed specific concerns about a pattern of behavior to the director of special education or other supervisory personnel (20 U.S.C. 1415[k][5][C]).

Social workers should become familiar with the basic law of suspension and expulsion of pupils with disabilities, because they may find themselves in the position of mediating disputes between schools and families of disabled students. Frequently, social workers are called on to act as impartial mediators as well as to utilize their skills in facilitating communication between the school and the family. Moreover, social workers are commonly called as experts in due process hearings for the purpose of establishing whether the behavior in question is or is not related to the pupil's disabling condition. Finally, current law relating to suspension and expulsion is a powerful tool for families of the disabled to persuade school authorities to consider more-restrictive alternatives for the child, such as private extended-day school programs or residential placement, when appropriate.

WHAT ARE PROVISIONS FOR A RESOLUTION SESSION, FOR MEDIATION, AND FOR AN IMPARTIAL DUE PROCESS HEARING?

It is not surprising that there could be differences between parents and others on the multidisciplinary team over a possible recommended placement for a child. In these circumstances, the due process protections of the Fifth and Fourteenth Amendments to the U.S. Constitution demand more-formal procedures. After all, a civil right is being defined. It was the intent of the framers of IDEIA (2004) that parents and educators be encouraged to "work out their differences by using nonadversarial means" (U.S. Government Printing Office [GPO], 1997, p. S4298). IDEIA (2004) provides for a resolution session to encourage resolution of complaints without the need for involvement of attorneys or hearing officers. Under 20 U.S.C. 1415(f)(1)(B)(ii), after a school district receives a request for a due process hearing, it is mandated to convene a meeting to try to resolve the complaint within fifteen days unless both parties agree to waive the meeting. If the parent attends the meeting without an attorney, the school district must be unrepresented as well. The parties may agree to use state mediation procedures instead of a resolution session. The next step would be an impartial due process hearing. In most cases, it is only after these steps have been taken, and the issue is still unresolved, that the case would go to court.

Mediation is a voluntary process conducted by a "qualified and impartial mediator who is trained in effective mediation techniques" (20 U.S.C. 1415 [e]). Mediation cannot be used to deny or delay a parent's right to an impartial due process hearing. The SEA usually has a list of approved mediators and carries the cost of the mediation process. Any agreement reached by the parties to the dispute would be set forth in a written mediation agreement. Discussions in the mediation process are confidential and cannot be used as evidence in subsequent due process hearings or civil proceedings. Both parties may be required to sign a confidentiality pledge prior to the mediation process (20 U.S.C. 1415 [e]).

The impartial due process hearing is conducted by either the SEA or the LEA, although not by an employee involved with the education of the child. It is a more formal process than mediation. Any evaluation completed in relation to the pupil must be disclosed at least five days prior to the hearing. There are procedural safeguards provided to the parents: the right to be accompanied or advised by counsel and by experts; the right to present evidence; the right to confront, cross-examine, and compel the attendance of witnesses; the right to a verbatim record; and the right to written findings of fact and decisions. If the hearing is conducted by the LEA, its outcome may be appealed to the SEA, where another hearing may take place. If the problem is not resolved at this point, it may be brought to court (20 U.S.C. 1415 [i]). During due process hearings, the child's placement would remain the same unless he or she has not been admitted to public school. In that case, the child would, with the parents' permission, be placed in the public school until the completion of the proceedings.

Several recent court decisions have clarified some of the procedures for due process hearings. In a court decision, *Schaffer v. Weast* (2005), the U.S. Supreme Court determined that the party that requested the hearing is the side to go first. The Court held that the burden of persuasion fell on the party that initiated the process. In a second case, *Arlington Central School District Board of Education v. Murphy* (2006), the Supreme Court held that, even if parents prevail in a due process case, they are not entitled to reimbursement to pay for any expert witnesses that they hire as part of their case. The prevailing parents are still entitled to reimbursement of reasonable attorney fees, however. Finally, in *Winkelman v. Parma City School District* (2007), the U.S. Supreme Court held that parents can represent themselves and their child in a due process hearing. The appellate court had dismissed the parents' claim for attorney fees because they had no attorney to represent them. The Supreme Court held that this would leave some parents, such as those who could not afford an attorney, without a remedy in the courts under IDEA.

WHAT ARE DUE PROCESS AND JUDICIAL REVIEW?

Once the due process hearing is completed, any party dissatisfied with the result may appeal it to either state or federal court (20 U.S.C. 1415 [i]) by filing a lawsuit against the other party, requesting appropriate relief. It is important to note that the stay-put provision operates while all proceedings are taking place (20 U.S.C. 1415 [j]). This provision requires that the child remain in his or her then-current placement while due process proceedings are pending. During this time, the district must pay for all educational services in the then-current placement. When certain behaviors occur, the school may place the student in an alternative education setting for up to forty-five calendar days. In these instances, the alternative setting is the stay-put placement.

In *School Committee of Town of Burlington, Massachusetts v. Department of Education of Massachusetts* (1985), parents and the school district disagreed about the adequacy of the district's placement for their child with specific learning disabilities. During the disagreement, the parents placed their child in a state-approved private school for special education and then sought reimbursement from the district for their expenses. The school district refused to reimburse the parents for the unilateral placement of their son in a private school, rather than the district's recommended placement, which was the last, agreed-on placement. The court decided in *Burlington* that parents who unilaterally change their child's placement during the pendency of the review process without the consent of the school officials do so at their own financial risk. The court ruled that if the school's placement ultimately is determined to be appropriate, then the parents would be barred from receiving reimbursement for any period that the child's placement violated the stay-put provision. Otherwise, the parents would be forced to leave their child in what may turn out to be an inappropriate educational placement. The stay-put provision is thus a powerful tool for parents if proceedings commence when the pupil is in an educational setting that satisfies the parents. Most commonly, the child will be in a school-funded residential placement while the district seeks to return him or her to a less-restrictive setting. If the parents request due process at this point, the child must remain in the residential setting at district expense during the pendency of all proceedings, through and including appellate court review.

Conversely, when the current placement is one that the parents believe is not appropriate, the stay-put provision operates to the benefit of the school district. In this instance, the parents' goal is to effect an alternative placement that they and their experts believe is more appropriate than the current setting, whereas the school district usually seeks to maintain the status quo. The school district continues to pay the cost of the child's educational placement, regardless of who requests due process. For younger pupils entering school for the first time, the current placement is interpreted by most states to be the setting in which the child would be placed in the absence of any disability. For a student with disabilities transferring from one school district to another, the current placement is determined by the student's most recent IEP.

Note here that it is not only parents who can request due process: schools also sometimes seek to provide a service that the parents oppose. For instance, the district may want to place the child in a classroom for children with retardation, while the parents may believe that their child is not a child with retardation but instead is a child with a learning disability. The parents' refusal to consent to the district's proposed placement may be met with the district's request for due process. From a liability point of view, this is the only alternative for districts in such a position. Parents are frequently unable to accept that their child has severe disabilities and has such low functioning. The social worker may be called on to assist the parents in working through their shame and guilt, among other feelings.

CONCLUSION

Legislation and case law on the civil right to a FAPE for children with disabilities have created new structures of service for these children. The social worker's services are framed in a developing body of law. It is important to understand that this law is not simply a set of procedures. It places a mandate on the school district and on the social worker to provide services that will enable children with disabilities and their families to survive in an initially unequal struggle. Here the language of the law can be translated into the language of service. The more familiar social workers are with both languages, the more able they will be to translate them into services that can redress this inequality.

References

Arlington Central School District Board of Education v. Murphy, 548 U.S. 291 (2006).

Board of Education of Hendrick Hudson Central School District, Westchester County, v. Rowley, 458 U.S. 176 (1982).

Education for All Handicapped Children Act of 1975, Pub. L. 94-142 (1975).

Honig v. Doe, 484 U.S. 305 (1988).

Individuals with Disabilities Education Act of 1990 (IDEA), Pub. L. 105-17, U.S.C. 11401 et seq. (1990).

Individuals with Disabilities Education Improvement Act of 2004 (IDEIA), Pub. L. 108-446 (2004).

Irving Independent School District v. Tatro, 468 U.S. (1984).

No Child Left Behind Act of 2001, Pub. L. 107-110 (2002).

Schaffer v. Weast, 546 U.S. 49 (2005).

School Committee of Town of Burlington, Massachusetts v. Department of Education of Massachusetts, 471 U.S. 359 (1985).

Timothy W. v. Rochester, New Hampshire School District, 875 F. 2d 954 (1st Cir., 1989).

Turnbull, H. R., & Turnbull, A. P. (1998). *Free appropriate public education: The law and children with disabilities* (5th ed.). Denver, CO: Love.

U.S. Government Printing Office (GPO). (1997, May 12). Individuals with Disabilities Education Act Amendments of 1997. *Congressional Record 143*(61). Retrieved from http://www.gpo.gov/fdsys/pkg/CREC-1997-05-12/html/CREC-1997-05-12-pt1-PgS4295-3.htm

Winkelman v. Parma City School District, 550 U.S. 516 (2007).

10

The School Social Work Contribution to Meeting National Standards for Social Emotional Learning

Brenda Lindsey
University of Illinois at Urbana Champaign

Kari Smith
University of Illinois at Chicago

Tory Cox
University of Southern California

Michelle Alvarez
Southern New Hampshire University

- ◆ State Adoption of Common Core
- ◆ Race to the Top
- ◆ Implementation of Common Core Standards: A Rocky Road
- ◆ Why School Social Workers Need to Know about Common Core Standards
- ◆ New Opportunities and Roles for School Social Workers in the Common Core State Standards Era
- ◆ National Social Emotional Learning Standards for School Social Workers and Common Core
- ◆ Development of National School Social Work Standards for Social Emotional Learning

Common Core state standards (CCSS) describe specific sets of skills that students should be able to demonstrate by the end of a particular grade level. Developed by teachers, researchers, parents, and school administrators, the CCSS are intended to promote rigor and equity in education (Common Core State Standards Initiative [CCSSI], 2013). CCSS are expected to bring about a uniform approach to education, regardless of school or teacher preferences. As with any educational initiative, there is also controversy surrounding the CCSS, ranging from the contention that the Standards are a top-down example of educational federalism to concern regarding the lack of clear assessments that actually demonstrate improved student academic performance (Manna & Ryan, 2011; Mathis, 2010; McShane, 2013).

Regardless of the controversy surrounding these standards, school social workers need to be prepared to carve out their place within them. One way to do this is to utilize states' well-established social-emotional learning (SEL) standards. This chapter will discuss the CCSS, implementation of these standards, why school social workers need to be familiar with them, and the link between these standards and SEL standards.

There is evidence to suggest that American students are often ill prepared for credit-bearing two- and four-year colleges, universities, and for entry-level positions (American College Testing [ACT], 2013; Kena et al., 2014; National Assessment of Educational Progress, 2013). Early in their educational careers, students already begin to lag. Fewer than half of all fourth and eighth graders in the United States demonstrate proficiency in mathematics and reading (National Assessment of Educational Progress, 2013). According to *The Condition of College and Career Readiness 2013* report (ACT, 2013), 64 percent of all students who took the ACT met the English college readiness benchmark, while 44 percent met the reading and mathematics benchmarks. Fewer than 30 percent of 2013 high school graduates met all four of the ACT's college readiness benchmarks in English, mathematics, reading, and science (ACT, 2013). These findings lead to what some call a "crisis" in literacy, particularly adolescent literacy (Jacobs, 2008; Shanahan & Shanahan, 2008).

The main goal of CCSS is to prepare students for college and career readiness within a global market. This goal directly addresses the concern that the current extensive need for postsecondary remedial courses is due to a lack of rigor and lack of quality in K–12 schools (Bettinger & Long, 2009). Students with below-par skills are often forced to take remedial courses and can become marginalized within the general college student population when they are placed in courses with other struggling students (Bettinger & Long, 2009; Shanahan & Shanahan, 2008).

The CCSS focus on learning standards for English language arts (commonly referred to as ELA) and mathematics for K–12 students. The ELA standards include standards for literacy in history/social studies, science, and technical subjects. Learning standards for technical subjects include skills such as the ability to understand and use information presented visually in a graph. The major components of the ELA standards are reading writing, speaking and listening, and language standards. The speaking and listening standards identify critical social, emotional, and communication skills students need to develop by the time they graduate from high school.

Effective social, emotional, and communication skills are also needed for students to know and understand how to manage emotions, deal with conflict, communicate their needs, advocate for themselves, and make responsible decisions (Cohen, 2006; Collaborative for Academic, Social, and Emotional Learning [CASEL], n.d.). Competency in communication skills is essential to ensure that students are prepared for post–high school success (Morreale, Osborn, & Pearson, 2000). SEL contributes to improved academic performance and a positive school climate, key tenets of a sound educational environment conducive to student learning (CASEL, n.d.; Cohen, 2006).

STATE ADOPTION OF COMMON CORE

Starting with Kentucky and New York in 2010, forty-five states and the District of Columbia have now committed to implementing both mathematics and ELA Common Core standards either as-is or using some variation of the standards (Association for Supervision and Curriculum Development [ASCD], 2013; Thompson, 2013). Standards for science, social studies, and the arts have not been formulated to date. Minnesota will be implementing the ELA, but not the mathematics standards, stating that its standards are equal to or higher than CCSS (ASCD, 2013). Additionally, the U.S. Department of Defense Education Activity (DoDEA) approved the standards for implementation in all schools working directly with children of military families, including those overseas (DoDEA, 2012). A map of the most up to date list of state adopters can be found at ASCD (n.d.).

These states value CCSS's emphasis on depth over breadth to ensure that students achieve readiness (Illinois State Board of Education [ISBE], 2012). The emphasis on critical thinking and preparing college and career-ready students by twelfth grade conceptually unites educators (Achieve and U.S. Education Delivery Institute, 2012). Four states, however (Alaska, Nebraska, Texas, and Virginia) will not be implementing these standards as of this writing (ASCD, 2013; Thompson, 2013).

These states' objections to CCSS share common themes:

1. CCSS are a top-down example of educational federalism that runs counter to these states' political views on the role of government.
2. There are no clear data showing improved aptitude on national tests due to increased standards brought about by the No Child Left Behind Act (USDOE, 2004).
3. There was very little input from educators in the formation of the standards.

4. CCSS had no field testing of the standards prior to adoption.
5. There are to date no clear assessments to assess the standards themselves.
6. The CCSS federal initiative has provided little federal support for states and local education agencies (LEAs) to build capacity with which to implement the standards (Manna & Ryan, 2011; Mathis, 2010; McShane, 2013).

Nationally, educators question whether the standards reflect the needs of the workforce and whether one set of standards is applicable to all segments of our diverse society (Mathis, 2010). Similar concerns have been raised by parents on social media and in popular news that describe CCSS as frustrating and puzzling (Richards, 2014; Rubikam, 2014).

An additional concern is that corrective measures for LEAs failing to meet the new standards are the same as the punitive measures of the No Child Left Behind Act (Mathis, 2010; USDOE, 2004). Contrary to expected corrective changes, LEAs may continue to be severely penalized if their students do not meet the standards despite a lack of funds, tools, or training for teachers to teach the new standards (Mathis, 2010; Sawchuk, 2012). Those penalties include firing of administrators and teachers, school closures, and conversion to charter schools (Manna & Ryan, 2011; Mathis, 2010).

The experiences of the early states in implementing CCSS have also not been very promising. Test scores remain low in Kentucky and New York, and there are no tangible results to indicate improvement (Thompson, 2013). These results could reflect low previous standards for each state, anticipated early implementation issues, or problems with the new standards (Sawchuk, 2012; Thompson, 2013). It will take several more years in these states to align the instruction with the new standards and produce reliable and accurate evaluations, which should coincide with the integration of national evaluative assessments (Thompson, 2013).

RACE TO THE TOP

Despite these struggles, the federal government included national standards in its Race to the Top (RTT) initiative in which LEAs vied for education grants from $4 to $30 million (Manna & Ryan, 2011). In August 2013 the request for proposals for the RTT at the district level (RTT-D) called for LEAs to "fully adopt a set of common college- and career-ready standards, along with 15 percent of their own standards" (Home School Legal Defense Association [HSLDA], 2013; see also USDOE, 2013a). Although the language did not explicitly mention Common Core standards, the initiative's rubric awarded extra points to states that adopted national standards, essentially ensuring that the winning states would be utilizing Common Core. Most states and LEAs interpreted this language as the federal government's desire to see Common Core reflected in the applications (HSLDA, 2013). This perception of veiled coercion led some states and LEAs to pull out of the competition, while others adopted the standards in order to compete for the dollars at stake. The competition carried with it political overtones connected to President Obama's administration that may have influenced the decision to remain in or withdraw from the competition (ASCD, 2013; HSLDA, 2013; Thompson, 2013).

Regardless of the politics of the competition, in December 2013 the winners of the RTT-D were announced. Selected from 31 finalists and dividing $120 million, the five winning districts or consortiums represented the states of Arkansas, Kentucky, South Carolina, Mississippi, and Texas (USDOE, 2013b).

IMPLEMENTATION OF COMMON CORE STANDARDS: A ROCKY ROAD

Thus far, implementation of CCSS has involved a composite of strategies addressing "teacher professional development, curriculum materials, and teacher-evaluation systems" (Education First and Editorial Projects in Education, Inc., 2012, p. 2). In a review of implementation efforts, Education First and Editorial Projects in Education surveyed state boards of education and found that most states have either developed a plan (twenty states) or have plans in development (twenty-five states) (Education First and Editorial Projects in Education, Inc., 2012). To support state implementation, the National Education Association (NEA) has created a toolkit for implementation of the standards (NEA, 2013). This resource contains materials, templates, and examples to aid states and educators (NEA, 2013). There is also a list of resources by state and instructional plans in various subjects (NEA, 2013).

Some states are playing a central role in preparing teachers for the new standards, while others are letting school districts take the lead. School districts in Tennessee, for example, have been preparing teachers through professional development activities, while in Idaho the Boise State Writing Project worked with teachers on ways to incorporate the standards through existing pedagogical methods in mathematics, physical education, and science (Wootton, 2013). In Illinois, a Web site was created as a resource for teachers to implement Common Core called the Professional Learning Series; it contains "more than fifty topics with over two hundred associated strategies, tools, and support materials" (ISBE, 2012, p. 1). Some LEAs are offering professional development activities for teachers to help them align their lessons and assessments with Common Core while others are struggling to assist teachers due to a lack of resources.

There is concern about the capacity of some districts throughout the nation to train teachers effectively to deliver the Common Core standards. "A national survey of school districts last fall by the Center on Education Policy found that fewer than half of districts had planned professional development aligned to the standards this school year" (Sawchuk, 2012, p. 17). For states and LEAs whose implementation plans have not been developed, teachers have expressed their frustration, saying that they feel ill-prepared for the implementation (Sawchuk, 2012).

Another area of criticism has been the lack of a comprehensive start-to-finish plan for implementing and assessing the CCSS. Despite the fact that Common Core standards have been adopted, there are no uniform assessment materials or approaches to evaluate the impact on student learning. Two different state collectives were formed to create assessments that began during the 2014–15 school year, although the numbers have been reduced since the RTT-D process reached its later stages (HSLDA, 2013). Because of concerns with cost, politics, and loss of local control with national assessments, some states have opted out of these collectives (Manna & Ryan, 2011; McShane, 2013). The Smarter Balanced Assessment Consortium (SBAC) and the Partnership for Assessment of Readiness for College and Careers (PARCC) are each working on new assessments to accurately measure proficiency of the new standards (ASCD, 2013). SBAC has twenty-five states in its consortium while PARCC has eighteen states plus the District of Columbia in its collaborative group (PARCC, 2013; SBAC, 2013). This fragmented approach is problematic in many ways and can only serve to deepen public cynicism toward educational reform.

Local schools are main sources of information about Common Core for students and parents. Nationally, organizations such as the National Parent Teacher Association (National PTA) and NEA have produced information to help families in their transition to Common Core. The National PTA has developed the "Parents' Guide to Student Success" that gives parents grade-by-grade information on the standards (National PTA, 2014). It also has information on its Web site that directs parents to SEAs to access information (National PTA, 2014). NEA, meanwhile, created the "Common Core State Standards Toolkit" that lists numerous resources, including links to more specific information under "Parent and Community Resources" (NEA, 2013).

WHY SCHOOL SOCIAL WORKERS NEED TO KNOW ABOUT COMMON CORE STATE STANDARDS

In its conceptualization, Common Core is a school reform effort intended to elevate the standards that determine proficiency across the nation and bring each state's standards in line with these expectations Because every state and district would need to adhere to these standards, the current inconsistent assessments of proficiency would theoretically dissolve (Mathis, 2010). Because "educational equity demands uniform, high-quality, standards-based curricula for all," all students should, in theory, receive the same standard-based instruction across the nation (Mathis, 2010, p. 6). This perspective aligns with the National Association of Social Workers's (NASW) Code of Ethics regarding social justice and the dignity and worth of all people (NASW, 2008).

RTT-D also sought districts advocating for "services that help meet students' academic, social, and emotional needs, outside of the classroom" (USDOE, 2013b, p. 1). For school social workers, "maximizing access to school-based and community-based resources" for students and families (Frey et al., 2013, p. 3) while responding to the diversity of human needs has the prospect of increased economic and social opportunities. According to the USDOE, RTT-D emphasized "making equity and access to high-quality education a priority" (USDOE, 2013b, p. 1). Ensuring equity in education underscores the dignity of each individual, family, group, and community, and helps guarantee "educational rights," part of a key construct governing school social work services (Frey et al., 2013, p. 4). Connecting the ethics of school social work services to the advent of Common Core theoretically aligns the two approaches in meaningful ways.

School social workers should also become conversant in Common Core because students who move or whose military parents are deployed during their K–12 years will be able to more easily adjust academically to a new school site (Mathis, 2010; Pfiffner, 2013). School social workers are aware of the deleterious effects of frequent moves on the educational outcomes of students, particularly for those most vulnerable, such as students experiencing foster care, children of military families, or youths experiencing homelessness. With more similarity in classroom environments and instruction across diverse schools and districts, transitional experiences for children or youths may improve (Mathis, 2010; Pfiffner, 2013).

NEW OPPORTUNITIES AND ROLES FOR SCHOOL SOCIAL WORKERS IN THE COMMON CORE STATE STANDARDS ERA

School social workers must take a leadership role in advocating for sufficient educational, social, and economic supports for children, especially those children that are neediest (Mathis, 2010). If Common Core is to successfully create college and career-ready students, more school-based mental health services are needed (Mathis, 2010). This approach is in line with the key construct for school social workers of home, school, and community linkages (Frey et al., 2013), as well as with the NASW ethical principles of service, empowerment, and self-determination (NASW, 2008).

The dual emphasis on college and career-readiness allows for a diverse pool of students to achieve success. The critical thinking and conceptual underpinning of Common Core is intended to develop life skills within students, regardless of the paths they take. Utilizing the principle of cultural competence and social diversity (NASW, 2008), school social workers can align their interventions with Common Core to facilitate student success.

In working with first-generation college students, educators often communicate that college is possible for them. The emphasis on college readiness opens up opportunities for strategic dialogue between students and educators, including school social workers. By reviewing the standards expected by twelfth grade, school social workers can connect students' present academic experience with a set of college-ready expectations. Emphasizing the home, school, and community linkage role (Frey et al., 2013), this conversation should also take place with parents and guardians to help them create the belief that college is an option for their children.

NATIONAL SOCIAL EMOTIONAL LEARNING STANDARDS FOR SCHOOL SOCIAL WORKERS AND COMMON CORE

School social workers can also play a key role in advocating for SEL standards to accompany the national mathematics and ELA standards. The identification of these SEL standards, already developed within the state of Illinois and developed nationally through the School Social Work Association of America (SSWAA) for school social workers, has the potential to create another level of equity in addressing these most critical areas of development for children and youths (ISBE, 2013). The often diffuse role of school social workers can be anchored to these SEL standards, providing clearer role definition as well as branding for school social workers. This underscores the ethical principle of competence and helps form a template for data-based decision making regarding students' progression in skill development (Frey et al., 2013; NASW, 2008). Utilizing SEL standards, school social workers can tailor their direct interventions with students, families, and teachers as well as system reform efforts to support these standards.

School social workers also have the opportunity to create a niche for future school social workers. Creating future roles in education could have a significant impact on the profession of school social work for years to come. School social workers should capitalize on this initiative and participate more fully in important decision-making processes that affect educational policy (Frey et al., 2013). Whether in advocacy for an individual student with an IEP or representing larger groups at the negotiating table, school social workers need to be active in site-based decision making, district administrative actions, and local, county, and state education leadership. Understanding Common Core, especially the politics surrounding the initiative (McShane, 2013), is essential in direct work with students and macro-oriented school reform efforts as identified in the NASW "Standards for School Social Work Services" (NASW, 2012).

Like teachers, school social workers will need to be trained in implementing Common Core and the SEL standards. After learning about both sets of standards, the first step is for them to understand how teachers are adapting to and implementing the new standards in the classroom. Key stakeholders will also need to be educated on the importance and relevance of the SEL standards. Finally, a link between the academic and SEL standards will need to be made so that all stakeholders can understand the importance of the SEL standards.

One area to review is the speaking and listening standards within ELA standards (CCSSI, 2013). These standards emphasize developing skill in understanding how to interact with others in social situations (CCSSI, 2013). Critical thinking skills that help individuals react to spontaneous situations are also found in ELA standards and could be utilized by school social workers in their interventions (CCSSI, 2013). Within the SEL standards, decision making could be strongly linked to the Common Core standards as a skill that can be generalized to all areas of life (ISBE, 2012).

As school social workers become familiar with and apply SEL standards consistently in their work with students, they can establish themselves as the professional experts on campus regarding SEL. Implementing standards that help ensure a student is emotionally and socially ready for college or career is an important complement to the Common Core. The highest academic standards will not likely result in college or career readiness if students are not emotionally or socially prepared to interact with others.

DEVELOPMENT OF NATIONAL SCHOOL SOCIAL WORK STANDARDS FOR SOCIAL EMOTIONAL LEARNING

The SSWAA coordinated the development of National School Social Work Standards for Social Emotional Learning. A task force comprising school social workers, school administrators, and university professors began by reviewing examples of SEL standards adopted by various states as well as best practices for implementation. Using a collaborative process, the task force identified key competencies that all students should possess: self-management, social awareness, relationship skills, and decision making. Each competency area includes learning standards that describe how students should demonstrate a particular skill at different levels: early childhood and early elementary, late elementary, middle/junior high, and high school. SSWAA will engage stakeholders in ongoing collaborative discussions regarding the SEL standards. Their insights and feedback will be invaluable to implementation of the initiative.

CONCLUSION

The National School Social Work Standards for Social Emotional Learning are aligned with the National School Social Work Practice Model©. School social workers provide evidence-based education, behavior, and mental health services. This includes interventions that are research-based SEL curriculums taught to all students (Lindsey, 2008). Such interventions promote school climate and culture conducive to student learning and are critical components of school social work practice. Thoughtful consideration should be given to evaluate SEL curricula against SEL standards. In this way, school social workers utilize advanced knowledge and technical skills to meet the needs of the communities, schools, families, and students served.

References

Achieve and U.S. Education Delivery Institute. (2012). *Implementing common core standards and assessments: A workbook for state and district leaders.* Retrieved from http://www.achieve.org/files/Common_Core_Workbook.pdf

American College Testing (ACT). (2013). *The condition of college and career readiness 2013.* Iowa City, IA: Author. Retrieved from http://www.act.org/research/policy makers/cccr13/improving.html

Association for Supervision and Curriculum Development (ASCD). (2013). *Common Core state standards: Myths and facts.* Retrieved from http://www.ascd.org/ ASCD/pdf/siteASCD/publications/policypoints/PolicyPoints_Common_Core_State_ Standards.pdf

Association for Supervision and Curriculum Development (ASCD). (n.d.). *Common core standards adoption by state.* Retrieved from http://www.ascd.org/common-core-state-standards/common-core-state-standards-adoption-map.aspx

Bettinger, E. P., & Long, B. T. (2009). Addressing the needs of underprepared students in higher education: Does college remediation work? *Journal of Human Resources, 44*(3), 736–771.

Cohen, J. (2006). Social, emotional, ethical, and academic education: Creating a climate for learning, participation in democracy, and well-being. *Harvard Educational Review, 76*(2), 201–237.

Collaborative for Academic, Social and Emotional Learning (CASEL). (n.d.). *The CASEL Forum, Educating all children for social, emotional, and academic excellence: From knowledge to action.* Chicago: Author. Retrieved from https://casel.square space.com/s/the-casel-forum.pdf

Common Core State Standards Initiative (CCSSI). (2013). *Development process.* Retrieved from http://www.corestandards.org/about-the-standards/development-process/

Education First and Editorial Projects in Education, Inc. (2012). *Preparing for change: A national perspective on common core state standards implementation planning.* Retrieved from http://www.edweek.org/media/preparingforchange-17standards.pdf

Frey, A. J., Alvarez, M. E., Dupper, D. R., Sabatino, C. A., Lindsey, B. C., Raines, J. C., Streeck, F., . . . & Norris, M. A. (2013). *School social work practice model.* School Social Work Association of America. Retrieved from http://sswaa.org/display common.cfm?an=1&subarticlenbr=459

Home School Legal Defense Association (HSLDA). (2013). *Common core issues: How is the federal government involved in common core?* Retrieved from http://www.hslda.org/commoncore/topic3.aspx

Illinois State Board of Education (ISBE). (2012). *College and career readiness: Illinois common core standards.* Retrieved from http://www.isbe.net/common_ core/default.htm

Illinois State Board of Education (ISBE). (2013). *Illinois learning standards: Social/ emotional learning (SEL).* Retrieved from http://www.isbe.net/ils/social_emotional/ standards.htm

Jacobs, V. A. (2008). Adolescent literacy: Putting the crisis in context. *Harvard Educational Review, 78*(1), 7–39.

Kena, G., Aud, S., Johnson, F., Wang, X., Zhang, J., Rathbun, A., . . . & Kristapovich, P. (2014). *The condition of education 2014* (NCES 2014-083). U.S. Department of Education, National Center for Education Statistics, Washington, DC. Retrieved from http://nces.ed.gov/pubsearch/pubsinfo.asp?pubid=2014083

Lindsey, B. (2008). Looking at positive behavior interventions and supports through the lens of innovations diffusion. *Innovation Journal, 13*(2), article 7.

Manna, P., & Ryan, L. L. (2011). Competitive grants and educational federalism: Pres. Obama's race to the top in theory and practice. *Publius: The Journal of Federalism, 41*(3), 522–546. doi:10.1093/publius/pjr021

Mathis, W. J. (2010). *The "common core" standards initiative: An effective reform tool?* Boulder, CO and Tempe, AZ: Education and the Public Interest Center & Education Policy Research Unit, 1–29. Retrieved from http://epicpolicy.org/publication/common-core-standards

McShane, M. Q. (2013). *The controversial common core*. American Enterprise Institute for Public Policy Research. *Education Outlook, 8*(November), 1–6.

Morreale, S. P., Osborn, M. M., & Pearson, J. C. (2000). Why communication is important: A rationale for the centrality of the study of communication. *Journal of the Association for Communication Administration, 29*, 1–25.

National Assessment of Educational Progress. (2013). *The nation's report card.* Washington, DC: National Center for Education Statistics. Retrieved from http://nationsreportcard.gov/about.aspx

National Association of Social Workers (NASW). (2008). *Code of ethics*. Retrieved from https://www.socialworkers.org/pubs/code/code.asp

National Association of Social Workers (NASW). (2012). *NASW standards for school social work services.* Washington, DC: Author.

National Education Association (NEA). (2013). *NEA common core state standards toolkit.* NEA Education Policy and Practice Department. Retrieved from http://www.nea.org/home/ccss-toolkit.htm

National Parent Teacher Association (National PTA). (2014). *Parents' guide to student success.* Retrieved from http://www.pta.org/parents/content.cfm?ItemNumber=2583

No Child Left Behind Act of 2001, Pub. L. 107-110 (2002).

Partnership for Assessment of Readiness for College and Careers (PARCC). (2013). *PARCC states.* Retrieved from http://www.parcconline.org/parcc-states

Pfiffner, E. (2013, January 29). *Common core standards benefit at-risk children* (written blog comment). Retrieved from http://www.wholechildeducation.org/blog/common-core-standards-will-benefit-at-risk-students

Richards, E. (2014, May). Uncommon frustration: Parents puzzled by common core math. *Milwaukee Journal-Sentinel.*

Rubikam, M. (2014, May). *Parents rail against "ridiculous" common core math homework.* FoxNews.com. Retrieved from http://www.foxnews.com/us/2014/05/15/parents-rail-against-ridiculous-common-core-math-homework/

Sawchuk, S. (2012). Many teachers not ready for the common core. *Education Week, 31*(29), p. S12–17.

Shanahan, T., & Shanahan, C. (2008). Teaching disciplinary literacy to adolescents: Rethinking content-area literacy. *Harvard Educational Review, 78*(1), 40–59.

Smarter Balanced Assessment Consortium (SBAC). (2013). *Member states.* Retrieved from http://www.smarterbalanced.org/about/member-states/

Thompson, C. (2013). *The big story: What are the Common Core standards?* Associated Press. Retrieved from http://bigstory.ap.org/article/what-are-common-core-state-standards

U.S. Department of Defense Education Activity (DoDEA). (2012). *DoDEA schools to adopt Common Core state standards.* Retrieved from http://www.dodea.edu/newsroom/pressreleases/06052012.cfm

U.S. Department of Education (USDOE). (2004). *The No Child Left Behind Act of 2001 executive summary.* Washington DC: Author. Retrieved from http://www2.ed.gov/nclb/overview/intro/execsumm.html

U.S. Department of Education (USDOE). (2013a). *Race to the Top–District (RTT-D).* Retrieved from http://www2.ed.gov/programs/racetothetop-district/index.html

U.S. Department of Education (USDOE). (2013b). *U.S. Department of Education names five winners of $120 million from Race to the Top-District grant competition.* Retrieved from http://www.ed.gov/news/press-releases/us-department-education-names-five-winners-120-million-race-top-district-grant-c

Wootton, J. (2013, July 7). Idaho teachers prepare for switch to common core. *Twin Falls Times-News.* Retrieved from http://magicvalley.com/news/local/idaho-teachers-prepare-for-switch-to-common-core/article_410f4ea7-75ba-598a-8610-1ecef88dbd3b.html

11

A History of the Education of African American Children

Cassandra McKay-Jackson
Jane Addams College of Social Work, University of Illinois at Chicago

Carol Rippey Massat
Indiana University School of Social Work, South Bend

- ◆ Pre–Civil War Schooling of African American Children
- ◆ Post–Civil War
- ◆ Constitutional Amendments
- ◆ Racial Discrimination and Segregation
- ◆ Shift toward Market Solutions
- ◆ Implications for Social Work Practice

Horace Mann, a pioneer education reformist of the twentieth century believed in the common school education being the great equalizer for all U.S. citizens. (We have chosen to focus on the population of African American students because of the critical importance of the history of race and racist practices in American education and the impact of racism on both the privileged and the oppressed populations in our society.) Mann believed that every child should receive a basic education funded by local taxes. Education was considered critical for the perpetuation of an active citizenry, democratic participation, and overall societal well-being. However a group of citizens were not included in this equation for equality, people of color, namely African Americans.

The history of African American education involves a centuries-long struggle in the United States to achieve educational opportunity. Efforts to limit the education of some citizens continue to be a concern for marginalized and oppressed groups in our society. The civil rights movement is a historic record of the struggle between oppression of a population through limits on education and basic rights and freedoms. Social work strives to be part of liberatory work that supports and strengthens all persons in our society through education, voting rights, and actions to prohibit and prevent discrimination and oppression. We focus this chapter on the emblematic history that focuses on one of the oppressed populations for which the National Association of Social Workers (NASW) Code of Ethics (2008) calls on the social work profession to advocate. This history, which includes violent struggles such as the Civil War and nonviolent movements such as the movement led by Dr. Martin Luther King Jr., involves political work, advocacy, and the fight for social justice that is a central focus of social work as a profession.

Before delving further into the history of education for African Americans, it is important to clarify race "as a social construct which has no rational basis of existence except to organize society based on skin pigment" (McKnight & Chandler 2009, p. 78) and later privilege. Plainly speaking, racial divide is promulgated within the United States via the privileging of white people over all others. In fact, whiteness as a category ceases to exist outside the boundaries of what it means to be a person of color; it is predicated on the existence of otherness (Fine, 1997). Yet the only ways that social reproduction of white privilege can be maintained is that (1) the privileged fail to examine what it means to be privileged, why they are privileged, and its impact on those who are not (Feagin & O'Brien, 2003); and (2) that the oppressed believe that "their station in life and its requisite benefits (or lack thereof) are the normal order of things" (McKnight & Chandler, 2009, p. 90). Truly effective school social work practice hinges on the active interrogation of such an insidious cultural exchange (on micro, mezzo, and macro levels) and the knowledge that the social construction of race, although pervasive, is still arbitrary, at best, for one-sided gain. It is with this understanding that the reader should examine the content of this chapter.

Finally, by reviewing this history, we observe historic opportunities and continuing struggles that affect one of the most historically oppressed populations served by school social workers: African American children. We learn the meaning of true policy change that can affect society as a whole and can open opportunities one child at a time. We observe the political and organizational skills discussed in other chapters, and see how they can be applied both for good and for ill.

At times in U.S. history education of African Americans has been outlawed, and at other times schools have been a means of social control through education for assimilation. Education for assimilation refers to efforts to use education as a tool to encourage members of diverse groups to adopt the characteristics and norms of a dominant group while relinquishing their own traditions and cultures. Education, as the traditional key to opportunity, continues to be a valued right for all citizens, and yet equal education has yet to be achieved for many members of minority groups. This fact is rooted in the history of African American schooling. For example, the state of Mississippi waited to ratify the Constitutional amendment prohibiting slavery until 2013, and the state of Kentucky did not ratify this amendment until 1976. History lives today, and the shadow of bigotry and racism continues to fall on American schools across the nation.

PRE–CIVIL WAR SCHOOLING OF AFRICAN AMERICAN CHILDREN

Pre–Civil War schooling of African Americans involved an extended struggle that is detailed in Carter Woodson's book *The Education of the Negro Prior to 1861* (1919).

In the beginning of American education of African American slaves, Protestants and Quakers followed the example of Catholics in providing education. From the inception of slavery until 1835, religious groups were the primary educators of African Americans. Initially, both Protestant and Catholic Christians who were proponents of slavery believed that by teaching Christianity to slaves they would be conferring a benefit to them that justified the institution of slavery (Woodson, 1919). The Anglican Church of London established a school in South Carolina in 1695, led by Rev. Thomas Goose. Elias Neau opened a second school in 1704 in New York. In the early 1700s, education of African Americans was established in Virginia, and later in North Carolina, also under Christian auspices.

Around 1700 the institution of slavery began to be attacked by a number of different Christian groups. No longer seeing slavery as a beneficial path to salvation, Christians of various denominations began to voice the opinion that slavery was in direct opposition to their faith. The abolitionist movement also advocated for education of African Americans, as right for both individuals and society (Woodson, 1919).

Yet, literacy laws were enacted prohibiting slaves to learn to read due to fear of insurrection. South Carolina prohibited the teaching of slaves in 1740 and in 1800 prohibited the education of all African Americans. Virginia and Georgia also made education of Negroes illegal, and North Carolina, Delaware, and Maryland passed laws requiring strict inspection and regulation of places where African Americans might gather, such as schools (Woodson, 1919). Nevertheless, slaves did participate in numerous rebellious acts and insurrections during this time. (See James [1969] for more information.) Only with the end of the Civil War were African Americans officially declared free to learn to read. Major events aided in this declaration: the establishment of the Freedmen's Bureau, and the passing of the Thirteenth, Fourteenth, and Fifteenth Amendments.

POST–CIVIL WAR

The Freedmen's Bureau was initially established to aid refugees of the Civil War, but was primarily known for its aid to newly freed slaves. One of the most widely recognized achievements of the Freedmen's Bureau was its establishment of public schools for newly freed slaves. The Freedmen's Bureau was abolished in 1872. At the end of 1870, 150,000 African American children were attending school. In addition, at the culmination of five years of educational effort, nearly $6 million were expended to establish schools of higher learning. Many of these institutions such as Fisk, Atlanta, Howard, and Hampton Universities remain in operation today (DuBois, 1901).

An important educator involved in this initiative was Brig. Gen. Samuel Chapman Armstrong. An agent of the Bureau, Armstrong later founded Hampton Normal and Agricultural Institute in 1868, and led that school until his death in 1893. Armstrong provided the educational architecture to acculturate and assimilate the newly freed slaves. His promotion of education for assimilation sought to "train and civilize" freed slaves in order to maintain a stratified social order, but it was shrouded in a cloak of humanitarianism. Girded by a moral conviction to save the "inferior Negro" from himself, the Hampton Institute sought to provide the African American a means of survival in a changed world. Hampton prepared African American teachers steeped in the Hampton Institute philosophy. These teachers furthered the promotion of Armstrong's educational ideology. Booker T. Washington was a firm believer in and advocate for the Hampton experiment. His influence would have deep and sustained implications for education for assimilation of African Americans (Watkins, 2001).

The racially tense climate that surrounded the establishment of Tuskegee Normal and Industrial Institute in 1881 convinced Booker T. Washington that education must dignify common labor for the African American. Washington believed that African Americans could achieve economic self-sufficiency through mass industrial education and vocational training, which he considered the best tactic in negotiating survival (Ogbu, 2004).

Washington, however, did not challenge the historical inequalities of wealth and power, and avoided confrontation between the races. His avoidance was criticized as legitimizing the status quo, providing respectability to the repressive tenets of education for assimilation, and creating a subjugated workforce disconnected from real political power (Potts, 2002). Furthermore, Washington's rhetoric of subservience to the old slave master brought more criticism. Washington (1900/1972) posited, "The wisest among my race understand that the agitation of questions of social equality is the extremest [sic] folly, and that progress in the enjoyment of all the privileges that will come to us must be the result of severe and constant struggle rather than of artificial forcing" (p. 76). This philosophy diminished progress toward a politically vital African American citizenry, and was critiqued by W. E. B. DuBois (1903/1994): "Mr. Washington's programme practically accepts the alleged inferiority of the Negro races" (p. 30), and, later, by Carter G. Woodson (1933/1998): "In our so-called democracy we are accustomed to give the majority what they want rather than educate them to understand what is best for them. We do not show the Negro how to overcome segregation; but we teach him how to accept it as final and just" (p. 101).

CONSTITUTIONAL AMENDMENTS

Three key amendments to the Constitution were passed soon after the Civil War. The Thirteenth Amendment ended slavery. The Fourteenth Amendment made black people citizens of the United States and prohibited state laws limiting their rights. The Fifteenth Amendment prohibited racial discrimination in voting. The Thirteenth Amendment was declared ratified on December 18, 1865. Delaware did not ratify the amendment until 1901, and Kentucky did not ratify it until 1976. The amendment was ratified by Mississippi in 1995, yet it was not sent to the Office of the Federal Register until February 7, 2013. As a result, the amendment was not officially approved until 148 years after slavery was abolished (Edelman, 2013).

The Fourteenth Amendment to the Constitution provides equal protection to all male citizens of the United States and prohibits states from passing laws that would restrict life, liberty, property, or the right to vote of U.S. citizens. This amendment was declared ratified July 28, 1868. Delaware did not ratify the amendment until 1901, Maryland waited until 1959, and Kentucky did not ratify the amendment until 1976, more than one hundred years after it was proposed (Martin Luther King Jr. National Historic Site Interpretive Staff, 1997).

The Fifteenth Amendment to the Constitution of the United States stated that the "right of citizens of the United States to vote shall not be denied or abridged by the United States or by any state on account of race, color, or previous condition of servitude." It was ratified on February 3, 1870, but Southern states circumvented the law to prevent African Americans from voting by the use of poll taxes, literacy tests, and other restrictions. The Voting Rights Act of 1965 finally led to the majority of African Americans in the South registering to vote. Temporary provisions within the Act are still subject to debate for reauthorization by members of Congress. In 2006, after extensive hearings, Congress reauthorized the Voting Rights Act for another twenty-five years (Leadership Conference, n.d.). However, in 2013 the Supreme Court ruled that a critical section of the Act, Section 4, was unconstitutional. Section 4 determined which states must receive clearance from the U.S. Justice Department or a federal court in Washington, DC, before any changes could be made to voting procedures such as moving a polling place or redrawing electoral districts. The Supreme Court's 5 to 4 ruling determined that the current political climate no longer requires such strict preclearance procedures (*Shelby County v. Holder,* 2013). The implications of this recent ruling may prove detrimental for historically marginalized voters in highly contested states (Liptak, 2013). The Supreme Court decision was predicated by an apparent belief that racial discrimination with regard to voting was a thing of the past. The original Voting Rights Act specified that certain regions demonstrated more racial discrimination in voting than others. This was determined by a formula in Section 4 of the Voting Rights Act. The first part of the formula was the presence of a practice that would tend to restrict voting rights of citizens, such as a literacy test, a poll tax, or character reference. The second part of the formula was whether 50 percent or fewer of eligible citizens in a region were actually registered to vote. If fewer than 50 percent were registered, this caused the federal government to consider a region as in need of additional scrutiny in regards to race discrimination in voting. Originally, the following states were deemed of need for this additional review: Alabama, Alaska, Georgia, Louisiana, Mississippi, South Carolina, and Virginia (U.S. Department of Justice, 2014). In addition, counties in Arizona, Hawaii, Idaho, and North Carolina were included. In 1970 counties in the following states were added: Alaska, Arizona, California, Connecticut, Idaho, Maine, Massachusetts, New Hampshire, New York, and Wyoming. Over time, the need for careful scrutiny of voting rights continued to be needed.

The Supreme Court, in its decision to strike down Section 4 of the Voting Rights Act, effectively eliminated Section 5 enforcement. This situation opens the door to a resurgence of restrictions on voting by minorities, the poor, and other disenfranchised populations. The potential limitation of the right to vote to the privileged few affects schools, school social workers, and children. Public schooling depends on taxes for funding. Those taxes are often determined by public referenda. School board policies are developed by elected members of the school board. Federal, state, and local laws that affect schools are determined by elected representatives and interpreted by (often) elected judges. Thus, policies that affect the right to vote of any sector of our population is of critical importance to schools and to school social work.

RACIAL DISCRIMINATION AND SEGREGATION

Racial discrimination was a part of federal law and case law before the Civil War. Before the Civil War, black men were not allowed to join militias, the U.S. Army, or the Navy. The federal government would not provide passports to free black persons.

After the Civil War, de jure segregation—that is segregation that is a matter of formal policy or law—spread across the United States. Black codes or Jim Crow laws were passed that limited the rights of African Americans, treating them as second-class citizens (PBS, 2002). In many states, such as Alabama, California, Indiana, Mississippi, and North Carolina, separate and unequal accommodations were maintained. Integration of educational facilities, lunch counters and restaurants, buses, trains, hotels, and prisons was prohibited, and interracial marriages were outlawed. Those who defied the laws were subject to fines, arrest, and violent retaliation (Constitutional Rights Foundation, 2015).

In the Southern states, sharecropping became a means to continue economic exploitation of African Americans. Plantation owners lost their labor force with the emancipation of slaves. In order to recoup their losses, they rented plots of land primarily to African Americans to plant and harvest crops. The African Americans had to purchase all their supplies to till the land, mostly on credit from the landowner at exorbitant prices. At harvest time the landowner decided what percentage of the crop's profit settled the debt. The sharecropper rarely saw a profit after paying rent and was usually more indebted to the landowner than he had been the previous year (Ochiltree, 2004).

Congress rebelled against the South in the Reconstruction period, when the Republican Party took control of Southern state governments. During this period, black people were first elected to public office in the South and much discriminatory state legislation was repealed. The Civil Rights Act of 1866, designed to grant citizenship to all male persons in the United States, despite a prior state of servitude, was passed, and the Civil Rights Act of 1875, designed to prohibit segregation in public places, was passed.

The Democrats had taken control of the South by 1877 and the gains made during Reconstruction were lost. Systematic efforts to stop African Americans from voting became routine, and a segregated society was created, including separate schools and separate public facilities. The Supreme Court in the *Civil Rights Cases* (1883) decided that African Americans had no right to be "special favorites" as citizens. As the Supreme Court withdrew, this allowed more and more discriminatory legislation to be passed. In the Supreme Court case of *Plessy v. Ferguson* (1896), the famous decision was made that "separate but equal" facilities were acceptable. The Supreme Court decision in *Williams v. Mississippi* in 1898 allowed a plan in Mississippi that would disenfranchise almost all black people in the state and keep black persons from serving on juries. De jure segregation grew, with Kentucky prohibiting the use by a white child of any textbook ever used by a black child, and Alabama prohibiting integrated checkers games. Segregation was supported both by the law and by terrorist organizations such as the Ku Klux Klan and the Knights of the White Camellia. These groups killed both blacks and whites who favored reform.

U.S. historical accounts testify that the Thirteenth, Fourteenth, and Fifteenth Amendments did not succeed in ending racial discrimination and segregation. Segregation is a problem that has affected both African American and other ethnic minorities, particularly Hispanic children. However, much of the existing case law has been established around issues of racial segregation of white and African American students.

For African Americans, schools began as segregated education. Woodson (1919) reports that this emerged both from views of white people attempting to organize such schools and from African Americans themselves. New York in 1864 included a provision in the state code that communities could offer separate schools for white children and "children of African descent" (Woodson, 1919, p. 121) as long as they were funded in the same manner. The case of *Roberts v. City of Boston* (1850), the first challenge to segregated schooling, took place in Massachusetts. Roberts lost the challenge, but the state of Massachusetts prohibited racial segregation of schools in 1855. However, the solidification of racial segregation of schools was not formally ended in federal policy until the Supreme Court decision *Brown v. Board of Education of Topeka* in 1954. This landmark case marked the change in federal policy from acceptance of a "separate but equal" doctrine to one that acknowledged that to be separate is to be inherently unequal.

Because of the great variability of local schools and conditions, the Supreme Court ordered that schools would desegregate "with all deliberate speed" (*Brown v. Board of Education II,* 1955, n.p.). Local schools were to develop desegregation plans under the supervision of local courts. This meant that states and communities had considerable latitude in the pace and timing of desegregation.

Local schools tried to delay or defeat the *Brown* decision through so-called freedom of choice plans and even the closing of public schools. Freedom of choice plans allowed parents to select the school their children would attend and did not explicitly require segregation (Fischer & Sorenson, 1996). Freedom of choice plans were not totally rejected by the Supreme Court, but in *Green v. County School Board of New Kent County* (1968), the Court stated that freedom of choice plans were unacceptable if other reasonable means are available to desegregate. Closing of public schools was tried in Virginia, which repealed compulsory attendance laws so that school attendance became controlled by local decisions. Prince Edward County closed the public schools and instituted private, whites-only schools that received governmental assistance. This effort to sustain de jure segregation of schools was struck down as unconstitutional by the Supreme Court in the 1964 *Griffin v. County School Board of Prince Edward County* (LaMorte, 2005).

Segregation in the South was the initial target of desegregation efforts. The video *Eyes on the Prize* (Public Broadcasting Service [PBS], 1987, Fighting Back [1957–62]) vividly chronicles the struggle to desegregate Southern schools. A notorious example is that of Little Rock, Arkansas, that the local school system attempted to desegregate. The governor of the state of

Arkansas defied that attempt, however, and ordered the National Guard to prevent black students from entering their assigned schools (LaMorte, 2005). The schools then sought to delay desegregation with the argument that the delay was necessary to preserve public peace. However, in the decision *Cooper v. Aaron*, 358 U.S. 1 (1958) the Supreme Court declared that desegregation could not be postponed.

In Mississippi, once called the "the closed society," the Council of Federated Organizations—a consortium of civil rights organizations including the Congress of Racial Equality, the Southern Christian Leadership Council, the National Association for the Advancement of Colored People, and the Student Non-Violent Coordinating Committee—spearheaded the 1964 Freedom Summer Project. This project was a social action endeavor established to challenge the unjust and unequal treatment of African American citizens in Mississippi. The Freedom Summer Project brought national attention to the violation of human rights, particularly the voting rights of African American citizens in Mississippi where African Americans were unfairly subjected to literacy laws that prohibited them from voting. If an individual could not read to the satisfaction of a registrar, he or she was denied the opportunity of voter registration. Although Mississippi was the last state of the union to enact compulsory education in 1918, education was still used as a means to perpetuate the myth of African American inferiority. In 1962 Mississippi paid $81.86 to educate each white student and $21.77 to educate each black student, and in many individual districts the discrepancies were much worse. In Yazoo County, with a 59.4 percent black population, white schools received $245.55 per student and black schools received $2.92 per student (Rothschild, 1982).

In order to address the inferior schools for African American children, Freedom Schools were established during the 1964 summer project. The Freedom Schools were set in motion by a letter from Charlie Cobb, a Howard University student, to Bob Moses, director of the Freedom Summer Project: "If we are concerned about breaking the power structure, then we have to be concerned about building our own institutions to replace the old, unjust, decadent ones which make up the existing power structure. Education in Mississippi is an institution, which must be reconstructed from the ground up" (as cited in Chilcoat & Ligon, 2004, p. 4). Volunteer Freedom School teachers, many of whom were white college students from the North, were expected to encourage

- honest and egalitarian relationships between themselves and students,
- the asking of open-ended questions,
- an authentic and empowering view of students and their history,
- skills applicable for action and effective participation in the world, and
- a direct line from classroom to community (Emery, Braselmann, & Reid Gold, 2004).

The Freedom Schools offered tools to African Americans to challenge discrimination. The Freedom School approach was based on three prevailing tenets: (1) problem-based education leading toward life application, (2) teaching for social justice, and (3) affirmation of African American identity (Aaronsohn et al., 1991; Chilcoat & Ligon, 1999; Perlstein, 1990; Rothschild, 1982). African American students were equipped with affirmed identities, tools of critical literacy, and skills to advocate for themselves and others. By the end of the summer of 1964, forty-one Freedom Schools had been established across the state of Mississippi.

On a national scale, fourteen years after the *Brown* decision, American citizens could no longer tolerate separate and unequal education for children of color. In *Alexander v. Holmes County Board of Education* 19 (1969) the Supreme Court decided that no additional delay was permissible and that all school districts were to end dual school systems immediately and to operate as unitary school districts.

In 1971 the Supreme Court made a definitive and detailed desegregation decision. In *Swann v. Charlotte-Mecklenburg Board of Education* (1971) the Supreme Court ordered (1) that teachers be assigned so as to achieve faculty desegregation, (2) that future school construction or school closings would not support a dual system of education, (3) that single-race schools were to be examined to make sure that present or past discrimination had not caused the lack of diversity, (4) that attendance zones be changed to undo segregation, (5) and that children be bused, if needed, to dismantle dual systems of education (LaMorte, 2005).

De jure segregation, which is segregation mandated by law, differs from de facto segregation. De facto segregation occurs when people choose to live in different neighborhoods and then send their children to neighborhood schools (Fischer & Sorenson, 1996). Only de jure segregation is illegal.

The Equal Educational Opportunities Act of 1974 solidified the federal commitment to equal educational opportunity and spelled out steps to be taken when court-ordered desegregation must occur due to a finding of denial of equal educational opportunity.

Busing as a Desegregation Tool. Busing of children from one part of a district to another to achieve racial integration has been a controversial tool. Given the long history of local control of schools and commitment to neighborhood schools, busing raised conflicting issues. In the *Swann v. Charlotte Mecklenburg Board of Education* (1971) case, the court ruled that busing was acceptable, since, in that case, assigning children to neighborhood schools would not result in dismantling the dual system of education. In a related case, *North Carolina Board of Education v. Swann* (1971) the Supreme Court affirmed an order that declared a North Carolina law unconstitutional. This law prohibited both racial assignment of students and busing based on racial assignment. This ruling was based on the Court's view that racial assignment was an essential tool of desegregation.

Desegregation in the North. Racial segregation was also occurring in the North, and illegal segregation has been found in many Northern cities. For example, statutes requiring separate-but-equal schools were present in New York until 1938, in Indiana until 1959, and in Wyoming until 1954 (LaMorte, 2005). Fischer and Sorenson (1996) write, "A key difference existed between southern and northern segregated schooling. Whereas it was done blatantly and through open official action in the South, it was usually accomplished in the North through complex and not-so-open arrangements between public officials and leaders in business and industry to control housing, real estate development, and finance as well as through the location of business, industry, and schools. Courts, however, ruled that such actions violate the fourteenth Amendment just as the more open official actions of the South had done" (p. 279). Because the Fourteenth Amendment prohibited only de jure segregation, it has been difficult to address segregation in the non-South, which often occurred through what appeared to be de facto segregation, or segregation based on housing patterns and local customs.

Interdistrict Integration. As "white flight" from urban schools continued, the problem of desegregation became one that crossed school district boundaries. In many instances urban school districts have become almost all black/Hispanic. In a challenge to this situation, a federal district court ordered that fifty-three independent school districts surrounding Detroit be consolidated with the Detroit public schools. Parents who had moved to the suburbs to attain greater educational opportunities for their children opposed this decision. The Supreme Court decided in *Milliken v. Bradley* (1974) that the only evidence of de jure segregation occurred in the Detroit public schools and that the fifty-three other districts had no violations. Therefore, they failed to uphold the district court's order. LaMorte (2005) states, "Many observers consider Milliken I as marking an end to the United States Supreme Court's unwavering support of desegregation efforts. Subsequent to this decision, the Court has been viewed decreasingly as a friendly and receptive forum for achieving school desegregation" (p. 307).

In another decision in 1996 (*Sheff v. O'Neill*, 1996) the Connecticut Supreme Court ruled that the state's school districting and attendance statutes were unconstitutional, since they produced segregation of minority students in Hartford schools and thus limited equal educational opportunity. In this case, the court determined that the state legislature was required to remedy segregation in public schools in Connecticut whether the segregation occurred due to de jure or to de facto segregation. Since then, another Connecticut decision, *Sheff v. O'Neill* (1999), laid out details of remedies to correct the educational inequity caused by racial segregation of minority students in the city of Hartford and white flight to suburban non-minority school districts (LaMorte, 2005). Such decisions by a state court may provide a model for addressing the seemingly intractable problem of segregation as it exists today.

On June 28, 2007, the Supreme Court made a significant step backward in its decision regarding plans by Seattle and Louisville to desegregate their schools (*Parents Involved in Community Schools v. Seattle School District* [2007] and *Meredith v. Jefferson County Board of Education* [2007]). The *New York Times* wrote,

> The nation is getting more diverse, but by many measures public schools are becoming more segregated. More than one in six Black children now attend schools that are 99 to 100 percent minority. This resegregation is likely to get appreciably worse as a result of the court's ruling.
>
> There should be no mistaking just how radical this decision is. In dissent, Justice John Paul Stevens said it was his "firm conviction that no Member of the Court that I joined in 1975 would have agreed with today's decision." He also noted the "cruel irony" of the court relying on *Brown v. Board of Education* while robbing that landmark ruling of much of its force and spirit. The citizens of Louisville and Seattle, and the rest of the nation, can ponder the majority's kind words about Brown as they get to work today making their schools, and their cities, more segregated. (*New York Times,* 2007, Editorial)

Eloquently stated more than a century ago, the color line continues to be the problem of the century (DuBois, 1903/1994) and education is still "the civil rights issue of our time." The United States cannot deny the systemic and ingrained nature of racism within its borders. Although the United States has "expressed guilt over racial injustice, the structural status quo and underlying roots, which founded a racist nation, have never been cut or radically revised" (McKnight & Chandler, 2009, p. 79), but merely replanted.

SHIFT TOWARD MARKET SOLUTIONS

Nationally, education policy has been affected by a shift in focus away from urban schools and desegregation and toward market solutions, such as school choice and charter schools. Mora and Christianakis (2011) describe this as a movement toward the privatization of education, with tax dollars being moved out of the public sector and into the market.

School vouchers and charter schools are supported by neoliberals and conservatives who believe that public education has failed and that a market-driven approach to education would be more successful in educating children. The business sector also perceives a new market, an opportunity for profit, through funneling tax dollars into the private sector. This movement strongly affects access to education for the most vulnerable and historically oppressed populations because public schools are required by law to serve all students. Movements to destroy or limit public education inherently limit access to education for these groups.

IMPLICATIONS FOR SOCIAL WORK PRACTICE

Recognizing that schooling represents a "racially situated and determined institution" (McKnight & Chandler, 2009, p. 94) that perpetuates white privilege, school social workers must adhere to the NASW Code of Ethics (2008) that calls for a commitment to social justice, because this history of injustice remains in practice today. The moves toward resegregation and the pressure to substitute market solutions that avoid protections afforded by national, state, and local policy for vulnerable students call for the use of the policy practice skills described in chapter 20, the organizational analysis skills described in chapter 21, and the understanding of research and evidence-informed practice, discussed throughout this book.

For individual school social workers and for school social work as a field of practice, this U.S. history calls for analysis of one's self and one's own settings, considering both the school and the community. Racism is embedded in the history of our nation and our schools, and this problem has not disappeared. The shooting of Michael Brown in Ferguson, Missouri, in the summer of 2014 illuminates the tragic persistence and violent threats that continue to be posed by our national history and by the nation's internalized and institutionalized racism.

Such a deeply embedded social problem cannot be solved or resolved by social workers alone, and actions of individuals to change ourselves and society must be based on an understanding of both oppression and privilege. Oppression involves the limitation of rights, reduction of power, silencing, and intentional discrimination against members of groups in society. African Americans have been a historically oppressed group throughout the history of our nation. The term "privilege" refers to the unearned benefits obtained through membership in a group or class that has higher status, greater resources, and greater power in society. Most individuals in American society are unaware of their own privilege, and individuals often prefer to believe that all they have is a result of their own hard work and individual merit. However meritorious individuals may be, their fates also depend on the good fortune and privilege they have experienced as a consequence of birth, geography, education, wealth, or other factors.

First, school social workers should make conscious and intentional efforts to consider all the sources of privilege that we have as individuals in various groups. For example, school social workers have privilege in our society based on the possession of a master's degree in social work. While attainment of such a degree is not easy, access to higher education is more available to persons with financial resources who have had the privilege of attending strong schools. Second, school social workers should consider the oppressive influences affecting their schools, students, and communities, considering race, ethnicity, gender, sexual orientation, income, social status, disability/ability, language, and other factors that are associated with privilege or oppression. With an awareness of privilege and oppression, school social workers can intentionally work to carry out antioppressive practice in schools, to promote social justice in schools and communities, and to work to address overt and covert discrimination wherever it occurs.

Effective practices do exist that work to reduce prejudice (Aboud & Fenwick, 1999), empower minority students and faculty (Upadyay, 2005), and strengthen academic achievement of members of oppressed groups (Haycock & Chenoweth, 2005). Chapter 20 in this volume describes antioppressive school practices. As school social workers, it is our responsibility to recognize and understand oppression and privilege, and to promote effective antioppressive practices.

CONCLUSION

On the surface, the nature of race relations within the U.S. educational system has evolved, yet the very core of racial relations remains unchanged. As we begin to examine the current status of law and policy relating to minority children in the next chapter, we must understand the historical context of schooling for African American children in this country. The struggle for education has been part of the historic struggle in the United States of African American citizens to gain the rights and privileges that all of our citizens need and deserve. School social workers therefore must challenge racist practices first within their own privileged or nonprivileged selves, and then within practices that are pervasive within the educational system. Only by understanding this historic struggle can we understand the issues of today, and can we make every effort to solve those issues for the generation of students to come.

References

Aaronsohn, L, Cobb, C., Lynd, S., Garrett, J., Lauter, P., O'Connell, B., . . . & Perlstein, D. (Contributors). (1991). Mississippi Freedom School curriculum 1964. *Radical Teacher, 40*, 19–22.

Aboud, F. E., & Fenwick, V. (1999). Exploring and evaluating school-based interventions to reduce prejudice. *Journal of Social Issues, 55*(4), 767–785.

Alexander v. Holmes County Board of Education 396 U.S. 19 (1969).

Brown v. Board of Education of Topeka, 347 U.S. 483 (1954).

Brown v. Board of Education II (1955). http://www.nationalcenter.org/cc0725.htm

Chilcoat, G., & Ligon, J. (1999). Helping to make democracy a living reality: The curriculum conference of the Mississippi Freedom Schools. *Journal of Curriculum and Supervision. 15*, 43–68

Chilcoat, G., & Ligon, J. (2004). Developing participatory democracy (and other wonderful "things"): Those "Bothersome" Educational Organizations (?) and their "Great Potential Curriculumers" at the New York Curriculum Conference for the Mississippi Freedom Schools. *Proceedings of the Freedom Summer conference*. Miami University, Oxford, OH, September 17–19.

Civil Rights Act of 1866, 14 Stat. 27 (1866).

Civil Rights Act of 1875, 18 Stat. 335 (1875).

Civil Rights Cases, 109 U.S. 3 (1883), (1).

Constitutional Rights Foundation. (2015). *A brief history of Jim Crow.* http://www.crf-usa.org/black-history-month/a-brief-history-of-jim-crow

Cooper v. Aaron, 358 U.S. 1 (1958).

DuBois, W. E. B. (1901). The Freedmen's Bureau. *Atlantic Monthly, 87,* 354–365.

DuBois, W. E. B. (1994). *The souls of black folk.* New York: Dover. (Original work published 1903)

Edelman, A. (2013). *After oversight, Mississippi ratifies 13th Amendment abolishing slavery almost 150 years after its adoption.* Retrieved from http://www.nydaily news.com/news/national/mississippi-finally-ratifies-slavery-ban-article-1.1267133#ixzz32sgiet7O

Emery, K., Braselmann, S., & Reid Gold, L. (2004). *Introduction: Freedom Summer and the Freedom Schools.* Retrieved from http://www.educationanddemocracy.org/FSCfiles/A_02_Introduction.htm

Equal Educational Opportunities Act of 1974, 20 U.S.C. § 1703 et seq. (1974).

Feagin, J., & O'Brien, E. (2003). *White Men on Race: Power, privilege, and the shaping of cultural consciousness.* Boston: Beacon Press.

Fine, M. (1997). Witnessing whiteness. In M. Fine, L. Powell, L.Weis, & M. Wong (Eds.), *Offwhite: Readings in race, power, and society* (pp. 57–65). New York: Routledge.

Fischer, L., & Sorenson, G. P. (1996). *School law for counselors, psychologists, and social workers* (3rd ed.). White Plains, NY: Longman.

Green v. County School Board of New Kent County, 391 U.S. 430 (1968).

Griffin v. County School Board of Prince Edward County, 377 U.S. 218 (1964).

Haycock, K., & Chenoweth, K. (2005). Choosing to make a difference. *American School Board Journal, 192*(4), 28–31.

James, C. L. R. (1969). *A history of the Negro revolt.* New York: Haskell House.

LaMorte, M. W. (2005). *School law: Cases and concepts.* Boston: Allyn & Bacon.

Leadership Conference. (n.d.). Voting Rights Act. http://www.civilrights.org/voting-rights/vra/?referrer=https://www.google.com/

Liptak, A. (2013). *Supreme Court invalidates key part of Voting Rights Act.* Retrieved from http://www.nytimes.com/2013/06/26/us/supreme-court-ruling.html

Martin Luther King Jr. National Historic Site Interpretive Staff (1997). *14th Amendment to the U.S. Constitution.* Retrieved from http://www.nps.gov/malu/documents/amend14.htm

McKnight, D., & Chandler, P. (2009). The complicated conversation of class and race in social and curricular analysis: An examination of Pierre Bourdieu's interpretative framework in relation to race. *Educational Philosophy and Theory, 44,* 74–97.

Meredith v. Jefferson County Board of Education, 551 US _Docket #05-915 (2007).

Milliken v. Bradley, 418 U.S. 717 (1974).

Mora, R., & Christianakis, M. (2011). Charter schools, market capitalism, and Obama's neoliberal agenda. *Journal of Inquiry and Action in Education, 4*(1), 93–111.

National Association of Social Workers (NASW). (2008). *Code of ethics.* Retrieved from https://www.socialworkers.org/pubs/code/code.asp

New York Times (2007, June 29). *Resegregation now.* [Editorial]. Retrieved from http://www.nytimes.com/2007/06/29/opinion/29fri1.html

North Carolina Board of Education v. Swann (1971). 402 U.S. 43.

Ochiltree, I. (2004). Mastering the sharecroppers: Land, labor and the search for independence in the U.S. South and South Africa. *Journal of South African Studies, 30*(1), 41–61.

Ogbu, J. (2004). Collective identity and the burden of "acting white" in black history, community and education. *The State Review, 35.*

Parents Involved in Community Schools v. Seattle School District, No. 1 551 U.S. 701 (2007). https://supreme.justia.com/cases/federal/us/551/701/

Perlstein, D. (1990). Teaching freedom: SNCC and the creation of the Mississippi freedom schools. *History of Education Quarterly, 30,* 297–324.

Plessy v. Ferguson 163 U.S. 537 (1896).

Potts, E. (2002).The DuBois–Washington debate: Conflicting strategies. In E. Peterson (Ed.), *Freedom road: Adult education for African Americans* (pp. 27–40). Malabar, FL: Krieger.

Public Broadcasting Service (PBS). (1987). *Eyes on the prize: America's Civil Rights Years 1954–1965.* DVD or VHS.

Public Broadcasting Service (PBS). (2002). *The rise and fall of Jim Crow.* Retrieved from http://www.pbs.org/wnet/jimcrow/

Roberts v. City of Boston 59 Mass. (5 Cush.) (1850).

Rothschild, M. A. (1982). The volunteers and the freedom schools: Education for social change in Mississippi. *History of Education Quarterly, 22,* 401–420.

Sheff v. O'Neill, 238 Conn. 1, 678 A.2d 1267 (1996).

Sheff v. O'Neill, 45 Conn. Sup. 630, 657 (1999).

Shelby County, Alabama v. Holder, 133 S.Ct. 2612, No. 12-96 (2013).

Swann v. Charlotte-Mecklenburg Board of Education, 402 U.S. 1 (1971).

U.S. Department of Justice. (2014). *Section 4 of the Voting Rights Act.* http://www.justice .gov/crt/about/vot/misc/sec_4.php

Upadyay, B. R. (2005). Practicing reform-based science curriculum in an urban classroom: A Hispanic elementary school teacher's thinking and decisions. *School Science and Mathematics, 105*(7), 343–352.

Voting Rights Act of 1965, Pub. L. 89-110, 79 Stat. 437 (1965).

Washington, B. T. (1972). The story of my life and work. In L. Harlan & J. Blassingame (Eds.), *The Booker T. Washington Papers,* Vol. 1, *The autobiographical writings* (pp. 1–206). Urbana: University of Illinois Press. (Original work published 1900)

Watkins, W. (2001). *The white architects of black education: Ideology and power in America 1865–1954.* New York: Teachers College.

Williams v. Mississippi, 170 U.S. 213 (1898).

Woodson, C. G. (1919). *The education of the Negro prior to 1861: A history of the education of colored people of the United States from the beginning of slavery until the Civil War.* Retrieved from http://andromeda.rutgers.edu/~natalieb/The_Education_Of_The_Negro_P.pdf

Woodson, C. G. (1998). *Miseducation of the Negro.* Trenton, NJ: Africa World Press. (Original work published 1933)

12

Policy and Law Affecting School Social Work with Vulnerable Populations

Cassandra McKay-Jackson

Jane Addams College of Social Work, University of Illinois at Chicago

Carol Rippey Massat

Indiana University School of Social Work, South Bend

◆ Current Policy Issues Affecting Racial and Ethnic Minority Children
◆ Native American Children and Educational Policy
◆ Gender and Educational Policy
◆ Lesbian, Gay, Bisexual, Transgender, and Questioning Students and Faculty
◆ Homeless Children and Schools
◆ Bilingual Education

In order to carry out effective policy practice, school social workers in every country must understand the history and policies that affect vulnerable groups in schools. In the United States this would include African American and other ethnic minority students; bilingual students; students with limited English proficiency (LEP); girls and women; lesbian, gay, bisexual, transgender, and questioning (LGBTQ) students; and homeless children. All of these groups have experienced discrimination in schools and in society. This history of discrimination has led to legislation and case law intended to protect members of such groups from additional oppression.

Core values and ethics create an ethical imperative of social justice for all social workers (National Association of Social Workers [NASW], 2008). School social work is becoming evidence informed. School social work has also long been grounded in core values and ethics that require all social workers to advocate for oppressed populations. Such advocacy requires that those with privilege remove the blinders created by their own privilege in order to see and understand the experience of the oppressed. Often students have learned only a Euro-white version of history, and they have not been exposed to the history of Native Americans, African Americans, or other people of color.

Good schools are crucial for the survival of any vulnerable group. The educational process itself has at times served as an oppressive force for members of vulnerable groups, and some theorists posit that schooling remains a pervasive and effective form of social control. For example, textbooks have often presented only European American male history, and have excluded the writings and histories of ethnic and racial minorities and women (Apple, 1998). Some educational curricula have implicitly focused on the development of a low-income work force that is likely to produce exploitive work conditions (Kliebard, 1998). Consumer-driven classroom media can also target the unsuspecting consumer (Kenway & Bullen, 2005). Education for assimilation, as discussed in chapter 11, is the use of schooling to teach members of oppressed groups to take on the characteristics of a dominant group, while abandoning their own cultures. Ferdman (1990) asserts an "assimilation perspective emphasizes the dysfunctionality of differences and the maintenance of the dominant culture, and so demands that subordinate groups acculturate" (p. 183). This perspective was realized in the historical origins of African American education, and in the education of Native American children and other vulnerable groups.

Education was seen as such a powerful tool in the hands of African Americans that it was prohibited in many places and times during the 246 years of American slavery. After the Thirteenth Amendment in 1865, education benefiting African Americans adopted an assimilationist stance, which is still in effect today. Pine and Hilliard (1990), proponents of integrating African themes within educational curricula, confront this assimilationist perspective because it does not address the history of Africans before slavery, the struggle against slavery, colonialism, segregation, apartheid, and domination, and common aspects of historic systemic racism (Hilliard, Payton-Stewart, & Williams, 1995).

CURRENT POLICY ISSUES AFFECTING RACIAL AND ETHNIC MINORITY CHILDREN

There are several current trends and policy issues that adversely affect many minority children. These include racism, resegregation, the persistent achievement gap between minority students and nonminority students, overrepresentation of minority children in special education, potentially biased tests, and issues around bilingual education.

Historically, African Americans were treated as inherently inferior to white Americans. However, even those holding this racist view often believed that African Americans could still be important in advancing the economic prosperity of the United States. They sought racial cooperation by minorities within an unequal society, giving birth to the Hampton Institute, Tuskegee Normal and Industrial Institute, and a myriad of other missionary schools for the black population, who were then called Negro. This influence lingers today.

Some members of American society assert that antiblack racism is a thing of the past and has no bearing on contemporary society. However, in schooling, income, arrests, employment, housing, education, entertainment, advertising, and in private and public discourse, racism persists, and the color line continues to be the problem of the century (DuBois, 1903/1998), with racially tinged public debates over issues that guide public policy such as affirmative action, crime, and the prison industrial complex (Giroux, 2003). One manifestation of this problem in schools lies in the negative pathological labels such as "at-risk," "cultural deficit," and "disadvantaged" often bestowed on African American children. Ramona Edelin (1995) challenges these labels that have become grounds for educational policymaking (Watkins, 1993).

Some assert that color blindness is the ideal for social policy makers and for society. While not denying the existence of race construction, color blindness denies that racial discrimination is responsible for injustices that support white privilege, replicate group inequalities, and negatively affect the economic mobility and the acquisition of political power of marginalized people (Giroux, 2003). Moreover, the logic of color blindness negates race as "a marker of identity or power when factored into the social vocabulary of everyday life and the capacity for exercising individual and social agency" (Giroux, 2003, p. 198).

Amidst neoliberalist education reform that promotes colorblind education for assimilation, two theoretical models can be employed to understand and confront racial discrimination and marginalization. The model of cultural reproductive systems and actions has been utilized to demonstrate how individual and institutional constitutive actions maintain hegemony, often without individuals being fully aware of their role in contributing to the inequity (Bowles & Gintis, 2011). Within the United States, white privilege is so embedded within the fabric of society that it is often not questioned or challenged. For example, curriculum is often presented as politically neutral and devoid of realism and interrogating a hegemonic view of society, which favors cultural whiteness (McKnight & Chandler, 2009a, 2009b). Critical Race Theory, on the other hand, provides a framework or a set of basic perspectives, methods, and pedagogy that seeks to identify, analyze, and transform those structural, cultural, and interpersonal aspects of education that maintain the subordination of students of color (Solorzano & Yosso, 2000, p. 42). However, a "structural racism approach to youth development and educational attainment . . . may [only] help youth do better *in spite of a* set of pernicious mechanisms that sort them by race" (Fullbright-Anderson, Lawrence, Sutton, Susi, & Kubisch, 2005, p. 13; emphasis in original). Therefore, it is critical that school social workers are committed not only to addressing emotional concerns of youths who are marginalized, but also to embracing the NASW core value of social justice in confronting the oppressive systemic conditions that further promote the racial marginalization and isolation of youths.

Resegregation

Despite years of vigorous federal efforts, many school districts are almost entirely made up of minority students, while other districts have little racial or ethnic diversity.

Kopels (2007) describes the "radical return toward resegregation" (p. 277) by the Supreme Court, citing several Supreme Court decisions of the 1990s, including *Board of Education of Oklahoma City v. Dowell* (1991), in which a school district had been given unitary status on a finding that past discriminatory practices had been redressed. She writes, "After a declaration of unitary status, the courts presume any government action creating racially segregated schools to be innocent, unless a plaintiff proves that the school district intentionally decided to discriminate" (p. 277). When new segregation problems emerged, the Court ruled that Court supervision had been effectively ended when the courts had determined that past discrimination had been eliminated to the extent possible. In *Missouri v. Jenkins* (1995), the Supreme Court ruled that the comprehensive plan ordered by a federal district court to integrate schools and improve student achievement in Kansas City schools went beyond the scope of constitutional limitations on court interventions. The Kansas City plan, which involved magnet schools and capital improvements to attract students from outside the district and from private schools, was ambitious, expensive, and, ultimately, not supported by the state of Missouri or the Supreme Court. Kopels summarizes these decisions and notes that they demonstrate a philosophy of less judicial involvement in education and a move away from desegregation. A decision of the Supreme Court, made on June 28, 2007 *(Parents Involved v. Seattle School District* [2007] and *Meredith v. Jefferson County Board of Education* [2007]) continues the trend toward resegregation.

The Continuing Shift toward Market Solutions

Because educational policies in the United States have been affected by the neoliberal and conservative shift toward market solutions, such as school vouchers and charter schools, public education for vulnerable groups is under threat (Mora & Christianakis, 2013).

School vouchers generally involve the concept of parents being granted a specific amount of money that they can use in choosing schools for their children. These funds can be used for private schools, most of which are faith-based. While this has developed into some controversy over separation of church and state, the voucher movement has moved forward.

Charter schools are publicly funded schools that are allowed to operate outside of the rules, policies, and constraints that normally govern public schools. For example, charter schools do not have to employ unionized teachers, or even certified school social workers. State mandates that are required of most public schools are not required of charter schools. The closing and reopening of schools as charter schools often becomes a sort of shell game. "The Consortium on Chicago School Research, a nonpartisan group at the University of Chicago, found that Duncan's closure of low-performing schools reshuffled 8 out of every 10 students into similarly low-performing schools, and that when math scores were compared with other urban school districts, charter students were not among the highest performers" (Gwynne de la Torre, 2009, as cited in Carr & Porfilio, 2011, p. 109). The pressure toward school vouchers and charter schools has been ideological, rather than evidence informed. Levine and Levine (2013) note that the privatization ideology is based on several beliefs:

1. Competition will inevitably lead to improved education.
2. Private enterprise is always superior to tax-based government sponsorship, even when a public good is concerned.
3. Public subsidies must be justified.
4. The benefits of private enterprise are self-evident. (p. 2)

Levine and Levine (2013) also note the "the hallmark of an ideology is imperviousness to evidence" (p. 3). There is a singular lack of evidence to support the claims of the privatization ideologists. Given the current focus on evidence-informed practice in school social work, this lack of evidence is dismaying, particularly for one of the major outgrowths of the market solutions/high-stakes testing movements, the Common Core state standards. (For more detail on Common Core state standards and critiques of Common Core, see chapter 10 in this volume.)

Achievement Gap

Despite many years of effort to desegregate schools, there are indicators that minority children have not been receiving adequate educational opportunities. This is reflected in a persistent achievement gap on standardized measures of achievement, high school graduation rates, and college attendance (Bybee & Stage, 2005; Fellmeth, 2005; Greene, 2003; Hemphill, Vanneman,

& Rahman, 2011; Vanneman, Hamilton, Baldwin Anderson, & Rahman, 2009). Many attribute this problem to the strong association between minority status and poverty.

Some research evidence suggests that curriculum varies by social class. Jean Anyon's (1980) critical ethnography of four Boston area elementary schools unveiled differing kinds of curricula and different functions of schooling for children of various socioeconomic classes. Curricula can be categorized in various ways (Anyon, 1980; Eisner, 1979; Schubert, 1981, 1986): taught curriculum (overtly communicated by instruction and materials), learned curriculum (what is internalized by the student about self and his or her world), null curriculum (absence may convey lack of access for future use by learner—for example, advanced mathematics curricula), hidden curriculum (often implicit instruction to stratify learners for future labor), and outside curriculum (ad hoc instruction experienced in the learner's home, and via peers, media, and formal organizations). In Anyon's study, class instead of race was the noted factor that determined the structure of taught, learned, null, hidden, and outside curricula:

- Children of working-class parents were taught to follow the steps of a procedure, usually mechanical procedures, involving rote behavior, with very little decision making or choice. Academic success was based on whether students followed the rules, not whether answers were right or wrong.
- Children of middle-class parents were encouraged to get the right answer. If one accumulates enough right answers, one gets a good grade. It was important to follow the directions in order to get the right answers, but there was allowance for some choices and decision making.
- Children of professional parents received more opportunity to be creative in their work. Students were encouraged to (1) work independently, engaging in critical thought and expressiveness, (2) expand and illustrate ideas, and (3) obtain the freedom to choose appropriate methods and materials to complete their work.
- Children of the executive/ruling class parents were expected to develop their own analytical intellectual powers. Children were continually asked to reason through a problem, and to produce intellectual products that were both logically sound and of top academic quality. A primary goal was to conceptualize rules by which elements may fit together in systems and then to apply these rules in solving a problem.

With its emphasis on high-stakes testing, the No Child Left Behind Act of 2001, as implemented, seems to subscribe to a working-class and middle-class standard of academic success. Creative programming goes unfunded for many schools in diverse communities, and children have limited opportunity to develop decision-making skills relevant to their future aspirations. Academic failure is attributed to the students' inability to perform well on standardized exams, which are often disconnected from the students' daily lives.

The No Child Left Behind Act can potentially call a school a "failing school" if any one of the demographic subgroups is not achieving at the level identified by each state as adequate. Thus the No Child Left Behind Act tends to have less impact on schools with small numbers of minority children or children with disabilities, since if there are fewer than forty students of an identified group in a school or member of a group that attend that school for fewer than 140 days, that group is not considered in the determination of annual yearly progress. Identified subgroups are (1) the school as a whole, (2) white, (3) black, (4) Hispanic, (5) Native American, (6) Asian, (7) multiracial, (8) economically disadvantaged, (9) LEP, and (10) students with disabilities.

Overrepresentation of Minority Children in Special Education

Minority children continue to be overrepresented in special education classes across the country. In one recent study of this issue, the investigators found that different and nonstandard procedures were being followed in the assessment of minority students for special education (Ebersole & Kapp, 2007). Others have speculated that this is the result of bias in testing (discussed below) or due to the relationship between minority status and poverty. In 1959 the American Association on Mental Retardation (AAMR) decided that too many individuals were being inaccurately categorized as mentally retarded due to an overreliance on IQ tests. The AAMR then decided to add adaptive behavior to its definition of mental retardation in order to add consideration of daily functioning to the evaluation. Later, the AAMR reduced the cutoff score for mental retardation from one standard deviation below the mean to two standard deviations below the mean, in order to address this continuing disparity (AAMR, 2002).

Despite these definitional changes, minority students continue to be overrepresented in special education. The National Center for Culturally Responsive Educational Systems (2007) was formed to address these issues; the Center reports on data on overrepresentation of racial, ethnic, or cultural minority students across the nation. They report disproportionate placement of African American students in all states. These varying rates strongly suggest that state policies and procedures contribute to the rates of overrepresentation of minority students in different states. Moreover, researchers assert that this disproportionality does not appear predicated on greater disability but rather on less understanding of cultural differences (Skiba, Poloni-Staudinger, Gallini, Simmons, & Feggins-Azziz, 2006).

Potentially Biased Tests

Two important federal district court cases have examined the question as to whether standardized tests can be used to determine placement of minority students. In *Larry P. v. Wilson Riles* (1984), Judge Peckham acknowledged controversy over what such tests actually measured. He decided to assume that such tests were accurate in measuring mental capacity of white students; he asked if they were also valid for black students. Expert testimony in that case demonstrated that the IQ tests being used had been developed and standardized only for use with white, middle-class students. Fischer and Sorenson (1996) write, "Despite the knowledge that a pioneer in developing I.Q. tests in the United States had said they were not valid for Black persons and that certain items were widely considered to be culturally biased, little effort had been made to investigate these issues. Furthermore, bias was not sought out; possible defects in the tests were not corrected; and there was little investigation of why Black children consistently scored lower, as a group, than White children" (p. 116). Judge Peckham stopped the use of IQ testing in the evaluation of black children for special education, and ordered that all black children then in placement be reevaluated without such tests.

In the second case (*Parents in Action on Special Education [PASE] v. Hannon,* 1980), Judge Grady, after listening to expert testimony, became convinced that the "experts" were not convincing enough in their credibility or expertise to base a decision on their testimony. Therefore, he decided to examine the standardized tests himself to determine whether the items were biased. He found in his personal examination of the Wechsler Intelligence Scale for Children (Revised) and the Wechsler Intelligence Scale for Children that there were eight biased items. He also found one biased item on the Stanford Binet test. Judge Grady believed that, since tests were only one component of the evaluation process, these biased items would be overcome by the expertise of those administering the tests and the multidisciplinary nature of the assessment. While Judge Peckham viewed the impact of these tests as substantial and often the primary determinant in the decision regarding placement in special education, Judge Grady saw the tests as only one component of a broad, multifaceted assessment. Judge Peckham, seeing the disproportionate number of minority children placed in special education and noting the absence of norming and validating such tests for minority children, put the burden of proof on the school system to show that the tests were not discriminatory. Judge Grady placed the burden of proof on the children's representatives to show that the tests were discriminatory (Fischer & Sorenson, 1996).

School social workers must be mindful that an ecological and team-based approach to evaluation requires that practitioners consider factors of culture, ethnicity and race, and socioeconomic status in assessments. Culture "affects the [individual's] display of language, behaviors, and beliefs"

(Raines & Van Acker, 2009, p. 436). An assessment devoid of a cultural understanding of the student creates the risk of improper identification and placement, and the potential for additional behavior and learning problems (Allen-Meares, 2008).

NATIVE AMERICAN CHILDREN AND EDUCATIONAL POLICY

The history of American policy on education of Native American children has shifted back and forth between assimilationist goals to those that respect and value Native American cultures. This history begins with the period from 1776 to 1926 that involved a policy of assimilation or education of Native American children into the white European culture and abandonment of their own cultures. Assimilationists used boarding schools as a mechanism to have Indian children adopt European values and beliefs. Col. Henry Pratt established the most well known of such schools in Carlisle, Pennsylvania, in 1879 (American Indian Education Foundation, 2007). Pratt sought to totally assimilate Native American students by mandating standard uniforms, the cutting of the boys' long hair, the imposition of new Anglo names, refusal to serve any traditional Native American foods, and prohibition of the use of native languages.

In 1905 a new direction began, deemphasizing assimilation and moving toward day schools rather than boarding schools. In the 1920s John Collier, the executive secretary for the Native American Defense Association, began reform efforts that led to the Meriam Report in 1926 (as cited in American Indian Education Foundation, n.d.) that recommended that younger Indian children should attend a school close to home, and that only older children should attend boarding schools, that the uniform course of study involving only white values and traditions be abandoned, and that Indian children should be given tools to work with both white and Indian cultures. Charles Rhoades, Indian commissioner, began to follow these recommendations in 1929, and in 1933 Franklin Delano Roosevelt appointed John Collier commissioner of Indian affairs. Under Collier, federal policies moved away from assimilation. Collier helped to draft the Indian Reorganization Act of 1934 (American Indian Education Foundation, n.d.). This period marked a beginning of policies that led to valuing Native American cultures, of nonassimilationist education, and of respect for Native American art and language. However, from the 1940s through the 1950s this movement went backward: funding was cut for services on reservations, and off-reservation boarding schools were again recommended. In the 1960s–1970s, this trend was reversed with substantial changes in public policy. For example, in 1965 the National Advisory Council on Indian Education was formed; in 1966 President Lyndon Johnson appointed Robert Lafollette Bennett, a Native American, as commissioner of Indian affairs; and in 1968 Johnson established the National Council on Indian Opportunity to facilitate Indian participation in federal decision making regarding Indian policy. In 1969 the Special Sub-committee on Indian Education, Senate Committee on Labor and Public Welfare, published the Kennedy Report. That report said, "The dominant policy of the federal government toward the Native American has been one of coercive assimilation" and the policy "has had disastrous effects on the education of Indian children" (quoted in National Center for Indian Education, n.d.).

The Indian Education Act of 1972, now known as Part A, Title IX, Education Amendments of 1994, provides federal support for education of Native American and Native Alaskan children in public schools, both tribal schools and Bureau of Indian Affairs schools. However, in the 1980s and 1990s the trend was again away from support of Native American cultures, and the Office of Indian Affairs was almost eliminated in 1995. President Clinton vetoed a budget that would have effectively eliminated the Office of Indian Affairs. The National Unity Task Force, a Native American political action committee, was formed and lobbied to change jurisdiction over the Office of Indian Affairs from the Department of the Interior to the Education Department. This effort was successful.

GENDER AND EDUCATIONAL POLICY

The primary federal legislation that relates to gender and schools is Title IX of the 1972 Education Amendments. This was the first major federal legislation to prohibit sex discrimination in schools that receive federal funds. This legislation includes prohibition against discrimination in employment, as well as with regard to the admission and treatment of students. Title IX applies to preschool through graduate-level education organizations that accept federal funds. Regulations for the legislation were published in 1975 (U.S. Department of Education [USDOE], 1975). This legislation also prohibits discrimination against pregnant students, who, in earlier years, may have been expelled or excluded from school on the basis of their pregnancy. According to Kopels (2007), most sex discrimination lawsuits based on Title IX have focused on athletic programs and admissions policies. She writes, "The very fact that public schools now have women's and girl's sports teams, like soccer or basketball, owes its origins to Title IX legislation" (p. 283). Title IX also has been used on behalf of those who are at risk of or who have experienced sexual harassment in schools.

Women have made much progress. On August 26, 1920, the Nineteenth Amendment to the Constitution at last gave women in the United States the right to vote. Illinois, Wisconsin, and Michigan were the first states to ratify this amendment, while Georgia and Alabama were the first to oppose it. Many occupations and professions, once barred to women, now admit women to their ranks, and in some traditionally male occupations, women have overtaken men in numbers. However, from 2003–5, college-educated women's median income was an average of 74 percent of that of college-educated men, with college-educated men earning a median income of $61,603, while the median income of college-educated women was $45,684. The disparity in income ranges from women earning 64 percent of men's salaries in Louisiana to 89 percent in West Virginia. According to the U.S. Census Bureau (2007), this disparity is found across all occupational categories that they list.

The Office for Civil Rights of the USDOE is responsible for enforcing Title IX in approximately 16,000 local school districts; 3,200 colleges and universities; as well as in libraries, museums, vocational rehabilitation agencies, state education agencies (SEAs), and about 5,000 for-profit schools in the United States. Anyone who believes there has been discrimination on the basis of sex against a person or group in one of these programs may file a complaint with the Office for Civil Rights under Title IX. The person filing the complaint may complain on behalf of another person or group. Usually, complaints must be filed within 180 days of the date of the alleged discrimination, unless the Office extends this time period. For filing procedures, see U.S. Department of Health & Human Services (n.d.). If discrimination is found, the case may be referred to the U.S. Department of Justice for court action. In some cases the USDOE may withdraw federal funding to the school or program after a hearing with an administrative law judge.

A second law that relates to gender and schools is the Civil Rights Act of 1964, Title VI. This Act prohibits discrimination in the workplace based on race, color, religion, sex, or national origin. Persons over age forty are also a protected category in regards to employment, due to a third law, the Age Discrimination in Employment Act of 1967.

LESBIAN, GAY, BISEXUAL, TRANSGENDER, AND QUESTIONING STUDENTS AND FACULTY

Sexual minority students and personnel are not a protected class under federal legislation. However, although sexual minorities are not named as a protected class, Title IX has been used as the foundation for case law that has established that schools cannot allow harassment of LGBTQ students (*Nabozny v. Podlesny*, 1996). Schools, however, are legally permitted to discriminate in employment against LGBTQ persons, and it remains legal to dismiss a school employee because he or she identifies as lesbian, gay, bisexual, or transgendered. A New Jersey court upheld the dismissal of a transgendered teacher due to "psychological harm to students" (In re Grossman, 1974). A federal court upheld the firing of a teacher for omitting to include on his application for employment the fact that he belonged to a group called "homophiles," a group that urges public acceptance of homosexuality (*Acanfora v. Board of Education*, 1974).

School districts have the right to include sexual minorities as a protected group in their nondiscrimination statements and many school districts have chosen to do so.

HOMELESS CHILDREN AND SCHOOLS

Due to the recent economic and housing crises in the United States, many school districts across the country report increases in the number of homeless students in the classroom. The National Association for the Education of Homeless Children and Youth and First Focus conducted a voluntary survey during the fall of 2008 and found that

- ◆ 330 school districts identified the same number or more homeless students in the first few months of this school year than they identified the entire previous year,
- ◆ 847 school districts identified half or more of last year's caseload in the first few months of this school year, and
- ◆ 459 school districts had an increase of at least 25 percent in the number of homeless students identified between the 2006–7 and 2007–8 school years.

School districts also reported many challenges associated with the increase in homelessness. These included

- ◆ Rising transportation costs and logistical challenges in making sure homeless children have access to school,
- ◆ Inadequate staff to identify and support children and youths experiencing homelessness,
- ◆ Lack of available shelter space and low-income housing, and
- ◆ Reduction in other community services and supplies (Duffield & Lovell, 2008).

All school social workers should be familiar with Title VII-B of the McKinney-Vento Homeless Assistance Act of 1986. This program was initially authorized in 1987 and was reauthorized with the No Child Left Behind Act of 2001.

The law defines "homeless children and youths" as individuals who lack a fixed, regular, and adequate nighttime residence, including (1) those who share housing with other persons due to lack of housing, financial hardship, or a similar reason; (2) those who live in motels, hotels, trailer parks, or camping grounds due to a lack of alternative adequate accommodations; (3) those who live in emergency or transitional shelters; (4) those who have been abandoned in hospitals; (5) those who are awaiting foster placement; (6) those who have a primary nighttime residence that is not designed or usually used as a regular sleeping accommodation for humans; (7) those who live in cars, parks, public spaces, abandoned buildings, substandard housing, bus or train station, or similar settings; and (8) those migratory children who are living in circumstances described above (USDOE, 2004). An "unaccompanied youth" is defined as a youth not in the physical custody of the parent or guardian, such as a youth living in runaway shelters, in cars, parks, or other inadequate housing.

If a family becomes homeless, the local education agency (LEA) must make school placement decisions on the basis of the best interest of the child. The LEA must continue the child's or youth's education in the school of origin for as long as the family is homeless, or the LEA must enroll the child in any public school that nonhomeless children living in the same attendance area as the homeless child are eligible to attend. To the extent possible, the LEA must keep the child in the school of origin unless this goes against the wishes of the parent or guardian.

No obstacles can legally be placed in the way of school enrollment of homeless children, even if the child is unable to produce documents usually required for enrollment, such as a birth certificate, immunization record, school records, or medical records. The LEA must provide transportation, if needed, to and from the school of origin if the child remains in that attendance area. If the child is living in another area, the two LEAs must either share equally the costs of transporting the child or agree on a method of apportioning financial responsibility. Additional guidance on the implementation of the McKinney-Vento Homeless Assistance Act is available at USDOE (2004).

BILINGUAL EDUCATION

Bilingual education has been a controversial issue, especially as immigration issues have intensified as divisive political topics. Proposition 227 that California voters approved in 1998 was intended to dismantle California's bilingual education program. This law was upheld in the *Valeria v. Davis* decision (2002), which determined that the law was constitutional (LaMorte, 2005). Arizona followed suit in 2000.

While not all states have carried out such extreme measures, the federal Bilingual Education Act of 1994, Title VII of the Elementary and Secondary Education Act of 1965, was eliminated in 2002 as one of the changes in the No Child Left Behind Act of 2001 (the most recent reauthorization of Elementary and Secondary Education Act). It was reborn as the English Language Learners Act of 2001, with the goal of rapid acquisition of English by LEP students. The word "bilingual" was expunged from the Act, and funding would no longer be made through competitive grants. Instead, formula grants to states would be made, based on the number of English language learners (Crawford, 2002).

The federal Bilingual Education Act of 1968, Title VII of the Elementary and Secondary Education Act, was first enacted in 1968 and provided strong support for bilingual learners. The first year no funds were appropriated to carry out the law, but the following year it was funded. The law provided funding to school districts to provide competitive grants directly to school districts that would be used to support the education of non-English-speaking students through (1) resources for educational programs, (2) training for teachers and teacher aides, (3) development and dissemination of materials, and (4) parent involvement projects. It did not require bilingual instruction or the use of the students' native language in the classroom. The Act focused on low-income students. Some states had barriers, such as English-only laws that created implementation problems.

The Supreme Court decision in the case of *Lau v. Nichols* (1974) provided important policy guidance for bilingual education. This Act, on behalf of San Francisco students of Chinese descent, found that it was not enough to provide non-English-speaking students equal access to English-only classrooms and reading materials: if the students could not read or speak English, the provision of English-only classes and materials prevented them from receiving an education. The court did not require a specific remedy, leaving that decision to educators (Fischer & Sorenson, 1996).

The Equal Educational Opportunities Act of 1974 also affected bilingual education policy, stating states may not "deny equal educational opportunity to an individual" because of "the failure by an educational agency to take appropriate action to overcome language barriers that impede equal participation by its students" (1982).

The Bilingual Education Act amendments of 1974 defined a bilingual education program as one that provided instruction both in the student's native language and in English. Programs for English as a second language alone were not enough. The amendments specified the goal of such a program as the preparation of LEP students to participate effectively in regular classrooms as soon as possible. The amendments included the removal of the low-income requirement of the 1968 Act. The amendments also established regional support centers to provide guidance and support to schools, required a national clearinghouse for bilingual education, and provided funding for capacity building for bilingual programs (Stewner-Manzares, 1988).

In 1975 and 1978 the law was amended again. The 1975 amendments were intended to assist schools in complying with the *Lau v. Nichols* court decision through what were called the Lau remedies or guidelines on implementing policy based on the *Lau v. Nichols* decision. The Lau remedies described educational strategies for teaching students with limited English-speaking ability. Schools were mandated to develop compliance plans if they were found to be noncompliant with Title VI of the Civil Rights Act and if they had twenty or more students of the same language group who had been identified as having a primary or home language other than English. These twenty students did not all have to have limited English language ability (Stewner-Manzares, 1988). The 1978 amendments expanded eligibility to LEP students and specified the goal of such programs as being the development of English skills as quickly as possible in order for students to be educated in English-only classrooms.

The Bilingual Education Act of 1984 Amendments awarded several grants for programs for LEP students, including

1. transitional bilingual education programs, in which structured English language instruction is combined with a native language component and up to 40 percent of the class may be non-LEP students;
2. developmental bilingual education programs, in which full-time instruction is given in both English and a second language with the goal of achieving competence in both English and a second language;
3. special alternative instructional programs in which the native language need not be used, but English language instruction and special instructional services are given to facilitate achievement of English competency. (Stewner-Manzares, 1988, n.p.)

The Bilingual Education Act of 1988 changed the formula for grants to schools to increase the percentage that could go to special alternative educational programs. This gave more flexibility to schools that found that transitional bilingual education programs were not feasible for them. The Act set a three-year limit on student participation in transitional bilingual programs, unless special circumstances existed, which would justify up to an additional two years. Family English literacy programs were to include provisions for instruction in English, U.S. history, and U.S. government for noncitizens eligible for temporary resident status under the Immigration and Naturalization Act of 1965. Information to parents or guardians was required to be in a language that they could understand. The Bilingual Education Act legislation emphasized training qualified personnel.

In 1994 the Bilingual Education Act was reauthorized as Title VII of the Improving America's Schools Act. The law cited numerous obstacles to education of LEP children. These obstacles included a shortage of qualified educators, overrepresentation of these children in special education, limited English skills of their parents, and segregation. This Act was positive regarding use of a child's native language in the classroom.

The elimination of the Bilingual Education Act of 1988 and creation of the English Language Learners Act of 2001 set high standards for the educational achievement of LEP children, but seriously backed off from support for bilingual education. This is a manifestation of the English-only trends that have been growing since the 1980s. Proponents of English-only classrooms believe that, in the past, immigrant groups had to learn English and to abandon their native languages and that this continues to be essential to the maintenance of a unified American language and culture. As of this writing thirty-one states have passed legislation declaring English as their states' official language.

CONCLUSION

Levine and Levine (2013) describe an ideology that is driving much current educational policy. We posit a competing ideology for the practice of social justice in school social work, based on five values:

1. Educational practice and policy must be based on evidence of effectiveness, insofar as evidence is currently available.
2. Educational practices must be based on the principle of equal access to free and appropriate education. While this is a value-based statement, it is in accordance with decades of policy development.
3. Educational practices are likely to differ, according to specific population and environmental contexts. Thus, the evidence used to develop policy and practice must be related to the needs and differences of the groups of students affected.
4. Educational achievement is related to a wide range of factors, including the evolution of race relations, structuralism, poverty, discrimination, disability, and other social factors. School social workers must be aware and active in working to affect the larger social context that affects the educational achievement of students.
5. School social workers are called to act within society to fight against social injustice, discrimination, and oppression, and to support the rights and opportunities of all students.

School social workers have a duty unique among school personnel to advocate for individuals and groups who belong to populations that have suffered historical discrimination and oppression. These groups include African Americans, Native Americans, bilingual students, girls and women, sexual minorities, and homeless children. The first step is to understand the current issues and how they are rooted in history and policy related to these vulnerable populations. These have been broadly outlined in this chapter, but the histories and contexts of groups are unique to each school and community, and specific community change involves learning about specific schools and communities and applying that knowledge in working with others to support students, families, and educators.

References

Acanfora v. Board of Education, 491F.2d 498, 4th Circuit (1974).

Age Discrimination in Employment Act of 1967, Pub. L. 90-202, 29 U.S.C. § 621–29, 29 U.S.C. § 634 (1967).

Allen-Meares, P. (2008). Assessing the adaptive behavior of youths: Multicultural responsivity. *Social Work, 53*, 307–316.

American Association on Mental Retardation (AAMR). (2002). *Mental retardation: Definition, classification, and systems of support* (10th ed.). Washington, DC: Author.

American Indian Education Foundation. (n.d). *History of Indian education.* Retrieved from http://www.nrcprograms.org/site/PageServer?pagename=aief_hist_main

American Indian Education Foundation. (2007). *1776–1926. Indian education means "assimilation."* Retrieved from http://www.nrcprograms.org/site/PageServer?page name=aief_hist_1776

Anyon, J. (1980). Social class and the hidden curriculum of work. *Journal of Education, 162,* 67–92.

Apple, M. (1998). The culture and commerce of the textbook. In L. Beyer & M. Apple (Eds.), *The curriculum: Problems, politics, and possibilities* (pp. 157–176). New York: SUNY Press.

Bilingual Education Act of 1968, Pub. L. 90-247, 81 Stat. § 816 (1968).

Bilingual Education Act of 1974, Pub. L. 93-380, 88 Stat. § 503 (1974).

Bilingual Education Act of 1984, Pub. L. 98-511, 98 Stat. § 2370 (1984).

Bilingual Education Act of 1988, Pub. L. 100-297 (1988).

Bilingual Education Act of 1994, Pub. L. 103-382 (1994).

Board of Education of Oklahoma City v. Dowell, 498 U.S. 237 (1991).

Bowles, S., & Gintis, H. (2011). *Schooling in a capitalist America: Educational reform and contradictions.* Chicago: Haymarket Books.

Bybee, R. W., & Stage, E. (2005). No country left behind. *Issues in Science & Technology, 21*(2), 69–76.

Carr, P. W., & Porfilio, B. (2011). *The phenomenon of Obama and the agenda for education: Can hope audaciously trump neoliberalism?* Charlotte, NC: IAC.

Civil Rights Act of 1964, Pub. L. 88-352, 78 Stat. § 241 (1964).

Crawford, J. (2002). Obituary: The Bilingual Education act: 1968–2002. *Rethinking Schools Online, 16*(4). Retrieved from http://www.rethinkingschools.org/restrict .asp?path=archive/16_04/Bil164.shtml

DuBois, W. E. B. (1998). *The souls of black folk.* New York, Dover. (Original work published 1903)

Duffield, B., & Lovell, P. (2008, December). The economic crisis hits home: The unfolding increase in child and youth homelessness. *First Focus,* 1–21.

Ebersole, J. L., & Kapp, S. A. (2007). Stemming the tide of overrepresentation: Ensuring accurate certification of African American students in programs for the mentally retarded. *School Social Work Journal, 31,* 1–16.

Edelin, R. (1995). Curriculum and cultural identity. In A. G. Hilliard, L. Payton-Stewart, & L. O. Williams (Eds.), *Infusion of African and African American content in the school curriculum: Proceedings of the First National Conference* (pp. 37–50). Chicago: Third World Press.

Education Amendments of 1994, Pub. L. 103-382 (1994).

Eisner, E. W. (1979). *The educational imagination.* New York: Macmillan.

Elementary and Secondary Education Act of 1965, 20 U.S.C. § 2701 et seq. (1965).

English Language Learners Act, No Child Left Behind Act of 2001, Pub. L. 107-110 (2002), Title III: Language instruction for limited English proficient & immigrant students program.

Equal Educational Opportunities Act of 1974, 20 U.S.C. § 1703 et seq. (1974).

Fellmeth, R. (2005). Child poverty in the United States. *Human Rights: Journal of the Section of Individual Rights and Responsibilities, 32*(1), 2–5.

Ferdman, B. (1990). Literacy and cultural identity. *Harvard Educational Review, 60,* 181–183.

Fischer, L., & Sorenson, G. P. (1996). *School law for counselors, psychologists, and social workers* (3rd ed.). White Plains, NY: Longman.

Fullbright-Anderson, K., Lawrence, K., Sutton, S., Susi, G., & Kubisch, A. (2005). *Structural racism and youth development: Issues, challenges, and implications.* Washington, DC: The Aspen Institute.

Giroux, H. (2003). Spectacles of race and pedagogies of denial: Antiblack racist pedagogy under the reign of neoliberalism. *Community Education, 52,* 191–211.

Greene, J. P. (2003). *Public high school graduation and college readiness rates in the United States.* New York: Manhattan Institute for Policy Research.

Hemphill, F. C., Vanneman, A., & Rahman, T. (2011). *Achievement gaps: How Hispanic and white students in public schools perform in mathematics and reading on the national assessment of educational progress.* National Center on Education Statistics. Retrieved from http://nces.ed.gov/nationsreportcard/pdf/studies/2011459.pdf

Hilliard, A. G., Payton-Stewart, L., & Williams, L. O. (Eds.). (1995). Introduction. *Infusion of African and African American content in the school curriculum: Proceedings of the First National Conference* (pp. xi–xxiv). Chicago: Third World Press.

Immigration and Nationality Act of 1965, Pub. L. 89-236 (1965).

Improving Americas Schools Act of 1994, Pub. L. 103-382 (1994).

In re Grossman, 316 A.2d 39, N.J. (1974).

Indian Education Act of 1972, Title IV, Pub. L. 92-318 (1972).

Kenway, J., & Bullen, E. (2005).Globalizing the young in the age of desire: Some educational policy issues. In M. Apple, J. Kenway, & M. Singh (Eds.), *Globalizing education: Policies, pedagogies and politics* (pp. 31–44). New York: Peter Lang.

Kliebard, H. M. (1998). *Schooled to work: Vocationalism and the American curriculum.* New York: Cambridge University Press.

Kopels, S. (2007). Securing equal educational opportunity. In P. Allen-Meares (Ed.), *Social work services in schools* (5th ed., pp. 262–292). Boston: Allyn & Bacon.

LaMorte, M. W. (2005). *School law: Cases and concepts.* Boston: Allyn & Bacon.

Larry P. v. Wilson Riles United States Court of Appeals, 1984, 793 F.2d 969 (9th Cir.) (1984).

Lau v. Nichols, 414 U.S. 563 (1974).

Levine, M., & Levine, A. (2013). Charters and foundations: Are we losing control of our public schools? *American Journal of Orthopsychiatry, 84* (1), 1–6.

McKinney-Vento Homeless Assistance Act of 1986, Pub. L. 100-77, 101 Stat. § 482, 42 U.S.C. § 11301 et seq. (1986).

McKnight, D., & Chandler, P. (2009a). The complicated conversation of class and race in social and curricular analysis: An examination of Pierre Bourdieu's interpretative framework in relation to race. *Educational Philosophy and Theory, 44,* 74–97.

McKnight, D., & Chandler, P. (2009b). The failure of social education in the United States: A critique of teaching the national story from "White" colourblind eyes. *Journal for Critical Education Policy Studies,* 7 (2), 218–248.

Meredith v. Jefferson County Board of Education, 551 US ____ (2007).

Missouri v. Jenkins 515 US 70 (1995).

Mora, R., & Christianakis, M. (2013). Feeding the school-to-prison pipeline: The convergence of neoliberalism, conservativism, and penal populism, *Journal of Educational Controversy,* 7(1), 1–10. Retrieved from http://cedar.wwu.edu/jec/vol7/iss1/5

Nabozny v. Podlesny, 92 F 3d 446, 7th cir. (1996).

National Association of Social Workers (NASW). (2008). *Code of ethics.* Retrieved from https://www.socialworkers.org/pubs/code/code.asp

National Center for Culturally Responsive Educational Systems. (2007). *About us.* Retrieved from http://www.nccrest.org/about.html

National Center for Indian Education. (n.d.). *History of Indian education*. Retrieved from http://www.nrcprograms.org/site/PageServer?pagename=aief_hist_1960

No Child Left Behind Act of 2001, Pub. L. 107-110 (2002).

Parents in Action on Special Education (PASE) v. Hannon. United States District Court, 1980. 506 F.Supp. 831 (N.D. Ill.) (1980).

Parents Involved v. Seattle School District. 551 U.S. (2007).

Pine, G. J., & Hilliard, A. G. (1990). Rx for racism: Imperatives for America's schools. *Phi Delta Kappan*, (April), 1–10.

Proposition 227 (1998). *Proposition 227: English language in public schools*. Retrieved from http://www.smartvoter.org/1998jun/ca/state/prop/227/

Raines, J., & Van Acker, R. (2009). The screening and assessment of adaptive behavior. In C. R. Massat, R. Constable, S. McDonald, & J. P. Flynn (Eds.), *School social work: Practice, policy and research* (7th ed., pp. 431–451). Chicago: Lyceum Books.

Schubert, W. H. (1981). Knowledge about out of school curriculum. *Educational Forum, 45*, 185–199.

Schubert, W. H. (1986). *Curriculum: Perspective, paradigm, and possibility*. New York: McMillan.

Skiba, R. J., Poloni-Staudinger, L., Gallini, S., Simmons, A. B., & Feggins-Azziz, L. R. (2006). Disparate access: The disproportionality of African American students with disabilities across educational environments. *Exceptional Children, 72*, 411–424.

Solorzano, D. G., & Yosso, T. J. (2000). Toward a critical race theory of Chicana and Chicano education. In C. Tejeda, C. Martinez, & Z. Leonardo (Eds.), *Charting new terrains of Chicana(o), Latina(o) education* (pp. 35–65). Cresskill, NJ: Hampton Press.

Stewner-Manzanares, G. (1988). *The Bilingual Education Act: Twenty years later*. Focus, 6. National Clearinghouse for English language acquisition. Retrieved from http://www.ncela.us/rcd/bibliography/BE021037

Title IX, Education Amendments of 1972, Title 20 U.S.C. Sec. 1681–1688 (1972).

U.S. Census Bureau (2007). *Occupation by sex and earnings in the past twelve months*. Retrieved from http://www.census.gov/compendia/statab/2009/tables/09s0627.pdf

U.S. Department of Education (USDOE). (1975). *Title 34 Education, Subtitle B Regulations of the Offices of the Department of Education, Chapter I Office for Civil Rights, Department of Education, Part 106 Nondiscrimination on the Basis of Sex in Education Programs or Activities Receiving Federal Financial Assistance*. Retrieved from https://www2.ed.gov/policy/rights/reg/ocr/edlite-34cfr106.html

U.S. Department of Education (USDOE). (2004). *Education for homeless children and youth program: Title VII-B of the McKinney-Vento Homeless Assistance Act*. Retrieved from http://www.ed.gov/programs/homeless/guidance.pdf

U.S. Department of Health & Human Services (DHHS). (n.d.). *Office for Civil Rights*. Retrieved from http://www.hhs.gov/ocr/office/

Valeria v. Davis, 307 F3d 1036, 9th Cir. (2002).

Vanneman, A., Hamilton, L., Baldwin Anderson, J., & Rahman, T. (2009). *Achievement gaps: How black and white students in public schools perform in mathematics and reading on the national assessment of educational progress*. National Center for Educational Statistics. Retrieved from http://nces.ed.gov/nationsreportcard/pdf/studies/2009455.pdf

Watkins, W. (1993). Black curriculum orientations: A preliminary inquiry. *Harvard Educational Review, 63*(3), 321–338.

13

Bullying and Sexual Harassment in Schools

Susan Fineran
University of Southern Maine

- ◆ Legal Distinctions between Bullying and Sexual Harassment
- ◆ Prevalence of Bullying and Sexual Harassment in U.S. Schools
- ◆ Bullying
- ◆ Peer Sexual Harassment
- ◆ Responses to Bullying and Sexual Harassment

This chapter defines bullying and sexual harassment and reviews the research on both topics. There are grave concerns that bullying and peer sexual harassment interfere with and inhibit personal development, prevent learning, and make the school into a hostile environment for many pupils. Experience as victim or perpetrator can negatively affect a student's life through adulthood. Each experience of bullying or sexual harassment needs to be understood as a complex set of transactions—involving not only a victim and a perpetrator, but also involving peers, parents, teachers, and the general school enrrironment. Assessment and intervention need to respond to this complexity, and social workers who are able to clearly identify the problems associated with bullying and peer sexual harassment strengthen their positions as advocates for improved school environments.

LEGAL DISTINCTIONS BETWEEN BULLYING AND
SEXUAL HARASSMENT

Although both bullying and sexual harassment are serious problems in schools, there are legal distinctions between them. It is important to understand these legal distinctions because although bullying is considered antisocial and aggressive behavior that is linked to criminal conduct (Nansel et al., 2001), it is not illegal according to federal law. Sexual harassment, however, is defined in the United States as a part of civil rights law (Title IX Education Amendments of 1972) where it is viewed as a form of discrimination. The following definitions clarify the legal meanings of these two terms:

> Bullying and/or intimidation of others, includes any aggressive or negative gesture, or written, verbal, or physical act that *places another student in reasonable fear of harm* to his or her person or property, or that has the effect of *insulting* or *demeaning* any student in such a way as to *disrupt* or *interfere* with *the school's educational mission*, or the education of any student. Bullying most often will occur when a student asserts *physical or psychological power* over, or is cruel to, another student perceived to be weaker. Such behavior may include but is not limited to pushing, hitting, threatening, name-calling, or other physical or verbal conduct of a belittling or browbeating nature. (Zuehl, Dillon, Schilling, & Oltmanns, 2002, n.p., emphasis added)

In 1997 the U.S Department of Education (USDOE) defined sexual harassment in schools as "unwelcome sexual advances, requests for sexual favors, and other verbal, nonverbal, or physical conduct of a sexual nature by an employee, by another student, or by a third party, that is sufficiently severe, persistent, or pervasive to limit a student's ability to participate in or benefit from an education program or activity, or to create a hostile or abusive educational environment" (USDOE, 1997, p. 12038).

The distinction between bullying and sexual harassment is important, because a child who identifies a behavior as bullying does not have the same protections as a child who calls the same behaviors sexual harasment.The following 2002 Vermont case illustrates the potential significance of this distinction.

> A parent filed a complaint against the St. Johnsbury School District claiming the district failed to protect her son from bullies on the bus and in homeroom. The parent claimed that the bullies sexually harassed him with taunts about being gay. The parent subsequently sued the St. Johnsbury School District under a new Vermont antibullying state law, and ultimately a jury sided with the school. Because this case was litigated in state court under a new antibullying law, federal civil rights laws, although accessible, were not invoked. Had the parent pursued this as a civil rights case in a federal court the outcome most likely would have been in favor of the son. (Stein, 2003)

Two concerns have arisen about the potential treatment of sexual harassment as bullying. One concern is that state laws do not offer the same protections as federal civil rights laws, and a failure to identify a case as one of sexual harassment rather than bullying could lead to a failure to provide all possible protections to victims (Stein, 2003). A second potential drawback to

the failure to identify sexual harassment and to call sexual harassment bullying is the potential personalization of the behavior to particular students,
whether bully or victim, thus pathologizing them as individuals. This perspective deflects the problem away from being a school climate issue that the
school has responsibility to solve under Title IX to an issue in which individual students are to blame for their behaviors. Under Title IX a school system can be held responsible when school personnel knowingly allow a hostile environment (*Bruneau v. South Kortright Central School District*, 1996).
Thus, legally, schools are responsible for the actions of both their employees
and their students in regard to sexual harassment, but when the allegation
is bullying it is more likely that the legal responsibility will revert to the individuals involved.

PREVALENCE OF BULLYING AND SEXUAL HARASSMENT IN U.S. SCHOOLS

Five national studies of bullying and sexual harassment provide statistics
regarding these behaviors in U.S. schools. The National Institute of Child
Health and Human Development (Nansel et al., 2001) found that one third
of children in grade 6 through grade 10 are directly involved in bullying,
with 10 percent as bullies, 13 percent as victims, and 6 percent as both. The
frequency of bullying was higher among sixth, seventh, and eighth graders
than among ninth and tenth graders. The USDOE School Crime Supplement
to the National Crime Victimization Survey (USDOE, 2011) reported that, in
2011, 38 percent of middle and high school students were bullied (25 percent of male students, 31 percent of female students). Grade level made a
difference, with 37 percent of sixth graders, 26 percent of ninth graders, and
22 percent of twelfth graders reporting bullying in school.

The American Association of University Women (AAUW) has conducted
three national studies of sexual harassment in U.S. schools. The first two
studies were conducted in 1993 and 2001 and had similar results: they
reported that 81 percent of students experienced some form of sexual
harassment during their entire school life. In 2011 AAUW repeated the
study, and using a shorter reporting period asked students to report only
sexual harassment they experienced during the current school year
2010–11. Accordingly, the reported rate was lower, with 48 percent of students (56 percent of girls and 40 percent of boys) reporting an experience
of sexual harassment. The 2011 survey also explored whether students were
harassed on the Internet. Nearly one third of students reported harassment
by text, e-mail, Facebook, or other electronic means. Not surprisingly, many
students reported being sexually harassed both in person and electronically.
Similar to the 1993 and 2001 studies, the 2011 study also showed girls experienced higher frequency of sexual harassment. Overall, 87 percent of those
students who experienced sexual harassment reported that it affected them
negatively.

BULLYING

Bullying has been well studied. Research on bullying covers the etiology of bullying, differential assessment of bullies, and outcomes for bullies.

There have been many attempts in the literature to define the developmental problems that lead to bullying behavior. Bullies have more psychiatric symptoms than other students (Kumpulainen, Raesaenen, & Henttonen, 1999). Nansel et al. (2001) stated that these youths suffer from insecurity, anxiety, depression, loneliness, unhappiness, physical and mental symptoms, and low self-esteem. Curtner-Smith (2000) suggested that bullying is learned from influential role models in the social environment of the child. Bullying is a significant indicator of risk for mental disorders in adolescence (Kaltiala-Heino, Pilla, Ruan, Simmons-Morton, & Scheidt, 2000). Parental maltreatment, both emotional and physical; physical discipline; and bullying in the home contribute to the prediction of bullying (Duncan, 1999; Smith & Myron-Wilson, 1998; Smith & Shu, 2000). Children from larger families are more likely to bully (Eslea & Smith, 2000).

Although the literature portrays a dim view of bullies, the picture is worse for the victims of bullying. A history of being victimized (being teased, hearing rumors spread about oneself, being or feeling deliberately excluded, experiencing violence or threats of violence) is associated with subsequent development of anxiety and depression in adolescence (Bond, Carlin, Thomas, Rubin, & Patton, 2001). Victims have a lower level of social acceptance than their peers (Haynie et al., 2001) and more serious mental and physical health problems and fewer support systems than others (Duncan, 1999; Nansel et al., 2001; Rigby, 2000). Finally, victimization is related to a greater incidence of suicidal ideation in young people (Carney, 2000; Rigby & Slee, 1999).

Victims of bullying do not always respond by suffering in silence. There is increasing concern about how these victims may express their frustrations and act them out in the school setting. McGee and DeBernardo (1999) studied sixteen students who committed homicide in schools and found fourteen of them to be bully victims. A study by Klein (2006) highlights the roles that bullying and sexual harassment played in school shootings. Many school shooters had been ostracized by peers, weathered homophobic attacks for months, and formulated revenge schemes. These students chose to retaliate against teachers, classmates, and the school, perhaps in a generalized rage against the school for not providing some protection to them. School was a dangerous place for them, but also a required place. Although not justified, their dilemma may have resulted in retaliatory violence.

Differential Assessment of Students Who Bully

Effective intervention planning calls for detailed assessment. A number of studies make a distinction between the bullies who are impulsive as a condition of an attention deficit disorder and those who are more calculating.

Arsenio and Lemerise (2001) argued that there are hot-blooded and cold-blooded bullies, concluding that the intervention and treatment strategies for school social workers should be differentiated on the basis of this differential assessment. Acting-out children who may be driven by attention deficit hyperactivity disorder (Wolke, Woods, Blomfield, & Karstadt, 2000) are referred to by Arsenio and Lemerise as the hot-blooded bullies. Treating this type of student strictly as a behavior problem (i.e., without taking attention deficit hyperactivity disorder into account) may have serious consequences.

There are also a number of studies that conclude that the bully may be a student who is very competent socially. They seem socially skilled, have a high level of self-esteem, and give the impression of being aloof and detached emotionally from others. These are identified by Arsenio and Lemerise (2001) as the cold-blooded bullies, and they are the most challenging to work with. Sutton, Smith, and Swettenham (1999) concluded that such bullies are likely to be cold, manipulative, and highly skilled in social situations; they may pose a higher risk to the safety of other children. They also have significantly higher levels of self-esteem than their classmates (Salmivalli, Kaukiainen, Kaistaniemi, & Kirsti, 1999). Failure to deal with this type of bully as a discipline problem will likely encourage continued bullying behavior. The first task of any intervention with this category of bully is the need to develop some motivation for change. The second task is to get the family involved in the intervention plan (Hoover & Oliver, 1996).

Outcomes for Children Who Bully

The long-term prediction for bullies is not good. Research shows that bullying is a strong predictor of juvenile delinquency and community violence (Baldry & Farrington, 2000; Colvin, Tobin, Beard, Hagan, & Sprague,1998). The most striking conclusions have been drawn from the work of Olweus (1993), who found that former bullies were four times more likely to engage in criminal behavior. At the age of twenty-four, 60 percent of former bullies in his study had one or more criminal convictions, and 35 percent of this sample had three or more convictions. Bullying is learned early in life. We must seek earlier identification and treatment.

PEER SEXUAL HARASSMENT

In contrast to the bullying research, sexual harassment research does not have detailed descriptions of harassers and victims and has been framed as more of an environmental issue located within schools. Students may be victimized by harassment or perpetrate it, but the behaviors are viewed as creating a hostile environment within the school rather than as negative individual personality traits.

The AAUW report *Hostile Hallways*, first conducted in 1993 and repeated in 2001 and 2011, lists examples of harassment:

♦ Made sexual comments, jokes, gestures, or looks
♦ Showed, gave, or left you sexual pictures, photographs, illustrations, messages, or notes
♦ Wrote sexual messages/graffiti about you on bathroom walls, in locker rooms, etc.
♦ Spread sexual rumors about you
♦ Said you were gay or lesbian
♦ Spied on you as you dressed or showered at school
♦ Flashed or "mooned" you
♦ Touched, grabbed, or pinched you in a sexual way
♦ Intentionally brushed up against you in a sexual way
♦ Pulled at your clothing in a sexual way
♦ Pulled off or down your clothing
♦ Blocked your way or cornered you in a sexual way
♦ Forced you to kiss him/her
♦ Forced you to do something sexual other than kissing (AAUW, 2001, p. 2)

The 2011 survey also included questions about sexual harassment through the use of Facebook, e-mail, and other electronic means.

In the 2011 AAUW study, approximately half of the students reported being sexually harassed by a peer. The 1993 AAUW study was the first to document a high level of sexual harassment experienced by boys as well as girls; these levels continue to hold true in the latest study (2011). In the 2011 study, 56 percent of the girls and 40 percent of the boys reported being sexually harassed by a peer at school. Thirty percent of students (36 percent of girls and 24 percent of boys) reported harassment through electronic means. Eighteen percent of all boys and 14 percent of all girls surveyed in the 2011 study admitted that they have sexually harassed someone in the school setting. Of the students in the 2011 AAUW study who said that they had sexually harassed someone in the school setting, 86 percent claimed they themselves had been harassed (92 percent of girls and 80 percent of boys). Additional findings from the AAUW (2011) and previous studies found that students who experience sexual harassment reported more school absence, lowered concentration, and less class participation. These studies also reported physical symptoms including sleep disturbance and appetite changes. Students reported feeling angry, upset, and threatened by sexual harassment, all of which contributed to lowered self-esteem and confidence (AAUW, 1993, 2001, 2011; Fineran & Bennett, 1999; Fineran & Bolen, 2006; Stein, Marshall, & Tropp, 1993; Strauss & Espeland, 1992).

Same-Sex Sexual Harassment

A certain amount of sexual harassment is same-sex harassment. In the AAUW (2001) study, 18 percent of girls reported being sexually harassed by other girls, while 45 percent of the boys reported being harassed by other boys. In the AAUW (2011) report, 16 percent of the students admitted targeting other students; 72 percent of the males targeted other males, while 41 percent of the females targeted other females. The negative implications of this are clear. Eighteen percent of all students surveyed stated that being labeled as "gay" or "lesbian" distressed them. For boys, this finding provoked the strongest reaction. Trigg and Wittenstrom (1996) state, "Boys were most disturbed by behaviors that threatened their masculinity, such as being called homosexual or being sexually harassed by other boys" (p. 59). They found that the only harassing behavior that boys experienced at a higher rate than girls was being called "gay."

In a study of 712 high school students Fineran (2001, 2002) found that sexual minority students experienced sexual harassment more frequently than heterosexual students. Sexual minority students and heterosexual girls reported being significantly more upset and threatened by peer sexual harassment victimization. In addition, sexual minority students were physically assaulted more frequently than were heterosexual students. Gruber and Fineran (2007) conducted a study on middle and high school students that examined sexual orientation, bullying, and sexual harassment. They found that lesbian middle school girls were more apt to experience ridicule (bullying) and sexual harassment than were their heterosexual classmates. Among high school students, lesbians experienced more sexual harassment than their heterosexual peers.

The AAUW (2011) study inquired about attributes students thought would lead to being sexually harassed. Girls viewed by peers as being physically well developed and pretty, girls who were considered unattractive, boys who were not considered athletic or masculine, and both sexes if overweight were viewed by peers as possible targets for harassment. The 2011 National School Climate Survey found that 35.5 percent of middle school students and 21.4 percent of high school students experienced physical harassment related to sexual orientation or gender expression (Kosciw, Greytak, Bartkiewicz, Boesen, & Palmer, 2012). Klein (2006) in an examination of school shootings theorizes that "gay bashing" is a related aspect of normalized masculinity, where "boys identified as homosexual as well as boys perceived as 'feminine' or 'weak' by others, but self-identified as heterosexual, are victims of unrelenting peer abuse" (p. 152).

Legal Issues in Sexual Harassment

Legislation and Regulation. Much of our understanding of sexual harassment in the schools has evolved from court decisions involving the workplace and Title VII of the Civil Rights Act of 1964. In general, the interpretation of what constitutes sexual harassment in the educational setting has followed the concepts developed under employment discrimination law. Title VII of the Civil Rights Act of 1964 (42 U.S.C. § 2000e-2[a]) provides the principal framework prohibiting discrimination on the basis of race, color, religion, national origin, and sex. This legislation defines peer sexual harassment as a sex discrimination issue (Fineran & Bennett, 1998).

In 1980 the Equal Employment Opportunity Commission (EEOC) issued a definition of sexual harassment, including specific guidelines to prohibit it (EEOC, 1980, pp. 74676–74677). Six years later, the U.S. Supreme Court upheld two categories of sexual harassment: quid pro quo and hostile environment (*Meritor Savings Bank v. Vinson,* 1986). The Office of Civil Rights, which oversees the enforcement of Title IX, restated these definitions in the 1997 release of *Sexual Harassment Guidance* (USDOE, 1997). Written expressly for schools, *Guidance* defines quid pro quo and hostile environment as follows:

> Quid pro quo harassment occurs when a school employee explicitly or implicitly conditions a student's participation in an education program or activity or bases an educational decision on the student's submission to unwelcome sexual advances, requests for sexual favors, or other verbal, nonverbal, or physical conduct of a sexual nature. Quid pro quo harassment is equally unlawful whether the student resists and suffers the threatened harm or submits and thus avoids the threatened harm.

> Hostile environment harassment, which includes unwelcome sexual advances, requests for sexual favors, and other verbal, nonverbal, or physical conduct of a sexual nature by an employee, by another student, or by a third party, is behavior that is sufficiently severe, persistent, or pervasive to limit a student's ability to participate in or benefit from an education program or activity, or to create a hostile or abusive educational environment. (USDOE, 1997, p. 12038)

It is the hostile environment definition that addresses peer sexual harassment, based on part three of the EEOC (2000) guidelines, which hold employers responsible for the actions of their employees. In education this definition has been expanded to include a school's responsibility for the actions of both its employees and students. According to the Office of Civil Rights' *Sexual Harassment Guidance,* "A school will be liable under Title IX if its students sexually harass other students if (1) a hostile environment exists in the school's programs or activities; (2) the school knows or should have known of the harassment; and (3) the school fails to take immediate and appropriate corrective action. . . . A school's failure to respond to the existence of a hostile environment within its own programs or activities permits an atmosphere of sexual discrimination to permeate the educational program and results in discrimination prohibited by Title IX" (USDOE, 1997, pp. 12039–12040).

Title IX requires that an institution receiving federal funds provide an environment free of discrimination and sexual harassment; it directs educational institutions to maintain a grievance procedure that allows for prompt and equitable resolution of all sex discrimination, including sexual harassment. Thus, a person experiencing sexual harassment has the following options: filing a grievance under Title IX within the school system, filing a complaint with the regional Office of Civil Rights of the USDOE, or suing in court for damages. Title IX does not make a school responsible for the actions of harassing students but rather for its own discrimination in failing to correct the situation once the school has been given notice.

Schools have been held accountable by Title VII and Title IX for over thirty years, and since 2000 the number of cases of sexual harassment filed by students has steadily increased. The USDOE recorded eleven sexual harassment complaints (including adult-to-student cases) by elementary and high school students in 1991 and twenty-five by college students. For the years 2000 to 2013, the combined number of Title IX sexual harassment complaints equaled 1,767 for elementary/secondary schools and 1,172 for postsecondary schools. Complaints now average approximately 126 per year for elementary/secondary schools and 83 for postsecondary schools (D. Campbell, Office for Civil Rights, personal communication, April 25, 2014).

The increase and reporting of behaviors called "bullying" prompted the Office of Civil Rights of the USDOE to advise schools in a "Dear Colleague" letter (USDOE Office for Civil Rights, 2010) to distinguish between behaviors that are inappropriate and harmful (bullying) from those that constitute a violation of Title IX (sexual harassment). They advised that "by limiting the school's response to a specific application of its antibullying disciplinary policy, a school may fail to properly consider whether the student misconduct also results in discriminatory harassment." They continued with the warning that such neglect "may lead to inadequate or inappropriate responses that fail to remedy violations of students' civil rights" (USDOE Office for Civil Rights, 2010). Unfortunately, bullying prevention training has frequently become the primary training tool used by school administrators while sexual harassment has slowly been subsumed under the expanding rubric of "sexual bullying" or "cyber bullying" (Stein, 2010). The "Dear Colleague" letter put schools on notice that many recent "bullying" cases were in fact sexual harassment and needed to be addressed as such.

Case Law. Court decisions have indicated that schools and school personnel who knowingly fail to respond to harmful conditions, such as peer sexual harassment, are made responsible and can be legally liable.

A landmark case decided by the Supreme Court in 1992, *Franklin v. Gwinnett County (GA) Public Schools,* made it clear that students who suffer sexual harassment and other forms of sex discrimination may seek monetary damages from their school districts and school officials for violation of their civil rights. Prior to that case damages were not included in the compensation awards, so schools had little incentive to address this issue.

In 1999 a Supreme Court decision concerning student-to-student sexual harassment, *Davis v. Monroe County Board of Education* (1994), found that schools are to be held responsible for student-to-student sexual harassment when the schools have been informed of the offending behaviors. The Court also ruled that schools would be liable for monetary damages "only if they were 'deliberately indifferent' to information about 'severe, pervasive, and objectively' offensive harassment among students" (Walsh, 1994, p. 10). In the state of New York, a sixth-grade girl was taunted with sexual comments and physically abused by boys in her class (*Bruneau v. South Kortright Central School District,* 1996). She filed charges under Title IX and recovered compensatory damages, punitive damages, and attorney fees. The school district was found liable because teachers and administrators knew of the assaults but took no action (Jones, 1994).

Many cases filed by students involve the sexual harassment of males by other males, and lawsuits have been dismissed because of the ambiguity of prior court decisions on whether same-sex sexual harassment is actionable. In Utah a sexual harassment lawsuit (*Seamons v. Snow,* 1994) filed by a male high school football player against his male teammates "was dismissed on the grounds that the boy failed to prove that he had been a victim of any concerted discriminatory effort" (Stein, 1999, p. 38). This football player had been taped naked to a towel rack by four of his teammates, who then brought in a girl (involuntarily) to view him. The school called it hazing and did not believe this was abnormal behavior for boys.

In two separate yet similar cases, one filed in California and the other in Massachusetts, two girls were harassed by female schoolmates. Both girls experienced sexual taunts, graffiti, and rumors of the girls' alleged sexual behavior with boys. In both cases the school had been notified of the sexual harassment but had not responded. In fact, the California school had decided that sexual harassment could occur only between students of the opposite sex. The Office of Civil Rights, which heard both of these cases, concluded that there had been "pervasive, persistent, and severe sexual harassment in violation of Title IX and that the school districts had inadequate grievance procedures for prompt and equitable resolution of complaints of sexual harassment" (Stein, 1995, p. 157).

Nabozny v. Podlesny (1996) concerned a gay male student who was harassed for four years. During this time he was called names, struck, spat on, and subjected to a mock rape. He brought suit under the equal protection clause, prevailed, and received substantial damages. The court ruled that the school was unjustified in allowing students to assault another student based on sexual orientation. He was entitled to an equivalent level of protection under 42 U.S.C. § 1983, claiming violation of his Fourteenth Amendment rights (*Nabozny v. Podlesny,* 1996).

These cases of same-sex sexual harassment if litigated today would most likely have positive outcomes due to the landmark Supreme Court decision, *Oncale v. Sundowner Offshore Services* (1998) that defined same-sex sexual harassment as actionable. Bringing suit under the Fourteenth Amendment is another venue that students (and adults) can pursue, although after the Oncale decision, the issue of same-sex sexual harassment should be clearer under Title VII, thus providing direction for Title IX cases. In addition, a bill under review by Congress as of this writing entitled the Safe Schools Improvement Act amends the Elementary and Secondary Education Act of 1965 to require schools receiving federal funds to adopt codes of conduct specifically prohibiting bullying and harassment based on sexual orientation and gender identity. Once signed into law, this bill would strengthen a student's right to an equal education under Title IX (Safe Schools Improvement Act).

RESPONSES TO BULLYING AND SEXUAL HARASSMENT

Policies will not work unless they reverberate with the culture of the school. A culture of violence, intimidation, and retaliation needs to be changed. This is a complex and difficult task. Many schools have developed sexual harassment policies and procedures that legislate behavior and are more reactive than proactive. This approach places the burden directly on the student to file a complaint and face the response. Stein (1995) pointed out that arbitrary rules can be problematic. One school district banned all physical touching due to numerous complaints from female students about being sexually assaulted by a football player. Lee, Croninger, Linn, and Chen (1996) pointed out that it is difficult to think that a policy of punishing the perpetrator and protecting the victim will be effective in eliminating (peer) sexual harassment in schools. The victim–perpetrator model breaks down when the majority of students are both perpetrator and victim (AAUW, 1993; Fineran & Bennett, 1998). Using the school as a courthouse with a jury of one's peers may also be questionable (Stein, 1995). Blaming the victim by "popular vote" can have perverse effects. A popular student accused of sexual harassment could paradoxically gain status as a victim, whereas the student who points the finger becomes the accuser and is blamed for provoking the behavior.

Although schools want to offer support to students affected by bullying and sexual harassment, the realities of a victim–perpetrator relationship complicate the situation enormously. This fact poses clinical and policy dilemmas. It would be easy to say that social workers need to provide support groups for victims or perpetrators, and in many circumstances this would be appropriate. However, some students who are victims may be retaliating or perpetrating in self-defense, and other students who are perpetrating may find themselves being victimized. Furthermore, the focus on the victim–perpetrator relationship alone has the effect of shifting the focus away from the normative culture of the school, which may implicitly permit, or even demand, interpersonal violence and retaliation.

One of the main complaints from students experiencing bullying and sexual harassment is that it occurs in front of school personnel who do nothing to stop it, and in these cases inaction supports interpersonal violence (AAUW, 1993, 2001, 2011; Stein et al., 1993). Teachers may be hesitant to intervene unless they are sure that consequences for the behavior are in place and will be enforced. A more direct course, recommended in the best practices guide (Dwyer et al., 1998), is for anyone in the school community who is present when students are being harassed or intimidated to intervene. Social workers would work closely with teachers and support them in providing immediate intervention when they observe bullying and sexual harassment. Students are encouraged to move away from their role as participant observer to band together and warn or report their peers when they see harassment. As civil rights attorney Catherine MacKinnon (1979) suggested, the unnamed should not be taken for the nonexistent. Students and teachers should be encouraged to name bullying and sexual harassment and not accept it as normal adolescent behavior.

Some policy approaches to the problem are bound to be ineffective because they do not address the basic issues, which are issues of moral and ethical solidarity. Denial of the existence of the problem, or its suppression, will not work. Neither will purely formal changes in the school's discipline code or grievance procedures. What Lee et al. (1996) identified as the ethical approach has a much broader and deeper focus. Shared values and ethical or moral concepts that bind members together as a community are most important. From Lee et al.'s perspective, sexual harassment is a sign of the failure of existing organizations to instill ethical coherence and integrity in their members. Schools need to take responsibility for teaching the basic tenets of respect for others, for self, and for a moral community. Lee et al. supported a cultural theory approach utilizing the ethical dimensions where "more discussion of basic democratic values" is encouraged and "moral and ethical questions are hotly debated" (p. 409). Stein and Sjostrom (1994) believed that sexual harassment needs to be considered a matter of social injustice, and schools should promote democratic principles.

CONCLUSION

Bullying and sexual harassment are both significant problems in schools, and public policies to address these issues have emerged both through legislation and regulation, and through case law. School social workers have opportunities to intervene to address these issues in schools today. Chapter 24 describes the development of safe and responsive schools, and the approaches in schools to address prevention and intervention with bullying, sexual harassment, and other forms of interpersonal violence.

References

American Association of University Women (AAUW) Educational Foundation. (1993). *Hostile hallways: The AAUW survey on sexual harassment in America's schools* (Research Rep. No. 923012). Washington, DC: Harris/Scholastic Research.

American Association of University Women (AAUW) Educational Foundation. (2001). *Hostile hallways: Bullying, teasing and sexual harassment in school.* Washington, DC: Author.

American Association of University Women (AAUW) Educational Foundation. (2011a). *Hostile hallways: Bullying, teasing and sexual harassment in school.* Washington, DC: Author.

American Association of University Women (AAUW) Educational Foundation. (2011b). *Crossing the Line: Sexual harassment at school.* Washington, DC: Author.

Arsenio, W. F., & Lemerise, E. A. (2001). Varieties of childhood bullying: Values, emotion processes, and social competence. *Social Development, 10*(1), 59–73.

Baldry, A. C., & Farrington, D. P. (2000). Bullies and delinquents: Personal characteristics and parental styles. *Journal of Community and Applied Social Psychology, 10*(1), 17–31.

Bond, L., Carlin, J. B., Thomas, L., Rubin, K., & Patton, G. (2001). Does bullying cause emotional problems? A prospective study of young teenagers. *British Medical Journal, 323,* 480–484.

Bruneau v. South Kortright Central School District, 935 F. Supp.162, N.D.N.Y. (1996).

Carney, J. V. (2000). Bullied to death: Perceptions of peer abuse and suicidal behavior during adolescence. *School Psychology International, 21*(2), 213–223.

Civil Rights Act of 1964, Pub. L. 88-352, 78 Stat. § 241 (1964), Title VII, 42 U.S.C. § 2000e-2(a) (1994).

Colvin, G., Tobin, T., Beard, K., Hagan, S., & Sprague, J. (1998). The school bully: Assessing the problem, developing interventions, and future research directions. *Journal of Behavioral Education, 8*(3), 293–319.

Curtner-Smith, M. E. (2000). Mechanisms by which family processes contribute to school-age boy's bullying. *Child Study Journal, 30*(3), 169–186.

Davis v. Monroe County (GA) Board of Education, 862 F. Supp. 863 (M.D. Ga. 1994), rev'd, 120 F.3d 1390 (11th Cir. 1997) (en banc). Rev'd and remanded to district court, 119 S Ct. 1661 (1999).

Duncan, R. D. (1999). Peer and sibling aggression: An investigation of intra- and extra-familial bullying. *Journal of Interpersonal Violence, 14*(8), 871–886.

Dwyer, K., Osher, D., Warger, C., Bear, G., Haynes, N., Knoff, H., . . . & Stockton, B. (1998). *Early warning, timely response: A guide to safe schools: The referenced edition.* Washington, DC: American Institutes for Research.

Elementary and Secondary Education Act of 1965, 20 U.S.C. § 2701 et seq. (1965).

Eslea, M., & Smith, P. K. (2000). Pupil and parent attitudes toward bullying in primary schools. *European Journal of Psychology of Education, 15*(2), 207–219.

Fineran, S. (2001). Sexual minority students and peer sexual harassment in high school. *Journal of School Social Work, 11*(2), 50–69.

Fineran, S. (2002). Sexual harassment between same-sex peers: The intersection of mental health, homophobia, and sexual violence in schools. *Social Work, 47*(1), 65–74.

Fineran, S., & Bennett, L. W. (1998). Teenage peer sexual harassment: Implications for social work practice in education. *Social Work, 43,* 55–64.

Fineran, S., & Bennett, L. W. (1999). Gender and power issues of peer sexual harassment among teenagers. *Journal of Interpersonal Violence, 14,* 626–641.

Fineran, S., & Bolen, R. M. (2006). Risk factors for peer sexual harassment in schools. *Journal of Interpersonal Violence, 21*(9), 1169–1190.

Gruber, J. E., & Fineran, S. (2007). The impact of bullying and sexual harassment on middle and high school girls. *Violence Against Women, 13*(6), 627–643.

Haynie, D. L., Nansel, T., Eitel, P., Crump, A. D., Saylor, K., Yu, K., & Simons-Morton, B. (2001). Bullies, victims, and bully/victims: Distinct groups of at-risk youth. *Journal of Early Adolescence, 21*(1), 29–49.

Hoover, J. H., & Oliver, R. (1996). *The bullying prevention handbook: A guide for principals, teachers and counselors*. Bloomington, IN: National Educational Service Press.

Jones, M. M. (1994). Student sues school for sexual harassment by other students. *Lawyer's Weekly USA, 94,* 12–13.

Kaltiala-Heino, R., Pilla, M., Ruan, W. J., Simmons-Morton, B., & Scheidt, P. (2000). Bullying at school: An indicator of adolescents at risk for mental disorders. *Journal of Adolescence, 23*(6), 661–674.

Klein, J. (2006). An invisible problem: Everyday violence against girls in schools. *Theoretical Criminology, 10*(2), 147–177.

Kosciw, J. G., Greytak, E. A., Bartkiewicz, M. J., Boesen, M. J., & Palmer, N. A. (2012). *The 2011 National School Climate Survey: The experiences of lesbian, gay, bisexual and transgender youth in our nation's schools*. New York: GLSEN.

Kumpulainen, K., Raesaenen, E., & Henttonen, I. (1999). Children involved in bullying: Psychological disturbance and the persistence of the involvement. *Child Abuse and Neglect, 23*(12), 1253–1262.

Lee, V. E., Croninger, R. G., Linn, E., & Chen, X. (1996). The culture of sexual harassment in secondary schools. *American Educational Research Journal, 33*(2), 383–417.

MacKinnon, C. A. (1979). *Sexual harassment of working women*. New Haven, CT: Yale University Press.

McGee, J., & DeBernardo, C. R. (1999, May/June). The classroom avenger: A behavioral profile of school shootings. *Forensic Examiner, 8,* 16–18.

Meritor Savings Bank v. Vinson, 106 S. Ct. 2399, 40 EPD ¶ 36,159 (1986).

Nabozny v. Podlesny, 92 F 3d 446 (7th cir. 1996).

Nansel, T. R., Overpeck, M., Pilla, R. S., Ruan, W. J., Simmons-Morton, B., & Scheidt, P. (2001). Bullying behaviors among U.S. youth: Prevalence and association with psychosocial adjustment. *Journal of the American Medical Association, 285*(16), 2094–2100.

Olweus, D. (1993). *Bullying at school: What we know and what we can do*. Cambridge, MA: Blackwell Press.

Oncale v. Sundowner Offshore Services, Inc., 523 U.S. 75 (1998).

Rigby, K. (2000). Effects of peer victimization in schools and perceived social support on adolescent well-being. *Journal of Adolescence, 23*(1), 57–68.

Rigby, K., & Slee, P. (1999). Suicidal ideation among adolescent school children, involvement in bully-victim problems, and perceived social support. *Suicide and Life-Threatening Behavior, 29*(2), 119–130.

Safe Schools Improvement Act, U.S. House (H.R. 1648) and U.S. Senate (S. 506).

Salmivalli, C., Kaukiainen, A., Kaistaniemi, L., & Kirsti, M. J. (1999). Self-evaluated self-esteem, peer-evaluated self-esteem, and defensive egotism as predictors of adolescents' participation in bullying situations. *Personality and Social Psychology Bulletin, 25*(10), 1268–1278.

Seamons v. Snow, 864 F. Supp. 1111, D. Utah (1994).

Smith, P. K., & Myron-Wilson, R. (1998). Parenting and school bullying. *Clinical Child Psychology and Psychiatry, 3*(3), 405–417.

Smith, P. K., & Shu, S. (2000). What good schools can do about bullying: Findings from a survey in English schools after a decade of research and action. *Childhood: A Global Journal of Child Research, 7*(2), 193–212.

Stein, N. (1995). Sexual harassment in K–12 schools: The public performance of gendered violence. *Harvard Educational Review, Special Issue on Violence and Youth, 65*(2), 145–162.

Stein, N. (1999). *Classrooms and courtrooms: Facing sexual harassment in K–12 schools.* New York: Teachers College Press.

Stein, N. (2003). Bullying or sexual harassment? The missing discourse of rights in an era of zero tolerance. *Arizona Law Review, 45,* 783–799.

Stein, N. (2010, June 4). Keynote address, Massachusetts General Hospital Conference on Bullying, Boston, MA.

Stein, N., & Sjostrom, L. (1994*). Flirting or hurting? A teachers guide on student to student sexual harassment in schools.* Washington, DC: National Education Association.

Stein, N., Marshall, N. L., & Tropp, L. R. (1993). *Secrets in public: Sexual harassment in our schools.* Wellesley, MA: Wellesley College Center for Research on Women.

Strauss, S., & Espeland, P. (1992). *Sexual harassment and teens.* Minneapolis, MN: Free Spirit.

Sutton, J., Smith, P. K., & Swettenham, J. (1999). Social cognition and bullying: Social inadequacy or skilled manipulation? *British Journal of Developmental Psychology, 17*(3), 435–450.

Title IX, Education Amendments of 1972, Title 20 U.S.C. Sec. 1681–1688 (1972).

Trigg, M., & Wittenstrom, K. (1996). That's the way the world goes: Sexual harassment and New Jersey teenagers. (Special Issue: Sexual Harassment). *Initiatives, 57*(2), 55–65.

U.S. Department of Education (USDOE). (1997). *Sexual harassment guidance 1997.* Retrieved from http://www.ed.gov/about/offices/list/ocr/docs/sexhar01.html

U.S. Department of Education (USDOE). (2011). *School crime supplement to the National Crime Victimization Survey.* Retrieved from http://nces.ed.gov/pubs2013/2013329.pdf

U.S. Department of Education (USDOE) Office for Civil Rights. (2010, October 30). *Dear colleague letter—bullying and sexual harassment.* Retrieved from http://www2.ed.gov/about/offices/list/ocr/letters/colleague-201010.html

U.S. Equal Employment Opportunity Commission (EEOC). (1980). *Guidelines on discrimination because of sex. Federal Register, 45,* 74676–74677.

U.S. Equal Employment Opportunity Commission (EEOC). (2000). Interim.

Walsh, M. (1994, Oct. 19). Harassment suit rejected. *Education Week, 14*(7), 10.

Wolke, D., Woods, S., Blomfield, L., & Karstadt, L. (2000). The association between direct and relational bullying and behavior problems among primary school children. *Journal of Child Psychology & Psychiatry & Related Disciplines, 41*(8), 989–1002.

Zuehl, J. J., Dillon, E., Schilling, J. L., & Oltmanns, J. K. (2002, January 26). Student discipline issues. In J. C. Franczek & P. C. Sullivan (Eds.), *Attorneys at Law Eighth Annual School Law Conference.* Unpublished paper.

Section III

Assessment and Practice-Based Research in School Social Work

The need for school social workers to engage in data-driven, evidence-informed practice has never been more pressing, and this section offers a number of practical tools for how school social workers can collect data to inform their assessment of student needs, and additionally collect intervention data to inform their practice going forward.

The first two chapters in this section are chapter 14, "School Social Workers and the Prereferral Process: Problem-Solving Teams and Data-Driven Decision Making," by Michele Capio, Laura Swanlund, and Michael S. Kelly; and chapter 15, "School Social Workers and the Special Education Process: From Assessment to Individualized Education Programs to School Social Work Services," by Michael S. Kelly, Michele Capio, Laura Swanlund, Robert Constable, Galen Thomas, and Erin Gleason Leyba. These chapters bring together new authors Michele Capio and Laura Swanlund (both expert practitioners in engaging in data-driven decision making and writing effective behavior plans) with other authors to further develop the material on these topics from the seventh edition. Finally, updated chapters 16 ("The Screening and Assessment of Adaptive Behavior," by James C. Raines), 17 ("Needs Assessment: A Tool of Policy Practice in School Social Work," by Lyndell R. Bleyer and Kathryn Joiner), and 18 ("Practitioner Research in the Schools: Becoming a Change Agent," by Nancy Farwell) offer practical tools and strategies for school social workers who are seeking to understand the needs of their school clients and then efficiently measure the impacts of their interventions.

Section III
Assessment and Practice-based Research in School Social Work

14

School Social Workers and the Prereferral Process: Problem-Solving Teams and Data-Driven Decision Making

Michele Capio
Laura Swanlund
Michael S. Kelly
Loyola University, Chicago

- ◆ Introduction to Problem-Solving Teams
- ◆ Tier 1: Problem Solving within Universal and Secondary Systems
- ◆ Tier 2: Secondary/Targeted
- ◆ Individual Student Problem-Solving Meeting
- ◆ Tier 3: Tertiary/Individualized (Interventions/Processes)
- ◆ Functional Behavior Assessment and Behavior Intervention Plans
- ◆ Critical Features of Behavior Intervention Plans
- ◆ Person-Centered Planning/Wraparound

INTRODUCTION TO PROBLEM-SOLVING TEAMS

Problem-solving teams involve multidisciplinary team members that use a systematic approach to solving problems with the use of data-based decision making.[1] Team members can include administration, general education teachers, school social workers, school psychologists, specialists, and parents. These teams identify interventions for students, monitor the interventions, and determine the success of the student supports. Interventions are evidence-based strategies and supports that are modified in order to assist students' improved performance (Schwanz & Barbour, 2005). Problem-solving teams are a part of a multitiered systems of support (MTSS), including core, tier 2, and tier 3 structures. The critical features of effective problem-solving teams include the use of student and systematic data; collaboration with staff, students, parents, and community; and following a step-by-step problem-solving model of intervention implementation (Burns, Wiley, & Viglietta, 2008). School social workers are integral members of the problem-solving teams.

Participating in the prereferral process is an important part of the role for school social workers (Kelly, 2008). Most schools have teams that examine student need within general education before considering special education services. Many times these needs are related to academic, social, and emotional concerns (Burns et al., 2008). This is where the role and expertise of the school social worker can be very valuable to ensure that students and their families are served effectively by the prereferral process (Capio, 2013; Kelly, 2008). This chapter will detail the various components of the problem-solving intervention process and locate the school social worker within each of these components.

A primary goal of the problem-solving process is to address student concerns and prevent more significant needs. When examining the social, emotional, and mental health needs for students, it is important to consider why we must have a prereferral process. The outcomes for students with mental health needs are often very poor, including for those who have and have not

---

1. *Editor's note:* This chapter is new for this eighth edition and reflects the changing landscape of intervention for at-risk students in school settings. It is meant to be seen as a complement to chapter 15, "School Social Workers and the Special Education Process: From Assessment to Individualized Education Programs to School Social Work Services," in this eighth edition. Following on the innovation of the three-tiered/response to intervention (RTI) policy changes embedded in the 1997 and 2004 reauthorizations of the special education Individuals with Disabilities Education Act (IDEA) law, the field is now seeing more and more schools adopting a two-part process for addressing student academic and behavioral problems: first, a problem-solving team model that employs data-driven decision making to assess and intervene with at-risk students, to be followed at some later point with the more traditional special education referral model that could result in a student being found eligible for special education services. This chapter discusses the first part of that process in detail and firmly situates this work within the RTI/MTSS framework commonly used in today's schools.

received individualized education program services (Benitez, Lattimore, & Wehmeyer, 2005; Koller & Bertel, 2006).

A school-wide prevention model that includes universal screening, school-wide instruction about social and emotional learning, and tertiary supports for at-risk students can address the mental health needs of children early in order to help prevent negative outcomes (Kutash & Duchnowski, 2006). Students may not have received support until their behaviors became problematic for the staff. By this time there have usually been a lot of negative emotions toward the child and family, and the common responses have usually been punitive, such as suspensions, detentions, and out-of-school placements. The role of mental health professionals was usually isolated. This means that school social workers would spend much of their time seeing students in their office either one on one or in a small group. They would also focus a lot on deficits, as opposed to creating clear and comprehensive plans (Burns et al., 2008).

Examples of systems that could help reverse the negative outcomes for these students include positive behavioral interventions and supports (PBIS), Children And Mentally Ill ParentS (or CHAMPS), wraparound, and systems of care. These are systematic practices that address behavioral and emotional needs (Kutash & Duchnowski, 2006). Through these systems all students receive preventive services, such as rewards for positive behaviors, school-wide celebrations, and a standardized social/emotional curriculum. The prereferral team and process is an essential component to these systems.

TIER 1: PROBLEM SOLVING WITHIN UNIVERSAL AND SECONDARY SYSTEMS

An MTSS offers up a framework to embed and root school social work interventions in systems, data, and practices. The three tiers of prevention are for both the academic and the social/emotional problems that students experience (Kelly, 2008). In this framework, the school social workers' primary focus is on the development and implementation of the three tiers to support students' social/emotional learning (Capio, 2013). Different states and school systems vary on the degree to which they are implementing MTSS in their schools; it is essential that social workers become fluent in the key concepts and practices as they become more and more integrated into our school settings. PBIS is often the behavior side of MTSS in schools.

Universal Behavior Expectations Implemented throughout the Entire School

The core of tier 1 involves defining common expectations and teaching, modeling, reinforcing, and reteaching the school expectations as needed. The outcome is to have at least 80 percent of the student body respond to the structure so that a lower percentage of students need additional supports. In the simplest terms, the school can prevent, teach, and reinforce school-wide expected behaviors. The core of classroom management mimics that of the school-wide implementation (Kelly, 2008). The critical features of universal behavior systems is to define and teach positive behavior, to have clear expectations, to employ a process of recognizing students for engaging in positive behavior, to clearly define what consequences are, and to have a data system to inform future practice (Kelly et al., 2010).

Since the school social worker in most cases has not been trained as a teacher or has no prior teaching experience, it is imperative to learn and understand evidence-based practices for classroom management (Oliver, Wehby, & Daniel, 2011). The school social worker will need to learn to coach these practices in an effort to get that same 80 percent response across each classroom setting so as to avoid overidentifying students with behavioral concerns when, in fact, the structure of the classroom environment is what is problematic. Box 14.1 identifies key evidence-based components to effective classroom management.

Universal Screening

In many mental health prevention systems there are school-wide data sources and/or a mental health screener who helps schools determine students who may need supports and who otherwise would have not been identified as in need of intervention. These screeners focus on behavioral, social, and emotional concerns. The goal is to identify students early and often before a student needs significant support. In all screeners, the staff provides information related to students who meet criteria for risk of mental health needs (Severson, Walker, Hope-Dolittle, Kratochwill, & Gresham, 2007).

In the use of universal screeners, the school uses data to identify students who are in need of additional social-emotional support (Severson et al., 2007). Decision rules are established consistent with community and school data patterns to determine when a student should be identified as

---

BOX 14.1   Evidence-Based Practices in Classroom Management

1. Maximize structure in the classroom.
2. Post, teach, review, monitor, and reinforce a small number of positively stated expectations.
3. Actively engage students in observable ways.
4. Establish a continuum of strategies to acknowledge appropriate behavior.
5. Establish a continuum of strategies to respond to inappropriate behavior.

SOURCE: Simonsen, Fairbanks, Briesch, Myers, & Sugai (2008).

one needing this support. The prereferral teams examine the school-wide systems and use data to determine student needs within the general education environment (Schwanz & Barbour, 2005). If a student needs additional support, he or she is typically scheduled to participate in secondary-level standard protocol group interventions (Schwanz & Barbour, 2005). The school social worker is an integral member of the team in terms of determining the appropriate screener, ensuring adequate administration, and leading data analysis and decision making based on the results (Capio, 2013; Kelly, 2008). Data sources that schools consider might include

- A specific number of office discipline referrals, sometimes called major discipline referrals, that exceeds the number of referrals that are within expected incidence rates for the student's age or grade placement;
- A pattern of repeated minor problem behaviors;
- Referral to the school social worker for social–emotional screening that indicates that additional supports are needed;
- A student who is not successful with standard classroom management procedures;
- A student who has chronic problems with tardiness or excessive absences;
- A student who frequently visits the nurse for nonmedical reasons; or
- A student who demonstrates peer or social interaction difficulties.

In addition to the above data sources, schools often also use a universal screener to determine mental health needs. A few examples include these:

- Systematic Screening for Behavior Disorders (Walker et al., 1990), http://store.cambiumlearning.com
- BASC-2/BESS (Kamphaus & Reynolds, 2007), http://www.pearson assessments.com
- Strengths and Difficulties Questionnaire (Goodman, 2001), http://www.sdqinfo.org
- Student Risk Screening Scale (Drummond, 1994), http://miblsi.cenmi.org/MiBLSiModel/Evaluation/Measures/StudentRiskScreeningScale.aspx
- Social Skills Improvement System (Gresham & Elliott, 2008), http://psychcorp.pearsonassessments.com/pai/ca/cahome.htm

TIER 2: SECONDARY/TARGETED

When student behavior problems spike in schools without MTSS and a strong tier 1 framework, the school social worker is called in to intervene, often cold without any additional information or previous interventions (Kelly, 2008). The expectation is that the social worker can do something to shape the behavior. However, within the framework of MTSS, while the social worker still responds to a teacher request for assistance, the request is usually funneled into the selection of an intervention that will be implemented for a minimum of four to six weeks to determine progress and the need to continue the intervention, modify the intervention, or discontinue it altogether will be determined by the MTSS team that includes both the teacher and the school social worker (Kelly et al., 2010). Tier 2 interventions typically should not be individuated but instead should be designed for groups of students so that students can easily access them and teachers can easily implement them. The group intervention takes place before a team meets to develop an individualized plan for a student. An intervention in tier 2 should be able to support roughly 10 percent of the student body at one time (Hawken, Vincent, & Schumann, 2008).

Some of the critical features involved in establishing effective tier 2 interventions follow:

- ◆ The interventions should be consistent with school-wide expectations and should incorporate similar language.
- ◆ Adequate resources and staff to support the interventions should be dedicated and available before the interventions are begun.
- ◆ The interventions should require low effort on the part of the teacher(s). The intervention(s) recommended should fit well within the classroom or other environments where it is implemented. Interventions that require too much time or too many resources will probably not be implemented consistently and with fidelity. It is important to have the teacher involved when deciding what interventions will be used so it or they will be workable.
- ◆ A system to refer and identify students should be in place, and procedures for referral and identification should be clear to all staff and families.
- ◆ A system should be in place to maintain data-based and timely monitoring of the intervention to decide if it should be maintained, revised, or restructured (Capio, 2013; Kelly et al., 2010).

Common interventions at tier 2 are check-in/check-out (CICO), social/academic instructional groups, and group or individual mentoring.

Check-in/Check-out

Students check in with designated CICO facilitator(s) before the beginning and at the end of each schoolday to receive positive contact, precorrects, reminders of school-wide expectations, and, if needed, basic school supplies. At the end of each class period, classroom teachers provide positive behavioral feedback, based on the school-wide expectations, on a daily progress report (DPR).

Social/Academic Instructional Groups

Youths are supported in a small group for direct instruction of school-wide expectations and/or replacement behaviors, including structured practice and direct behavioral feedback. Teachers provide youths with positive behavioral feedback on a DPR related to their transference of newly learned skills that has been taught during group sessions.

Group or Individual Mentoring

Mentoring involves one adult meeting with one or more students at a time, one or more times per week, to provide precorrects and a positive connection with the school through a supportive relationship (PBISWorld.com, 2014).

At tier 2 the social worker acts primarily as a coordinator. Consider a school that has multiple simple secondary interventions in place, CICO, skills groups, and mentoring. A school social worker could sit on the team that oversees all intervention development and implementation but be the coordinator only for skills groups. That school social worker would oversee the curriculum selection, grouping of students, data tracking, and training of the group facilitators, but not facilitate or lead all groups because time is limited and youths with the highest needs might require more school social worker attention.

Intervention Group Progress Monitoring

Interventions are considered effective when at least 70 percent of students in an intervention meet the criteria for success (Capio, 2013). Each school establishes decision rules consistent with community and school data patterns to determine when a student is successful or when she or he should be identified as someone needing additional tier 2 supports. Finally, the teams examine how all students are responding to the social and emotional supports through a monthly examination of how many students are receiving interventions and how many are responding to the interventions. The problem-solving team discusses these results and makes changes to the practices with intervention implementation as needed.

Prereferral/Individual Problem-Solving Meeting

Sometimes students do not respond to the supports received at tier 1 and tier 2, which may result in an individual problem-solving meeting. At this multidisciplinary meeting, the team engages in the problem-solving process in order to determine individualized supports for students within the general education environment using general education resources. This model involves asking four questions:

1. Is there a problem? If so, what is it?
2. Why is the problem happening?
3. What can be done about the problem?
4. Did the intervention work? (Tilly, 2008).

Parents are essential team members of the problem-solving team.

To fully answer the first question, team members, with the social worker, collect data in order to have a strong understanding of the student's strengths and needs. Data can come from a variety of sources and have different, but essential, purposes for the decision-making process. It is important for the school social worker to be a leader with data when discussing students with social and emotional needs. Without the multiple sources of data available, teams are at risk of making uninformed decisions that would not benefit the child and family (Tilly, 2008).

Assessment before the Problem-Solving Meeting

Strong problem analysis involves analyzing multiple domains using multiple modes of assessment. The domains include examining the student strengths and needs in regard to Instruction (I), Curriculum (C), Environment (E), and Learner (L). This is referred to as the ICEL domains for assessment (Christ, 2008). For each domain, the team members gather information through Review of records (R), Interview (I), Observe (O), and Test (T), referred to as RIOT data collection (Christ, 2008). The ICEL and RIOT assessment data provide key information about student history, what has and has not produced positive outcomes, and environmental factors that should be considered in identifying antecedents and consequences that could be triggering or maintaining problem behaviors (Christ, 2008). Meeting time can be used more efficiently for problem solving rather than to gather data when team members review the information in advance. Figure 14.1 provides guidelines for how to complete the ICEL and RIOT assessment (Christ, 2008).

CASE EXAMPLE

Mark was a third-grade student who was demonstrating difficulties with disruptive behaviors, physical aggression, and inappropriate and disrespectful comments. He had received the tier 1 PBIS instruction and recognition since kindergarten. Due to difficulties with acting-out and disruptive behaviors, tier 2 CICO and individual mentoring were added during kindergarten through third grade. Due to a significant number of office referrals as well as teacher and parent concerns, the problem-solving team met to examine Mark's needs and intervention through the data-based problem-solving process. The team included Mark's teacher, his parents, the school social

FIGURE 14.1   The RIOT and ICEL Process for Problem Analysis

	Review	Interview	Observe	Test
Instruction	*Review instruction* through past report cards and documents	*Interview about instruction* through teacher interviews of classroom management practices	*Observe instruction* through classroom observations	*Test instruction* through examining student functioning with different modes of instruction
Curriculum	*Review curriculum* through work products	*Interview about curriculum* through student and teacher interview about social and emotional skills	*Observe curriculum* through classroom observations	*Test curriculum* through examining student response to diagnostic test of foundational skills
Environment	*Review environment* through folder reviews, office referrals, social or emotional concerns in different settings	*Interview about environment* through parent, teacher, and student interview of social and emotional functioning in different settings	*Observe environment* through behavioral observations in multiple settings	*Test curriculum* through functional behavior assessment
Learner	*Review learner* through history of documented social and emotional supports	*Interview learner* through parent and student interviews about mental health history and functioning	*Observe learner* through behavior-based observations	*Test learner* through behavioral ratings and peer comparison

SOURCE: Christ (2008).

worker, the school psychologist, and the school principal. Before the team meeting, the team worked together to complete the ICEL and RIOT in order to have the data needed to determine if there was a problem and, if so, what the problem was.

Case Example: Part 1, Review of Records

♦ Document series of parent contacts to inform parents of interventions and results of these interventions that led up to the current problem-solving meeting.
♦ Document current vision and hearing screening results (within the past six months).
♦ Record current diagnoses and medication history, and list current outside medical/mental health providers.

Past Interventions

In order for the team to have a complete picture of what interventions the student has received, a team member will document all of the interventions recorded in the student's cumulative or any other temporary student files.

Review should include information from all electronic records, teacher grade books, hard copies of cumulative records, and special education files. Record *all* achievement scores recorded for the student, including scores from interventions.

Current Interventions

The prereferral team documents all current interventions (academic and behavioral) that the student is receiving including the following information:

Case Example: Part 1, Review of Records

The review of records indicated that Mark did not have any academic concerns. All of his academic areas were within the average range. He demonstrated no difficulties with curriculum or instruction in regard to his academic skills.

In reviewing his history in relation to social and emotional functioning, the school social worker reviewed Mark's file. She found that in kindergarten he had had difficulty staying seated and following directions. The social worker worked with the family and teacher during kindergarten to create a sticker chart based on the school-wide values of being safe, respectful, and responsible. The data indicated that this intervention had worked. Mark then moved to another school for first grade. In second grade Mark returned to the first school and, due to his level of functioning, had an individualized mentoring plan until April. He received four office referrals through April, and three more in May. The average student received one or none in a year. A simple behavior plan was created in May of second grade.

Figure 14.2 demonstrated his daily response to the intervention in second grade. Each month shows the average percentage of points he received on his DPR. The goal was to have 80 percent of his points. In April the plan was adjusted to be more targeted with the aggressive and acting-out behaviors.

Case Example: Part 2, Interviews

After the review of the records, the social worker would interview teachers, the student, and the parents. Typically interviews involved unstructured, semistructured, and structured formats. The purpose is to gain understanding of teacher, parent, and student perspectives of the student's strengths and weaknesses within the classroom, school, community, and multiple learning environments (Christ, 2008).

Interviews with the teacher found that there were no concerns with Mark's academic skills within the classroom. He performed well with the general education curriculum and instruction. Mark struggled, however,

FIGURE 14.2   Average Percent of Points Mark Made on the Daily Progress
Report Each Month with a Goal of 80 Percent and Note of
When the Intervention Was Adjusted in April

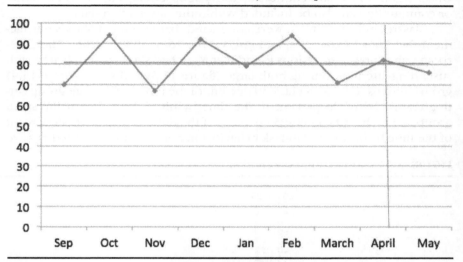

NOTE: Following the creation of the behavior plan, the prereferral continued to examine his response to intervention. In the beginning of second grade, Mark continued to receive the behavior plan, but he did not respond. Therefore, by November there had been multiple parent meetings and the team created a more-intensive plan for Mark.

with different environments. His teachers indicated that when in the large group he often was disruptive and engaged in peer-seeking behaviors. In smaller academic settings, such as in groups of no more than five students, Mark's behavior improved. Acting-out behaviors was still noted, however, by the teachers in the small group. Interviews with the nurse indicated that he was taking medication daily to assist with emotional regulation, and that the nurse frequently communicated with home in regard to his medication. Finally, the interviews with the parents indicated significant concern with Mark's behavior at home as well as at school. His mom stated that he does better with more discipline at home.

Case Example: Part 3, Observations

The multidisciplinary team engages in observations of the student within multiple settings and environments. The team member records the observations that have been completed. Teams include a summary of observations from previous classroom teachers that might inform the problem-solving team of early indicators of similar patterns of student performance. These indicators include teacher observations on the report card comment section from the student's previous teachers.

School social workers often include observations from nonacademic settings, such as during lunch, recess, or small group social work sessions. Observations of the student outside the school setting, such as in the home or community, can also be included within the observation data.

Classroom observations were conducted that examined Mark's engagement, behavior frequencies, and interval recording of behaviors. The classroom behavioral observations found that Mark had significant difficulty with sustaining attention during both large (figure 14.3) and small (figure 14.4) group settings. He was on task 30 percent of the time in the large group setting compared to 90 percent of the time by his male peers. In the small group setting he was on task 50 percent of the time compared to 95 percent of the time by his peers. Off-task behaviors in both settings included passive

FIGURE 14.3   Large Group Observation

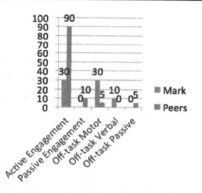

NOTE: Percent of time each behavior was observed for Mark and male peers in a large group setting.

FIGURE 14.4   Small Group Observation

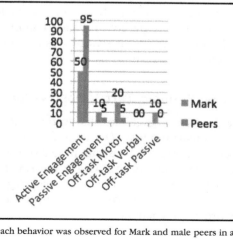

NOTE: Percent of time each behavior was observed for Mark and male peers in a small group setting.

disengagement, movement, and talking with peers. His behaviors were significantly more disruptive than were behaviors of other students.

In addition to examining Mark's time on task during the twenty-minute observations, a count of behaviors was also taken. A recording of the behavior frequencies during large groups (figure 14.5) and small groups (figure 14.6) found that he required a significant amount of individual teacher support, he did not follow directions during the large group setting, and he talked out and touched peers multiple times during the observation.

FIGURE 14.5   Large Group Observation

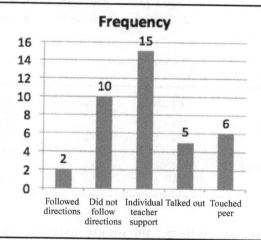

NOTE: Frequency of Mark's behavior that was observed in a large group observation.

FIGURE 14.6   Small Group Observation

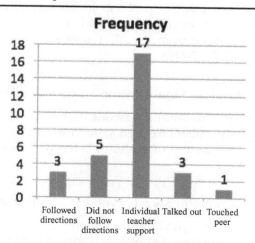

NOTE: Frequency of Mark's behavior that was observed in a small group observation.

Case Example: Part 4, Test

For the final process, the team determines a hypothesis as to why the problem behavior is occurring from information collected through the record review, interviews, and observations. Additional student assessment may be determined as part of this process. Individual assessment is provided as needed.

Given that there were no concerns with Mark's academic skills, the only assessment provided was in relation to social and emotional functioning. Mark's parents provided permission to complete the *Behavior Assessment of Children in Schools,* 2nd Edition (BASC-2) to further understand his level of need in relation to same-aged peers. The data from the teacher rating indicated clinically significant concerns with acting out and internalizing behaviors (table 14.1).

TABLE 14.1   Mark's T Score, Percentile Rank, and Clinical Range on the Parent BASC-2 Rating Scale

Composites	T Score	Percentile	Clinical Range
Externalizing problems	80	98	Clinically significant
Internalizing problems	70	96	Clinically significant
School problems	58	81	Average
Behavioral symptoms	72	96	Clinically significant
Adaptive skills	35	7	At Risk

INDIVIDUAL STUDENT PROBLEM-SOLVING MEETING

Once the prereferral teams collaborate to gather data through the RIOT model, the teams engage in the student problem-solving process. This is a data-based system that involves problem identification, problem analysis, plan development and interventions, and implementation. The team reviews the data provided from the RIOT review and follows the process seen in figure 14.7 (Tilly, 2008).

Step 1: Problem Identification/Statement of Problem

The problem-solving team uses the baseline data from the ICEL and RIOT to provide a description of initial frequency, intensity, and severity of the problem behavior(s). Comparisons of student's behavioral data are made to that of a typical peer.

Case Example: Step 1, Problem Identification

Based on the information gathered through the RIOT assessment, the team determined that the problem was with following directions, keeping hands

FIGURE 14.7   The Problem-Solving Process

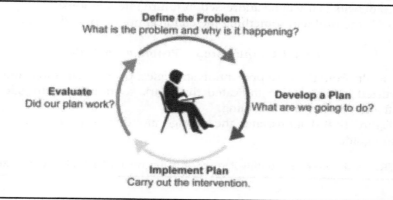

Define the Problem
What is the problem and why is it happening?

Evaluate
Did our plan work?

Develop a Plan
What are we going to do?

Implement Plan
Carry out the intervention.

SOURCE: Tilly (2008).

and feet to self, respectful actions toward adults and peers, and independently functioning in the classroom. Based on this information, the prereferral team examined why the problem was occurring.

To determine why Mark was having difficulty, the team first examined if his difficulty was due to a performance or skill deficit. This means that the team wanted to assess if he had the skills to be respectful, responsible, and safe. Through this the team created a hypothesis for why Mark was struggling. With help from the school social worker, the team determined the following problem analysis.

The problem occurs when he is given directions, is with peers, and has unstructured interactions with others. Functions are to gain peer and adult attention and avoid a task.

Step 2: Problem Analysis/Strengths and Weaknesses

Why Is This Problem Happening?

The problem-solving team describes the student's skill strengths and weaknesses in the identified area(s) of concern within the relevant domains. The team includes data that demonstrate the student's strengths and weaknesses. The information gathered attempts to identify why the problem exists. The data from the ICEL and RIOT process assist with this process.

The problem-solving team addresses the following questions:

1. What were the results of interventions that were tried?
2. Which parts of the interventions resulted in progress and which were not successful?
3. What are the team's hypotheses about why any interventions did not work?

4. Does the team need any additional information to identify skill deficits that will be addressed in future interventions?
5. Is the problem something the child cannot do or will not do?

Case Example: Step 2 Problem Analysis

The results from the core prevention strategies, CICO, mentoring, and individualized behavior plan indicated that Mark continued to struggle with social and emotional functioning:

Figure 14.8 demonstrates the average monthly percent of his DPR in second grade.

FIGURE 14.8   Average Monthly Percent of Points on Mark's Daily Progress Report

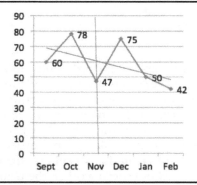

NOTE: Average monthly percent of points on Mark's DPR with a trend line and indication of when the intervention was adjusted in November.

Figure 14.9 provides the number of major office discipline referrals Mark received in second grade.

FIGURE 14.9   Number of Major Office Discipline Referrals Mark Received Each Month

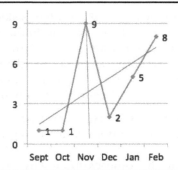

NOTE: The number of major office discipline referrals Mark received each month with a trend line over time and notification of intervention change in November.

An analysis of Mark's DPR in relation to his target behaviors found that the concerns were more likely to occur in the afternoon (figure 14.10), when there was a larger class size and with less adult support.

FIGURE 14.10   Scatterplot of the Amount of Problem Behavior from His Daily Progress Report for Each Behavior and Time Period

	8:35-9	9-9:30	9:30-10	10-10:30	10:30-11	12:15-12:45	12:45-1:15	1:15-1:45	1:45-2:15	2:15-2:50	2:50-3:20	Total
Respect: Follow directions Peer relations Respectful tone	*** *** **	*** ***	***	***	****	**** **** **** *	**** **** **** **	**** **** **** **	**** **** **** **	*** *** *** **	*** *** *** ***	105
Safe: Hands and feet to self	*** *** *	*** **			****	**** **** ***	**** **** ***	**** **** ***	**** **** ***	*** *** *	*** *** ***	77
Responsible: Has all materials Organized Materials	*** *** *** **	*** ***	***	***	**** *	**** **** **** *	**** **** **** **	**** **** ****	**** **** **** **	*** *** *	*** *** *** *** ***	104

Therefore, the plan was more successful when Mark was in a smaller, more-structured environment where he could receive more-frequent opportunities for adult feedback and correction. The team hypothesized that if he were provided with more support throughout the afternoon then he would be able to demonstrate respect, responsibility, and safety throughout the day. Based on the information collected through the RIOT assessment, the team did not need any more details in order to develop further interventions for Mark. They determined that he was able to demonstrate the skills when provided with scaffolding and feedback.

Step 3: Plan Development and Interventions

Once the team has identified and analyzed the problem, the problem-solving team determines further intervention plans including core/tier 1, supplemental/tier 2, and intensive/tier 3 supports. With the information gathered from the problem identification and analysis, the team determines what new interventions will be used to support skill development and/or performance of those skills. Using the data, the team provides a rationale for why the intervention was chosen.

The following areas are addressed with the plan development:

A. How will the success of the intervention be monitored? (Progress monitoring plan)
B. How will fidelity of intervention be documented?

TIER 3: TERTIARY/INDIVIDUALIZED (INTERVENTIONS/PROCESSES)

At tier 3 the social worker is facilitating person-centered or function-based comprehensive planning for an individual student. Because there is a foundation in the school and efficient and effective tier 2 interventions, there are fewer students that show a need for tier 3 interventions and the school social worker has some time freed up to do this work. As a lead facilitator, the school social worker can take ownership of the process while maintaining the integrity of the selected tier 3 process.

FUNCTIONAL BEHAVIOR ASSESSMENT AND BEHAVIOR INTERVENTION PLANS

Functional behavioral assessment (FBA) and behavior intervention plans (BIP) are the most researched and proven processes within the PBIS continuum of interventions/processes (Office of Special Education Programs, 2013). The primary purpose of FBA is to define and understand a behavior that is currently interfering with a child's ability to access his or her education or is prohibiting other children from accessing theirs. The process needs to be teacher driven, beginning with interviews and often leading to observations. Using established tools to support the building of a hypothesis statement adds structure to the process and provides reassurance to the team that they are on the right track. The purpose in conducting an FBA is to identify an observable and measurable behavior, common triggers, and the best guess of what is maintaining and encouraging the behavior to continue (figure 14.11). A hypothesis statement (including triggers, observable behavior, and maintaining consequence/function) must be established before the school social worker moves to the next step of determining an alternative behavior and writing the BIP (Capio, 2013; Crone & Horner, 2012).

CRITICAL FEATURES OF BEHAVIOR INTERVENTION PLANS

When moving toward writing a BIP it is imperative that the problem-solving team referenced earlier in this chapter is called on to support the teacher or team of teachers to write the plan. Writing a BIP alone as a social worker will not produce the impact needed to reshape the behavior of a child in a classroom. The person that owns the environment (teacher) must be in the driver's seat. Facilitating and guiding a team through the process of identi-

FIGURE 14.11   Functional Behavior Assessment Paperwork

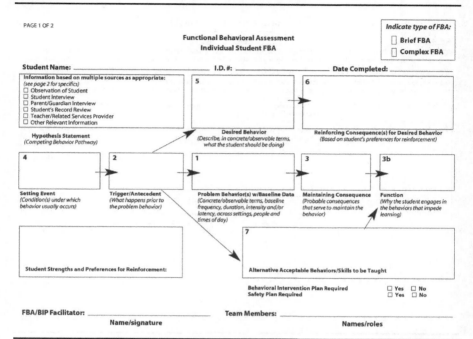

SOURCE: Adapted from Anderson & Borgmeier (2007); and Todd, Horner, Sugai, & Sprague (1999).

fying what will work and what will not work requires a professional trained in group work process and negotiating the needs of multiple stakeholders. Once a team is established and a working hypothesis statement is agreed on, the team can begin to create the plan. The critical components are the following:

1. Replace problem behavior by teaching a socially acceptable and efficient behavior that allows the student to obtain the pay-off/function.
2. Prevent problem behaviors by directly addressing triggers and prompting alternative behaviors based on the function of the behavior.
3. Reinforce the alternative and desired behaviors based on pay-off/function for the student.
4. Redirect problem behaviors by quickly and effectively redirecting students to alternative behavior.
5. Minimize reinforcement by ensuring that the problem behaviors do not pay off for the student.

The behavior plan (figure 14.12) must also include a safety plan if the student is exhibiting dangerous behaviors that put either him- or herself or others at risk (Loman, Strickland-Cohen, Borgmeier, & Horner, 2013).

FIGURE 14.12   Behavior Intervention Plan Paperwork

Behavorial Intervention Plan (BIP)

Student name: _____   **Referred by:** _____   **Date** _____

Hypothesis statement: Describe problem behavior in concrete terms and provide baseline measure, including frequency, duration, and intensity across activities, settings, people, and times of day, as well as the global or specific hypothesis as to why the problem behavior occurs. Fill in blanks below to complete an accurate statement for this youth.

When (setting event) and (antecedent) (student) does (problem behavior for how long, how many times, at what intensity) to get/avoid _____

Brainstorm possible elements of behavior support; select strategies that are contextually appropriate for final plan, and list them below. Provide 1 or more strategies for each section. Multiple stakeholders should be included in providing these supports. *Remember to reference the corresponding sections of the FBA to ensure alignment.*

Setting Event Strategies	Antecedent Strategies Behavior	Teaching Strategies	Consequence Strategies
Prevent or neutralize setting event's	Prevent problem behavior	Teach alternative behavior	Reinforce use of desired behavior Reinforce use of alternate behavior
	Prompt alternative behavior	Teach desired behavior/academic/social skills Academic:	Response to problem behavior that minimizes reinforcement (i.e. extinction)

SOURCE: Adapted from Anderson & Borgmeier (2007) and Todd et al. (1999).

Now that the FBA and BIP are complete the team needs to be guided through the process of determining contextual fit of the plan and what planning needs to take place for implementation. Contextual fit refers to the extent to which support strategies "fit" with

◆ The skills and values of the implementers,
◆ The available resources, and
◆ Administrative structure/support.

Strategies with good fit are more likely to be implemented accurately and consistently (Loman et al., 2013). When considering implementation planning, a good action planning system will help in determining who will do what by when for each strategy. Consider

◆ Specific activities that will be involved,
◆ Developing materials (e.g., reinforcement system),
◆ Designing and teaching curriculum,
◆ Data collection design,
◆ Identification of personnel that is responsible for implementing each part of the intervention, and
◆ Times for when each part of the plan will be implemented.

The last step of completing this process will be determining how the plan will be evaluated. There are two components with any intervention that must be reviewed: the degree to which the intervention was actually implemented and the impact that the intervention had on the student. Fidelity measures for the plan could include reviewing each strategy four weeks into the plan as a team and rating the degree to which the team followed through on the strategy (figure 14.13).

FIGURE 14.13   An Implementer's Checklist and Evaluation Plan from Basic Functional Behavior Assessment to Behavior Support Plan Trainer's Manual

FBA-BPI
Sample Implementer's Checklist & Evaluation Plan

Question	Yes (every day this week)	Kind of (2–3 days this week)	No (0 days this week)	Notables *
1. With each strategy that is listed on the behavior plan you state as a question and ask the team if it occurred. For example. Did we meet with Mark each morning as planned?		X		We missed M/W because the teacher was caught in a crisis.
2. Insert Strategy				
3. Insert Strategy				
4. Insert Strategy				
5. Insert Strategy				
6. Insert Strategy				
7. Insert Strategy				
TOTALS				

SOURCE: Loman et al. (2013).

How social workers measure the student outcome data will be a team decision, however; again, social workers need to consider the ease of the teachers' ability to track the data. Progress-monitoring the plan will aid the team when making decisions about what strategies to keep, modify, or discontinue.

PERSON-CENTERED PLANNING/WRAPAROUND

There is more than one method for community or school-based wraparound. However, the process of school-based wraparound is primarily centered on the same values of self-determination and the voice of the person the plan is centered around. Wraparound is a process for developing family-centered teams and plans that are strength and needs based, which is in contrast to the deficit-based problem solving that schools often engage in. School-based wraparound is a meaningful process when all of the adults involved are having a difficult time getting on the same page and the reshaping of behavior is not going to touch the bigger need of the child and family. This process will serve as a holistic, family-centered process that allows for the rebuilding of trust and working together.

The Ten Principles of Wraparound

The ten principles of wraparound are discussed next (Eber et al., 2009; National Wraparound Initiative, 2014; PBIS, 2014).

1. Family Voice and Choice. Family and youth/child perspectives are intentionally elicited and prioritized during all phases of the wraparound process. All planning includes family members' perspectives, and the team strives to provide options and choices to ensure the plan reflects family values and preferences. Family involvement comes with accountability and responsibility.

2. Team-Based Decision-Making. The wraparound team consists of individuals, agreed on by the family or through mandates, who are committed to the family through either informal or formal community support and service relationships.

3. Natural Supports. The team actively seeks out and encourages the full participation of team members drawn from family members' networks of interpersonal and community relationships. The wraparound plan reflects activities and interventions that draw on sources of natural support.

4. Collaborative Teaming. Team members work cooperatively and share responsibility for developing, implementing, monitoring, and evaluating a single wraparound plan. The plan reflects a blending of team members' perspectives, mandates, and available resources. The plan guides and coordinates each team member's contribution toward meeting the team's (and family's) goals.

5. Community-Based Interventions. The wraparound team implements service and support strategies that take place in the most inclusive, most responsive, most accessible, and least restrictive settings possible; and that safely promote child and family integration into home and community life.

6. Culturally Competent Planning and Intervention Implementation. The wraparound process demonstrates respect for and builds on the values, preferences, beliefs, culture, and identity of the child/youth and family, and their community.

7. Individualized Strategies. To achieve goals laid out in the wraparound plan, the team develops and implements a customized set of strategies, supports, and services unique to the youth's and family's identified needs.

8. Strengths-Based Interventions. The wraparound process and the wraparound plan identify, build on, and enhance the capabilities, knowledge, skills, and assets of the child and family, their community, and their team members.

9. Unconditional Care. Despite challenges, the team persists in working toward the goals included in the wraparound plan until the team reaches agreement that a formal wraparound process is no longer required.

10. Outcome-Based Processes and Progress Monitoring. The team ties the goals and strategies of the wraparound plan to observable or measurable indicators of success, monitors progress in terms of these indicators or outcomes, and revises the plan accordingly.

Four Phases of Wraparound

The four phases of wraparound are discussed next (Eber et al., 2009; National Wraparound Initiative, 2014; PBIS, 2014).

Phase 1: Engagement. The goals of this phase are to

◆ Establish a rapport with student and family that is transparent and based on trust;
◆ Educate the family about the process so they can make an informed decision to participate;
◆ Explore individual and family strengths, needs, culture across life domains;
◆ Identify the family's big needs;
◆ Identify and engage team members that will support the youth(s) and family through the process; and
◆ Prepare family (and team members) for the first meeting.

Phase 2: Initial Plan Development. The goals of this phase are to

◆ Facilitate initial wraparound meeting;
◆ Develop a team culture;
◆ Develop a family mission;
◆ Develop an action plan;
◆ Complete FBA/BIP—safety plan; and
◆ Integrate the plan across classroom settings and different environments.

Phase 3: Wraparound Implementation. The goals of this phase are to

◆ Ensure that plans are implemented with ongoing monitoring and support;
◆ Ensure the plan works and achieves outcomes;
◆ Review and update the plan over time; and
◆ Improve team cohesion and effectiveness.

Phase 4: Transition. The goals of this phase are to

◆ Ensure there is continuing support after professional facilitation ends;
◆ Update the action and crisis plans; and
◆ Prepare the family to manage its own process.

Case Example: Step 3, Plan Development

The team determined interventions to address the problem and how it would be monitored. Mark continued to receive the tier 1 instruction, social and emotional instructional groups, and the tier 2 CICO with mentoring interventions. Based on the data, the team created a complex behavior plan in order to address his disrespectful behaviors, aggression, and classroom functioning. This plan involved the creation of an FBA and a BIP with the problem-solving team. Through this tier 3 plan the problem-solving team added intensive tier 3 supports that included individual social work. Important features of this plan included a schedule for more adult assistance within the afternoon, structured activities during lunch and recess periods, a hallway escort, and more social work minutes. A daily communication system was developed with the parent in order to have consistent communication with home. This was done through a DPR; Mark's teachers monitored how Mark responded to each target behavior at different times of the day. Mark's DPR is shown in figure 14.14.

FIGURE 14.14   Mark's Daily Progress Report

MARK'S DAILY PROGRESS REPORT

Name: _____   Date: _____   Goal: _____   80% _____

Teachers please indicate: without prompting (2), 1 to 2 prompts (1), No (0) regarding the student's achievement for the following goals.

Goals	1	2	3	4	5/6	7	8	9
Followed teacher directions	2 1 0	2 1 0	2 1 0	2 1 0	2 1 0	2 1 0	2 1 0	2 1 0
Used a respectful tone	2 1 0	2 1 0	2 1 0	2 1 0	2 1 0	2 1 0	2 1 0	2 1 0
Hands and feet to self	2 1 0	2 1 0	2 1 0	2 1 0	2 1 0	2 1 0	2 1 0	2 1 0
Has all materials	2 1 0	2 1 0	2 1 0	2 1 0	2 1 0	2 1 0	2 1 0	2 1 0
Is ready for class	2 1 0	2 1 0	2 1 0	2 1 0	2 1 0	2 1 0	2 1 0	2 1 0
Appropriate peer interactions	2 1 0	2 1 0	2 1 0	2 1 0	2 1 0	2 1 0	2 1 0	2 1 0
Total Points								
Teacher Initials								

Daily Points/112 Parent signature _____

NOTE: Mark's DPR, indicating the replacement behaviors and possible points for each period of the day.

Case Example: Step 4, Schedule a Progress Review Meeting for Progress Four to Six Weeks

After four to eight weeks, the prereferral team meets to review the data and to examine the student's response to the intervention supports received. Student progress in response to secondary interventions is measured using data collected with a DPR. Feedback on the DPR includes a short teacher rating that serves as feedback and provides a way to monitor students' behavior at regular intervals during each day. Student scores and teacher comments on the DPR are collected daily and tracked weekly to monitor progress. Data from student DPRs are used to measure individual student outcomes to determine adjustments that might be warranted when observable change in student behavior that would indicate progress does not occur within a reasonable time frame. Most schools will evaluate student progress within a four- to eight-week time frame or at other regular intervals as determined by the individual student's needs. DPR data are also examined in aggregate across all students in an intervention to evaluate how effective the program is in changing behavior for all students in the intervention.

Often the school social worker helps create, collect, and analyze the data from the DPR. Often spreadsheets such as Excel, or tools such as Google Forms, assist the school social worker in managing the data. Through this the school social worker is able to create charts that demonstrate (1) percentage of points received over time, (2) percentage of points received by target behaviors, (3) percentage of points received by time of day, and finally (4) percentage of points received by location. When these data are used in conjunction with other data frequency measures such as office referrals, problem behavior noted, attendance, or any specific areas of concern, the prereferral team is able to examine the students' responses over time and areas of strength and need.

The following data sources are often used to progress-monitor response to intervention supports for both individual students and groups of students:

◆ DPR data
◆ Data graphs from percentage of time or frequency within a time frame in which student engages in replacement behaviors per BIP
◆ Office discipline referrals and frequency of minor discipline referrals when secondary interventions are in place
◆ Number of tardies or absences when secondary interventions are in place
◆ Results of Standardized Behavior Rating Scales (e.g., BASC-2, BRIEF, or Connors Rating Scale)

Case Example: Step 4, Progress Review

For six weeks the team monitored Mark's progress through his DPR, office referrals, and parent and teacher interviews. The data indicated that in some areas Mark demonstrated improvement, but overall he needed more time to demonstrate the expected behaviors. The social worker interviewed the teacher and parent, who both indicated that they had seen some improvement but were still concerned with Mark's interaction with adults and peers.

First, the team examined the percent of points he earned from the DPR over time. Figure 14.15 shows that his trend moved from about 60 percent to 70 percent, but did not meet the goal of 80 percent.

FIGURE 14.15   Mark Complex Functional Behavioral Assessment/
Behavior Intervention Plan Daily Progress Report Percent

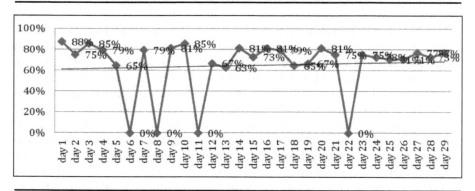

NOTE: Percent of total points Mark received each day on the complex behavior plan with a trend line indicating progress over time.

Next, the team examined how many office referrals Mark received during the time period. The team noted that he received ten major office referrals during the period, which was significantly more than his peers. Most of the referrals were for defiance and inappropriate peer interactions (figure 14.16).

FIGURE 14.16   Office Discipline Referrals Percent by Category (ten total)

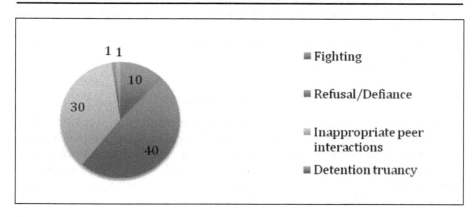

NOTE: Percent of office referrals Mark received by behavior over thirty days.

Finally, the school social worker completed an in-depth analysis of Mark's behavior throughout the day. She first examined how many points he received during each feedback period, and then she examined how many points he received for each behavior (figure 14.17). Finally, she looked for a pattern with the time of day and behavior (figures 14.18 and 14.19). Overall the results demonstrated that for some areas Mark was able to make 80 percent of his points on average (e.g., to follow teacher directions and be ready for class). He continued to struggle, however, with showing respect and with appropriate behavior with peers. The end of the day continued to be the most difficult for Mark. In all, the areas where he lost most of his points were the least structured, due to class size and lack of additional adult support.

FIGURE 14.17   Complex Functional Behavioral Assessment/Behavior Intervention Plan Average Percent

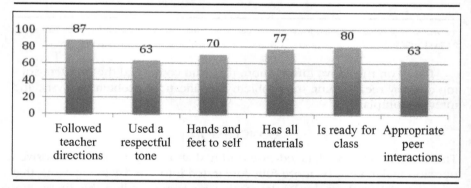

NOTE: Average percent of points Mark received for each behavior on his complex behavior plan.

FIGURE 14.18   Average Percent by Time of Day

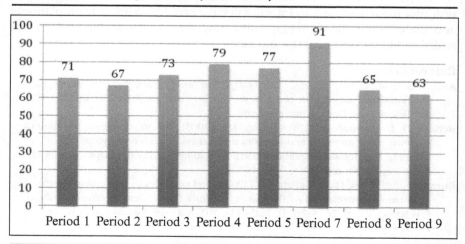

NOTE: Average percent of points Mark received during each time period on his complex behavior plan.

FIGURE 14.19   Average Percent of Points Made by Behavior and Time of Day

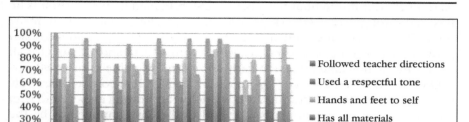

NOTE: Average percent of points Mark received during each time period for each behavior on his complex behavior plan.

Based on the above information, the team continued the problem-solving cycle by reexamining the problem identification, problem analysis, and intervention plan.

CONCLUSION

This chapter, and the detailed case outlined above, shows how data-driven decision making can be more fully integrated into the day-to-day work that school social workers do. We know that for some reading this these concepts may seem more suited to other members of the faculty (e.g., the school psychologist or the team case manager), but it is our strong conviction that the use of data to inform effective problem-solving team planning and interventions is absolutely something that school social workers can and should be doing in 2015 and beyond.

References

Anderson, C. M., & Borgmeier, C. (2007). *Efficient functional behavior assessment: The functional assessment checklist for teachers and staff (FACTS)*. Eugene, OR: Educational and Community Supports.

Benitez, D. T., Lattimore, J., & Wehmeyer, M. L. (2005). Promoting the involvement of students with emotional and behavioral disorders in career and vocational planning and decision-making: The self-determined career development model. *Behavioral Disorders, 30*(4), 431–447.

Burns, M., Ives Wiley, H., & Viglietta, E. (2008). Best practices in implementing effective problem-solving team. In A. Thomas & J. Grimes (Eds.), *Best practices in school psychology* V (pp. 1633–1644). Bethesda, MD: National Association of School Psychologists.

Capio, M. (2013, Summer). *The reality of implementation: School social workers and a three-tiered model of support.* School Social Work Section Connection. Retrieved from http://www.socialworkers.org/sections/areas/archives.asp?sVal=approaches& print=1

Christ, T. (2008). Best practices in problem analysis. In A. Thomas & J. Grimes (Eds.), *Best practices in school psychology* V (pp. 159–176). Bethesda, MD: National Association of School Psychologists.

Crone, D. A., & Horner, R. H. (2012). *Building positive behavior support systems in schools: Functional behavioral assessment.* New York: Guilford Press.

Drummond, T. (1994). *The student risk screening scale (SRSS).* Grants Pass, OR: Josephine County Mental Health Program.

Eber, L., Hyde, K., Rose, J., Breen, K., McDonald, D., & Lewandowski, H. (2009). Completing the continuum of schoolwide positive behavior support: Wraparound as a tertiary-level intervention. In W. Sailor, G. Dunlap, G. Sugai, & R. Horner (Eds.), *Handbook of positive behavior support* (pp. 671–709). New York: Springer.

Goodman, R. (2001). Psychometric properties of the strengths and difficulties questionnaire. *Journal of the American Academy of Child & Adolescent Psychiatry, 40*(11), 1337–1345.

Gresham, F., & Elliott, S. N. (2008). *Social skills improvement system (SSIS) rating scales.* Bloomington, MN: Pearson Assessments.

Hawken, L. S., Vincent, C. G., & Schumann, J. (2008). Response to intervention for social behavior. *Behavioral Disorders, 16*(4), 213–225.

Kamphaus, R. W., & Reynolds, C. R. (2007). *BASC-2 behavioral and emotional screening system manual.* Circle Pines, MN: Pearson.

Kelly, M. S. (2008). *The domains and demands of school social work practice: A guide to working effectively with students, families, and schools.* New York: Oxford.

Kelly, M. S., Frey, A. J., Alvarez, M., Berzin, S. C., Shaffer, G., & O'Brien, K. (2010). School social work practice and response to intervention. *Children & Schools, 32*(4), 201–209.

Koller, J. R., & Bertel, J. M. (2006). Responding to today's mental health needs of children, families and schools: Revisiting the preservice training and preparation of school-based personnel. *Education and treatment of children, 29*(2), 197–217.

Kutash, K., & Duchnowski, A. (2006). *School-based mental health: An empirical guide for decision-makers.* The Research and Training Center for Children's Mental Health, Florida Mental Health Institute, University of South Florida.

Loman, S., Strickland-Cohen, M. K., Borgmeier, C., & Horner, R. (2013). *Basic FBA to BSP trainer's manual.* Retrieved from http://pdxscholar.library.pdx.edu/sped_fac/1/

National Wraparound Initiative. (2014). *Resource guide to wrap-around.* Retrieved from http://nwi.pdx.edu/NWI-book/

Office of Special Education Programs (OSEP). (2013). *OSEP Technical Assistance Center on Positive Behavioral Interventions and Supports: Project overview.* Retrieved from http://www.pbis.org/about-us

Oliver, R., Wehby, J., & Daniel, J. (2011). Teacher classroom management practices: Effects on disruptive or aggressive student behavior. *Campbell Systematic Reviews.* doi:10.4073/csr.2011.4

PBISWorld.Com. (2014). *Guide to tier 2 interventions.* Retrieved from http://www.pbis world.com/tier-2/

Positive Behavioral Interventions and Supports (PBIS). (2014). *Wraparound service and positive behavior support.* Retrieved from https://www.pbis.org/school/tertiary-level/wraparound

Schwanz, K. A., & Barbour, C. B. (2005). Problem-solving teams: Information for educators and parents. *NASP* [National Association of School Psychologists] *Comuniqué, 33*(8). Retrieved from http://www.nasponline.org/publications/cq/mocq338glbt.aspx

Severson, H. H., Walker, H. M., Hope-Dolittle, J., Kratochwill, T. R., & Gresham, F. M. (2007). Proactive, early screening to detect behaviorally at-risk students: Issues, approaches, emerging innovations, and professional practices. *Journal of School Psychology, 45,* 193–223.

Simonsen, B., Fairbanks, S., Briesch, A., Myers, D., & Sugai, G. (2008). Evidence-based practices in classroom management: Considerations for research to practice. *Education and Treatment of Children, 31*(3), 351–380.

Tilly, D. (2008). The evolution of school psychology to science-based practice: Problem solving and the three-tiered model. In A. Thomas & J. Grimes (Eds.), *Best practices in school psychology* V (pp. 17–36). Bethesda, MD: National Association of School Psychologists.

Todd, A. W., Horner, R. H., Sugai, G., & Sprague, J. R. (1999). Effective behavior support: Strengthening school-wide systems through a team-based approach. *Effective School Practices, 17*(4), 23–37.

Walker, H. M., Severson, H. H., Todis, B. J., Block-Pedego, A. E., Williams, G. J., Haring, N. G., & Barckley, M. (1990). Systematic Screening for Behavior Disorders (SSBD): Further validation, replication, and normative data. *Remedial and Special Education, 11*(2), 32–46.

15

School Social Workers and the Special Education Process: From Assessment to Individualized Education Programs to School Social Work Services

Michael S. Kelly
Robert Constable
Loyola University Chicago

Michele Capio
Oak Park Elementary School District 97

Laura Swanlund
Loyola University School of Education

Galen Thomas

Southern Illinois University

Erin Gleason Leyba

University of Illinois at Chicago

- Special Education and the School Social Work Role
- What Are Individualized Education Programs and What Is the Special Education Individualized Education Program Team?
- The Importance of Assessment in the Special Education Process
- Assessment and the Strengths Perspective
- The Case Study Assessment and the Social Developmental Study
- Components of a Case Study Assessment
- A Final Note on School Social Workers' Special Education Assessment
- After the Case Study Assessment and Determining Eligibility: Writing the Individualized Education Program
- Early Childhood Special Education: The Individualized Family Service Plan
- Additional Specific Components of an Individualized Education Program: Functional Behavioral Assessments and Behavior Intervention Plans
- Writing Measurable Individualized Education Program Goals for School Social Work Services: The Process of Setting Goals and Objectives

Many school social workers are involved in determining student eligibility for special education, and many are also involved in providing social work services after a student has been found eligible for special education services. This chapter provides details about each facet of this process from the perspective of a school social worker serving as part of a multidisciplinary team.

SPECIAL EDUCATION AND THE SCHOOL SOCIAL WORK ROLE

The right to a free appropriate public education (FAPE) for a child with disabilities demands a more formalized assessment process (a complete multifaceted nondiscriminatory evaluation) and an individualized education program (IEP) for educational placement. Multidisciplinary teamwork is mandated in special education as part of this process. The team should at least include the parents of the child, a regular education teacher, a school administrator, and a person to interpret the results of testing. The parents are expected to be equal participants along with school personnel in developing, reviewing, and revising the IEP for their child (U.S. Government Printing Office [GPO], 2003, Appendix A, Question 5). School social workers are often members of this team. Their services are defined in the federal regulations to include

1. Preparing a social or developmental history on a child with a disability;
2. Group and individual counseling with the child and family;
3. Working in partnership with parents and others on those problems in a child's living situation (home, school, and community) that affect the child's adjustment in school;
4. Mobilizing school and community resources to enable the child to learn as effectively as possible in his or her educational program; and
5. Assisting in developing positive behavioral interventions and supports (PBIS). (GPO, 2003, 300.24[b][13])

This chapter describes the various components of the special education assessment and intervention process, and locates the specific tasks of the school social worker within the context of the IEP, the IEP team, and the provision of school social work services. Specific components of the special education process, including the case study assessment (CSA), social developmental study (SDS), adaptive behavior assessment, functional behavioral analysis (FBA), and behavior intervention plan (BIP) will also be addressed (Department of Defense Education Activity [DoDEA], 2014; Illinois Legal Aid, 2012).

WHAT ARE INDIVIDUALIZED EDUCATION PROGRAMS AND WHAT IS THE SPECIAL EDUCATION INDIVIDUALIZED EDUCATION PROGRAM TEAM?

School social workers are regularly involved in the special education eligibility/IEP process. Social workers often offer services to students with disabilities within the context of an IEP (DoDEA, 2014; Kelly, 2008). Their unique contribution to the IEP process takes place in at least four major areas. (1) The social worker participates in the IEP team to conduct a case study evaluation, and writes a report called an SDS. (2) If the student is found eligible for special education, the school social worker participates in the process of setting annual goals (and intermediate objectives) as part of the IEP, (3) helps the multidisciplinary team to develop sufficient consensus among itself and with parents to proceed, and (4) is involved with case management and integration of school and outside agency resources (Kelly, 2008). For a detailed case example of the case study/IEP process, see appendix C, "Putting it All Together: A Hypothetical Case Study (Devin)."

The IEP is a program of service that is cocreated by the IEP team to assist a student who has been identified as being eligible for special education services. The IEP team is a group of individuals comprising (1) the parents of a child with a disability, (2) a regular education teacher of the child (if the child is, or may be, participating in the regular education environment), (3) at least one special education teacher of the child, (4) a representative of the local educational agency (LEA) who provides or supervises special education and who is knowledgeable about the general education curriculum, and (5) an individual who can interpret the instructional implications of evaluation results (Illinois Legal Aid, 2012). Parents, as part of the multidisciplinary team, must be included in the decision-making process that determines these resources. The term "parents" may include a biological or adoptive parent, an individual who may have special knowledge of the child such as a foster parent, a guardian (but not the state), a person who is acting in the place of the parent (e.g., a grandparent, stepparent, or other relative) with whom the child lives, or a legally appointed surrogate parent (GPO, 2003, 300.30[a])

Also, whenever appropriate, the students themselves should be included, especially when postsecondary transition is part of the IEP considerations. The emphasis on self-determination would require participation whenever the student is going to be able to manage appropriately in the meeting. Recent reviews of best practices suggest preparation of the student for the meeting when necessary. This preparation may involve some form of verbal rehearsal, role-playing, or the use of verbal, visual, and/or physical prompts as part of this. In addition, student involvement in the meeting can be facilitated by avoiding jargon, using understandable language and vocabulary, and directing questions to the student (Test et al., 2004).

THE IMPORTANCE OF ASSESSMENT IN THE SPECIAL EDUCATION PROCESS

Assessment is a systematic way of understanding what is happening in the student's relations within the classroom, within the family, with peers, and between family and school. It provides a basis for deciding which interventions will be most effective. Thus, it is an individualized effort to identify and evaluate the interrelations of problems, people, and situations (Siporin, 1975). Assessment is more than a one-time, required procedure, or a formal evaluation. It is a continuous, ongoing process in which school social workers engage as they work with students, their families, school personnel, and community agencies. Its power is its focus on the identification of strengths in individuals and systems rather than on deficits alone (Gleason, 2007). Because assessments are individualized to the purpose and context of the assessment, the worker needs to develop a systematic way to gather and evaluate information, sifting out significant details from the potentially vast universe of information available.

ASSESSMENT AND THE STRENGTHS PERSPECTIVE

Because assessment procedures are often used to determine whether a student has a disability and is eligible for special education, they often concentrate on documenting limitations in student performance. Although some information about deficit or risk areas is needed, attending to a student's strengths and talents can ensure that the assessment provides a holistic, balanced perspective of overall functioning (Gleason, 2007). A strengths-based assessment focuses on a student's resiliencies, talents, connections, skills, and gifts (Cowger, Anderson, & Snively, 2006). It attempts to understand the supportive elements in the environment that help a student grow or respond effectively to stress. It explores how a student has been resilient or has adapted successfully when faced with challenges (Wang, Haertel, & Walberg, 1999). In a strengths-based assessment, questioning strategies attempt to identify what works and how it works. During assessment interviews, the social worker might use

- Exception questions ("When things were going well, what was different?");
- Survival questions ("How have you managed to survive this far?");
- Support questions ("What people have given you special understanding, support, and guidance?"); and
- Esteem questions ("What accomplishments in your life have given you pride?") (Parton & O'Byrne, 2000; Saleebey, 2006).

The relationship-oriented process of eliciting examples of a student's strengths and talents builds trust among the social worker, the student, and the family (Gleason, 2007). When the social worker communicates a student's strengths in reports and at meetings, the interdisciplinary team is able to acknowledge the student's progress, existing skills, humanity, heroism, and courage. The team can use detailed information about previously successful supports and interventions to advocate that these effective strategies be replicated and further developed (Gleason, 2007; Kelly, 2008). The team can also use information about a student's strengths and talents to address problems and risk areas through creative methods.

The approaches proscribed in special education laws, detailed here and elsewhere in this book, have created profound changes in the entitlements of children with disabilities to a FAPE (Illinois Legal Aid, 2012; Kelly, 2008). These changes in entitlements have been linked to overrepresentation (in relation to their expected frequency in a population) of students in certain categories, such as specific learning disability, and overrepresentation of minority students. Additionally, a deficit approach to assessment regularly leads school teams to categorize the student with a special education label, resulting in placement outside of general education when it is not clear that special education services are needed (Bean, 2011; Mallett, Stoddard-Dare, & Workman-Crewnshaw, 2011).

In many ways the issues presented in this chapter exemplify some of the limitations of a deficit approach. Students can be caught in categories. Well-intentioned special educators and related service professionals can unintentionally ignore strengths because of the push for categorization. Power struggles develop. Members of the team might stay within their specialties and lose the student and the meaning of the situation. Students believe they are trapped in special education no matter what they do. Parents, particularly minority parents or parents of high school students, can be left out (Bean, 2011; Kelly, 2008). These concerns have led to the gradual development of an approach that would focus on strengths, outcomes, and collaboration. To do this strengths-based collaboration in schools requires school social workers to make their way into the complicated dynamics of the classroom (Gleason, 2007).

THE CASE STUDY ASSESSMENT AND THE SOCIAL DEVELOPMENTAL STUDY

Assessment brings everything together by creating a picture of how students function in a learning situation, with their families, with their peers in their school, and in the larger community. CSA is a more formal assessment process in which school social workers participate (DoDEA, 2014; Kelly, 2008). The CSA is a compilation and analysis of information concerning those life experiences of the child, both past and present, that pertain to his or her problems in school. The CSA includes information from many sources, including the student, parents/foster parents, teachers, other school personnel, involved agency personnel, and other significant people outside the school, such as extended family or other caretakers (DoDEA, 2014; Illinois Legal Aid, 2012). When the CSA is used as part of the evaluation for services for a child with a disability, it should include an assessment of the student's adaptive behaviors, discussed briefly in this chapter and more fully in chapter 16. Although the CSA is sometimes referred to as the social history, a tool often used by social workers to understand client dynamics, the CSA has additional components that make it more comprehensive than a social history. The CSA includes a basic description of the following:

1. The student
2. The student's current social functioning and the presenting problem
3. Observations in classroom(s) as well as other less-structured school environments
4. An individual interview with the student

5. The student's sociocultural background
6. Any events or stressors possibly contributing to the problem
7. Other significant life experiences
8. Current abilities of the student

The CSA is an assessment of the whole child in his or her environment. It focuses on identified strengths as well as on areas in need of support. It brings into focus the developmental systems and ecological factors that affect the child's learning and behavioral patterns (DoDEA, 2014; Illinois Legal Aid, 2012). By involving the family in this information gathering, the school social worker can begin a cooperative working relationship between parents or guardian and the school that may not have been present earlier. The relationship with the family formed by the social worker when he or she compiles a CSA can continue through the development and implementation of an educational plan. Even if it is a brief contact, this relationship frequently can have a positive impact on the parents or guardians, helping them to address feelings of anxiety or alienation from their child's educational experience. Parents may also be eager to share positive information about their children. Social workers can ask, "What is your son or daughter good at?," "What does your son or daughter do that makes you proud?," and "What time do you enjoy most with your son or daughter?" By eliciting positive stories and examples of the child's resiliency from parents, the social worker can build trust and help the team further understand the child's gifts and needs (Gleason, 2007).

COMPONENTS OF A CASE STUDY ASSESSMENT

The CSA assembles the evaluations done by the school social worker into a single written statement. With the addition of professional judgment, the foundations for the social worker's recommendations emerge. We outline ten components that contribute to the gathering of information for a CSA:

1. Student interview(s)
2. Parent interview(s)
3. Social history and current functioning
4. Significant health history and current health needs
5. Socioeconomic and cultural background
6. Assessment of the student's learning environment
7. Observation of the student in the school (in classrooms, in individualized tasks, in a structured group, in the playground, and ideally in the home environment)
8. Consultation with the student's current and (preferably) previous teachers
9. Review of student files (grades, discipline, achievement testing)
10. Consultation with other staff and agencies when necessary

Although the potential wealth of descriptive information gathered through this process may go beyond the scope of one's assessment focus, only information directly pertinent to the child's educational progress that does not breach the right to confidentiality of the parent or child may be included in the written report. As a useful concrete framework, we can outline nine components of the CSA:

1. Identifying Information

A. The child's name, birth date, school, grade, and teacher
B. Each family member's name, age, relationship to the child, educational background, occupation, employment, address, and marital status
C. Names of other persons living in the home and their relationship to the child
D. Race/ethnicity of the family
E. Brief impression of the child at your initial meeting

2. Reasons for Referral

A. The stated reasons for the referral and any specific questions that should be addressed
B. The problem (the child's learning or behavior) as described by the teacher, parent, or others
C. At least three significant interventions that have been used to try to correct the situation
D. The immediate precipitating events that prompted the referral
E. A checklist of specific behaviors that interfere with the learning process

3. Sources of Information. A list of dates and sources of data obtained should include, but not be limited to, the following:

A. Home visit(s) or alternative modes of interviewing parents, guardians, or other relatives
B. Social worker's or others' interview(s) with the child
C. Review of school records
D. Outside evaluations
E. Observations of the student ideally in various settings, but at least in the classroom and one unstructured situation (e.g., recess)
F. Review of health history
G. Teacher interviews

4. Developmental History

Developmental milestones may be significant and can include problems that occurred during pregnancy and delivery, or any unusual conditions at birth.

This information conveys an understanding of the child over time to determine whether development is progressing appropriately. Developmental history from infancy forward should include tolerance of frustration, sources of frustration, and what parental coping strategies have been employed. Emotional development includes the ability to successfully get needs met and to develop satisfying age-appropriate relationships.

The CSA can include any traumas, hospitalizations, accidents, health problems, or chronic conditions, disabilities, unusual problems, or chronic need for medication, if relevant to the child's educational functioning. The school social worker needs to consider the reasons for absences from school. The child's stamina, energy level, and length of attention span in specific situations or times of day can be significant. The child's physical appearance and conduct while in the company of the social worker should be noted in the CSA. This information can form the basis for an evaluation of the child's strengths and areas of need, and will be useful for the team, particularly if the information provides a different perspective on the student. Significant health issues can provide important clues to why children have developed learning or behavioral problems.

5. School History

The school history for young children begins with day care, nursery school, preschool, and early childhood classes and experiences. Increasingly, children experience group learning and day-care facilities from infancy forward. The section on school history should include a chronological account of informal and formal learning experiences, including their changes and interruptions and the child's progress or lack of progress to date. School records are quite useful. For an experienced school social worker, a cumulative record can give a clear indication of the issues and directions in the student's life, learning patterns, and what appears to work and to not work. The record would reveal attendance patterns, progress rates, special instructional assistance, testing results, and remarks of teachers. In addition, the parents' attitudes toward early learning situations, their involvement with their child's learning, and their expectations of the school are all important data. The school history can also include a current classroom observation to explore how the school history matches current behavior in the classroom.

6. Cultural Background, Family History, and Current Issues

The assessment of cultural background is done to determine how the child's culture or background affects his or her ability to function in school as well as whether the school and community are responding appropriately. All children have a cultural background. It includes the family's ethnicity and primary language spoken in the home, the degree of English-speaking proficiency, the usual mode of communication (spoken, sign, etc.) utilized by the student and the family, and the family's socioeconomic status relative to the community. In a dynamic sense, how do the family and the student process the meanings from their culture and from the broader culture? Children's understanding of their cultural background may include ethnic customs, special observances, and unique dress or food not shared by others their age, as well as how they come to experience the larger society. An appropriate assessment might read in part as follows:

> Ranjit's family is of East Indian origin, and they observe Sikh traditions. They currently reside in a community with about 25 percent minority population; however, only one other family is of East Indian background, and is also of Sikh tradition. Fluent in English and in their own language, both of Ranjit's parents come from professional families in India. Economically, Ranjit's family seems to be about average in this solidly middle-class community. Though the family is close knit, they feel well respected and comfortable with their neighbors. Ranjit speaks only English and in many ways appears more adapted to the culture of his peers than to the culture of his parents.

In addition, this section on cultural background may include information specific to this family's history or dynamics—for example, length of marriage, separations, divorces, deaths, remarriages, moves, transfers, changes in child care, presence or absence of various family members, and other significant events. Observations of the child's role in the family, family expectations, opportunities for friends outside of school, and sense of humor can all contribute to understanding the child as a person in the environment. The atmosphere within the family (which may be temporarily in crisis) should be noted, along with the family's methods and abilities, individually and as a unit, to cope with stressful situations. Because, as previously mentioned, some of this information may be highly sensitive and confidential, an agreed-to substitute statement may be needed, such as, "Some current difficulties in the home make consistent parental support difficult at this time." Because the focus is on the student's functioning, the impact of the situation on the student's functioning is more important than what actually happened in the family.

7. Assessment of Current Functioning

Sensitivity of family members to the child's problem and the family's ability, time, temperament, and willingness to be helpful are important. The parents' view of the child's personality, the interrelationships between family members, the family's interests, activities, hobbies, and leisure activities all give clues to possible recommendations to help the child. Special attention is given to a child's interests at home, how he or she seems to learn best, areas of giftedness, hobbies, and special opportunities the child has for learning. Any maladaptive tendencies toward temper tantrums, fears, impulsivity, enuresis, sleep disturbances, stealing, or other difficulties should be noted. Additionally, some students may require a more in-depth assessment of their adaptive behavior: How age-appropriate is their behavior in relation to peers? How do their behavioral issues in school affect their learning? (Those latter issues are often described through an FBA, discussed more fully later in this chapter.) Though not all students will have an adaptive behavior component or FBA completed as part of their case study, we offer some detail here to show how these parts fit into the overall assessment.

Functions of Behavior. Normally students are expected to behave in class in ways that address the tasks of their own learning and do not interfere with the learning of others. When students are off-task or interfere with others, it is assumed that their behaviors may serve functions of seeking attention from the teacher or others in the class, communicating their needs to teacher or peers, or avoiding academic tasks (Zuna & McDougall, 2004). These functions cover motivations for a wide range of behavior and are a good beginning. Raines (2002) goes farther to suggest needs from the perspective of normal development: for autonomy, individuation, and control; for self-esteem; to regulate stimulation; and to set some structure in what may be perceived as an unstructured environment. Other functions of behavior, maladaptive and less amenable to immediate change, may be a need to repeat a learned scapegoat role, to create safety from imagined threats, to display grandiose invulnerability, to be punished, to have revenge, or to derive pleasure from the discomfort of others (Raines, 2002).

Antecedents in the Classroom. Each classroom is different, reflecting the teacher's preferred style and the composition of the classroom group. To begin to understand these differences we need to consider

1. The number of students in the classroom;
2. The resources available;
3. The amount of freedom a teacher has to individualize and modify curriculum or select alternative behavior management techniques;
4. The amount of time to individualize for one student's needs;
5. The degree of pressure placed on teachers for accountability through state and district high-stakes testing and the effect of that on the learning process;
6. The group composition and atmosphere of the class: How many prosocial students? How many students with difficulties? How much time is available on task? How much distraction is there? and
7. The teacher's preferred style and repertoire of teaching approaches to respond to a situation or to the needs of particular students (Barnhill, 2005).

Understanding the learning environment demands that we first understand the realities a particular teacher is facing. We cannot really advocate for an individual student without advocacy for the teacher's needs, and without empathy for the teacher's reality. Without some understanding of the pressures on teachers, social workers will have difficulty developing a working relationship with them or even gaining their acceptance of the assessment information (Berzin et al., 2011; Bradshaw, Pas, Goldweber, Rosenberg, & Leaf, 2012). Teachers have different styles that can be effective with certain types of students. Some teachers are very comfortable with their firmness and can work compassionately with students needing limits. Others do better with youngsters by using patience, warmth, and nonpossessive concern. We believe it is important for school social workers to practice with teachers the same attitudes they typically are trained to use with students and parents. They should exhibit a nonjudgmental attitude, start where the teacher is, exercise positive regard, and assume teachers are doing their best given the amount of support they have, available resources, and the extent of their experience.

The Importance of the Student Interview. An understanding of the student's perspective often comes with experience, from the teacher's account, and from observation, but there is hardly a substitute for the learning contained in a direct interview with the student. In the interview, the social worker can explore whether personal or family factors are supporting, assisting, discouraging, or distracting the student. The social worker might ask the student about his or her interests and supports through questions such as, "If you had to join one sport, hobby, or club, what would it be?" "What is one way you're a good friend?" "What is your favorite part of the day?" "What are you most proud of?" "How has your family helped you out?" (Gleason, 2007). Answers can offer rich clues as to how to potentially rekindle the student's motivation, build on talents, and capitalize on existing supports.

Adaptive Behavior Assessment and Other Standardized Measures. In some cases, students show social, communication, and daily living deficits that are maladaptive and pose challenges to their functioning with age-peers in school. In these cases, school social workers may elect to assess the student's overall adaptive behavior related to their functioning in school, home, and community. We outline multiple resources and strategies for doing this in chapter 16 in this book.

In addition to tools that are used to assess adaptive behavior, school social workers should consider using standardized measures to establish possible clinically significant areas of concern (e.g., depression, anxiety, autism, attention deficit disorder). While not the sole diagnostician in the IEP team, school social workers should avail themselves of useful assessment tools when considering these issues as part of their SDS. A useful resource for reviewing the strengths and weaknesses of any specific instrument is the Mental Measurements Yearbook (Geisinger, Spies, Carlson, & Blake, 2007), which is available in most university libraries and online. Raines and Van Acker (2009), Van Acker, Boreson, Gable, and Potterton (2005), and chapter 16 in this volume also provide guidelines on how to identify which instrument may be best suited to the evaluator's needs. It is particularly important to consider issues such as whether the instrument has data to demonstrate that the scales are reliable and valid for the characteristics being assessed, and whether it is possible to triangulate information from more than one informant. It is also essential to consider whether the social worker has the educational background and training to use the instrument being considered. Some instruments specify that the user is expected to have the background and training of a psychologist. Others qualify the instruction with the admonition that it is ultimately the responsibility of the evaluator to determine whether he or she has the training to adequately administer, report, and interpret the results of the assessment instrument.

The necessary training to administer and report the results of an instrument is often available from others in the district or through workshops. The person administering will usually make a report to the team. Here there must be some selection of relevant findings from a mass of quantitative scores, but the qualitative information gathered as part of the SDS will make a considerable difference. Interpretation is best done by the team as a whole, particularly persons with graduate training in tests and measurements and day-to-day familiarity with the instrument. In any case, the key element in the SDS is the social worker's analysis and synthesis of significant information from a variety of sources using multiple methodologies. This requires going well beyond the computer-generated reports produced by some assessment instruments.

8. Evaluation, Summary, Conclusions, and Recommendations

The final part of the CSA is a concise summary of the meaningful information, including how these experiences affect the child's educational progress. This forms the basis for the social worker's recommendations regarding the educational needs of the child, the best learning environment, parent counseling, available school-based services, and further diagnostic evaluations. Specific recommendations about how parents can be helpful and supportive are appropriate. Because the CSA is a diagnostic tool and is often essential in assessing the severity of emotional problems and mental retardation, school social workers must carefully collect and evaluate the data to ensure their accurate contribution to a differential assessment.

9. Signature

The CSA ends with the name and professional qualification of the writer (e.g., Susan Smith, MSW and/or LCSW) and the date of completion of the document.

Confidentiality is a frequent concern in writing a CSA. The social worker may be given sensitive information that has a direct bearing on the student's presenting issues, but it may be inappropriate to share the information with other school personnel. "Sometimes social data is very personal and its potential prejudicial effect may outweigh its diagnostic values" (Byrne,

Hare, Hooper, Morse, & Sabatino, 1977, p. 52). If the assessment focuses more on a student's strengths and coping mechanisms rather than on the details of his or her so-called problems, then confidentiality quandaries can dissipate (Gleason, 2007). Another important approach to managing confidentiality in the CSA is to assure the parents early in the initial interview that this confidential information will not be shared with the school unless the parents give their permission or unless withholding it would endanger the health or welfare of the child. One procedure in keeping with this approach is to prepare the study in the form in which it will be presented and give the parent(s) the opportunity to read it and correct factual inaccuracies. This procedure gives the parents concrete emotional assurance that confidentiality will be honored and adds trust to the social worker–parent relationship. Often the social worker and parent can collaborate on wording that will convey concern without revealing sensitive details. In rare cases, information to which the parents object may need to be included. Such information is included only if it is accurate and critical to decisions to be made about the child's educational needs.

A FINAL NOTE ON SCHOOL SOCIAL WORKERS' SPECIAL EDUCATION ASSESSMENT

The SDS contributes to the overall CSA, and assists in evaluating a student's possible eligibility for special education services. The SDS is the social worker's contribution to the complete, multifaceted, and nondiscriminatory evaluation of the student's needs as required by law. This complete evaluation becomes the basis for the team's planning for and with students with special needs through development of IEPs. The SDS is an analysis and synthesis of the information gathered from various sources into a concise presentation of those life experiences of the child, both past and present, that pertain to the child's educational experiences. It needs to address cultural, environmental, and familial influences on the student's behavior and learning processes. It should contain an adaptive behavior assessment of the youngster's behavior patterns and functional abilities both in and outside of the learning environment. In the case of youngsters with discipline problems, it may need to include an FBA, the basis for a behavioral intervention plan (both of which we discuss in detail below, this chapter). The SDS provides information to the team that can guard against inappropriate labeling or placement of a child. The SDS is written in educational language (behavioral descriptions, not psychological diagnoses) and should not include the social worker's recommendations for interventions that address the stated concerns. These will be developed later at the team meeting and by the entire team. Thus, specific identification of a special education category or recommendation for placement is not appropriate. A special education category designation, such as behavior disorder, learning disability, and so forth, is the result of the compilation of the findings of the full multidisciplinary team, including the parents, as an outcome of the multidisciplinary conference. Only when the child's learning needs have been identified from a variety of different perspectives in the meeting can the multidisciplinary team determine potential special education eligibility and the most appropriate and least restrictive environment (or placement; LRE) in which the student's needs can be met.

AFTER THE CASE STUDY ASSESSMENT AND DETERMINING ELIGIBILITY: WRITING THE INDIVIDUALIZED EDUCATION PROGRAM

Once the team has determined that a student meets the criteria for a specific disability, the team writes an IEP. The IEP is the central management tool used to ensure the child with disabilities receives a FAPE. The IEP assembles recent evaluation, present decision making, and future expectations in one document. It is a synopsis of the service efforts of the IEP team. It reflects the assessment effort that has previously taken place and the areas of need identified by a team of qualified professionals and the parents of the child. It involves the people who have interest in the child's education and who attend the IEP staffing: the parents, various members of the IEP team (e.g., the teacher, administrator, psychologist, and other specialized personnel) when appropriate, and the child.

The IEP goes beyond a simple report or a plan. It is the living record of a complex evaluation and goal-setting process, which has taken place among parents, school, and child. The IEP is also a program that outlines the educational resources necessary to accomplish the goals. And these become the basis for the civil right of the child with disabilities to FAPE. If signed and not contested, it is concrete evidence that consensus has been reached. The decision-making process aims for an agreement in seven crucial areas:

1. The child's present level of academic achievement and functional performance. The social work SDS has studied the relation between appropriate social and developmental tasks, present functional performance, and academic achievement. The school social worker establishes baselines in different areas on which measurable goals and objectives can be constructed. The school social worker will mainly contribute to the child's IEP in the areas of functional performance.
2. How the child's disability affects the child's involvement and progress in the general education curriculum. This begins to align the assessment with the general education curriculum and its district-wide assessment processes. When a child cannot participate in the regular assessment, there must be an appropriate alternative assessment, aligned to alternative achievement standards, selected by the team.

3. Measurable annual goals. Goals are measurable academic and behavioral (functional) outcomes achievable over a period of one year or less. Goals are made up of short-term objectives, the measurable steps or benchmarks that may lead to the achievement of goals.
4. The program—that is, the special education and related services to be provided for or on behalf of the child. This includes program modifications to enable the child to make progress in general education and/or supports for school personnel. For school social workers, direct individual or group work with the student can be a related service. Consultation on behalf of the student can be a support or involve a program modification.
5. A statement of the extent to which the child will not participate with children without disabilities in the regular class, with or without support services. This underlines the importance of the LRE for the child with disabilities. The negative wording ("not participate") is meant to bring the team to justify nonparticipation in a general education environment, rather than to assume an environment that is directly matched to the child's learning needs but is more restrictive. School social workers have important responsibilities assisting the team to develop this optimal match.
6. The projected dates for initiation of services, planned modifications, and the anticipated frequency, location, and duration of those services and modifications.
7. Beginning at age sixteen, goals of postsecondary transition to training, education, employment and, where appropriate, independent living skills, as well as the needed transition services to reach these goals (GPO, 2003, 300.320; 20 U.S.C. 1414 et seq.).

Transition services are a coordinated set of activities for a student, designed within an outcome-oriented process that promotes movement from school to postschool activities. The coordinated set of activities is based on the individual student's needs, taking into account the student's preferences and interests. It includes instruction, community experiences, the development of employment and postschool adult-living objectives, and, when appropriate, acquisition of daily living skills and a functional vocational evaluation. If a participating agency other than the educational agency fails to provide agreed-on services, the educational agency would reconvene the IEP team to identify alternative strategies to meet the transition objectives.

Although the law specifies an individualized transition plan for students sixteen or older with certain variations as the student grows older, the term "transition" has also been applied to all movement from one level to another. For example, as a five-year-old child with severe disabilities moves from early childhood special education to kindergarten, school social workers and their problem-solving teams should develop an appropriate transition plan. Whenever there is a delicate transition from one environment to another, there needs to be planning, and the social worker probably should be involved. To do good transition planning, the school social worker needs a broad, ecological perspective on the relations of the student to the home, the school, and the community resources. She needs to understand the possible process of transition, and the supports needed to make the transition successful.

EARLY CHILDHOOD SPECIAL EDUCATION: THE INDIVIDUALIZED FAMILY SERVICE PLAN

Another separate but related aspect of the K–12 IEP process involves early childhood students and their families. The individualized family services plan (IFSP) grows out of early intervention programs for infants and toddlers and the obvious necessity of family involvement with children from birth through two years of age, especially children with multiple disabilities. Many of the principles underlying the IEP are also applicable to the IFSP and need not be repeated. There are several differences, however, because the IFSP is more comprehensive than the IEP and takes in a wider universe. The IFSP has first of all a focus on development, rather than a more static focus, appropriate to the older child. The IFSP is evaluated through a variety of means and instruments. In addition, a statement of the family's strengths and needs relating to enhancing the child's development is needed. A statement of the family's strengths and needs requires a family assessment and is best carried out by the school social worker. An agreement on goals, objectives, and tasks needs to emerge from this mutual assessment between social worker and family. In addition, the coping and adaptation of parents, siblings, and support systems in an extended family and friendship network need to be assessed.

The IFSP must contain

1. A statement of the child's present levels of development (cognitive, speech/language, psychosocial, motor, and self-help);
2. A statement of the family's strengths and needs relating to enhancing the child's development;
3. The measurable outcome criteria, procedures, and timelines for determining progress;
4. The specific early intervention services necessary to meet the unique needs of the child and family, including the method, frequency, and intensity of service;
5. The projected dates for the initiation of service and the expected duration;
6. The name of the case manager; and
7. Procedures for transition from early intervention into the preschool program (Bruder, 2010).

Schools must evaluate the IFSP at least once a year and must review it every six months or more, where appropriate. The family is of crucial importance at the earliest stages of dealing with the possibility that a child has a disability. There is often a heavy involvement with the health-care system, and this is confusing at a time when parents are just beginning to bond with a child: Whose child is this, ours or the health-care system's (or the school's)? The health-care system and the school actually have similar concerns with families. If either system seeks to displace the family, the result can be chaos. When there are multiple specialists, parents often have a great deal of case management to do at a time when they are most uncertain of their role. Working with the parents, when care patterns have not been completely solidified, may prevent the most crippling effects of these disrupting patterns on the family and especially on the child with a disability.

Expected Outcomes. The IFSP, a statement of expected outcomes and an agreement on a type of partnership, can be used as the basis for the social worker's intervention with the child and the family. Based on the assessment and the particular contacts developed with the family, major expected outcomes now can be stated in a way that reinforces the primary roles of parents as educators as well as caregivers and the appropriate assistance of the school in carrying out its related mission. A key outcome will be the family's participation in the teaching and caregiving roles and ability to use the case management process. The expected outcomes are largely based on (1) the assessments previously made of the child's present levels of development, and (2) the new coping and adaptation patterns becoming established in the family. Although educational and medical specialists have an important role in setting achievable developmental outcomes, social workers should also be involved in setting such family outcomes and showing their relation to the student's developmental outcomes.

Service Coordination. The IFSP must contain the name of the service coordinator from the profession most immediately relevant to the infant's, toddler's, or family's needs who will be responsible for the implementation of the plan in coordination with other agencies or persons. She coordinates services to the family of an infant or toddler with a disability to assist in gaining access to early intervention services identified in the IFSP. Service coordination includes

1. Coordinating assessments and participating in the development of the IFSP;
2. Assisting families in identifying available service providers;
3. Coordinating and monitoring the delivery of services, including coordinating the provision of early intervention services with other services that the child or family may need or is receiving, but that are not required under this part; and
4. Facilitating the development of a transition plan to preschool services where appropriate. (*Federal Register,* 2000)

The coordinator then assists parents in gaining access to these services. The social worker's role places him or her closest to the parents in carrying out service coordination responsibilities. The final part of the IFSP is that of the child's transition from an early intervention program to the preschool program. Although this is frequently the domain of the educational specialists, the process and the timing of the entry of the child from a family context into a new program with new demands may be an area in which the school social worker needs to participate.

The family involvement projected in the IFSP need not be confined to infants and toddlers. When children present complex vulnerabilities and long-established patterns that inevitably affect the educational process, it is simply good practice to involve the parents in the work of the school. The IEP and the IFSP can be no better than the process of thinking, communicating, and decision making they represent. They certainly are accountability documents, but they also are vehicles for collaboration with parents and for coordination of resources and development of the working agreements necessary for complex goals to be achieved. The IFSP and the IEP are challenges for social workers in developing clarity about what they will be offering students, parents, and the school, while providing an opportunity to work systematically with all of the influences on the full educational process. It is an opportunity that we cannot afford to let pass.

Summary

The IEP encapsulates the entire provision of special education and related services as well as the evaluation of the effectiveness of those services. It is ultimately a list of services to be provided to reach agreed-on goals. Although the IEP cannot guarantee the child will actually reach these particular goals, it is an agreement on the school's part to provide or purchase (if it cannot directly provide) the special education and related services listed in the document. If necessary resources are unavailable within the school district, the school must contract with outside agencies, individuals, or other school districts to ensure their provision—thus the importance of listing the program and setting measurable goals for each program component.

ADDITIONAL SPECIFIC COMPONENTS OF AN INDIVIDUALIZED EDUCATION PROGRAM: FUNCTIONAL BEHAVIORAL ASSESSMENTS AND BEHAVIOR INTERVENTION PLANS

FBAs are often made of the student's academic and behavioral performance as part of the CSA. From there, an FBA can lead the team to draft a BIP to include in the student's IEP. We will describe next in this section how these two important and related components are carried out.

The key questions in FBAs are these: How is the student currently performing? How does the student respond to interventions suggested by the problem-solving team? What is the relation between students, educational environments, and students' behavior? (Raines, 2002).

Assessments of the learning environment start with observation and concrete description. To look further for patterns and sequences, a good model to follow is the antecedent-behavior-consequences (ABC) model. Here you, as an observer, record in anecdotal form in each instance of (A) significant antecedent events, (B) the behavior of concern, and (C) the immediate and longer-term consequences of the behavior. From repeated observations and interviews with the teacher and parents, you can begin to map out the times and conditions where the student did or did not exhibit the particular behavior of concern (Raines, 2002; Repp & Horner, 1999; also see chapter 14 on the prereferral process). You can then begin to develop some hypotheses about the possible functions or purposes of the behavior. Hypotheses are plausible explanations of the function of the behavior that predict the general conditions under which the behavior is most likely to occur, as well as the possible consequences that serve to maintain the behavior (Raines, 2002). The key is to develop a conceptual language for nonacademic, developmental learning, such as those illustrated in the sampler of developmental (functional) learning objectives in table 15.1. With this approach, you can begin to explain classroom behavior and develop a positive BIP, changing the antecedents and/or consequences of the behavior and/or assisting students to develop skills to deal with certain situations. We will say more later on the specific components of classroom observation and suggest specific tools and measures to use to complete this part of the assessment.

TABLE 15.1   Developmental Learning Objectives Sampler

Area of Learning	Measurement
I. Motivation	
A. Profile: Poor homework completion, weak organization skills, poor study skills	
1. Student will learn the importance of completing homework assignments and being prepared for class.	Tests (content based)
2. With an incentive plan, student will complete homework as assigned and be prepared for class.	Charting (contracting, incentive plans) Daily log (teacher's records, assignment notebooks)
3. Independently, student will complete homework as assigned and will be prepared for class (receive passing grades in (x) class, maintain credits to graduate with class).	Charting (contracting incentive plans) Daily log (teacher's gradebook) Other (midterm reports, report cards)

B. Profile: Off-task behavior

   1. Student will learn the importance   Tests (content based)
     of listening and being on task
     at school.

   2. With an incentive plan, student   Charting (contracting, incentive plans)
     will begin in-class assignments   Observations (documented)
     and (with appropriate cues from   Other (formal classroom observations)
     the teacher) will be on task for (x)
     minutes (until work is completed).

   3. Independently, student will be   Charting (contracting, incentive plans)
     consistently and appropriately   Observations (documented)
     on task.   Other (consultations, formal classroom
     observations)

C. Profile: Poor school attendance, truancy

   1. Student will learn the importance   Tests (content based)
     of daily school attendance.

   2. With an incentive plan, with a   Charting (contracting, incentive plans)
     behavior modification schedule,   Other (attendance records)
     student will decrease school
     absences to fewer than one (two)
     per month.

   3. Independently, student will be at   Other (attendance records)
     school each attendance day unless
     ill (excused, etc.).

II. Behavior

A. Profile: Poor listening skills, not following directions

   1. Student will learn why paying   Charting (contracting, incentive plans)
     attention and following directions   Observations (documented)
     are important in the classroom
     (on the playground, in the
     cafeteria, etc.).

   2. With an incentive plan, student   Other (consultations, formal classroom
     will listen for and follow directions   observations)
     in the classroom (with appropriate
     cues from the teacher).

   3. Independently, student will listen   Tests (content based)
     for and follow directions.   Observations (documented)
     Other (consultations, formal classroom
     observations)

B. Profile: Chronic classroom misbehavior

   1. Student will understand the   Tests (content based)
     importance of rule systems in
     school and will know the classroom
     (school, playground, cafeteria)
     rules and consequences of
     noncompliance.

2. Student will learn the purpose of time-out and will learn and practice correct time-out behavior.

Tests (content based)
Daily log (record of practice sessions)

3. With an incentive plan, student will take time-out correctly in the classroom in compliance to the classroom behavior plan.

Charting (schedules, contracting)
Daily log (teacher's behavior records)
Observations (documented)

4. Independently, with an incentive plan, student will accept and follow the classroom behavior plan (increase acceptable class-room behaviors, decrease class-room disruptions to (x) or fewer per (x)).

Charting (schedules, contracting)
Daily log (teacher's behavior records)
Observations (reports from teachers, staff)
Other (office discipline records)

C. Profile: Bothering others, aggressive behaviors

1. Student will learn why every student should feel safe and be safe at school.

Charting (contracting, incentive plans)
Daily logs (teacher's behavior logs)
Other (office discipline records)

2. Student will learn to identify motivations and causes of aggres-sive behavior (teasing, baiting).

Tests (content based)

3. With a conflict resolution program, student will learn and practice a conflict resolution strategy (assertive, nonaggressive problem-solving techniques).

Tests (content based)

4. Independently, with an incentive plan, student will decrease incidents of physical aggression at school (in the classroom, in the cafeteria, to fewer than (x) per (x)).

Daily log (record of practice sessions)

D. Profile: Accepting consequences, respecting authority

1. Student will understand cause and effect relationships as they relate to behavior and prescribed negative consequences.

Tests (content related)

2. Student will be able to explain how his or her behavior precipitates a prescribed negative consequence.

Tests (content related)
Observations (reports from staff)

3. Independently, student will cooperatively accept prescribed negative consequences of his or her behavior.

Charting (contracting, incentive plans)
Observations (reports from staff)

4. Independently, student will accept legitimate direction, criticism, and/or negative consequences.

Observations (reports from staff)
Daily log (daily record of incidents)

III. Social Skills
A. Profile: Uncooperative, dysfunctional social behavior

1. Student will learn the importance of cooperative social behavior.
   Tests (content based)

2. Using a conflict resolution strategy, student will learn and practice a conflict resolution (problem-solving) strategy.
   Tests (content based)
   Daily log (record of practice sessions)

3. Independently (with an incentive plan), student will decrease incidents of social conflict in the classroom (school environment, on the playground) to one (two) or fewer per day (week).
   Charting (contracting)
   Daily log (teacher's behavior records)
   Other (office discipline records)

B. Profile: Poor social skills, difficulties making friends

1. With group work intervention, student will learn and practice basic social skills (taking turns, waiting politely, saying nice things, sharing, respecting differences, accepting others, good manners, controlling teasing and name calling).
   Tests (content based)
   Daily log (content based)

2. Independently, student will use (increase) positive, cooperative interpersonal social skills in the classroom (on the playground, at school, that can be observed by (x)).
   Observations (documented)

C. Profile: Anger control

1. Student will be able to identify telltale feelings and body signals when becoming angry.
   Tests
   Charting

2. Student will develop a understanding of reactions to and perceptions of anger.
   Tests
   Charting

3. Student will learn a self-talk (cool-down) technique to reduce angry feelings.
   Tests (content based)
   Charting

4. Independently, student will use a self-talk (cool-down) technique to reduce and control his or her anger.
   Observations (documented)

Functional Behavior Assessment

When Individuals with Disabilities Education Improvement Act (IDEA; 1990) was reauthorized in 1997 and again in 2004 (the last time it was reauthorized) it specified that when disciplinary action is being considered, students who receive special education services are to be provided with some additional procedural safeguards. A multidisciplinary team in the school is directed to conduct an FBA. This in turn assists in developing a behavioral intervention plan for (and with) the student. The assessment is based on

- An objective, detailed, and behaviorally specific definition or description of the behaviors of concern;
- A description of the frequency, duration, intensity, and severity of the behaviors of concern and the settings in which they occur;
- A description of other environmental variables that may affect the behavior (e.g., medication, medical conditions, sleep, diet, schedule, social factors, etc.);
- An examination and review of the known communicative behavior and the functional and practical intent of the behavior;
- A description of environmental modifications made to change the target behavior; and
- An identification of appropriate behaviors that could serve as functional alternatives to the target behavior (Clark, 2001).

In many ways the FBA is not very different from the way social workers ordinarily think, except that it is quite behaviorally specific. It does not explicitly compare or classify the student in relation to an abstract norm of the behavior of other students. Rather it begins where the student is and looks at what may trigger a behavior and what might be workable next steps and goals for social participation. What antecedent conditions might possibly trigger the behavior? What functional payoff might there have been for the student? What did he get or avoid? Multiple methods such as interviews, observations, checklists, and so on should be used to gather the information. This process would then result in the development of a behavioral intervention plan (BIP) with interventions linked to the functional assessment.

The Behavior Intervention Plan

When disciplinary action is being considered, it is important to develop an FBA (discussed in chapter 14), the basis for a behavioral intervention plan (BIP). The BIP is the responsibility of the entire team, and, in particular, the teacher, who may have the most contact with the student. It is an integral part of teamwork and consultation. Social workers may assist in the construction of the plan and in its implementation. They may have responsibilities in skill development and in modifying antecedent conditions and consequences.

The BIP should be designed to fulfill the original function of the student's negative behavior (i.e., power and control, task avoidance, attention, belonging, fun) through positive interventions so the negative behavior can be diminished. For example, if a student constantly talks out in class to achieve a sense of belonging, the interventions listed in the BIP should include positive alternatives to help the student belong, such as giving the student a special role in the class, linking the student with a peer buddy, or helping the student feel more included in small-group work. One of the most important aspects of the BIP is that its interventions should provide the same payoff (serve the same function) as the negative behavior, but through appropriate means (Van Acker et al., 2005).

The BIP should focus on the behaviors of concern. Building on the ABC FBA, described in more detail in chapter 16, a plan would specify

+ Needs for development: motivation, behavior, social skills, self-esteem (see figure 15.1);
+ Antecedent conditions (these might be modified); and
+ Consequences (these might be modified).

BOX 15.1   Involving Children in the Individualized Educational Program

It is a good practice to involve the schoolchild in IEP plans. Sometimes the plan's goals may seem abstract to the child, and so a mechanism, such as the car-in-the-garage technique developed by Fairbanks (1985; see figure 15.1, this volume), is useful. This technique involves the following steps:

1. The school social worker draws a rough sketch of a garage on a piece of paper, connects it to a road, indicates that the garage is to be the child's destination, and asks the child to identify what should be placed in the garage as goals.
2. The child tells the school social worker what the changes are that he or she desires, and the social worker or the child writes these goals inside the garage.
3. The child places one or more cars at various points along the road to the garage, symbolizing how far away from the goals and objectives he or she is. Sometimes the child leaves one or more cars off the road completely, indicating extreme lack of progress toward the goals represented by those cars.
4. The social worker asks the child for additional information about the cars and records the responses. The child's stated goals and objectives then become part of the IEP that is formally drafted at the planning team meeting.
5. The child draws new cars on the road as treatment progresses, relocating the cars on the road either closer to or farther away from the garage.
6. The child places one or more cars inside the garage when particular objectives are attained and either establishes a new set of objectives or terminates treatment. Figure 15.1 illustrates use of the technique in clarifying initial objectives for Mike, age twelve, and Jerry, age eight, in a public school day treatment program. Following the clarification of objectives, the technique can be used to measure progress and change objectives. In some cases, it can be used with a group because the technique becomes a visual and verbal metaphor for their accomplishments.

FIGURE 15.1   Using the Car-in-the-Garage Technique to Clarify Objectives

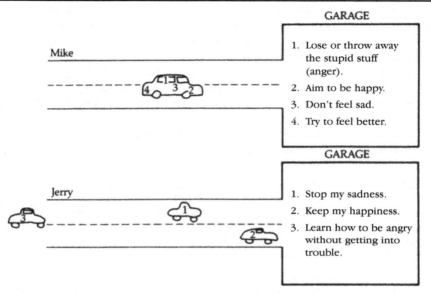

SOURCE: Fairbanks (1985).

Antecedent conditions that could be modified might include task or instructional modifications, incorporation of student interests, chunking or reduction of assignments, use of advance organizers, peer tutors or models, student choices, instruction in alternative forms of communication, or limitation of homework to tasks that the student has mastered (Raines, 2002; Zuna & McDougall, 2004).

The BIP should have measurable goals and objectives along with a clear description of how to increase positive behaviors rather than simply trying to reduce the undesirable ones. These measurable goals and objectives should clearly describe the desired improvement or remedy for the problem. Here the charts of functional behavior objectives in this chapter may be a useful beginning in assessment and treatment planning. The plan should include strategies for generalizing and maintaining positive behavior outside of the educational situation and planned disciplinary procedures, if necessary. The BIP would have a list of responsible participants and resources to access. Evaluation can take place by comparing a measure of the initial target behavior with a later period. When the plan is developed, it should be monitored regularly, and modified when necessary. It should be documented in a way that conveys to parents and others whether the student is making progress (Clark, 2001).

WRITING MEASURABLE INDIVIDUALIZED EDUCATION PROGRAM GOALS FOR SCHOOL SOCIAL WORK SERVICES: THE PROCESS OF SETTING GOALS AND OBJECTIVES

The final (and in some ways most challenging) components of the IEP involves the writing of measurable goals for students receiving social work services. Goals and achieved objectives provide a way for educators and parents to track the child's progress in special education. They should be milestones in the student's expected progress. They should be measurable, even if by "measurable" we mean the presence or absence of an observed behavior, such as making a friend. Such objectives for children with disabilities reflect the confluence of academic and functional (social) goals (Bateman & Herr, 2011; Bouris & Guilamo-Ramos, 2012). The concept of education is broad and includes social skills, life skills, problem-solving skills, and developmental steps. For children with disabilities these skills and steps are often the most important parts of their education. The education of the child with disabilities is in large part a preparation for his or her best level of social functioning outside of the school situation. Particularly for children with severe disabilities, a large part of this preparation has to do with the learning of life skills—those skills that promote appropriate independence, appropriate and satisfying interpersonal relationships, problem-solving skills, an appropriate self-image, and tolerance for unavoidable stress. These are areas where social workers have particular expertise and can make a crucial contribution to the educational process (Kelly, 2008; Stanley, 2012).

CONCLUSION

The special education planning and service delivery process, formalized in documents like the IEP, BIP, and the IFSP, builds on strengths-based assessments, discussed earlier in this chapter. In the United States, the IEP and the IFSP are the chief documents for the child's right to a FAPE. They are formal planning instruments under the IDEA (1990) and central to the school social worker's work with any child or infant with a disability. The IEP deals with children aged three through twenty-one; the IFSP generally deals with infants and toddlers, from birth to three years of age, and their families, although Individuals with Disabilities Education Improvement Act (IDEIA; 2004) permits the use of the IFSP for children until they enter kindergarten under certain circumstances. Although the family is important in both, in the IFSP the family is a principal agent to manage and implement a plan using a variety of resources to meet the young child's educational needs.

The greater the need and complexity of family involvement, the more important the social worker's role becomes.

Strengths are the starting point for assessment and planning. The strengths-based perspective assists students to discover and develop capabilities where they often lack authentic confidence and belief in themselves. Social work or educational interventions that make use of strengths minimize resistance to change by capitalizing on things the student enjoys and by creating positive (constructional) behaviors rather than simply eliminating negative behaviors. (See table 15.2 for examples of this process.) As social workers reframe stories in a strengths-based manner, such stories eventually become accepted as the dominant understanding (Dietz, 2000). Positive reframing can occur while brainstorming IEP goals and objectives, services, accommodations, scheduling, strategies for professionals, or placement options. Although formal accommodations are usually made on the basis of deficits, social workers can advocate that they also be based on strengths.

TABLE 15.2   Examples: Using Strengths to Solve Problems Creatively

Protective Factor/Strength	Key Risk Factor/Need	Creative Problem Solving
Parent indicates that child is a real leader around younger children. Child loves to help younger kids around the neighborhood.	Child is highly disruptive during art class.	Arrange for child to be a helper/model/coteacher for younger children's art classes one to two times per week.
Child loves to watch music videos and sing along at home.	Child has low self-esteem.	Arrange for child to sing a holiday song over the PA system.
Child loves to make things, to put things together.	Child cannot follow classroom routine.	Post daily or weekly classroom routine on puzzle. Have child put it together (in order) for the class.
Child is on-task and alert during the morning.	Child has difficulty with social studies and tends to tune out during lessons.	Arrange a schedule change so child has social studies in the morning.
Child knows a significant amount of historical facts.	Child makes bullying comments to others during morning announcements.	Arrange for child to formulate a history question/riddle during morning announcements to be presented daily to the history class.
Child is close to uncle and loves animals.	Child does not practice reading at home.	Arrange for child to read with uncle about animals.
Child scored high on adaptive behavior scale for community orientation, or "knowing where things are."	Child's adaptive behavior scale weaknesses are in socialization, peer interaction, and expressive language.	Arrange for child to be a school tour guide with another peer for children who are new to the school.

References

Barnhill, G. P. (2005). Functional behavioral assessment in schools. *Intervention in School and Clinic, 40*(3), 131–143.

Bateman, B. D., & Herr, C. M. (2011). *Writing measurable IEP goals and objectives.* Verona, WI: Attainment.

Bean, K. F. (2011). Social workers' role in the disproportionality of African American students in special education. *Advances in Social Work, 12*(2), 363–375.

Berzin, S. C., O'Brien, K. H. M., Frey, A., Kelly, M. S., Alvarez, M. E., & Shaffer, G. L. (2011). Meeting the social and behavioral health needs of students: Rethinking the relationship between teachers and school social workers. *Journal of School Health, 81*(8), 493–501.

Bouris, A., & Guilamo-Ramos, V. (2012). Writing strategies for school social workers. In W. Green & B. L. Simon (Eds.), *The Columbia guide to social work writing* (p. 236). New York: Columbia University Press.

Bradshaw, C. P., Pas, E. T., Goldweber, A., Rosenberg, M. S., & Leaf, P. J. (2012). Integrating school-wide positive behavioral interventions and supports with tier 2 coaching to student support teams: The PBIS plus model. *Advances in School Mental Health Promotion, 5*(3), 177–193.

Bruder, M. B. (2010). Early childhood intervention: A promise to children and families for their future. *Exceptional Children, 76*(3), 339–355.

Byrne, J. L., Hare, I., Hooper, S. N., Morse, B. J., & Sabatino, C. A. (1977). The role of a social history in special education evaluation. In R. J. Anderson, M. Freeman, & R. L. Edwards (Eds.), *School social work and PL 94-142: The Education for All Handicapped Act* (pp. 47–55). Washington, DC: National Association of Social Workers.

Clark, J. (2001). *Functional behavioral assessment and behavioral intervention plans: Implementing the student discipline provisions of IDEA '97. NASW school social work hot topics.* Washington, DC: National Association of Social Workers. Retrieved from http://www.naswdc.org/sections/ssw/hottopics/schalark.htm

Cowger, C. D., Anderson, K. M., & Snively, C. A. (2006). Assessing strengths: The political context of individual, family, and community empowerment. In D. Saleebey (Ed.), *The strengths perspective in social work practice* (4th ed., pp. 93–115). Boston: Allyn & Bacon.

Department of Defense Education Activity (DoDEA). (2014). *Parent handbook on special education.* Retrieved from http://www.am.dodea.edu/knox/fkcsco/pages/Parent_Handbook_on_Special_Education.pdf

Dietz, C. A. (2000). Reshaping clinical practice for the new millennium. *Journal of Social Work Education, 36,* 503–520.

Fairbanks, N. M. (1985). Involving children in the IEP: The car-in-the-garage technique. *Social Work in Education, 7*(3), 171–182.

Federal Register. (2000). *Early intervention program for infants and toddlers with disabilities.* Retrieved from https://www.federalregister.gov/articles/2000/09/05/00-21969/early-intervention-program-for-infants-and-toddlers-with-disabilities

Geisinger, K. E., Spies, R. A., Carlson, J. F., & Blake, B. S. (Eds.). (2007). *Mental measurements yearbook* (17th ed.). Lincoln, NE: Buros Institute.

Gleason, E. T. (2007). A strengths-based approach to the social developmental study. *Children & Schools, 29*(1), 51–59.

Illinois Legal Aid (2012). *Special education law.* Retrieved from http://www.illinois
legalaid.org/index.cfm?fuseaction=home.dsp_content&contentID=311#Domain_
Meetings_and_Evaluations

Individuals with Disabilities Education Act of 1990 (IDEA), Pub. L. 105-17, U.S.C. 11401
et seq. (1990).

Individuals with Disabilities Education Improvement Act of 2004 (IDEIA), Pub. L. 108-
446, 118 Stat. 2647 (2004).

Kelly, M. S. (2008). *The domains and demands of school social work practice: A guide
to working effectively with students, families, and schools.* New York: Oxford.

Mallett, C. A., Stoddard-Dare, P., & Workman-Crewnshaw, L. (2011). Special education
disabilities and juvenile delinquency: A unique challenge for school social work.
School Social Work Journal, 36(1), 26–40.

Parton, N., & O'Byrne, P. (2000). *Constructive social work: Towards a new practice.*
New York: St. Martin's Press.

Raines, J. C. (2002). Brainstorming hypotheses for functional behavior assessment:
The link to effective behavioral intervention plans. *School Social Work Journal,
26*(2), 30–45.

Raines, J. C., & Van Acker, R. (2009). The assessment of adaptive behavior. In C. R.
Massat, R. Constable, S. McDonald, & J. P. Flynn (Eds.), *School social work:
Practice, policy and research* (7th ed., pp. 431–451). Chicago: Lyceum Books.

Repp, A. C., & Horner, R. H. (1999). *Functional analysis of problem behavior: From
effective assessment to effective support.* Belmont, CA: Wadsworth.

Saleebey, D. (2006). The strengths approach to practice. In D. Saleebey (Ed.), *The
strengths perspective in social work practice* (4th ed., pp. 77–92). Boston:
Allyn & Bacon.

Siporin, M. (1975). *Introduction to social work practice.* New York: Macmillan.

Stanley, S. G. (2012). Children with disabilities in foster care: The role of the school
social worker in the context of special education. *Children & Schools, 34*(3),
190–192.

Test, D. W., Mason, C., Hughes, C., Konrad, M., Neale, M., & Wood, W. (2004). Student
involvement in individualized education program meetings. *Exceptional Children,
70*(4), 391–412.

U.S. Government Printing Office (GPO). (2003). *Title 34: Education. C.F.R. 34.* Retrieved
from http://www.gpo.gov/fdsys/pkg/CFR-2002-title34-vol1/content-detail.html

Van Acker, R., Boreson, L., Gable, R. A., & Potterton, T. (2005). Are we on the right
course? Lessons learned about current FBA/BIP practices in schools. *Journal of
Behavioral Education, 14*(1), 35–56.

Wang, M. C., Haertel, G. D., & Walberg, H. J. (1999). Psychological and educational
resilience. In A. J. Reynolds, H. J. Walberg, & R. P. Weissberg (Eds.), *Promoting
positive outcomes: Issues in children's and families' lives* (pp. 329–366).
Washington, DC: CWLA Press.

Zuna, N., & McDougall, D. (2004). Using positive behavioral support to manage avoidance of academic tasks. *Teaching Exceptional Children, 37*(1), 18–24.

16

The Screening and Assessment of Adaptive Behavior

James C. Raines
California State University Monterey Bay

- Reasons for Screenings of Adaptive Behavior
- Reasons for Assessing Adaptive Behavior
- Why Social Workers Are Qualified to Assess Adaptive Behavior
- Defining Terms
- The Assessment of Adaptive Behavior
- Common Instruments Used to Measure Adaptive Behavior
- Using Clinical Judgment in the Assessment of Adaptive Behavior

For decades, social workers have attempted to identify and measure accurately those behaviors related to competence that distinguish individuals as they interact with their environments—that is, social workers have attempted to assess individuals' adaptive behavior (Schmidt & Salvia, 1984). Adaptive behavior assessments fall into two major types: formal and informal. This chapter will discuss primarily the formal, which use semistructured interviews or standardized scales. Understanding how individuals adapt themselves to the requirements of their physical and social environment is the goal of many of our social sciences. The ability to function effectively across a range of adaptive skill areas is essential for personal success and adjustment in life. Maximizing adaptive behavior skills for individuals with physical, mental, or emotional challenges is often a goal for social work intervention. Thus, the construct of adaptive behavior is becoming increasingly important in the identification and treatment of individuals with various disabilities, such as cognitive impairments, emotional disturbance, and mental impairments. The American Association on Intellectual & Developmental Disabilities (AAIDD) is the international and multidisciplinary leader in the conceptualization, definition, and classification of mental retardation (see www.aaidd.org). Founded in 1876, this organization has included adaptive behavior as a critical factor in defining mental retardation since the late 1950s (Heber, 1959).

REASONS FOR SCREENINGS OF ADAPTIVE BEHAVIOR

There are three major reasons for social workers to screen for adaptive behavior. First, the Individuals with Disabilities Education Act (IDEA; 1990) requires that all states have policies and procedures in place to find children who are in need of special education regardless of whether they are homeless, attend private schools, or are a ward of the state. Therefore schools require quick and accurate ways to determine which children require further evaluation and which children do not. Second, as more school districts adopt a response-to-intervention model of services (see figure 16.1), related

FIGURE 16.1   A Response-to-Intervention Model

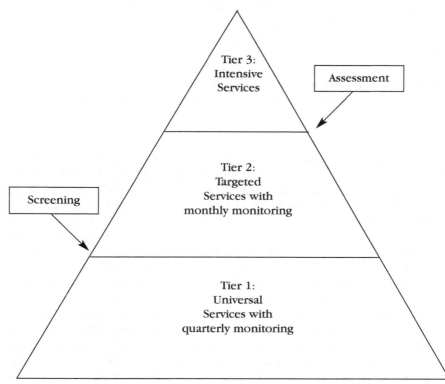

service providers need to be able to identify which children require more-intensive services than general education, but less-intensive services than special education (National Association of State Directors of Special Education, 2006). For these children, screening instruments can be an efficient way of monitoring which children are responding to intervention and which are not (Torgesen, 2004). Finally, early screening can lead to early intervention and ultimately save the government from having to fund costly remediation programs (Barnett, 2000). Early intervention programs are cost-efficient when one realizes that for every $1 spent, society saves $17 in remedial costs (Glascoe, 2006).

REASONS FOR ASSESSING ADAPTIVE BEHAVIOR

There are a number of reasons for assessing adaptive behavior. Federal regulations and state school codes began to require that adaptive behavior be assessed before a pupil could be considered eligible for special education services under the category of mental retardation, developmental disability, or autism. The latest reauthorization of the Individuals with Disabilities Education Act (IDEA) in 2004 (i.e., the Individuals with Disabilities Education Improvement Act [IDEIA]) clarified that any evaluation of a child's school performance was meant to be inclusive of both academic achievement and functional performance (Raines, 2006). Another reason for assessing adaptive behavior relates to program planning. The reauthorization of the IDEA in 1997 specified the need to develop educational objectives and behavior management plans for students with disabilities whose behavior interferes with their own learning or that of others. Thus, the assessment of both adaptive and maladaptive behavior has an increased level of importance in the identification of target behaviors. This legislation also specified increased responsibility in the development of educational objectives to promote the transition of students with disabilities into the workplace. Again, the assessment of adaptive behavior can play an important role in the identification of appropriate goals and objectives.

WHY SOCIAL WORKERS ARE QUALIFIED TO ASSESS ADAPTIVE BEHAVIOR

Social workers have assessed people's functioning in their various environments throughout the history of the profession. Assessments are made in comparison to others in the same cohort, controlling for age, gender, ethnicity, community, environment, socioeconomic status, and any perceived or suspected disabilities, as well as other defining characteristics. For most people, functional abilities are relatively stable across various settings, but for some people there is significant variation. Describing this variability is an essential component of a social developmental study, and is identified as the adaptive behavior assessment. It is important that in school settings the social worker take responsibility for adaptive behavior assessments, for three reasons:

1. Social workers are well trained in the interviewing process.
2. The professional focus of social work is the functioning of persons in their environment. The central theme of social work practice is improving the fit between the person and the environment.
3. Finally, one of the requirements of the IDEIA (2004) is the multidisciplinary approach to assessment and decision making in determining the academic, developmental, or functional needs of each referred student. Thus, the adaptive behavior assessment falls well within the professional responsibility of the social worker.

DEFINING TERMS

There are three terms that require definition before we continue. The term "mental retardation" has been discarded for the more accurate and current term "intellectual disability." According to the AAIDD Ad Hoc Committee on Termination and Classification (2010), the word "intelligence" is defined as "general mental ability. It includes reasoning, planning, solving problems, thinking abstractly, comprehending complex ideas, learning quickly, and learning from experience" (p. 15). The term "adaptive behavior" is "the collection of conceptual, social, and practical skills that have been learned and are performed by people in their daily lives" (p. 15). "Conceptual skills" include language; reading and writing; and money, time, and number concepts. "Social skills" include interpersonal skills, social responsibility, self-esteem, gullibility, naivete, the ability to follow rules or obey laws, the ability to avoid being victimized, and social problem-solving. "Practical skills" include activities of daily living, occupational skills, use of money, safety, health care, travel/transportation, schedules/routines, and use of the telephone.

Adaptive Behavior as a Function of Age

The age of the target individual must be considered when assessing adaptive behavior. The person completing the measure must take care to be sensitive to the realities of child development when assessing adaptive behavior. As most assessment measures call for the respondent to rate the frequency with which the target individual displays a given behavior, knowledge of what is developmentally appropriate is assumed. Only a subset of the adaptive skill areas identified by the AAIDD may be relevant at a given age. The nature of the expectations placed on the individual for the display of adaptive behavior changes dramatically over the life span. As children grow, assessment of adaptive behavior targets learned behavior. We expect young children to communicate socially with others and to demonstrate social skills as they play together. We anticipate that children will demonstrate increased independence in self-care, community use, self-direction, and engagement in leisure time activities as they mature. With adolescence come expectations for eventual transition into the adult world of work.

Adaptive Behavior as a Function of Cultural Expectations

Cultural awareness and sensitivity play a critical role in the assessment of adaptive behavior. Culture, by definition, affects the display of language, behavior, and beliefs. For example, some cultures support personal independence and individual achievement more than others do. The age at which children are expected to display specific behaviors related to self-care, self-direction, and independent community use differ dramatically across cultures. The respondent must be aware of the cultural expectations of the individual being assessed. Moreover, the validity of the score obtained will depend on the similarity or difference of the person being assessed to those individuals included within the normative sample of the measure being employed (Eikeseth, 2006; Zhang & Yao, 2003).

Adaptive Behavior and the Environment

Successful adaptation requires a good person-in-environment fit. The individual's capabilities must match the environmental demands. The concept of environment in the assessment of adaptive behavior includes those specific settings in which the individual functions, in particular the home, school, work, and community environments. What is considered adaptive in one environment may prove maladaptive in another. A behavior that proves adaptive in a rural setting may have quite a different outcome in an urban setting (Bornstein et al., 2005).

Not only can the environment affect the individual's pattern of adaptive behavior, but the opposite is true as well. Children's adaptative abilities can change the environmental climate in which they develop. For example, Weiss, Sullivan, and Diamond (2003) found that children with lower adaptive functioning increased parental stress. Given the relationship between parental stress and child abuse, it should come as no surprise that children with disabilities experience a higher rate of abuse than those without disabilities (Sullivan & Knutson, 2000). In conclusion, adaptive behavior and the environment have a complex and reciprocal relationship.

The Assessment of Maladaptive Behaviors

The inclusion of maladaptive behavior in measures of adaptive behavior often increases the confusion and difficulty in the interpretation of findings.

For obvious reasons, the identification of maladaptive behavior is important in its own right. The relation of adaptive to maladaptive behavior, however, is not that of behaviors at opposite ends of a continuum. Most children with disabilities have both strengths and weaknesses that need to be assessed (Geschwind & Dykens, 2004). In fact, these behaviors can appear to exist quite independently of one another and both can increase as a function of age (Cohen, Schmidt-Lackner, Romanczyk, & Sudhalter, 2003). An individual can display both adaptive and maladaptive behavior in the same area. Moreover, the absence of maladaptive behavior does not imply the presence of adaptive behavior.

THE ASSESSMENT OF ADAPTIVE BEHAVIOR

Adaptive behavior is measured across multiple environmental settings using typical, everyday functioning rather than optimal performance. Adaptive behaviors are those that are performed regularly, spontaneously, and without prompting or assistance from others. When assessing adaptive behavior, we are not interested in what the target individual can do, but rather what the individual typically does. This is an important and often misunderstood distinction. Individuals who have the knowledge and skills necessary to perform a given response often fail to do so routinely in their everyday interactions with their environment. For example, a student might know how to solve a given social problem in an acceptable fashion. When confronted with a peer conflict, however, the student might routinely respond with aggression. The assessment of his adaptive behavior is not aimed at the discovery of his potential response, but rather at a measure of his typical response. Behaviors are rated as performed regularly. Moreover, behaviors must be displayed spontaneously without prompting or assistance from others.

Adaptive behavior information may be gathered either through a standardized measure or through observations and interviews as a more qualitative assessment. IDEA does not specify that standardized measures are required to make an adaptive behavior assessment. Informal adaptive behavior assessments can bring an understanding of the effect of environmental conditions on behavior. Informal or qualitative assessments can be used to assess a child's functioning in the classroom and compare this to his or her functioning in other settings. The child's age and sociocultural background are essential ingredients in such an informal assessment, as they are in formal assessments. Areas of functioning include independent functioning, personal responsibility, and social responsibility. For each of these areas, the school social worker needs to determine whether the child has necessary skills to function at his or her grade level.

Adaptive behavior is most often assessed using a formal, standardized instrument. The report usually comes from a third person and this in turn generates a standardized rating of a target individual. Rather than employing systematic observation of the behavior of the target individual, the examiner relies on the cumulative observations of a respondent who is familiar with the target individual. This method of assessment is susceptible to various types of limitations, errors, and biases. The respondents are limited to those behaviors they have had the opportunity to observe. Often different respondents will observe individuals in only a limited number of contexts. Some of these environments have different demands on students, so children will often display different behavior in these various contexts. This is why Achenbach, McConaughy, and Howell (1987) concluded that the best way to get a three-dimensional view of the child within his or her environment was to use multiple informants and multiple methods.

There also is a concern that respondents can differ significantly in their awareness and/or tolerance for some behaviors. Most assessments of adaptive behavior ask respondents to rate on a scale the frequency or seriousness of various behaviors with an underlying assumption that respondents will employ a similar standard. Thus, there is an assumption that one respondent's "sometimes" is assumed to differ from another respondent's "usually." This may not be a safe assumption. A related problem results from the fact that these ordinal level measurements are often treated as interval-level measurements to calculate the target individual's scores. These scores are obtained by assigning numbers to the various ratings and manipulating these numbers mathematically. Remember, what are really being added are subjective ratings. This is why clinical judgment is required whenever one interprets the results of either formal or informal assessments (AAIDD, 2010).

Another concern with the traditional approach to assessing adaptive behavior is that the individual being assessed may conceal important behaviors from the respondent, perhaps due to cultural demands, fear of consequences, or other personal agendas. Thus, the respondent may not report the presence of a potentially important adaptive or maladaptive behavior, or a respondent might be less than truthful when completing an assessment. This is especially true if the respondent has a stake in the outcome. For example, parents might be more willing to give their child the benefit of the doubt if they are concerned that their child might be stigmatized as having an intellectual disability. On the other hand, a teacher might be inclined to magnify the frequency of a maladaptive behavior if it will increase the likelihood of removing a challenging child from her classroom.

Given these potential limitations, errors, and biases, the examiner is advised to seek information and assessments of adaptive behavior from multiple people across a variety of settings within which the target individual interacts. The goal of multiple measurements of adaptive behavior is the identification of patterns in responding and the development of a reliable understanding of the target individual's adaptive and maladaptive behavior. Best practice involves multiple data collection strategies that can be recalled using the acronym, RIOT, for Reviewing records (R), Interviewing primary caregivers (I), Observing the child within multiple contexts (O), and Testing for mastery (T). One has to keep in mind that disparate ratings do not necessarily indicate error but could signal the differential behavior of an individual in distinct settings and/or its impact on different people.

COMMON INSTRUMENTS USED TO MEASURE ADAPTIVE BEHAVIOR

It has been estimated that there are more than 200 instuments designed to measure adaptive behavior (Spreat, 1999). In the next section of this chapter, both screening instruments (see table 16.1) and assessment instruments (see table 16.2) used to measure adaptive behavior are reviewed. The 2002

TABLE 16.1   Common Screening Measures of Adaptive Behavior

Instrument (Authors)	Age Range	Informant	Type of Measure
Ages & Stages Questionnaire (Bricker & Squires, 1999)	4 mos.–5 yrs.	Parent	Rating Scale
Battelle Developmental Inventory Screener (Newborg, 2005)	Birth–7 yrs.	Parent	Rating Scale
Parents' Evaluation of Developmental Status (Glascoe, 2002)	Birth–8 yrs.	Parent	Rating Scale
Prescreening Developmental Questionnaire (Frankenburg et al., 1992)	1 mo.–6 yrs.	Parent	Rating Scale

TABLE 16.2   Common Assessment Measures of Adaptive Behavior

Measure (Authors)	Age Range	Informant(s)	Type of Measure
Adaptive Behavior Assessment System, 2nd ed. (Harrison & Oakland, 2003)	Birth–21 years	Parents and teachers	Rating scale
Adaptive Behavior Evaluation Scale, 2nd revised ed. (McCarney & Arthaud, 2006)	4–18 years	Parents and teachers	Rating scale
Bayley Scales of Infant Development, 3rd ed. (Bayley, 2005)	1–42 months	Professional	Rating scale
Diagnostic Adaptive Behavior Scale (Balboni et al., 2014)	4–21 years	Parents and teachers	Rating scale
Scales of Independent Behavior, Revised (Bruininks, Woodcock, Weatherman, & Hill, 1996)	3 months–90 years	Parents and teachers	Interview questionnaire
Vineland Adaptive Behavior Scale, 2nd ed. (Sparrow, Ciccheti, & Balla, 2005)	Birth–90 years	Parents and teachers	Interview or rating scale

American Association on Mental Retardation (AAMR) manual clearly states that a valid determination of adaptive skills requires that "adaptive behavior should be measured with a standardized instrument that provides normative data on people without mental retardation" (2002, p. 83). The purpose of this section, therefore, is to familiarize the reader with some of the most commonly used measures and to point out some of the important features related to scoring the measure, the normative samples available for interpretation, and critical psychometric properties of the measure. This information should help the reader select the appropriate measure for a specific need and aid in the interpretation of results.

Screening Measures

Screening measures are broad measures that attempt to uncover multiple risk factors with a minimum of effort. All the measures below cover five standard domains for developmental disabilities, including personal-social, adaptive, motor, communication, and cognitive functioning. Hamilton (2006) identified a number of screening measures that were brief, reliable, and easy to administer. The ideal amount of time for screening is ten to fifteen minutes per child. Good screening measures strike a balance between sensitivity and specificity (Jenkins, 2003). Sensitivity is the degree to which the instrument correctly identifies those children who are at risk for future problems. Specificity is the degree to which the instrument also correctly identifies those children who are not at risk (Raines, 2008). Too much sensitivity can lead to false positives—those children who score poorly but are really doing well. Too much specificity can lead to false negatives—those children who score well, but really need help. The following four scales are widely employed and possess good sensitivity and specificity.

Ages and Stages Questionnaire

The Ages and Stages Questionnaire (ASQ) was revised in 2009 (Bricker, Squires, & Clifford, 2010). The ASQ has been adapted into Chinese (Tsai, McClelland, Pratt, & Squires, 2006) and Korean (Heo & Squires, 2012). It covers five standard domains with six questions for each domain. It is appropriate for ages three months to four years and is available in English and Spanish from Brookes Publishing (www.brookespublishing.com).

Battelle Developmental Inventory Screener (Second Edition)

The Battelle Developmental Inventory Screener (Second Edition; BDI-2S) was developd in 1984 and revised in 2005 (Newborg, 2005). It can also be used for children on the autism spectrum (Sipes, Matson, & Turygin, 2011). The BDI-2S screening test takes ten to thirty minutes prior to employing the full BDI. It is appropriate for ages birth to seven years and is available in English and Spanish from Riverside Publishing (www.riverpub.com).

Parents' Evaluation of Developmental Status

The Parents' Evaluation of Developmental Status (PEDS) was developd in 1997 (Glascoe, 2002). The PEDS relies solely on parent report and covers the same five domains with ten questions per age level, making it the shortest of the screening measures. Similar to the the BDI, the PEDS is appropriate for ages birth to eight years and is available in English and Spanish (www.pedstest.com). The publisher also licenses translations into thirty more languages.

Prescreening Developmental Questionnaire (Second Edition)

The Prescreening Developmental Questionnaire (Second Edition; PDQ-II) is based on the longer Denver Developmental Screening Test (Second Edition; DDST-II) (Frankenburg, Dodds, Archer, Shapiro, Bresnick, 1992). While the DDST-II uses direct observation and has 125 questions, the PDQ-II relies on parent report and can be administered in only ten minutes. The DDST-II and the PDQ-II are appropriate for ages one month to six years; both are available in English and Spanish (www.denverii.com).

Asessment Measures

Assessment measures perform a more in-depth function of pinpointing specific problems and even aiding in the diagnosis of specific disorders. All of the scales below focus specifically on adaptive functioning. Most of these scales are longer, more expensive, and better researched than the screening instruments above. Due to the time and expense of administering these scales, they probably should not be used on a wide basis, but only when previous measures have alerted the school social worker to the need for greater clarity about the problem or the child has failed to respond to targeted interventions.

Adaptive Behavior Assessment System (Second Edition)

The Adaptive Behavior Assessment System (Second Edition; ABAS-II) was revised in 2002 to meet the new standards set by the AAIDD. It has five forms depending on the age of the child and who does the rating. There are two parent forms for ages birth to five years, and five to twenty-one years, and two teacher forms for ages two to five years and five to twenty-one years There is also a self-report form for ages sixteen to eighty-nine years. The ABAS-II measures functioning in the eleven skills areas of communication, community use, health and safety, leisure, self-care, self-direction, functional preacademics, home (or school) living, social skills, work, and motor skills. These skills are then translated into four domain scores: conceptual, social, practical, and general adaptive composite to conform with the AAIDD's definition of adaptive behavior. The ABAS-II is available only in English (http://www.proedinc.com).

Adaptive Behavior Evaluation Scale (Second Revised Edition)

The Adaptive Behavior Evaluation Scale (Second Revised Edition; ABES-R2) comes in two versions—one for children four to twelve years of age and one for adolescents thirteen to eighteen years of age (McCarney & Arthaud, 2006). Like the ABAS-II, it is designed to meet the AAIDD's tripartite definition for adaptive behavior: conceptual, social, and practical. The ABES-R2 is available only in English (http://www.hawthorne-ed.com).

Bayley Scales of Infant Development (Third Edition)

The Bayley Scales of Infant Development (Third Edition; Bayley-III) has been one of the most widely used instruments for early identification of infants and toddlers with special needs. The Bayley-III is appropriate for children between one month and forty-two months (Bayley, 2005). There are five scales used to measure cognitive, language, motor, social-emotional, and adaptive behavioral development. The Bayley-III is available only in English (http://pearsonclinical.com).

Diagnostic Adaptive Behavior Scale

As an organization, the AAIDD has developed its own rating scale, titled Diagnostic Adaptive Behavior Scale (DABS). The new scale is meant to be used with people ages four to twenty-one years old and with an IQ score of 55–80. The DABS has seventy-five items. Assessed individuals receive a composite score as well as three subscale scores: Conceptual, Practical, and Social Skills. The DABS is administered via a face-to-face interview with a caregiver and requires about thirty minutes. Ratings are based on the respondent's direct observation or knowledge of the adaptive behavior of the individual assessed. Its reliability and validity are still being investigated (Balboni et al., 2014).

Scales of Independent Behavior (Revised)

The Scales of Independent Behavior (Revised; SIB-R) is an individually administered test to be used with individuals aged three months through ninety years (Bruininks et al., 1996). There are three forms of the SIB-R available: the full-scale form, the short form, and the early development form. The short form of the SIB-R is intended to serve as a screening device and consists of forty items. The early development form has been developed to assess "the development of preschoolers and the adaptive skills of youths or adults with serious disabilities" (Bruininks et al., 1996, p. 16). The SIB-R is specifically intended to be used to assess independent functioning within various settings such as the home or school. The SIB-R lends itself well to purposes such as the establishment of appropriate instructional goals, making placement decisions, and evaluating program outcomes. The SIB-R is available only in English (http://www.riverpub.com).

Vineland Adaptive Behavior Scales (Second Edition)

The Vineland Adaptive Behavior Scales (Second Edition; VABS-II) was completed in 2007. The VABS-II is administered individually and is completed by a respondent familiar with the target individual (Sparrow et al., 2005). There are now four separate forms, each with its own technical manual. Two of the forms are termed interview versions. The survey form includes fewer items than the expanded interview form and consequently requires less administration time. Interviews are conducted in a semistructured format with the interviewer asking questions in her own words to probe the respondent about the target individual's functioning (rather than simply reading the interview items).

Thus, the VABS requires that the interviewer gain familiarity with the instrument before administering it and provides a manual with a good deal of data about scoring the items. Two of the forms are rating scale versions: the parent/caregiver form and the teacher rating form. The interview forms and parent form are designed for assessment of individuals from birth to ninety years. The teacher form can be completed by a teacher or daycare provider in approximately twenty minutes. This version is suitable for children ages three to twenty-one years. The VABS-II is available in English and Spanish (http://www.pearsonclinical.com).

USING CLINICAL JUDGMENT IN THE ASSESSMENT OF ADAPTIVE BEHAVIOR

Test results do not interpret themselves; they require a clinically skilled and perceptive examiner to make sense and derive educationally relevant implications. The AAIDD (2010) defines "clinical judgment" as "a special type of judgment rooted in a high level of clinical expertise and experience. It emerges directly from extensive data and is based on the training, experiences, and specific knowledge of the person and his or her environment" (p. 85).

The AAIDD (2010) discusses ten guidelines for clinical judgment.

1. Social workers must ensure a match between the evaluation's purpose and the assessment measure chosen.

2. Social workers must review the appropriateness and psychometric properties of the measures in terms of the client's age, gender, ethnic-racial group, primary language, and sensory-motor limitations.
3. Social workers must be sensitive to the instrument's examiner qualifications and ensure that they have been properly trained in its use. Most of the publishers' Web sites provide training materials for their instruments.
4. Social workers must administer the instrument with fidelity to its directions and avoid taking liberties in its application. Remember that an instrument's reliability and validity depend on consistent application.
5. Social workers must stay abreast of the scientific literature and ethical concerns regarding available instruments. As new editions of instruments become available, clinicians should dispose of their old forms and utilize the latest versions (Raines, 2003).
6. Social workers should choose informants carefully by determining how well they know the client and the likelihood that they can provide reliable and valid information.
7. When interpreting test results, social workers should consider the client's experiences as they relate to participation, interactions, and roles. For example, children born with very low birthweights should be measured against their due date rather than their birth date (Pritchard, Coldwitz, & Beller, 2005).
8. When interpreting test results, social workers should be sensitive to physical or mental health contributants that influence their responses.
9. Social workers should utilize other members of the multidisciplinary team as resources. Psychologists may be especially useful in understanding an instrument's psychometric qualities.
10. Social workers should follow published guidelines for the interpretation of the specific test used. Clinical judgment should never be a justification for setting aside test results in favor of subjective hunches or impressionistic generalizations.

CONCLUSION

The assessment of adaptive behavior is an increasingly important activity for teachers, social workers, and psychologists. When assessing adaptive behavior, the examiner is generally interested in how well a target individual meets the needs of his or her physical and social environment. Does the individual function well enough not to represent a significant risk to self or others? Unfortunately, there is a lack of agreement as to exactly which behaviors need to be assessed. Adaptive behavior is greatly influenced by societal expectations. The social worker must take the developmental level and cultural heritage of the individual into consideration when assessing adaptive behavior.

Adaptive behavior is usually not measured directly, but rather through information provided by a third-party respondent familiar with the target individual. When assessing adaptive behavior, one is interested in what the target individual does on a regular basis. The assessment of adaptive behavior suffers from a lack of adequate measures. There is a lack of reliability across many of the subscales in the various measures that results in serious error measurement. Moreover, the norms available are often inadequate.

Care must be taken when selecting measures for assessing adaptive behavior. Examiners may wish to select scales, or subscales, from any number of measures to maximize the validity and reliability of the results. When conducting an assessment of adaptive behavior, seek multiple respondents who are very familiar with the target individual. Look for patterns of behavior displayed in the target individual as reported across respondents. When behavior varies across respondents the evaluator attempts to identify elements in the contexts assessed that might affect behavior. The ultimate goal of an assessment of adaptive behavior is to identify both the strengths and weaknesses displayed by individuals as they interact with the world. With care and understanding of the potentials as well as the limitations of current measures of adaptive behavior, one can proceed to identify possible areas of both adaptive and maladaptive behavior.

References

Achenbach, T. M., McConaughy, S. H., & Howell, C. T. (1987). Child/adolescent behavioral and emotional problems: Implications of cross-informant correlations for situational specificity. *Psychological Bulletin, 101*(2), 213–232.

American Association on Intellectual & Developmental Disabilities (AAIDD) Ad Hoc Committee on Termination and Classification. (2010). *Intellectual disability: Definition, classification and systems of supports* (11th ed.). Washington, DC: Author.

American Association on Mental Retardation (AAMR). (2002). *Mental retardation: Definition, classification, and systems of supports* (10th ed.). Washington, DC: Author.

Balboni, G., Tassé, M. J., Schalock, R. L., Borthwick-Duffy, S. A., Spreat, S., Thissen, D., . . . & Navas, P. (2014). The Diagnostic Adaptive Behavior Scale: Evaluating its diagnostic sensitivity and specificity. *Research in Developmental Disabilities, 35*(11), 2884–2893.

Barnett, W. S. (2000). Economics of early childhood intervention. In J. P. Shonkoff & S. J. Meisels (Eds.), *Handbook of early childhood intervention* (2nd ed., pp. 589–610). New York: Cambridge University Press.

Bayley, N. (2005). *Bayley scales of infant and toddler development* (3rd ed.) (Bayley-III). San Antonio, TX: Harcourt Assessment.

Bornstein, M. H., Giusti, Z., Leach, D. B., & Venuti, P. (2005). Maternal reports of adaptive behaviours in young children: Urban-rural and gender comparisons in Italy and the United States. *Infant and Child Development, 14*(44), 403–424.

Bricker, D., Squires, J., & Clifford, J. (2010). Developmental screening measures: Stretching the use of the ASQ for other assessment purposes. *Infants & Young Children, 23*(1), 14–22.

Bruininks, R., Woodcock, R., Weatherman, R., & Hill, B. (1996). *Scales of independent behavior, revised, comprehensive manual.* Chicago: Riverside.

Cohen, I. L., Schmidt-Lackner, S., Romanczyk, R., & Sudhalter, V. (2003). The PDD Behavior Inventory: A rating scale for assessing response to intervention in children with pervasive developmental disorder. *Journal of Autism and Developmental Disorders, 33*(1), 31–45.

Eikeseth, S. (2006). The Vineland Adaptive Behavior Scale in a sample of Norwegian second-grade children: A preliminary study. *Tidsskrift for Norsk Psykologforening, 43*(10), 1036–1039.

Frankenburg, W. K., Dodds, J., Archer, P., Shapiro, H., & Bresnick, B. (1992). The Denver II: A major revision and restandardization of the Denver Developmental Screening Test. *Pediatrics, 89,* 91–97.

Geschwind, D. H., & Dykens, E. (2004). Neurobehavioral and psychosocial issues in Klinefelter syndrome. *Learning Disabilities Research & Practice, 19*(3), 166–173.

Glascoe, F. P. (2002). *Collaborating with parents: Using Parents' Evaluation of Developmental Status (PEDS) to detect and address developmental and behavioral problems.* Nashville, TN: Ellsworth & Vandermeer Press.

Glascoe, F. P. (2006). *Talking points on developmental-behavioral problems.* Retrieved from http://www.pedstest.com/Training/OverviewofTraining/TalkingPoints.aspx

Hamilton, S. (2006). Screening for developmental delay: Reliable, easy-to-use tools. *Journal of Family Practice, 55*(5), 415–422.

Harrison, P. L., & Oakland, T. (2003). *Adaptive behavior assessment system* (2nd ed.). San Antonio, TX: Harcourt Assessment.

Heber, R. (1959). A manual on terminology and classification in mental retardation. *American Journal of Mental Deficiency,* Monograph Supplement (rev.), 56.

Heo, K. H., & Squires, J. (2012). Cultural adaptation of a parent completed emotional screening instrument for young children: Ages and Stages questionnaire—social emotional. *Early Human Development, 88*(3), 151–158.

Individuals with Disabilities Education Act of 1990 (IDEA), Pub. L. 105-17, U.S.C. 11401 et seq. (1990).

Individuals with Disabilities Education Improvement Act of 2004 (IDEIA), Pub. L. 108-446, 118 Stat. 2647 (2004).

Jenkins, J. R. (2003, December). *Candidate measures for screening at-risk students.* Paper presented at the National Research Center on Learning Disabilities Responsiveness-to-Intervention symposium, Kansas City, MO.

McCarney, S. B., & Arthaud, T. J. (2006). *Adaptive behavior evaluation scale*—Revised (2nd ed.). Columbia, MO: Hawthorne Educational Services.

National Association of State Directors of Special Education. (2006). *Response-to-intervention.* Retrieved from http://www.betterhighschools.org/docs/NASDSE_RtI_AnAdministratorsPerspective_1-06.pdf

Newborg, J. (2005). *Battelle developmental inventory* (2nd ed.). (BDI-2). Rolling Meadows, IL: Riverside.

Pritchard, M. A., Coldwitz, P. B., & Beller, E. M. (2005). Parent's evaluation of developmental status in children born with a birthweight of 1250 grams or less. *Journal of Paediatrics and Child Health, 41*(4), 191–196.

Raines, J. C. (2003). Rating the rating scales: Ten criteria to use. *School Social Work Journal, 27*(2), 1–17.

Raines, J. C. (2006). The new IDEA: Reflections on the reauthorization. *School Social Work Journal, 31*(1), 1–18.

Raines, J. C. (2008). *Evidence-based practice in school mental health: A primer for school social workers, psychologists, and counselors.* New York: Oxford University Press.

Schmidt, M., & Salvia, J. (1984). Adaptive behavior: A conceptual analysis. *Diagnostique, 9,* 117–125.

Sipes, M., Matson, J. L., & Turygin, N. (2011). The use of the Battelle Developmental Inventory—2nd Edition (BDI-2) as an early screener for autism spectrum disorders. *Developmental Neurorehabilitation, 14*(5), 310–314.

Sparrow, S., Ciccheti, D. V., & Balla, D. A. (2005). *Vineland Adaptive Behavior Scales* (2nd ed.). Survey forms manual. Circle Pines, MN: American Guidance Service.

Spreat, S. (1999). Psychometric standards for adaptive behavior assessment. In R. A. Schalock (Ed.), *Adaptive behavior and its measurement: Implications for the field of mental retardation* (pp. 103–117). Washington, DC: American Association on Mental Retardation.

Sullivan, P. M., & Knutson, J. F. (2000). Maltreatment and disabilities: A population-based epidemiological study. *Child Abuse & Neglect, 24*(10), 1257–1273.

Torgesen, J. K. (2004). Avoiding the devastating downward spiral: The evidence that early intervention prevents reading failure. *American Educator, 28,* 6–19.

Tsai, H-L. A., McClelland, M. M., Pratt, C., & Squires, J. (2006). Adaptation of the 36-month Ages and Stages Questionnaire in Taiwan: Results from a preliminary study. *Journal of Early Intervention, 28*(3), 213–225.

Weiss, J. A., Sullivan, A., & Diamond, T. (2003). Parent stress and adaptive functioning of individuals with developmental disabilities. *Journal on Developmental Disabilities, 10*(1), 129–135.

Zhang, Q., & Yao, S. (2003). Development of Adaptive Skill Rating Scale for school age children. *Chinese Mental Health Journal, 17*(3), 161–163.

17

Needs Assessment: A Tool of Policy Practice in School Social Work

Lyndell R. Bleyer
Western Michigan University

Kathryn Joiner
Western Michigan University

◆ What Is Needs Assessment?
◆ Why Conduct a Needs Assessment?
◆ Planning Your Needs Assessment
◆ Implementing the Assessment
◆ Analyzing Your Data
◆ Reporting Your Findings
◆ Sources for Data and Other Resources
◆ State Government Resources
◆ Federal Government Resources
◆ Private and Nonprofit Resources

WHAT IS NEEDS ASSESSMENT?

The ability to conduct a needs assessment is a crucial skill in school social work. A needs assessment provides a systematic means of gathering data about a problem experienced by more than a few students in the school. It provides a broader context for the problems that students are experiencing. It provides a data-based means of communicating about this broader context in a way that school administrators, teachers, and community members can understand. It provides school social workers with a powerful, data-based means of customizing their roles to fit the needs of a particular school or district.

A human need is any identifiable condition that limits a person in meeting his or her full potential. Human needs are usually expressed in social, economic, or health-related terms. From a research perspective they are frequently qualitative statements. Needs of individuals may be aggregated to express similar needs in quantified terms (United Way of America, 1999).

A needs assessment is a data-gathering and planning activity to inform decision making. The data describe the characteristics, achievements, knowledge, behaviors, desires, needs, and/or opinions of a group of persons or an entire community. Many have attempted to define human need in a more specific way than the previous definition. These definitions have ranged from Erikson's (1968/1994) eight critical stages of development, to Maslow's concept of motivation based on a hierarchy of needs (Maslow, 1970). J. A. Ponsioen (1962) stated that every society's first duty is to take care of the basic survival needs of its citizens, which include biological, emotional, social, and spiritual needs. According to this view, each society must establish a level below which no person must be allowed to fall. These levels vary from society to society and change over time within the same society. Therefore, need is a normative concept involving value judgments and is greatly influenced by social, political, and economic conditions. For example, in the early 1950s a family was considered fortunate if it had a television. Today, a student whose family does not have a computer might be considered academically disadvantaged.

WHY CONDUCT A NEEDS ASSESSMENT?

The data obtained through a needs assessment process are used to
- Help understand the nature of a problem, its characteristics, magnitude, or consequences;
- Provide clues about causes and possible interventions;
- Compare students with other students or other schools;
- Identify and monitor trends (academic achievement, graduation rates, etc.);
- Document a need to be included in the problem statement of a grant proposal;
- Convince school officials that a problem exists that warrants the allocation of resources;
- Demonstrate the need for programs threatened by budget cuts;
- Document the support for new programs or interventions;
- Determine if and where additional resources are needed;

♦ Provide information to assist with planning or developing new services/programs; and
♦ Influence legislation.

A needs assessment can be as simple as examining existing data, and it can be as complex as a multiyear, multiphase study involving strategies to collect new data, through questionnaires or holding community forums. Designing and administering surveys is time consuming and expensive. It is generally wise to first explore and use existing data before considering any type of new data collection. Analyzing existing data can be very effective, and schools generally have a wealth of data on hand. Data are collected on attendance, test scores, demographic characteristics, free lunch eligibility, enrollment in specific programs, grades, results of standardized tests, and many other issues.

♦ Characteristics describe the group or population being studied and include ascribed features such as age, gender, race, and achieved characteristics like family income, poverty status, highest grade completed, and so on.
♦ Counts and rates provide data on the incidence and prevalence of conditions. For instance, the teen birthrate incidence is a measure of the number of births to teenage mothers compared to the number of female teenagers. Prevalence is the number of cases in a given population at a point in time, such as the number of teen suicides that occurred during a particular period in your community (Simons & Jablonski, 1990).
♦ Knowledge might include mathematics proficiency, reading comprehension levels, standardized test scores, street smarts, and so on.
♦ Beliefs and opinions range all the way from thoughts about one's self, such as self-esteem, to views about behavior, such as moral or cultural values, and stereotypes about others, such as gender or ethnic stereotypes.
♦ Behaviors might include frequency of talking out in class, the duration of study time, eating habits, use of alcohol, participation in sports, number of hours worked per week by full-time students, absences, number of students suspended or expelled by reason, and so on. Normative behaviors fall within culturally expected/acceptable ranges.
♦ Desires are what people want (or think they want) but do not have, whereas needs can encompass things missing that are self-perceived or perceived by others. Needs might be determined by directly asking the intended audience, or might be observed or inferred from available data. Desires and opinions are usually gathered directly from questions on a survey and/or are gathered through observation, interviews, focus groups, or community forums.

PLANNING YOUR NEEDS ASSESSMENT

Determining What You Need to Know

The first step is determining what you need to know, and then deciding what information is needed to make an informed decision. The second step is determining the best source, and balancing accuracy and reliability against cost and time constraints. Often as you begin to explore doing a needs assessment, the list of questions to be answered keeps growing. To expedite the process, make a checklist and decide which data are critical to your goal, which data would be helpful to clarifying issues, which would be interesting to have, and which will not add any insight to the problem being studied. As part of your checklist, include a source column: this may help you narrow your choices. Remember to look at existing data first before gathering new data.

For example, if a school district wants to know if a school breakfast program is a worthwhile pursuit, extensive research has already been done nationally indicating that behavior and academic performance of most students improve in school systems where breakfast programs have been established. So what would be studied is not the relationship between breakfast and performance, but rather the need for a breakfast program in a particular school district.

The information needed is found by answering these questions: (1) What percentage of students currently do not eat a nutritious breakfast? (2) How many children would be eligible for a subsidized breakfast program? And (3) for those children not eligible, but not having a nutritious breakfast, how many parents would buy into a breakfast program? Other factors influencing academic performance might also be interesting to study such as adequacy of sleep and parental involvement in study habits. Table 17.1 provides a grid to help frame the data needed, sources, methods of data collection, and level of usefulness.

To answer these questions, you might employ two tactics. First, have students keep a breakfast log or journal for three weeks in which they record everything they ate for breakfast each morning. To be effective, the students should update their journal as soon as possible after arriving at school (during homeroom or the first class of the day). The social worker would analyze these journals, using a nutritional guide, to give positive points for healthy foods consumed. If a question at the end of the journal asked if the student was eligible for free or reduced-price lunches and/or Medicaid, the response would answer the eligibility question. If a survey were developed for parents, it would also ask about eligibility, and for those not eligible, whether the parent would like nutritious breakfasts to be available for purchase. Do not forget to ask each family the grade level of the students in their family, in case your school system can phase in a new program only a few schools at a time.

TABLE 17.1   Types of Data or Questions and Associated Sources or Methods

Type of Data or Questions	Source and Method	Essential	Helpful	Interesting	No Use
Breakfast's impact on learning—does it make a difference?	Literature review, e.g., Nutrition & Learning www.nal.usda.gov/fnic/service/learnpub.htm	✓			
How many of our students eat a nutritious breakfast?	Students and/or parents via log, diary, or question	✓			
What are eligibility guidelines for subsidies?	U.S. Dept. of Health & Human Serv.; census		✓		
How many of our school's students are eligible?	School records: i.e., now eligible for free milk or lunch subsidy; census data on poverty		✓		
Are there any differences in achievement between:	*Grades and test scores plus:*				
Our students who do and don't eat breakfast?	students &/or parents, teacher observation	✓			
Our students who get <7 vs. >7 hours sleep?	students &/or parents log/diary, teacher observation			✓	
Our students with parental review of homework ?	parent signature on homework or not			✓	

Once the data are summarized, the school district can then look at need (students not currently eating nutritious breakfasts) and examine the cost of starting a breakfast program (the number of students eligible for free and reduced-price meals, and the number of students for whom parents are willing to pay). Eliminating barriers to participation is important, too. Schools that use a prepaid meal card that does not distinguish between family-paid and subsidized meals have had the greatest success in getting eligible students to participate in meal programs without the stigma of being identified by peers as low income.

Your school may have other topics that need answers. Some examples of information that may be useful in planning school services or child-related programs are the following:

- The number of children living in your community and the percentage of the total population that those children represent
- The number of children living in poverty
- The number of children experiencing homelessness (number using shelters and doubled-up with other families)
- Mobility/transience or the number and percentage of students who attend the same school in June that they attended in September
- The number of children with disabilities or special needs by type
- The number of children living in single-parent families or families in which both parents work outside the home
- The reported incidence of violent, serious, and misdemeanor juvenile crimes
- The services and resources already available to meet the specific need you are addressing

A thorough analysis could also look at other factors that might influence performance, such as amount of sleep, family income (access to reading materials, access to a home computer, educational toys, etc.), and parental involvement such as regular parental review of homework and encouragement of reading in the home.

Build a Base of Support by Getting Others Involved

Discuss the project with school administrators, teachers, parents, and student representatives to develop a clear idea of the purpose of the needs assessment and what you hope to learn or achieve. One way to encourage cooperation among all the concerned parties is to form a small committee to help you formulate an action plan. In addition to promoting ownership of the project, involving others in the planning stage is a good way to make sure you have not overlooked important details. Having the scope of the activity agreed on by a majority of those involved will reduce hurdles.

Write a Proposal or Plan

After you have determined the scope of the needs assessment, develop a written plan. In the proposal, include the following:
- Methodology of the needs assessment.
- Tasks to be performed and by whom.
- Projected time line. Do not set short deadlines. Give yourself enough time to collect data, review it, and produce a well-written summary.
- Budget for the project. Base this on the activities and time needed to carry them out. In addition to personnel, other expenses might include copying of questionnaires and summary reports, computer time, phone, postage, and resource materials.

In writing your plan, be realistic about whether you have the time and the expertise to carry out all elements of the project. Keep in mind the impact school breaks will have on your project. It may be that you will want to perform certain tasks but will need to engage additional help from other professionals to perform certain functions. If there are colleges or universities close by, you may be able to work out a plan for a graduate-level or upper-level undergraduate class to take on all or portions of your study as their semester project. Many colleges and universities have research centers that provide technical assistance and consultation to nonprofit organizations at cost. Large corporations may have research staff that they are willing to loan for committee work or consultation. If you intend to carry out the needs assessment yourself, consider whether you will need or can get release time.

IMPLEMENTING THE ASSESSMENT

Accurate information is key to successful planning. Having reliable data can help you make your point and persuade others. Think of the group or groups that will be the beneficiaries of the needs assessment and also think of the groups that will be potential funding sources or will make the decision to allocate resources to address the need. Gather data with both audiences in mind.

You are concerned about the need for enhanced substance abuse prevention education. You provide a number of statistics from existing data (see Centers for Disease Control Youth Risk Behavior Surveillance System under U.S. Census Bureau Publications, below) regarding substance use and abuse. These could be the age at which children begin to smoke or use drugs and alcohol, the number of teenagers and young adults who smoke or use alcohol, gender differences in who uses drugs, changes in use/abuse patterns over time, the number of automobile crashes attributed to substance abuse by age of driver, and so on. Some data may be readily available only at state or national levels. You may cite the data as found, or you could provide a rough estimation of local incidence by applying state or national rates to local populations. In addition, you may gather local incidents and estimates from key observers. You might use an anonymous questionnaire with the caution that the resultant information could be under- or overstated.

Gathering Existing Data

Be sure to make use of your own organization. Most school districts have data on absences, suspensions, number repeating a grade, standardized test scores, student turnover (migration in and out of school district or building), immunization records, and so on. Also check with the regional or intermediate school district and the state department of education. Local libraries possess a wealth of data. If materials are not available at your library, the librarian may be able to assist with interlibrary loans, searches of other libraries' catalogs, and computer searches of various databases, including educational associations, census data, and federal and state resources. A local college or university library may provide access to the most current literature.

♦ Do a literature review or search to find out what other studies or data exist.
♦ Establish a profile of the student population affected by the problem.
♦ Describe your organizational structure, goals, and objectives.
♦ List programs, services, and resources currently in place to meet the need.

Identify sources of existing data (see list at end of chapter for additional ideas and resources):

♦ Federal: U.S. Census Bureau, Department of Education, Department of Health and Human Services, and other federal agencies.
♦ State: Department of Education, Department of Public Health, state data centers, state human service leagues, special interest/lobby groups, and so on.
♦ Local: Public, college, and university libraries; police or public safety departments; chambers of commerce; school boards; technical consulting with local universities; and computer-based/Internet searches. Many hospitals maintain medical libraries that may be open to the public.
♦ Other national: Children's Defense Fund, Child Welfare League of America, and many nonprofit foundations that fund programs and research about children and teens.
♦ Your organization: teacher and guidance counselor records, evaluation forms, reports done for accreditation reviews, and standardized test scores.

Gathering New Data

Exhaust existing sources of data before determining if you need to collect any new data. If you determine that you need additional data that can only be gathered firsthand, several methods are possible: (1) observation, (2) focus groups, (3) key informant interviews, and (4) surveys.

The following methods might be used to collect new data for your project:

Observation. The classroom observation methods can be adapted for your needs assessment. Observation involves counting the frequency of events, their duration, the context of schooling, or interactions between persons. Observation of behavior is often the clearest method of measurement available. An example of data gathered through observation would be to count the number of aggressive behaviors during passing periods in a high school. To do so, it would be necessary to clearly define aggressive behavior and to develop codes for behavior that are exhaustive and mutually exclusive. Piloting the coding scheme with more than one observer and then checking for interrater reliability is helpful in developing your observation method.

Focus Groups. These small informal groups, led by a facilitator, gather information from audiences who fill out a questionnaire (e.g., teachers, students, parents, school administrators). You usually have a script or a short questionnaire to serve as a guide; however, the advantage of a focus group is that people build on the ideas of others (brainstorm, think tank) and therefore the group may explore ideas that you or the committee never anticipated. The groups need to be audiotaped or transcribed or the school social worker needs to take careful notes of responses.

Key Informant Interviews. Key informants are persons in a position to know or be aware of the problem you are studying. They may include the same people you would invite to a focus group (e.g., teachers, administrators, parents, other professionals, and/or students). A questionnaire is used, but the format enables the interviewer to follow up and clarify responses as well as explore areas that were not on the original questionnaire. This procedure is best when there are a limited number of issues to be discussed, a limited number of people to interview, and when there are interviewers available who are well trained not to be judgmental or to allow their own opinions to influence the outcome.

Surveys. If an appropriate instrument or questionnaire already exists and has been tested, it may be the best use of time to obtain permission to use that instrument. Instruments may be found in the review of the literature or through searches of collections of measures.

Surveys may be used with in-person or phone interviews or can be distributed by mail or in person at meetings or other gatherings, including focus groups. If you decide to design a new instrument, develop your questions with data analysis and output in mind. Try to make it as easy as possible for respondents to answer. Keep in mind that a large number of open-ended questions requiring the person to write answers (rather than circle answers on a provided list) will add considerable time to your data analysis process as you will have to categorize and then synthesize these responses. However, if you do not want to lead or limit the respondent by providing checklists or multiple-choice answers, an in-person or telephone interview, in which the interviewer reads the questions but not the checklist of answers, is often a good compromise.

If time permits, pilot test your questionnaire on a small group (12 to 30 people) to help you anticipate the range of responses for checklists, and to see if some questions are too ambiguous or poorly worded. At the very least, have the person who will analyze the data look at the questionnaire from the perspective of data analysis. The ideal situation is to envision the type of data you want in a report, then build a good questionnaire that addresses those topics.

Suggestions for Getting the Most Out of Each Method

Observation. Direct observation can be carried out in classrooms, lunch rooms, play areas, school buses, and at school meetings. Observation can be one of the most useful forms of data collection if the context of the observation is described, the target of observation is clearly defined, and recording methods are determined in advance. At the beginning of an observation session, the setting, time, date, and environment should be noted. Aspects of the environment that should be briefly described include the space, the furniture, temperature, noise level, number of people in the room, the arrangement of furniture, and the observer's general impression of the physical space. For example, when observing on a playground, one would describe the play equipment, the size of the space, the apparent level of maintenance of the equipment, the number of children at play, and the number and apparent roles of supervising adults. The observation should be timed, with beginning and ending times noted.

The target of the observation should be determined in advance, and it should be measurable and observable. For example, when observing a child in a classroom setting, one might look for off-task and on-task behaviors. It would be important to define off-task and on-task in advance, so that the behaviors can be quickly tallied during the observation period. Off-task behaviors might be the student getting out of his or her desk, talking to other students, or playing rather than working on an assignment. On-task behaviors might include listening to the teacher, following directions, and appearing to concentrate on the assignment given. It is also critical to decide in advance how the observation will be recorded. Often a standard observation sheet is used that includes spaces for the time, the location, and markings for time periods; a student's behavior, however, can be tallied on a simple piece of paper. As long as the recording method can be clearly understood after the event, many forms and approaches are workable. By describing the context of an observation, defining the target of observation, and determining recording methods in advance, the school social worker can make the most of observation as a form of data collection (Massat & Sanders, 2009).

Focus Groups. Carefully identify those you want included to be as representative as possible and to reduce bias or skewing. Schedule in advance. Hold the sessions at a location convenient for those who will be attending. Offer an incentive for attending (e.g., food, beverages, on-site child care for those with young children, drawing for a prize or gift certificate). Have someone lead the focus group who is experienced. If possible, tape-record your sessions so you will not have to concentrate on note taking; have a backup tape recorder.

Key Informant Interviews. Schedule the interviews in advance and have your questions prepared. Let those being interviewed know how long the interview will take and stick to that time frame.

Surveys. For mailed surveys, allow adequate time for the return mail, and possibly time to do follow-up if your initial response rate is low. Including a business-reply envelope or stamped self-addressed reply envelope will increase your response rate. This tends to be the least expensive method. However, response rates are lower in this method than other methods, unless you offer an incentive or have a hot topic on which people want to express their opinion.

For phone surveys, try to schedule your phone calls at the most likely time to reach your specific population. For example, schedule interviews during the day for stay-at-home moms or retirees, or evenings for working parents. This method tends to be expensive, unless you have volunteers, such as PTA members, to make the calls. Phone interviewers must be trained so that they ask the questions and record answers in a standard format. You will need approximately ten phone numbers for every three surveys you hope to complete, and this is if you attempt each phone number at least three times on different days and different times. It takes approximately six nights with twelve interviewers to complete 300 to 350 four-page questionnaires.

For in-person surveys, use interviewers who are friendly and outgoing. Keep the questions short so those being interviewed do not have to remember long sentences or lists of things. Use 3 x 5 index cards for answer scales; the interviewer can hand these to the person who completes them (i.e., 1 = strongly agree, 5 = strongly disagree). Carry out the surveys at a time when those you want to reach are not rushed. Pick your interview location carefully. For example, if you want to talk to students, a good place might be a quiet room located near a study hall or the library. Bad timing for students would be during midterm or final exams.

ANALYZING YOUR DATA

Unless your study is funded by a major foundation or a federal or state agency, which requires detailed documentation, you may be able to analyze your data by looking primarily at the frequency or prevalence of conditions. How many students are not eating a nutritional breakfast more than three times a week? How many students come from families with incomes below the poverty level? How many parents attend parent-teacher conferences? You may examine the frequency of opinions, such as these: How many parents believe their children are receiving a strong foundation in the three Rs? How many parents believe it is important to review their child's homework?

If, however, you need to provide more-extensive data analysis, many of today's computerized software packages will provide you with an assortment of statistical measures and tests that are appropriate for various types of data. If you feel your data-analysis skills are rusty, consider using a consultant to provide this level of analysis for you. Remember, it is important for the consultant to review your data-collection methodology, including the questionnaire, before you begin collecting data. Contact local colleges and universities for consultants within educational leadership, social work, statistics, and other disciplines that specialize in research.

Your data can be hand tabulated (for fewer than fifty respondents), entered into a spreadsheet such as Excel (for 50 to 500 respondents), or entered into and analyzed by a statistical analysis software package such as SPSS (Statistical Package for Social Sciences), SAS (Statistical Analysis System), or other software packages. Your method of tabulation depends on the size of the sample and the resources available to you.

Tips on Using Excel

For small sample sizes (50 to 500 respondents), you may manually enter the responses in Excel and calculate totals and percentages for each question or set of answers. The easiest way to get clean results is to enter each survey (with, e.g., subject, student, parent, or respondent) as a separate row. Enter each answer as a separate column. Then simply sum or total each column to get the frequency or number who answered yes or no, strongly agree, and so on, to each question. Table 17.2 represents the results of a few questions.

TABLE 17.2 Example Format for Data Entry and Analysis Using Excel Spreadsheet

ID	Eat Nutritious Breakfast 3x/Wk		Eligible for Free Lunch		Important for me to review my child's homework				
	Yes	No	Yes	No	Strongly Agree	Agree Somewhat	Undecided	Disagree Somewhat	Strongly Disagree
270	1		1		1				
271		1		1		1			
272	1			1			1		
273	1			1				1	
274		1	1				1		
275		1	1			1			
276		1		1	1				
277		1	1			1			
278	1			1		1			
279		1	1				1		
Total	4	6	5	5	2	4	3	1	0
%	40.0%	60.0%	50.0%	50.0%	20.0%	40.0%	30.0%	10.0%	0.0%

Another tip is to freeze the column headings. In that way as you enter more and more rows of data, the headings will remain at the top of the page, helping ensure that you are entering the data for the matching question. ID numbers are important for going back and finding data entry errors or tracing inconsistent answers back to a survey. Write the ID number on the survey as you begin to enter each questionnaire in the Excel file.

An important reminder when using Excel is that you have to block or highlight all the data in your rows before sorting data. If you sort without highlighting all the data, it sorts just that column and the tie or relationship to the rest of the questions for each individual is lost.

Optical Scanning

For larger samples (501 or more respondents), you may want to consider using an optical scan form for questionnaire responses. With this method, answer sheets are optically scanned instead of typed manually into a computer file. The optical scan format for data gathering and analysis generally saves time and money with large size samples. Customized scan forms, which allow the respondent to read the question and mark their answer next to each question, have the highest degree of accuracy. However, the minimum fee for printing customized forms is likely to be $1,000, making it more cost-efficient for surveys involving 501 or more respondents.

If your school has a software program that scans and produces results for teacher-designed student tests and quizzes, especially multiple-choice style questions, you may be able to adapt your questionnaire to use that software. Make sure such use does not violate the software's purchase agreement.

REPORTING YOUR FINDINGS

This is a critical element to the success of your needs assessment. Present your results in a manner that is easy to understand. Do not lose sight of your audience. Focus your attention on the specific issue you have been studying and use your data to show that the changes you are proposing will make a difference. If you want to convince your audience that there are programs or services that are effective, you should cite examples of successful programs or efforts.

Lengthy narratives are often not the best way to report your findings. You may find that a simple summary accompanied by charts, graphs, or tables showing your data in easy-to-interpret formats is the best way to present the results. Table 17.3 illustrates one method of displaying standardized test scores. The key statistic is the percentage of students with satisfactory test scores. School districts evaluate strengths and weaknesses in their curricula by looking at these data over time. Comparing your own school or

TABLE 17.3   Comparing Our School with State Proficiency Test Scores

Percentage of Students with Satisfactory Proficiency Test Scores: 2003–2004

Grade Level	4th		7th		11th	
Geographic Area	State	ZPS	State	ZPS	State	ZPS
Reading	47.5%	48.5%	44.2%	46.2%	43.5%	44.5%
Math	49.9%	50.2%	46.8%	48.4%	33.0%	32.7%
Science	70.0%	70.0%	61.9%	63.5%	58.1%	57.5%

State = State-wide average. ZPS = Average for our local public school
SOURCE: Fictitious Educational Assessment Program: 2003–2004

school district with others in your county or state provides a measure of where your district stands in relation to others.

Graphical Presentation

Sometimes it is easier to get a point across by providing the data in a graphic format (figure 17.1). For example, the difference in family income is very different for single-parent households in which the parent is a male or a female. Instead of wading through paragraphs of narrative, the reader can see at a glance how dramatically different economic circumstances can be for children living with two parents versus a single, female parent.

FIGURE 17.1   Impact of Family Type on Family Income

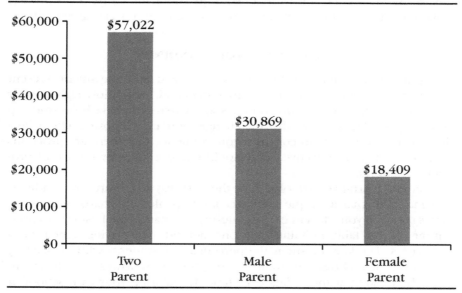

SOURCE: http://www.census.gov/hhes/income/histinc.html 8/9/2000

Conclusion

Needs assessment is a systematic data collection and analysis process. Its purposes are (1) to discover and identify the resources the community is lacking in relation to generally accepted standards, and (2) to transmit that information to those who make resource allocation decisions. The choice of data collection methods will depend on several factors, including availability of existing data, the topic of need being explored, and time and cost constraints. Using existing data will help conserve time and funds. Using focus groups and/or key informants will provide information on the level of support and help rank needs by your audience's opinion of their importance. Questionnaires, although more costly and time intensive, enable you to directly measure the desires, beliefs, knowledge, and opinions of your intended beneficiaries and benefactors.

SOURCES FOR DATA AND OTHER RESOURCES

The Internet has a wealth of information, including results of studies, how-to guides, and data. Many reports are available on the Internet, and some can be downloaded. Often the reports are in Adobe or PDF format. You can download the Adobe Reader software at the census.gov site and also at many of the sites that publish reports in the Adobe format. If you do not have a computer with a Web browser, try your school library or computer lab, your community's public library, or a local college or university computer center. Some of the federal, state, and private sources have data down to the local county level, as well as at state and federal levels.

STATE GOVERNMENT RESOURCES

U.S. Department of Education (relevant department for your state). School demographics, enrollment. http://firstgov.gov/Citizen/Topics/ Education_Training.html
State Government Sites

FEDERAL GOVERNMENT RESOURCES

National Contact Center: (800) 333-4636 toll-free between 8 A.M. and 8 P.M. Eastern time, Monday through Friday, except federal holidays.
Bureau of the Census Customer Services. Bureau of the Census, U.S. Census Bureau, 4600 Silver Hill Road, Washington, DC 20233. (301) 763-4636. Customer services has phone numbers for the following data sources:
Depository Libraries: 1,400 libraries (college and public) that have selected publications and computer files from the U.S. Government Publishing Office and Census Bureau

State Data Centers: Usually state government agencies (and assorted affiliates—often state universities) with data services. Centers receive Census Bureau data for their areas and make them available to the public.

Bureau of the Census Publications

2010 Census of Population Reports, Characteristics of the Population. (County and City Data Book: 2010 provides selected characteristics about counties and cities above 50,000 in population.)

Demographic data via the Census Bureau. http://www.census.gov

Centers for Disease Control Youth Risk Behavior Surveillance System: Youth risk-taking behavior such as cigarette use, social drinking, binge drinking, use of drugs, nonuse of seat-belts, riding with a driver who is drunk, suicidal ideation and attempts, being the victim of bullying, intimidation, or violence at school, getting into a physical fight, carrying a weapon, etc. http://www.cdc.gov/HealthyYouth/yrbs/index.htm

Library of Congress. http://www.loc.gov/

USA Services links to federal government sites, including Pueblo Publications. http://fic.info.gov/

The White House Social Statistics Briefing Room. http://www.whitehouse.gov/fsbr/ssbr.html Assessments and Evaluation

PRIVATE AND NONPROFIT RESOURCES

The University of Maryland Practical Assessment Research and Evaluation (PARE). http://pareonline.net/

Center for Schools and Communities, 275 Grandview Avenue, Suite 200, Camp Hill, PA 17011, (717) 763-1661. Committed to improving outcomes for children and families through training, technical assistance, program evaluation, research, and resource development. http://www.center-school.org/

Children's Defense Fund, 25 E Street N.W., Washington, DC 20001, (202) 662-3652. The State of America's Children Yearbook 2004. http://www.childrensdefense.org/

Council of Chief State School Officers, One Massachusetts Avenue, N.W., Suite 700, Washington, DC 20001-1431, (202) 336-7000. http://www.ccsso.org/

Harvard Family Research Project. Harvard Graduate School of Education, 50 Church Street, 4th Floor, Cambridge, MA 02138. Online publications. http://www.gse.harvard.edu/hfrp/

Kids Count. National Statistics for all 50 states, updated annually by Annie E. Casey Foundation. http://www.aecf.org/kidscount/. There may also be a Kids Count for your state that provides more-detailed county-level information. Example: Kids Count in Michigan: Data

Book 2004: County profiles of child well-being. (Produced annually). Michigan League for Human Services, 1115 S. Pennsylvania Avenue, Suite 202, Lansing, MI 48912, (517) 487-5436. http://www.milhs.org

National Association for the Education of Young Children (NAEYC) leads and consolidates the efforts of individuals and groups working to achieve healthy development and constructive education for all young children. Primary attention is devoted to ensuring the provision of high-quality early childhood programs for young children. http://www.naeyc.org/

National Campaign To Prevent Teen Pregnancy works to prevent teen pregnancy by supporting values and stimulating actions that are consistent with a pregnancy-free adolescence. http://www.teenpregnancy .org/

National Dropout Prevention Network provides linkages to and among educators, communities, researchers, parents, and the private sector to find solutions to the common goal of preventing and recovering dropouts. http://www.dropoutprevention.org/

National Foundation for the Improvement of Education. The National Education Association, 1201 16th Street, NW, Washington, DC 20036. http://www.nfie.org/

United Way of America. 701 N. Fairfax Street, Alexandria, VA 22314. http://national.unitedway.org

Youth Crime Watch (violence prevention programs). http://www.ycwa.org/

References

Erikson, E. H. (1994). *Identity, youth and crisis.* New York: W. W. Norton. (Original work published 1968)

Maslow, A. H. (1970). *Motivation and personality.* New York: Harper & Row.

Massat, C. R., & Sanders, D. (2009). Classroom observation. In C. R. Massat, R. Constable, S. McDonald, & J. P. Flynn (Eds.), *School social work: Practice, policy, and research* (7th edition, pp. 452–463). Chicago: Lyceum.

Ponsioen, J. A. (1962). *Social welfare policy: Contributions to theory.* The Institute of Social Studies, Vol. 3. The Hague: Mouton.

Simons, J., & Jablonski, D. (1990). *An advocate's guide to using data.* Washington, DC: Children's Defense Fund.

United Way of America. (1999). *Community status reports and targeted community interventions: Drawing a distinction.* Alexandria, VA: Author.

18

Practitioner Research in the Schools: Becoming a Change Agent

Nancy Farwell
University of Washington

◆ Conducting Research in Schools
◆ Applications of School-Based Research
◆ Connecting to Unrecognized Constituencies
◆ Improving Home–School–Community Partnerships
◆ Promoting Inclusion and Involvement
◆ Beginning Your Research
◆ Low-Cost, Straightforward Methods

School social workers are uniquely situated to work collaboratively within interconnected networks of students, families, communities, and educational institutions to help improve educational experiences, processes, and outcomes in authentic ways.[1] As schools become key public institutions fostering social and economic development, educational systems face increased demands to respond to the changing nature of a knowledge-based economy. New trends and policies have brought profound changes for education, notably the increasing requirements that schools provide knowledge and skills linked to economic production needs. Entrepreneurial approaches, concerned with profit and micro-focused knowledge instead of

1. *Author's note:* The author wishes to thank Professor Sung Sil Lee Sohng and Professor Richard Weatherly for their substantial contributions to earlier versions of this chapter.

a broad and humanistic understanding of our surrounding world, are becoming more prevalent in public education. Increasingly, school restructuring, accountability, testing, standardization, and measurement of educational activities have been framed as solutions to both social and educational problems (Gorlewski & Porfilio, 2013; Lipman, 2004). Changes in the global economy require educational administrators and practitioners to examine closely the interlinked imperatives of productivity, accountability, and community in the processes and management of public education (Katz & Rose, 2013). Under conditions of increasing social, economic, and political inequalities, inclusion is ever more crucial to the mission of both public education and social work, ensuring that those who have been marginalized or excluded have the opportunity to participate fully.

As a practitioner-researcher, one views oneself as having the potential to build knowledge, an act of learning as well as a form of professional practice. Information is everywhere. One must learn to be attentive to information, which sheds light on issues and processes that can promote creative and collaborative ways of identifying and addressing changing needs, challenges, and opportunities. Being a practitioner-researcher also means that one becomes disciplined: one learns to account for one's reasons for gathering information, for structuring questions in particular ways, for how one gathers information, and for how one uses it.

This chapter demystifies a process generally considered the exclusive domain of professionally trained researchers. It suggests low-cost research approaches that can be carried out by school social workers. Practitioner research is a unique genre of research. Experimental researchers strive for valid and reliable measures to ensure generalizability of their results, and naturalistic researchers seek trustworthiness and authenticity to uncover the social rules for the situations they describe. In contrast, practitioner-researchers seek to understand individual actions, policies, and events in their work environment in order to make professional decisions. As practitioner-researchers, school social workers participate in improving educational outcomes for students, and restructuring schools and influencing curriculum. They have the potential to transform school social work practice, develop on-site prevention programs, involve students in networks of community-based supports, and foster social and political change to ensure that schools become more inclusive. Practitioner research helps legitimate knowledge produced within the lived realities of professionals. It reaches both within and beyond educational institutions to facilitate collaborative efforts with communities and families to support students' social development needs, and to contribute to the social work knowledge base.

A number of concurrent forces have advanced the growth and legitimacy of practitioner research. First, the conduct of research has been linked to the professionalization of social work practice. Second, following the postmodern challenge of objective truth, narratives, self-studies, cases, biographical methods, vignettes, and other writings, as well as oral histories, have been recognized as potentially significant sources for the knowledge base (Chamberlayne, Bornat, & Wengraf, 2000; Harold, Palmiter, Lynch, & Freedman-Doan, 1995; Holland, 1991; Josselson, 1996; Martin, 1995). Third, the interest in practitioner research has also increased in response to the movement to create reflective, critical practitioners (Altrichter, Posch, & Somekh, 1993; Dodd & Epstein, 2012; Jay, 2003; Pearlmutter, 2002). Fourth, educational reformers have recognized that the success of reforms is dependent on an understanding of the context in which they are to be implemented. Using inquiry processes such as action research, practitioners can bridge the gulf between policies and the actuality of everyday lives, adapting the reforms to suit particular work situations (Armstrong & Moore, 2004). Emphases on the complex interrelated contextual factors that are the reality of students' lives as well as the interconnections of these with educational processes and outcomes have fueled a shift to qualitative research methods in education since the 1970s (Hammersley, 2000). Practitioner research can also underscore the importance of connective pedagogies that flexibly link individual learning styles and needs with the curriculum as well as with relationships, values, and experiences in the wider community (Corbett, 2001; Simpson, 2004). Finally, the work of Paolo Freire (1973) and others (Brydon-Miller & Maguire, 2009; Carr, 1995; Hick, 1997; Noffke & Stevenson, 1995; Sohng, 1996) has forged a link between practitioner research and critical pedagogical thought. Practitioner inquiry and other forms of action research are seen as emancipatory tools to help practitioners to become aware of the often hidden hierarchical institutional structures that govern their work.

Following an introductory discussion of research in the schools, the author considers a range of alternative applications and discusses their relevance for the school-based practitioner. The chapter outlines guidelines for initiating research, and identifies several low-cost methods for gathering data and using research.

CONDUCTING RESEARCH IN SCHOOLS

The impact of the research explosion on local schools is well known, showing itself in constantly growing bureaucratic requirements. School personnel spend much of their time completing forms and reports, usually providing data for research conducted elsewhere. The bulk of research, evaluation, and data-gathering efforts in the schools is a response to federal and state legislative mandates. Legislative bodies demand strict accounting for the funds they appropriate, and impose heavy reporting and evaluation requirements. Legislation may also mandate regulations for what is legitimate research. For example, the No Child Left Behind Act of 2001 specifies that the majority of research funded under federal law utilize experimental designs and methods, randomized control groups, and models of causality (Christ, 2014; Lather, 2004; No Child Left Behind Act of 2001), methods that are also stipulated in the 2009 Race to the Top Initiative (Gorlewski & Porfilio, 2013).

Such methodological requirements can make research the domain of academics, whose specialized language and methods are assumed to be necessary conditions for scientific validity. In fact, the use of complex statistical methods often limits the communication of research results, shutting out practitioners and the public. All too often esoteric language and methods are worn as a badge of expertise and rationalized as necessary for scientific precision. Local school personnel, parents, and community members are rarely involved in designing research, assessing research products, or suggesting applications. More often, these potential partners are considered instruments for achieving organizational objectives. They are, in this sense, passive receivers of information and objects of administrative control. Furthermore, even the most rigorous research, designed from afar, may yield statistically significant findings that have little practical application.

APPLICATIONS OF SCHOOL-BASED RESEARCH

If externally driven research is so often irrelevant to practice as suggested above, then why should school social workers be concerned with research at all? There are compelling reasons, both defensive and affirmative, for school social workers to conduct their own research. In this age of accountability, implementation of performance-based accountability systems can bring about complex reactions in school systems. These reactions may also affect families and communities. Externally imposed performance-based accountability systems are rarely adequate for producing significant changes in program delivery at individual schools, beyond an emphasis on test performance, and they may even promote a false sense of accountability (Elmore & Fuhrman, 2001; Kwalwasser, 2012).

Practitioner-based research can support a bottom-up change process, warding off top-down bureaucratic measures, and supporting a collegial form of accountability. Student engagement and learning are nested within complex contextual family and community networks that practitioner-based research can help illuminate. Educational reforms emphasize working toward institutionalization of cooperative principles as the focus of school renewal (Board on Children, Youth and Families, Division of Behavioral and Social Sciences and Education [BCYF], 2003; Holy, 1991). Studies of educational innovations suggest that involving the local school community in collaborative research helps mobilize the capacity for internal regeneration of policies and strategies for school-driven improvement (Beatty, 2007; Broussard, 2003; Herr, 1995; Jones, 1991; Sirotnik, 1989). Rather than being passive consumers or clients, parents and community members can become active partners in the collaborative network (Anderson-Butcher, et al., 2010; Armstrong & Moore, 2004).

Because school social workers spend their working lives with students, they are in an excellent position to identify educational issues firsthand. They are interested in what works and are sensitive to the practical constraints of school settings in ways that outside researchers may not be. The utilitarian, participatory, and localized nature of school-based research significantly reduces the gap between the discovery of what works and practical applications of this knowledge (deMarrais, 2004; Elliott, 1991; Hammersley, 2000). School-based research is the antithesis of externally generated and externally imposed change. Just as administrators and policy makers use research as a political resource, school social workers can do the same. Teachers, school social workers, psychologists, and others can use research to ward off new programs and requirements that are unfeasible, impractical, or harmful to students. On the other hand, they can use research in a positive way to gain support for new program initiatives, to improve school climate, to demonstrate the effectiveness of their services, to obtain additional resources, or to find out what kinds of interventions work best. School social workers can use research to move beyond traditional clinical roles to enlarge the arena of practice. Research can be used as an adjunct to consultation and as a way of demonstrating the potential of a more ecological social work role.

Fostering Collaborative Practice

School social workers are in an especially advantageous position to develop collaborative school-based research. The profession has long been interested in effecting change through the empowerment, participation, and action of the people involved. A collaborative approach calls on interactive skills, cultural sensitivity, group decision making, and mediation and conflict management skills (Brydon-Miller & Maguire, 2009). This kind of collaborative research is characterized by (1) participation in problem posing, (2) practitioner participation in data gathering that answers questions relevant to their concerns, and (3) collaboration among members of the school community as a critical community. Here, research is aimed at generating data, which can guide and direct planned change. It involves observing, assessing, interviewing, reading, analyzing reports and documents, and writing findings. These skills are already within the behavioral repertoire of school social workers. We will review how to carry out research tasks. However, first we will examine some of the uses and potential benefits of practitioner-initiated school-based research.

Developing Multicultural Resources: Fostering Inclusion

Consciousness of multiple realities lies at the heart of postmodern thinking, spurring us to accomplish the vision of social inclusion that lies at the heart of equity in public education. Schools must incorporate diverse voices into their communities and their curricula, as well as in the discernment and formulation stages of the policy-making process, with particular attention to those who have been silenced (C. Banks, 2005; J. Banks, 1996; Sleeter,

1996). For example, a social worker at a predominantly white school noted that students of color continued to drop out at a high rate. She formed a multiethnic team in collaboration with an administrator and a teacher to conduct an action research project examining the experiences of students of color at the school. The project helped focus attention on the larger institutional processes that silenced students' experiences of exclusion and alienation (Herr, 1995). The key concept in this endeavor is the deliberate, thoughtful development of research that illuminates the diversity of perspectives and interests, accompanied by an analytical and implementation process that is inclusive of these interests. School-based research can offer a promising vehicle for assessing cultural diversity in curriculum, classroom, and school practices, and improving the campus climate for a diverse student body.

To make the case for improving multicultural resources and building a more inclusive approach, you might begin by taking a look at how the composition of the student population at your school has changed over the years. To get an overall picture, you might examine student characteristics over the past ten years, comparing two different years for which you can get good demographic data. In considering diversity at your school, you should also familiarize yourself with both official and informal institutional policies and procedures, academic programs, and instructional support. Have these policies and programs kept pace with the changing student population? Are they being implemented fairly and effectively? A social worker in a large urban school district received many complaints from parents that their English-speaking children were placed in English as a second language (ESL) classes for no apparent reason other than assumptions about their language abilities, because they had Latino surnames. Similarly, bicultural instructional assistants in another district noted that recently arrived East African children were being placed inappropriately in special education classes, instead of in ESL classes. Social workers in these instances can collaborate with teachers, instructional aides, and assessment personnel in a self-study to investigate processes within the school, such as assessment and placement of students in remedial, special education, and ESL classes. Such processes may be affected by bias with regard to student ethnicity, immigration status, age, or gender. Combined with an analysis of changing demographics, policies, and available resources, this self-study can make the case for in-service training for staff and improved bilingual-bicultural resources such as student mentoring, tutoring, and support programs.

CONNECTING TO UNRECOGNIZED CONSTITUENCIES

The constituent base of multicultural education in this society consists of disenfranchised people, particularly parents and children of color and/or of low-income backgrounds; immigrants and refugees; children with different abilities; youths transitioning to schools from juvenile justice programs; and youths who self-identify as lesbian, gay, bisexual, transgender, or questioning (LGBTQ), as well as their parents. However, in many arenas of multicultural activity, professionals sometimes act as if they were the constituents. Professionals can certainly be allies, but they need to recognize their power and their self-interest, which may lead them to shape multicultural education to fit their own needs. As Sleeter (1996) observed, much of the literature on multicultural education and inclusion is directed toward professionals, often substituting for dialogue between school personnel and community people. Research redirected toward, and in collaboration with, parents and community activists from diverse groups can serve as an empowering resource for those who are often unheard and uninvolved. A community needs assessment, for example, provides an instrument whereby community people can make their educational needs known, and can express an action agenda for school change (Delgado-Gaitan, 1993; Williams, 1989).

IMPROVING HOME–SCHOOL–COMMUNITY PARTNERSHIPS

School social workers are in a good position to facilitate the involvement of family members in their children's education, a critical factor in student and family success (Broussard, 2003). Practitioner research can provide avenues for the involvement of immigrant and refugee parents and other marginalized families in the schools through parent support groups, multicultural policy advocacy groups, and facilitation of direct parent–school communication, as well as by ensuring that the school provides a welcoming environment for families (Coats & Xu, 2013; Delgado-Gaitan, 2001, 2004; Witherspoon, 2002). Practitioners concerned about community violence and personal safety of students can use action research to assess the impact of local programs such as Neighborhood Watch in protecting youths from violence as they walk to and from school. Such research can identify methods of retaining students who live in potentially dangerous neighborhoods (Salcido, Ornelas, & Garcia, 2002). Collaboration with public housing and community-based youth programs can be an excellent means for the practitioner-researcher to understand and address student concerns regarding contradictions between their self-perceived strengths, obstacles in their actual community contexts, and the norms and missions of mainstream institutions such as the schools (Gran-O'Donnell et al., 2001).

PROMOTING INCLUSION AND INVOLVEMENT

Creating and sustaining inclusive education involves the school social worker as cultural agent (Blair, 2002). Practitioner research can be instrumental in promoting an agenda for inclusion, through the process itself, as well as by transforming school culture, curricula, practices, and community relationships. Action research involving students of color or other marginalized populations such as GLBTQ youths can be designed to educate the school community about diversity and homophobia, encouraging student engagement through activism and advocacy (Herr, 1995; Lunt & Fouche, 2009; Peters, 2003). For example, students of First Nations from West Seattle High School formed a community of inquiry to examine the use of Native American mascots, nicknames, and logos within the public school system, and the impact of that use on Native American youth cultural identities. Supported by the school social worker and the Native American community, they identified sixty-five schools in Washington State that have Indian mascots or logos. Their research indicates that Indian imagery within schools not only disrespects Native Americans by buying into historical stereotypes and caricatures, but also perpetuates cultural ignorance and insensitivity within what is purported to be a supportive learning environment. The students who were originally interviewees became collaborators in a passionate change process, leading the campaign to change racist school practices and the school environment (Beeson, 2002). Another example is a community youth mapping project carried out by Latino and Southeast Asian students in Seattle. This project was supervised by one of the authors and a school social work intern in collaboration with key community-based social service agencies in 2003. Youth mapping provided a guided forum for youths to identify and critically examine assets and deficits in their community, and to find ways to build on the assets and articulate actions to address the deficits.

Demonstrating the Effectiveness of Services

As practitioners, we generally know, or think we know, the effectiveness of the services we provide. We sometimes assume that because we are professionals, others should take us at our word when we make claims about the need for and benefits of our services. However, in the absence of convincing evidence, such claims can be dismissed by others as self-serving.

One school social worker, for example, was valued by the principals and teachers of the schools she served for her effectiveness in handling crisis situations—episodes of students acting out, students' threatening violent and destructive behavior, or confrontations between students and teachers. She was frequently called on to handle emergencies. She believed that this disruption of her regular work schedule was well worth the price, because her availability to handle crises gave her the credibility needed to get into the schools to do some of the more routine work. However, the principal did not officially recognize her crisis work. It was not part of her job description, nor did her superiors know how much time it took or how much the principals appreciated it. Had she taken the time to document the number of such cases per month, to describe the circumstances and outcomes, and to record the feedback from the students and teachers, she could have used these data to gain official acknowledgment of an enlarged work role. She might also have gained greater insights into her work, recognition of her contribution, additional resources or decreased demands, or authorization for training school personnel in crisis intervention. As it stood, her work was appreciated by many but unacknowledged and unrewarded by administrators.

Fostering Collegial Accountability

School-based research conducted by practitioners on practical concerns can foster a greater congruence between research and practice and help to demystify the research process. It can also contribute to building greater collegial, shared accountability. Let us assume, for example, that a social worker and a group of teachers have developed an alternative tutorial strategy, adding adult helpers to the classroom to work with a group of students, rather than taking these students out of class for remedial instruction. The team wants to examine the effect of this experiment. They could measure the results by outcomes such as students' progress, increase/decrease of tutoring time, or student and teacher assessments of the new procedures. Here, the purpose of research does not necessarily require rigorous research procedures but rather calls for collegial problem identification and problem solving. The process of observing students and gathering data may also be an occasion for the team to examine and reflect on their interaction and behaviors with students. By having the opportunity to experience and experiment with the research process, team members may gain an increased appreciation of research and come to demand more of themselves, by being more clear about learning objectives, and more parsimonious and specific in data they collect.

Establishing the Need for New Services

Arguments for the establishment of new services are all the more persuasive when supported by research data. Let us assume, for example, that the social worker and teachers believe that there is a need for a school breakfast program. School administrators resist this idea, concerned about the cost as well as the administrative problems of implementing a program for which there may be little constituent demand. In the absence of any other compelling reasons, administrators can easily deflect teachers' and social workers' requests for the program. When the request for such a program is accompanied by data showing support from students and parents, the number of children who come to school without breakfast, well-documented reports of behavioral problems and the lack of attentiveness of children who have not had breakfast, information on effects of nutritional deficits on learning, and data on the costs of the program, administrators would more seriously consider the request. In another example, the social worker is concerned about reports of bullying across multiple age groups on and near the school grounds, and advocates for the implementation of an antibullying and conflict resolution curriculum. The principal discourages this due to lack of funds and concerns about workload. The social worker surveys parents, children, and teachers about the school climate and documents serious instances of bullying experienced by a significant percentage of children. The social worker then identifies bullying as a priority area for intervention, and the principal adopts a curriculum used in other district schools, with support from the Parent-Teacher Association.

Establishing the Need for Additional Resources

School personnel are constantly seeking increased resources or reduced workloads to accomplish their work in keeping with professional standards. Administrators hear such requests so often that they are routinely discounted. Administrators like to sidestep conflicts between professional standards or official policy requirements and the limited resources available to meet them. This forces the practitioner to reconcile conflicting demands as best he or she can. For example, with the requirements of the Individuals with Disabilities Education Act (IDEA; 1990), school social workers, psychologists, special education class teachers, and other educational specialists are often expected to carry out their regular work while accommodating time-consuming and cumbersome assessment and paperwork requirements for increased numbers of children. Administrators, themselves caught between federal and state requirements and limited resources, often thrust the problem downward, leaving it to school-based personnel to figure out how best to meet the new demands. School personnel work harder, take paperwork home with them, forgo planning and preparation time, or routinize work tasks. A more proactive approach would be to conduct team-based data gathering, documenting carefully the time required to perform specific tasks, thereby demonstrating the impossibility of completing the tasks without sacrificing quality and deferring other responsibilities. Furthermore, the group involved in such data gathering and analysis can identify ways to reduce duplication and redundancy and can recommend new procedures more relevant to the school community.

Testing New Programs or Procedures

Often administrators develop new procedures in response to mandates from Congress, the state legislature, or the local school board. This top-down approach often results in new requirements being imposed with insufficient sensitivity to actual conditions within the schools. School-based personnel cope as best they can. However, it makes more sense to test new programs and procedures before they are implemented throughout the system. As an advocate for and participant in pilot tests, school social workers can expand their role while indirectly contributing to the empowerment of all school-based staff.

Illuminating Practices Normally Hidden from View

In all organizations, schools being no exception, there generally are some practices tacitly accepted but at variance with official policy and not openly discussed. Research offers a way of bringing such practices out into the open by guaranteeing anonymity and confidentiality, thereby depersonalizing what may be very emotional issues. Examples include disciplinary practices, cultural sensitivity, discrimination, or concerns about student-to-student sexual harassment and harassment based on actual or perceived sexual orientation. Teachers may be reluctant to discuss their own practices because such policies may violate official policy or because of the divisive nature of the issue. Such emotion-laden issues may be driven underground and beyond the scope of discussion. An anonymous survey might elicit responses that would otherwise never be openly discussed; administrators, however, might prefer not to hear some responses or to know about some practices.

A favorite method of politicians to avoid taking action is to call for a study of the issues. Although outright opposition to an undesirable policy may be viewed by the administration as insubordination, proposing a study is a more constructive and conciliatory step that is harder for recalcitrant administrators to oppose. If, in fact, a study is undertaken, the results may help resolve differences about implementing a proposed policy.

BEGINNING YOUR RESEARCH

We have discussed a number of ways in which research can be used to enhance the role of the school social worker and to support organizational change in an inclusive process initiated from below. We turn now to the more difficult question of how to do research. In this section of the chapter, we offer guidelines for getting started and suggest ways to augment limited resources. The concluding section provides a discussion of readily available data sources and methods of conducting research that do not require special research training.

Questions for Focus

The most important part of research is your thinking process while planning and carrying out the research. Here are six questions to help you put your research process together. When you work through these questions, you end up with a research design.

1. What do you want and need to know? Why do you want to know this? Right from the start you will have to be clear about how you will use the information you collect.
2. What do you already know? Answering this question lets you use the information you already have, or that is available in the published literature.
3. Where do you go to find out? Where are the answers to your questions? Are you going to ask people? Are you going to review reports and documents?
4. Whom do you ask? If you are going to ask people to give you information, whom are you going to ask? If you need certain documents, where are you going to find them?
5. What kind of information do you need? Do you need descriptive information? Do you need some numbers? Do you need stories? Do you need information that tells you what others think? Answering these questions will help you make decisions about what research tools to develop.
6. Do you need help? If so, what kind of help do you need? Advice about the topic? Help with research tools? Help in deciding whom to interview? Help with language translation or interpretation? Help from colleagues, students, parents, or supervisors?

Be Clear about Objectives

The first step in contemplating any research is clarity of objectives, both political and substantive. What are the specific group or organizational goals to be accomplished by undertaking the research? Will these objectives be realized if the research is carried out? What are the costs in terms of both resources and possibly strained relations? If, for example, the objective is to encourage the implementation of a free breakfast program, would research findings in fact bring about that result?

It is important to distinguish between broad goals and specific objectives. A frequent error of practitioner-researchers is to undertake a study with only vague objectives, hoping to make some sense out of the findings later. This approach is time consuming and wasteful for researcher and participants alike. For example, in approaching the issue of discipline, one could try to find out about teacher, student, and parent attitudes as well as actual practices in the schools. However, if current practices are the focus of concern, then that is what should be studied. If teachers' support for a particular policy is at issue, then their attitudes and opinions may be a more appropriate focus. The objectives, framed as precisely as possible, should determine the direction of the research, not vice versa.

Don't Try for Too Much

When thinking in research terms, everything becomes a potential subject of research. One must guard against being overly ambitious and be realistic about the adequacy of the resources available to do the job. If one is planning to do a study without additional help, how much time can one realistically spend? Will this be sufficient to complete the study? One should estimate the time needed to accomplish each specific step. Even if it can be done, are the results likely to be worth the effort? If the answer to the latter two questions is "no," then the social worker should not undertake the research.

Involve Others at an Early Stage

There are two reasons to involve others at the early stage of a project. First and most important, the contributions of others enlarge the scope of issues considered and provide an essential source of new ideas. Second, some potential collaborators and/or stakeholders might feel slighted, and justifiably so, if asked to join a project after the major directions have already been decided by others. On the one hand, group process may complicate the orderly formulation and achievement of objectives, and groups are subject to groupthink, which may constrain the consideration of alternatives. On the other hand, research aimed at changing current practices should be undertaken with a view of building constituencies of support to help implement the findings.

Ask for Help

One way of extending available resources is to get additional help. This might mean seeking release time or volunteer assistance from colleagues and students. If the research objective is to bring about change, it is desirable to bring about the greatest possible involvement of both colleagues and school community. Additional resources are available outside the school system. These include academics, student researchers, retired teacher associations, Parent-Teacher Associations, community organizations, and advocacy groups. Advocacy groups have their own particular interest in practices within the schools, although their advocacy position may itself increase suspicions of administrators. Academics are often interested in consulting on practical issues and may even be willing to undertake the research themselves if offered an interesting research issue and access to a site. University students are often available from a number of academic disciplines such as social work, education, psychology, sociology, political science, and public administration to carry out research that satisfies their practicum requirements under academic supervision.

LOW-COST, STRAIGHTFORWARD METHODS

Most social research is an extension of logical processes used in everyday life. In shopping for new clothes, getting estimates for car repair or home improvement, or planning a vacation, the customary first step is to gather data on the reliability of the seller, the quality of the merchandise or service, and its availability and price. Prior to the data-gathering stage, there may be some assessment of the need and ability to pay. Similarly, when contemplating research in the work setting, a first step is to specify the objectives of the research and then develop a research plan. This involves a determination of the information needed, its availability, the methods required to obtain it, and the relative costs of time, materials, and other resources. At this point, you may also wish to review documents, data, and literature that are relevant to your research questions.

Use of Readily Available Data

There are several research approaches that require a minimum of time, some of which may be undertaken using readily available data. Although it is generally desirable to enlist the support of administrators and colleagues in undertaking research, there occasionally may be situations in which some administrators are threatened by the proposed research and withhold permission or seek in other ways to block it. In such instances, it is still possible to gather data using records and documents that are public information. Perhaps the most straightforward kind of research involves the analysis of existing data. Schools are constantly compiling reams of data on every conceivable activity. Much of this information is funneled to state and federal agencies to meet reporting requirements but is not necessarily analyzed for local administrative purposes. Examples include aggregate data on pupil characteristics, family income, attendance, grades, achievement test scores, the numbers of students receiving free lunches, the incidence of visual or dental problems, the prevalence of handicapping conditions, the numbers in special classes or programs, the incidence of problems requiring disciplinary action, and so forth. Other data are available with respect to class size and caseloads of social workers and other educational specialists. Frequently, when scholars examine caseload sizes in relation to performance requirements, a discrepancy between expectations and the reality of the workload is immediately apparent. The fact that a class for children with special needs includes fifteen children of differing ages and levels of ability and is taught by one teacher with no aide offers prima facie evidence of a resource deficiency. Alternatively, if a particular school has an unusually high incidence of violence, then there may be cause to investigate further.

Use of Public Documents

Another invaluable source of information is the school district's budget. The budget is a planning document that paints a good picture of what the district actually does and what its priorities are, as represented by the commitment of resources. An examination of the budget permits a comparison of the stated objectives with the actual allocation of resources to achieve those objectives. Other public documents that may shed light on local practices are federal and state laws, administrative codes and regulations, court decisions, state agency policy and procedural statements, and state and local education agency reports. (Many of these public documents and data are available on the Internet.) A reading of the state or federal laws and regulations may reveal a discrepancy between these requirements and local practices. Some administrators intentionally keep information about the specific state and federal requirements from those school personnel who must implement them. Knowledge of deliberate violations of law can give school-based staff a powerful tool for advocating change. School practices with regard to discipline, suspensions, expulsions, and the notification and involvement of parents in placing children in special programs may be at variance with the law and/or district policy. If so, a range of interventions can encourage change, all the way from judicious questioning to encouraging advocacy groups to file suit.

Calculations of Costs and Procedural Practices

Another powerful kind of analysis is estimating the costs of procedures and practices. For example, it is a humbling exercise to calculate the cost of a single meeting in relation to its objectives and results. When one counts the dollar value of the participants' time, the costs can be quite substantial. Certain reporting requirements are expensive, yet the costs are rarely calculated or compared with costs of actual instructional time. In processing paperwork, one must consider both the actual cost of completing the forms and reports as well as other hidden costs. These hidden costs include the costs of printing the forms, moving the paper through the organization, handling and storing it, and the time of those who must read it, comment on it, and analyze it. Similarly, use of digitalized documents requires computer hardware, software, and technical support. Cost comparisons of alternative procedures can be used to support one alternative over another.

Seeking out Library, Internet, and Other Agency Resources, Records, and Research

Chances are good that most problems have been encountered elsewhere and subjected to some kind of analysis or research. Therefore, good starting points in any research activity are the library and the Internet. A review of the literature provides an essential foundation for any research you plan to do. Reviewing the literature establishes what is already known on the topic and forms the basis for the research focus. The existing literature can also suggest methods for carrying out the research. Published measures and questionnaires can make the job a lot easier by providing an established means of collecting data. The key is to familiarize oneself with the literature before finalizing any research questions or design. You may find that your question can be answered primarily by using existing studies, rather than by collecting original data.

When reviewing the literature, it is important to examine the most recent studies, especially since they will generally include summaries of earlier work in their review of the literature. However, classic studies must not be ignored. Often these classics can be identified by examining the reference lists of the articles you find when a particular author or study is repeatedly studied. This would indicate that their work is significant in the field and should be read. For example, someone who is interested in studying the role of the school social worker would not ignore the work of Lela Costin or Paula Allen-Meares.

University librarians are generally helpful in locating studies and reports. There are a number of excellent computerized reference files that can produce a list of titles and abstracts on specific subjects at nominal cost. Using online databases, practitioners from large and small schools, and from urban and rural communities, can gain access to a range of popular and specialized periodicals, government publications, historical resources, and newspapers. Some excellent databases that can assist in a literature search are The Educational Resources Information Center (ERIC), PsycINFO, EBSCO Host, Expanded Academic Index, Social Work Abstracts, Sociological Abstracts, JSTOR, and many others available at libraries or through an Internet search engine. Census data, historical resources, government documents, and newspapers can also be accessed using databases such as International Data Base, Historical Abstracts, GPO Access, PAIS International, and LexisNexis. Many of these databases include online, full-text copies of articles in important journals. Access may be limited to patrons of libraries that have purchased access to these resources. However, gaining access through a local university or through your university alumni association makes a wide range of electronic resources available to you. Partnering with a university faculty member or graduate student, or a professional association, can also make these resources more accessible to the school social worker. In some states, all citizens of the state have the right to use the state university libraries, including their electronic resources.

Academic specialists in schools of education and social work, and departments of psychology and sociology may be familiar with specific bodies of literature and be willing to share their expertise with practitioners. For just about any problem that can occur in a public school setting, there are likely to be some interested specialists. In addition to academic departments of universities, educational specialists are found in the U.S. Department of

Education, in state departments of education, in contract research firms, and on the staffs of interest groups such as state chapters of the Children's Defense Fund, Council for Exceptional Children, National Association of School Boards, Council of Chief State School Officers, National Association of Social Workers (NASW), National Alliance for the Mentally Ill (NAMI), state school social work associations, and so on. A few phone calls or a quick visit to organizational Web sites are generally sufficient to access such networks and learn what work has already been done in a specific problem area. For example, if one is investigating student discipline, the Children's Defense Fund might provide a number of references to completed studies, summaries of legal opinions and pertinent laws, and suggestions about model programs. The state teachers' union may maintain a research staff and have access to information on many school issues. Newspaper articles provide another source of data about school policies. In larger cities, local newspapers often have reporters who specialize in educational concerns and who develop expertise in particular educational areas. The papers themselves frequently maintain clipping files, as does the school administration. This is an important documentary record that one should not overlook. The school board minutes are available to the public; they supply a documentary record of actions taken and contemplated.

Methods for Gathering New Data

Other methods for gathering data about school activities include surveys, structured observation, interviews, focus groups, action research, and online databases. Questionnaires are advantageous for gathering information that safeguards anonymity and for providing a structured format for analysis of responses. The disadvantages are that they restrict the amount of data that can be gathered and analyzed, and responses may be at variance with actual behavior. Face-to-face interviews offer an opportunity to gather information in greater depth. The interviewer can probe, ask additional questions, and clarify responses. Furthermore, some structure may be maintained through an interview schedule, a listing of topics, or questions. Structured observations are those in which there is some purposeful gathering of data according to predetermined categories. Observational techniques can become very sophisticated and complicated, as with the use of interaction scales to record information about who initiates and responds in a group meeting or in a class. More-straightforward, simple observational methods will usually suffice. For example, classroom observation methods are readily adaptable to research purposes. Very simple categorization and computations will sometimes reveal profound meanings. Sometimes it is also possible to enlist others in making observations. For example, all school social workers may agree to keep records of certain activities or to record observations of meetings in which they participate for subsequent analysis.

Letting the Facts Speak for Themselves:
Compiling Data and Preparing Reports

A final stage in the process is the compilation of data and the preparation of a report or position paper. The format will depend on the purpose of the research and the objectives sought. If one is attempting to block the initiation of a new policy or procedure, the report would necessarily differ from that used in attempting to compare two alternative procedures, neither of which is particularly preferred. Those guidelines offered earlier for initiating the research will also serve in planning the report; one should be clear about objectives, avoid being overly ambitious, keep it simple, involve others, and seek the help of those with expert knowledge. In writing the report one should avoid pejorative language, cast the findings in objective or neutral terms, and let the facts make the argument. Brevity and clarity are the watchwords. Graphic programs and materials, music, and multimedia sources enhance research presentations. Using technology can make dry materials interesting, colorful, and appealing. Dissemination of research reports to the constituent communities through community centers and local organizations is important to enlist their involvement with the school.

The following example illustrates a collaborative practitioner research effort utilizing a number of the methods and resources described above:

A school social worker observed that communications between staff and parents of incoming refugee and immigrant children were often strained and incomplete. Using existing school data and public documents, she noted the increasing diversity within the school population. She then initiated informal conversations with newcomer parents, who explained that, although they were concerned about their children's education and well-being at school, there were many barriers to participation in parent-teacher conferences, and to discussions about educational and disciplinary concerns. These barriers were linguistic, cultural, and logistical—for example, timing of appointments, adequate notification of activities at the school, differing cultural expectations on the part of both parents and teachers, need for language interpretation, and transportation. It was also apparent that, even with the presence of bilingual classes, ESL teachers, students, and bilingual instructional aides, school personnel envisioned family within a narrow construction of mainstream, educated, middle-class, English-speaking parents. The practitioner brought these concerns to a course on empowerment practice with refugees and immigrants taught by one of the authors. For her course project, she developed a participatory action research project in collaboration with staff at a local agency serving refugees and immigrants, and with an intern who worked with school-age youths at a local multiethnic service organization. Through interviews with parents and school personnel, focus groups with parents and youths, and meetings with agency staff and parents, the research team developed a needs statement, and designed a parent advocate project to help bridge the gap between newcomer families and schools. The practitioner-researchers further informed the project by reviewing the educational and social work literature, searching for model interventions that had been effective in other school districts working on similar issues. They also sought the expertise of parents who had successfully involved themselves in the schools, and school personnel and staff at other refugee service agencies. They thus brought together multifaceted resources with which to facilitate the problem solving and creative work of the project participants. The team successfully submitted a proposal for funds for a three-year project to form and mentor parent advocate groups. The practitioner-researcher as an agent of change successfully mobilized family and community collaboration to improve children's educational experiences by building mutual cultural understanding and better school–family–community relationships.

CONCLUSION

Research is too important to be left entirely to researchers. This chapter shows some of the ways practitioners can conduct and use research and, in the process, enhance their practice roles. Perhaps the most difficult step is getting started, particularly in view of the widely held perception that the proper conduct of research requires expertise that comes only from years of specialized training and experience. Such a view effectively rules out many of the more relevant applications of research in schools. However, as shown in this chapter, the school social worker can rescue research from researchers and, by so doing, assume a more affirmative role in fostering collaboration, making space for diverse perspectives, and shaping school policy.

References

Altrichter, H., Posch, P., & Somekh, B. (1993). *Teachers investigate their work: An introduction to the methods of action research.* New York: Routledge.

Anderson-Butcher, D. Lawson, H. A., Iachini, A., Flaspohler, P., Bean, J., & Wade-Mdivanian, R. (2010). Emergent evidence in support of a community collaboration model for school improvement. *Children & Schools, 32*(3), 160–171.

Armstrong, F., & Moore, M. (2004). Action research: Developing inclusive practice and transforming cultures. In F. Armstrong & M. Moore (Eds.), *Action research for inclusive education: Changing places, changing practices, changing minds* (pp. 1–16). London: Routledge/Falmer.

Banks, C. A. M. (2005). *Improving multicultural education: Lessons from the intergroup education movement.* New York: Teachers College Press.

Banks, J. (Ed.). (1996). *Multicultural education, transformative knowledge and action.* New York: Teachers College, Columbia University.

Beatty, B. (2007). Going through the emotions: Leadership that gets to the heart of school renewal. *Australian Journal of Education, 51*(3), 328–340.

Beeson, J. (May 2002). We are not your mascot. *Colors North West,* 12–14.

Blair, K. (2002). School social work, the transmission of culture, and gender roles in schools. *Social Work, 21*(1), 21–33.

Board on Children, Youth and Families, Division of Behavioral and Social Sciences and Education (BCYF). (2003). *Engaging schools: Fostering high school students' motivation to learn.* Washington, DC: National Academies Press. Retrieved from http://www.nap.edu/books/0309084350/html/

Broussard, C. A. (2003). Facilitating home-school partnerships for multiethnic families: School social workers collaborating for success. *Children & Schools, 25*(4), 211–222.

Brydon-Miller, M., & Maguire, P. (2009). Participatory action research: Contributions to the development of practitioner inquiry in education. *Educational Action Research, 17*(1), 79–93.

Carr, W. (1995). *For education: Towards critical educational inquiry.* Bristol, PA: Open University Press.

Chamberlayne, P., Bornat, J., & Wengraf, T. (2000). *The turn to biographical methods in social science: Comparative issues and examples.* London: Routledge.

Christ, T. W. (2014). Scientific-based research and randomized controlled trials, the "Gold" standard? Alternative paradigms and mixed methodologies. *Qualitative Inquiry, 20*(1), 72.

Coats, L., & Xu, J. (2013). No Child Left Behind and outreach to families and communities: The perspectives of exemplary African-American science teachers. *Research Papers in Education, 28*(5), 609–627.

Corbett, J. (2001). *Supporting inclusive education: A connective pedagogy.* London: Routledge/Falmer.

Delgado-Gaitan, C. (1993). Researching change and changing the researcher. *Harvard Educational Review, 63*(4), 389–411.

Delgado-Gaitan, C. (2001). *The power of community: Mobilizing for family and schooling.* Lanham, MD: Rowman & Littlefield.

Delgado-Gaitan, C. (2004). *Involving Latino families in schools: Raising student achievement through home-school partnerships.* Thousand Oaks, CA: Corwin.

deMarrais, K. (2004). Elegant communications: Sharing qualitative research with communities, colleagues, and critics. *Qualitative Inquiry, 10*(2), 281–297.

Dodd, S., & Epstein, I. (2012). *Practice-based research in social work: A guide for reluctant researchers.* New York: Routledge

Elliott, J. (1991). *Action research for educational change.* Milton Keynes, UK: Open University Press.

Elmore, R. F., & Fuhrman, S. H. (2001). Research finds the false assumption of accountability. *Education Digest, 67*(4), 9–14.

Freire, P. (1973). *Education for critical consciousness.* New York: Seabury Press.

Gorlewski, J. A., & Porfilio, B. J. (2013). *Left behind in the race to the top: Realities of school reform.* Charlotte, NC: Information Age.

Gran-O'Donnell, S., Farwell, N., Spigner, C., Nguyen, C., Ciske, S., Young, T., . . . & Krieger, J. (2001). *Perspectives of multicultural youth on community building: A participatory approach.* Unpublished manuscript.

Hammersley, M. (2000). Evidence-based practice in education and the contribution of educational research. In L. Trinder & S. Reynolds (Eds.), *Evidence-based practice: A critical appraisal* (pp. 163–183). Thousand Oaks, CA: Sage.

Harold, R. D., Palmiter, M. L., Lynch, S. A., & Freedman-Doan, C. R. (1995). Life stories: A practice-based research technique. *Journal of Sociology and Social Welfare, 22,* 23–44.

Herr, K. (1995). Action research as empowering practice. *Journal of Progressive Human Services, 6*(2), 45–58.

Hick, S. (1997). Participatory research: An approach for structural social workers. *Journal of Progressive Human Services, 8*(2), 63–78.

Holland, T. P. (1991). Narrative, knowledge and professional practice. *Social Thought, 17*(1), 32–40.

Holy, P. (1991). From action research to collaborative inquiry: The processing of an innovation. In O. Zuber-Skerritt (Ed.), *Action research for change and development* (pp. 36–56). Brookfield, VA: Gower Publishing.

Individuals with Disabilities Education Act of 1990 (IDEA), Pub. L. 105-17, U.S.C. 11401 et seq. (1990).

Jay, J. (2003). *Quality teaching: Reflection as the heart of practice.* Lanham, MD: Scarecrow Press.

Jones, J. (1991). Action research in facilitating change in institutional practice. In O. Zuber-Skerritt (Ed.), *Action research for change and development* (pp. 207–223). Brookfield, VA: Gower.

Josselson, R. (1996). *Ethics and process in the narrative study of lives.* Thousand Oaks, CA: Sage.

Katz, M., & Rose, M. (2013). *Public education under siege.* Philadelphia: University of Pennsylvania Press.

Kwalwasser, H. (2012). *Renewal: Remaking America's schools for the twenty-first century.* Lanham, MD: Rowman & Littlefield.

Lather, P. (2004). This *is* your father's paradigm: Government intrusion and the case of qualitative research in education. *Qualitative Inquiry, 10*(1),15–34.

Lipman, P. (2004). *High stakes education: Inequality, globalization, and urban school reform.* New York: Routledge/Falmer.

Lunt, N., & Fouche, C. (2009). Action research for developing social workers' research capacity. *Educational Action Research, 17*(2), 225–237.

Martin, R. (1995). *Oral history in social work: Research, assessment, and intervention.* Thousand Oaks, CA: Sage.

No Child Left Behind Act of 2001, Pub. L. 107-110 (2002).

Noffke, S., & Stevenson, S. (1995). *Educational action research: Becoming practically critical.* New York: Teachers College Press.

Pearlmutter, S. (2002). Achieving political practice: Integrating individual need and social action. *Journal of Progressive Human Services, 13*(1), 31–51.

Peters, A. (2003). Isolation or inclusion: Creating safe spaces for lesbian and gay youth. *Families in Society, 84*(3), 331–337.

Salcido, R., Ornelas, V., & Garcia, J. (2002). A neighborhood watch program for inner-city school children. *Children and Schools, 24*(3), 175–187.

Simpson, L. (2004). Students who challenge: Reducing barriers to inclusion. In F. Armstrong & M. Moore (Eds.), *Action research for inclusive education: Changing places, changing practices, changing minds.* London: Routledge/Falmer.

Sirotnik, K. A. (1989). The school as the center of change. In T. J. Sergiovanni & J. H. Moore (Eds.), *Schooling for tomorrow: Directing reforms to issues that count* (pp. 89–113). Boston: Allyn & Bacon.

Sleeter, C. (1996). *Multicultural education as social activism.* Albany: State University of New York.

Sohng, S. (1996). Participatory research and community organizing. *Journal of Sociology and Social Welfare, 23*(4), 77–97.

Williams, M. R. (1989). *Neighborhood organizing for urban school reform.* New York: Teachers College Press.

Witherspoon, R. (2002). The involvement of African American families and communities in education: Whose responsibility is it? In S. Denbo & L. Beaulieu (Eds.), *Improving schools for African American students: A reader for educational leaders* (pp. 181–191). Springfield, IL: Charles C Thomas.

Section IV

Policy Practice

Policy practice is a central element of all social work practice. In fact, a commitment to social justice is one of the core values of the social work profession. Whether we work with individuals or communities, social workers always maintain an awareness of policy issues that affect individuals and society. Members of the social work profession work toward a just society. This section focuses on policy practice, beginning with an overview of the methods of influencing policy in chapter 19, "Policy Practice for School Social Workers," by Carol Rippey Massat and Elizabeth Lehr Essex. In chapter 20, "Tackling Oppression in Schools: Skills for School Social Workers," Andrew Brake and Leon Livingston focus directly on addressing and fighting oppression in schools. One of the essential skills in creating change at the organizational level—one type of policy practice—is skill in analyzing the school as an organization, which is covered in chapter 21, "Schools as Organizations," by Emily Shayman and Carol Rippey Massat. Once the school as an organization has been analyzed, the school social worker can work on developing policy in schools, as Annahita Ball describes in chapter 22, "Policy Development and the School Social Worker." The field of school social work is currently challenged to grow and expand into all fifty states, the District of Columbia, and around the world. Elizabeth Lehr Essex, Noriko Yamano, and Carol Rippey Massat describe strategies for promoting and developing the field of school social work in chapter 23, "Making School Social Work Visible, Viable, and Valued."

19

Policy Practice for School Social Workers

Carol Rippey Massat
Indiana University School of Social Work

Elizabeth Lehr Essex
Governors State University

- ◆ The School Social Worker's Role in Policy Practice
- ◆ Tasks and Skills of Policy Practice
- ◆ Policy Practice in Action

In a rural Midwestern community, a large, impoverished farm family had a daughter, Sarah, with differences from other children. As she grew, her walking was delayed, and she had stiff movements. Her speech development was slow and hard to understand, and yet her family delighted in the bright intelligence shining in her eyes. When Sarah was six, her mother carefully dressed her in a freshly ironed school dress and sent her to school with the other children, excited about the first day of school. Within a few days, this little girl returned home with a note pinned to her dress that read, "This child cannot learn. Do not send her to school." Saddened and disappointed, the family kept Sarah at home, loving her, caring for her, and helping her to learn what she could at home. After a few years, the first teacher left the one-room school, and a new teacher was appointed. She came to visit all the families, and asked, "What about this little girl? Why isn't she in school?" The mother explained about the note, and the new teacher said, "Send her to school." Despite her cerebral palsy, Sarah eventually went to college and became a special education teacher, destined to help hundreds of children with disabilities.

This true story occurred before the 1975 Education for All Handicapped Children Act. (Identifying information has been changed to protect privacy.) The 1975 legislation meant that never again would a child like Sarah be denied an education. The power of policy worked and continues to work to assist children with disabilities to reach their potential and to contribute to society. The *Brown v. Board of Education* Supreme Court (1954) decision had a similar sweeping impact on education, with the determination that separate education was inherently unequal. Policy in all its forms has the power to change lives, for good or for ill. Schools as social institutions are inherently linked to public policy. There is little that the school social worker does that is disconnected from policy. This fact is basic to social work practice within the school community.

It is an ethical requirement of the profession that social workers promote social justice and social change on behalf of clients and work to end discrimination, oppression, poverty, and social injustice—to involve themselves in policy and to participate in implementing policy. The preamble to the National Association of Social Workers (NASW) Code of Ethics reads, in part,

> Social workers promote social justice and social change with and on behalf of clients. "Clients" is used inclusively to refer to individuals, families, groups, organizations, and communities. Social workers are sensitive to cultural and ethnic diversity and strive to end discrimination, oppression, poverty, and other forms of social injustice. These activities may be in the form of direct practice, community organizing, supervision, consultation, administration, advocacy, social and political action, policy development and implementation, education, and research and evaluation. Social workers seek to enhance the capacity of people to address their own needs. Social workers also seek to promote the responsiveness of organizations, communities, and other social institutions to individuals' needs and social problems. (NASW, 2008, Preamble)

No other profession working in schools has this professional mandate. This focus is absent in the codes of ethics of teachers, nurses, psychologists, school counselors, and school administrators.

This ethical mandate may be carried out in different forms and at different levels of the environment. It may take place through advocacy on behalf of individuals and families, through organizational change, through community development, through research, or through policy development at the school, community, state, or federal levels. In school social work these methods come to fruition in making the educational process effective for children who are having difficulty using what schools offer.

While progress is being made toward universal basic education, there are obstacles that prevent many children from having access to and benefiting from education. School social work, developing throughout the world because the demands on education have amplified, seeks to deal with these obstacles (Huxtable & Blyth, 2002). Internationally, there is an increasingly level playing field provided by information technologies, and in every country economic survival is related to education (Friedman, 2005). Education has become key to social development (Midgeley, 1997). With greater demands for educational achievement, American school reform is shifting toward outcome-based education, higher standards for school personnel, and greater accountability for effective practice. For school social workers, state education agencies are beginning to require specialized preparation prior to employment and a period of performance assessment as a school social worker afterwards (Constable & Alvarez, 2006). Although there has been a movement toward national certification of school social workers (Alvarez & Harrington, 2004), little progress has been made toward this goal in the past decade.

THE SCHOOL SOCIAL WORKER'S ROLE IN POLICY PRACTICE

Schools and families hold the keys to participation of future generations in society. Schools face social injustice in the form of economic inequality, inequitable school funding, racial and ethnic school segregation, gender inequities, sexual harassment, and oppression of marginalized groups in schools. Chapters 11, 12, and 20 in this book expand on a historic struggle in the United States to rectify inequities in education for racial and ethnic minorities, women, and sexual minorities. Through statutes, administrative regulations, and case law, groups have engaged in a long struggle to eradicate social injustice in schools. Those forces seeking to oppress others have utilized public policy to impede the education of minorities, to limit the right to vote to the favored few, or to limit funding for education of minority or impoverished students. Others, also recognizing the power of policy, have crafted policies to combat segregation, to eliminate discrimination, and to provide opportunities.

A school social worker's opportunities for involvement in the creation and implementation of policy at the school, community, state, and federal levels permit client group advocacy and engagement in this historic struggle. Section IV of the book is intended to give school social workers the background and tools to be policy practitioners. We describe skills and information needed to carry out policy practice. We define the context for policy practice by school social workers, the role of the school social worker in policy practice, and the skills and competencies for policy practice, with examples of policy reform.

The role of the school social worker includes participation in program and policy development at the local school and community level. This broader role demands a deep understanding of the school as an organization, of policy analysis, and of research geared to program development and evaluation.

Policies are often pictured as developing through federal, state, and local statutory, regulatory, and case law (court decisions) that take place from the top down, but this is only one part of policy and program development in school social work. At the federal and state levels, policies may prescribe and suggest common goals and means. However, it is up to the grassroots level, the level of implementation, the level of the school community, and the levels of the local education agency and the local school to develop ways to carry out policies and develop programs.

When the connection between policy and practice is not acknowledged, there would appear to be little basis for a practitioner role in policy development. Furthermore, the limits of policies are becoming all too clear. Any policy's success depends on the real environment of service and the capabilities of those implementing it. Some policies exist mainly on paper because no one has found a way to implement them successfully. Other policies may even work against their initial purposes. For example, a national dress code for schools would not likely be helpful to local schools. Regional variation, local and school commitment to school colors, and other factors would render such a policy useless and possibly detrimental. However, many schools have found dress codes that meet their specific needs in addressing gang control, issues of class, and school solidarity.

School social workers do participate in policy and program development, particularly in the school community. Indeed practice itself often creates policy. There are thus two necessary directions of policy development—from the top down, often expressed as public policy, and from the bottom up, often expressed as locality development. The inherently complex organization of the local school makes room for policy practice, even at the local school level. Policies may originate from grassroots programs that resonate with needs and empower consumers to take action on these needs. Initiatives may develop as experiments from points where need and service are defined. In developing programs to meet the needs of the school community, school social workers are both developing and implementing policies. School social workers are well situated to have access to both levels. Unfortunately, recent research on the role of the school social worker indicates that many school social workers do not currently take advantage of the opportunities to carry out policy practice, even when they express a desire to do so (Kelly et al., 2010).

For school social workers, the common thread in all of this is a need to understand the language and theory of policy as well as of practice. For example, it is part of their role to help develop and implement crisis plans as members of the school crisis team. A crisis plan is both policy and prescribed practice. Social workers work with teachers, parents, and pupils to develop solutions to include youngsters with disabilities in general education classes, thus creating avenues for implementation of special education mandates. Since social workers work in the most difficult areas of education, their role inevitably can become an innovative one that goes beyond the givens of the institution or the situation. The distance from such innovation to policy and program development is not great. The two directions of policy, from the top down and from the bottom up, are beginning to mesh, particularly in recent legislation and school reform initiatives. It is important that school social workers see policy and program development as their participation in the school's response in its own community context to societal conditions and mandates. When school social workers have the freedom to develop their role, the school can become more responsive to societal and community conditions, conditions that inevitably affect the educational process (Meenaghan & Gibbons, 2000; Meenaghan & Kilty, 1994).

TASKS AND SKILLS OF POLICY PRACTICE

Bruce Jansson (2014) spells out an action framework for policy analysis and development of tasks and skills necessary for effective policy practice. There are six components in his framework, now applied to school social work policy practice. First, a policy framework for practice must include the context of the policy. Ball describes a framework that includes careful analysis of policy context in chapter 22. The context includes the location of the policy and its bases for legitimacy. Is it a local, school, community, state, or federal policy? Is it based on legislation, case law, or regulations? What is the state of communication, and what are the boundaries of the system in which this policy occurs? What authority is needed to carry out this policy? Second, what is the perspective of stakeholders and policy advocates? Stakeholders, or those with a "vested interest in a specific policy or issue being contested" (Jansson, 2014, p. 73), can include members of interest groups, advocacy groups, administrators, consumers, and others. The third element of Jansson's framework includes the patterns of participation related to proposed policies. The fourth element is the identification of key tasks that policy advocates undertake, the fifth is identification of the fundamental skills of policy advocates, and the sixth is the identification of key competencies of policy advocates.

There are eight tasks that policy practitioners engage in (Jansson, 2014). Several of these tasks may occur at the same time, rather than in a step-by-step progression, and individual policy practitioners do not necessarily carry out all eight tasks.

> When *deciding what is right and wrong* [the foundational policy task], they use ethics and analysis to decide if specific policies are meritorious. . . .
>
> When they decide how to *navigate policy and advocacy systems*, they decide where to focus and position their policy intervention, such as whether to seek changes at the local, state or federal level. . . .
>
> In the *agenda setting task*, practitioners gauge whether the context is favorable for a policy initiative, and they evolve early strategy to place it on policy maker's agendas. . . .
>
> In the *problem-analyzing task*, practitioners analyze the causes, nature, and prevalence of specific problems. . . .

In the *proposal-writing task*, practitioners develop solutions to specific problems. Proposals may be relatively ambitious, such as a piece of legislation, or relatively modest, such as incremental change in existing policies. . . .

In the *policy enacting task*, practitioners try to have policies approved or enacted by using various influence and power resources, as well as strategy. . . . Once a policy has been enacted, policy advocates undertake the policy-implementing task. . . .

Policy practitioners evaluate programs when they undertake the *policy-assessing task*. (pp. 76–77; emphasis in original)

In chapters 19, 21, and 22, several tools for policy analysis are described: organizational analyses, use of a policy analysis framework, and policy development. In chapters 9, 11, 12, and 13 information on existing policies is given as part of the policy context for practice and as information needed for advocacy on behalf of vulnerable individuals and groups. In chapter 18 the use of research as part of the role of change agent is described. Research skills assist in the analysis of the needs of groups and organizations, and in carrying out evaluations of programs and policies. Chapter 23 applies the eight tasks to advocacy aimed at strengthening the school social work profession.

There are four skills that policy practitioners need (Jansson, 2014):

◆ They need analytic skills to evaluate social problems and develop policy proposals, to analyze the severity of specific problems, to identify the barriers to policy implementation, and to develop strategies for assessing programs.

◆ They need political skills to gain and use power and to develop and implement political strategy.

◆ They need interactional skills to participate in task groups, such as committees and coalitions, and to persuade other people to support specific policies. . . .

◆ They need value clarifying skills to identify and rank relevant principles when engaging in policy practice. (Jansson, 2014, p. 78)

Skills needed for policy analysis are described in chapters 21 and 22. The political and interactional skills needed for policy practice by school social workers are inherent in the tasks of collaboration as a member of a school team. No school social worker will be able to bring about policy change alone. Fortunately, school social workers are comfortable with these skills, and develop strong communication and interactional skills as part of their foundation and specialized training.

Policy competencies are specific actions that policy practitioners carry out utilizing the four kinds of policy skills. Competencies needed for policy practice thus include political competencies, analytic competencies, interactional competencies, and value-clarifying competencies (Jansson, 2014).

Political competencies include the ability to use mass media, take personal positions, seek positions of power, empower others, orchestrate pressure on decision makers, find funding, use personal power, donate time/resources, advocate for clients, participate in demonstrations, initiate litigation, and work on electoral change. School social workers can carry out most of these activities as part of their professional role, but must carry out some of them during nonwork hours, or personal time. For example, working on a political campaign during working hours would be considered unethical for public school employees. Initiating litigation is also unlikely to be appropriate for a school social worker. As an example of the use of political competencies, a school social worker may work as part of a school social work association legislative committee to develop policies supporting increased mental health services in schools. In this role, the school social worker may work with legislators, testify to the state legislature, and develop policy statements to disseminate to members of the organization.

Analytic competencies include proposal development, calculating trade-offs, using existing research, using the Internet, budgeting, finding funding, designing presentations, diagnosing implementation barriers, developing political strategies, analysis of policy context, and design of policy assessments. School social workers may use analytic competencies in developing a specific proposal to increase mental health services in schools. What services should be provided? What models of service provision should be used? How many school social workers might be necessary to meet the needs of students? What does the body of evidence tell us about the best way to address these needs?

Interactional competencies include building coalitions, making presentations, building personal power, forming task groups, and managing conflict. In promoting increased mental health services in schools, the school social worker would use interactional competencies in building coalitions locally and statewide to support such an initiative. Since the Newtown, Connecticut, shootings, there has been increased support for mental health services across the aisle. Both conservatives and liberals have shared a reawakening that could have potential for coalition building among diverse groups. Coalition building is challenging, since it is necessary to bring groups together that may not be accustomed to being allies. Beginning at the point of shared interests and working from there can be the beginning of a continuing partnership, at least on specific issues.

Value-clarifying competencies involve ethical reasoning to determine the identity and relative importance of values driving policy development, advocacy, and implementation (Jansson, 2014). This competency could be quite important in furthering a movement toward more mental health services in schools. Some of the values supporting such services would include social control of student behavior as well as more altruistic concerns for individual student well-being. Would services reflect a value of the dignity and worth of persons with mental health concerns? If more services are desired, would mental health issues be valued as highly as other school priorities, such as improved test scores?

A most important skill in policy development is the ability to work with others, often having different beliefs and investments in the policy development process. No policies are ever developed by one person. Policy development is often a matter of the right connections with other possible allies in a common effort. This political process means that none of the participants in change efforts will get all that they want. Policy development is often a matter of the right timing, the right place, the right network, the will to overcome inevitable obstacles, and the ability to compromise and to get things done. Social workers can apply all of the skills they learn from other sectors of their practice to the vision of how things might be, the will to get things accomplished with others, and the flexibility to develop a workable common proposition and fall-back positions when initial strategies fail. Here the work they can do in the school and in the school community is analogous to what they can do in larger forums, such as when they help to develop state educational policy in relation to a particular issue.

POLICY PRACTICE IN ACTION

School social workers can engage in policy practice as citizens and professionals outside of work hours or as change agents within their place of employment. As social work professionals, school social workers should maintain membership in professional and advocacy organizations, such as state school organizations, School Social Work Association of America, NASW, and other relevant groups. Such organizations maintain legislative updates and policy issues of concern to social workers, so that pending legislation, policy changes, and court cases of interest can be easily accessed. Such groups also maintain easy to use links to respond to these issues through e-mail or phone calls to legislators. Subscriptions to Internet sites such as Education Week (www.edweek.org), also provide rapid notification of issues relevant to school social work. It is critical that every social worker know the identity and contact information for his or her state and federal legislators, as well as local government and school board members. As a citizen, a school social worker may also choose to run for public office, run for a seat on a local school board, or participate directly in forums for policy development. The presence of a school social worker in a school, with the distinctive NASW Code of Ethics and unique professional perspective, can, in and of itself, influence the climate and policies of a school. In the roles of consultant, team member, and collaborator, the school social worker constantly has the opportunity to influence others in the school. It is also possible to take deliberate action to bring about organizational change that will benefit the students, teachers, and administration. When analysis has occurred and information has been gathered, the first steps to organizational change have begun.

No school social worker or other member of the team will bring about such change alone. Even if one were to grant the social worker the individual authority to create a change, implementation of that change would require the cooperation of all the stakeholders. In this sense, the power of relationship is essential in creating a climate for needed change, and in building coalitions of interested persons to work for change. Often change is derailed more by apathy or lack of time than by active opposition. Finding others who care and are willing and able to commit time and energy to a project may be the primary element needed.

The development of a school breakfast program could be the goal of policy change. Such a program is easy to support and may well be embraced by almost everyone who is part of the school community. Other desired programs could include after-school programs, tutoring, violence prevention programs, social and emotional learning programs, or other initiatives to benefit the school and community (table 19.1).

Haynes and Mickelson (2010) and Cummins, Byers, and Pedrick (2011) have written excellent guides for social work advocacy and policy practice. The reader may want to consult their books to learn more about how to carry out a wide range of policy practice activities. The following will touch on a number of available options for the school social worker.

TABLE 19.1   Potential Policy Practice Goals

Goal	Stakeholders	Potential Allies
School breakfast program	Students Teachers Community members	Social service agencies Health-care providers
After-school program	Parents Students School personnel	Law enforcement Local churches Social service agencies
Tutoring program	Parents Teachers Students School personnel	Local churches Mentoring programs Local colleges or universities The business community
Violence prevention program	Parents Students School personnel Community members	Law enforcement Community groups Social service agencies

The Policy-Making Process

Cummins et al. (2011) describe stages of policy practice that move from identifying a policy problem to evaluating a policy that has been developed. For example, a school social worker may notice a pattern of interpersonal violence in the school. Cummins et al. (2011) would identify this as the first stage, which is problem identification and case finding. The school social worker may then determine, through collecting data from students, teachers, and parents, the sense of safety of students in the school and the number of violent incidents that students experience, perpetrate, or witness. This is the second stage, which involves systematic data collection and analysis about the issue.

The data collection phase is extremely important. In order to effectively address a concern, the school social worker must understand the extent of the issue and the number of people affected. The data guide us in understanding whether our perceptions reflect the reality in the school. It is all too easy to make a leap from observing one incident of a problem to generalizing from it without checking the facts and determining whether there is an actual need for policy change. Just as school social workers carry out evidence-informed practice with individuals and groups, evidence-informed policy practice is critical to the development and formation of policies that are truly needed. Data collection may begin with an organizational analysis, discussed in chapter 21. A needs assessment, as discussed in chapter 17, may be conducted to gather data regarding the needs of the school. Existing research may be reviewed or new data collected, as discussed in chapter 18.

In the third stage of the policy-making process, policy practitioners identify stakeholders and inform the public. Stakeholders include everyone who is potentially affected by the problem and those who can contribute to change. If members of a school community are concerned about school violence, stakeholders would include students, teachers, school administrators, school social workers, parents, and local police. A committee with representatives from these groups could form a task force to move toward a policy change. That group of stakeholders could inform the school and community about the issue and then move on to consider potential policies and develop policy goals, the fourth stage of the Cummins et al. (2011) approach.

A review of the literature would reveal a number of effective violence prevention approaches in schools. One such evidence-informed model is PEACE POWER, described by Mattaini (2000). This approach focuses on changing school culture by influencing the school community to adopt principles of respect, affirmation, shared power, and making peace. To implement this model, it would be necessary to find support within and around the school and to develop coalitions united to address the cause of interpersonal violence in schools (the fifth stage in Cummins et al., 2011).

The final stages of policy development in schools involve implementing the newly developed policy and then evaluating and making changes in response to the data collected in the evaluation process. Once again, data collection skills are critical for school social workers who plan to develop and carry out effective policy practice. The use of existing data in schools, such as discipline records before and after the new approach, could be used to determine the impact of the new policy. Surveys of parents, students, and teachers could be done to assess students' sense of safety. If the new policy/program is working, we can expect to see postive changes in school climate, sense of safety, and reduction in disciplinary incidents. If desired changes are not occurring, the school social worker and other team members may need to consider aspects of policy implementation, the appropriateness of the selected approach for the specific setting, and other issues that may affect success.

Tools of Policy Advocacy

School social workers also carry out policy advocacy activities to support broader societal change on issues that affect students and schools. Such policy advocacy may involve writing letters, e-mailing, or telephoning elected officials or other policy makers; using social media to promote a cause; or providing testimony at public hearings.

A carefully crafted letter to a policy maker is an important tool of policy advocacy. A letter or e-mail written about a policy should be no longer than one page, and should be legible. You should identify yourself and state the subject in the first paragraph. You should address only one issue per letter. The specific issue or bill number should be clearly identified. In a second paragraph, you should clearly state an opinion, and should include reasons for that opinion and relevant personal experiences or examples. In the third paragraph, request specific action, such as voting yes or no on a bill. You should include your contact information, including an address and phone number. Some legislators will respond only to constituents. Other legislators may wish to contact you for further information (Haynes & Mickelson, 2010).

Sending an e-mail is also a useful expression of opinion to a policy maker. Many organizational Web sites have links to legislators and make it easy to send e-mails on important issues. Such e-mails must also be carefully done. If you send the letter as an e-mail, you should use a clear and descriptive subject line. For example, you might say, "Vote yes on HB 123." As in a letter, you should include your street address and phone number(s). If e-mailing legislators, send it only to those who represent your state or district. If you e-mail the chair of a committee who is not your representative, send a copy to your representative. Do not send attachments with your e-mail. An attachment, as a potential source of a virus, will rarely be opened and can overload an e-mail system (Haynes & Mickelson, 2010).

Telephone calls to legislators can also be helpful. When making a call, do not expect to speak with a legislator. The call will likely be taken by a staff member. If using the telephone, call about forty-eight hours before a specific vote. Be ready to present your position on an issue in a concise format. Be ready to give identifying information, since legislators especially want to know if you are a constituent (Haynes & Mickelson, 2010).

CONCLUSION

As professionals, school social workers may also be called to present testimony regarding proposed legislation or administrative regulations affecting schools or children. If so, you should provide written testimony in addition to the oral statement given. Such written testimony ensures that the record will be accurate and professional (Haynes & Mickelson, 2010).

Wallace Stevens (1972), in his poem "The Man with the Blue Guitar," writes about someone who does not "play things as they are." Social workers, like the man with the blue guitar, do not need to accept existing inequities, oppressive practices, or ineffective approaches to meeting student needs. School social workers have the capacity to envision and to bring into practice effective new policies and programs. The development of policy practice skills and the use of those skills can change the lives of individuals, families, schools, and communities. Our profession challenges us in the NASW Code of Ethics to promote social justice. By developing the skills of policy practice, school social workers can meet this challenge.

References

Alvarez, M. E., & Harrington, C. (2004). A pressing need for acceptance of an advanced national school social work certification. *School Social Work Journal, 29*(1), 18–27.

Brown v. Board of Education 347 U.C. 483 (1954).

Constable, R., & Alvarez, M. (2006). Moving into specialization in school social work: Issues in practice, policy, and education. *School Social Work Journal, 31*(3), 116–131.

Cummins, L. K., Byers, K. V., & Pedrick, L. (2011). *Policy practice for social workers: New strategies for a new era.* Boston: Allyn & Bacon.

Education for All Handicapped Children Act of 1975, Pub. L. 94-142 (1975).

Friedman, T. L. (2005). It's a flat world, after all. *New York Times.* Retrieved from http://www.nytimes.com/2005/04/03/magazine/its-a-flat-world-after-all.html?_r=0

Haynes, K. S., & Mickelson, J. S. (2010). *Affecting change: Social workers in the political arena* (7th ed.). Boston: Allyn & Bacon.

Huxtable, M., & Blyth, E. (2002). *School social work worldwide.* Washington, DC: National Association of Social Work Press.

Individuals with Disabilities Education Act of 1990 (IDEA), Pub. L. 105-17, U.S.C. 11401 et seq. (1990).

Jansson, B. S. (2014). *Becoming an effective policy advocate: From policy practice to social justice* (7th ed.). Pacific Grove, CA: Brooks/Cole, Cengage Learning.

Kelly, M. S., Berzin, S. C., Frey, A., Alvarez, M., Shaffer, G., & O'Brien, K. (2010). The state of school social work: Findings from the national school social work survey. *School Mental Health, 2*(3), 132–141.

Mattaini, M. (2000). *PEACE POWER.* New York: National Association of Social Workers.

Meenaghan, T., & Gibbons, W. E. (2000). *Generalist practice in larger settings: Knowledge and skill concepts.* Chicago: Lyceum Books.

Meenaghan, T., & Kilty, K. (1994). *Policy analysis and research technology.* Chicago: Lyceum Books.

Midgeley, J. (1997). *Social welfare in global context.* Thousand Oaks, CA: Sage.

National Association of Social Workers (NASW). (2008). *Code of ethics.* Retrieved from https://www.socialworkers.org/pubs/code/code.asp

Stevens, W. (1972). *The palm at the end of the mind.* New York: Vintage.

20

Tackling Oppression in Schools: Skills for School Social Workers

Andrew Brake
Northeastern Illinois University

Leon Livingston
Morehouse College

◆ Defining Oppression in School Policy and Practice
◆ Orienting Our Professional Compass: Authentically Supportive Relationships and School Social Work Ethical Standards
◆ Six Skills for Tackling Oppression in Schools
◆ Tackling Oppression in Schools: Reflections on an Authentically Supportive Relationship
◆ Discussion Questions

This chapter provides school social workers with six skills for tackling oppression in schools. Oppression in schools takes many forms, including structural barriers such as insufficient funding for mental health services for youths in urban public schools, and interpersonal barriers, such as discrimination that students with disabilities often experience in classrooms. We stress that school social workers must make tackling oppression their top professional priority.

We begin with a commitment to building authentically supportive relationships (Stanton-Salazar, 2011) with oppressed youths and families. These relationships are complemented by ongoing efforts to continuously strengthen professional capacities and to expand our network of allies who share this priority. The six skills described in this chapter sketch a roadmap for all school social workers to follow in working to develop antioppressive policies and practices in schools.

DEFINING OPPRESSION IN SCHOOL POLICY AND PRACTICE

Tackling oppression has long been a central goal of school social work. Oppression is broadly defined as a process of domination and subordination of one group over another, across one or more dimensions of human society, such as race, class, gender, age, sexual orientation, and dis/ability (Ward & Mullender, 1991). Whether enacted actively or passively, oppression can be created and reinforced by the policies and practices of school professionals themselves. School social workers work with oppressed youths and families from communities who experience many intersecting and compounding effects of historical and contemporary political and economic discrimination, exclusion, and marginalization. School social workers are advocates for youths and families from oppressed communities. As such, it is our central role to challenge the belief that tackling oppression in society is beyond the reach of school social workers. Instead, we must work to ensure that the policies and practices that we enact in our schools do not reinforce oppression. By tackling oppression in schools we take important steps toward tackling oppression in society.

To begin tackling oppression in schools, school social workers must first engage in an honest, critical, and ongoing assessment of our professional roles in schools. This assessment will help us examine what is unique about how each of our schools is organized and what priorities matter most. It helps to identify what motivates and drives our core practices and what challenges us to honestly reflect on each of our roles and responsibilities in shaping the day-to-day policies, practices, and interactions that affect the youths and families we serve.

To begin the process of assessing oppressive policies and practices in our schools it is important to have a working framework with which to examine the different ways in which each of our school's policies and practices facilitate or resist oppression. Recent educational policy and practice research suggests that each school is unique in how oppression operates in its policies and practices. In broad terms, schools tend to fall into one of three types: (1) actively oppressive schools, (2) passively oppressive schools, and (3) antioppressive schools. Factors such as schools' discipline policies, their ability to be responsive to the social-emotional needs and culturally distinct backgrounds of their students and families, and the ways in which they allocate resources and set priorities to provide academic and social supports for their most vulnerable populations are all important signals of how schools facilitate or resist oppression. Moreover, while each school and district is distinct, it is also important to remember that no school is oppressive in every dimension of its service provision. Furthermore, simply because a school may be broadly classified as one type, it can shift over time with changes in its priorities, policies, and practices. With this in mind, the three broad types of schools defined in this chapter aim to serve as working definitions to help school social workers examine how their own schools reinforce or resist oppression for the youths and families they serve.

The first type of school, actively oppressive schools, are those whose policies and practices actively reinforce oppression and further limit the school success, well-being, and life chances of oppressed youths. Schools that actively rely on zero tolerance discipline policies, that disproportionately criminalize youths who commit minor infractions of school policy, and that excessively use law enforcement within their walls to monitor and enforce strict punitive behavior policies are examples of actively oppressive schools. Additionally, school professionals who frequently enact punitive behavior interventions and classroom management strategies, who teach course material that is not inclusive of all students or who fail to regularly assess and reflect on the impact of their policy and practice approaches on the social-emotional needs of different subgroups of students typify actively oppressive schools.

Research on the school-to-prison pipeline and its disproportionate criminalization and negative impact on the school performance of low-income youths of color, particularly males, as well as youths receiving special education services, highlights the profoundly negative implications for youths who attend actively oppressive schools (Bahena, Cooc, Currie-Rubin, Kuttner, & Ng, 2012; Christle, Jolivette, & Nelson, 2005; Noguera, 2003; Wald & Losen, 2003). In the Chicago Public Schools (CPS), for example, where 86.9 percent of the 384,909 students enrolled in kindergarten through twelfth grade received federal free lunch and 87.0 percent identified as African American or Latino during the 2009–10 school year, there were 5,651 arrests of CPS youths aged seventeen and under on school property in 2009 and 5,574 arrests in 2010 (CPS, 2014; Patterson & Kaba, 2011). Moreover, nearly two out of every five of these arrests (38.6 percent) were made in schools in just five of the city's twenty-five police districts, districts with among the poorest African American and Latino communities in the city (Patterson & Kaba, 2011). These alarming numbers underscore how disproportionately concentrated particularly punitive school policies and practices can be in schools within a district's most oppressed communities. Moreover, given the increasingly constrained life chances associated with school-based arrests (Christle et al., 2005), school social workers face a broad set of policy and practice challenges in actively oppressive schools, challenges that this chapter aims to help school social workers and school professionals to begin to tackle. (See also chapters 11 and 12 for more information on the history of oppressive policies and practices in schools in the United States.)

The second type of schools, those classified as passively oppressive schools, often recognize that particular policies and practices in their schools are facilitating oppression for youths. However, professionals in these schools avoid making tackling oppression a top school-wide priority. Passively oppressive schools may not actively utilize zero-tolerance policies or law enforcement personnel in the same ways that actively oppressive schools do. However, a distinguishing feature of passively oppressive schools is a heavy reliance on the myth that schools' failure is rooted in the skill deficits of their students more so than a critical self-assessment of school professionals' day-to-day biases and assumptions that reinforce oppression and inequality (Goodlad, 2002). Examples of passively oppressive schools are those that concentrate more resources on academic remediation without either raising academic performance expectations for all students or allocating resources for targeted social-emotional supports for struggling learners. In so doing, these schools may in fact reinforce oppression for certain students simply by overlooking or underserving their needs. Furthermore, while passively oppressive schools may be willing and able to identify signs and dimensions of oppression in their buildings, they either fail to implement changes in the policies, practices, and resources that challenge oppression such as reallocating resources toward enhancing supports for their most vulnerable populations, or they work to reframe their deficit-perspectives of youths. In turn, while some efforts of passively oppressive schools may serve to reduce inequality and oppression across some of its policies and practices, when school professionals' priorities and decisions do not closely examine the root causes of oppression in their schools they effectively reinforce oppressive policies and practices.

Finally, the third type of schools, antioppressive schools, are those that recognize and actively work to tackle oppression in their policies and practices. In short, antioppressive schools make tackling oppression a top priority in policy and practice at every level of the school's operation. Antioppressive schools continuously assess and identify various dimensions of oppression in their building and strive to understand and tackle how oppression works and how it affects youths on a daily basis. In antioppressive schools all members of the school community talk openly about their struggle and commitment to tackle oppression in their school and regularly organize explicit and intentional efforts for how to do this well. They accomplish this through a clearly articulated vision and mission, led by school leaders who sustain an ongoing commitment and focus on antioppressive goals and continuously assess their progress toward these goals. Members of antioppressive school communities also recognize and value the mutual benefits of working toward these goals and are invested in efforts to improve student engagement and performance, as well as to encourage an honest and reflective process for monitoring and improving antioppressive policies and practices with all stakeholders. Together, these efforts serve to create a community of faculty, staff, students, and families who openly work with one another to develop policies and practices that aim to be antioppressive and to create new opportunities for engagement, learning, and growth for all members of the school community.

As school social workers, we are particularly well positioned to lead schools in tackling oppression. However, finding ways to engage our colleagues and school community in developing antioppressive policies and practices in each of our schools is no easy task. Moreover, when we are unsuccessful we still will likely find ourselves on the front lines, bearing witness to the negative effects of oppressive school policies and practices on youths and families. However, in order to develop skills to more effectively lead our schools toward the goal of becoming antioppressive, it is important to carefully understand our professional roles within schools, and to draw on the ethical guidelines that can focus our antioppressive efforts.

ORIENTING OUR PROFESSIONAL COMPASS: AUTHENTICALLY SUPPORTIVE RELATIONSHIPS AND SCHOOL SOCIAL WORK ETHICAL STANDARDS

After determining the type of school in which we work, effectively tackling oppression in schools also means examining how well we forge relationships with oppressed youths and families. Stanton-Salazar (2011) highlights the key role of school professionals in working with oppressed youths through our efforts to help them gain access to the social capital to which all students should have equal access in schools. Stanton-Salazar defines social capital as consisting of "resources and key forms of institutional support embedded in a multilayered system of social structures—beginning with a fundamental network-analytic structure (i.e., relationships, networks, and associations as social mediums) which, in turn, is embedded in complex and usually hierarchical structures found in formal and complex organizations and institutions (e.g., schools, universities, firms, corporations)" (Stanton-Salazar, 2011, p. 1067). In order to forge authentically supportive relationships, Stanton-Salazar contends that school professionals should use a specific set of actions, enact various roles, and demonstrate particular relational qualities as institutional brokers of social capital in schools, particularly in working with oppressed youths. Through a process he describes as counterstratification, school professionals can work with oppressed youths to help them gain access to resources embedded in the structures of society and schools by creating authentically supportive relationships. These relationships are characterized by school professionals' ability to (1) demonstrate their trustworthiness with youths, (2) develop a shared meaning of the oppressive contexts in which youths and school professionals interact, and (3) express solidarity with oppressed youths in helping them attain social capital. Through these relationships, youths not only gain access to critical knowledge and information, but they also develop a set of "problem-solving capacities, help-seeking orientations, networking skills, and instrumental behaviors which are directed toward overcoming stressful institutional barriers and harmful ecological conditions" (Stanton-Salazar, 2011, p. 1093). One example of how school social workers might work to create opportunities and increase access to social capital for oppressed youths may be when social workers, teachers, administrators, and counselors collaborate to provide targeted supports for students with disabilities and first-generation college students to receive added access to technology, resources, and college advising during the school day in order for them to understand, apply, and navigate the college application and financial aid processes that they may not have access to at home.

Dedicating ourselves to the ongoing process of counterstratification, through our efforts to build authentically supportive relationships, also calls school social workers to look to specific ethical standards for guiding our policies and practices. The National Association of Social Workers (NASW) Code of Ethics (2008) is one example of resources available to help guide core social work practices by providing clear and specific language that aligns with many dimensions of counterstratification. Specifically, our ethical guidelines that focus on cultural competence, respect, discrimination, and social and political action provide a concrete and useful set of professional priorities that school social workers can use in their antioppressive efforts. Being guided by these four ethical standards, continuously orienting our professional compass toward a critical understanding of our roles in the process of conterstratification, and creating authentically supportive relationships, school social workers can begin to create antioppressive policies and practices in schools. Moreover, readers are also strongly encouraged to regularly review these standards (NASW, 2008), to join national and local social work and school social work professional organizations, and to regularly discuss and revisit these standards with fellow social workers, colleagues, and school leaders.

SIX SKILLS FOR TACKLING OPPRESSION IN SCHOOLS

Drawing on the guidelines and priorities that orient our ethical compasses, and our commitment to forging authentically supportive relationships with youths and families, we offer six specific skills for social workers to use to tackle oppression in schools. These six skills are (1) recognizing and acknowledging our privilege, (2) critically reflecting on our policy and practice priorities, (3) strategically using data and multitiered interventions, (4) owning our unique roles as school social workers, (5) aligning with antioppressive allies, and (6) actively involving oppressed youths, families, and community members. Together, by working to develop these skills, school social workers can help direct each of our school's collective priorities toward developing robust antioppressive policies and practices in schools.

1. Recognizing and Acknowledging Our Privilege. Antioppressive school social work begins with a critical reflection of one's own position within the social and political hierarchy of schools. As a deeply relational practice, antioppressive social work recognizes and acknowledges one's privileges within a given social structure, and maintains a steadfast commitment to reducing the negative effects of oppressive structures and relationships (Strier & Binyamin, 2013). Often, as educated, well-trained school professionals, particularly when we work in schools serving low-income communities, we have many privileges in relation to the youths and families we work with, particularly along such dimensions as age, education, income, and employment. Thus, the first step in tackling oppression for school professionals is to recognize and acknowledge how our own individual and collective privileges have the potential to reinforce oppression for youths in schools.

The ways in which we understand and reflect on our privileges often begin in our training as school professionals, and continue forward in how we identify, acknowledge, and act on those privileges in our practice. Abrams and Gibson (2007) argue that in seeking to deeply understand and value the complex cultural and demographic differences that often exist within our schools, social work training programs and the students in those programs must be deeply dedicated to teaching and learning about the impact of privilege. So, too, should all school professional training programs and students. Solomona, Portelli, Daniel, and Campbell (2005), for example, highlight how white candidates in teacher training programs often adopt a discourse of denial about their privilege. Specifically, they rely on strategies that include an acceptance of ideological incongruence between themselves and "others," a belief in liberalist notions of individualism and meritocracy, and a continuous negation of white capital (Solomona et al., 2005). In so doing, they find that this denial also becomes evident in the curricular emphasis that teachers choose to adopt as they prepare to become school teachers. Picower (2009) similarly found that through a series of protective actions, which trainee teachers employ when developing curricula and making classroom practice decisions, these beginning teachers use various emotional, ideological, and performative tools of whiteness that either consciously or subconsciously perpetuate their privilege in schools.

Thus, in order to begin to effectively tackle oppression in schools, it is vital for school social work training programs and their students to learn how to critically examine our own identity formation and privileges across multiple social dimensions. Moreover, it is essential to continuously create specific learning time, language, training, practices, and curricula to guide us toward this effort. By doing so, future school social workers can begin to take steps toward being prepared to work alongside teachers and administrators to tackle school structures, policies, and practices that perpetuate oppression from the beginning through the end of our careers (Solomona et al., 2005).

2. Critically Reflecting on Our Policy and Practice Priorities. Tackling oppression in schools also means being able to acknowledge that, across the wide and diverse landscape of schools, many specific forms of oppression exist. Thus, it is up to us as school professionals to determine the unique, dominant language, assumptions, policies, and practices that undergird oppression for youths in each of our school buildings. Given our unique position as school social workers, as one of the few professionals in schools with such a broad network of collegial working relationships, extensive access to school data, and great flexibility in our professional roles and tasks, we are well positioned to identify key sources of oppression in our schools and to begin developing strategies to tackle them. Certainly assessing whether one's school is actively, passively, or antioppressive in its policies and practices is an important step in this process. As well we must critically and continuously reflect on whether our schools are developing specific strategies for identifying and organizing steps toward tackling various forms of oppression. This effort begins with bringing together individuals and groups, who may have had little previous exposure to one another to collectively examine our professional roles and responsibilities across the various positions, curriculum tracks, and extracurricular responsibilities that make up our school. Given the historically segregated, stratified, and oppressive ways in which school policies, practices, and interpersonal dynamics are often rooted, however, Goldsmith (2004) notes that schools must critically and continuously consider ways of engaging their school's communities to reflect on both the negative and positive effects of promoting antioppressive interactions, dialogue, and action. In fact, failure to do so may actually work to increase intergroup conflict and reinforce oppression in schools. Yosso (2005), for example, calls for schools to draw on critical race theory to help reframe deficit-oriented assumptions that frequently pervade school policy and practice. They challenge all school members to instead find ways to identify and learn about the various aspirational, navigational, social linguistic, familial, and resistance wealth that exists within all the youths, families, and communities we serve. Doing so can enable us to draw on historically oppressed youths' strengths, and begin to tackle the structural inequalities and practice orientations that reinforce oppression in each of our schools.

Another way to reflect on our schools' priorities is to use tools that can serve as accountability checks for regularly assessing our antioppressive policies and practices. The National School Social Work Evaluation Framework for School Social Work Practice (Sabatino et al., 2013) is one such tool. School social workers can use this framework to continuously reflect on and improve their level of performance across four domains of practice: (1)

planning and preparation, (2) the school environment, (3) service delivery and resources, and (4) professional responsibilities. Woven throughout this framework, multiple subdomains offer explicit guidance for school social workers to continuously assess their antioppressive policies and practices, particularly those that appear in the second domain, school environment. Focusing on approaches that contribute to creating a safe and healthy school environment, examining the effects of various forms of inequality and oppression on the learning context, developing culturally sensitive, strengths-based approaches to school practice, and engaging in efforts that promote social and economic justice, this domain calls on school social workers to provide specific and practical benchmarks for tackling oppression alongside clear, ethical standards that are at the center of our work. Using this framework to self-assess one's practice, to guide our supervision, and to organize dialogue with colleagues about oppression in our schools are just a few practical ways in which this tool can help school social workers continuously develop skills to lead schools in making reflective, antioppressive policies and practices our top priority.

   3. Strategically Using Data and Multitiered Interventions. Creating antioppressive policies and practices in schools also requires school social workers to thoughtfully and strategically make sense of the enormous amount of data available to us in schools, and to decide which data receive the most attention and scrutiny for the goals we set. Using data-driven, evidence-informed, and multitiered, response-to-intervention (RTI) approaches, school professionals can systematically develop interventions at all levels of a school (Barnett, Daly, Jones, & Lentz, 2004; Gresham, 2005; Kelly, 2010). Using an RTI approach in tackling oppressive structures, policies, and practices, school professionals begin by asking a series of critical questions related to the school's role in facilitating oppression. These questions include the following:

+ Who experiences oppression in our school?
+ In what ways, and under what circumstances, does oppression occur?
+ What antioppressive policies and practices can we implement?
+ What evidence can we gather to determine if progress is being made?
+ How can we continuously improve our efforts to be antioppressive?

   In following an RTI approach to tackling oppression, we first identify potentially oppressive school conditions, events, policies, and practices as targets for intervention. We then develop antioppressive interventions, track their progress, and assess their effectiveness in reducing oppression for various groups and individuals. Readers should also be encouraged that a number of school social work practice tools already exist that can be effective in this effort. Functional behavior assessments, behavior intervention plans, and restorative justice and positive behavioral interventions and supports, for example, have all shown effectiveness in countering policies and practices associated with oppression and disproportionality in schools (Filter,

Alvarez, & Zammit, 2013; Moreno & Bullock, 2011; Moreno & Gaytán, 2013; Peguero & Shekarkhar, 2011; Skiba et al., 2008; Skiba et al., 2006; Van Acker, Borenson, Gable, & Potterton, 2005). As members of schools' problem-solving, intervention, and leadership teams, it is also important for school social workers to provide effective consultation to classroom teachers and school leaders to maximize the positive impact of these tools and to continuously make them a central part of a school's intervention framework (Sabatino, 2009). Together, through a data-driven, multitiered approach, school social workers can work to focus, assess, and prioritize which school policies and practices are most effective toward tackling oppression.

4. Owning Our Unique Roles as School Social Workers. Beyond being equipped with effective intervention tools, it is also important for school social workers to develop skills that reflect our unique professional identities and positions within schools' complex organizational structures. Historically, school social workers have experienced many turning points in the development of our professional roles, responsibilities, and priorities (Allen-Meares, 2010; Constable, 1992). Even today, our profession may be unfairly perceived as lacking clearly marked professional job responsibilities and tasks, particularly compared to other school professionals such as classroom teachers. In an attempt to provide clarity about the unique and critical professional roles of social workers in schools, Phillippo and Blosser (2013) draw on interstitial emergence theory. Developed by Morrill (2006) to assess professionals' roles within changing organizations, Phillippo and Blosser describe how social work practice has followed a historic and contemporary trajectory in its professional evolution, characterized by three distinct professional features: (1) innovation, (2) mobilization, and (3) structuration. ("Structuration" is a term originally used by sociologist Anthony Giddens to highlight the interconnected relationship that human agency and social structures have with one another. Structuration suggests that through their actions social actors concurrently are shaped by and influence the shaping of their relationships and their environment. For further explanation, see Giddens [2013].) The authors argue that school social workers must continuously offer a clearly defined commitment to being responsive to the unmet challenges that schools face in meeting the needs of their most marginalized youths. In doing so, we often find ourselves seeking innovative solutions, and mobilizing improved resources, priorities, policies, and practices to guide and support schools in improving their structures and systems to better meet student needs. At the same time, school social workers should also embrace having a responsive role in order to remain closely attuned and adaptively skilled in responding to the needs of oppressed youths in schools. Thus, in our interstitial role we are well positioned as unique leaders in schools to closely monitor a school's priorities, identify its students' needs, and advocate for developing antioppressive policies and practices wherever the need is greatest.

5. *Aligning with Antioppressive Allies.* School social workers' ability to be responsive to the changing, unique, and context-specific forms of oppression in our schools also means being thoughtful and intentional about allying with school professionals who share a similar commitment to developing antioppressive policies and practices. The development of collaborative skills (Bronstein, 2003) is a time-honored hallmark of effective school social work practice. Collaborative skills facilitate collective, involved, and mutually invested partnerships with colleagues, families, and community partners. Such skills are also essential for antioppressive social work practice (Strier & Binyamin, 2013). Research on collegial trust in schools suggests that the more effective school professionals are at demonstrating respect, competence, personal regard for others, and integrity in their work, the more likely they are to effectively build trusting relationships with youths and families, to effectively work with one another, and to see their students' engagement and performance improve over time (Bryk & Schneider, 2002). Additionally, Daly, Moolenaar, Bolivar, and Burke (2010) find that building trusting relationships with fellow school professionals does not simply occur out of an organic, collective commitment to do so. Rather, trust emerges through a tireless, ongoing, and task-centered approach in working together with fellow school professionals toward a school's commonly agreed-on and clearly defined goals. In schools, collegial trust may emerge through a shared and mutually invested commitment to working together toward developing a school-wide instructional focus, by focusing on and fully developing a school's antioppressive mission across every dimension of its functioning, or by agreeing to collectively tackle a particular problem facing a school community. Thus, in working collaboratively with professional allies in our schools, particularly aligning with those who share the same commitment to making antioppressive policy and practice a top priority in our schools, we can begin the process of bringing our school's collective goals into focus, and in organizing resources, advocates, and efforts to identifying key challenges and opportunities that oppressed youths in each of our schools face. In doing so we also lay that groundwork for building trusting collegial relationships with our fellow school professionals.

6. *Actively Involving Youth, Families, and Community Members.* Finally, and perhaps most importantly, the ways in which we engage all members of a school community, both inside and outside of schools, calls on school social workers to develop skills that actively involve youths, families, and community members in the ongoing processes of problem-solving, program development, and community-building in schools. Developing effective skills toward this effort first means that school social workers must have a clear sense of who we are in relation to others. As well, we must also be able to balance our individual, autonomous, and authentic identities with a respect and appreciation for the various cultural values, collective goals, and common assets and challenges we share, even when they

might stand in tension and contradiction with our own (Johnson & Munch, 2009). Writing on the use of self in social work, Arnd-Caddigan and Pozzuto (2008) highlight that using the self is an ongoing process whereby the most skilled practitioners recognize that our own identity is, at its core, a function of our relationships with others. Therefore, the effectiveness of our efforts in tackling oppression in schools might best be measured by closely examining the quality of relationships and partnerships we forge with youths, families, and community members.

Describing school professionals who effectively forge high-quality relationships with youths as employing "developmentally responsive practice," Fusco (2012, p. 33) returns us to the critical role of relationships, and the power of working relationally, as a means of replacing our notions of others with the more common understandings of *us*. Calling on school social workers to develop skills that are effective within a social and supportive milieu as our most valuable method of school social work practice, Fusco argues that school social workers can learn to invite positive social change in schools through shaping the conditions and spaces we create in our relationships with all members of our school community. Echoing this call, and targeting parent and family involvement, Bunting, Drew, Lasseigne, and Anderson-Butcher (2013) recommend key steps for recruiting parents to be more involved in schools. This process starts with (1) assessing and addressing parent and family needs, then (2) encourages us to continuously build relationships with families, then (3) calls us to view parents as experts and leaders, and (4) ends with creating dedicated space and involving parents in meaningful and engaging activities within the school. In the classroom, shifting teaching priorities to first focus on becoming trustworthy and culturally responsive advocates and supports for students is also a critically important step in forging lasting and impactful relationships between youths and educators (Phillippo, 2012). Thus, by regularly and continually involving youths, family, and community members in the assessment, ideas, and tasks of schooling, we can work to bring together a larger, stronger, and more invested community of allies for working together to tackle oppression in schools.

TACKLING OPPRESSION IN SCHOOLS: REFLECTIONS ON AN AUTHENTICALLY SUPPORTIVE RELATIONSHIP

In light of the six skills for tackling oppression in schools outlined in this chapter, the following case aims to provide an example of the authors' own authentically supportive mentor-mentee relationship. Our aim is to show how school social workers can forge such relationships with youths and colleagues by drawing on the six skills for tackling oppression in schools outlined in this chapter. In writing this reflection, the authors each separately identified key moments that we experienced with one another that we believed were formative in developing our relationships; we also identified the motivations, practices, and actions that each of us used in those moments. We then discussed how these experiences contributed to shaping how our relationship has developed over time and how it helped in the process of tackling oppression in the school where we worked together. After reviewing this case we encourage readers to use the questions provided to reflect on how similar relationships, policies, and practices can be developed in your own school.

The First Two Years: Recognizing Privileges, Identifying Barriers, Forging Our Relationship

The authors of this chapter first met at a student-faculty/staff football game organized by the director of admissions of a public selective enrollment high school in Chicago.

At the time of that friendly football game, Leon was fourteen years old and about to begin ninth grade. Mr. Brake was employed as a full-time social worker with a youth-serving organization that partnered with the school. In his role, Mr. Brake developed leadership and mentorship programs for the school, forged community partnerships to provide services to meet the extracurricular and social emotional needs of students and families, and case-managed a group off-track students to help them access additional academic, mental health, and extracurricular supports.

The mission of the high school, which served a student body of 800 students from throughout Chicago, centered around six values of student leadership and learning that were reinforced by the school's deep commitment to developing strong, supportive relationships with their students. Faculty and staff regularly and openly talked about how their policies and practices could be improved to strengthen their instruction, improve their relationships with their students and families, and limit oppression for those most vulnerable. However, in many ways the school struggled to move beyond a deficit-oriented perspective in viewing its students' challenges and in reflecting on how to improve its policies and practices. The director of admissions, who was charged by the school's principal to recruit a student body that mirrored the diversity of the city, focused much of his efforts on recruiting and helping to retain low-income African American and Latino students, particularly males, once the school began noticing significant declines among these groups of students attending the school in recent years. One strategy the director used was to develop a male mentoring program at the school. The football game that day was the mentor program's kick-off event.

At this event, the twenty predominantly African American and Latino ninth and tenth-grade male student mentees met their faculty and staff mentors. That day, Mr. Brake and the other mentors also learned two valuable lessons: (1) our mentees were absolutely determined to win the football game, and (2) Leon's strength, determination, and leadership set the tone and led the way. One time in particular, marked by a failed attempt by Mr. Brake to tackle Leon was punctuated by a confident stiff-arm delivered by Leon directly to Mr. Brake's face. This moment not only left the staff mentors down yet-another touchdown, but also sent the jubilation of the mentees soaring. It also set the tone for how Leon and Mr. Brake's mentor-mentee relationship would develop in the years ahead. Through Leon's tireless drive to be successful in school and Mr. Brake's determined efforts to continuously find ways to create supports and opportunities for Leon and the other mentees, in that one failed tackle, Leon had sent a message—he knew where he was headed in life and it was Mr. Brake's job not to tackle Leon, but rather to find effective ways to tackle oppression in the school that might stand in Leon's way.

For Leon, during the first two years of high school there were a number of ways that Mr. Brake accepted his challenge. The first was how Mr. Brake worked to overcome the interpersonal barriers that initially existed between the students and the faculty and staff at the school. Leon quickly came to value how Mr. Brake demonstrated a genuine concern for his and other students' learning, for ensuring their sense of belonging at the school, and for his ability to help them access the resources and supports he needed to be successful at the school. Leon especially appreciated how Mr. Brake targeted his support efforts after school during their time together in the school's student learning center to make sure Leon was completing his homework, improving his writing skills, getting his questions answered by his various teachers, and advocating for him and his needs with faculty and staff who were unaware of his strengths. These efforts showed Leon that Mr. Brake was committed to his success early on in ninth grade and that he was always willing to make extra efforts on his behalf.

In addition to his individual and group efforts with students Mr. Brake also positioned himself to participate in important school-wide leadership roles and influential team and committee meetings. His aim in doing so was to help the school continuously focus on reforming its policies and practices to better support students across the school, particularly those most vulnerable to its oppressive policies and practices. As a member of the school development team Mr. Brake helped the school create and analyze new and existing data sources such as student and parent school climate surveys, student attendance, grades, achievement, discipline, retention, graduation, and college-going data, in order to identify which groups of students were most in need of supports and to determine how changes in policy and practices could target these efforts. The school development team became the key faculty and staff team for developing, managing, and monitoring the school's multitiered interventions, for organizing instructional and intervention priorities, and for identifying needed changes in school-wide, grade-level, and classroom-level policies and practices. Mr. Brake also worked to identify additional community resources and partnerships, as well as to develop greater family engagement, input, and leadership opportunities toward creating further supports for the school's most vulnerable youths, such as many of the students who participated in the male mentor program.

The Second Two Years: Developing Leaders, Aligning Allies, and Planning for the Future

For Leon, in his first two years of high school it was important for him to have a strong academic foundation with which to take on new extracurricular and leadership opportunities during his second two years in high school. Mr. Brake constantly reinforced this message and supported Leon's goal throughout his first two years of high school. By the end of his first year, with the support of Mr. Brake and other mentors at the school, Leon had gained comfort in seeking help from other adults in the high school, had found a supportive network of peer and adult allies, and was developing a strong academic record and set of skills that enabled him to take on new challenges, address personal or academic concerns, and to help advocate for his and others' needs. In recognition of his emerging leadership skills and potential, in his second year of high school, Leon was selected by Mr. Brake and the director of admissions to be a school ambassador. In this leadership position Leon and eight other student ambassadors helped promote positive student life school-wide through events and activities that built community across students' many interests and backgrounds. Ambassadors also helped the school develop common language, values, and commitment to promoting a culture of positive youth development by building positive peer relationships and deepening and appreciation of cross-cultural community-building activities and dialogue.

Continuing to improve his academic record each year, in his second two years of high school Leon began to take on more student leadership roles in the school. By his third year, he also began to focus on his goal to attend college. By using the self-advocacy skills he had developed, he worked closely with his college counselors to articulate his extreme financial needs so that they could help him find scholarships throughout his extensive college search and application process. During his senior year, Leon was selected as a mentor for a yearlong peer mentorship and leadership program that Mr. Brake and the school's freshman counselor had developed to support ninth graders in their transition into the high school. The peer mentors also often worked closely with school leaders to lead discussions on critical issues affecting the student body. As well, they spoke at various colleges, universities, and community organizations about how their experiences were shaping their leadership skills and contributing to the supportive climate for which the school had become well known in the city. Meanwhile, not only did Leon graduate as one of the most valued and respected student leaders at one of the top high schools in Illinois, but he was also headed to Morehouse College on a full scholarship. Proud of Leon's accomplishments and the impact he and Mr. Brake had in positively shaping the school's policies and practices, we continue to take these experiences, and the authentically supportive relationship we have developed, into our continued studies and professional endeavors.

College and Beyond: Mutual Benefits, Building Our Personal and Professional Networks

Now in his third year of undergraduate studies, Leon is excelling academically at Morehouse, each term earning a spot on the school's dean's list. As well, he holds a number of key leadership positions on campus, has founded and developed his own college scholarship program for low-income Morehouse students, and has been offered a number of internships at large accounting firms throughout the country. Mr. Brake earned his doctorate in social work and now teaches as an assistant professor at Northeastern Illinois University in Chicago. Whenever we are in Chicago together we continue to meet, to discuss our personal and professional goals, and to reflect on the lessons we are learning and skills we are continuing to develop. Authoring this chapter was one result of these meetings, the authentically supportive relationship we have developed, and our continued effort to create antioppressive supports for youths and families in schools. In many ways, the two of us seemed like a mentor-mentee match that might struggle to develop an authentically supportive relationship. On the surface, we appeared to have little in common in terms of age, race, class, and educational background—a fifteen-year-old African American male who had grown up in public housing on the south side of Chicago and a thirty-year-old white school social worker who grew up middle-class in Louisville, Kentucky. However, through Leon's strength, determination, and leadership, and Mr. Brake's commitment to antioppressive school social work policy and practice, over the years we have developed a relationship that has overcome many potential barriers and reinforced the lesson that by working together to tackle oppression in schools we can mutually strengthen our skills and relationships while also helping to build strong, supportive, antioppressive schools that mutually benefit all community members.

CONCLUSION

This chapter has outlined six skills to guide social workers in tackling oppression in schools. Doing so begins with having a clear understanding of the unique forms of oppression that characerize your school and making the tackling of these forms of oppression your top priority. Next, by drawing on our ethical standards as well as setting out to develop authentically supportive relationships with oppressed youth and families, developing these six skills—to be clear about your own privileges, to critically reflect on your school's policies and practices, to strategically use data and multitiered interventions, to own your unique role as a social worker, to align with antioppressive allies, and to actively involve the most marginalized in your school—can position school social workers to take the lead in tackling oppression and orienting a new direction for schools to become the antioppressive and equalizing institutions they have always had the potential to be.

DISCUSSION QUESTIONS

◆ What are the most valuable lessons for tackling oppression in schools that this chapter highlights?
◆ How would you classify the type of school (actively oppressive, passively oppressive, antioppressive) featured in this case study? Why?
◆ Which of the six skills for tackling oppression did Mr. Brake appear to be the most effective in his social work practice? Why?
◆ How did Mr. Brake demonstrate the three components of counter-stratification in his work with Leon?
◆ Are there additional skills that social workers should develop for tackling oppression in schools?
◆ What is unique about the role of school social workers as advocates for oppressed youths and families in schools?
◆ In light of this chapter, how would you collaborate with your colleagues to begin to tackle oppression in your school?

References

Abrams, L. S., & Gibson, P. (2007). Teaching notes: Reframing multicultural educations: Teaching white privilege in the social work curriculum. *Journal of Social Work Education, 43*(1), 147–160.

Allen-Meares, P. (2010). School social work: Historical development, influences, and practices. *Social work services in schools.* Boston: Allyn & Bacon.

Arnd-Caddigan, M., & Pozzuto, R. (2008). Use of self in relational clinical social work. *Clinical Social Work Journal, 36*(3), 235–243.

Bahena, S., Cooc, N., Currie-Rubin, R., Kuttner, P., & Ng, M. (2012). *Disrupting the school-to-prison pipeline.* Cambridge, MA: Harvard Education

Barnett, D. W., Daly, E. J., Jones, K. M., & Lentz, F. E. (2004). Response to intervention: Empirically based special service decisions from single-case designs of increasing and decreasing intensity. *Journal of Special Education, 38*(2), 66–79.

Bronstein, L. R. (2003). A model for interdisciplinary collaboration. *Social Work, 48*(3), 297–306.

Bryk, A., & Schneider, B. (2002). *Trust in schools: A core resource for improvement.* New York: Russell Sage Foundation.

Bunting, H., Drew, H., Lasseigne, A., & Anderson-Butcher, D. (2013). Effective strategies for involving parents in schools. In C. Franklin, M. B. Harris, & P. Allen-Meares (Eds.), *The school services sourcebook:A guide for school-based professionals* (2nd ed., pp. 633–644). New York: Oxford University Press.

Chicago Public Schools (CPS). (2014). *Racial ethnic survey.* Retrieved from http://cps .edu/Performance/Documents/DataFiles/FY14_Racial_Ethnic_Survey.xls

Christle, C. A., Jolivette, K., & Nelson, C. M. (2005). Breaking the school-to-prison pipeline: Identifying school risk and protective factors for youth delinquency. *Exceptionality, 13*(2), 69–88.

Constable, R. T. (1992). The new school reform and the school social worker. *Children & Schools, 14*(2), 106–113.

Daly, A. J., Moolenaar, N. M., Bolivar, J. M., & Burke, P. (2010). Relationships in reform: The role of teachers' social networks. *Journal of Educational Administration, 48*(3), 359–391.

Filter, K. J., Alvarez, M. E., & Zammitt, K. A. (2013). Functional behavior assessment in a three-tiered prevention model. In C. Franklin, M. B. Harris, & P. Allen-Meares (Eds.), *The school services sourcebook: A guide for school-based professionals* (pp. 25–36). New York: Oxford University Press.

Fusco, D. (2012). Use of self in the context of youth work. *Child & Youth Services, 33*(1), 33–45.

Giddens, A. (2013). *The constitution of society: Outline of the theory of structuration.* New York: John Wiley & Sons.

Goldsmith, P. A. (2004). Schools' role in shaping race relations: Evidence on friendliness and conflict. *Social Problems, 51*(4), 587–612.

Goodlad, J. I. (2002). Kudzu, rabbits, and school reform. *Phi Delta Kappan, 84*(1), 16–23.

Gresham, F. M. (2005). Response to intervention: An alternative means of identifying students as emotionally disturbed. *Education and Treatment of Children,* 328–344.

Johnson, Y. M., & Munch, S. (2009). Fundamental contradictions in cultural competence. *Social Work, 54*(3), 220–231.

Kelly, M. S. (2010). An evidence informed process for school social workers. In M. S. Kelly, J. C. Raines, S. Stone, & A. Frey (Eds.), *School social work: An evidence informed framework for practice* (pp. 42–51). New York: Oxford University Press.

Moreno, G., & Bullock, L. M. (2011). Principles of positive behaviour supports: Using the FBA as a problem-solving approach to address challenging behaviours beyond special populations. *Emotional and Behavioural Difficulties, 16*(2), 117–127.

Moreno, G., & Gaytán, F. X. (2013). Reducing subjectivity in special education referrals by educators working with Latino students: Using functional behavioral assessment as a pre-referral practice in student support teams. *Emotional and Behavioural Difficulties, 18*(1), 88–101.

Morrill, C. (2006). *Institutional change through interstitial emergence: The growth of alternative dispute resolution in American law, 1965–1995.* Unpublished manuscript. University of California, Irvine.

National Association of Social Workers (NASW). (2008). *Code of ethics.* Retrieved from http://www.socialworkers.org/pubs/code/code.asp

Noguera, P. A. (2003). Schools, prisons, and social implications of punishment: Rethinking disciplinary practices. *Theory into Practice, 42*(4), 341–350.

Patterson C., & Kaba, M. (2011). *Arresting justice: A report about juvenile arrests in Chicago 2009 & 2010.* Chicago: First Defense Legal Aid and Project NIA.

Peguero, A. A., & Shekarkhar, Z. (2011). Latino/a student misbehavior and school punishment. *Hispanic Journal of Behavioral Sciences, 33*(1), 54–70.

Phillippo, K. (2012). "You're trying to know me": Students from nondominant groups respond to teacher personalism. *Urban Review, 44*(4), 441–467.

Phillippo, K., & Blosser, A. (2013). Specialty practice or interstitial practice? A reconsideration of school social work's past and present. *Children & Schools, 35*(1), 19–31.

Picower, B. (2009). The unexamined whiteness of teaching: How white teachers maintain and enact dominant racial ideologies. *Race Ethnicity and Education, 12*(2), 197–215.

Sabatino, C. A. (2009). School social work consultation models and response to intervention: A perfect match. *Children & Schools, 31*(4), 197–206.

Sabatino, C. A., Alvarez, M., Frey, A., Dupper, D., Lindsey, B., Raines, J., . . . & Norris, M. (2013). *National evaluation framework for school social work practice.* School Social Work Association of America. Retrieved from http://www.sswaa.org/associations/13190/files/SSWAANationalEvalFrameworkFINAL10_14_2013.docx

Skiba, R. J., Simmons, A. B., Ritter, S., Gibb, A. C., Rausch, M. K., Cuadrado, J., & Chung, C. G. (2008). Achieving equity in special education: History, status and current challenges. *Council for Exceptional Children, 74*(3), 264–288.

Skiba, R. J., Simmons, A. S., Ritter, S., Kohler, K., Henderson, M., & Wu, T. (2006). The context of minority disproportionality: Practitioner perspectives on special education referral. *Teachers College Record, 108*(7), 1424–1459.

Solomona, R. P., Portelli, J. P., Daniel, B. J., & Campbell, A. (2005). The discourse of denial: How white teacher candidates construct race, racism and "white privilege." *Race, Ethnicity and Education, 8*(2), 147–169.

Stanton-Salazar, R. (2011). A social capital framework for the study of institutional agents and their role in the empowerment of low-status students and youth. *Youth & Society, 43*(3), 1066–1109.

Strier, R., & Binyamin, S. (2013). Introducing anti-oppressive social work practices in public services: Rhetoric to practice. *British Journal of Social Work.* Bct049. doi:10.1093/bjsw/bct049

Van Acker, R., Borenson, L., Gable, R., & Potterton, T. (2005). Are we on the right course? Lessons learned about current FBA/BIP practices in schools. *Journal of Behavioral Education, 14*(1), 35–56.

Wald, J. M., & Losen, D. J. (2003). *Deconstructing the school-to-prison pipeline.* Indianapolis, IN: Jossey-Bass.

Ward, D., & Mullender, A. (1991). Empowerment and oppression: An indissoluble pairing for contemporary social work. *Critical Social Policy, 11*(32), 21–30.

Yosso, T. J. (2005). Whose culture has capital? A critical race theory discussion of community cultural wealth. *Race Ethnicity and Education, 8*(1), 69–91.

21

Schools as Organizations

Emily Shayman
Loyola University Chicago

Carol Rippey Massat
Indiana University School of Social Work

- ◆ Organizational Analysis
- ◆ Formal Organizational Structure
- ◆ The School as an Organizational Culture
- ◆ People-Processing and People-Changing Perspectives
- ◆ Routinized Action Perspective
- ◆ Diversity Change Perspective
- ◆ Postmodern Perspective
- ◆ Strengths Perspective

School social workers are change agents in schools.[1] The model of school social work described in this book involves interventions at multiple levels of practice: individual, family, group, classroom, school, community, and state and national policy levels. While current practice discussed in this chapter is deeply rooted in the history of school social work, it is also a good fit with the tiered model of school social work intervention discussed throughout this volume (Kelly, 2008).

School social workers practice in host settings where most other professionals identify as educators. It is therefore challenging to present and discuss change relating to social/emotional development. School social work goals are not always the same as the goals of educators: school social

---

1. *Editor's note:* An earlier version of this chapter was written by Pawlak and Cousins (2009).

workers focus on mental and emotional health, social skills, school culture, social justice, and survival needs (Mumm & Bye, 2011).

Other school stakeholders may not understand the relevance or necessity of these issues, because they concentrate on academic goals. Therefore, school social workers must articulate the value of social work goals in supporting the learning process for students. In order to collaborate with teachers, school social workers must first understand how they themselves fit into the community, district, and school. This understanding evolves through an organizational perspective (Kahn, 2005).

This chapter is designed to assist school social workers in analyzing and understanding their school settings from an organizational perspective. We describe the elements of an organization through the language of organizational analysis, then describe how social work services fit into a host organization, and how the mission of the school affects school social workers. Finally, we consider a range of theoretical lenses that can help us to build new vision for a school as an organization.

ORGANIZATIONAL ANALYSIS

Organizational analysis is the first step in developing a clear understanding of a specific school's culture and functioning. Every school social worker should carry out such an analysis of his or her own school setting. Such analysis provides the information needed to form effective collaborative teams and to establish support for future change. Organizational analysis helps school social workers develop conceptual maps of the system and its operations. Any organization has structures, processes, policies, and cultures, and schools are no exception. These elements affect all school participants: teachers, staff, administration, students, and families. School social workers have a responsibility to understand and influence these factors. Most school social workers explain that everyone in the school is their client, but some students and families may have direct services while others have indirect support, such as through school-wide programs or policy development. School social workers have a responsibility to understand and influence these factors, especially on behalf of students and families who may be direct clients. Such an analysis begins with an understanding of formal organizational structure and informal organizational structures; it is enhanced with the addition of additional theoretical lenses. Understanding the school as an organization also helps school social workers to avoid costly errors in working within the organization. For example, one of the authors narrowly missed some potential errors when she began a new job without the knowledge that one of the faculty was married to the head of the school. This dynamic could have led to faux pas in faculty meetings or casual conversation. Learning about the structure of the organization and both formal and informal relationships helps to avoid missteps in working with the system, and to facilitate the construction of helpful networks.

FORMAL ORGANIZATIONAL STRUCTURE

Formal structure refers to official, established, and documented patterns of functioning within an organization. Several dimensions can be used to describe the formal structure of organizations: formalization, standardization, centralization/decentralization, and horizontal and vertical complexity (Hall, 1996). These dimensions can be manipulated or altered such that aspects of the organization or its programs can be designed to be more or less formalized, standardized, centralized, or complex. Variations in organizational and program structure lead to variations in consequences (that can be positive or negative) for school administrators, teachers, students, or parents. Although some school organizational and program structures are not accessible to school social workers, it is important to note the various aspects of schools that can be influenced or changed.

Formalization refers to the degree to which rules, policies, and procedures that govern behavior in the organization are officially codified and set forth in writing. Examples include rules governing how individualized education program meetings are conducted, criteria governing discipline of students, guidelines for conducting locker searches, or protocols for recording and reporting unexcused absences. Formalization prescribes behavior and should reduce discretion (e.g., in some school districts principals may suspend students, but only the superintendent can expel students). However, in some instances formalization may legitimate discretion (e.g., in one school district a school social worker is charged to solely help children in their roles as students, but in another district she or he may provide counseling to parents if such assistance will facilitate the child's school adjustment).

Standardization is a type of formalization in which organizations carry out uniform ways of dealing with uniform situations; rules or definitions are established to cover a particular set of circumstances and apply invariably. For example, schools have standardized forms and practices to record student absences and report them to parents. School officials often follow a series of steps in which the frequency and intensity of interventions increase as absences increase. Each of these concepts can be used to analyze several aspects of an organization's formal structure, and these analyses are useful for several reasons.

Some people are comfortable only with formalization and standardization. Maintaining formalization and standardization may help schools to maintain roles for school personnel that are more clearly defined. Documenting rights, duties, and expectations holds school officials, staff, teachers, students, and parents accountable for specific actions. For example, formal structures that permit students and parents to appeal class schedules dictated by a school guidance counselor may ease strong student reactions. Without these formal procedures, parents or students are more likely to cast school professionals as authoritarian and arbitrary, which creates anger and tension. Therefore, formalization and standardization within organizations can eliminate or constrain arbitrariness, and can promote equitable treatment and equal opportunity for programs, services, or benefits. Standardization can promote consistency among staff members with similar decision making or processing tasks; for example, this can be in the form of a rubric so that all junior mathematics teachers have consistent expectations, and all students are held to the same standards.

Of course formalization and standardization can be dysfunctional. Some staff members within an organization may say that such mandates promote bureau pathologies such as red tape, inflexibility, devotion to method, and discouragement of innovation and appropriate discretion (Patti, 1982; Walker & Brewer, 2008). When school rules and procedures are contested, a school social worker could speak with the appropriate person(s) to ask about the extent that such rules are formalized and if there is any amount of discretion available. For example, teachers have probably heard a student or parent ask, "Where does it say that she can't do that?"

Formalization and standardization may be dysfunctional when these lead to routinization or ritualistic behavior, when a situation calls instead for individualizing the interpretation and implementation of a policy. For example, some states have zero tolerance for weapons on school grounds with severe consequences for violating the rule (e.g., automatic expulsion with no exception). A fourth-grade student in a small town brought a knife to school in order to cut brownies for her classmates. Her behavior came under the stipulations of the law, and she was barred from school. Some proponents were concerned that a precedent might be set if an exception was made, whereas others advocated that an exception does not drive the rule.

Centralization refers to the concentration of power, authority, and decision making at the top of the organization. As applied to a school district or system, centralization refers to the board, superintendent, or what is commonly known as the central office or central administration. As applied to a particular school building, centralization refers to the principal, assistant principal, and other office staff. Decentralization refers to the distribution of power, authority, and decision making throughout the organization. As applied to a school district or system, decentralization refers to arrangements such as regional offices or centers, or the delegation of some functions to local school principals and faculty. As applied to a particular school building, decentralization refers to the delegation of some functions to individual teachers, faculty committees, parent–teacher advisory councils, or teacher–student work groups. Within some school buildings, principals can make decisions about discipline, suspension, and access to services, or they can involve staff and parents in developing guidelines for such decisions or rely on a faculty advisory committee. Whatever the case may be, school social workers must first learn what is centralized or decentralized before they can engage in organizational change.

Centralized and decentralized structures can be functional or dysfunctional. For example, centralizing decisions regarding expulsion in the superintendent's office is functional, because dismissal has profound consequences for the student and could lead to litigation; decentralizing decisions to local school officials regarding which students should be referred for school social work services is functional, because the predominant needs of students vary from school to school. Generally speaking, centralization of authority, power, and decision making may be functional when schools have to manage boundary relationships with the external environment (e.g., the press, police, juvenile court, community advocacy groups), when scarce resources have to be rationed and carefully allocated, or when there are threats to the school (e.g., protests, litigation, complaints). Decentralization enables teachers, students, or their parents to gain ownership of policies and programs and increases the likelihood of their legitimacy and successful implementation. For example, a decentralized decision-making structure such as a joint faculty–student committee on student conduct might promote student ownership of the code of conduct, whereas a centralized top-down imposition of the code might generate resistance. Decentralization also facilitates the management of change and uncertainty at the front lines of the organization, and bottom-up innovation and adaptation (Wagoner, 1994).

Horizontal complexity refers to the type and degree of organizational segmentation, such as departmentalization, and to the specialization of positions, roles, jobs, or duties. The degree of specialization and departmentalization can be functional or dysfunctional. High specialization sometimes leads to fragmented and uncoordinated delivery of services, but it also might contribute to efficiency and the availability of high levels of expertise.

If teachers themselves are attempting to understand the horizontal complexity in their daily jobs, then parents must also learn how to navigate the environment. School social workers might find themselves supporting students and parents who are overwhelmed with their problems and the bureaucratic maze of services.

Vertical complexity refers to the number of levels in the hierarchy from the top to the bottom of the organization. Vertical complexity may be functional or dysfunctional from the standpoint of a school social worker or parent interested in promoting change. If a change proposal has to traverse many hierarchical levels for approval, the structure may not be functional; if officials are accessible, and there are few levels between the top and the bottom, organizational change may be more easily influenced.

In some districts, classroom teachers report to an instructional coach, who then reports to a teacher on assignment, who then reports to an assistant principal, who then reports to the principal. Although instructional coaches are meant to support teachers in designing curriculum, they do not have expertise in behavior management or social-emotional well-being of students. Therefore, teachers must learn how to find the social workers who can explain how mental health affects learning ability and learning style. However, these ideas must align to the mandated curriculum that comes from both building administration as well as governmental laws. Therefore, the maze of services within the building becomes more complex after accounting for the power differentials between various departments within the building.

As school social workers begin employment at a new school, they should devote time to comprehending the school's horizontal and vertical complexity, or its negotiated political order, often found in school manuals or handbooks. If such documentation is not available, school social workers are advised to be observant, check out the arrangements with opinion leaders, and map the structure or negotiated order for themselves. Such understanding is important because school social workers are required to integrate, coordinate, link, and communicate throughout various departments, positions, and roles within the organizational structure.

The role of a school social worker gives practitioners legitimate and unique access. In other words, school social workers find structural mobility to most, if not all, segments and roles within schools. Thus, school social workers must figure out their niche within the organization—within the district and/or within a specific school—and which individuals in which positions might facilitate or hinder work goals or tasks.

Staff members within schools—and, in fact, in all organizations—develop social relationships that are not prescribed by organizational administration or management. These social relationships evolve into patterned group processes and social structures that are known as informal organizations or informal structures and relations. These social relationships are informal in that they are unofficial, not mandated, and not planned. Informal structure is rarely, if ever, documented. For example, you cannot ask your school principal for a copy of the school's informal organization chart because it does not exist (but, as we will point out shortly, you can draw one yourself). There are four types of informal structure: relationship structure, communication structure, decision-making structure, and power structure.

Relationship structure refers to patterns of social relationships based on friendship, mutual attraction, similar interests, and common experience. Relationship structure manifests itself in several ways: for example, two or more staff members frequently have coffee break or lunch together, sit next to each other at meetings, attend professional conferences together, and perhaps even socialize off the job.

Communication structure refers to patterns of social interaction among staff members based on giving and getting information, opinions, viewpoints, or feelings—even when those individuals do not have a formal or informal relationship. Some common metaphors for communication structure include the rumor mill, the talk on the street, the grapevine, or inside information. Informal communication structure can be detected by observing who talks with whom after a controversy or a staff meeting. Who are the confidants, the listeners? Who do teachers depend on to figure out and report "what's going on"?

Decision-making structure refers to patterns of social interaction among school personnel based on the solicitation or provision of analysis, insights, and advice leading up to a decision. Decision-making structure can be detected by observing who consults with whom during deliberations. For example, is there a small group of experienced teachers with whom the principal often consults on the side? Do particular teachers meet informally before a meeting in an attempt to sway opinion prior to a formal meeting?

Power structure refers to patterns of social interaction based on ability to create influence. There are four types of power: referent, expertise, reward, and coercive (French & Raven, 1968). A teacher may have referent power because she is liked, and another may have expertise power because she is a respected English instructor. Some teachers have reward power because they support colleagues and praise them for their contributions, and others have coercive power because they have years of experience, are abrasive, or intimidate colleagues.

School social workers must strive to discern informal structure because they will inevitably become a part of it; this can work for or against each individual social worker. In attempt to better understand surroundings, social workers can use flow charts for informal structure, just as if using an organizational flow chart of structure—though they themselves will have to create the flow chart based on observation and interpretation of the social structure. If mapping relevant informal structures and relations is essential or desirable, school social workers can easily do so with a formal organization chart and highlighters of different colors. Let's assume that the school has an organizational chart in which each school official, staff member, and teacher name/position are posted within a rectangular box. Let's assume that an assistant principal and two teachers are part of a relationship structure, and the principal relies on the school secretary and head of the physical plant to "keep their ears to the ground and keep her posted on goings-on." You can use different-colored highlighters to visually map these two informal structures. Such mapping may help demystify the complex informal operational structure and relations within a school and their congruence with formal structure.

Several factors can contribute to the development and maintenance of informal structure and relations. These include, but are not limited to

1. Characteristics or attributes of individuals (e.g., gender, race, or age);
2. Common life experiences (e.g., being a single parent, caring for an adult parent, or being alumni of the same university);
3. Shared values and interests (e.g., conservative orientation, quilting, or fishing);
4. Common memberships in organizations external to the school (e.g., a church or political party); or
5. Sharing a common fate (e.g., working under an authoritarian director).

Understanding such contributing factors can help the school social worker determine what creates or restricts the informal structures within the building.

Informal structures involve not only administrators, teachers, and staff in varying combinations, but also may include students and their families. Teachers may have favorite students or parents. Some students and their families might be insiders due to high participation rates in school activities: some students, teachers, and family volunteers could be involved in clubs together or play basketball in the school gym together. Students themselves detect and maintain an informal structure and have names for its variations such as jock, band geek, prep, emo, and so on.

Informal structure serves several functions within organizations:

1. It provides informal linkages between departments, positions, and roles (e.g., the school social worker and attendance officer worked together in another school district).
2. It compensates for problems in the formal structure (e.g., when the principal was of little help to teachers who had to manage classroom behavior problems, the teachers turned to an experienced teacher for assistance).
3. It socializes and orients new school personnel and students to life in the organization (what are the do's and don'ts?).
4. It provides a network for the circulation of information.
5. It provides social support and alleviates stress and frustration.
6. It meets interpersonal and associational needs.

In examining a school's informal structure, school social workers should try to determine the functions that it serves in order to decide whether the informal structure supports or undermines students, who are ultimately the direct clients.

THE SCHOOL AS AN ORGANIZATIONAL CULTURE

Cultures within schools can be defined as the beliefs, values, traditions, and attitudes that are the basis of the frames of reference or meanings people use to organize reality and direct their behavioral actions. In short, culture within a school comes down to the general intonation of the people within the building. If students and/or parents and/or teachers are frustrated, the culture becomes negative. If administration is unhappy with the work ethic, the culture may become more structured. When most students are completing homework and attempting to learn, then staff members may become more flexible about rules, which can allow for an independent and positive culture.

The organizational culture of a school affects all school functions. This fact is particularly relevant to social workers who practice in schools where there is difficulty in understanding the mutual influence and effect on intraschool relationships of social and academic processes occurring between schools and the rest of the community (see McWhorter, 2001; Perry, Steele, & Hilliard, 2003). Posing several questions might bring the issues into focus: What is the nature of organizational culture in schools? Why is this information important to social workers? What do social workers need to know about organizational culture in schools to function effectively? In deciphering the culture in how schools work as organizations, two pathways are important: formal structure and informal structure.

Organizational Culture as It Relates to the Formal Structure

Schools are transmitters of dominant cultural standards, norms, and values emanating from society at large. Dominant cultural norms are infused into schools through federal regulations, state and local boards of education, and universities as institutions for knowledge development and training. These institutions define, design, and organize academic materials that become a part of the educational and social activities that have to be administered in a school. This means that the selection and enforcement of reading, writing, and arithmetic curricula, as well as the methods to teach these subjects, are artifacts of Western cultural beliefs about learning and socialization, and are not universal facts of human nature.

Interpersonal transactions occurring between students and teachers or staff provide another pathway for culture to permeate schools as organizations. Culture provides a blueprint for the meaning and interpretation of acceptable and unacceptable behavior, attitudes, emotions, and beliefs. For example, students generally understand that when they enter the classroom the teacher is in charge. The teacher makes the rules and enforces them. He or she decides who can talk and when. When a student violates the rules, the consequences generally fit the sanctioned norms in school. As such, school culture manifests in an organized way based on various frames of reference or meanings associated with compliance and violations of policies and regulations.

Both pathways of culture in the organization of schools are alike in reflecting varying degrees of influence by dominant culture norms in society at large. When there is a high degree of compatibility and homogeneity among students and school officials, there is likely to be less conflict within the organizational milieu of the school. However, nonwhite students rarely experience schools in which the dominant culture is the same as their own. Homogenous school cultures are becoming less common because of the increasing ethnic, religious, and economic diversity of groups residing in the United States and participating in the school system.

Disciplinary guidelines and actions are largely based on white European culture; therefore, we should carefully examine implications surrounding the diverse ethnic groups in American schools. School social workers reflect and can influence the organizational culture that is demonstrated through dominant beliefs, values, attitudes, and behaviors embedded in customs, traditions, and notions of common sense that form the basis of administrative policy and regulations in schools. For example, social workers should examine disciplinary and evaluative activities occurring between social workers and students; between students and staff; and among parents, staff, and social workers. When observing disciplinary activities in school, social workers can ask themselves the following questions: "Do the infractions that led to disciplinary action reflect commonly held beliefs, values, and attitudes between the student and school official? If so, did the disciplinary action occur because there was a lack of cultural commonality? When there is a lack of commonality, are the differences labeled as dysfunctional rather than as variations in how people understand the multiple meanings of the standards being enforced?" These questions are especially important to consider when the outcomes of the disciplinary action are detrimental to the social, emotional, and/or academic well-being of students.

While teachers bring academic integrity to the school organization, social workers bring social skills and cultural competence. Therefore, social workers are a key component in ensuring that organizational policy and culture do not conflict with student values relating to culture. Social workers can advocate for students' needs and rights. For example, many African Americans have experienced strain in relation to dominant cultural norms in schools, and have responded with resistance. Many African Americans have questioned the relevance of the subjects taught in school in relation to their plight as an oppressed group. While mastery of academic skills can help, it cannot resolve larger societal influences on a student's life. When frames of reference operating in the organizational culture of a school are juxtaposed, compliance and noncompliance are better understood.

One Latina faculty member said to one of the authors, "My husband says our faculty parties are like funerals!" School norms based on cultures that limit expression may not be a good fit for all students or faculty. Members of diverse groups may have been socialized in cultures that value a high degree of expressiveness and animation through language and the body in communicating with people. However, school etiquette generally requires that students sit still when speaking, stay in their seats, and address only the teacher. When students do not or cannot comply with these social and behavioral norms, they are punished or labeled as dysfunctional.

School social workers can address cultural dissonance through advocacy regarding school policies that may inhibit the success of culturally or ethnically diverse students. Social workers must participate in public education through school in-service training on cultural diversity, community dialogues, and political actions that address official policy-making bodies. School social workers can attend staff meetings, board meetings, state education association meetings, or legislation meetings. More on this topic that specifically addresses antioppressive policies is available in chapter 20.

The understandings and actions regarding the organizational culture of schools proposed in this discussion offer a way in which school social workers can become transformative professionals. They can begin by refusing to submit to the notion that academic and social functions in schools are neutral transactions in organizational culture. Acting as such, social workers contribute to the realization of the overall interdependence between U.S. institutions such as schools, as well as social, economic, political, and cultural processes within the society at large.

Organizational Culture as It Relates to Informal Structure

Just as the formal culture affects student functioning, so does the informal culture. Informal culture is present in all organizations and can largely depend on the formal culture designated to the school. Informal culture shows itself through various scenarios within a school building. One key example to understanding the informal culture is circumnavigating the impact of personal relationships between staff members. When teachers are friends with one another outside of the workplace, their interactions are naturally more cohesive. When administrators know their teachers or other staff members from outside of the workplace, their relationships potentially create informal power dynamics due to the higher frequency of interactions. Yet another unique culture exists when none of the employees befriend one another beyond professional gatherings. Humans form relationships; while not all relationships will be positive, all relationships will affect the work culture. When teachers are frustrated with one another, students may experience this frustration second-hand.

Furthermore, informal culture is strongly related to the general job satisfaction of the employees of the school. Job satisfaction may well relate to better performance. Teachers who are happy to be in the school may advance student learning in a better way than unhappy teachers will do. Job satisfaction is a large factor in the overall informal culture within a school. It is therefore also important to understand that job satisfaction comes from more than just a good salary. School administrators that demonstrate their appreciation for employees are likely to retain individuals within the workplace who are more highly qualified. Emmert and Taher (1992) explain, "Public professionals seem to derive their attitudes more from the social relations on the job and from the extent to which their intrinsic needs are met. The dimensions of the work itself appear to be a secondary consideration" (p. 44). An optimistic, positive culture will attract and retain the best social workers, teachers, and other staff members.

In order to influence school culture, several organizational lenses and conceptual frameworks can be used to manage and influence organizational structures, processes, policies, and culture (Netting & O'Connor, 2005). Rather than review all possible organizational frameworks, we have selected some (both general perspectives on schools as organizations and more specific organizational theories) that we believe can be particularly useful to school social workers.

PEOPLE-PROCESSING AND PEOPLE-CHANGING PERSPECTIVES

While all organizations have common elements, human services organizations are different from profit-making enterprises (Hasenfeld, 2010; Kahn, 2005). Human services agencies rely on people-processing and people-changing operations (Hasenfeld, 2010). People processing involves, for example, rules that govern behavior that set limits or create admissions criteria. For example, a school may have an honors policy that limits membership to the honors society to students who have taken a certain number of honors-level courses in high school. A transfer student from a school lacking such programs would not be eligible to join the honors society.

As applied to the school as an organization, these perspectives direct attention to several processing tasks and decision-making procedures (Lauffer, 1984). Key elements that a school social worker must address are organizational decision making, school modes of operation, patterns of student processing, student change, and whether these patterns are appropriately or inappropriately different among students with particular attributes.

For example, school social workers can use the people-processing perspective to explore several questions, such as these:

1. What are the rules and procedures used by school officials and faculty in transactions with students and their families?
2. Are these rules and procedures applied equitably among students facing discipline, suspension, or expulsion?
3. Do students with particular characteristics experience different and less-favorable school career paths (e.g., low-income vs. upper-income students, girls vs. boys, white students vs. minority students)?
4. Do students with particular attributes have equal access to academic curricula, programs, and activities? Is stigma attached to participation in some school programs and activities? Which teachers or staff members are working with which students? (Hasenfeld, 2010).

Knowing the answers to these questions can affect school procedures and decision making for school administrators, school social workers, and other professionals. Asking these questions might lead school social workers to engage in interventions (Jansson, 2011).

The people-processing perspective provides another lens with which to view school policy and procedures, and can lead to new ways to move schools forward. Asking these new questions can bring new approaches that consider the ways that groups and individuals are treated using current procedures and ways to create new, more-inclusive, more-supportive, and more-productive practices. Similarly, the concept of routinized actions gives us a new vision to view old patterns in schools.

ROUTINIZED ACTION PERSPECTIVE

Routines create consistency within everyday patterns of human behavior. Organizational routine is considered part of the structure of the organization. Whether a conscious decision or not, members of an organization can easily fall into routines. Districts and schools all have their own routines that are created and emphasized by participating members. Routinization is common when it comes to making class lists, scheduling, or assigning substitute teachers. Routines can also be broken or modified as needed through policy or management strategy. "By applying routinized action theory, [the school administration] is able to examine, analyze, and initiate changes in routines and can help their organizations better address challenges from the environment" (Conley & Enomoto, 2009, p. 382).

An example of routinized action theory could be the development of a school honors assembly. In one school the same teacher volunteered for ten years to organize and manage this assembly at the end of the year, and the rest of the staff was appreciative of this contribution. However, because she was an AP English teacher, she did not work with many students in special education or with at-risk students. Therefore, her plans for this assembly never included students whose talents were outside of academic achievement. A group of students approached the administration about their feelings of dread related to this assembly. They felt excluded from the potential to be honored. The principal called the school social worker. After talking, they realized that the honors assembly was rooted in tradition and failed to encompass emerging values, such as honoring the whole student and not simply academic intelligence. Finding more staff members to create an honors assembly committee allowed for new recognition through the addition of recognition for arts, music, and even skateboarding and tumbling exercises. Everyone was glad to include many more students in this all-school event that had simply become a routine.

There are questions to ask stemming from this approach:

- ◆ Why is this the way it is?
- ◆ Is anything different this year compared to last year?

- When was the last time we thought about changing the way we run this activity?
- Does the general student population feel success with the way we currently run things?
- If we could change one thing about this programming, what would it be?

The routinized action lens creates a new perspective on the organization that allows us to take a fresh look at traditions and patterns that could be strengthened in order to enhance the experience of all students in schools (Conley & Enomoto, 2009). Another force that moves us toward organizational change is that of demographic shifts in neighborhoods, schools, and communities. With an ever-changing economy, shifting immigration patterns, and regional change, schools often must respond to exciting changes in the demographic characteristics of students, families, and communities. The diversity change perspective can assist school social workers in addressing these developments.

DIVERSITY CHANGE PERSPECTIVE

Schools in the United States are going through consistent demographic change and growth. Diversity change in an organization occurs when the demographics of the participants shift (Gonzalez, 2010). As the student body shifts to become more multicultural, the school must adapt to the changing demographics. For example, schools may find that a large Asian population has developed in the community. This requires greater cultural competence on the part of students, teachers, and all school personnel. This also provides opportunities for learning and celebrating diverse cultures on a regular basis. Schools in which students self-segregate by ethnicity may need to be mixed up in ways that bring diverse students together. Potential cultural conflicts can become teachable moments. School social workers can anticipate needed organizational changes through a diversity change perspective. A postmodern perspective also provides a novel way of looking at school practices, a view that includes power, culture, and ideology.

POSTMODERN PERSPECTIVE

The social work profession has embraced postmodernism through research, clinical designs, interventions, and organizational analysis. Postmodernism is essentially an alternative way of thinking about scientific claims. Because of this, postmodernists are skeptical of generalizations, especially about groups of people. What is true for one person may not be true for another, even if they appear to have similar characteristics.

A postmodern perspective relating to organizational analysis allows for significant changes in perspectives and attitudes of school personnel. Postmodernism "emphasizes the role of power in structuring organizational relations. Like institutional theory, it proposes that culture influences organizational structures and practices" (Hasenfeld, 2010, pp. 48–49). When using a postmodern perspective, you have to be careful to avoid unconsciously adhering to the dominant point of view. Postmodernism does not allow for assumptions or automatic adoption of the prevailing situation.

A postmodern approach recognizes that different people experience life in different ways. An athlete's experience of high school will differ from a nonathlete's experiences. Both sets of lived experiences are real and important. A female student's experience of elementary school will vary from that of a male student. Both experiences are real and important. The same event—a school assembly, a school crisis, an art class—will be experienced as somewhat different realities based on the differing characteristics of individuals. Seeking to understand these multiple realities is complex and difficult, but rewarding.

This means that the functioning of an organization and its members could be understood through quantitative as well as qualitative explanations. Thus, even though student test scores are an accepted source of quantitative information about students, postmodernism asserts that student or faculty narratives and stories are also valuable information to guide school practices. Listening, recording, and understanding students' own perceptions of their academic experiences may tell us a great deal about how different students value and approach learning and assessment. For example, one group of students may believe that academic success is not compatible with the culture of their social group. A student may fear the testing process and consequently do poorly on standardized tests. Other students may find collaborative and experiential learning most useful, while others may prefer the banking model of instruction through a lecture format (Freire, 1993).

Organizational analysis of a school can incorporate this postmodernism through recognition of social problems, power differentials, and individual and cultural variance that affect student learning. Postmodernism accepts the fact that bureaucratic decisions are made in school settings but challenges the actions taken in response to these decisions (Hasenfeld, 2010; Thorne-Beckerman, 1999). A social worker taking a postmodern perspective is able to step back from the existing organization and policies and work to understand the separate realities of the students described above: the athlete and the nonathlete, the male student and the female student, members of oppressed groups and members of groups with more privilege. Consider the view of the school of an honors student who graduated from a strong middle school and enters high school with high achievement test scores and good grades. How might this student perceive high school? How might the view of school be different for a student transferring in from a weak school district, with low achievement test scores, and a history of good grades? Each reality is true and real. Each experience is a piece of the truth about that high school, and each is valid. Understanding these multiple realities is part of the social construction aspect of postmodernism.

The strengths perspective easily fits into a postmodern approach. Many strengths-based approaches in school social work, such as solution-focused brief therapy and motivational interviewing, presume a social construction-ist view of reality, one that can be cocreated with the client. While relative to the organization and its current status, the strengths perspective is a signif-icant component when undergoing organizational analysis. It is important to expand on the characteristics that already work well.

STRENGTHS PERSPECTIVE

You will always find needs and weaknesses within an organization. For this reason, schools are constantly and consistently working to improve. There-fore, organizational analysis can focus on further development of the exist-ing positive elements. For example, some teachers may have a strong class-room management system that encourages positive behavior and critical thinking. Future initiatives relating to behavior can then resemble the strong programming that is already in place.

Furthermore, schools have the advantage of having an inherently strong clientele. Students naturally contribute to the strengths perspective, but it is up to individual members of the school to both recognize unique strengths and then remember this recognition in times of chaos or frustration.

The use of a strengths perspective can help bring to light the many diverse gifts and talents that students bring to school (Saleebey, 2002). Rec-ognizing them is not costly, but the results can be priceless. For example, a high school student with a severe and persistent mental illness may also have extraordinary musical gifts that are rarely highlighted. Including this student in musical performances or talent shows can demonstrate the spe-cial gifts of this student to the rest of the school. A shy student may never be noticed, despite unusual contributions to the community through volunteer service in leading projects to feed the hungry. Featuring this student in a brief announcement in the morning on the school's PA system may bring substantial results for that students and similar students who observe that their contributions are also valued. A student identified as having a learning disability may also exhibit strengths and abilities, such as spatial intelli-gence, that would surprise many. Using a strengths approach and support-ing student strengths can change school culture in longlasting ways.

All of these theoretical windows give us new ways of developing a fresh vision of schools as organizations. These perspectives are applied in organi-zational analysis, including analysis of formal and informal organizational structures.

CONCLUSION

Organizational analysis is usually done for a reason—for better understanding of structures, which can then allow for modifications and adjustments to strengthen the inner workings of teams and individuals within the organization. Knowing the strengths and weaknesses of the school allows for continued planning and implementation of change efforts. The following vignette focuses on management of organizational change.

Mason Cooper is a fictive school social worker in an urban high school who notes a concern in the school regarding lesbian, gay, bisexual, transgendered, and questioning (LGBTQ) students who appear to feel isolated, who experience outdated school rules that do not fit their situations, and who are being bullied. First, Mason must describe the organizational problem, condition, or opportunity for change. She may ask herself about the features of the problem: How common is it throughout the school? Who is most affected? What are the consequences? (Pawlak & Vinter, 2004). She may find that rules about school functions effectively exclude same-sex couples from important social events. She may learn that about 10 percent of the student body is directly affected by this systemic concern, while others are affected as witnesses or complicit partners in discrimination against LGBTQ students. Mason may then ask what factors are sustaining this discrimination. Are embedded homophobic attitudes or local cultural factors supporting heterosexist policies in the school? Are there traditions that have simply been unexamined for years?

She may then begin to work with others and create a group in the school to create change. The group would work together to develop goals for the proposed changes. Such goals may be to recognize the experiences of LGBTQ students, to create a more welcoming environment, and to create new, more-inclusive traditions that support the social development of all students. This group may seek to understand how changes could be effectively implemented, what strengths they each bring to the table, and what challenges may be present.Understanding these strengths and weakness can help to facilitate organizational change, as Mason's group asks the question, "What are the financial, psychological, and emotional costs of heterosexist school policies?" They may talk to students about the academic impact of stigma, personal pain, and lack of recognition of LGBTQ youths.

Mason's group would need to identify possible approaches to change. There may be resistance from an administration entrenched in long-term patterns. Some simple changes, such as allowing same-sex couples to attend prom, or ending the requirement for specific gendered attire (white dresses at graduation, for example) for important events, may have a powerful impact and help recognize the lived realties of LGBTQ youths.

The group may want to launch a larger, educational strategy, and would need to explore the advantages and disadvantages of each approach and to consider the potential negative or positive outcomes (Packard, 2001). Mason's group would need to get ideas—perhaps through focus groups—on strategies for change. They would need to explore the resources needed to carry out change. For a large, school-wide educational intervention, costs may be greater than small policy changes regarding, for example, rules for social events to be changed to be more inclusive of LGBTQ students. Ultimately, through an analytic process, school change can be developed in order to support students' social and emotional development.

When organizational conditions contribute to or sustain student problems, interventions must be directed toward the school as an organization. The roles and status of school social workers, as well as their professional education, enable them to take holistic perspectives and to legitimately engage the structures, culture, units, roles, and personnel within schools. School social workers have more opportunities to leverage change than they might realize. Use it well and do good things. Carpe diem.

References

Conley, S., & Enomoto, E. (2009). Organizational routines in flux. *Education and Urban Society, 41*(3), 364–386.

Emmert, M., & Taher, W. (1992). Public sector professionals: The effects of public sector jobs on motivation, job satisfaction and work involvement. *American Review of Public Administration, 22*(1), 37–48.

Freire, P. (1993). *Pedagogy of the oppressed.* New York: Continuum.

French, J., & Raven, B. (1968). *The bases of social power.* In D. Cartwright & A. Zander (Eds.), *Group dynamics* (3rd ed., pp. 215–235). New York: Harper & Row.

Gonzalez, J. (2010). Diversity change in organizations: A systemic, multilevel, and nonlinear process. *Journal of Applied Behavioral Science, 46*(2), 197–219.

Hall, R. (1996). *Organizations: Structure, process, and outcomes* (6th ed.). Englewood Cliffs, NJ: Prentice Hall.

Hasenfeld, Y. (2010). *Human services as complex organizations.* (2nd ed). Thousand Oaks, CA: Sage.

Jansson, B. (2011). *The reluctant welfare state* (7th ed.). Belmont, CA: Brooks/Cole.

Kahn, W. (2005). *Holding fast: The struggle to create resilient caregiving organizations.* Hove, UK: Brunner-Routledge.

Kelly, M. (2008). *The domains and demands of school social work practice: A guide to working effectively with students, families, and schools.* New York: Oxford University Press.

Lauffer, A. (1984). *Strategic marketing for not-for-profit organizations: Program and resource development.* New York: Free Press.

McWhorter, J. (2001). *Losing the race: Self-sabotage in black America.* New York: Perennial.

Mumm, A., & Bye, L. (2011). Certification of school social workers and curriculum content of programs offering training in school social work. *Children & Schools, 33*(1), 17–23.

Netting, F. E., & O'Connor, M. K. (2005). Teaching organization practice: A multi-paradigmatic approach. *Administration in Social Work, 29*(1), 25–43.

Packard, T. (2001). Enhancing staff commitment through organizational values. *Administration in Social Work, 25*(3), 35–52.

Patti, R. (1982). Book review: Administration in the human services: A normative systems approach. *Social Service Review, 56*(3), 472–473.

Pawlak, E., & Cousins, L. (2009). School social work: Organizational perspectives. In C. Massat, R. Constable, S. McDonald, & J. P. Flynn (Eds.), *School social work: Practice, policy, and research* (7th ed., pp.176–192). Chicago: Lyceum Books.

Pawlak, E., & Vinter, R. (2004). *Designing and planning programs for nonprofit and government organizations.* San Francisco: Jossey-Bass.

Perry, T., Steele, C., & Hilliard, A. (2003). *Young, gifted, and black: Promoting high achievement among African-American students.* Boston: Beacon Press.

Saleebey, D. (2002). *The strengths perspective in social work practice.* Boston: Allyn & Bacon.

Thorne-Beckerman, A. (1999). Postmodern organizational analysis: An alternative framework for school social workers. *Social Work in Education, 21*(3), 177–188.

Wagoner, R. V. (1994). Changing school governance: A case for decentralized management. *Planning and Change, 25*(3–4), 206–218.

Walker, R., & Brewer, G. (2008). An organizational echelon analysis of the determinants of red tape in public organizations. *Public Administration Review, 68*(6), 1112–1127.

22

Policy Development and the School Social Worker

Annahita Ball

University at Buffalo, State University of New York

- ◆ Social Policy Defined
- ◆ Policy and Social Work Practice in Schools
- ◆ Millerville School District Case Example
- ◆ Policy Practice
- ◆ Policy Analysis
- ◆ Policy Landscape
- ◆ Policy Solutions
- ◆ Advocacy

Practice within the policy arena is specifically focused on social problems, which are public issues that have implications for society as a whole (Reisch, 2013). While these problems are large and affect a number of people, they are rooted in the issues that individuals face. School social workers frequently engage in activities across the micro, meso, and macro practice levels (Kelly et al., 2010). As such, multilevel social work practice in schools is well-aligned with Popple and Leighninger's (2010) model of a "policy-based profession" (p. 12) in which social work comprises the client system, professional system, and policy system that, together, shape social work practice and service delivery for clients. Their model acknowledges the complexity of social work practice within broader macrosystems. For instance, while a social worker provides services to a client, it is often the policy system that defines the problem, prescribes the scope of interventions, and pays the professional (Popple & Leighninger, 2010).

This policy-based profession model also is evident within the National Association of Social Workers (NASW) Code of Ethics (2008), which requires all social workers to pursue social change that addresses the needs of vulnerable and oppressed populations. It is only through efforts that reach across the micro, meso, and macro systems that social workers will effect long-lasting change. School social workers utilize a variety of strategies to address individual and social problems (Kelly, 2008). The use of multilevel practice places school social workers in an especially unique position to have a broad impact on children and families. In fact, the NASW (2012) Standards for School Social Work Practice identify school social workers as "systems' change agents" (p. 13) who are charged with creating and advocating for services that address the needs of children and families. Likewise, a number of school social work scholars emphasize the ways in which practitioners may have meaningful and long-lasting impacts on school systems through policy (e.g., Anderson-Butcher, Lawson, Iachini, Flaspohler, & Bean, 2010; Teasley, 2004). In turn, it is imperative that policy is a vital component of school social workers' practice. This chapter will provide an overview of the specific components of policy practice in relation to school social work, including a case example of the Millerville School District.

SOCIAL POLICY DEFINED

"Policy" is a term often used to describe a number of laws, actions, and mandates that are frequently rooted in government intervention. To be clear, school social work practice is most often related to social policy, which is a public response to the social problems of society (Reisch, 2013). Policies guide intervention and determine the goals of service, the client population, available funding sources, benefits and services, mechanisms of service delivery, and the focus of services (Popple & Leighninger, 2010; Segal, 2010). Collectively, social policy may be broadly conceptualized to include federal, state, local, and organizational policies that take the form of laws, guidelines, regulations, or benefits and services designed to meet the needs of society and maintain social order (Popple & Leighninger, 2010). Additionally, policies may be expressed formally as written documents (e.g., bylaws, executive agendas, standardized operating procedures, etc.) or informally as unwritten rules or norms that guide processes or services.

Disciplinary policies and procedures in schools offer a salient example highlighting the multiple aspects of social policy in relation to school social work. Many school districts have formal policies that specify disciplinary procedures for their students; school social workers are frequently responsible for implementing or upholding these policies. Recently, the federal Department of Education (USDOE, 2014) issued policy guidelines that discourage the use of harsh discipline in schools; as a result, local districts may need to modify their own policies to align with the guidance provided by the federal government. This example highlights the varying forms of social policy, and the many influences that shape policy development in schools.

POLICY AND SOCIAL WORK PRACTICE IN SCHOOLS

Table 22.1 provides a list of current federal policies organized under four primary categories of interest to school social workers: student and family support services; education reform and civil rights; school and child safety; and professional practice. Together, these policies largely govern schools and social work practice in school settings. In many instances, the federal government provides guidelines that then guide state-level policy. These

TABLE 22.1   Policies Related to School Social Work Practice

Student and Family Support Services	Education Reform and Civil Rights
◆ Individuals with Disabilities Education Improvement Act (IDEIA) of 2004	◆ The Elementary and Secondary Education Act of 1965 (reauthorized by the No Child Left Behind Act of 2001) includes provisions for low-income schools, accountability and assessment, parent involvement, supplemental education services, and vulnerable student subgroups
◆ Section 504 of the Rehabilitation Act of 1973	
◆ McKinney-Vento Homeless Assistance Act of 1986	
◆ Personal Responsibility & Work Opportunity Reconciliation Act of 1996	
◆ Patient Protection and Affordable Care Act of 2010	◆ Race to the Top Fund
◆ Child Care Development Block Grant of 2014	◆ American Recovery and Reinvestment Act of 2009 (School Improvement Grants and Investing in Innovation Fund)
◆ Title XX of the Social Security Act	
School and Child Safety	◆ Title VI of the Civil Rights Act of 1964
◆ Bullying Policies and Guidelines*	◆ Title IX of the Education Amendments of 1972
◆ Child Abuse Prevention and Treatment Act of 1974	◆ Americans with Disabilities Act of 1990
◆ Safe and Drug Free Schools and Communities Act of 2004	**Professional Practice**
◆ School Climate and Discipline Guidelines (federal guidelines are available and many states have state-specific policies)	◆ Family Education Rights and Privacy Act of 1974 (FERPA)
	◆ Corporal punishment and discipline*
◆ Truancy and dropout ordinances*	◆ Confidentiality and informed consent (NASW Code of Ethics)
	◆ Protection of Pupil Rights Amendment of 1978
	◆ Social work credentialing*
	◆ Mandatory reporting procedures*

NOTE: All policies are federal policies unless noted with an asterisk (*) to indicate that these policies are often made at the state level. Only policies that are currently adopted are listed.

state-level policies include specific provisions that may, in turn, guide local and organizational policies as well. Each of the policies listed in table 22.1 is a federal policy (unless noted), but all of the policies hold implications for social workers at the state and local levels as well.

Within social work practice, policy is expressed across a multilevel practice framework that includes micro-, mezzo-, and macrolevel policy practice. First, microlevel policy practice includes smaller-scale, direct-practice policy decision making. Second, mezzolevel policy practice is expressed at the organizational and administrative level. Third, macrolevel policy practice is located at the local, state, or federal level and has a far-reaching impact on school social work service delivery. Likewise, school social work practice activities may differ across levels of practice in relation to any one policy. Table 22.2 provides two detailed examples of the ways in which policies affect multilevel school social work.

TABLE 22.2   Examples of Multilevel School Social Work Practice Activities

Policy	Individuals with Disabilities Education Interventions Act (IDEA) of 1990	State-Level School Climate Standards
Purpose	Identifies specific assessment and intervention procedures and protocols for students with disabilities	Establishes expectations for school safety, teaching and interpersonal relationships, and the organizational environment
Practice Level	*Practice Activities*	
Macro	Create school–family–community partnerships that support students with disabilities; advocate for local, state, and national policy; and ensure that transitions for students throughout the district and the community support students with disabilities	Advocate for district-wide strategies to address school climate, create and maintain partnerships with community agencies to support positive climate-building activities in the school, and engage parents to create consistent expectations for behavior
Meso	Meet with IEP teams; coordinate services for special education students across the school; create or monitor the referral process; and lead or develop school-wide policies and procedures in relation to special education referrals, assessments, and interventions	Sit on building-level committees to establish and monitor policies and procedures for school climate, such as bullying; provide professional development for school staff
Micro	Establish services; write IEPs; coordinate IEP teams for one student; provide supports or related services to individual students; consult with teachers; conduct assessments	Consult with teachers and school staff to provide professional development on building positive, supportive relationships with students; provide universal interventions to support positive school climate; and provide individual counseling

MILLERVILLE SCHOOL DISTRICT CASE EXAMPLE

The case example of the Millerville School District (MSD) that follows will highlight policies at the federal, state, and local levels. In addition, the case example will be used to exemplify multilevel policy practice in school social work. The MSD's student handbook outlines a uniform policy indicating that all students must wear uniforms; it also outlines disciplinary procedures to address students' noncompliance with the uniform policy. It indicates that first and second offenses result in conferences with the principal and students' parents, respectively. The third offense results in an in-school suspension, and the fourth results in a two-day out-of-school suspension.

Jaclyn is a school social worker at a middle school within MSD. Many of her clients receive numerous infractions for uniform noncompliance, thus they are frequently removed from class. In addition, her clients are frequently absent and receive several other types of disciplinary infractions. In fact, an analysis of her records indicates that nearly 25 percent of her caseload received in-school and out-of-school suspensions for uniform infractions within the past year. This is especially concerning because many of her clients are at high risk for school failure. Jaclyn is aware that her school district is increasingly focused on positive behavior support techniques to address student behavior concerns and to promote positive school climate. Moreover, her state recently passed a law that requires schools to utilize positive behavior supports in discipline policies. After researching this issue further, she learns that a new bill is being debated by her state's legislature that would require schools to utilize out-of-school suspensions as a last resort in school discipline.

POLICY PRACTICE

Policy practitioners apply their understanding of policy to individual clients or social service contexts. As such, social workers in schools engage in policy practice. As outlined in figure 22.1, policy practice includes four components: (1) policy analysis, (2) the policy landscape, (3) policy solutions, and (4) advocacy. Multiple actions are necessary within each of these components, including those that require analytical, direct practice, and advocacy knowledge and skills. Each component will be described in detail as it relates to the MSD case.

POLICY ANALYSIS

Policy analysis involves the use of analytic techniques to understand policy. Policy analysis in school social work helps practitioners critically examine the benefits and services available for children and families in schools and communities. A number of frameworks are available to guide social workers in their efforts to analyze social policies (e.g., Gilbert & Terrell, 2010; Reisch, 2013). A select set of key elements within these frameworks (see figure 22.1)

FIGURE 22.1   A Guide to Policy Practice

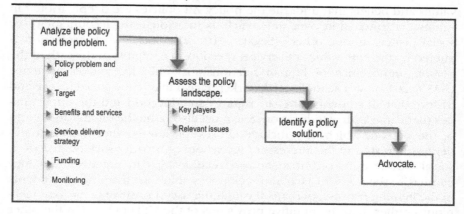

will be discussed here to allow for the greatest flexibility in applying these concepts to a wide scope of policies.

Policy Problem and Goals

Understanding policy must begin with critical analysis of the policy problem. This is best initiated by outlining the concrete and observable signs of the problem. In the MSD case, the problem may be defined as, "Twenty-five percent of high risk students at MSD middle school received in-school or out-of-school suspensions for uniform infractions within the past year." While this problem statement outlines the observable signs of the problem, the definition of the problem is still somewhat unclear. Jaclyn is concerned with how much instructional time students miss as a result of this policy, rather than the high numbers of students receiving infractions. To further define the problem, Jaclyn could indicate, "As a result of uniform infractions, this group of students has missed over 100 hours of instructional time in total." The problem in this case is not simply high infraction rates, but rather missed instructional time for high-risk students.

Once Jaclyn defines the problem, she must identify the purpose of the policy. In this case, MSD's policy is designed to establish expectations for uniforms and to hold students accountable for these expectations, yet a deeper analysis of the policy goal may be facilitated by considering who benefits and who loses in relation to this problem. A number of stakeholders may benefit from MSD's policy, such as teachers who are able to remove the students from their classrooms or administrators who may need evidence that they are enforcing the policy. A number of stakeholders may lose as well, such as the students who receive suspensions and miss class and the parents who spend valuable time attending conferences about uniform infractions.

Another helpful way to identify the purpose of policy is to consider the values and beliefs that underlie the policy. All policies are deeply rooted in values that often shift over time, such as individualism, accountability, or social justice, among others (Segal, 2010). The social work profession is guided by the core values of service, social justice, dignity and worth of the person, importance of human relationships, integrity, and competence (NASW, 2010). As a school social worker, Jaclyn may value social justice and believe that all students have the right to an education and the opportunities that come with an education. She must also value the dignity and worth of the person, which may include addressing any conflicts between students' interests and the interests of the school or broader society. Moreover, social work values prioritize human relationships in practice. This may emphasize the need for Jaclyn to seek policy solutions that engage students in the helping process, perhaps through the use of positive behavioral techniques rather than the punitive provisions of the MSD policy. On the other hand, the school system may value personal responsibility and accountability, which suggests that students and parents should be responsible for following the uniform policy and must be held accountable when they are noncompliant. It is critical that school social workers recognize and consider the interprofessional nature of practice in schools. Various professions may be guided by differing values, beliefs, and theoretical assumptions that will likely influence the development and implementation of policy (Mellin, 2009). School social workers will benefit from understanding these varying value systems and utilizing an inclusive approach to policy practice in schools (Bronstein, Ball, Mellin, Wade-Mdivanian, & Anderson-Butcher, 2011).

Flynn (2009) identified an important step in policy analysis: the application of the GRADES (Gender, Race, Age, Disability, Ethnicity, and Socioeconomic) test for all policy analyses. This step involves examining the impact of the policy on issues of GRADES status. This step is particularly important for school social workers whose profession involves a commitment to social justice.

Benefits and Services

If we understand the goals of a policy, then the benefits and services of a policy are best identified by considering what it is that individuals or groups may obtain to achieve the policy goal. Benefits may be in the form of cash, or they may be in-kind (i.e., concrete commodities such as clothing, food, etc.; Gilbert & Terrell, 2010). Services are benefits that are "activities performed on the client's behalf, such as counseling, job training, transportation, case management" (Gilbert & Terrell, 2010, p. 135). In addition, policies may also provide power, such as more influence or control over decision making or opportunities, such as increased choice or options in service delivery. It is not uncommon for one policy to include multiple types of benefits and services. In the MSD case, the benefits that students gain from the policy are in the form of clear expectations for behavior along with remedial actions to address uniform issues. These provisions provide the benefit of structure and perhaps safety to the entire study body and staff as well.

Target

The target of a policy specifies who the policy or program is intended to affect (i.e., eligibility). The MSD policy states, "All MSD students are required to wear the approved school uniform daily. Students who are not in compliance with the uniform will receive the following consequences." An analysis of the target in relation to this policy is rather vague if one considers the conditions under which a student would fall into the noncompliance group. For instance, is a student with only one item of clothing that is not part of the uniform considered noncompliant, or must a majority of the student's uniform be incorrect? Decisions about compliance will determine which students (and how many students) receive disciplinary action. These decisions are seemingly subjective as the policy provides little specificity. Likewise, it is unclear what constitutes an infraction (i.e., Must the offense be documented to count?). Since these questions are unclear, the policy may be implemented and enforced differently for each student. Differences in the interpretation of the target (i.e., eligibility criteria) may result in an overutilization (too many students are identified for disciplinary action) or an underutilization (extremely small numbers of students are identified for uniform infractions) of the policy.

Service Delivery Strategy

The structures and processes in which benefits and services are delivered is another element of policy. These structures and processes bridge the service providers (e.g., individual professionals, public and private agencies, schools, community centers, hospitals) and clients in the implementation of the policy or program to address how clients will receive the benefits or services. There are a number of strategies that could be used to deliver services, and each strategy has unique implications and impacts on clients. Services may be privatized, faith-based, for-profit, governmental, or nonprofit (Gilbert & Terrell, 2010). Gilbert and Terrell suggest that service providers should focus on coordinating and integrating services by utilizing effective communication and referral strategies, eliminating duplicated services, and creating a means for stakeholders to have input and decision-making power. For a policy to be effective, it must be clearly published and clearly implemented. That means that policies must be accessible and understandable.

The policy also must be clearly communicated to all stakeholders and feedback must be incorporated into the policy process. The MSD policy might be most effective if Jaclyn considers the extent to which MSD students, parents, teachers, and school administrators have a shared understanding of the uniform rules.

Funding

In relation to policy, funding is ultimately about resources to sustain programs. Funds may be provided by legislators, foundations, agencies, schools, government agencies, and private donors, among others. Schools are largely financed through state funds and local property taxes, but they also receive funds from the federal government, local and state grants, philanthropic contributions, fees, and community partnerships (Poirier & Osher, 2012). Collectively, these funds drive the services that schools offer. In order for policies and programs to achieve their goals, financial resources must be available to support the initiatives.

Monitoring

The implementation of the policy must be monitored to ascertain any unintended consequences. Monitoring may include ongoing data collection in the form of tracking, verbal or written feedback, or process analyses. Some policies include provisions that assign monitoring responsibilities to a specific person or entity. For instance, MSD's current uniform policy does not specify who will monitor offenses and disciplinary actions: Jaclyn performs this task informally in her role as a school social worker. A more clear delineation of this duty would be written explicitly in the policy statement. As a result of her monitoring, Jaclyn has identified unintended consequences of the uniform policy. That is, students who do not comply with the uniform policy receive consequences that deny them instructional time, and large numbers of students are missing from class. The policy was intended to address a problem of uniform compliance, but now the uniform policy has created a new problem.

POLICY LANDSCAPE

Policy is largely a political process and it is important to understand the "politics of policy-making" (Popple & Leighninger, 2010, p. 98) to maximize the impact of change efforts. In contemplating a change-making endeavor, social workers should assess the policy landscape. This includes an understanding of the key players related to and engaged in the policy. Jaclyn would want to consider the following questions as she assesses the policy landscape: "Who is involved in the system and how is power distributed among them? What offices or agencies are involved in this policy? And who might oppose or support changes in this context?" In this case, the key players would include students, parents, the school principal and other administrators, school staff, Jaclyn, and any community businesses that supply school uniforms. Additionally, Jaclyn is aware of a current bill under debate in the state legislature that would require schools to utilize out-of-school suspensions as a last resort in school discipline. It is critical to identify the key players associated with both the current policy at her school and the proposed bill as well. In this case, Jaclyn also finds that a local advocacy group was very active in drafting the new bill.

Relevant issues entrenched in the problem and policy are important to note as well. The history of the problem, the community, or the organization may provide insight into current actions and policies. For example, perhaps MSD had a history of poorly enforcing the uniform policy that resulted in the strict policy in place today. In addition, any controversial issues at the time the policy was developed may be critical. Today, discipline policies are the topic of considerable debate in school social work and education (e.g., Osher, Bear, Sprague, & Doyle, 2010). As such, the advocacy group in the MSD case example brought the issue to the forefront of the local community's attention. After conducting an assessment of the key players and the relevant issues involved with this policy problem, Jaclyn is much more equipped to begin considering potential policy solutions.

POLICY SOLUTIONS

Potential policy solutions may strengthen, improve, or totally replace existing policies and programs (Gilbert & Terrell, 2010). The task at this stage of policy practice is to develop several alternatives that may be used to address or ameliorate any existing issues that were uncovered during the analysis stage. One way to identify potential policy solutions is to consider any existing policies that may be informative, such as those within other districts, states, or countries. During the policy-making process, it also is important to consider the available evidence-base for the social problem. It is likely that several policy solutions are available, but a number of solutions may be supported by existing research. School social workers should engage in evidence-informed policy making, which involves careful analysis and consideration of the research evidence available to support or refute possible policy solutions and alternatives.

After Jaclyn conducted her analysis of the MSD uniform policy, she discovered that there are multiple parties with interest in this problem, that the current policy has unintended consequences, and that potential policy solutions have already been suggested within her state. Some potential solutions include introducing a new bill that would encourage the use of positive behavior supports, eliminating school uniforms entirely, or issuing less-punitive consequences for uniform offenses. Jaclyn may investigate the uniform policies of other nearby districts and consider their effectiveness. In addition, she may want to consider how effective schools have been in their adoption of positive behavior supports. Perhaps some of the potential solutions are more effective, feasible, supported, or cost-effective than others.

ADVOCACY

After selecting a policy solution, it will be necessary to advocate for change within the system. Advocacy is defined as action on behalf of vulnerable individuals, groups, or communities, those who experience oppression, discrimination, or injustice (Richan, 1973). Social workers are frequently engaged in professional advocacy to create change for the profession. This is a critical aspect of advocacy, yet it is qualitatively different from advocacy on behalf of clients. Advocacy for clients is an imperative of social work practice (NASW, 2010) and, at a minimum, involves an understanding of the complexity of policies that affect clients (McIntosh, 2004).

Advocating for change involves a number of steps and activities that may not unfold in a linear fashion (Jansson, 2013). Several resources provide considerable guidance for social workers engaged in advocacy, such as the advocacy resources available from NASW, American Council of School Social Work, School Social Work Association of America, and the National Association of School Psychologists. In sum, social workers advocate by mobilizing communities, gathering research and collecting data to support a policy solution, communicating a clear message to critical parties (via media, conferences, meetings, or written documents), educating policy makers about the issue, and building relationships with key stakeholders. In the MSD case, Jaclyn has analyzed the problem and policy, assessed the policy landscape, and identified a policy solution. Now it is time to craft a clear message and advocate for the policy solution she has identified. In this case, Jaclyn wants to utilize more positive behavioral interventions for discipline and exclude suspensions as a disciplinary option for uniform infractions. She may mobilize the community by garnering support from parents, students, teachers, and other community members, including the local advocacy group that has already started to advocate for this change. They may use media outlets such as the local newspaper, flyers, radio, television, and social media to share their message with the community. In addition, Jaclyn may work with the local advocacy group and other community members to draft an informational brief for policy makers. Together, Jaclyn and the other stakeholders could have a significant impact on the legislators' perceptions of the new bill and, ultimately, change policy at the district or state level.

CONCLUSION

School social workers are in a unique and powerful position to create positive change for children, families, and communities. As social work practice in schools requires policy practice across micro-, meso-, and macropractice levels, it is essential for practitioners to understand how to analyze policy and engage in advocacy. Moreover, practitioners are not alone in their efforts. A number of advocacy and policy resources are available through professional organizations, such as NASW, the School Social Work Association of America, and the American Council of School Social Work. Policy practice occurs at all levels of practice and will vary in different contexts. Because school social workers are change agents, it is necessary for them to continually identify, analyze, and address social policy issues in schools.

References

Americans With Disabilities Act of 1990, Pub. L. No. 101-336, 104 Stat. 328 (1990).

Anderson-Butcher, D., Lawson, H. A., Iachini, A., Flaspohler, P., & Bean, J. (2010). Emergent evidence in support of a community collaboration model for school improvement. *Children & Schools, 32*(3), 160–171.

Bronstein, L., Ball, A., Mellin, E. A., Wade-Mdivanian, R. L., & Anderson-Butcher, D. (2011). Advancing collaboration between school- and agency-employed school-based social workers: A mixed methods comparison of competencies and preparedness. *Children & Schools, 33*(2), 83–95.

Child Abuse Prevention and Treatment Act (CAPTA) of 1974, Pub. L. 93-247; 42 U.S.C. § 5101 et seq. (1974).

Civic Impulse. (2015). H.R. 3734, 104th Congress: Personal Responsibility and Work Opportunity Reconciliation Act of 1996. Retrieved from https://www.govtrack.us/congress/bills/104/hr3734

Civic Impulse. (2015). H.R. 1, 111th Congress: American Recovery and Reinvestment Act of 2009. Retrieved from https://www.govtrack.us/congress/bills/111/hr1

Civic Impulse. (2015). S. 1086, 113th Congress: Child Care and Development Block Grant Act of 2014. Retrieved from https://www.govtrack.us/congress/bills/113/s1086

Civic Impulse. (2015). H.R. 6442, 112th Congress: To amend title XX of the Social Security Act to repeal the program of block grants. Retrieved from https://www.govtrack.us/congress/bills/112/hr6442

Civil Rights Act of 1964, Pub.L. 88-352, 78 Stat. 241 (1964).

Elementary and Secondary Education Act of 1965, 20 U.S.C. § 2701 et seq. (1965).

Family Educational Rights and Privacy Act of 1974 (FERPA), Pub. L. 93-380, 88 Stat. 571 (1974).

Flynn, J. (2009). School policy development and the school social worker. In C. R. Massat, R. Constable, S. McDonald, & J. P. Flynn (Eds.), *School social work: Practice, policy and research* (7th ed., pp. 193–216). Chicago: Lyceum Books.

Gilbert, N., & Terrell, P. (2010). *Dimensions of social welfare policy* (7th ed.). Boston: Allyn & Bacon.

Individuals with Disabilities Education Act of 1990 (IDEA), Pub. L. 105-17, U.S.C. 11401 et seq. (1990).

Individuals with Disabilities Education Improvement Act of 2004 (IDEIA), Pub. L. 108-446, 118 Stat. 2647 (2004).

Jansson, B. (2013). *Becoming an effective policy advocate*. Pacific Grove, CA: Brooks/Cole.

Kelly, M. (2008). *The domains and demands of school social work practice: A guide to working effectively with students, families, and schools.* New York: Oxford University Press.

Kelly, M. S., Berzin, S. C., Frey, A., Alvarez, M., Shaffer, G., & O'Brien, K. (2010). The state of school social work: Findings from the National School Social Work Survey. *School Mental Health, 2,* 132–141.

McIntosh, D. (2004). Taking no action is an action. *New Social Worker, 11*(2), 6–8.

McKinney-Vento Homeless Assistance Act of 1986, Pub. L. 100-77, 101 Stat. § 482, 42 U.S.C. § 11301 et seq. (1986).

Mellin, E. A. (2009). Unpacking interdisciplinary collaboration in expanded school mental health service utilization for children and adolescents. *Advances in School Mental Health Promotion, 2,* 5–15.

National Association of Social Workers (NASW). (2008). *Code of ethics.* Retrieved from https://www.socialworkers.org/pubs/code/code.asp

National Association of Social Workers (NASW). (2010). *Code of ethics of the National Association of Social Workers.* Washington, DC: NASW Press.

National Association of Social Workers (NASW). (2012). *Standards for school social work services.* Washington, DC: Author.

No Child Left Behind Act of 2001, Pub. L. 107-110 (2002).

Osher, D., Bear, G. G., Sprague, J. R., & Doyle, W. (2010). How can we improve school discipline? *Educational Researcher, 39,* 48–58.

Patient Protection and Affordable Care Act, 42 U.S.C. § 18001 (2010).

Poirier, J. M., & Osher, D. (2012). Understanding the current environment of public school funding: How student support services are funded. In C. Franklin, M. B. Harris, & P. Allen-Meares (Eds.). *The school services sourcebook: A guide for school-based professionals* (2nd ed., pp. 935–950). New York: Oxford University Press.

Popple, P. R., & Leighninger, L. (2010). *The policy-based profession: An introduction to social welfare policy analysis for social workers* (5th ed.). Boston, MA: Pearson.

Protection of Pupil Rights Amendment (PPRA) (20 U.S.C. § 1232h; 34 CFR Part 98).

Reisch, M. (2013). U.S. social policy in the new century. In M. Reisch (Ed.), *Social policy and social justice* (pp. 5–42). Thousand Oaks, CA: Sage.

Richan, W. (1973). Dilemmas of the social work advocate. *Child Welfare, 52*(4), 220–226.

Safe and Drug-Free Schools and Communities Act of 2004. Title IV, Part A, Subpart 1 Elementary and Secondary Education Act of 1965 as amended by the No Child Left Behind Act of 2001 Public Law 107-110 (2004).

Section 504 of the Rehabilitation Act of 1973, 34 C.F.R. Part 104 (1973).

Segal, E. A. (2010). *Social welfare policy and social programs: A values perspective* (2nd ed.). Belmont, CA: Brooks/Cole.

Teasley, M. (2004). School social workers and urban education reform: Realities, advocacy, and strategies for change. *School Community Journal, 14*(2), 19–39.

Title VI of the Civil Rights Act of 1964, Pub. L. 88-352, 78 Stat. § 241 (1964).

U.S. Department of Labor. (1972, June 23). Office of the Assistant Secretary for Administration and Management. *Title IX, Education Amendments of 1972.* Retrieved from http://www.dol.gov/oasam/regs/statutes/titleIX.htm

U.S. Department of Education (USDOE). (2014). *Guiding principles: A resource guide for improving school climate and discipline.* Washington, DC: Author.

23

Making School Social Work Visible, Viable, and Valued

Elizabeth Lehr Essex
Governors State University

Noriko Yamano
Osaka Prefecture University

Carol Rippey Massat
Indiana University School of Social Work

- ◆ Challenges to the Profession
- ◆ Addressing the Challenges
- ◆ School Social Work in Illinois: Building the Profession
- ◆ Building School Social Work in Japan

School social work is one of the oldest social work specialties, dating back to 1906 in the United States. It has grown immensely since the early beginnings, with school social workers now present in all fifty U.S. states (Altshuler & Webb, 2009), Washington, DC (Alvarez, Bye, Bryant, & Mumm, 2013), Puerto Rico (School Social Work Association of America [SSWAA], n.d.), Guam (University of Guam, n.d.), and at least forty-nine countries (International Network for School Social Work, n.d.). As noted by Huxtable and Blyth (2002), school social workers throughout the world share common principles: "The rights of children (especially the right to appropriate education and equal opportunity) and the goal of helping all children reach their potential" (p. 234). Among school-related professions, school social work lays claim to the most holistic stance, with its person-in-environment, ecological perspective. An increasing body of research supports the effectiveness of social work interventions in schools (Allen-Meares, Montgomery, & Kim, 2013; Franklin, Kim, & Tripodi, 2009) and the vital role of school social workers as primary providers of mental health services in many communities (Kelly et al., 2010).

In spite of these many strengths, school social work continues to face challenges to its strength and legitimacy as a profession. For example, in the United States there are wide disparities in requirements for school social workers across states and disproportion in the numbers of school social workers (Altshuler & Webb, 2009). In many other countries, school social work is still in the beginning stages of development or nonexistent (Huxtable & Blyth, 2002). In her 1981 article, included in this book as appendix B, "The Wonderland of Social Work in the Schools or 'How Alice Learned to Cope,'" Sally Goren (1981) emphasized the importance for a school social worker to establish his or her visibility, viability, and value in the school setting. More recently, Altshuler and Webb referred to these three Vs in reference to the legitimacy of school social work as a profession in the United States. This chapter focuses on the standing of the profession both nationally and internationally. We first review challenges to school social work, and then delineate an approach to addressing the challenges. This discussion sets the stage for examining the development and legitimizing of school social work in two case examples: Illinois, a state with a strong school social work presence, and Japan, where social work in schools was only recently established.

CHALLENGES TO THE PROFESSION

There is much variability in how school social work is conceptualized and implemented by different countries, reflecting different economic, social, cultural, and political contexts. Reviewing the specific situation within a number of different nations would be an enormous task, and also difficult given a dearth of literature on school social work across the globe (Allen-Meares et al., 2013). In this section, we therefore review challenges to school social work in the United States, followed by a less in-depth discussion of challenges to its strength and legitimacy as an international profession.

Challenges in the United States

As Altshuler and Webb (2009) point out, school social work is at a competitive disadvantage, because it "lags behind school counseling and school psychology in carving out a self-defined niche with consistent expectations and responsibilities" (p. 215). This difficulty in achieving a clear national role definition continues to be a challenge for the field of school social work.

There are incomplete data on the total number of school social workers in the nation and in each state. Estimated numbers of school social workers for twenty-six states, available from Minnesota State University Mankato (n.d.), indicate a range across states from 5 to 2,500. The twenty-six states in this data set do not include Illinois and New York, which reportedly have the highest numbers of school-based mental health professionals (Lueck & Kelly, 2010). What data exist suggest wide discrepancies between states in the number and relative proportions of school social workers. Across states, there are widely varying definitions for school social workers' roles; achieving a consistent national definition remains a work in progress. School social work is inherently state-based and local in this country, so local conditions, policies, and budgets dictate practice in ways that might be different in other countries where education is more federally based.

While economic standing of states may play a role, this does not adequately account for the discrepancies. Some relatively poor states (e.g., Mississippi and West Virginia) have a disproportionately low number of school social workers (Minnesota State University Mankato, n.d.; see Bureau of Business & Economic Research, University of New Mexico, 2013, for rankings of states by per capita income). However, Alaska, a relatively wealthy state, has few school social workers in proportion to its population, and Illinois has more school social workers than California (Alvarez et al., 2013; Kelly, 2008; Lueck & Kelly, 2010; Minnesota State University Mankato, n.d.).

In their national survey of school social workers, Kelly et al. (2010) found a wide range in the number of schools respondents served. With outliers removed, findings indicated that only 38 percent served a single school and 31.5 percent served four or more schools. In addition, the school social workers reported serving children with high needs related to social and behavioral issues; few of them reported that "most or all of the children they serve" receive outside counseling or therapeutic services (p. 137). On average, they also spent 30 percent of their time on administrative tasks. On the other hand, most respondents indicated that they ideally would like to spend more time on prevention activities. In discussing their results, the researchers suggest that the many demands on school social workers may impede their ability to engage in school leadership activities and prevention initiatives. Thus, school social workers are finding it difficult to truly utilize an ecological approach. A clear implication is the need for more school social workers, particularly in states and localities where they are disproportionately low.

School social workers in the United States face the challenge of token status (i.e., constituting less than 16 percent of the workforce) in a host setting (Dane & Simon, 1991). This can lead to a lack of visibility, marginality in the school, and difficulty maintaining the unique identity as a social worker. A related issue is competition and role overlap with other specialized instructional support personnel, particularly school counselors and psychologists (Altshuler & Webb, 2009; Kelly, 2008). As suggested by the Kelly et al. (2010) findings, it does not appear that school social workers fully claim and implement the person-in-environment approach that social work views as its distinct domain.

Regulation through licensure or certification gives status and recognition to a profession and also provides some degree of protection to the clients served (Donaldson, Hill, Ferguson, Fogel, & Erickson, 2014).). However requirements for school social workers vary by state, and some states, although not the majority, have no certification process at all. Among states with certification/licensure for school social work, many do not specify all the hallmarks of an advanced-level specialization—that is, graduate-level training with specialized internships and curricula that reflect disciplinary standards, discipline-related tests, and professional development after employment (Altshuler & Webb, 2009; Mumm & Bye, 2011). Compared to requirements for school social workers, certification requirements for school psychologists are much more consistent and rigorous across states, in line with the standards of the National Association of School Psychologists. In addition, school psychologists must receive their degree from a state-approved psychology program that includes content areas reflecting the standards of the National Association of School Psychologists. State certification requirements for school counselors are generally more stringent and uniform than they are for school social workers; all states have school counselor certification standards (Altshuler & Webb, 2009).

In conducting a recent research study, Alvarez et al. (2013) found that many school districts had employees with social work degrees employed with job titles other than "school social worker." The titles used appeared to reflect the funding source for the particular position. This practice likely decreases the visibility and professional identity of school social workers, as well as the ability to carry out research to show their value.

A final challenge, related to standards and training, is solidifying the knowledge and research base for school social work. Theory from the sociology of professions literature describes a fully established profession as being able to provide training in specific, shared, theoretical and empirical knowledge and skills (Kelly, 2008). Although school social work claims major perspectives (e.g., person-in-environment, strengths approach), it needs to make clear how these perspectives are expressed in terms of specific practices (Raines, 2006). In addition, to gain respect in the current context for professions, school social work needs to demonstrate its use of research-based practices and provide evidence of its effectiveness through ongoing research (Alvarez et al., 2013; Franklin et al., 2009; Kelly, 2008).

International Challenges

Although circumstances vary by national context, the kinds of concerns described above for the United States are relevant and often magnified in relation to social work across the world. School social work still does not exist in the majority of countries. In those countries that have school social work, funding is always a challenge, and the number of school social workers is generally far from optimal, particularly in less-developed nations. Compared to the United States, school social work is a more recent development in most other countries that have school social workers (Huxtable & Blyth, 2002), so there has been less time for them to establish a professional identity and presence. Few countries require graduate-level training (Kelly, 2008). School social workers often have less training and credentials than teaching staff do, impeding their ability to be viewed as collaborative partners (Huxtable, 1998; Huxtable & Blyth, 2002).

There is no common international definition of school social work or common set of professional requirements. The titles given to school social workers vary, reflecting differences in historical development as well as the specific activities that are emphasized the most. For example, school social workers are called education welfare officers in the United Kingdom and school curators in Finland. In a number of European countries, there is overlap, blending, or no distinction between social work and the older profession of social pedagogy (Huxtable & Blyth, 2002). As noted previously, the title "school social worker" is not always used for social workers in U.S. schools. Huxtable and Blyth identify the need for "a stable title that carries a positive image and a clear meaning to the international community, as do other well-established professions" (p. 235).

The knowledge base for school social work in most countries is even more problematic than in the United States. Textbooks on school social work are available in few countries, and specialized training in school social work is often meager or nonexistent (Huxtable & Blyth, 2002).

ADDRESSING THE CHALLENGES

Ultimately, strengthening the school social work profession will require changes in policy within multiple systems and at multiple levels. For example, in the United States funding for public school personnel is established by local, state, and federal public policies; regulation of school social work is related to policies set by state governments and professional organizations, which are in turn influenced by federal policies, such as requirements of the Individuals with Disabilities Education Act (IDEA; 1990) and the No Child Left Behind Act of 2001. Preparation for well-qualified school social work practitioners and researchers is also related to university policies. How to bring about policy change to address each of the challenges reviewed above requires complex analysis that would entail more than this one chapter. Instead, we will show how applying elements of a specific framework developed by Jansson (2014) may assist in pursuing change. We find Jansson's framework particularly useful because it can be applied to any kind of policy change (e.g., whether aimed at an organization, a community, or higher governmental entity); moreover Jansson's well-known text on policy advocacy was developed for social workers and is utilized by many social work academic programs.

First, Jansson (2014) notes that "policy advocates seldom act alone" (p. 26). They work with other stakeholders through groups, organizations, networks, and coalitions. This enables the sharing of knowledge, skills, and other resources. Power resources (i.e., resources that can be drawn on to gain approval for particular initiatives) are central to policy practice. For example, an advocacy organization can mobilize its members; raise money to hire a professional lobbyist; and draw on the knowledge, skills, and contacts of particular individuals in the organization. Professional associations have been identified as a strength of school social work in the United States (Raines, 2006). These associations include but are not limited to state associations (e.g., the Illinois Association of School Social Workers [IASSW]), regional associations (e.g., the Midwest School Social Work Council), and the SSWAA. School social work practitioners and academics may also join and/or network with other organizations, such as the National Association of Social Workers (NASW), the Council on Social Work Education (CSWE), and the National Education Association. Expertise is a kind of power resource. School social workers gain power when they are viewed as expert professionals, with specialized and beneficial knowledge and skills.

Jansson (2014) delineates eight policy practice tasks and assigns them specific numbers (task 1, task 2, etc.), but they do not always occur in that specific order. Below, we identify the tasks and discuss how each is relevant for strengthening school social work.

Task 1. In the foundational task, deciding what is right and wrong, policy practitioners use ethics and analysis to determine the merits of existing policies and possible policy change. It is essential that school social workers consider both the values of their profession and the research base on school social work before embarking on a change initiative. To do otherwise would be unethical and could also be counterproductive. For example, policies to increase school social workers' involvement in individual counseling and to limit opportunities for broader interventions would be inconsistent with the body of research supporting the efficacy of wider, school-based initiatives, and the three-tiered model that has been adopted in the field.

Task 2. In the navigating policy and advocacy systems task, practitioners determine "where to focus and position their policy intervention" (Jansson, 2014, p. 76). An example of this for school social workers is determining which system or systems to focus on in order to bring about changes in certification policies. Since certification and licensure in the United States are determined by individual states, school social workers in a particular state may decide to focus on changing state policy. On the other hand, to create more uniform professional preparation it may be more appropriate to first focus on policy set by educational gate-keepers, such as CSWE.

Task 3. In the agenda-setting task, practitioners consider whether the context is or can be made favorable for a policy initiative, and, if so, how to develop and utilize strategies to place the initiative on the agendas of decision makers. An important aspect of agenda setting is bringing decision makers' attention to the particular issue. This may include use of mass media, presentations, and other means of communication. For example, the IASSW, along with the school psychologist and school counselor associations, presents at the annual conference of school boards, school administrators, and school business officials (Raines, 2006). School social workers and their allies should be ready to take advantage of windows of opportunity—periods of time where the context is advantageous for particular kinds of policy initiatives (Jansson, 2014). For example, the 2012 Sandy Hook Elementary School shooting created a window of opportunity for school social workers to join with other specialized instructional support personnel in advocating for more mental health service providers (including social workers) in schools. The 2014 shooting and protests in Ferguson, Missouri, provided a window of opportunity for school social workers to address issues of racial discrimination and prejudice in schools.

Task 4. In the problem-analyzing task, practitioners analyze the nature, causes, and prevalence of specific problems. This chapter has engaged in some initial problem-analyzing in discussing the challenges facing the profession. To strengthen the ability to carry out this task, school social work researchers should engage in data collection, and practitioners can advocate for increased data collection by state and federal governmental entities. For example, there is a need for systematic data on the number of school social workers in the United States, in specific states and localities, and the kinds of school programs they work in (Alvarez et al., 2013; Sabatino, Alvarez, & Anderson-Ketchmark, 2011). Recently, as this book goes to press, a research team led by eighth edition coeditor Michael S. Kelly in early 2014, built the first-ever collaboration between all the national and state school social work associations to conduct an update to the 2008 National School Social Work Survey; these data will be made available to the national and state partners as well as policy makers in legislatures around the country.

Task 5. In the proposal-writing task, "practitioners develop solutions to specific problems" (Jansson, 2014, p. 76). The major focus of this task is not simply the mechanics of writing, but also deciding exactly what content the proposal should include. Policy practitioners may use criteria (e.g., cost-effectiveness, equity) to determine which aspects are most important to include in a policy. For major policy proposals (e.g., bills, national position statements), school social work should draw on the expertise of professionals relevant to the particular proposal-writing task, such as policy analysts and researchers. It is also important to involve major stakeholders in fashioning the content of proposals. Along these lines, Altshuler and Webb (2009) suggest the involvement of NASW, SSWAA, and CSWE in developing and fine-tuning nationally recommended requirements for professional preparation and certification. Involving all three of these major organizations representing social work practitioners and academics, rather than just one of them, could result in a stronger, more applicable proposal and could also gain these organizations' commitment to rally state support for the new standards.

Task 6. In the policy-enacting task, practitioners seek to have policies approved or enacted. Skillful use of power resources is particularly relevant to this task. SSWAA hires experienced lobbyists to increase its effectiveness in gaining support for a policy change; lobbyists are used by many state school social work associations as well.

Task 7. In the policy-implementing task, practitioners attempt to influence how policies are carried out after they have been enacted. School social workers can do this on an individual level in carrying out publically mandated activities (e.g., IDEA) and programs adopted by the school (e.g., social and emotional learning programs). School social work associations should develop positions on policy implementation and advocate for their stance; many do so already.

Task 8. In the policy-assessing task, practitioners assess the outcomes of an implemented policy. For example, researchers have evaluated the impact of social emotional learning programs on social and emotional skills, attitudes, behavior, and academic performance (Durlak, Weissberg, Dymnicki, Taylor, & Schellinger, 2011). All school social work preparatory programs should include training in evaluation of both processes and outcomes of interventions. Involvement in research builds the knowledge base for a profession and establishes its expertise.

Additional aspects of the Jansson (2014) framework are described in chapter 19, and can also be useful in devising strategies to strengthen school social work.

SCHOOL SOCIAL WORK IN ILLINOIS: BUILDING THE PROFESSION

Illinois has long been considered the national leader in school social work (Morrison, 2006; Raines, 2006). As of 2009 there were almost 4,000 school social workers in Illinois—approximately twice the number of school psychologists and a sixth more than school counselors (Lueck & Kelly, 2010). The state has one of the best ratios of students to school social workers in the United States (Morrison, 2006), with most Illinois school social workers working in one or two schools (Kelly, 2008). Endorsement as a school social worker in the state requires a master's degree from an Illinois State Board of Education (ISBE)–approved social work program, an internship in a school site, and passing two state tests. In addition, school social workers are required to submit periodic evidence of continuing education.

The strong position of school social work in Illinois likely reflects in part the overall political, social, and economic context related to education and social services in the state. However, as Kelly (2008) has pointed out, the strength of a profession also depends on the action and advocacy of its members. School social work in Illinois has benefited from visionary leaders who established strong organizations and networked with key organizational systems. Many of these individuals undertook multiple professional roles (e.g., school social work practice, university instruction and research, and elected positions in social work associations), giving them expertise, authority, and connections power (Jansson, 2014). We highlight here some of the individuals and organizations that established Illinois as a national leader in school social work. Much of the information is based on an article by Vaughn Morrison (2006), a school social work leader himself and an expert on school social work history in Illinois. In accord with the previous section, we conclude by linking this discussion to the Jansson policy practice framework.

Illinois became one of the first states to employ school social workers when Chicago Public Schools employed their first three school social workers in 1919. Two women from Illinois, Wilma Walker and Gladys Hall, served as national presidents of the American Association of Visiting Teachers (the original title for school social workers) in the 1930s (Morrison, 2006). That organization was eventually renamed the National Association of School Social Workers (NASSW) in 1945 (Raines, 2008).

Morrison (2006) considers Ray Graham to be "the father of Illinois school social work" (p. 12). As ISBE director of the Department of Exceptional Children, Graham convened a meeting for all public school administrators in

1945 and urged them to hire school social workers. He then organized the first statewide Illinois school social work conference in 1948. Graham also served on the NASSW board of directors in the late 1940s.

Having school social workers positioned within ISBE, the state's education department, was important to the success of the profession in Illinois. From 1949 until 2001, ISBE employed a school social work consultant, who was able to influence the department's work. The particular individuals hired as consultants were actively involved in the profession on a regional and national level as well. The first consultant, Opal Boston, later became a social work instructor and a key national figure in school social work. Boston represented NASSW on the committee that worked out the merger of seven social work professional organizations to form NASW in 1955, was chairperson of the first NASW school social work section, participated in writing the first NASW school social work standards, and helped form the Midwest School Social Work Council (Morrison, 2006; Raines, 2008). The most recent consultant, Vaughn Morrison, served as president of the National Council of State Consultants for School Social Work Services. Under his leadership in 1980 and 1981, that organization published four articles in the *School Social Work Journal* that helped set the agenda for NASW's School Social Work Standards (Morrison, 2006). In his article on school social work in Illinois, Morrison lists examples of Illinois policies that resulted from the work of the ISBE school social work consultants. Among these are Medicaid reimbursement for school social work services, the ability for school services personnel (including social workers) to obtain an Educational Administrative Certificate, regulations giving equal status to school social workers and psychologists, and inclusion of a definition of school social work in Illinois law.

The IASSW, founded in 1970, was one of the first state associations organized after the formation of NASW in 1955, when the NASSW and its state organizations ceased to exist (Morrison, 2006). IASSW launched its monthly newsletter in 1970 and the *School Social Work Journal* in 1976. To this day, the *School Social Work Journal* continues to have wide circulation and influence in the profession. In 1984 IASSW became the first school social work state association to hire a paid lobbyist, and in 1999 became the first to employ an executive director (Morrison, 2006). Solidifying the structure of the organization and its ability to lobby strengthened the organization's stature and advocacy ability. For example, Morrison notes that IASSW was the major driving force behind Illinois's enactment of a 1985 statute outlawing corporal punishment in schools and a 1992 behavioral interventions statute; behavioral intervention requirements were not incorporated in IDEA until 1997.

Illinois also played a major role in the founding of the Midwest School Social Work Council, a regional association with representatives from Midwest states. Geraldine Tosby, then ISBE school social work consultant, was the first chair; Illinois obtained funding for and hosted the association's first regional conference in 1968. The Council's advocacy work related to special education legislation had a major impact on the future of the school social work profession. The Education for All Handicapped Children Act of 1975 did not include a role for school social workers. The Midwest Council mobilized a campaign to include school social work in the regulations passed subsequent to the Act. Through numerous meetings and a petition campaign, the Council convinced NASW to lobby for the regulations. The Council also spearheaded a national letter-writing campaign to the Department of Education. As a result, the term "social work services in schools" was included in the regulations and has been included in reauthorizations of the IDEA statute (Morrison, 2006; Raines, 2008). Illinois in particular capitalized on this special education legislation to solidify its position in schools (Kelly, 2008). IASSW advocated for social workers' inclusion in special education service provision and, along with university MSW programs, prepared school social workers to participate in the special education process (S. McDonald, past president and former board member of IASSW, personal communication, July 17, 2014).

The national SSWAA was founded in 1994, in part due to dissatisfaction with NASW in representing school social workers. Randy Fisher of Illinois was the first president, and other prominent school social workers in Illinois, such as Vaughn Morrison, have served on the SSWAA board (Morrison, 2006).

Illinois has also been a leader in school social work scholarship and research. As noted by Morrison (2006), "More school social work text-book authors and editors have either earned an MSW and/or doctorate, practiced school social work, or taught school social work at the university level in Illinois than in any other state" (p. 22). Many of the school social work university scholars in Illinois are former school social work practitioners, and bring that understanding to their scholarship. For example, in recent years Michael Kelly, professor at Loyola University and former school social worker, has been involved in analyzing the direction and activities of school social work in Illinois.

Using the Jansson (2014) framework, we observe that school social work leaders and organizations in Illinois have skillfully engaged in policy practice tasks. They have determined where to focus advocacy and policy efforts (task 2). They have created agendas favorable to school social work, particularly in Illinois. They have also engaged in problem-analyzing (e.g., making a case for national NASW school social work standards), participated in the creation of policy proposals (e.g., state and national bills and regulations), and mobilized support for the enactment of state and federal policies. Participation in the policy implementation task is exemplified by their attention to school social work's role in the implementation of IDEA. Research by Illinois school social workers brings attention to school social work outcomes (task 8), and enriches the knowledge base and expertise of the school social work profession.

BUILDING SCHOOL SOCIAL WORK IN JAPAN

Although it began one hundred years later than in the United States, school social work in Japan is undergoing rapid development. In 2013 the Japanese Ministry of Education, Culture, Sports, Science and Technology (MEXT) reported that 76 of 110 local governments large enough to receive MEXT funding were employing a total of 1,008 school social workers (MEXT, 2014). Currently school social work positions may be funded by the national government (through MEXT) and prefecture; by the national government, prefecture, and local community; or by the local community only.

As school social work has become more prevalent in Japanese society, several empirical studies have reported the effectiveness of school social work in Japanese schools. For example, school social work intervention was found to be effective in preventing negative outcomes for children who experienced maltreatment (Nishino, 2009). School social workers have helped students experiencing truancy issues (Okumura, 2009), and have supported connections between schools and families (Akao, Yamano, & Zushi, 2011; Zushi & Yamano, 2011). The body of research on school social work practice is new and developing in Japan, but it is playing a role in establishing the visibility, viability, and value of school social work as it develops in Japan,

Numerous challenges exist for the development of school social work in Japan. There are no national guidelines for school social work practice, which varies between communities. Local governments and schools often do not understand the differences between school social workers and counselors, how to involve school social workers, or the benefits of using school social workers. Without a clear national definition, the school social worker may be viewed by others simply as a professional who deals with social welfare programs and issues.

Current Status of School Social Work in Japan

Given the evolving status of school social work in Japan, Noriko Yamano decided to carry out a national study of school social work practice (Yamano, 2012). The study surveyed education board personnel and school social workers in 155 local communities, including prefectures, cities, towns, and villages that utilized school social work services. Findings indicated that, where it exists, the practice of school social work in Japan is perceived as an effective support for students and schools.

One focus of the study was on certification status and employment practices related to school social work. Yamano found that professional preparation for school social work in Japan is quite diverse. The majority of respondents had teaching licenses (52.2 percent), followed by a smaller number who were certified social workers (39.5 percent), with an even smaller percentage having certificates related to psychology, mental health, or other welfare-related certificates. (Some respondents had more than one kind of certificate.) In addition, of those with past experience, more than half (52.7 percent) had experience in education prior to becoming a school social worker, whereas fewer (28 percent) had experience in social work. Most (62.6 percent) were employed part-time, and 35.4 percent self-identified as temporary employees. The majority of respondents worked fewer than 150 days a year; 26.3 percent worked only 50 to 100 days a year, and nearly 20 percent worked fewer than 50 days a year (fewer than two days per week). School social workers were rarely housed in a single school, but instead were dispatched to schools by education boards.

An important study finding suggests that social work preparation strengthens the work of personnel carrying out school social work tasks in Japan. Workers with social work certificates demonstrated significantly greater skill when carrying out case consultations in schools than workers who lacked social work certificates. Specifically, personnel with social work training were better able to collaboratively assess case conferences with the participants and had greater ability to incorporate children's backgrounds in the case conference.

Utilizing findings from the Yamano (2012) study and the national U.S. study (Kelly et al., 2010) allows for tentative comparison of school social work practice tasks in the two countries. Due to methodological differences in the studies and differences in the specific tasks, such as home visits that are mandatory for teachers in Japan, it is difficult to simply compare, but we can examine trends. In the United States the task carried out the most was individual counseling, whereas meeting with parents was the most frequent task reported in Japan. The least frequent task in the United States was consultation with teachers, but this was the third-most frequent task in Japan. Group work was the second-most frequent task in the United States, but it was much less common among Japanese personnel carrying out school social work tasks (only 1.5 percent of time was reported as allocated to this task).

One similarity in the two studies is that respondents frequently engaged in consultation with children and parents. On the other hand, indirect approaches, such as teacher consultation, appear to be utilized more by Japanese than by U.S. school social workers. The emphasis on indirect practice, particularly case conferences, in Japan is related to the conditions under which school social workers are employed. As noted previously, most school social workers are part-time workers employed by local education boards, and are dispatched to consult with teachers and designated schools.

There are advantages to the use of case conferences by school social workers in Japan. Unlike one-on-one practice with children and their parents, followed by a report to teachers, the case conference system in schools may help participants and entire schools change their perspectives. Whereas a micro approach is prevalent in the United States (Kelly et al., 2010), Japanese practice is strong in mezzo- and macrolevel approaches such as work with teachers and education boards. Since school social work is not currently treated as essential in Japan, evidence of effectiveness is increasingly important, and emerging evidence suggests that school social work practice in Japan has led to positive effects. This is enhanced when education board personnel strategically work with school social workers. In fact, an increasing number of local communities are adopting school social workers without funding from the national government and prefecture.

The focus on macro practice may assist the future development of school social work in Japan. School social work is in a period of rapid development in Japan, and macrolevel practice is likely to continue to influence the teachers and education boards who create policies. Thus work at the macrolevel is a critical focus for school social workers in Japan who are working to create this new field of practice.

Challenges and Opportunities for School Social Work in Japan

School social work practice is an emerging discipline in Japan. Its first five years, as reported above, have included wide variations in employment status and training of personnel carrying out school social work–types of tasks. Almost immediately, Japanese scholars began to evaluate the impact of school social work practice, with promising results. Both the national ministry and local education boards are now supporting further development of school social work in Japan. Under the Child Poverty Prevention Act (Japan) of 2013, the national government committed to increasing the number of school social workers to 10,000 by 2020, ten times the current number for which the national government provides one third of funding.

Practice is different in Japan than in the United States. It is expected that differences in funding for services, cultural differences, and varying traditions would lead to different foci in the two nations. However, school social work leaders can learn from the rapid growth and development of school social work in Japan. In the United States, many states still do not have an active school social work presence. The focus on macrolevel practice, the immediate emphasis on evaluation of practice and programs, and the involvement of both local and national agencies have resulted in an impressive growth of school social work in Japan.

Change is messy. The invention of a new field of practice involves rapidly evolving roles and practices. However, the Japanese model demonstrates the impact of intense collaborative efforts across local, national, and university systems. Critical to this rapid development has been a vision for the future and the use of macrolevel strategies to develop this new field. Although such beginnings are difficult and fraught with risk and hazard, leaders in Japan have worked to visualize mezzo and macro practices and to demonstrate the feasibility and effectiveness of these practices.

A priority for the continued development of school social work in Japan is to consciously focus on mezzo- and macrolevel practices. School social work in Japan places a primary emphasis on support for teachers because this approach is ultimately beneficial for children and their parents. If a teacher has a broad social welfare perspective and looks at a child's background, it is possible for his or her entire class of forty children to be helped. Thus, case conferences can bring change into schools. It is important to conduct such conferences based on the values of school social work. This is a great challenge in Japan where most school social workers possess teaching certificates.

An additional challenge to school social work in Japan involves development of a consistent and unique role. Collaboration with teachers is one important piece of that developing role. School social workers themselves may lack a clear understanding of their own role in schools and believe they should act like the school principal. By taking on a mezzo-practice approach in mediating between teachers and between teachers and parents, school social work tasks become broadly defined. In the long run, school social workers may need to define their role and create boundaries instead of taking on all the tasks currently available to them.

Finally, through macro practice school social workers promote the value of the profession and assist education boards in planning for school social work services. Much important work is needed at broader levels of practice. However, the boundaries and role definition of school social work are evolving. Therefore, it is necessary to create consistent guidelines for practice to be utilized not only by individual school social workers, but also by education boards.

Similar to the development of school social work in Illinois, a strong future for the profession in Japan will require the kinds of policy practice tasks delineated by Jansson (2014). Advocates for the profession in Japan can continue to network, organize, and build the body of expertise for school social work practice. In considering policy and program change, those advocates should take into account social work values and ethics (Jansson's task 1) and the optimal system(s) to focus on (e.g., MEXT, education boards, or individual schools) for their advocacy (Jansson's task 2). Effective change efforts will also require continued analysis of problems related to the profession, creating strategies for influencing decision makers' agendas, developing policy proposals, and advocating for policy enactment (Jansson's tasks 3 through 6). School social workers in Japan need to consider how they should and can influence the implementation of policies in schools and should continue to assess the outcomes of school social work practices and programs (Jansson's tasks 7 and 8). The rapid development of school social work in Japan would not be possible without the skillful policy practice already undertaken by advocates for the profession.

CONCLUSION

The history and development of school social work practice in one state and the emerging development of school social work in Japan have been framed within the Jansson (2014) framework for policy practice. School social work, as a field of practice, continues to need national and international development, which calls for policy practice skills and macrolevel interventions by school social workers. School social work needs to clarify its role in order to fully communicate its value, visibility, and viability. To achieve wider recognition and support, school social workers must engage in collaborative efforts with members of the profession, state and local governments, professional associations, universities, and schools. These broad partnerships have created success in the past, but more is needed to strengthen our field both in the United States and around the world.

References

Akao, K., Yamano, N., & Zushi, K. (2011). Empirical study of school social work practice: Process of reconnecting teachers and families. *Child and Family Welfare Study, 10,* 59–68.

Allen-Meares, P., Montgomery, K. L., & Kim, J. S. (2013). School-based social work interventions: A cross-national systematic review. *Social Work, 58,* 253–262. doi:10.1093/sw/swt022

Altshuler, S. J., & Webb, J. R. (2009). Social social work: Increasing the legitimacy of the profession. *Children & Schools, 31,* 208–218.

Alvarez, M. E., Bye, L., Bryant, R., & Mumm, A. M. (2013). School social workers and educational outcomes. *Children & Schools, 35,* 235–243. doi:10.1093/cs/cdt019

Bureau of Business & Economic Research, University of New Mexico. (2013, April 2). *Per capita personal income by state.* Retrieved from https://bber.unm.edu/econ/us-pci.htm

Child Poverty Prevention Act (Japan) of 2013 (2013).

Dane, B. O., & Simon, B. L. (1991). Resident guests: Social workers in host settings. *Social Work, 36,* 208–213.

Donaldson, P. D., Hill, K., Ferguson, S., Fogel, S., & Erickson, C. (2014). Contemporary social work licensure: Implications for macro social work practice and education. *Social Work, 59,* 52–61. doi:10.1093/sw/swt045

Durlak, J. A., Weissberg, R. P., Dymnicki, A. B., Taylor, R. D., & Schellinger, K. B. (2011). The impact of enhancing students' social and emotional learning: A meta-analysis of school-based university interventions. *Child Development, 82,* 405–432. doi:10.1111/j.1467-8624.2010.01564.x

Education for All Handicapped Children Act of 1975, Pub. L. 94-142 (1975).

Franklin, C., Kim, J. S., & Tripodi, S. J. (2009). A meta-analysis of published school social work practice studies: 1980–2007. *Research on Social Work Practice, 19,* 667–677. doi:10.1177/1049731508330224

Goren, S. G. (1981). The wonderland of social work in the schools, or how Alice learned to cope. *School Social Work Journal, 6,* 19–26.

Huxtable, M. (1998). School social work: An international profession. *Social Work in Education, 20,* 95–109.

Huxtable, M., & Blyth, B. (Eds.). (2002). *School social work worldwide.* Washington, DC: National Association of Social Workers.

Individuals with Disabilities Education Act of 1990 (IDEA), Pub. L. 105-17, U.S.C. 11401 et seq. (1990).

International Network for School Social Work. (n.d.). *Countries.* Retrieved from http://internationalnetwork-schoolsocialwork.htmlplanet.com/Countries.html

Jansson, B. S. (2014). *Becoming an effective policy advocate: From policy practice to social justice* (7th ed). Belmont, CA: Brooks/Cole, Cengage Learning.

Kelly, M. S. (2008). *The domains and demands of school social work practice: A guide to working effectively with students, families and schools.* New York: Oxford University Press.

Kelly, M. S., Berzin, S. C., Frey, A., Alvarez, M., Shaffer, G., & O'Brien, K. (2010). The state of school social work: Findings from the National School Social Work Survey. *School Mental Health, 2,* 132–141. doi:10.1007/s12310-010-9034-5

Lueck, C., & Kelly, M. S. (2010). *School based mental health in Illinois: Assessing the present and looking toward the future.* Chicago: Illinois Mental Health Partnership. Retrieved from http://icmhp.org/icmhpproducts/files/ICMHP-SBMH-Report Final11-19-10.pdf

Ministry of Education, Culture, Sports, Science and Technology (MEXT). (2014). *2013 summary of school social work project* [Handout]. Osaka: Author.

Minnesota State University Mankato. (n.d.). *US school social work information.* Retrieved from http://sbs.mnsu.edu/socialwork/schoolswcertificate/

Morrison, V. (2006). History of school social work: The Illinois perspective. *School Social Work Journal, 30*(3, special issue), 1–23.

Mumm, A. M., & Bye, L. (2011). Certification of school social workers and curriculum content of programs offering training in school social work. *Children & Schools, 33,* 17–23.

Nishino, M. (2009). Effectiveness and challenges of school social workers as school staff based on helping process of school social worker for children in abusive nurturing environments. *School Social Work Study, 4,* 28–41.

No Child Left Behind Act of 2001, Pub. L. 107-110 (2002).

Okumura, K. (2009). A discussion of improving the situations of children in tardiness through family support: School social work based on power exchange model. *School Social Work, 4,* 2–15.

Raines, J. C. (2006). SWOT! A strategic plan for school social work in the twenty-first century. *School Social Work Journal, 30*(3, special issue), 132–150.

Raines, J. C. (2008). A retrospective chronicle of the Midwest School Social Work Council: Its vision and influence after forty years. *School Social Work Journal, 33*(1), 1–15.

Sabatino, C. A., Alvarez, M. E., & Anderson-Ketchmark, C. (2011). "Highly qualified" school social workers. *Children & Schools, 33,* 189–192.

School Social Work Association of America (SSWAA). (n.d.). *Second National School Social Work Survey results*. Retrieved from http://www.sswaa.org

University of Guam. (n.d.). *Bachelor of social work*. Retrieved from http://www.uog.edu/degree-programs/social-work

Yamano, N. (2012). Study of school social worker allocation program. In M. Shirasawa (Ed.), *Study of how to evaluate school social work and creation of evaluation manual* (Report No. 2, pp. 38–91). Tokyo: MEXT.

Zushi, K., & Yamano, N. (2011). Factors that influence the practice process of school social workers: Focus on school social workers in the area where the parties concerned do not have awareness of their issues. *Japanese Journal of Social Welfare, 52*(2), 32–42.

Section V

Tier 1 Interventions

Response to intervention (RTI) has evolved to multitiered system supports (MTSS). This framework includes three tiers of interventions, with tier 1 interventions focusing on school-wide intervention aimed at all students, as opposed to interventions that target at-risk students or those focused on students who have been identified as having problems. The three tiers of RTI remain central in MTSS. This section of the book provides two examples of tier 1 interventions: chapter 24 by Aidyn Iachini, "Developing Safe, Responsive, and Respectful School Communities: Evidence-Informed Tier 1 Interventions," that focuses on school safety; and chapter 25 by Michael Valenti, Mary Margaret Kerr, and Garry King, "Evidence-Informed Suicide Prevention in Schools," that focuses on suicide prevention.

24

Developing Safe, Responsive, and Respectful School Communities: Evidence-Informed Tier 1 Interventions

Aidyn L. Iachini
College of Social Work, University of South Carolina

- ◆ Defining School Climate: Safe, Responsive, and Respectful School Communities
- ◆ Importance of Developing Safe, Responsive, and Respectful School Communities
- ◆ A Data-Informed Process for School Climate Decision Making
- ◆ Evidence-Informed Tier 1 Interventions to Develop Safe, Responsive, and Respectful School Communities
- ◆ Other Key Considerations for School Social Workers

The development of safe, responsive, and respectful school communities is a growing priority for schools. National data estimate that one high school youth in five experiences bullying on school grounds, and 12 percent are involved in physical fights at school (Centers for Disease Control and Prevention, 2012). Many more youths also experience other barriers to learning such as trauma, abuse, unmet mental health needs, homelessness, feelings of disconnect from teachers, and unstable family environments (Richman, Bowen, & Wooley, 2004). Schools must aim to foster feelings of safety, be responsive in addressing these nonacademic barriers to student learning, and respect differences and diversity. School social workers are essential leaders and change agents in developing these types of school communities (Hopson & Lawson, 2011).

This chapter focuses on evidence-informed tier 1 interventions that aim to develop safe, responsive, and respectful school communities. Specifically, this chapter describes the important role for school social workers in promoting positive school climates through data-driven decision-making processes. This chapter then conceptualizes potential efforts to foster these climates within a three-tiered framework and offers considerations in the selection of evidence-informed tier 1 interventions. The chapter then offers a case example, and shares other important considerations for school social workers leading and engaging in these efforts in their school communities.

DEFINING SCHOOL CLIMATE: SAFE, RESPONSIVE, AND RESPECTFUL SCHOOL COMMUNITIES

Students oftentimes experience numerous nonacademic barriers that can impede their overall healthy development and ability to be successful in school (Adelman & Taylor, 2002). Imagine children who are bullied at school most days and feel unsafe when they walk into their school buildings. Imagine those youths whose families are homeless and enter school tired and hungry. Imagine children who experience significant emotional and behavioral difficulties and who are not receiving the help and support needed from their teachers and other school staff to be successful in school. Then imagine how difficult it might be for these same students to engage in classroom learning. Together, these examples highlight salient risk factors that many students face that can increase their risk for poor academic achievement (Richman et al., 2004). These examples also illustrate how factors that influence learning are complex, and can span a variety of domains—individual, peer, family, school, and community—in a youth's ecological context.

As a school social worker, one primary role in helping to address these barriers to learning is to provide individual, group, and/or family interventions. Providing these interventions, however, is oftentimes only one part of a complex solution. Many school social workers may need to initiate and implement systemic efforts to promote comprehensive school-wide climate change and help develop school environments that are safe, responsive, and respectful in meeting students' needs (Frey & Dupper, 2005). These latter efforts are the focus of this chapter.

In general, a "positive school climate" is the term used to capture this idea of a safe, responsive, and respectful school environment. Although definitions may vary (Kohl, Recchia, & Steffgen, 2013; Zullig, Koopman, Patton, & Ubbes, 2010), school climate is oftentimes defined as "the quality and character of school life" (Cohen, McCabe, Michelli, & Pickeral, 2009, p. 182). Cohen et al. indicate that a school's climate "is based on patterns of students', parents' and school personnel's experience of school life and reflects norms, goals, values, interpersonal relationships, teaching and learning practices, and organizational structures" (Cohen et al., 2009, p. 182). Perceptions of school climate are based on collective experiences of students, families, school personnel, and community members as they interface with each other and the school system.

School climate is oftentimes conceptualized according to four primary dimensions (Cohen et al., 2009):

1. One primary dimension of school climate is safety. A healthy school climate is one in which students, family members, and others feel physically, psychologically, and emotionally safe.
2. Teaching and learning is a second dimension of school climate. Here, a key aspect of school climate relates to stakeholders' perceptions regarding the strength of administrative leadership, the support for quality teaching, the support for the professional development and growth of school staff, and the value placed on social and emotional learning.
3. A third dimension of school climate is relationships. It is important that students and adults feel welcomed, respected, connected to each other, and involved as important collaborators in the school community.
4. Environmental-structural is the last dimension of school climate. A positive school climate is one where the facilities are perceived to be clean, adequate, and safe for teaching and learning to occur.

Together, these four school climate dimensions are important to consider in the creation of a healthy school community. School social workers' attention to each dimension can help foster a school environment that is perceived as safe, responsive, and respectful by those who work and learn within it. The next section synthesizes research on the positive impact of these types of school environments, as well as recent policy initiatives that support the importance of school climate as an important pathway to school improvement and improved student outcomes.

IMPORTANCE OF DEVELOPING SAFE, RESPONSIVE, AND RESPECTFUL SCHOOL COMMUNITIES

Recent studies, along with comprehensive reviews of school climate research (see Cohen et al., 2009; and Thapa, Cohen, Guffey, & Higgins-D'Alessandro, 2013), continue to demonstrate the critical impact of school climate on students' learning, healthy development, and overall academic success. Kidger, Araya, Donovan, and Gunnell (2012), for example, found that students' perceived connectedness to school and perceived support from teachers—two aspects of school climate—related to better emotional health among students. McCoy, Roy, and Sirkman (2013) found that students' perceptions of safety and respect in their school community, along with perceptions of social and emotional learning, related to improved academic achievement. A recent meta-analysis also documented that positive perceptions of school climate negatively related to school violence (Steffgen, Recchia, & Viechtbauer, 2013).

Given these documented benefits and positive outcomes, school climate is now recognized as one of many important pathways to school improvement and student success in school (Anderson-Butcher et al., 2010; Hopson & Lawson, 2011; Iachini, Dorr, & Anderson-Butcher, 2008; Thapa et al., 2013). Federal policies and reports (e.g., the Safe and Drug-Free Schools and Communities Act of 2004, the president's safety and gun violence plan titled *Now is the time to do something about gun violence* [White House, 2013], and Cowan, Vaillancourt, Rossen, & Pollit's [2013] *A Framework for Safe and Successful Schools*), along with federal funding streams (e.g., Safe and Supportive Schools grants) continue to advance this pathway as foundational for school safety and broader school improvement initiatives. National organizations, such as the National School Climate Center (www.schoolclimate.org/), also have been created to offer technical assistance, along with resources and strategies, to support schools engaged in these efforts.

Yet, despite this emerging focus on school climate, the reality is that many schools feel the pressure to achieve the academic accountability benchmarks to which they are accountable through the No Child Left Behind Act of 2001. As such, school climate can oftentimes be viewed as peripheral, but not central, to school improvement efforts. Schools are realizing, however, that a sole focus on quality instruction and teaching, along with implementation of academic intervention strategies, are not enough to improve academic outcomes for all students in a school community. Many schools are now expanding their school improvement priorities, and related data collection and intervention strategies, to include a focus on school climate.

As schools continue to broaden their school improvement efforts, understanding this research and policy context around school climate and school improvement is critical. As advocates for change, school social workers can use this knowledge in advocacy efforts aimed at inclusion of school climate priorities within their own school community. Likewise, school social workers can support data collection and intervention strategies that help promote healthier school climates. The next section of this chapter identifies key ways school social workers can help lead and mobilize these efforts.

A DATA-INFORMED PROCESS FOR
SCHOOL CLIMATE DECISION MAKING

As schools continue to expand their school improvement priorities to focus on school climate, two processes are important. First, similar to how academic outcomes are systematically monitored and tracked per the requirements of the No Child Left Behind Act, there needs to be a process for monitoring, assessing, and identifying school climate priorities (Cohen, 2006; Cohen et al., 2009; Hopson & Lawson, 2011; Wang, Berry, & Swearer, 2013). Second, a process also needs to be in place for selecting and implementing evidence-informed interventions to address those identified school climate needs. This section focuses on the first process—assessing and monitoring school climate as part of a data-informed process for identifying school climate priorities.

Similar to assessing the needs of individual students to target individually based interventions, it also is important to assess the needs of the school in relationship to school climate to drive decision making. To do this, many schools utilize a survey or a battery of surveys to assess school climate needs (Kohl et al., 2013). Because surveys allow for the collection of a large quantity of data, and can be used to assess multiple stakeholder perspectives (e.g., students, families, school staff, etc.), surveys are oftentimes preferable to other data collection strategies (e.g., focus groups, interviews, etc.) for assessing school climate.

Many survey tools exist to help school social workers assess school climate priorities. While a review of all of these tools is beyond the scope of this chapter, table 24.1 provides an example of a few select school climate tools available for use in schools. Each tool is unique in terms of the dimensions that are assessed, the target respondent for which the survey was designed, and the availability of the survey in the public domain. The National Center on Safe and Supportive Learning Environments (2013) has

TABLE 24.1   Select Examples of School Climate Measures

Name of School Climate Measure	Select Examples of Dimensions Assessed	Target Respondent(s)	Web site
Comprehensive School Climate Inventory	Sense of social-emotional security Respect for diversity School connectedness/engagement	School personnel Parents Students (elementary, middle, and high school)	http://www.schoolclimate.org/programs/csci.php
Community and Youth Collaborative Institute School Experience Family of Surveys	Academic press Safety Support for learning School connectedness	School personnel Parents Students (elementary, middle, and high school)	http://cayci.osu.edu/surveys/
School Success Profile	Learning climate School safety School behavior expectations	School personnel Parents Students (elementary, middle, and high school)	http://www.uncssp.org/
American Institutes for Research: Conditions for Learning Survey	Safe and respectful climate Student support Social and emotional learning	Students	http://www.air.org/expertise/index/?fa=viewContent&content_id=383

created one of the most comprehensive lists of valid and reliable measures of school climate in their *School Climate Survey Compendia*. Other lists of select school climate measures are also available. Please see Clifford, Menon, Gangi, Condon, and Hornung (2012) and Kohl et al. (2013) for lists of these other measures.

Because of the plethora of school climate survey tools that exist, selecting a tool for use in a specific school community can be challenging. Here are several important considerations when selecting a tool:

◆ What dimensions of school climate are most relevant to your school community? Because each tool assesses different dimensions of school climate, school social workers in partnership with other key stakeholders in the school community should select a tool that assesses aspects of school climate that are most relevant to your specific school community. For example, if safety is a primary concern, then it is important to select a tool that assesses this dimension of school climate. If both safety and social/emotional learning are a concern, then a school would want to select a school climate measure that assesses both dimensions.

◆ Which stakeholder groups will participate in the survey? Some tools are available that assess school climate from the perspective of multiple stakeholder groups (e.g., students, families, school staff, etc.). While some schools might be interested in gaining only the student perspective, other schools might want to assess both student and school staff perceptions. Here again, school social workers in partnership with stakeholders in the school community should select a tool that is available for the stakeholder group(s) interested in being assessed in your own school community.

◆ Is the tool available in the public domain or is there a fee associated with use of the tool? Some school climate tools are publicly accessible and therefore are free to use, whereas others have a cost associated with their use. Keeping in mind the available resources and funding in a school community is important when determining a tool to use.

◆ What survey format will work best for your school community? Some school climate surveys are available to complete online, some are available in paper-and-pencil forms, and yet others are available in both forms. Because of this, it is important to consider the technology resources in your school community and whether computers are available for an online survey option.

◆ What are the language preferences of the stakeholder group(s) being assessed? Some tools are available in English, as well as in other languages (e.g., Spanish, French, etc.). It is important to consider the primary language of the school community population when selecting a tool.

As school social workers and other school community stakeholders consider and answer these key questions, it becomes easier to identify a school climate tool that might best fit a particular school community. Once a school climate measure has been selected and data are collected and analyzed, the next critical step in the process is for school social workers and other relevant stakeholders to identify and prioritize the areas of school climate that might be important to target through intervention strategies. This step ultimately requires sifting through the data and determining which aspects of school climate are perceived most favorably and which seem to be perceived least favorably by respondents. Those aspects, once identified, can then be prioritized in order to determine which intervention strategies may be important to implement first. Keeping in mind available school and community resources is again important here, particularly as it can help identify areas that might be the most feasible to initially target.

Deciding which school climate survey to use and which aspects of school climate to address first is not easy. Formation of a school climate team may be important here. This team may be made up of building leaders, school social workers, teachers, youths, and other community stakeholders important to school climate improvement efforts. In this way, collaborative decisions can be made regarding what might work best for the school community. School social workers, trained in leadership and group-facilitation, are well-suited to provide leadership for these school climate teams.

EVIDENCE-INFORMED TIER 1 INTERVENTIONS TO DEVELOP SAFE, RESPONSIVE, AND RESPECTFUL SCHOOL COMMUNITIES

As mentioned above, the second important process for school climate improvement efforts is the identification and selection of evidence-informed interventions to address identified school climate priorities. Consistent with the three-tiered framework that many schools use to conceptualize the range of services and supports they offer, this chapter focuses only on those evidence-informed interventions that are categorized as tier 1 strategies. Sometimes referred to as prevention and promotion strategies, tier 1 strategies include those that are provided to all students through school-wide or classroom-based efforts. The aim of tier 1 strategies is often to prevent problematic student behavior and/or promote prosocial behavior (Allen-Meares, Montgomery, & Kim, 2013). These are in contrast with tier 2 (early intervention) or tier 3 (treatment) strategies that provide progressively more-targeted and individualized support to identified students.

Many evidence-informed tier 1 strategies exist that target various dimensions of school climate. Bullying and violence prevention programs, social and emotional learning programs, behavioral management strategies, and character education programs all represent different types of tier 1 strategies schools might implement to help foster safer, more responsive, and more respectful school communities. Many specific evidence-informed programs exist, however, within each of these different broader program types. This oftentimes can make it a bit more challenging for schools to decide which specific evidence-informed tier 1 program or strategy to implement in a school community.

Key Considerations in Selecting an Evidence-Informed Tier 1 Strategy

Because the needs of each school community are unique, there is no prescriptive approach to selecting an evidence-informed tier 1 strategy to enhance school climate. Related to this, there is oftentimes no one "right" tier 1 strategy to implement in a school. Schools often arrive at decisions through discussions focusing on a host of key issues, including the following:

- ◆ Evidence of effectiveness: When deciding on a strategy to implement, it is important to review the research base documenting its effectiveness (or lack thereof). Again, a lot of Web sites are available to help synthesize this research, but it is always important to ask the question and review the research regarding whether the program has been found effective, ineffective, or even harmful to students.
- ◆ Student population: Beyond considering program effectiveness, it also is important to keep in mind the student population that the program will serve. For example, is the program designed for elementary school students or is it designed for high school students? Has the program been found effective for the diverse population you are serving? Is the program available in the language needed to best serve your student population?
- ◆ Cost and resources: It also is important to consider a range of issues related to the cost of the program and resources needed to implement it. For example, how much does the program cost to use and implement? Are training and technical assistance available? How much time is required of school staff? Are the resources available to implement the program? Is there a curriculum provided?
- ◆ School and community context: Consideration of the school and community context is also important. Is this program or strategy something that easily integrates with existing programs and initiatives? Is the program redundant of another program being offered in the school or in the community? Is there an aspect of the program that might not fit well with our school needs that could be adapted if necessary? Is there one program that might meet several related needs in the school community (e.g., bullying prevention and social and emotional learning)?

As these questions are answered, it becomes easier to determine which tier 1 program or strategy to implement. Regardless of the strategy selected, though, it is always important to evaluate both the implementation and the impact of that strategy in your own school community to ensure that it is effective in meeting identified school needs. Data and information from these evaluation efforts can then be used to guide continuous refinement of the program over time. Evaluation findings also might lead to the decision that another program might better suit the needs of the school community. Here again, there are important leadership opportunities for school social workers within these selection, implementation, and evaluation processes.

A case example is shared next to illustrate the two processes identified above as central for school climate improvement efforts. Please note that mention of specific tier 1 programs in the case example does not serve as an endorsement of those programs. These programs were selected merely for illustrative purposes.

Case Example: ABC Middle School

The principal of ABC Middle School was interested in understanding students' and teachers' perceptions of safety in the school community. The principal also was concerned about the extent to which bullying was occurring on school grounds. She tasked the school social worker to lead these efforts to further understand these challenges in the school community. As a first step, the school social worker formed a team called the ABC School Climate Team, knowing that it was critical to have a variety of perspectives available to help understand and address any school climate concerns. The team's first task was to identify a way to assess perceptions of safety that would be feasible for the school. After examining a variety of school climate tools, the team decided that the Community and Youth Collaborative Institute (CAYCI) School Experience Surveys (SES), specifically the middle/high school youth version and the teacher/staff version, would best meet their needs. These surveys assessed two key dimensions of interest (safety and externalizing behaviors, including bullying) to the school, were in the public domain, and were available for both key stakeholder audiences. The surveys also could be completed online, which was important for the school given that the technology was available.

Once the ABC School Climate Team selected the survey and devised a data collection plan that included the days and times the surveys would be completed, the team collected the data from both youths and teachers. The school social worker then descriptively analyzed these data, and shared them back with the ABC School Climate Team to help identify areas of concern. From the team discussions, it became clear that perceptions of bullying and safety were of utmost concern among students and teachers/school staff. From the data collected via the surveys, 31 percent of students reported that they had bullied someone at school, and 65 percent of students reported that they did not feel safe at school. Teachers and staff in the middle school also expressed safety concerns, with 52 percent reporting they thought students did not feel safe at school. Anecdotally, the school social worker and several teachers on the team also noted their concerns with bullying at the school and believed that this may be a contributing factor to feelings of safety. As a result, the ABC School Climate Team decided that bullying was the top priority that needed to be addressed first. They reported that if this was addressed first, perhaps perceptions of safety also would be enhanced in the school community.

Once this priority was identified, the next step was for the ABC School Climate Team to identify an evidence-informed tier 1 strategy to address this school climate issue in the middle school. As an initial step, the school social worker searched a variety of evidence-based practice Web sites (table 24.2) to see if there was an already established program that might fit the school's needs. From this initial search, more than fifteen programs were listed that had evidence supporting their effectiveness. These included programs such as Steps to Respect, Positive Action, Fourth R: Skills for Youth Relationships, and Second Step, among others. The school social worker also reached out to other local middle schools to identify any programs or strategies they were using that might be effective.

From here, the ABC School Climate Team was faced with the ultimate decision of determining which program or strategy would be the most feasible and effective to implement. Through several meetings, the ABC School Climate Team worked through answering the key questions outlined above in this chapter. First, they were able to narrow down programs based on target population and age range. Some programs were designed specifically for elementary school students, and not the middle school population targeted through these efforts. Other programs had not been implemented in a

TABLE 24.2   List of Resources to Identify School Climate Tier 1 Interventions

Name of Resource	Web Site
Blueprints for Healthy Youth Development	www.blueprintsprograms.com
Coalition for Evidence-Based Policy	www.toptierevidence.org
Office of Justice Programs	www.crimesolutions.gov
Office of Juvenile Justice and Delinquency Prevention Model Programs Guide	www.ojjdp.gov/mpg
SAMHSA's National Registry of Evidence-based Programs and Practices	http://nrepp.samhsa.gov/SearchResults New.aspx?s=b&q=school+climate
What Works Clearinghouse	http://ies.ed.gov/ncee/wwc/findwhat works.aspx

diverse student population, such as the one served through this school. Some programs also were too costly, given the available resources in the school, and required a significant time commitment from school staff and teachers. The ABC School Climate Team then discussed the available evidence of effectiveness for the remaining programs. Discussions also occurred regarding how the program fit into the existing programs and services offered in the school, ensuring that implementation of this strategy would not be duplicative of other efforts. Together, these important discussions ultimately led to a decision about a program that might work best in this school community. The ABC School Climate Team then shifted its responsibility from planning to implementing and evaluating this selected tier 1 strategy over time.

OTHER KEY CONSIDERATIONS FOR SCHOOL SOCIAL WORKERS

As school social workers engage in these processes to improve the climate in their own school community, it is important for them to remember that addressing school climate oftentimes requires the support and resources of many key school and community stakeholders. As such, and mentioned above, formation of a school climate team—or expansion of an existing school team—can be an important first step in addressing these priorities. In addition, it is critical that school administrators are involved in these efforts, particularly because their buy-in can help ensure that school climate efforts are prioritized within school improvement plans, that sufficient resources are allocated to the process, and that school climate issues are considered in the development and refinement of school policies and procedures.

Second, it is important to remember that school climate does not only affect the students in a school, but also greatly influences teachers and school staff. School social workers can serve an instrumental role in this area, both through offering professional development for teachers around school climate and through advocacy. In particular, school social workers can advocate for policies and opportunities that help foster a sense of connectedness and build a sense of community among school staff.

Finally, it also is important to consider how community organizations can support school climate efforts. In collaboration with schools, community-based organizations oftentimes have staff, resources, or other forms of support that might be critically important for improving a school's climate. Knowledge and experience in partnership building and coordination make school social workers particularly well suited to lead and support this outreach.

CONCLUSION

Development of a school climate characterized by safety, respect, and responsiveness is foundational to support student learning. As policy makers and scholars continue to prioritize this important school improvement pathway, school social workers have the potential to serve as critical leaders, change agents, and advocates in these efforts. Hopefully, the processes and key considerations around data-driven decision making and selection of evidence-informed tier 1 strategies discussed in this chapter help prepare school social workers to embrace this role and and to make the climates in their own school community more safe, more responsive, and more respectful for those they serve.

References

Adelman, H. S., & Taylor, L. (2002). Building comprehensive, multifaceted, and integrated approaches to address barriers to student learning. *Childhood Education, 78*(5), 261–268.

Allen-Meares, P., Montgomery, K. L., & Kim, J. S. (2013). School-based social work interventions: A cross-national systematic review. *Social Work, 58*(3), 253–262.

Anderson-Butcher, D., Lawson, H., Iachini, A. L., Flaspohler, P., Bean, J., & Wade-Mdivanian, R. (2010). Emergent evidence in support of a community collaboration model for school improvement. *Children & Schools, 32*(3), 160–171.

Centers for Disease Control and Prevention (CDC). (2012). *Understanding youth violence: Fact sheet.* Retrieved from http://www.cdc.gov/violenceprevention/pub/yv_factsheet.html

Clifford, M., Menon, R., Gangi, T., Condon, C., & Hornung, K. (2012). *Measuring school climate for gauging principal performance: A review of the validity and reliability of publicly accessible measures.* Washington DC: American Institutes for Research.

Cohen, J. (2006). Social, emotional, ethical and academic education: Creating a climate for learning, participation in democracy and well-being. *Harvard Educational Review, 76,* 201–237.

Cohen, J., McCabe, E. M., Michelli, N. M., & Pickeral, T. (2009). School climate: Research, policy, practice, and teacher education. *Teachers College Record, 111*(1), 180–213.

Cowan, K. C., Vaillancourt, K., Rossen, E., & Pollitt, K. (2013). *A framework for safe and successful schools* [Brief]. Bethesda, MD: National Association of School Psychologists.

Frey, A. J., & Dupper, D. R. (2005). A broader conceptual approach to clinical practice for the 21st century. *Children & Schools, 27*(1), 33–44.

Hopson, L., & Lawson, H. (2011). Social workers' leadership for positive school climates via data-informed planning and decision making. *Children & Schools, 33*(2), 106–118.

Iachini, A. L., Dorr, C., & Anderson-Butcher, D. (2008). Fostoria Community Schools' innovative approach to refining and coordinating their school-based mental health service delivery system. *Report on Emotional and Behavioral Disorders in Youth, 8*(3), 69–75.

Kidger, J., Araya, R., Donovan, J., & Gunnell, D. (2012). The effect of the school environment on the emotional health of adolescents: A systematic review. *Pediatrics, 129*(5), 925–949.

Kohl, D., Recchia, S., & Steffgen, G. (2013). Measuring school climate: An overview of measurement scales. *Educational Research, 55*(4), 411–426.

McCoy, D. C., Roy, A. L., & Sirkman, G. M. (2013). Neighborhood crime and school climate as predictors of elementary school academic quality: A cross-lagged panel analysis. *American Journal of Community Psychology, 52*, 128–140.

National Center on Safe and Supportive Learning Environments. (2013). *School climate survey compendia.* Retrieved from http://safesupportivelearning.ed.gov/topic-research/school-climate-measurement/school-climate-survey-compendium

No Child Left Behind Act of 2001, Pub. L. 107-110 (2002).

Richman, J. M., Bowen, G. L., & Wooley, M. E. (2004). School failure: An eco-interactional developmental perspective. In M. W. Fraser (Ed.), *Risk and resilience in childhood: An ecological perspective* (2nd ed., pp. 133–160). Washington, DC: National Association of Social Workers.

Safe and Drug-Free Schools and Communities Act of 2004. Title IV, Part A, Subpart 1 Elementary and Secondary Education Act of 1965 as amended by the No Child Left Behind Act of 2001 Pub. L. 107-110 (2004).

Steffgen, G., Recchia, S., & Viechtbauer, W. (2013). The link between school climate and violence in school: A meta-analytic review. *Aggression and Violent Behavior, 18,* 300–309.

Thapa, A., Cohen, J., Guffey, S., & Higgins-D'Alessandro, A. (2013). A review of school climate research. *Review of Educational Research, 83*(3), 357–385.

Wang, C., Berry, B., & Swearer, S. M. (2013). The critical role of school climate in effective bullying prevention. *Theory Into Practice, 52,* 296–302.

White House. (2013). *Now is the time to do something about gun violence.* Retrieved from http://www.whitehouse.gov/issues/preventing-gun-violence

Zullig, K. J., Koopman, T. M., Patton, J. M., & Ubbes, V. A. (2010). School climate: Historical review, instrument, development, and school assessment. *Journal of Psychoeducational Assessment, 28*(2), 139–152.

25

Evidence-Informed Suicide Prevention in Schools

Michael Valenti
Pressley Ridge

Mary Margaret Kerr
University of Pittsburgh

Garry King
Australian Institute for Suicide Research and Prevention, Griffith University

- ◆ Translational Challenges
- ◆ What Do We Know About Youth Suicide?
- ◆ Data Collection
- ◆ Identifying and Referring Students at Risk
- ◆ Formal Mental Health Promotion and Suicide Prevention Programs

"Rhonda, hurry! Meet me in the gym. There's a suicide note on the locker-room mirror," Professor Garcia, Rhonda's principal, shouted over the phone.

Rhonda had worked in the high school as a school social worker for only six months, but already Professor Garcia had come to depend on her during crises. This time was no different. As Rhonda scrambled to identify the author of the note, she realized how unprepared the school was. Teachers looked confused when she asked them about students who might be depressed or suicidal. Mr. Lu's response was typical of what she heard all morning: "I'm just not sure. . . . I'd like to be helpful but how would I know if somebody was suicidal? You know teenagers. They *all* seem stressed out at some point. I'd hate to be wrong about something like this," he said.

In a faculty meeting later that afternoon to review the school's crisis plan, it became clear that the plan was inadequate to address suicide. Walking back to her office, Rhonda overheard a group of ninth-grade teachers talking.

"Sure, I'd tell somebody if I *knew* a kid was suicidal, but sometimes, I think these kids are just trying to get my attention."

"Isn't that the truth? There's a whole lot of drama in ninth grade . . . especially with the girls."

"Yeah. . . . Like the way they rub those erasers into their skin until it bleeds. What's that about, anyway? You can't tell me all *those* kids are suicidal. They keep coming back to school like everyone else."

As the teachers turned to head down the stairs, one stopped walking and turned to Rhonda.

"Now do you see what we've been telling you? Somebody's got to get this suicide plan together. It's not that we don't want to. We are just slammed with all this testing on top of everything else we do."

Later that week, Professor Garcia charged Rhonda with the task of organizing a school-based suicide prevention plan and response. Her initial search uncovered dozens of suicide prevention resources. Rhonda quickly became overwhelmed.

"If *I'm* overwhelmed, how on earth will the faculty respond to all these ideas?" she asked herself.

Rhonda's perplexing situation is not unique. All school-based mental health practitioners face the grave responsibility of preventing youth suicide (Miller & Eckert, 2009). In particular, school social workers often play central leadership roles in the design, coordination, and implementation of suicide prevention programs and policies. School social workers often possess highly influential roles concerning school-based suicide prevention due to several contributing factors. First, school leaders and teachers typically possess limited knowledge regarding mental health and therefore seek the advice of those with specialized training and skills (Caparelli, 2012; Scouller & Smith, 2002). Second, social workers are identified by school personnel with leadership roles in crises, including suicides (Issurdatt, 2013), so school administrators naturally turn to them. Third, school counselors may be unavailable to assist suicide prevention efforts due to a reduction in their numbers (Hurwitz & Howell, 2013) or the reallocation of their time to academic tasks (College Board Advocacy and Policy Center, 2012), leading to an increased workload for school social workers in regards to prevention efforts. Finally, school social workers and social workers in community mental health centers may be the clinicians with whom school-aged youths in treatment may have the most contact.

Despite the centrality of their role, school social workers may be hampered by the knowledge-action gap in suicide prevention (Wilkins et al., 2013), and often fail to recognize risk factors and warning signs of suicide (Osteen, Jacobson, & Sharpe, 2014). A recent study of school social workers indicated that most social workers report low levels of training to work with suicidal youths (Singer & Slovak, 2010). Fewer than 25 percent of social workers in a nationwide survey reported receiving any training in suicide prevention, while a majority reported that their training had been inadequate (Feldman & Freedenthal, 2006). Therefore, this chapter outlines specific recommendations for school social workers engaged in suicide prevention. Our recommendations reflect research in the assessment, treatment, and crisis management of suicidal students, are responsive to school culture (Kerr, 2009), and are reflective of the role of school social workers.

Implementing comprehensive, school-based suicide prevention practices is a complex effort requiring collaboration of professionals within and outside of the school ecosystem. Effective prevention involves multiple levels of influence and addresses multiple risk factors (Nation et al., 2003). Therefore, a comprehensive review of youth suicide prevention and clinical intervention is beyond the scope of this chapter. For a review of current research on youth suicide interventions, see Brent et al. (2013). For a detailed guide to suicide prevention in schools, see Substance Abuse and Mental Health Services Administration (SAMHSA; 2012). Rather, this chapter has four specific goals:

1. To highlight the important translational role of the school social worker when collaborating with school faculty and staff unfamiliar with this field
2. To identify evidence-informed prevention practices suitable for the school context
3. To share easily accessed, yet reliable resources for ongoing professional growth and program design
4. To highlight unresolved questions in school-based suicide prevention, including popular and/or promising approaches for which more research is needed

First, we review the many translational challenges that school social workers face when implementing suicide prevention efforts, including the need to interpret for school personnel the terminology associated with youth suicide and to help them grasp the complexity of suicide. Next, we present a brief review of the literature concerning youth suicide, including prevalence, risk factors, and common behavioral indicators. The third part of this chapter offers guidance on data collection to inform the school's prevention programming. After all, each community has its own culture; youths living in those communities engage in risk behaviors and access supports differently. Finally, the chapter offers examples of formal mental health promotion and suicide prevention programs that school social workers can implement.

TRANSLATIONAL CHALLENGES

School personnel have been asked to play a greater role in promoting students' mental health and wellness (Miller, Gilman, & Martens, 2007), particularly in the area of suicide prevention (Power, DuPaul, Shapiro, & Kazak, 2003). Yet, as our opening case illustrated, school personnel may be unprepared to use the technical language that characterizes this field. For this reason, school social workers may first need to articulate key terms, especially when those terms connote specific protocols in a crisis. In a critical incident, the response hinges on clear communication. For example, a suicide completion calls for one set of actions, whereas a suicide threat calls for a different protocol.

Defining Key Terms

Suicide prevention work is often highly specialized. Trained professionals often use terminology specifically related to suicide; those who are not trained in mental health may have heard these terms but may be unclear as to their precise meanings. Three key terms are "suicide threat," "suicide attempt," and "suicide completion" (U.S. Surgeon General and the National Action Alliance for Suicide Prevention, 2012). A suicide threat is a verbal or nonverbal communication that the individual intends to harm him- or herself with the intention to die but has not acted on the threat. A suicide attempt is a potentially self-injurious behavior for which there is evidence that the person probably intended to kill him- or herself. A suicide attempt may result in death, injuries, or no injuries. The term "self-harm" refers to an individual's acts that result in physical harm, but not death. These may or may not be suicidal. However, nonsuicidal self-harm has emerged as a strong predictor of both attempted and completed suicide (Asarnow, Porta et al., 2011; Brent, 2011). Finally, a suicide completion is death from injury, poisoning, or suffocation where there is initial indication or evidence that a self-inflicted act may have led to the person's death.

It is important for school staff to understand the distinction between these terms to avoid confusion during times of crisis. In addition, school policies, procedures, and communications regarding completed suicides should avoid describing the deceased in these ways: "committed suicide," "killed him- or herself," or "took his or her own life." These terms may be harmful to loved ones because they imply that the individual was making a rational decision. An alternative is to say that the person "died by suicide."

Interpreting Three Fundamental Concepts

Contagion. Research supports a contagion factor associated with suicidal behavior in adolescents, making it fundamentally different from other school crises (Gould, Jamieson, & Romer, 2003). Spatial or temporal clustering of suicides is more common among adolescents than among other age groups (Hawton, Hawton, Niedzwiedz, & Platt, 2013; Kutcher & Szumilas, 2008) and may account for up to 10 percent of all youth suicides (Shaffer, 2004).

School social workers should help colleagues understand that exposure to a classmate's suicide attempt may prompt suicidal behavior in other students, calling for immediate and decisive action on the part of school personnel. Young people most vulnerable to contagion immediately following a suicide generally are characterized as more isolated, not close to the suicide victims, and exhibiting the risk factors identified later in this chapter. Surveillance of those at risk continues long after the initial crisis. Therefore, school personnel need to understand the concept of contagion and why a suicide crisis response—unlike many other school crises—warrants personnel's vigilance over time.

Even indirect exposure to social media, TV programs, and news stories on suicide may prompt suicidal behavior in vulnerable adolescents. Therefore, prevention extends beyond the school to include educating reporters, editors, and producers about contagion to minimize harm and emphasize the media's positive role in educating and shaping attitudes about suicide (Pirkis, Blood, Beautrais, Burgess, & Skehan, 2006).

Mental Illness as a Primary Risk Factor. Many factors increase the risk of suicide, but the most reliable and robust risk factor is the presence of mental illness. Estimates indicate that approximately 90 percent of young people who die by suicide had at least one mental illness at the time of their death (Fleischmann, Bertolote, Belfer, & Beautrais, 2005).

The Influence of Stressful Events. If left unchecked, a one-dimensional mental model of "Too much stress causes suicide" can result in perceptions such as "He has everything going for him, why would he try suicide?" or "She's the valedictorian and got into her first-choice school. . . . You don't need to worry about her." Framing suicide risk solely as a response to stressful life events can undermine efforts to identify other risk factors that are harder to discern such as depression, anxiety, family violence, and substance abuse. Without question, stressful life events can contribute to suicidal behavior in a vulnerable student. However, "There is now ample evidence that suicidal behavior is not an understandable response to adversity but is rather a fatal complication of an underlying mental illness that has gone untreated, has been inadequately treated, or, in some instances, is untreatable" (Shaffer, 2004, p. 517). Therefore, social workers must help colleagues conceptualize suicide more appropriately. Providing education, as well as debunking misinformation or myths in the workplace is but one process the school-based social worker can commence to assist others in this broader understanding of mental illness and its impact on students.

WHAT DO WE KNOW ABOUT YOUTH SUICIDE?

Suicide is the third leading cause of death for American young people aged ten to twenty-four years, killing 4,600 young people each year (Centers for Disease Control and Prevention [CDC], 2012). Children younger than twelve years old are a growing cause for concern, and suicide is the twelfth leading cause of death in this age group (Tishler, Reiss, & Rhodes, 2007). The most recent available data suggest that 2,014 teens between the ages of thirteen and nineteen die by suicide in one year in the United States (CDC, 2014a), and 16 percent of students in grades nine to twelve report having seriously considered suicide (Substance Abuse and Mental Health Services Administration [SAMHSA], 2011). These data stress that youth suicide is an important concern, especially for secondary school personnel. School social workers can familiarize educators with demographic characteristics, risk factors, and warning signs; together these factors help school personnel identify those at risk.

Demographic Characteristics

In America, completed suicide is four times higher among males (CDC, 2012), although females experience suicidal ideation and make more suicide attempts (males use more lethal means). In the United States, youth suicide rates are highest among Native Americans and lowest among those classified by the U.S. government as black (CDC, 2012). Concerning sexual orientation, studies have identified "a two- to six-fold increased risk of non-lethal suicidal behavior for homosexual and bisexual youths" (Gould, Greenberg, Velting, & Shaffer, 2003, p. 390).

Risk Factors

In this part of the chapter, we review key risk factors and their implications for those working in schools. Risk factors are characteristics that have been associated with (but do not necessarily cause) suicide. These include

- Depression and other mental disorders;
- Substance abuse disorder (often in combination with other mental disorders);
- Prior suicide attempt;
- Family history of suicide;
- Family violence including physical or sexual abuse;
- Firearms in the home;
- Incarceration or being imprisoned and
- Exposure to suicidal behavior of others, such as family members or peers (National Institute of Mental Health, 2014).

Mental Illness. As mentioned above, mental illness is a major underlying risk factor for suicide. If not identified and treated, mental health disorders (in isolation or comorbid with other mental health disorders) can increase the risk for suicidal thoughts and/or behaviors in vulnerable individuals. Unfortunately, educators typically receive little training in mental illness, so the school social worker may want to review symptoms of mood disorders, anxiety disorders, and substance abuse disorders with school staff. In the later part of this chapter on formal mental health promotion and suicide prevention programs, we include resources to assist students in learning about mental health disorders. Moreover, the school social worker should remain vigilant to the fact that there are very likely staff who themselves are struggling with these disorders.

Prior Attempts. According to the *Youth Risk Behavior Surveillance System* (CDC, 2015), during the prior twelve months,

- 17 percent of American high school students reported having seriously considered suicide,
- 13.6 percent had made a plan about how they would attempt suicide,
- 8 percent had attempted suicide, and
- 2.7 percent made a suicidal attempt that required medical treatment (CDC, 2014b).

Studies have shown that 15 percent to 30 percent of adolescent attempters reattempt within one year (Bridge, Goldstein, & Brent, 2006; Hawton et al., 2012). These data can help the school social worker assess the general level of case finding, or how many cases are coming to the school's attention. Such case finding is important, because young people with a history of prior suicide attempts are at much higher risk of suicide completion than those who have no history of attempts. School social workers will no doubt be called on to monitor students after hospitalizations for attempts, because the risk of a repeated attempt is greatest then (Brent et al., 2013). Research shows that between 30 percent and 50 percent of youth attempters do not adhere to treatment recommendations (Asarnow, Baraff, et al., 2011; Trautman, Stewart, & Morishima, 1993). School-based social workers face significant challenges, therefore, in reducing risk factors and increasing protective factors for these students returning after an attempted suicide. We recommend that school social workers formally develop and establish a safety plan with the student and the family.

Family History of Suicide. A two- to six-fold increase of suicidal behavior is found in the relatives of adolescent suicide victims and suicide attempters (Agerbo, Nordentoft, & Mortensen, 2002; Borowsky, Ireland, & Resnick, 2001; Fergusson, Beautrais, Horwood, 2003; Rey-Gex, Narring, Ferron, & Michaud, 1998). Acquiring knowledge about students' family history of suicidal behavior requires not only working with and monitoring the school cohort, but also engaging actively with parents.

Family Violence, Including Physical and Sexual Abuse. Violence and suicidality mutually affect each other from adolescence into young adulthood. One study confirmed previous findings by demonstrating that violence is a risk factor for future suicide (Van Dulmen et al., 2013). An increased risk for ideation and suicide attempts are associated with childhood abuse (Gal, Levav, & Gross, 2012).

Substance Abuse. Substance abuse prevention is critical to suicide prevention. An increased prevalence of drugs or alcohol is a factor accounting for why older adolescents are more likely to attempt and complete suicide compared to younger adolescents. Some adolescents use drugs and alcohol to cope with depressive feelings. Alcohol also does not seem to inhibit suicidal behavior. A high percentage of young people who attempt suicide do so either during or immediately after their use of drugs or alcohol (Bagge et al., 2013). We know that adolescents who are depressed and use alcohol are also more likely to use a firearm (Bridge et al., 2006).

Access to Firearms. Because access to firearms is a major risk factor, school social workers may want to engage in parent education about safeguarding weapons when their children are identified for other problems such as depression or substance abuse. Educating parents to keep guns locked and unloaded, and to store ammunition in a locked compartment in a separate location are all practical strategies in the reduction of suicide risk (Grossman et al., 2005). While this may appear to be common sense, previous efforts at getting parents to remove firearms have had mixed results (Brent, Baugher, Birmaher, Kolko, & Bridge, 2000; Grossman et al., 2000). In addition, school social workers may be called on to create interview protocols for school counselors and others who screen students of concern. These interviews should ask about access to lethal weapons, including firearms. For specific weapons interviewing guidance, see Pittel (1998).

Additional risk factors include social isolation, limited access to mental health facilities, poor problem-solving and coping skills, child abuse and other trauma, parental psychopathology (Kuramoto, Brent, & Wilcox, 2009; Runeson & Asberg, 2003), and repeated engagement in or exposure to violence.

Warning Signs

Warning signs signal the need to get help from a staff member trained to detect and refer those at risk for suicide. Here are some signs that school personnel could observe and report:

- Talking about wanting to die or to take one's life
- Searching for a lethal weapon, pills, or suicide instructions
- Expressing hopelessness about the future or about a situation (e.g., feeling trapped)
- Talking about having no options, or not being able to bear the pain
- Claiming to be a burden to others (e.g., "My parents would be better off without me")
- Talking about harming others
- Increasing alcohol or drug intake
- Appearing highly anxious or agitated
- Engaging in reckless behavior
- Withdrawing from typical activities and relationships
- Displaying extreme mood swings (Rudd et al., 2006)

Youths considering suicide may also exhibit behaviors that may indicate their intentions. Suicidal teens may begin writing or talking about death and suicide. Clues may also appear in art and music projects, essays, diaries, or journals. Occasionally, suicidal teens begin giving away prized possessions, perhaps mentioning that "You can have this. I won't be needing it anymore." Other warning signs include writing wills, suicide notes, or saying "good-bye" in an untimely way (Kerr, 2009).

DATA COLLECTION

Because suicidal youths may never seek treatment or share their plans with others, school personnel face the daunting task of trying to identify who may be at risk. Formal, purposeful data collection, including data about risk-taking behaviors, can inform prevention efforts. Another use for data collection is to evaluate how well prevention programs are working. Yet many school social workers may find that their schools do not have data on student risk behaviors or outcomes associated with classroom prevention programs.

Gathering data on the behaviors that place youths at heightened risk is an essential component of school-based suicide prevention. Therefore, it is suggested that schools use an established anonymous survey to gather information that can

- ◆ Inform schools about the risk-taking behaviors of youths in the community,
- ◆ Aid schools in successful grant applications for additional funding for prevention and intervention, and
- ◆ Inform strategic planning and staffing of prevention and intervention efforts.

One such assessment is the Youth Risk Behavior Surveillance System, available at no cost from the CDC (2015). Schools and districts may modify the questionnaire depending on community needs and interests. The standard Youth Risk Behavior Surveillance System questionnaire takes about thirty-five minutes to complete. Ideally, the survey should be completed prior to selecting prevention and response measures, because information gathered via the questionnaire should be used to select intervention services and personnel. "The process of introducing data allows each school to identify its specific needs, limitations, strengths, and resources so choices can be made regarding which specific interventions and components to implement" (Astor, Benbenishty, & Meyer, 2004, p. 40). For example, if results indicate that an alarming number of middle school students are experimenting with prescription drugs or alcohol, then a prevention program could target those students while the high school partners with intervention and recovery resources in the community.

IDENTIFYING AND REFERRING STUDENTS AT RISK

Assessing the prevalence of risk behaviors across the student population serves as an initial step to help identify students at risk; however, most experts suggest that successful prevention programs also include student screening to identify students struggling with mental health problems (Gould, 2009). Because mental illness underlies most suicides, many prevention approaches include screening as a part of the program. Formal screening programs can identify mental health problems and suicidal intent in students that may not be recognized by school staff members (Scott et al., 2009). A screening program may also assist in identifying any students who have made previous attempts or who are depressed and facilitate their evaluation and treatment (Shaffer, 2004). Suicide screening programs have been found to be safe (Gould, Marrocco, & Kleinman, 2005), and a large body of research (Guiterrez, Watkins, & Collura, 2004; Mazza, 1997; Miller & DuPaul, 1996) advocates their use in prevention. On the other hand, there are limited data at this time in regards to their effectiveness for reducing suicidal behavior (Miller, Eckert, & Mazza, 2009).

For example, the Columbia TeenScreen Program uses a multistage screening process that (1) teaches teens about depression and treatment, and encourages them to identify and refer themselves; and (2) systematically screens each teen for anxiety, depression, substance abuse, and suicidality. When faced with an at-risk student, school district personnel often use different (or informal) interview questions. We recommend that school social workers review how personnel are talking with at-risk students and also consider adopting a uniform protocol.

Assessing the needs and risk of the student population is important, but educators must also respond to crises. Often, the first response of a school staff member is to refer the student to a school social worker (Kelly, Moses, Ornstein, & Massat, 2009). Interventions known as "gatekeeper" training programs are designed to help staff members make the appropriate referral. Gatekeeper training refers to educating staff members of the school and community in how to interact with youths who may be at risk for suicide. Research has demonstrated that training gatekeepers can improve competencies for intervening and that these skills can be retained over time (Davidson & Range, 1999; Tompkins, Witt, & Abraibesh, 2009; Wyman et al., 2008). Gatekeeper training programs teach school staff members to (1) recognize individuals at risk for suicidal behavior and (2) make a referral to the appropriate mental health service or professional. All employees must be alerted to those at highest risk—males sixteen to nineteen, teens with mental health or substance abuse problems, teens who are lesbian, gay, bisexual, transgender, and questioning (LGBTQ), and those who have attempted suicide or engaged in self-harm. Additionally, it is helpful to address the plethora of myths and misinformation that often exists within communities.

Whether schools adopt formal or informal gatekeeper training, the training should explain specific suicide-related concepts such as contagion, how to identify warning signs for suicidal behavior and other high-risk behavior, and how to refer students. One example of an effective gatekeeper training program is QPR (Question, Persuade, and Refer) Gatekeeper Training for Suicide Prevention (Quinnett, 1995). The QPR training consists of three actionable steps:

1. Question the student's desire or intent regarding suicide.
2. Persuade the student to seek and accept help.
3. Refer the student to the appropriate resources.

Staff members can be trained online in one to two hours for general training (or three to four hours for specialized training), making QPR a highly accessible intervention. Those who complete the training receive wallet cards that serve to reinforce their roles and describe actions to take when detecting a suicidal student. Gatekeeper training programs such as QPR are effective if gatekeepers obtain the knowledge to identify those at risk and have confidence in their ability to use their skills (Goldston et al., 2010).

To expand their screening and gatekeeper training efforts, school social workers in the United States can publicize the National Suicide Prevention Lifeline (1-800-273-TALK) and its Web site (www.suicidepreventionlifeline .org). This free network of 162 crisis centers in fifty states is staffed twenty-four hours a day, seven days a week, and serves as anonymous outreach for individuals experiencing suicidal thoughts. Individuals in crisis or those concerned about them can also use the online chat to contact a counselor. The Web site offers free wallet cards, posters, and other materials for dissemination in schools.

FORMAL MENTAL HEALTH PROMOTION AND SUICIDE PREVENTION PROGRAMS

Suicide prevention models often stress very different approaches, making it difficult for school social workers to determine the most effective ways to prevent youth suicide. The first category of suicide prevention approaches emphasizes protective factors and peer support networks (e.g., Kalafat, 2003; Mazza & Reynolds, 2008). The second category derives from child psychiatry or public health and tends to focus on risk factors, identification, referral, and treatment (e.g., Bridge et al., 2006). Finally, a third category of suicide prevention methods stems from the direct personal experiences of those who have lost a loved one to suicide (Yellow Ribbon Suicide Prevention Program). Also see chapters 32 and 33 in this volume for additional information regarding mental health issues in schools and crisis intervention in schools.

Many formal prevention programs adhere to one or more of these theoretical orientations and generally include presentations and/or curricula designed for reducing suicide in the school setting. Informal programs may include suicide-focused classroom or large-group instruction that does not emphasize mental health promotion or treatment and other components such as screening. School social workers should be cautious about programs that focus exclusively on suicide (e.g., testimonials from suicide attempters) because the content may be disturbing to vulnerable students and thereby increase their risk. In fact, the American Academy of Child and Adolescent Psychiatry (2001) recommends that prevention efforts focus not specifically on suicide, but rather on characteristics of mental illness and substance abuse that may predispose one to suicidality.

Lack of information about the critical role of mental illness was demonstrated in a recent study indicating that fewer than 20 percent of students thought that mental illness was a major contributor to suicide (Lake, Kandasamy, Kleinman, & Gould, 2013). This attitude may be influenced by the prevalence of negative and inaccurate media portrayals of mental illness. To summarize, "In light of the risk of normalizing suicide on the one hand, and of stigmatizing attitudes toward mental illness on the other, youth suicide prevention programs might best leave aside the complex question of the etiology of suicidal behavior and focus instead on promoting positive messaging regarding the possibility of getting help and the use of positive coping mechanisms by students in distress" (Lake et al., 2013, p. 701). School social workers might encourage communities to adopt campaigns to reduce the stigma of help seeking for mental health problems.

Fortunately, school social workers can turn to the National Registry of Evidence-based Programs and Practices to learn about peer-reviewed programs with defined outcomes, including improved ability of adults to identify youths in need of mental health services, increased knowledge of mental health conditions and/or suicidal indicators, increased knowledge of prevention resources, and reductions in suicide attempts. A matrix of school-based suicide prevention programs from the National Registry is included in *Preventing Suicide: A Toolkit for High Schools* (SAMHSA, 2012).

A common concern about any district's prevention programs is whether the programs are being implemented with fidelity. Implementation fidelity is important because it assures districts that the program is being implemented in the manner in which the reported positive outcomes were achieved in evaluation studies. Though not the responsibility of the school social worker, districts should find a way to monitor implementation of any prevention curricula.

Informal Curricula, Textbooks, and Library Books

Misinformation about suicide can creep into classes such as health, psychology, and English, so a school-based suicide prevention plan should include a review of curricula and a discussion with teachers about how they cover this topic in class. Curriculum supervisors may want to monitor any informal activities that might expose students to the suicidality of others (e.g., autobiographical activities in which a student might disclose suicidal ideation or attempts). While one should discourage the use of a stress model to explain suicide, instructors should endorse high-quality efforts to teach students healthy approaches to managing stress.

If a suicide completion occurs, the school social worker may recommend that the district pull from circulation textbooks that show the names of the deceased students (i.e., the student's name appears in the front of the textbook because the student was issued that book for the year). Districts should not merely cover over these names, lest students uncover them.

Similarly, district librarians might be alerted to evaluate holdings of non-fiction books regarding suicide, substance abuse, and other mental health topics. Mental health treatment has changed dramatically during the past two decades, offering far more hope than in prior years. Older volumes may not contain accurate information or may contribute to the stigma of help-seeking for mental health or substance abuse problems.

As an alternative, excellent texts for professionals, parents, and youths can be found on the CopeCareDeal Web site (www.copecaredeal.org). This site is funded by the Annenberg Foundation Trust through its Adolescent Mental Health Initiative and is extensively reviewed by experts. The Web site "synthesize[s] and disseminate[s] scientific research on the prevention and treatment of mental disorders in adolescents. This initiative produced the award-winning *Treating and Preventing Adolescent Mental Health Disorders: What We Know and What We Don't Know*, a definitive guide book for mental health professionals; a series of four books for parents, counselors and others concerned with the prevention and treatment of mental disorders in adolescents; and eight books for teens designed to help them cope with prevalent mental health disorders, including depression and substance abuse" (www.copecaredeal.org), which school social workers may find useful to recommend to students and families.

Drug and Alcohol Services

Many students are struggling with drug and alcohol problems themselves or within their families. Support groups for students who are in recovery or who are coping with substance issues in their families are important to recovery and can be hosted in the community. In addition, school leaders should consider designating a drug and alcohol coordinator (typically someone already on staff) for each of its middle and high schools. A district may also want to institute and disseminate a directory of families who pledge not to serve alcohol to minors. Families who participate or read about this may feel supported in their attempts to limit their children's underage use of alcohol.

Parent Education

District communications with parents constitute an opportunity for important psychoeducation. Communications include conversations with parents, parent forums, parent handbooks, parent letters, and communications to the public that may be heard or read by parents. School social workers should review such communications to ensure that they convey helpful and accurate information. (SAMHSA [2012] has examples and templates for communications.)

Despite outreach efforts, many parents do not know how to access quality mental health services. School social workers can partner with community providers to provide information for all parents on when and how to access mental health services for crisis and noncrisis situations, including nights, weekends, and over school breaks. This may require collaboration with commercial insurers as well. The National Suicide Prevention Lifeline (1-800-273-TALK) is a good resource to share with parents.

CONCLUSION

Though we know much about effective suicide prevention, many questions remain unanswered. These unanswered questions and the ensuing debates can be overwhelming to a school social worker trying to make good decisions and to guide less-knowledgeable colleagues. To heighten the challenge further, the school-based suicide prevention field is advancing rapidly, as we accumulate new knowledge that confirms or offers alternatives to contemporary approaches.Finally, some promising prevention practices remain to be fully evaluated (Robinson et al., 2013). This includes better understanding of protective factors, including the promotion of sobriety, healthy sleep, and positive affect (Brent et al., 2013).

The role of social workers in preventing suicide is well documented, indicating a critical need for school social workers to possess the knowledge, skills, and resources required to work with those who may be at risk for suicide (Osteen et al., 2014). Across the country, schools have begun to require suicide prevention training for all staff (American Foundation for Suicide Prevention, 2014). Most of these trainings recommend referral to a qualified mental health professional such as a school social worker (Schmitz et al., 2012). Without question, school social workers will continue to play an important role not only in today's suicide prevention efforts, but also in creating the knowledge that will unlock a brighter future for vulnerable youths.

References

Agerbo, E., Nordentoft, M., & Mortensen, P. B. (2002). Familial, psychiatric, and socio-economic risk factors for suicide in young people: Nested case–control study. *British Medical Journal, 325,* 74.

American Academy of Child and Adolescent Psychiatry. (2001). *Practice parameter for the treatment of children and adolescents with suicidal behavior.* Retrieved from http://www.jaacap.com/article/S0890-8567(09)60355-5/pdf

American Foundation for Suicide Prevention. (2014). *State laws on suicide prevention training for school personnel.* Retrieved from http://www.afsp.org/content/download/7133/130923/file/School%20Personnel%20Training%20Overview.pdf

Asarnow, J. R., Baraff, L. J., Berk, M., Grob, C. S., Devich-Navarro, M., Suddath, R. . . . & Tang, L. (2011). An emergency department intervention for linking pediatric suicidal patients to follow-up mental health treatment. *Psychiatric Services, 62*(11), 1303–1309.

Asarnow, J. R., Porta, G., Spirito, A., Emslie, G., Clarke, G., Wagner, K. D., . . . & Brent, D. A. (2011). Suicide attempts and non-suicidal self-injury in the treatment of resistant depression in adolescents: Findings from TORDIA study. *Journal of the Academy of Child and Adolescent Psychiatry, 50*(8), 772–781.

Astor, R. A., Benbenishty, R., & Meyer, H. A. (2004). Monitoring and mapping student victimization in schools. *Theory into Practice, 43,* 39–49.

Bagge, C. L., Lee, H. J., Schumacher, J. A., Gratz, K. L., Krull, J. L., & Holloman, G. (2013). Alcohol as an acute risk factor for recent suicide attempts: A case-crossover analysis. *Journal for Study of Alcohol and Drugs, 74*(4), 552–558.

Borowsky, I. W., Ireland, M., & Resnick, M. D. (2001). Adolescent suicide attempts: Risks and protectors. *Pediatrics, 107*(3), 485–493.

Brent, D. A. (2011). Nonsuicidal self-injury as a predictor of suicidal behavior in depressed adolescents. *American Journal of Psychiatry, 168*(5), 452–454.

Brent, D. A., Baugher, M., Birmaher, B., Kolko, D. J., & Bridge, J. (2000). Compliance with recommendations to remove firearms in families participating in a clinical trial for adolescent depression. *Journal of the American Academy of Child and Adolescent Psychiatry, 39*(10), 1220–1226.

Brent, D. A., McMakin, D. L., Kennard, B. D., Goldstein, T. R., Mayes, T. L., & Douaihy, A. B. (2013). Protecting adolescents from self-harm: A critical review of intervention studies. *Journal of the American Academy of Child and Adolescent Psychiatry, 52*(12), 1260–1271.

Bridge, J. A., Goldstein, T. R., & Brent, D. A. (2006). Adolescent suicide and suicidal behavior. *Journal of Child Psychology and Psychiatry, 47*(3–4), 372–394.

Caparelli, S. M. (2012). *School leadership and school mental health: An exploratory study of SMH content in the preparation of principals.* (Doctoral dissertation). Retrieved from http://d-scholarship.pitt.edu/13476/1/FINALDissCaparelli080712.pdf

Centers for Disease Control and Prevention (CDC). (2012). *Youth risk behavior surveillance—United States, 2011.* Retrieved from http://www.cdc.gov/mmwr/pdf/ss/ss6104.pdf

Centers for Disease Control and Prevention (CDC). (2014a). *WISQARS: Leading causes of death.* Retrieved from http://webappa.cdc.gov/sasweb/ncipc/leadcaus10_us.html

Centers for Disease Control and Prevention (CDC). (2014b). *Youth risk behavior surveillance—United States 2013.* Retrieved from http://www.cdc.gov/mmwr/pdf/ss/ss6304.pdf

Centers for Disease Control and Prevention (CDC). (2015). *Youth risk behavior surveillance system (YRBSS).* Retrieved from http://www.cdc.gov/healthyyouth/data/yrbs/index.htm

College Board Advocacy and Policy Center. (2012). *National survey of school counselors and administrators.* New York: College Board.

Davidson, M. W., & Range, L. M. (1999). Are teachers of children and young adolescents responsive to suicide prevention training modules? Yes. *Death Studies, 23,* 61–71.

Feldman, B. N., & Freedenthal, S. (2006). Social work education in suicide intervention and prevention: An unmet need? *Suicide and Life-Threatening Behavior, 36*(4), 467–480.

Fergusson, D. M., Beautrais, A. L., & Horwood, L. J. (2003). Vulnerability and resiliency to suicidal behaviours in young people. *Psychological Medicine, 33,* 61–73.

Fleischmann, A., Bertolote, J. M., Belfer, M., & Beautrais, A. (2005). Completed suicide and psychiatric diagnoses in young people: Examination of the evidence. *American Journal of Orthopsychiatry, 75*(4), 676–683.

Gal, G., Levav, I., & Gross, R. (2012). Child/adolescent abuse and suicidal behavior: Are they sex related? *Suicide and Life-Threatening Behavior, 42*(5), 580–588.

Goldston, D. B., Walrath, C. M., McKeon, R., Puddy, R. W., Lubell, K. M., Potter, L. B., & Rodi, M. S. (2010). The Garrett Lee Smith Memorial Suicide Prevention Program. *Suicide and Life-Threatening Behavior, 40*(3), 245–256.

Gould, M. S. (2009, January). Preventing youth suicide: A review of school-based strategies. Symposium conducted at the Garrett Lee Smith Suicide Prevention Grantee Meeting, Phoenix, AZ.

Gould, M. S., Greenberg, T., Velting, D. M., & Shaffer, D. (2003). Youth suicide risk and preventive interventions: A review of the past 10 years. *American Academy of Child & Adolescent Psychiatry, 42*(4), 386–405.

Gould, M. S., Jamieson, D., & Romer, D. (2003). Media contagion and suicide among the young. *American Behavioral Scientist, 46*(9), 1269–1284.

Gould, M. S., Marrocco, F. A., & Kleinman, M. (2005). Evaluating iatrogenic risk of youth suicide screening programs: A randomized controlled trial. *Journal of the American Medical Association, 293,* 1635–1643.

Grossman, D. C., Cummings, P., Koepsell, T. D., Marshall, J., D'Ambrosio, L., Thompson, R. S., & Mack, C.(2000). Firearm safety counseling in primary care pediatrics: A randomized, controlled trial. *Pediatrics, 106*(1 Pt 1), 22–26.

Grossman, D. C., Mueller, B. A., Riedy, C., Dowd, M. D., Villaveces, A., Prodzinski, J., . . . & Harruff, R. (2005). Gun storage practices and risk of youth suicide and unintentional firearm injuries. *Journal of the American Medical Association, 293*(6), 707–714.

Guiterrez, P. M., Watkins, R., & Collura, D. (2004). Suicide risk screening in an urban high school. *Suicide and Life Threatening Behavior, 34*(4), 421–428.

Hawton, C., Hawton, K., Niedzwiedz, C., & Platt, S. (2013). Suicide clusters: A review of risk factors and mechanisms. *Suicide and Life-Threatening Behavior, 43*(1), 97–108.

Hawton, K., Bergen, H., Kapur, N., Cooper, J., Steeg, S., Ness, J., & Waters, K. (2012). Repetition of self-harm and suicide following self-harm in children and adolescents: Findings from the Multicentre Study of Self-harm in England. *Journal of Child Psychology and Psychiatry, 53*(12), 1212–1219.

Hurwitz, M., & Howell, J. (2013). *Measuring the impact of high school counselors on college enrollment.* New York: College Board.

Issurdatt, S. (2013, April). The school social worker in crisis situations: The right skills, the right profession, *Practice Perspectives, Spring.* Retrieved from http://www.social workers.org/assets/secured/documents/practice/schoolsocialworkerincrisis.pdf

Kalafat, J. (2003). School approaches to youth suicide prevention. *American Behavioral Scientist, 46,* 1211–1223.

Kelly, M. S., Moses, H., Ornstein, E. D., & Massat, C. R. (2009). Mental health and school social work. In C. R. Massat, R. Constable, S. McDonald, & J. P. Flynn (Eds.), *School social work: Practice, policy and research* (7th ed., pp. 464–493). Chicago: Lyceum Books.

Kerr, M. M. (2009). *School crisis intervention and prevention,* Upper Saddle River, NJ: Pearson Education.

Kuramoto, S. J., Brent, D. A., & Wilcox, H. C. (2009). The impact of parental suicide on child and adolescent offspring. *Suicide and Life-Threatening Behavior, 39*(2), 137–151.

Kutcher, S. P., & Szumilas, M. (2008). Youth suicide prevention. *Canadian Medical Association Journal, 178*(3), 282–285.

Lake, A. M., Kandasamy, S., Kleinman, M., & Gould, M. S. (2013). Adolescents' attitudes about the role of mental illness in suicide, and their association with suicide risk. *Suicide & Life-Threatening Behavior, 43*(6), 692–703.

Mazza, J. J. (1997). School-based suicide prevention programs: Are they effective? *School Psychology Review, 26,* 382–396.

Mazza, J. J., & Reynolds, W. M. (2008). School-wide approaches to prevention of and treatment for depression and suicidal behaviors. In B. Doll & J. A. Cummings (Eds.), *Transforming school mental health services* (pp. 213–241). Thousand Oaks, CA: Corwin.

Miller, D. N., & DuPaul, G. J. (1996). School-based prevention of adolescent suicide: Issues, obstacles, and recommendations for practice. *Journal of Emotional and Behavioral Disorders, 4*(4), 221–230.

Miller, D. N., & Eckert, T. L. (2009). Youth suicidal behavior: An introduction and overview. *School Psychology Review, 38*(2), 153–167.

Miller, D. N., Eckert, T. L., & Mazza, J. J. (2009). Suicide prevention programs in the schools: A review and public health perspective. *School Psychology Review, 38*(2), 168–188.

Miller, D. N., Gilman, R., & Martens, M. P. (2007). Wellness promotion in the schools: Enhancing students' mental and physical health. *Psychology in the Schools, 45,* 5–15.

Nation, M., Crusto, C., Wandersman, A., Kumpfer, K. L., Seybolt, D., Morrissey-Kane, E., & Davino, K. (2003). What works in prevention: Principles of effective prevention programs. *American Psychologist, 58*(6), 449–456.

National Institute of Mental Health (NIMH). (2014). *Suicide prevention: Who is at risk for suicide?* Retrieved from http://www.nimh.nih.gov/health/topics/suicide-prevention/index.shtml

Osteen, P. J., Jacobson, J. M., & Sharpe, T. L. (2014). Suicide prevention in social work education: How prepared are social work students? *Journal of Social Work Education, 50*(1), 349–364.

Pirkis, J., Blood, R. W., Beautrais, A., Burgess, P., & Skehan, J. (2006). Media guidelines on the reporting of suicide. *Crisis: The Journal of Crisis Intervention and Suicide Prevention, 27*(2), 82–87.

Pittel, E. M. (1998). How to take a weapons history: Interviewing children at risk for violence at school. *Journal of the American Academy of Child & Adolescent Psychiatry, 37*(10), 1100–1102.

Power, T. J., DuPaul, G. J., Shapiro, E. S., & Kazak, A. E. (2003). *Promoting children's health: Integrating school, family, and community.* New York: Guilford Press.

Quinnett, P. (1995). *QPR: Ask a question, save a life.* Spokane, WA: The QPR Institute.

Rey-Gex, C., Narring, F., Ferron, C., & Michaud, P. A. (1998). Suicide attempts among adolescents in Switzerland: Prevalence, associated factors and comorbidity. *Acta Psychiatrica Scandinavica, 98,* 28–33.

Robinson, J., Cox, G., Malone, A., Williamson, M., Baldwin, G., Fletcher, K., & O'Brien, M. (2013). A systematic review of school-based interventions aimed at preventing, treating, and responding to suicide-related behavior in young people. *Journal of Crisis Intervention and Suicide Prevention, 34*(3), 164–182.

Rudd, M. D., Berman, A. L., Joiner, T. E., Nock, M. K., Silverman, M., Mandrusiak, M., . . . & Witte, T. (2006). Warning signs for suicide: Theory, research, and clinical applications. *Suicide and Life-Threatening Behavior, 36*(3), 255–262.

Runeson, B., & Asberg, M. (2003). Family history of suicide among suicide victims. *American Journal of Psychiatry, 160*(8), 1525–1526.

Schmitz, W. M., Allen, M. H., Feldman, B. N., Gutin, N. J., Jahn, D. R., Kleespies, P. M., . . . & Simpson, S. (2012). Preventing suicide through improved training in suicide risk assessment and care: An American Association of Suicidology Task Force Report addressing serious gaps in U.S. mental health training. *Suicide and Life-Threatening Behavior, 42*(3), 292–304.

Scott, M. A., Wilcox, H. C., Schonfeld, I. S., Davies, M., Hicks, R. C., Turner, J. B., & Shaffer, D. (2009). School-based screening to identify at-risk students not already known to school professionals: The Columbia Suicide Screen. *American Journal of Public Health, 99,* 334–339.

Scouller, K. M., & Smith, D. I. (2002). Prevention of youth suicide: How well informed are the potential gatekeepers of adolescents in distress? *Suicide and Life-Threatening Behavior, 32,* 67–79.

Shaffer, D. (2004). The suicidal adolescent. *Focus, 2*(4), 517–523.

Singer, J. B., & Slovak, K. (2010). School social workers' experiences with youth suicidal behavior: An exploratory study. *Children & Schools, 33*(4), 215–228.

Substance Abuse and Mental Health Services Administration (SAMHSA). (2011). *Utilization of mental health services by adults with suicidal thoughts and behavior.* Retrieved from http://www.samhsa.gov/data/2k11/web_sr_014/web_sr_014_html.pdf

Substance Abuse and Mental Health Services Administration (SAMHSA). (2012). *Preventing suicide: A toolkit for high schools* (HHS Publication No. SMA-12-4669). Retrieved from http://store.samhsa.gov/shin/content/sma12-4669/sma12-4669.pdf

Tishler, C. L., Reiss, N. S., & Rhodes, A. R. (2007). Suicidal behavior in children younger than twelve: A diagnostic challenge for emergency department personnel. *Academic Emergency Medicine, 14*(9), 810–818.

Tompkins, T. L., Witt, J., & Abraibesh, N. (2009). Does a gatekeeper suicide prevention program work in a school setting? Evaluating training outcome and moderators of effectiveness. *Suicide and Life-Threatening Behavior, 39*(6), 671–681.

Trautman, P. D., Stewart, M., & Morishima, A. (1993). Are adolescent suicide attempters noncompliant with outpatient care? *Journal of the American Academy of Child and Adolescent Psychiatry, 32,* 89–94.

U.S. Surgeon General and the National Action Alliance for Suicide Prevention. (2012). *2012 national strategy for suicide prevention: Goals and objectives for action.* Retrieved from http://www.surgeongeneral.gov/library/reports/national-strategy-suicide-prevention/full_report-rev.pdf

Van Dulmen, M., Mata, A., Claxton, S., Klipfel, K., Schinka, K., Swahn, M., & Bossarte, R. (2013). Longitudinal associations between violence and suicidality from adolescence into adulthood. *Suicide and Life-Threatening Behavior, 43*(5), 523–531.

Wilkins, N., Thigpen, S., Lockman, J., Mackin, M., Madden, M., Perkins, T., . . . & Donovan, J. (2013). Putting program evaluation to work: A framework for creating actionable knowledge for suicide prevention practice. *Translational Behavioral Medicine, 3*(2), 1–13.

Wyman, P. A., Brown, C. Hendricks, Inman, J., Cross, W., Schmeelk-Cone, K., . . . & Pena, J. B. (2008). Randomized trial of a gatekeeper program for suicide prevention: 1-year impact on secondary school staff. *Journal of Consulting and Clinical Psychology, 76,* 104–115.

Section VI

Tier 2 Interventions in Schools: Working with At-Risk Students

In response to intervention and multitiered systems of supports, tier 2 interventions address the needs of students who have been identified as being at risk. In this section, we cover interventions that can be used to address at-risk students. In chapter 26, Brenda Lindsey writes about "Evidence-Informed Tier 2 Behavioral Interventions for At-Risk Students." Craig Winston LeCroy describes the teaching of social skills in schools in chapter 27, "Teaching Social Skills in School Settings." Joan Letendre and Kendra J. Garrett describe the use and evaluation of groups in schools in chapter 28, "Working with Groups in Schools: Planning for and Working with Group Process," and chapter 29, "Evaluation of School-based Counseling Groups," respectively.

26

Evidence-Informed Tier 2 Behavioral Interventions for At-Risk Students

Brenda Lindsey

University of Illinois at Urbana Champaign

◆ Critical Features of Tier 2 Interventions
◆ Tier 2 Interventions
◆ Structured Psychotherapy for Adolescents Responding to Chronic Stress
◆ Cognitive Behavioral Interventions for Trauma in Schools
◆ Peaceful Alternatives to Tough Situations
◆ Homework, Organization, and Planning Skills
◆ Motivational Interviewing

Response to intervention (RTI)/multitiered system supports (MTSS) systematic school-wide approaches provide a continuum of academic and behavioral assessment and intervention to students at risk of academic failure (Batsche et al., 2006; Ridgeway, Price, Simpson, & Rose, 2012). Sugai and Horner (2002) recommend that schools develop a uniform set of academic and behavioral expectations for students. Schools should do this with support from school and district leaders through team-based problem-solving approaches, evidence-informed practices, and data-based decision-making processes. These components bring about a consistent school-wide approach to prevent academic failure and encourage students to display socially appropriate behaviors while reducing the likelihood that challenging behaviors will occur (Lindsey, 2008).

RTI/MTSS use a multitiered framework of academic and behavioral support (Batsche et al., 2006; Brown-Chidsey & Steege, 2005; Sugai & Horner, 2002). Tier 1 interventions are designed to prevent academic and behavioral problems and are provided to all students. Examples of tier 1 interventions include research-validated social-emotional learning curricula taught in general education classrooms to all students. The tier 1 interventions provide instruction on how to display expected behaviors, precorrect students, and reward students for exhibiting desired behaviors. It is estimated that 80 to 90 percent of students will respond to tier 1 interventions (Lindsey, 2008).

Tier 2 interventions include short-term individualized interventions and specially designed small group counseling interventions provided by school social workers and other specialized instructional support personnel (Alvarez & Anderson-Ketchmark, 2010; Crone, Hawken, & Horner, 2010; Lindsey, 2008). About 10 to 15 percent of students will need tier 2–level interventions to be successful in school. Students at this level may exhibit externalizing behavior problems such as classroom disruption, work refusal, tardiness, and absenteeism (Beard & Sugai, 2004; Yong & Cheney, 2013). However, the problems are not severe enough to require intensive interventions (Walker et al., 1996). Examples of tier 2 interventions that can be implemented by school social workers are discussed in this chapter.

Tier 3 interventions are designed for students with intensive academic and behavioral needs that require long-term individualized plans (Eber, Lindsey, & White 2010; Malloy, Sundar, Hagner, Pierias, & Viet, 2010; Scott & Eber, 2003). Examples of tier 3 interventions include Rehabilitation, Empowerment, Natural supports, Education, and Work (RENEW; Eber, Malloy, Rose, & Flamini, 2013). RENEW applies the wraparound planning process to student strengths and needs across home, school, and community. RTI/MTSS anticipates that 1 to 5 percent of students will require tier 3–level interventions. An MTSS that relies on effective interventions at lower tiers results in fewer students requiring more-intensive interventions at higher tiers (Allen & Philliber, 2001).

School social workers work through all three tiers to provide a continuum of school-wide instructional and behavioral support. Although school social workers typically focus on the behavior side of RTI, they also should be familiar with academic components of the approach (Johnson, 2012). They should have a basic understanding of reading and mathematics curricula and instructional strategies adopted by schools, as well as knowledge of the available interventions for students experiencing learning problems. This background provides a way for school social workers to identify links between behavioral interventions and social skills needed for school success.

CRITICAL FEATURES OF TIER 2 INTERVENTIONS

There are a number of significant features to consider when implementing tier 2 interventions (Anderson et al., 2012; Yong & Cheney, 2013). These include the following:

1. Interventions are provided within a multitiered framework of academic and behavioral support (Anderson et al., 2012; Hawken, Adolphson, MacLeod, & Schumann, 2009; Yong & Cheney, 2013).

2. New programs are embedded into existing school policies and practices (Domitrovich et al., 2010; Massey, Armstrong, Boroughs, Henson, & McCash, 2005; Nelson et al., 2009).

3. Students are identified for tier 2 by using consistent criteria and are given systematically delivered interventions (Yong & Cheney, 2013).

4. Students know how to get started and what to do when problems arise through standardized orientation procedures and materials (Anderson et al., 2012).

5. Interventions can be quickly accessed and are continuously available to students (Anderson et al., 2012).

6. All school staff are trained on how to refer and support students in need of tier 2 interventions (Yong & Cheney, 2013).

7. Student progress is monitored via ongoing data collection and analysis. For shorter interventions that last two to six months, weekly data review is recommended. Student progress can be assessed through a variety of methods including behavior rating scales, direct observation, procedural checklists, and daily/weekly progress reports. The results from these assessment tools are used to evaluate the degree to which the intervention is or is not working (Yong & Cheney, 2013).

8. A variety of intervention approaches are used to address different problem behaviors and student needs (Yong & Cheney, 2013).

9. Interventions that are selected have multiple components, target more than one social skill and setting, and involve essential persons such as parents and teachers (Hawken et al., 2009; Horner, Sugai, & Anderson, 2010).

10. To increase the likelihood that the intervention is implemented as intended, follow-up training and coaching is provided (Fairbanks, Sugai, Guardino, & Lathrop, 2007; Fuchs & Fuchs, 2006; Nelson et al., 2009).

11. Parents and caregivers are involved so they can support the intervention at home and thus help students maintain and generalize positive behaviors outside of school (Yong & Cheney, 2013).

12. Students are assisted to maintain positive behavior changes over time by incorporating specific strategies such as teaching self-management skills and/or gradually reducing powerful reinforcers (Yong & Cheney, 2013).

Tier 2 interventions should be incorporated into a multitiered framework of support that reflects the unique needs of particular schools. It is important that tier 2 interventions incorporate the critical features described above. The remainder of this chapter will highlight effective tier 2 interventions that school social workers can implement.

TIER 2 INTERVENTIONS

The Behavior Education Program (BEP) is a daily check-in/check-out (CICO) system that is continuously available for students in need of additional support (Crone et al., 2010; Myers, Briere, & Simonsen, 2010; Simonsen, Myers, & Briere, 2011). Students begin each day by checking in with an adult to receive encouragement and a goal sheet. Throughout the day, teachers use the goal sheet to provide written and verbal feedback to students. Students check out again with an adult at the end of the day. The student takes the goal sheet home and gives it to a parent or caregiver for their signature, then returns it the following morning at check in. Individual performance percentage goals are determined in advance and calculated daily; results are shared with students and parents. Students may earn tokens that can be exchanged for rewards such as prizes, extra privileges, or special activities. Schools are encouraged to modify BEP procedures, target behaviors, and rewards to fit the needs of students and staff. The BEP includes critical tier 2 features such as regular communication with parents or caregivers and training for teachers and staff on how to refer students and ways to provide effective feedback. The BEP incorporates school-wide behavior expectations and requires regular meetings to review data and monitor student progress (Crone et al., 2010; Myers et al., 2010; Simonsen et al., 2011).

The BEP has been shown to be effective with elementary, middle, and high school students (Crone et al., 2010). It is most successful with students who act out to get attention but less so for students who act out to avoid work (Hawken & Horner, 2003). Detailed information including step-by-step instructions on how to implement BEP and reproducible daily progress reports can be found in Crone et al. for about $37, as of this writing. A training DVD is also available at an approximate cost of $76 (Hawken, Pettersson, Mootz, & Anderson, 2006).

STRUCTURED PSYCHOTHERAPY FOR ADOLESCENTS RESPONDING TO CHRONIC STRESS

SPARCS is a trauma-focused group intervention for adolescents experiencing ongoing stress and problems in multiple areas of their lives. Groups of six to ten members discuss how trauma has affected their lives, with particular emphasis on understanding within the context of their culture. The SPARCS program consists of sixteen one-hour sessions that can be divided into two segments and conducted twice a week to accommodate school schedules. A combination of effective therapeutic approaches are used such as cognitive behavioral therapy, dialetical behavior therapy, and other trauma-focused interventions (Amaya-Jackson & DeRosa, 2007). Sample lesson topics consist of managing emotions, improving communication skills, understanding impact of stress, and building supportive relationships. There are also six additional sessions for parents/caregivers to practice communication and emotional regulation skills. SPARCS materials include a manual and student workbook (M. Habib, SPARCS director, personal communication, January 7, 2014). They are available for purchase at an approximate cost of $75 for the manual and $10 to $20 per student workbook. SPARCS training is highly recommended to ensure the intervention is implemented with fidelity. More information is available at http://sparcstraining.com.

COGNITIVE BEHAVIORAL INTERVENTIONS FOR TRAUMA IN SCHOOLS

The Cognitive Behavioral Intervention for Trauma in Schools (CBITS) program is a school-based group intervention for children who have experienced significant traumatic events and are exhibiting associated emotional and behavioral problems (Jaycox, 2004; Jaycox, Kataoka, Stein, Langley, & Wong, 2012; Jaycox et al., 2010; Kataoka et al., 2003; Stein et al., 2003). Although it has demonstrated effectiveness with children aged eleven to fifteen, it has been expanded for use with children in grades three through twelve. CBITS has also been validated for use with diverse student populations. Only school staff with clinical training such as school social workers should provide the intervention (Jaycox et al., 2002).

The CBITS program includes components for students, parents, and teachers. It includes ten one-hour group sessions, one to three individual student sessions, two parent sessions, and one teacher training (Jaycox, 2004; Jaycox et al., 2012). It is best suited for students with moderate symptom levels of posttraumatic stress disorder. Some of the skills covered in the CBITS curriculum include linking thoughts and feelings, social problem solving, and relaxation training. Optimal student group size is five to eight students. The parent/caregiver and teacher component presents an overview of the program and typical reactions to trauma. School social workers and other mental health professionals can complete a free CBITS training course and gain access to other free resources at www.cbits program.org. The CBITS intervention manual can be purchased for an estimated cost of $44.95 plus shipping/handling (Jaycox, 2004).

PEACEFUL ALTERNATIVES TO TOUGH SITUATIONS

Peaceful Alternatives to Tough Situation (PATTS) is an evidence-based small group intervention that can be implemented by school social workers (Williams, Johnson, & Botts, 2008.) The goal of the intervention is to decrease aggressive behavior and increase conflict mediation skills among students. PATTS (n.d.) offers separate curricula for grades K to 2, 3 to 5, and middle/high school that are delivered in nine weekly, one-hour sessions. Skills taught include peer refusal, conflict mediation, anger triggers, and forgiveness. Group sessions use a format that introduces a featured skill followed by role-play and discussion. Parents and teachers are also trained on the skills emphasized in the PATTS curricula with emphasis on how to reinforce ways that students can display highlighted skills at home and at school (Williams et al., 2008). Program materials are available at an estimated cost of $675 or $825 plus shipping and handling per curriculum (PATTS, n.d.).

HOMEWORK, ORGANIZATION, AND PLANNING SKILLS

Homework, Organization, and Planning Skills (HOPS) is a research-validated intervention developed for students in grades 3 to 10 with attention problems, ADHD, or experiencing difficulties in planning and organization (Langberg, 2011; Langberg, Epstein, Becker, Girio-Herrera, & Vaughn, 2012). It consists of sixteen brief individual sessions (twenty minutes or less) provided by school social workers. Three main skill sets are emphasized in the HOPS program: (1) organization of school materials, (2) time management, and (3) planning. Students learn specific strategies to organize school binders, backpacks, and lockers as well as suggestions of how to get homework to and from school. The time management component teaches students helpful techniques on how to split up bigger assignments into smaller chunks of work. Students learn self-monitoring skills in session 12 that enable them to maintain progress over time (Langberg, 2011, p. 7). The HOPS program is an effective school-based intervention for improving the organizational skills associated with school success (Langberg et al., 2012).

HOPS uses a point system that provides immediate rewards when students demonstrate appropriate organizational and planning behaviors (Langberg, 2011, p. 8). A series of checklists are provided for teachers, administrators, or other school staff to assess student skills in selected areas and award points when the student demonstrates desired behaviors. Students can accumulate points and then redeem them for prizes or other rewards. Two parent meetings are an integral part of the HOPS intervention and provide training on how to implement the checklist and reward system at home thus establishing a plan for ongoing transfer of skills. The manual contains information on how to implement the HOPS interventions. It is available from the National Association of School Psychologists for $52 for members or $65 for nonmembers (Langberg, 2011).

MOTIVATIONAL INTERVIEWING

Motivational interviewing (MI) is a promising practice that can be used to help students address feelings of uncertainty related to making positive behavior changes (Enea & Dafinoiu, 2009; Strait et al., 2012; Terry, Smith,

Strait, & McQuillin, 2013) The underlying premise of the approach is for clinicians to acknowledge client resistance to change without direct confrontation. Basic tenets of MI include establishing rapport, asking open-ended questions, acknowledging client efforts to change, asking permission prior to giving advice or information, and developing a plan for change based on the level of client commitment. As an intervention, MI has been used to address a host of problem behaviors such as substance abuse. It has also been applied in schools to reduce truancy and improve academic performance (Enea & Dafinoiu, 2009; Strait et al., 2012; Terry et al., 2013; Villiger, Niggli, Wandeler, & Kutzelmann, 2012). The evidence suggests that a limited number of MI sessions can bring about positive behavior changes in several areas.

School social workers interested in becoming proficient at using MI techniques in their practice must complete training and follow-up coaching to ensure fidelity of the approach (Barwick, Bennett, Johnson, McGowan, & Moore, 2012; Madson, Loignon, & Lane, 2008). A list of training opportunities and other resources are available through the Motivational Interviewing Network of Trainers Web site (n.d.).

CONCLUSION

School social workers provide services within a multitiered framework of support. When evaluating and selecting two interventions, it is important to keep in mind the critical features that should be embedded within selected approaches. This chapter highlighted a variety of evidence-based and promising-practice tier 2 interventions that promote behavioral and social skills associated with school success. By using these and other effective tier 2 interventions, school social workers can greatly improve learning outcomes for students experiencing poor academic performance.

References

Allen, J., & Philliber, S. (2001). Who benefits most from a broadly targeted prevention program? Differential efficacy across populations in the teen outreach program. *Journal of Community Psychology, 29*(6), 637–655.

Alvarez, M., & Anderson-Ketchmark, C. (2010). Review of an evidence-based school social work intervention: Check & connect. *Children & Schools, 32*(2), 125–127.

Amaya-Jackson, A., & DeRosa, R. (2007). Treatment considerations for clinicians in applying evidence-based practice to complex presentations in child trauma. *Journal of Traumatic Stress, 20*(4), 379–390.

Anderson, C., Lewis-Palmer, T., Todd, A., Horner, R., Sugai, G., & Sampson, N. (2012). *Individual Student Systems Evaluation Tool 3.0.* Educational & Community Supports, University of Oregon. Retrieved from http://www.pbis.org/common/pbisresources/publications/ISSET_TOOL_v_3_March_2012.pdf

Barwick, M., Bennett, L., Johnson, S., McGowan, J., & Moore, J. (2012). Training health and mental health professionals in motivational interviewing: A systematic review. *Children & Youth Services Review, 34*, 1786–1795.

Batsche, G., Elliott, J., Graden, J. L., Grimes, J., Kovaleski, J. F., Prasse, D., . . . & Tilly, W. D. (2006). *Response to intervention: Policy considerations and implementation.* Alexandria, VA: National Association of State Directors of Special Education.

Beard, K., & Sugai, G. (2004). First step to success: An early intervention for elementary children at risk for antisocial behavior. *Behavioral Disorders, 29,* 396–409.

Brown-Chidsey, R., & Steege, M. W. (2005). *Response to intervention: Principles and strategies for effective practice.* New York: Guilford Press.

Crone, D., Hawken, L., & Horner, R. (2010). *Responding to problem behavior in schools: The Behavior Education Program* (2nd ed.). New York: Guilford Press. Retrieved from http://www.guilford.com/cgi-bin/cartscript.cgi?page=pr/crone2.htm&dir=edu/PIS_series

Domitrovich, C., Bradshaw, C., Greenberg, M., Embry, D., Poduska, J., & Ialongo, N. (2010). Integrated models of school-based prevention: Logic and theory. *Psychology in the Schools, 47*(1), 71–88.

Eber, L., Lindsey, B., & White, M. (2010). Tier 3 case example: Wraparound. In J. Clark & M. Alvarez (Eds.), *Response to intervention: A guide for school social workers* (pp. 167–190). New York: Oxford University Press.

Eber, L., Malloy, J., Rose, J., & Flamini, A. (2013). School-based wraparound for adolescents: The RENEW model for transition-aged youth with or at-risk of EBD. In H. Walker & F. Gresham (Eds.), *Handbook of evidence-based practices for emotional and behavioral disorders: Applications in schools* (pp. 378–393). New York: Guilford Press.

Enea, V., & Dafinoiu, I. (2009). Motivational/solution-focused intervention for reducing school truancy among adolscents. *Journal of Cognitive & Behavioral Psychotherapies, 9*(2), 185–198.

Fairbanks, S., Sugai, G., Guardino, D., & Lathrop, M. (2007). Response to intervention: Examining classroom behavior support in second grade. *Exceptional Children, 73,* 288–310.

Fuchs, D., & Fuchs, L. (2006). Introduction to response to intervention: What, why, and how valid is it? *Reading Research Quarterly, 41,* 93–99.

Hawken, L., Adolphson, S., MacLeod, K., & Schumann, J. (2009). Secondary-Tier interventions and supports. In W. Sailor, G. Dunlap, G. Sugai, & R. Horner (Eds.), *Handbook of positive behavior support* (pp. 395–420). New York: Springer.

Hawken, L., & Horner, R. (2003). Evaluation of a targeted intervention within a school-wide system of behavior support. *Journal of Behavioral Education, 12,* 225–240.

Hawken, L., Pettersson, H., Mootz, J., & Anderson, C. (2006). The Behavior Education Program: A check-in, check-out intervention for students at risk. [DVD]. Retrieved from http://www.guilford.com/cgi-bin/cartscript.cgi?page=pr/hawken.htm

Horner, R., Sugai, G., & Anderson, C. (2010). Examining the evidence base for school-wide positive behavior support. *Focus on Exceptional Children, 42,* 1–14.

Jaycox, L. (2004). *Cognitive behavioral intervention for trauma in schools.* Voyager Sopris http://www.voyagersopris.com/curriculum/subject/school-climate/cognitive-behavioral-intervention-for-trauma-in-schools

Jaycox, L., Kataoka, S., Stein, B., Langley, A., & Wong, M. (2012). Cognitive behavioral intervention for trauma in schools. *Journal of Applied School Psychology, 28,* 239–255.

Jaycox, L., Stein, B., Kataoka, S., Wong, M., Fink, A., Escudera, P., & Zaragoza, C. (2002). Violence exposure, PTSD, and depressive symptoms among recent immigrant school children. *Journal of the American Academy of Child and Adolescent Psychiatry, 41*(9), 1104–1110.

Jaycox, L., Stein, B., Kataoka, S., Wong, M., Fink, A., Escudera, P., & Schonlau, M. (2010). Children's mental health care following Hurricane Katrina: A field trial of trauma-focused psychotherapies. *Journal of Traumatic Stress, 23*(2), 223–231.

Johnson, A. (2012). For school social workers: The changing role of the school social worker. *The Networker.* Retrieved from http://naswil.org/news/chapter-news/featured/for-school-social-workers-the-changing-role-of-the-school-social-worker/

Kataoka, S., Stein, B., Jaycox, L., Wong, M., Escudero, P., Tu, W., . . . & Fink, A. (2003). A school-based mental health program for traumatized Latino immigrant children. *Journal of the American Academy of Child and Adolescent Psychiatry, 42*(3), 311–318.

Langberg, J. (2011). *Homework, Organization and Planning Skills (HOPS) interventions: A treatment manual.* National Association of School Psychologists: Bethesda, MD. Retrieved from http://www.nasponline.org/publications/booksproducts/N1108.aspx

Langberg, J., Epstein, J., Becker, S., Girio-Herrera, E., & Vaughn, A. (2012). Evaluation of the Homework, Organization, and Planning Skills (HOPS) Intervention for middle school students with Attention Deficit Hyperactivity Disorder as implemented by school mental health providers. *School Psychology Review, 41*(3), 342–364.

Lindsey, B. (2008). Looking at positive behavior interventions and supports through the lens of innovations diffusion. *Innovation Journal, 13*(2).

Madson, M., Loignon, A., & Lane, C. (2008). Training in motivational interviewing: A systematic review. *Journal of Substance Abuse Treatment, 36,* 101–109.

Malloy, J. M., Sundar, V., Hagner, D., Pierias, L., & Viet, T. (2010). The efficacy of the RENEW model: Individualized school-to-career services for youth at risk of school dropout. *Journal of At-Risk Issues, 15*(2), 19–26.

Massey, O., Armstrong, K., Boroughs, M., Henson, K., & McCash, L. (2005). Mental health services in schools: A qualitative analysis of challenges to implementation, operation, and sustainability. *Psychology in the Schools, 42,* 361–372.

Motivational Interviewing Network of Trainers (MINT). (n.d.). *Welcome to the motivational interviewing website.* Retrieved at www.motivationalinterviewing.org

Myers, D., Briere, D., & Simonsen, B. (2010). Lessons learned from implementing a Check-in/Check-out behavioral program in an urban middle school. *Beyond Behavior,* Winter, 21–27.

Nelson, J., Hurley, K., Synhorst, L., Epstein, M., Stage, S., & Buckley, J. (2009). The child outcomes of a behavior model. *Exceptional Children, 76,* 7–30.

Peaceful Alternatives to Tough Situations (PATTS). (n.d.). *Order PATTS.* Retrieved from http://www.patts.info/

Ridgeway, T. R., Price, D. P., Simpson, C. G., & Rose, C. A. (2012). Reviewing the roots of response to intervention: Is there enough research to support the promise? *Administrative Issues Journal: Education, Practice & Research, 2*(1), 83–95.

Scott, T., & Eber, L. (2003). Functional assessment and wraparound as systemic school processes: Primary, secondary, and tertiary systems examples. *Journal of Positive Behavior Interventions, 5*(3), 131–143.

Simonsen, B., Myers, D., & Briere, D. (2011). Comparing a behavioral Check-In/Check-Out (CICO) intervention to standard practice in an urban middle school setting using an experimental group design. *Journal of Positive Behavior Interventions, 13*(1), 31–48.

Stein, B., Jaycox, L., Kataoka, S., Wong, M., Tu, W., Elliott, M., & Fink, A. (2003). A mental health intervention for school children exposed to violence. *Journal of the American Medical Association, 290*(5), 603–611.

Strait, G., Smith, B., McQuillin, S., Terry, J., Swan, S., & Malone, P. (2012). A randomized trial of motivational interviewing to improve middle school students' academic performance. *Journal of Community Psychology, 40*(8), 1032–1039.

Sugai, G., & Horner, R. (2002). The evolution of discipline practices: School-wide positive behavior supports. *Child & Family Behavior Therapy, 24*(1/2), 23–50.

Terry, J., Smith, B., Strait, G., & McQuillin, S. (2013). Motivational interviewing to improve middle school students' academic performance: A replication study. *Journal of Community Psychology, 41*(7), 902–909.

Villiger, C., Niggli, A., Wandeler, C., & Kutzelmann, S. (2012). Does family make a difference? Mid-term effects of a school/home-based intervention program to enhance reading motivation. *Learning & Instruction, 22*(2), 79–91.

Walker, H., Horner, R., Sugai, G., Bullis, M., Sprague, J., Bricker, D., & Kaufman, M. (1996). Integrated approaches to preventing antisocial behavior patterns among school-age children and youth. *Journal of Emotional and Behavioral Disorders, 4*(4), 194–209.

Williams, E., Johnson, J., & Botts, C. (2008). Evaluation of a program for reduction of childhood aggression. *Psychological Reports, 103,* 347–357.

Yong, M., & Cheney, D. (2013). Essential features of tier 2 social-behavioral interventions. *Psychology in the Schools, 50*(8), 844–861.

27

Teaching Social Skills in School Settings

Craig Winston LeCroy
Arizona State University

◆ Defining and Conceptualizing Social Skills
◆ Group Format and the Social Skills Training Method
◆ Practical Considerations in Conducting Social Skills Groups
◆ Guidelines for Practitioners
◆ Social Skills Training Illustrated
◆ Classroom Social Skills Approaches

School is the major socializing institution for children. An important function of school is a place where children learn social behavior as well as academic skills. Schools focus on children's educational and cognitive skills and capabilities, but they recognize an important but neglected area of concern—the healthy social development of children. The National Mental Health Association Commission on the Prevention of Mental-Emotional Disabilities recommended, "Programs should be developed in schools (preschool through high school) that incorporate validated mental health strategies and competence building as an integral part of the curriculum" (as cited in Long, 1986, p. 828). In general, the public supports a broader educational agenda that includes enhancing children's social and emotional competence (Rose & Gallup, 2006).

Without proper social skills, children face numerous negative consequences later in life. For example, poor social skills are linked to later psychiatric disorders, externalizing problems, and internalizing problems. Self-regulation skills (e.g., being able to communicate thoughts and needs, being sensitive to others, and following instructions) are critical to school readiness (Blair, 2002). Teachers most often cite the self-regulation of pupils as being more important than academic skills because it is easier to help a child catch up academically when he or she has the expected and needed self-regulation capabilities.

Lela Costin (1969) in a well-known study of the tasks of school social workers argued more than thirty years ago that social workers should apply group work methods more broadly in school settings. A focus on children's social skills provides the strategy for using effective group work skills to improve the lives of children. Social skills groups can equip children with prosocial skills to help them replace aggressive or withdrawn behaviors with appropriate coping strategies. For example, interpersonal skills can be taught to enhance communication with peers, parents, and authority figures. Self-regulation skills can be taught to enhance classroom processes such as taking turns and following instructions. Numerous opportunities exist for the implementation of various skill-based programs that can help facilitate the successful socialization of children and adolescents in our schools. School social workers can play an important role in the design and implementation of social skill programs that (1) enhance children's ability to learn and interact successfully with others, and (2) enable teachers to focus on and better accomplish educational goals.

DEFINING AND CONCEPTUALIZING SOCIAL SKILLS

Social skills can be defined as a complex set of skills that facilitate successful interactions between peers, and among parents, teachers, and other adults (LeCroy, 2008). The word "social" refers to interactions between people; the word "skills" refers to making appropriate discriminations—deciding what would be the most effective response and using the verbal and nonverbal behaviors that facilitate interaction. The conceptualization of social skills as training suggests that problem behaviors can be viewed as remediable deficits in a child's response repertoire. This perspective focuses on building prosocial responses as opposed to eliminating excessive antisocial responses. Children learn new options in coping with problem situations. Learning how to respond effectively to new situations produces more positive consequences than using behaviors that the child may have used in similar situations in the past. This model focuses on the teaching of skills and competencies for day-to-day living rather than on understanding and eliminating defects. This model is an optimistic view of children and is implemented in an educative-remedial framework.

Research supports the relationship between various problem behaviors and the lack of social skills. For example, adolescents with depression have less-satisfying peer relationships than adolescents without depression do; this problem exacerbates isolation and feelings of loneliness for adolescents with depression (Weisz, 2004). Social skill deficits also play a role in the difficulties faced by children with conduct disorder and oppositional defiance disorder. It is estimated that up to 40 percent of children who are rejected because of poor social skills have problems with aggression (Fonagy, Target, Cottrell, Phillips, & Kurtz, 2002) and children who are both rejected and who have problems with aggression are at the highest risk of developing antisocial behavior in adolescence (Coie, Underwood, & Lochman, 1991). Children with attention deficit hyperactivity disorder are well known for their social deficits and their struggle to modulate their behavior in demanding social interactions (Mikami, Jack, & Lerner, 2009).

There is a growing body of research supporting the use of social skills training as an evidence-based treatment strategy (LeCroy, 2002, 2008). In a comprehensive review, Tobler et al. (2000) examined outcome studies with children and adolescents over a twenty-year period. The greatest benefits were found with programs that included life skills models, refusal skills, goal setting, assertiveness, communication, and coping strategies—all aspects of different social skills programs. Other studies (see, e.g., Hinshaw, Buhrmester, & Heller, 1989; Kazdin, Siegel, & Bass, 1992; LeCroy & Rose, 1986; Lochman & Wells, 2002; Wilson, Gottfredson, & Najaka, 2001) have documented the effectiveness of social skills training. However, it is important to note that often social skills training is only one component of a multi-faceted program.

GROUP FORMAT AND THE SOCIAL SKILLS TRAINING METHOD

Social skills training is usually conducted in a group format. The group format provides support and a reinforcing context for learning new responses and appropriate behaviors in a variety of social situations. The group is a natural context for social skills training because of the peer interactions that take place as the group members work together. In addition, the group allows for extensive use of modeling and feedback, which are critical components of successful skills training. However, it is important to note that not all children do well in group settings, and on some occasions certain children experience negative effects from working in groups. In these situations, social skills are best taught one on one.

PRACTICAL CONSIDERATIONS IN CONDUCTING SOCIAL SKILLS GROUPS

Group Composition

Conducting group prevention and intervention services is an efficient use of a school social worker's time, because social workers can see several students at one time. However, groups must be recruited and constructed with certain key factors in mind. First, recruitment for social skills training groups will depend on the goals of the particular program. It may be necessary to limit the number of participants involved, in which case the social worker must use procedures to help identify students most likely to benefit from the program. This screening process can be accomplished by administering assessment devices, identifying students who meet specified risk criteria, conducting pregroup interviews, or designing a referral system for teachers and other professionals to use to refer children directly to the group. On the other hand, limiting groups only to children who meet certain risk criteria may not be best in some groups. Often including participants who do not have social skills difficulties but who are highly socially competent can have positive implications. Because some groups will contain children who act out antisocially, a higher degree of poor social skill modeling could initially take place. By including high-functioning children in an antisocial group, the opportunity for prosocial modeling increases. Moreover, it may be less difficult to maintain order (Merrell & Gimpel, 1998).

Finally, group composition will be influenced by factors such as how well the group participants know one another, how heterogeneous the group is, how large the group is, the age and developmental level of the participants, and their gender. It is important that all members of a group have the time and attention they need to practice skills and receive important feedback; social skills groups should have between six and ten members, and there should be a low leader-to-participant ratio. Two group leaders are recommended, especially if the group has as many as ten participants. Merrell and Gimpel (1998) proposed that the members in the group should not vary in age by more than two or three years, and suggested that, depending on the developmental level of the group, the level of structure and language used may need to be altered. Presenting social skills that require a high level of cognitive ability will not be effective for group members who are either too young or who are functioning at a lower developmental level than the skill requires. For certain purposes, mixed-gender groups may provide a realistic context for interaction and increase the possibilities of generalization of particular skills.

Developing Program Goals

The first step in the development of a successful social skills training program is to identify the goals of the program based on the needs and strengths of the target population. A program goal, for example, might be for withdrawn children to be able to initiate positive social interactions. Once the goals of the program are clearly defined, the next step is to select the specific skills that are to be taught. Then you may help the group get ready for the skills by discussing with them the details of the skills as well as when, where, and why they should use this skill.

Selecting Skills

Depending on the type of problem to be addressed, a number of different skills may be appropriate. Skills for withdrawn and isolated children include greeting others, joining in ongoing activities, managing a conversation, and sharing/cooperating around things (e.g., toys) and ideas (Painter, 2008; Weiss & Harris, 2001). Barth (1996) elaborated assertiveness skills needed for preventing teen pregnancy, including problem solving and refusing unacceptable demands. The basic principles are to (1) break the preferred behavior down into a number of skills, and (2) assist the group in practicing those skills.

It is important to remember each member's developmental level of communication, motor skills, and cognition. This is especially important when working with children who have disabilities (Nevil, Beatty, & Moxley, 1997; Weiss & Harris, 2001).

Refining Selected Skills

The process of social skills training requires continual attention to refining each skill that is to be taught. After identifying the broad social skills, it is important to divide each broad skill into its component parts so that they can be more easily learned. For example, LeCroy (2008) breaks down the skill of beginning a conversation into six component parts (see also Cartledge & Milburn, 1995; Elias & Tobias, 1996):

1. Look the person in the eye and demonstrate appropriate body language.
2. Greet the person, and say one's own name.
3. Ask an open-ended question about the person. Listen attentively to the response.
4. Make a statement to follow up on the person's response.
5. Ask another open-ended question about the person. Listen attentively to the response.
6. Make another statement about the conversation.

Depending on the program, the same basic skill, such as starting a conversation, may be broken down differently. It is important to remember that social skills are more complex than they appear to be on the surface.

Major Skill Areas for Healthy Development

Five major social skill areas have been identified that children and adolescents need for healthy development. Following is a list of major skill areas and the most important skills within those areas. Each specific skill can be further broken down into subskills:

Peer Relationship Skills

1. Compliments, praises, or applauds peers
2. Offers help or assistance to peers when needed

3. Invites peers to play or interact
4. Participates in discussions; talks with peers for extended periods
5. Stands up for rights of peers; defends a peer in trouble
6. Is sought out by peers to join activities; everyone likes to be with him or her
7. Has skills or abilities admired by peers; participates skillfully with peers
8. Skillfully initiates or joins conversations with peers
9. Is sensitive to feelings of peers
10. Has good leadership skills; assumes leadership role in peer activities
11. Makes friends easily; has many friends
12. Has sense of humor; shares laughter with peers

Self-Management Skills

1. Remains calm when problems arise; controls temper when angry
2. Follows rules; accepts imposed limits
3. Compromises with others when appropriate; compromises in conflicts
4. Receives criticism well; accepts criticism from others
5. Responds to teasing by ignoring peers; responds appropriately to teasing
6. Cooperates with others in a variety of situations.

Academic Skills

1. Accomplishes tasks or assignments independently; displays independent study skills
2. Completes individual seatwork and assigned tasks
3. Listens to and carries out teacher's directions
4. Produces work of acceptable quality for ability level; works up to potential
5. Uses free time appropriately
6. Is personally well organized
7. Appropriately asks for assistance as needed; asks questions
8. Ignores peer distractions while working; functions well despite distractions.

Compliance Skills

1. Follows instructions and directions
2. Follows rules
3. Appropriately uses free time
4. Shares toys, materials, and belongings
5. Responds appropriately to constructive criticism or correction
6. Finishes assignments, completes tasks
7. Puts toys, work, or property away

Assertion Skills

1. Initiates conversations with others
2. Acknowledges compliments
3. Invites peers to play
4. Says and does nice things for self; is self-confident
5. Makes friends
6. Questions unfair rules
7. Introduces self to new people
8. Appears confident with opposite sex
9. Expresses feelings when wronged
10. Appropriately joins ongoing activity/group

Constructing Realistic Social Situations

It is important to construct realistic social situations that demand the use of social skills being taught, and it is important that the social situations and skills are determined empirically. Okamoto, LeCroy, Dustman, Hohmann-Marriott, and Kulis (2004) constructed problematic or difficult situations that American Indian youths encounter involving drugs and alcohol. The process involved conducting a series of focus groups and recording the kinds of situations that American Indian youths typically face when confronted with situations that involve substance use. The researchers then put these difficult situations into a survey and asked American Indian youths to rate each situation in terms of frequency and difficulty. At the end of the survey there is a list of common and difficult situations with social validity (in this case, cultural validity) that can be used for skills training. For example, in this study we found that many of the difficult situations for American Indian youths revolved around family interactions and social gatherings. When conducting substance abuse prevention groups with this population, we include these exact situations and help young people learn appropriate skills for handling relevant situations in their social context.

Due to the uniqueness of each interpersonal interaction, most practitioners must develop their own problematic situations or elicit them from the group during social skills training. For example, a substance abuse prevention program could address the following problem situation:

> You ride to a party with someone you've been dating for about six months. The party is at the house of a boy whose parents are gone for the weekend. There is a lot of beer and drugs, and your date has had too much to drink. Your date says, "Hey, where's my keys? Let's get going."

This situation ends with a stimulus for applying the skills of resisting peer pressure. An effective response to this situation would include the steps involved in resisting peer pressure: name the trouble, say no quickly, suggest alternatives, and leave the situation.

Social skills programs must be sensitive to racial and ethnic considerations. Cultural differences are often also differences in communication. Thus, the goals that are targeted in social skills groups must be culturally sensitive and depend on the major cultural values of the participants in the program. The selection of social skills must be tailored to become an effective social interaction in a variety of cultures.

GUIDELINES FOR PRACTITIONERS

After program goals are defined and skills are selected, there is a sequential process for teaching social skills. The seven basic steps in table 27.1 delineate the process that leaders can follow (based on LeCroy, 2008). These guidelines were developed for social skills groups with middle school and high school students. Social skills groups with younger children would use modified guidelines (see King & Kirschenbaum, 1992). Table 27.1 presents these steps and outlines the process for teaching social skills. In each step there is a request for group member involvement because it is critical that group leaders actively involve the participants in the skill training. In addition, such requests keep the group interesting and fun for the group members.

TABLE 27.1   Steps in Teaching Social Skills Training

1. Present the social skill being taught.
   A. Solicit an explanation of the skill.
   B. Get group members to provide rationales for the skill.
2. Discuss the social skill.
   A. List the skill steps.
   B. Get group members to give examples of using the skill.
3. Present a problem situation and model the skill.
   A. Evaluate the performance.
   B. Get group members to discuss the model.
4. Set the stage for role-playing the skill.
   A. Select the group members for role-playing.
   B. Get group members to observe the role-play.
5. Have group members rehearse the skill.
   A. Provide coaching if necessary.
   B. Get group members to provide feedback on verbal and nonverbal elements.
6. Practice using complex skill situations.
   A. Teach accessory skills such as problem solving.
   B. Get group members to discuss situations and provide feedback.
7. Train for generalization and maintenance.
   A. Encourage practice of skills outside the group.
   B. Get group members to bring in their problem situations.

1. Present the Social Skill Being Taught

The first step for the group leader is to present the skill. The leader solicits an explanation of the skill, for example, "Can anyone tell me what it means to resist peer pressure?" After group members have answered this question, the leader emphasizes the rationale for using the skill. For example, "You would use this skill when you're in a situation where you don't want to do something that your friends want you to do. You should be able to say no in a way that helps your friends to be able to accept your refusal." The leader then requests that group members voice additional reasons for learning the skill.

2. Discuss the Social Skill

The leader presents the specific skill steps that constitute the social skill. For example, the skill steps for resisting peer pressure are good nonverbal communication (including eye contact, posture, and voice volume), saying no early in the interaction, suggesting an alternative activity, and leaving the situation if there is continued pressure. Leaders then ask group members to state examples of times they used the skill, or examples of times they could have used the skill but chose not to.

3. Present a Problem Situation and Model the Skill

The leader presents a problem situation. For example, the following is a problem situation for resisting peer pressure.

> After seeing a movie, your friends suggest that you go with them to the mall. It is 10:45 and you are supposed to be home by 11:00. It is important that you get home by 11:00 or you will not be able to go out next weekend.

The group leader chooses members to role-play this situation and then models the skills. Group members evaluate the model's performance. Did the model follow all the skill steps? Was his or her performance successful? The group leader may choose another group member to model if the leader believes he or she already has the requisite skills. An alternative to live role-plays is to present videotaped models to the group. This has the advantage of following the recommendation by researchers that the models be similar to trainees in age, sex, and social characteristics.

4. Set the Stage for Role-Playing the Skill

For this step the group leader needs to construct the social circumstances for the role-play. Leaders select group members for the role-play and give them their parts. The leader reviews with the role-players how to act out their roles. Group members not in the role-play observe the process. It is sometimes helpful if group members not in the role-play are given specific instructions for their observations. For example, one member may observe the use of nonverbal skills, and another member may be instructed to observe when "no" is said in the interaction.

5. Have Group Members Rehearse the Skill

Rehearsal or guided practice of the skill is an important part of effective social skills training. Group leaders and group members provide instructions or coaching before and during the role-play and provide praise and feedback for improvement. Following a role-play rehearsal the leader will usually give instructions for improvement, model the suggested improvements, or coach the person to incorporate the feedback in the subsequent role-play. Often the group member doing the role-play will practice the skills in the situation several times to refine the skills and incorporate feedback offered by the group. The role-plays continue until the trainee's behavior becomes more and more similar to that of the model. It is important that overlearning takes place, so the group leader should encourage many examples of effective skill demonstration followed by praise. Group members should be taught how to give effective feedback before the rehearsals. Throughout the teaching process the group leader can model desired responses. For example, after a role-play the leader can respond first and model feedback that starts with a positive statement.

6. Practice Using Complex Skill Situations

The next-to-last phase deals with more difficult and complex skill situations. Complex situations can be developed by extending the interactions and roles in the problem situations. Another possible and relevant way to construct complex social situations is to ask group members to describe a situation in their own lives or in the lives of their friends, which relates to the skill the group is working on. Most social skills groups also incorporate the teaching of problem-solving abilities. Problem solving is a general approach to helping young people gather information about a problematic situation, generate a large number of potential solutions, evaluate the consequences of various solutions, and outline plans for the implementation of a particular solution. Group leaders can identify appropriate problem situations and lead members through the seven steps. Problem-solving training is important because it prepares young people to make adjustments as needed in particular situations. It is a general skill with large-scale application. (For a more complete discussion on the use of problem-solving approaches, see Manassis [2012].)

7. Train for Generalization and Maintenance

The success of the social skills program depends on the extent to which the skills young people learn transfer to their daily lives. Practitioners must always be planning for ways to maximize the generalization of skills learned and promote their continued use after training. There are several principles that help facilitate the generalization and maintenance of skills. The first is the use of overlearning: the more overlearning that occurs in the group the greater likelihood that there will be a later transfer of skills. Therefore, it is important that group leaders insist on mastery of the skills. Another important principle of generalization is to vary the stimuli as skills are learned. To accomplish this, practitioners can use a variety of models, problem situations, role-play actors, and trainers. The different styles and behaviors of the people used produce a broader context in which the students can apply the skills learned. Perhaps most important is to require that young people use the skills in their real-life settings. Group leaders should assign and monitor homework to encourage transfer of learning. This may include the use of written contracts to do certain tasks outside of the group. Group members should be asked to bring to the group examples of problem situations where the social skills can be applied. Finally, practitioners should attempt to develop external support for the skills learned. One approach to this is to set up a buddy system whereby group members work together to perform the skills learned outside the group.

SOCIAL SKILLS TRAINING ILLUSTRATED

This methodology may be applied to a whole range of problem areas. Table 27.2 illustrates some common focus areas for social skills training in the schools, along with general skills to be developed and resources for information that is more specific about these focus areas.

Although the examples in table 27.2 examine particular aspects of social skills training interventions, many practitioners use multiproblem social skills training in groups with children experiencing a variety of problems. For example, groups could include children with such problems as acting-out behavior, withdrawn behavior, fear, and so forth.

In groups designed for prevention purposes, the goal is to promote positive prosocial alternative behaviors (LeCroy, 2001, 2008). Such programs may be tailored to meet the needs of specific populations. Although social skills training will likely be the major component of the treatment, other treatment procedures also can be used; for example, a social skills training program may be enhanced by the addition of a psychoeducational component. A specific example of the development of one such prevention program follows.

TABLE 27.2 Problem Behaviors and Related Social Skills Training

Type of Program and Resources	*Social Skills Focus*
Aggressive behavior Feindler & Gerber, 2008 Olweus, 2007 Lochman & Wells, 2002 Waterman & Walker, 2001	*Skills to work on* Recognizing interactions likely to lead to problems Learning responses to negative communications Learning to request a behavior change
Depression Clarke, Lewinsohn, & Hops, 2001 Stark et al., 2004	*Skills to work on* Conversation skills Planning social activities Making friends Increasing pleasant activities Reducing negative cognitions
Anxiety or withdrawn, isolated behavior Painter, 2008 Hops, Walker, & Greenwood, 1979 Kearney, 2008 Kendall, Choudhury, Hudson, & Webb, 2002 Chorpita, 2007 Weiss & Harris, 2001	*Skills to work on* Greeting others Joining in ongoing activities Starting a conversation Sharing things and ideas
Substance abuse prevention Botvin, 2000 Hohman & Buchik, 1994 Henggeler, Clingempeel, Brondino, & Pickrel, 2002	*Skills to work on* Identifying problem situations Learning effective refusal skills Making friends with nonusing peers Learning general problem-solving techniques
Teen pregnancy and HIV prevention Barth, 1996 Jermmott & Jermmott, 1992 Wang et al., 2000 Wingood & DiClemente, 2008	*Skills to work on* Identifying risky situations Refusing unreasonable demands Learning new interpersonal responses Learning problem-solving techniques
Peer mediation for interpersonal conflict Schrumpf, Crawford, & Bodine, 2014 Tindall, 2008	*Skills to work on* Learning communication skills Focusing on common interests Creating options Writing an agreement
Children with cognitive and other disabilities Myers, 2013 Giler, 2011 Weiss & Harris, 2001	*Skills to work on* Gaining teacher attention Following classroom rules Being organized Drinking from the water fountain appropriately (and other skills appropriate for this population)

A Prevention Program for Early Adolescent Girls

A social skills training psychoeducational prevention program called Go Grrrls (LeCroy & Daley, 2001) was developed specifically for early adolescent girls. Program goals were identified through empirical investigation of problems common to this population and through direct interaction with middle-school girls. In response to these identified problems, a group of core social skills—for example, assertiveness skills and basic conversational skills—are presented and taught during the first half of a twelve-session program. Participants are then asked to build on core skills by applying them to more-specific situations, such as substance abuse refusal, during the latter half of the program.

Two examples of program goals for the Go Grrrls program are to equip girls with assertiveness skills, and to equip them with the skills necessary to build healthy peer relationships.

Building a Solid Foundation of Skills

For the focus area of assertiveness, the Go Grrrls program provides three sessions that help girls to learn this skill. In one of the early group meetings, girls are introduced to the general concept of assertiveness and are given practice using this skill. In two later sessions, girls are given additional practice using assertiveness skills in the context of refusing substances and unwanted sexual advances. As the program progresses, girls are able to combine several of the core social skills they learned in early sessions to help them deal with more-specific problem areas in the later curriculum. For example, by the time participants reach the curriculum section dealing with substance abuse, they have already completed sessions on the core social skills of being assertive and starting conversations. They can draw from both of these areas in learning to effectively deal with peer pressure to use drugs. Table 27.3 illustrates how social skills may be combined in a complementary fashion to help participants build strengths. Research studies (LeCroy, 2004) have found this program produced significant outcomes in comparison to a control group of participants who did not receive the program.

CLASSROOM SOCIAL SKILLS APPROACHES

Although few evidence-based interventions have been developed specifically for teaching social skills in the classroom, such efforts are gaining greater appeal in order to target a large number of students. (See Webster-Stratton & Taylor [2001] for an exception.) Practitioners can take many of the same methods as used in teaching child management skills to parents

TABLE 27.3 Go Grrrls Skill Building

Go Grrrls Program Goal	*Related Social Skills Training*
Core skill: assertiveness Goal: To teach girls to act assertively rather than passively or aggressively. Rationale: Teaching girls basic assertiveness skills will help them speak up in classrooms and withstand peer pressure, and will serve as a foundation for learning more-specific refusal skills.	1. Discuss the skill of assertiveness. 2. Group leaders demonstrate assertive, passive, and aggressive responses to sample situations. 3. Group members practice identifying assertive behavior. 4. Group members practice assertiveness skills. 5. Group leaders and other members provide feedback. Sample scenario: You are in science class, and the boy you are partners with tells you that he will mix the chemicals and you will be the secretary. What do you do?
Core skill: Making and keeping friends Goal: To equip girls with the tools they need to establish and maintain healthy peer relationships. Rationale: Disturbances in peer relationships are among the best predictors of psychiatric, social, and school problems. Teaching friendship skills can reduce these problems.	1. Discuss the components of a successful conversation, including the beginning, middle, and end. 2. Group leaders demonstrate both ineffective and effective conversational skills. 3. Group members practice identifying effective conversational skills such as making eye contact and asking questions of the other person. 4. Group members practice conversation skills in role-play situations. 5. Group leaders and other members provide feedback. Sample scenario: It is your first day of junior high and you don't know anyone in your homeroom. Start a conversation with the girl who sits next to you.
Specific skill: Avoiding substance abuse Goal: To teach girls coping strategies and skills they may use to avoid using alcohol, tobacco, and other drugs. Rationale: More girls are using drugs, and at earlier ages, than ever before. Early drug use may place girls at risk for serious health and psychological problems.	1. Discuss the reasons why some girls use drugs. (Reasons may include: They don't know how to say no, they don't have friends and get lonely, etc.) 2. Discuss reasons why some girls don't use drugs. 3. Group members practice refusing drugs in role-play situations. They build on the core skill of assertiveness learned earlier. 4. Group members list coping strategies they can use instead of turning to drugs. They build on the core skill of starting conversations, by recognizing that they can build healthy friendships with nonusing friends to help them stay drug free.

and apply them in classroom settings with teachers. Studies have found that modifying teacher-child interactions can have an impact on child engagement and behavior (Howes, 2000). Such classroom-based interventions are more typically established with younger children. Teachers are taught skills in promoting positive social behavior using attention, praise, and encouragement (Webster-Stratton & Taylor, 2001).

Additionally teachers can be taught the specific skills of helping improve students' self-regulation. Research is documenting that self-regulation and its component parts (working memory, executive attention, and emotional regulation) can be harnessed to improve children's mental health and social functioning (Buckner, Mezzacappa, & Beardslee, 2003). This may be accomplished by guiding students in tasks that require higher-order cognitive skills, such as successfully negotiating situations that heighten negative emotional arousal and that require higher-order reasoning and executive function skills to successfully resolve.

CONCLUSION

As school social workers work toward the goal of enhancing the socialization process of children, methods for promoting social competence, such as social skills training, have much to offer. Social workers can make an important contribution to children, families, and schools through preventive and remedial approaches such as those described in this chapter. As we have seen, children's social behavior is a critical aspect of successful adaptation in society. The school represents an ideal place for children to learn and practice social behavior. It provides the needed multipeer context and offers multiple opportunities for newly learned behaviors to be generalized to other situations and circumstances.

Social skills training provides a clear methodology for providing remedial and preventive services to children. This direct approach to working with children has been applied in numerous problem areas and with many child behavior problems. It is straightforward in application and has been adapted so that social workers, teachers, and peer helpers can successfully apply the methodology. Although we have emphasized the group application, social skills training also can be applied in individual or classroom settings.

References

Barth, R. P. (1996). *Reducing the risk: Building skills to prevent pregnancy, STD, and HIV* (3rd ed.). Santa Cruz, CA: ETR Associates.

Blair, C. (2002). School readiness: Integrating cognition and emotion in a neurobiological conceptualization of children's functioning at school entry. *American Psychologist, 57*, 111–127.

Botvin, G. J. (2000). *Life skills training: Promoting health and personal development.* New York: Princeton Health.

Buckner, J. C., Mezzacappa, E., & Beardslee, W. R. (2003). Characteristics of resilient youths living in poverty: The role of self-regulatory processes. *Development and Psychopathology, 15*, 139–162.

Cartledge, C., & Milburn, J. F. (1995). *Teaching social skills to children and youth: Innovative approaches* (3rd ed.). Boston: Allyn & Bacon.

Chorpita, B. F. (2007). *Modular Cognitive-Behavior Therapy for childhood anxiety disorders.* New York: Guilford Press.

Clarke, G. N., Lewinsohn, P. M., & Hops, H. (2001). *Instructor's manual for the Adolescent Coping with Depression course.* Retrieved from http://www.kpchr.org/public/acwd/acwdl.html

Coie, J. D., Underwood, M., & Lochman, E. (1991). Programmatic intervention with aggressive children in the school setting. In D. J. Pepler & K. H. Rubin (Eds.), *The development and treatment of childhood aggression* (pp. 389–410). Hillsdale, NJ: Lawrence Erlbaum.

Costin, L. B. (1969). An analysis of the tasks of school social work. *Social Service Review, 43,* 247–285.

Elias, M. J., & Tobias, S. E. (1996). *Social problem solving: Interventions in the schools.* New York: Guilford Press.

Feindler, E. L., & Gerber, M. (2008). TAME: Treatment Anger Management Education. In C. LeCroy (Ed.), *Handbook of evidence-based child and adolescent treatment manuals.* New York: Oxford University Press.

Fonagy, P., Target, M., Cottrell, D., Phillips, J., & Kurtz, Z. (2002). *What works for whom? A critical review of treatments for children and adolescents.* New York: Guilford Press.

Giler, J. Z. (2011). Socially *ADDept: Teaching social skills to children with ADHD, LD, and Asperger's.* San Francisco: Jossey-Bass.

Henggeler, S. W., Clingempeel, W. G., Brondino, M. J., & Pickrel, S. G. (2002). Four-year follow-up of Multisystemic Therapy with substance-abusing and substance-dependent juvenile offenders. *Journal of the American Academy of Child and Adolescent Psychiatry, 41*(7), 868–874.

Hinshaw, S. P., Buhrmester, D., & Heller, T. (1989). Anger control in response to verbal provocation: Effects of stimulant medication for boys with ADHD. *Journal of Abnormal Child Psychology, 17,* 393–407.

Hohman, M., & Buchik, G. (1994). Adolescent relapse prevention. In C. LeCroy (Ed.), *Handbook of child and adolescent treatment manuals* (pp. 200–239). New York: Lexington.

Hops, H., Walker, H. M., & Greenwood, C. R. (1979). PEERS: A program for remediating social withdrawal in school. In L. A. Hamerlynch (Ed.), *Behavior systems for the developmentally disabled: I. School and family environments* (pp. 224–241). New York: Brunner/Mazel.

Howes, C. (2000). Social-emotional classroom climate in child care, child-teacher relationships, and children's second-grade peer relations. *Social Development, 9,* 191–204.

Jermmott, L. S., & Jermmott, J. B. III (1992). Increasing condom-use intentions among sexually active inner-city adolescent women: Effects of an AIDS prevention program. *Nursing Research, 41,* 273–278.

Kazdin, A. E., Siegel, T. C., & Bass, D. (1992). Cognitive problem-solving skills training and parent management training in the treatment of antisocial behavior in children. *Journal of Consulting and Clinical Psychology, 60,* 733–747.

Kearney, C. A. (2008). Manualized treatment for anxiety-based school refusal behavior in youth. In C. LeCroy (Ed.), *Handbook of evidence-based child and adolescent treatment manuals* (pp. 286–313). New York: Oxford University Press.

Kendall, P. C., Choudhury, M., Hudson, J., & Webb, A. (2002). *The C. A. T. project workbook for the cognitive-behavioral treatment of anxious adolescents.* Ardmore, PA: Workbook.

King, C. A., & Kirschenbaum, D. S. (1992). *Helping young children develop social skills.* Pacific Grove, CA: Brooks/Cole.

LeCroy, C. W. (2001). Promoting social competence in youth. In H. E. Briggs & K. Corcoran (Eds.), *Social work practice: Treating common problems.* Chicago: Lyceum Books.

LeCroy, C. W. (2002). Child therapy and social skills. In A. R. Roberts & G. J. Greene (Eds.), *Social work desk reference* (pp. 406–412). New York: Oxford University Press.

LeCroy, C. W. (2004). Experimental evaluation of the "Go Grrrls" preventive intervention for early adolescent girls. *Journal of Primary Prevention, 25,* 457–473.

LeCroy, C. W. (2008). Social skills training. In C. LeCroy (Ed.). *Handbook of evidence-based child and adolescent treatment manuals.* New York: Oxford University Press.

LeCroy, C. W., & Daley, J. (2001). *Empowering adolescent girls: Examining the present and building skills for the future with the Go Grrrls program.* New York: W. W. Norton.

LeCroy, C. W., & Rose, S. D. (1986). Evaluation of preventive interventions for promoting social competence in adolescents. *Social Work Research and Abstracts, 22,* 8–17.

Lochman, J. E., & Wells, K. C. (2002). *The coping program for preadolescent aggressive boys and their parents.* Unpublished manuscript.

Long, B. B. (1986). The prevention of mental-emotional disabilities: A report from a National Mental Health Association Commission. *American Psychologist, 41,* 825–829.

Manassis, K. (2012). *Problem solving in child and adolescent psychotherapy: A skills based collaborative approach.* New York: Guilford Press.

Merrell, K. W., & Gimpel, G. A. (1998). *Social skills of children and adolescents: Conceptualization, assessment, treatment.* Mahwah, NJ: Lawrence Erlbaum.

Mikami, A. Y., Jack, A., & Lerner, M. D. (2009). Attention-deficit/hyperactivity disorder. In J. L. Matson (Ed.), *Social behavior and skills in children* (pp. 76–93). New York: Springer.

Myers, H. N. F. (2013). *Social skill deficits in students with disabilities: Successful strategies from the disabilities field.* New York: Rowman & Littlefield Education.

Nevil, N. F., Beatty, M. L., & Moxley, D. P. (1997). *Socialization games for persons with disabilities: Structured group activities for social and interpersonal development.* Springfield, IL: Charles C Thomas.

Okamoto, S. K., LeCroy, C. W., Dustman, P., Hohmann-Marriott, B., & Kulis, S. (2004). An ecological assessment of drug-related problem situations for American Indian adolescents in the southwest. *Journal of Social Work Practice in the Addictions, 4,* 47–64.

Olweus, D. (2007). Bullying at school: Knowledge base and an effective intervention program. *Annals of the New York Academy of Sciences, 794,* 265–276.

Painter, K. K. (2008). *Social skills groups for children and adolescents with Asperger's syndrome: A step-by-step program.* London: Jessica Kingsley.

Rose, L. C., & Gallup, A. M. (2006). The 38th annual Phi Delta Kappa/Gallup Poll of the public's attitudes toward the public schools. *Phi Delta Kappan, 88,* 41–56.

Schrumpf, F., Crawford, D. K., & Bodine, R. J. (2014). *Peer mediation: Conflict resolution in the schools: Student manual.* Champaign, IL: Research Press.

Stark, K. D., Schnoebelen, S., Simpson, J., Hargrave, J., Glenn, R., & Molnar, J. (2004). *Therapist's manual for ACTION.* Broadmore, PA: Workbook.

Tindall, J. A. (2008). *Peer power: Workbook: Applying peer helper skills.* New York: Routledge.

Tobler, N. S., Roona, M. R., Ochshorn, P., Marshall, D. G., Streke, A. V., & Stackpole, K. M. (2000). School-based adolescent drug prevention programs: 1998 meta-analysis. *Journal of Primary Prevention, 20,* 275–337.

Wang, L. I., Davis, M., Robin, L., Collins, J., Coyle, K., & Baumler, E. (2000). Economic evaluation of safer choices: A school-based human immunodeficiency virus, other sexually transmitted diseases, and pregnancy prevention program. *Archives of Pediatric Adolescent Medicine, 154,* 1017–1024.

Waterman, J., & Walker, E. (2001). *Helping at-risk students.* New York: Guilford Press.

Webster-Stratton, C., & Taylor, T. (2001). Nipping early risk factors in the bud: Preventing substance abuse, delinquency, and violence in adolescence through interventions targeted at young children (0–8 years). *Prevention Science, 2,* 165–192.

Weiss, M. J., & Harris, S. L. (2001). *Reaching out, joining in: Teaching social skills to young children with autism.* New York: Woodbine House.

Weisz, J. R. (2004). *Psychotherapy for children and adolescents: Evidence-based treatments and case examples.* New York: Cambridge University Press.

Wilson, D. B., Gottfredson, D. C., & Najaka, S. S. (2001). School-based prevention of problem behaviors: A meta-analysis. *Journal of Quantitative Criminology, 17,* 247–272.

Wingood, G. M., & DiClemente, R. J. (2008). HIV prevention with African American females. In C. W. LeCroy (Ed.), *Handbook of evidence based child and adolescent treatment manuals* (pp. 85–98). New York: Oxford University Press.

28

Working with Groups in Schools: Planning for and Working with Group Process

Joan Letendre
University of Connecticut

- ◆ Evidence-Informed Practice and Group Work
- ◆ Planning the Group
- ◆ Stages of Group Process
- ◆ Group Facilitation: From Beginning Stage through Working Stage to Ending Stage

This chapter focuses on principles of social work groups in schools. It puts special emphasis on the four stages of work with groups in schools: (1) the planning stage, (2) the initial engagement stage, (3) the work stage, and (4) the ending stage, and provides examples of groups that illustrate processes of planning for and facilitating groups. In one example in this chapter, the social worker plans a group for socially shy third and fourth graders. In another example, the school social worker plans a group for seventh-grade girls, referred for fighting behaviors, and facilitates the group through beginning, working, and ending stages of group development.

The use of groups historically has been and continues to be a method used by school social workers. In a 1959 survey by the practice committee of the School Social Work Section of the National Association of Social Workers (NASW), school social workers reported requests from school staff for group services for children, an interest in combining individual and group work, and yet a lack of education and training in leading groups (Johnson, 1962). Requests from school staff for group services and school social worker interest in combining group and individual services continue to be factors in implementation of groups in school. Besides the obvious benefit to busy school social workers of serving numerous children simultaneously, the group offers a real-life experience in which children are guided and reinforced for offering mutual aid and support to their peers. Groups provide multiple opportunities to experience positive peer reinforcement and camaraderie as well as to engage in mutual sharing and problem solving that modifies beliefs and behaviors toward children of different statuses (Bierman & Furman, 1984; Letendre, 2003). A lonely child, unskilled in friendship, can practice social skills through the use of fun activities with same-aged children in a safe and structured environment. A preadolescent child experiencing a difficult family situation that involves divorce, incarceration, military service, or illness or death of a family member can share the experiences with peers and realize that he or she is not alone with the situation. An adolescent girl struggling with anger can develop positive peer relations in an all-girl group where she can practice effective skills to calm angry thoughts and develop more-adaptive ways of coping with situations that generate strong emotional reactions (Letendre & Smith, 2011).

EVIDENCE-INFORMED PRACTICE AND GROUP WORK

Pawlak, Wozniak, and McGowan (2006) report that school social workers facilitate groups to address a wide variety of issues including substance abuse, attention deficit hyperactivity disorder, race and culture, socialization and peer interaction skills, adolescent parenting, trauma, drop-out prevention, and grief and loss. Garrett (2004) reported on the findings of a survey of the members of the School Social Work Association of America in which members reported that groups were used to serve multiple needs of children and adolescents and that the majority of groups (87 percent) taught social skills. Fifty-nine percent of the groups focused on peer difficulties, including bullying or aggression. The groups focused on a variety of social-emotional and behavioral issues affecting self-esteem, emotional regulation, and self-management of behaviors. Other groups addressed grief and loss, as well as changes in families such as divorce or remarriage. Some groups involved pupils with specific diagnoses such as attention deficit hyperactivity disorder, anxiety disorder, substance abuse, and eating disorders.

In an increasingly evidence-informed world, it is imperative for school social workers to have knowledge of group models that have been demonstrated to be effective in addressing specific problem behaviors (LeCroy, 2009). Such models provide a knowledge base and content for working with specific problems such as social anxiety, anger control, or grief and loss.

Social group work contributes the knowledge base of group process and methods to the content of the groups. The effective school social worker must integrate the evidence related to specific problem areas, with a general understanding of group processes and related intervention skills (Letendre & Wayne, 2008).

Group methodologies that focus on specific skill-set development and that use empirically tested curricular models to help children model and practice new ways of thinking and behaving (LeCroy, 2009) are readily accepted in school settings, where behavior change is important to learning and to the development of positive peer interactions. Behavioral changes learned in the group can be readily observed, measured, and documented. When the school social worker integrates the process of the group within the sessions children simultaneously learn how to interact positively with the other children by practicing new behaviors and by helping each other (Letendre & Wayne, 2008). Informed facilitation ensures that school social workers understand the current knowledge base for working with specific social-emotional problems as well as understanding group factors that contribute to helping members feel comfortable sharing concerns, offering mutual aid, and practicing different ways of thinking and behaving. Knowledge of how to evaluate group interventions with multiple stakeholders (children, teachers, parents) provides important data that support the efficacy of groups as well as factors that need to be modified to better fit the populations and problems.

PLANNING THE GROUP

Planning provides a road map for the trajectory of the group sessions, yet careful attention to the planning stage is an often-overlooked aspect of group work in schools. All too often groups are haphazardly developed with no attention to the factors affecting group functioning. Lack of prior planning, sometimes fostered by the pressure that school social workers feel to provide immediate services to troubled children can create barriers to the ongoing work of a group (Kurland, 2005; Letendre, 2007a). A systematic planning process prepares the worker and members for the group. This planning process includes attention to need, purpose and goals, structure, composition, content, and a pregroup interview. This section of the chapter will use the example of a group for shy, elementary school–aged children to illustrate the planning process.

Need

The first element to which school social workers must attend is need. A need for a group can be identified by the various stakeholders (students, teachers, support staff, parents, administrators) who raise concerns about a specific problem that is surfacing or populations of children who need a service. In our example, several teachers at an elementary school asked the school social worker to facilitate a group for children who are shy and apparently friendless. Two of the children are known to the school social worker who has been working with them in individual sessions because of their refusal to go to the cafeteria for lunch with the other children. The parents and teachers of the students are in support of the group because they recognize their children's anxiety about social relationships.

Agency Context: The Group within the School

The structure of the group is often determined by the specifics of its setting. With the growing emphasis on academic proficiency and accountability, teachers are increasingly less willing to release their students for support services such as social work groups. School social workers must become proficient at discussing with teachers the connections between social emotional proficiency and academic success, a topic that has not been emphasized in current No Child Left Behind Act of 2001 mandates (Zeng et al., 2013). If teachers can see the relationship between a group work intervention for shy children and the children's ability to attend school with less fear and to interact more easily with peers, the teachers may be more likely to support group attendance (Pawlak et al., 2006). When teachers and school social workers support the same purposes for the group, the recruitment and ongoing implementation of the group is facilitated (Malekoff, 2014; Toseland & Rivas, 2012).

Evidence-based work with socially unskilled children includes components of (1) modeling, (2) coaching in conversational skills, (3) peer-mediated interventions, and (4) group contingencies (Bierman & Erath, 2006; Gresham & Evans, 1987). Sharing this information with teachers helps strengthen the collaborative relationship that includes classroom/playground skill building as well as small group activities of peer coaching, peer pairing, highlighting of accomplishments, and giving low-risk tasks that promote conversation. Teacher involvement is key to the success of these interventions (Bierman & Erath, 2006; Bierman & Powers, 2009; Brophy, 1996).

Purpose

Developing a clear and convincing rationale guides the purpose of the group and informs members about its focus and direction of the work of the sessions (Kurland, 2005). With a clearly defined purpose, the social worker is better able to develop clear objectives that are specific, measurable, and attainable within a specified period of time (Corey, Corey, & Corey, 2013). The purpose of the group is described in a clear and concise statement that informs the members and referral sources of the reason that the group is being formed. An example of a purpose statement for the group of shy students is, "The purpose of the group is to provide a safe place where children can learn how to talk to and play with other children." The objectives for the group in our example are to teach children specific conversational skills with regard to initiating conversation, asking questions of peers, and developing the ability to take the lead in conversations. Additionally, the school social worker plans to assess how the child interacts in the larger school context of classroom and playground. Weekly assessment of skill development within the group sessions and in classroom and school environments allows for inclusion of a progression of tasks that respond to each child's ability to integrate and use what he or she has learned.

Composition: Group Membership

The composition of the group refers to number and characteristics of the group leaders and group (Kurland, 2005). The social worker in our example decides to include a teacher in the groups to support generalization of the new behaviors to the classroom setting. Cofacilitation of groups offers additional input on group dynamics and support in working with the group members (Doel, 2006). In the group for shy children, this can be helpful as it provides opportunity to observe group interactions as well as to teach specific skill sets. Recognizing that the number and characteristics of group members affect how much time each member will have to take part in group learning, the worker decides that the group will comprise five shy children and two socially competent peer mentors.

In our example of a group for shy children, combining children from grades 3 and 4 enhances the heterogeneity of skills and age level and responds to the referrals by the third- and fourth-grade teachers. Among the fourth graders is a child who has limited social interaction and an individualized education program with objectives to develop social skills in a group. This child has been working on social skills in a dyad with another student for several months, and the social worker is confident that he is now capable of learning in a structured small group. Differences in characteristics of group members provide opportunities to learn different perspectives and ways of interacting (Toseland & Rivas, 2012). In our example, the school social worker also includes two same-age peer mentors to model peer socialization skills and to promote acceptance in social situations outside of the group (Bierman & Furman, 1984; Brophy, 1996). The mentors are chosen by teacher recommendations for strong social skills and helpful relationships with classmates.

Structure of Group

The structure of the group refers to the concrete arrangements that will define the group (Kurland, 2005) including when and where it will meet, the number of sessions, the duration of each session, and whether the groups will be closed or open to new members. Coordination of the structure of the group is complicated, particularly when group members are being recruited from different classrooms. The number of sessions, as well as the duration of each session, are influenced by teacher and school schedules, necessitating flexibility from the school social worker. Teachers may be reluctant to allow students to leave the classroom during certain academic subjects. Many times the only available time for meeting is during the lunch hour, which includes getting food from the cafeteria and taking it to the meeting location, which takes time away from the session.

When the school social worker fails to communicate the importance of the closed group composition, he or she can be coerced by late requests for someone to join a group already established and comfortable for its members. In our example, the plan is to close the group to new members for the ten-session curriculum, allowing the children to become comfortable with one another and adept in progressive social skill development. Depending on teacher schedule (with children coming from two classrooms), it may be preferable for a five-week program to conduct two thirty-minute weekly sessions rather than one sixty-minute weekly session. Such exposure increases the comfort of group members and the learning of new skills and may be easier for teachers to accommodate. In our example, the worker alternates group sessions between an early morning group that accommodates the needs of two of the children who have frequent absences triggered by fear of coming to school, and a lunchtime group that allows group members opportunities to practice social interactions on the playground with the help of their peer mentors.

Content of the Sessions: What Will Be Done to Achieve Goals?

Planning for each session includes defining a structure with flexibility to change as the session demands. The social worker examines several skill-building curricula, because development of specific skill-sets is essential in improving peer interactions of shy, somewhat fearful children (LeCroy, 2009). The curricular models provide the worker with current evidence-based practices for socioemotional and behavioral change, specifying the content to be delivered over a set number of sessions and ensuring that the designated skills are being delivered across settings and practitioners (Galinsky, Terzian, & Fraser, 2006). Bierman and Furman (1984) recommend focusing on three conversational skills with shy and withdrawn children: (1) sharing information about self, (2) asking others about themselves, and (3) giving help, suggestions, invitations, and advice. Keeping in mind that generalization of social skills to settings outside of the groups is essential if the children are to master the skills and have opportunities to interact with peers (Bierman & Erath, 2006; Bierman & Powers, 2009; Frey & George-Nichols, 2003), the social worker chooses as program a school-wide poster project related to kindness. Kindness would be a theme for conversational practice in the groups. The theme was also chosen because the teachers have noted that two of the shy children are quite artistically talented.

Skills would be learned through pairing a shy child with a socially skilled peer who models each skill and role-plays a situation in which the skill could be used. Each exercise is directed by the group facilitator with ample opportunities for both child and mentor to be rewarded. Praise and/or concrete rewards for even small behavioral changes (Frey & George-Nichols, 2003; Mattaini, 2001) are recommended. Group members can also be reinforced for praising other children. In our example, the mentor might initially demonstrate beginning a conversation about a poster contest with one of the shy children. The shy child then would be coached in initiating a similar conversation with the mentor. Finally, the child would be coached to have conversations about the poster project (with the support of his or her peer mentor) with other children in the classroom and on the playground.

Evaluation

Assessment and evaluation of both individuals and group interactions are an ongoing part of the group experience. Chapter 29 specifically focuses on evaluating outcomes of group interventions, but we will also review group evaluation here.

The social worker preassesses each individual's conversational skills of sharing information about self; asking questions of others; and giving help, suggestions, and advice to others. Specific development of each skill may be evaluated after each training session with a simple list of behaviors learned. Use of a goal attainment scale (Toseland & Rivas, 2012) with three points of measurement evaluates skill acquisition over time. Sample rating questions for this project are, How often (1 = never; 2 = 1–2 times; 3= 3 or more times) in the past week has the student

- Asked the peer buddy questions about his or her art project?
- Asked another group member questions about his or her art projects?
- Offered ideas or help to the peer buddy about his or her art project?
- Offered ideas or help to the other group members about his or her art project?

Evaluation after each group session allows the social worker to assess the level of skill development and to target and reinforce specific behaviors that the child must continue to practice. The social worker also evaluates whether the children are interacting more easily and more comfortably in the group as they learn the various conversational skills. Teacher evaluation of the child's acquisition of skills is also measured with a similar simple checklist that monitors how children interact in the classroom and on the playground. It is important for the social worker to keep the classroom teachers informed about the various skills practiced in the group to support reinforcement in the classroom. For instance, the social worker could report that the children are discussing a poster contest with the theme of kindness and suggest that the teacher could arrange for the shy child to talk about it in a small group of supportive peers (with the help of the peer mentor). Chapter 18 also has useful ideas for research skills and evaluation in schools.

Pregroup Contact: Mutual Conversation and Getting to Know Each Other

An important step in recruiting members to any group is the pregroup interview that allows prospective group members to more fully understand the purpose of the group, to ask clarifying questions, and to form an initial bond with the leaders. Pregroup contact eases transition to the group. This is especially important for children who have anxiety about social situations because they can experience considerable trepidation at the idea of joining a group of peers. As the school social worker presents the group as a way for them to have fun, learn how to make friends, and work with other students on a project that they enjoy, their anxiety may decrease. The pregroup interview allows the worker to assess the strengths and challenges of each member. It will also allow prospective members to decide whether they are ready for a group experience at this time. The social worker can invite children to participate and, if they are reluctant, can encourage them to try the group for several sessions. If they find that they do not like the group, children have the option of dropping out. Pregroup interviews may also lead to exclusion of potential members who are not appropriate at this time for the group intervention, such as children who are vehement that they do not want to take part in the group, children whose parents are opposed to the group, or children who are highly anxious about interacting with more than one peer at a time.

STAGES OF GROUP PROCESS

After careful planning and recruitment of members for the group, the social worker's next task is to understand the needs of individual members and the group process as the group progresses through beginning, working, and ending stages (Corey et al., 2013). The role of the school social worker is to lead the group in such a way that positive group experiences for members are maximized. The social worker facilitating the group must have a clear understanding of the purpose of the group and be ready to help members become comfortable sharing concerns and changing behaviors that interfere with optimal group interactions. In order to do this, school social workers must be knowledgeable about group work principles and must develop awareness of the skills used to further positive group movement at various stages of group development.

The school social worker must be a keen observer of interactions between group members and must actively intervene in encouraging members to focus on both the session theme and on their relationships with each other within the group. Each group—whether it is a structured, time limited, curricular-based group with the same core group of members meeting for several weeks, or an open-ended support group that invites members for support for a common issue—goes through predictable stages that mirror the members' comfort levels in working on specific themes. When the worker is aware of the meaning of various behaviors at each stage of group development, he or she will be more able to support group members in positive interactions with peers, to encourage use of mutual aid, and to facilitate learning of new behaviors that will lead to more-satisfying interactions in the school and community.

The following is an example of how the worker intervenes in processes and helps the members to engage productively in different stages of the group's development. The group involves seventh-grade girls referred by the assistant principal for fighting.

Principal's Request

The principal of an urban middle school has asked the school social worker to convene a group for seventh-grade girls who have had disciplinary actions for fighting with classmates. Some girls have had only verbal battles where staff has intervened to deescalate the conflict, while others have had physical altercations that resulted in suspension from a school that has a zero tolerance rule for fighting. The principal believes that this group of girls needs additional intensive intervention to learn new ways of managing conflict and has requested that the school social worker develop a group for six to eight girls identified as having fighting behaviors.

Evidence-Based Practice for Group Work with Girls Who Are Aggressive

Girl fighting is a multifaceted problem that is influenced by several contexts, including family, school, and peer group (Chamberlain, 2003; Dellasega & Adamshick, 2005; Talbott, Celinska, Simpson, & Coe, 2002). Gender-specific methods for working with girls have fine-tuned the interventions to respond to the unique needs that girls have for methods that respond to female socialization and its influence on the ways that girls have learned to express anger, solve conflict, and protect themselves from physical and sexual victimization (Dellasega & Adamshick, 2005; Letendre, 2007b). Group interventions are an ideal method of working with young adolescent girls because of the importance of relationships and connectedness to others in the lives of females (LeCroy & Daley, 2001; Letendre & Smith, 2011) and cognitive-behavioral curricula are commonly used to teach the skills in schools (Garrett, 2004). The challenge of using the cognitive-behavioral curricular model is in allowing time to also attend to the interactions among members (Letendre & Wayne, 2008). An all-girls' group can teach methods for calming hurt and angry feelings and developing better coping skills for problem solving the interactional challenges faced by middle school girls. Helping the girls to practice the skills in the group as situations arise will further enhance learning. Keeping teachers and parents aware of the various themes of the curriculum allows for discussion with members and reinforcement of the skills outside of the group.

The Plan

In pregroup interviews and beginning sessions it is important to carefully assess the specific strengths and challenges that each girl brings to the group (Toseland & Rivas, 2012). An individual assessment will enable the school social worker to understand how each girl's strengths and challenges will affect the group process. School social workers must be aware that to compose a homogenous group (girls with fighting behaviors) without attending to the heterogeneity of the group members (race/ethnicity, comfort with participation, personal characteristics, coping styles) misses an opportunity to focus on the strengths of the group members that will contribute to an effective group interaction rather than to a group experience where the girls have verbal and physical altercations. Conversations with the administrator and teachers related to the importance of learning nonaggressive skills as prevention of behaviors that will lead to greater violence is an essential part of the planning process. Ideally, the ten-week group will meet for a class period (e.g., forty minutes), but the schedule is often dictated by the academic demands, and teachers will want to know how the groups will improve the girls' behavior in ways that will contribute to learning. It may be necessary to facilitate the groups during the lunch hour or elective classes (which are not always the most favorable time for middle school students). Skill building with an empirically tested curriculum will be combined with ample opportunities to modify the generic curriculum to the needs of this group of urban girls with integration of cultural components throughout the sessions (Letendre, 2007a; Peeks, 1999; Scott, 2002). The social worker recruits two eighth-grade girl mentors recommended by teachers and peers for their ability to interact positively with peers and model prosocial ways of behaving. Inclusion of mentors who do not use aggression in interactions is important since research indicates that aggressive behaviors are encouraged in homogenous groupings of peers (Bierman & Powers, 2009). The worker should maintain biweekly contact with families to inform parents of the skill-building topics that are focuses of the group sessions.

GROUP FACILITATION: FROM BEGINNING STAGE THROUGH WORKING STAGE TO ENDING STAGE

Engaging Group Members in the Beginning

When members first come together in a group, they experience typical fears and exhibit predictable behaviors associated with entering new situations (Corey et al., 2013). Young adolescent girls who see each other daily in school may fear appearing foolish, being rejected by peers, having their participation in the group known by other students, being talked about outside of group, or not being competent to perform the tasks of the group. Such fears may be masked by behaviors that interfere with the work of the group such as monopolizing group time when a topic is raised, giving advice without waiting for discussion of the problem, putting other members down, clowning, refusing to participate, acting superior, socializing with one or two other members, and allying with other group members against the leader (Corey et al., 2013). Members who have not voluntarily sought the group but who have been sent to sessions by the principal or urged to attend by a teacher/parent may remain silent, hostile, and withdrawn. The worker's ability to refrain from taking such behaviors personally and to actively provide structure in the early sessions allows the girls to discuss their feelings and to calm their fears.

In the beginning stage of the group the emphasis is on (1) helping members to get to know one another by identifying commonalities and concerns, (2) connecting the purpose of the group with individual needs and goals of members, and (3) developing group norms that assure members of a safe experience where positive interactions are reinforced and every voice is heard (Corey et al., 2013). Inclusion of the many activities of curricular-based models can be useful here. Use of a positive, nonpunitive behavioral system is also helpful to facilitate the work of the group for students with challenging behaviors (Mattaini, 2001).

The following process illustrates how group members can be engaged in the group process, and can be taught skills of active listening, empathy, and problem solving while setting norms for confidentiality.

> In the first meeting of the group, the social worker introduced the discussion of confidentiality. This is particularly important to encourage open sharing of the many concerns that might lead to aggressive behaviors. The worker stated that she has responsibility to protect the girls in the group from harm and therefore would need to intervene if a girl were to say that she or someone else could be hurt. She also said that there are ways other than physical harm by which the members can be hurt in the group. Rather than authoritatively dictating "What is said in the group, stays in the group," the worker modeled active listening when she asked each member how she might feel if her personal story about a friend, boyfriend, or family member was shared with

peers outside the group. She repeated each girl's statements as a way of underscoring the hurt, betrayal, and ensuing anger that might result from this breach of confidentiality. Next the social worker led a discussion on ways to problem solve and prevent girls from sharing stories outside of the group. Finally, the school social worker helps the girls to discuss appropriate consequences if sharing outside the group should occur.

By sharing a group problem with its members, the worker provided an opportunity for the girls to listen to each other, to develop empathy for their peers, and to engage in a problem-solving method that encourages brainstorming nonaggressive solutions to a problem. By encouraging active involvement of this group of girls, who are frequently disempowered in the school setting, the worker has demonstrated that their input is a valued part of this group intervention. It is important to recognize, however, that some girls in the group could be reluctant to trust other girls. The school social worker must assure the group members that they are only expected to share information that they are comfortable with other girls knowing. Trust may take several sessions to develop.

Since schools often fail to provide the support and encouragement that aggressive students need to change their behaviors, it is important to avoid allying with administration as disciplinarians when discussing how girls were referred to the group. It is critical to be honest with the girls about why they were chosen and to clarify the purpose of the group, what they might gain from attending, and the specific content of the sessions. Members must be involved in the discussion of how specific issues and skills that are discussed in the group may be helpful in their lives. The rare opportunity for the young adolescent girls to be heard and understood by a caring, nonjudging adult furthers the work of trust building and connection to the group as a helpful place to meet and solve problems (Letendre & Smith, 2011).

Working Stage: Encouraging Interaction

Once the girls are more comfortable with other members, the group moves to the working stage. In this stage, the school social worker is looking for opportunities to help each girl to try out different roles and ways of thinking and behaving. For many of the girls in the group who habitually react rather than communicate their needs calmly and assertively, changing roles is difficult. The group offers opportunities for this kind of practice and includes role-playing of situations that are common themes for the girls' lives and that often result in hurt feelings and subsequent fighting. Such an activity can be both enjoyable and instructive as the girls are encouraged to take different roles and give feedback on the particular skills used in the scenarios. As the school social worker and student mentors model new skills (e.g., methods of calming down when angry and generating cool thoughts) for practice and role-play situation, he or she is scanning the group to observe how members are reacting to the material and to each other and using group facilitation skills to encourage open communication. The worker can challenge members in a caring and respectful way to talk about issues that may be painful and/or difficult. It may be hard for one girl to apologize to another after a putdown and she may need much support from the group for gradually being able to see the other girl's point of view. Gently encouraging exploration of feelings and actions related to sharing hurtful situations offers opportunities for empathy building and mutual support among the girls. Making observations as "hunches" allows the girls to either accept or reject interpretations of their actions and behaviors. Demonstrating sensitivity to racial, cultural, and oppressive attitudes can set the tone for girls to express to the group ways that they have felt put down because of their skin color or ethnicity (e.g., being followed by a clerk in a store, being laughed at for an accent) (Letendre & Smith, 2011; Letendre & Werkmeister-Rozas, 2015). Encouraging listening and step-by-step problem solving trains members to think before acting. Inviting members to share positive and negative feedback in caring, nonaggressive ways increases their repertoire of skills for showing appreciation and asking for what they need, which are all skills that have been poorly developed and reinforced in this group of girls.

Conflict around Difference (during the working stage)

As the girls become more comfortable within the group and begin to share differences conflict may emerge. When a conflict arises in the group related to stereotyping or lack of comfort with differences, the worker invites exploration of the issue. When one member, a recent immigrant, is scapegoated by the other members for her "funkiness" (hygiene) and the "dumb" statements that she makes to the members and leaders, the group worker provides guidance in helping the girls talk openly with each other about the specific reasons that the girls are shunning this group member and the normally taboo subject of hygiene. This is an opportunity for the worker to reframe existing concerns around female socialization and stereotypical behaviors and roles, an important topic in the curriculum. Throughout the discussion, the worker encourages the girl to express how being shunned makes her feel. The worker asks the other group members whether any of them had ever experienced not knowing what to do in a situation and having others make fun of them. This discussion helped the girls to be empathic with the plight of the excluded member and to understand the impact of this practice on other girls within the middle school. The worker also asks other group members to share with the shunned member some ways that she might behave differently and bring greater acceptance from her peers. Finally, the worker asks the members if they would like to do anything to help the girl to fit in more easily in this new social setting. Such a discussion, although difficult, teaches the girls to listen to another's point of view, put themselves in her place, and even offer support to someone who is different from them. Helping members to talk to each other models ways of interacting that are more adaptive and less destructive than the girls have previously learned. This is quite a different scenario than one that might have occurred before the girls entered the group, and the leader commends them for the way they have handled the situation.

Ending the Group with Good-byes, Gains, and Next Steps

The ending of the group involved sharing feelings about leaving the group, saying good-bye, celebrating gains, and planning for using the newly learned skills and behaviors outside the group. The most important part of ending is that the group members need to be helped to wrap up the group. For this group of girls, many of whom have not had satisfying relationships with other girls, the ending of a group experience that was fun and where they felt accepted and valued can be difficult. The worker must help members to discuss their feelings of loss as well as the gains that they have made while in the group. When the curriculum specifies a set number of sessions it can be useful to remind the members of the session number and how many sessions remain. As the group nears ending (sessions 7 and 8) the social worker can remind the girls that they will be finishing in three, two, or one week. Revisiting the initial purpose of the group as well as the goals that each girl set for herself can help to consolidate the gains. Changes observed in the group and in the other school contexts are praised. The group members also discuss plans for continuing to use their newly acquired skills, challenges that might interfere with their successes, and plans for possibilities for periodic booster groups. Since the group has been facilitated in the school with eighth-grade mentors, contact with the girls will continue informally as they see each other in the school setting. This interaction with socially skilled peers may influence acceptance by other girls in the school (Bierman & Furman, 1984; Bierman & Powers, 2009). A celebration with food chosen by the girls and certificates of achievement that are individualized for each member brings a formal closure to the group.

CONCLUSION

School social workers have long known that group work is a powerful method for helping children to solve problems and learn to interact with peers in ways that promote positive social and emotional growth. In current school climates, school social workers are using evidence-based group models that build specific skill-sets to prevent or intervene in problem behaviors. School social workers must attend to the specific content of the curriculum as well as the planning and facilitation if the group interventions are to be effective. As school social workers continue to become trained and educated in group work models of practice as well as best practices for different populations, problems, and stages of group development, they can continue to provide the group work services that children and adolescents need for skill development, belonging, mutual support, and problem solving. The next chapter builds further on this model to focus on monitoring of group processes and outcomes.

References

Bierman, K. L., & Erath, S. A. (2006). Promoting social competence in early childhood: Classroom curricula and social skills coaching programs. In K. McCartney & D. Phillips (Eds.), *Blackwell handbook on early childhood development* (pp. 595–615). Malden, MA: Blackwell.

Bierman, K. L., & Furman, W. (1984). The effects of social skills training and peer involvement on the social adjustment of preadolescents. *Child Development, 55*(1), 151–162.

Bierman, K. L., & Powers, C. J. (2009). Social skills training to improve peer relations. In K. H. Rubin, W. M. Bukowski, & B. Laursen (Eds.), *Handbook of peer interactions, relationships, and groups* (pp. 603–621). New York: Guilford Press.

Brophy, J. (1996). *Working with shy or withdrawn students* (Report No. EDO-PS-96-14). Washington DC: Office of Educational Research and Improvement (ED). (ERIC Document Reproduction Service No. ED402070 1996-11-00.)

Chamberlain, P. (2003). *Treating chronic juvenile offenders: Advances made through the Oregon multidimensional treatment foster care model.* Washington, DC: American Psychological Association.

Corey, M. S., Corey, G., & Corey, C. (2013). *Groups: Process and practice* (9th ed.). Belmont, CA: Thomson/Brooks Cole.

Dellasega, C., & Adamshick, P. (2005). Evaluation of a program designed to reduce relational aggression in middle school girls. *Journal of School Violence, 4*(3), 63–76.

Doel, M. (2006). *Using group work.* New York: Routledge.

Frey, A., & George-Nichols, N. (2003). Intervention practices for students with emotional and behavioral problems. *Children & Schools, 25*(2), 97–103.

Galinsky, M., Terzian, M. A., & Fraser, M. W. (2006). The art of group work practice with manualized groups. *Social Work with Groups, 29*(1), 11–26.

Garrett, K. J. (2004). Use of groups in school social work and group processes. *Social Work with Groups, 27*(2/3), 75–92.

Gresham, F. M., & Evans, S. E. (1987). Conceptualization and treatment of social withdrawal in the schools. *Special Services in Schools, 3*(3–4), 37–51.

Johnson, A. (1962). *School social work: Its contribution to professional education.* New York: National Association of Social Workers.

Kurland, R. (2005). Planning: The neglected component of group development. *Social Work with Groups, 28*(3/4), 9–16.

LeCroy, C. W. (2009). Social skills training through groups in school settings: Some practical considerations. In C. R. Massat, R. Constable, S. McDonald, & J. P. Flynn (Eds.), *School social work: Practice, policy, and research* (7th ed., pp. 621–637). Chicago: Lyceum Books.

LeCroy, C. W., & Daley, J. (2001). *Empowering adolescent girls: Examining the present and building skills for the future with the Go Grrrls Program.* New York: W. W. Norton & Company.

Letendre, J. A. (2003). Led by the children: Modification of an urban violence prevention project based on insights learned from the group members. *School Social Work Journal, 28*(1), 36–50.

Letendre, J. (2007a). "Take your time and give it more": Supports and constraints to success in curricular school based groups. *Social Work with Groups, 30*(3), 65–84.

Letendre, J. (2007b). Sugar and spice but not always nice: Gender socialization and its impact on development of aggression in adolescent girls. *Child and Adolescent Social Work Journal, 24*(4), 353–368.

Letendre, J., & Smith, E. (2011). "It's murder out today": Middle school girls speak out about factors contributing to girl fighting. *Children and Schools, 33*(1), 47–57.

Letendre, J., & Wayne, J. (2008). Integrating process interventions into a school-based curriculum group. *Social Work with Groups, 31*(3/4), 289–305.

Letendre, J., & Werkmeister-Rozas, L. (2015). "She can't fight cuz she acts White": Identity and coping for girls of color in middle school. *Children and Schools, 37*(1), 46–53.

Malekoff, A. (2014). *Group work with adolescents: Principles and practice* (3rd ed.). New York: Guilford Press.

Mattaini, M. (2001). *PEACEPOWER for adolescents: Strategies for a culture of non-violence.* Washington, DC: National Association of Social Workers.

No Child Left Behind Act of 2001, Pub. L. 107-110 (2002).

Pawlak, E., Wozniak, D., & McGowan, M. (2006). Perspectives on groups for school social workers. In C. R. Massat, R. Constable, S. McDonald, & J. P. Flynn (Eds.), *School social work: Practice, policy, and research* (7th ed., pp. 598–617). Chicago: Lyceum Books.

Peeks, A. L. (1999). Conducting a social skills group with Latina adolescents. *Journal of Child and Adolescent Group Therapy, 9*(3), 139–153.

Scott, C. C. (2002). The sisterhood group: A culturally focused empowerment group model for inner city African-American youth. *Journal of Child and Adolescent Group Therapy, 11*(2/3), 77–85.

Talbott, E., Celinska, D., Simpson, J., & Coe, M. (2002). "Somebody else making somebody else fight": Aggression and the social context among urban adolescent girls. *Exceptionality, 10*(3), 203–220.

Toseland, R. W., & Rivas, R. F. (2012). *An introduction to group work practice* (7th ed.). Boston, MA: Allyn & Bacon.

Zeng, G., Boe, E. E., Bulotsky-Shearer, R. J., Garrett, S. D., Slaughter-Defoe, D., Brown, E. D., & Lopez, B. (2013). Integrating U.S. federal efforts to address the multifaceted problems of children: A historical perspective on national education and child mental health policies. *School Mental Health, 5*(3), 119–131.

29

Evaluation of School-Based Counseling Groups

Kendra J. Garrett

School of Social Work, St. Catherine University and University of St. Thomas

- ◆ Determining Evidence-Informed Group Interventions
- ◆ Monitoring and Implementation of Interventions
- ◆ Monitoring Group Dynamics
- ◆ Monitoring Individual and Group Outcomes
- ◆ Methods for Monitoring Groups

School social workers are increasingly being asked to show that their practice with students is effective and to link social work intervention with student academic progress. The No Child Left Behind Act of 2001 created external mandates to ensure that methods used in working with students have positive and demonstrable results. Ongoing proposals to reform the No Child Left Behind Act, while becoming more flexible, continue the quest for student achievement, generally documented in the form of academic testing (U.S. Department of Education, 2015). This emphasis on evaluation fits well with the social work emphasis on monitoring practice outcomes identified in the National Association of Social Workers (NASW) Code of Ethics (2008), the NASW Standards for School Social Work Services (2002), and the International Association for Social Work with Groups (2006). Effective practice has been defined in terms of evidence-based practice (Franklin & Kelly, 2009). As described in chapter 4, the term "evidence-informed practice" (EIP) is preferred in this volume.

DETERMINING EVIDENCE-INFORMED GROUP INTERVENTIONS

EIP requires identification of the best empirically supported interventions to meet student needs. Decisions on what interventions to apply are determined in collaboration with the student, parents/guardians, and other members of the school team. When school social workers implement interventions, they monitor both that the intervention is administered as intended and that students are making appropriate progress (Franklin & Kelly, 2009; Franklin, Kim, & Tripodi, 2009; Raines, 2008; Roberts & Yeager, 2004).

In the case of school social workers, the discernment process regarding evidence-informed interventions often results in identifying group strategies as the treatment of choice, because there are a number of group interventions that have been shown to be effective in schools. School social workers have successfully addressed academic outcomes through group interventions. For example, Harris and Franklin (2003) found that an eight-session cognitive-behavioral skills training group improved grades and attendance significantly in Mexican American pregnant and parenting teens. Newsome (2005) found that an eight-week solution-focused group of at-risk eleven- to fourteen-year-old students significantly improved homework completion and maintained the gains through six-week follow up. Larkin and Thyer (1999) found that an eight-session cognitive-behavioral counseling group for disruptive elementary students significantly improved grades, and improvements remained at three-month follow up.

Social workers have also been successful in helping students improve emotional and behavioral skills in school-based groups. In their study described above, Larkin and Thyer's (1999) group intervention helped students make significant gains in self-control, self-esteem, and classroom behavior, and the students maintained the gains on follow up. Newsome's (2005) solution-focused groups demonstrated significantly improved classroom behavior, which also was maintained on follow up. Hilliard (2007) found that a social work group that addressed grief in elementary children improved behavior ratings significantly in comparison to the pretest and a control group.

Social work group interventions to address social skills have also been shown to be empirically effective. Mishna, Muskat, and Wiener (2010) found student improvement through a qualitative study that evaluated a twelve-session manual-based group whose goal was to help students with learning disabilities develop increased understanding of their disabilities and improve their self-advocacy skills. LeCroy (2004) developed a twelve-session group curriculum for adolescent girls. Participants significantly increased in peer esteem and helping others, and decreased irrational beliefs, compared to a control group. Spencer, Brown, Griffin, and Abdullah (2008) found that a year-long group that taught mediation and dialogue skills to high school juniors significantly improved ratings of social identity and critical social awareness; these students expressed improved understanding of communication across differences and resolution of intergroup conflict. Harris and Franklin's (2003) groups significantly improved their members' coping and problem-solving skills, and those skills were maintained through thirty-day follow up. Newsome's (2005) group members showed significant growth in social skills and maintained this growth on follow up.

MONITORING AND IMPLEMENTATION OF INTERVENTIONS

EIP requires that social workers use critical thinking regarding existing research. Workers must critically evaluate the research to determine if it is of high quality, and they must consider the extent to which the research applies to their clients' specific situations. Sometimes school social workers may need to adapt programs slightly to meet unique developmental, cognitive, or cultural needs (Raines, 2008). Garrett (2004) found that school social workers freely adapt manual-based group curricula to meet needs of students in their groups and to fit with stages of group development. While fidelity to evidence-informed treatments is imperative, social workers must, at the same time, implement programs with enough flexibility to meet client needs or to fit with school resources (Frankin & Kelly, 2009; Kendall, Gosch, Furr, & Sood, 2008). Raines noted that changes that social workers make to evidence-based interventions should remain faithful to the intervention's theoretical concepts and should include all of its principal components; in addition, social workers should fully implement all components without truncating length or number of sessions.

When keeping track of group records, the school social worker should, therefore, describe the session-by-session implementation of the intervention; doing so allows the worker to identify his or her efforts to maintain treatment fidelity. When the social worker makes changes, he or she should record the adjustments to the intervention and the reasoning behind them. This documentation of changes, together with information on outcomes, can be used to evaluate the effectiveness of the adapted intervention. Raines (2008) suggested that workers communicate changes and the results to the developers of evidence-supported treatments.

MONITORING GROUP DYNAMICS

In addition to monitoring fidelity of the intervention, the school social worker also monitors what is happening within the group as it develops (Northen & Kurland, 2001; Wayne & Cohen, 2001). We know, for example, that groups that function effectively together are more effective in accomplishing tasks and meeting goals. For example, group-centered communication leads to increased commitment to goals and improved morale; cohesiveness, effective group norms, and positive climate lead to improved outcomes (Toseland & Rivas, 2012).

"Knowing what are normative behaviors at each stage [of group development] can help the worker to assess whether the group is making progress toward achieving its goals" (Toseland & Rivas, 2012, p. 93). Monitoring the development of group dynamics is important in determining if the group is headed in a positive direction. When a worker gathers data on group dynamics on an ongoing basis, he or she should let members know that the purpose of gathering those data is to share them with the group, in service of improving the functioning of the group (Rose & Tolman, 1989).

Any process monitoring needs to be minimally intrusive and time efficient. Rose (1998) suggested using a postsession questionnaire in groups for children and adolescents. Such a questionnaire may be a rating scale that asks members to comment on member perception of the usefulness of the group, the member's own involvement, the degree of mutual help and self-disclosure, cohesion, on-task behavior, and anxiety. These can be quickly summarized to track member satisfaction as the group progresses. When the social worker identifies concerns, she or he can take them to the group for discussion. Mackenzie (1990) suggested that group records should note major issues for each member; a sociogram of interaction; and summaries of major themes, critical incidents, therapist issues, supervision comments, and notes for the next session. Another recording approach is to record groups in a consistent format that includes session number, a seating chart, notes on communication flow, and a brief summary of group content, processes, developmental stage, and a practice reflection of the group, including plans for the future (Cohen & Garrett, 1995).

MONITORING INDIVIDUAL AND GROUP OUTCOMES

In addition to choosing empirically supported treatments, assessing their relevance to the problem at hand, collaborating with clients and others to determine the most appropriate intervention to address a situation, and monitoring fidelity of the intervention, EIP requires that school social workers monitor their own practice outcomes to determine if the work they are doing is helpful in meeting client needs. While use of research-based methodologies is essential, it will never substitute for the school social worker's monitoring outcomes for all clients in his or her caseload, including, of course, clients receiving services in groups. Monitoring of groups is complicated by the need to monitor the experiences of each individual member and the group as a whole.

Members need to understand the purpose of the group, and the purpose needs to be congruent with what members hope to accomplish (Toseland & Rivas, 2012). Sometimes younger students are not aware of reasons they are participating in a group. The school social worker may initially need to help students understand the concept of goals, perhaps by discussing them in a concrete way (e.g., by talking about goals in sports) before the group can move on to actually discussing the goals of the group (Rose & Edleson, 1987). Goals for students in social work counseling groups need to be congruent with the educational purposes of the school, and group members need to be able to articulate, consistent with their developmental levels, the purposes of the groups in which they are participating as well as what they will accomplish as part of the group.

Goal setting in groups may be complicated by the fact that goals may be group goals, common to everyone in the group, or individual, with each student carrying different goals (Toseland & Rivas, 2012). When the entire group is working on a collective project, goals are generally clear to the members. In such a situation, it is often quite easy to evaluate group goals because the completed project defines the successful outcome of the group. When all members of a group are working on similar goals (as they might in a group in which all students are working on increasing their self-esteem, managing their anger, or coping with a divorce in the family), measurements can often be the same for all students in the group. Goal monitoring is most complicated when each member has a different goal. This might happen when group members are working on similar but slightly different goals. For example, a group might be working on increasing social skills, but each member might have different skill goals. One student might be working to be more assertive, another may be improving impulse control, and yet another may be managing anger. In a situation such as this, each student's goals would need unique measurement strategies, and the group would also need frequent reminders of the various member goals so that they can give each other support and help. In this example, the group might want to be particularly tolerant of an angry statement from the student wanting to become more assertive, while giving a student who wanted to manage anger gentle feedback to be more patient. Setting the stage in a group with a number of individual goals will take good organization and communication skills on the part of the school social worker.

Good goals are measurable, attainable, and specific (Raines, 2002; Toseland & Rivas, 2012). Making goals measurable requires that the school social worker (and group members) are able to articulate what they are trying to accomplish together in the group so they can recognize when they have been successful. In making goals specific, members understand what the goals are and how they will go about attaining them. Clearly goals need to be attainable, so that members can reasonably hope to be successful without setting unrealistic hopes.

Setting goals with members can have considerable therapeutic merit, especially for students who have not previously been involved in their own goal setting. Students often gain clearer understanding of why they are participating in the group as they talk about teachers' and parents' concerns. But they are often surprised to learn that they might have a say in what they are to work on in the group. The process of negotiating a student-stated goal of "getting the teacher off my back" might lead to discussions on what the student can change (e.g., his own behavior) in order to, perhaps, in turn change the way the teacher relates to him. This contracting around goals is extremely important because interventions are more likely to be successful when there is a shared understanding between members and the social worker about what they are working to accomplish (Toseland & Rivas, 2012). In other words, treatment is more likely to be effective when the group leader and the group members are all on the same page about what the group hopes to accomplish.

School social workers working with students who have individualized education programs (IEPs) may have an advantage in measuring goals, since goals and objectives are clarified in the IEP. These goals may not be specific enough to constitute group goals, however, or the purpose of the group may not fit exactly with the IEP. In this situation, and for all other students who do not have IEP goals, the school social worker should specify the goals with members as part of the beginning stage of the group.

Monitoring Outcomes

It is wise to use a variety of strategies to monitor goals (Dibble, n.d.; Monette, Sullivan, & DeJong, 2014; Toseland & Rivas, 2012). Quantitative measures require the worker to identify a way to count or assign numbers to measure the goal. Qualitative methods use words, pictures, or descriptions to explain changes in goals over time. Both can be useful in monitoring the success of group work in schools. Additional strategies can be found in chapter 20.

One important caveat in monitoring goals, whether through numbers or with narratives, is that measurements and markers used must be reliable and valid. Reliable measurements are those that are stable (Monette et al., 2014). This means that there is shared understanding among all parties about what the goals are, they are defined well enough that everyone understands what they mean, and they are consistent from one measurement to the next and from one observer (e.g., teacher, parent, student, social worker) to another. Measurements must also be valid, meaning that the measurement adequately measures what it is intended to measure (Monette et al., 2014). For example, a goal of increasing self-esteem cannot be measured validly by monitoring the number of times the student volunteers to help other students in the classroom, even though there may be a presumption that students with high self-esteem volunteer more often to help others.

Another consideration in choosing measurements for goals is that the unit of analysis must match the measurement strategy (Monette et al., 2014). For example, if the members have individual goals (e.g., changes in individual behavior), it would not make sense to analyze changes made by the group (e.g., group cohesion) or school-wide changes (e.g., total number of discipline incidents).

Quantitative Measurement

There are a number of quantitative ways to measure goals for group members. Perhaps the easiest way is to count behaviors that are to be targets for change. Students who have angry outbursts, are sent out of class for discipline purposes, receive detentions, get into fights, disrespect others, or fail to do homework have countable behaviors that can be used as measures of group outcomes. These behavioral goals are, perhaps, the easiest kind of goal to identify and monitor, as long as the people who monitor the behaviors (school social worker, group members, teachers, and parents) have a shared understanding of what those behaviors mean. If parents define a behavior in one way and the teacher defines it in another, the measurement is not clear or specific enough to be an effective marker of a student's behavior change. So part of the goal-setting discussion is to clarify what constitutes the behavior to be counted, and who will observe the behavior. If, for example, the target behavior is for the student to do homework, the worker and group members (and maybe also the teacher) need to discuss what constitutes homework, what quality of work is acceptable, and whether it is sufficient for the student to do the homework and leave it at home, or if the student must also turn it in on time.

A second way to quantify individual change is through standardized measurements. These measurements are those that have been administered to large numbers of students to determine the range and average scores for students at various ages. A large number of these standardized measurements are readily available to school social workers for use with students, although some have restrictions that require coursework in psychometrics for those who administer or score them (Raines, 2003). A complete discussion of these scales is beyond the scope of this chapter, but some commonly known standardized measures are the Multi-Dimensional Self-Concept Scale (Pro Ed, n.d.), the Child Behavior Checklist (Achenbach & Rescorla, 2001), the Beck Youth Inventories (Beck, Beck, & Jolly, 2005), and Connors's Comprehensive Behavior Rating Scales (Connors, 2008). One advantage of standardized scales is that their reliability and validity are known and clearly discussed in the manuals that accompany the tests. Some have subscales so that school social workers can limit the time needed to administer and score the tests to the specific areas that relate to group goals.

A third quantitative way of measuring goals is through the use of available data. Student records are rich sources of information on group members (Dibble, n.d.). Cumulative files contain standardized test scores, attendance information, discipline reports, and grades. Teacher records may be additional sources of such information. A teacher's grade book, for example, may have information on homework completion rates and daily grades.

The fourth measurement strategy is to find or develop measurement scales. School social workers may find that they need to search for other measurements of their group members' goals. Fischer and Corcoran (2007) have compiled a sourcebook of measurements for children and families that may fit the goals of group members. The Hudson Scales (parental attitudes, children's attitudes toward parents, and peer relations, among other psychosocial measures) (see www.walmyr.com/) are considered rapid assessment instruments, so named for their ease in administration and scoring (Monette et al., 2014).

If specific measurements are not readily available, it may be necessary for school social workers to develop their own set of questions or self-anchored scales to assess progress. Group members may be involved in this process, and some wonderful therapeutic work can be done in the process by identifying what work the group will be doing and how the worker and members will know if it is successful. One such strategy is to measure the goal on a scale of 1 (very poor success in meeting the goal) to 10 (very excellent success in meeting the goal). For example, a member whose goal is to manage his anger more effectively could rate his anger management for the past week numerically from 1 to 10 as very poor, very successful, or somewhere in between. This quick scale could be used weekly as a check in, providing data that can be tracked from week to week. If group members are working on a common goal, the worker, with the aid of the group members, can develop this ten-point scale and use it to track both individual progress and the weekly aggregate progress of the group by averaging the scores of all members. If group members have different individual goals, it would still be possible to aggregate group members' weekly ratings to provide a combined group measure of growth, as the scale is the same for everyone, even though members' goals are different.

A goal attainment scale (GAS) (Toseland & Rivas, 2012) is another good example of an individualized scale. A GAS is similar to the ten-point scale described above, but instead of identifying only the end points, it defines markers of success and describes the behavior that the levels represent. While this scale takes more time and effort to develop, it has the advantage of helping group members to identify behaviors that are happening in the present and examples of behaviors that would show improvement. The goals are, therefore, clearer to students and more concrete. This GAS would have three to five levels of markers. So, for example, a member who is working on anger management might identify his current level of anger management as losing his temper no more than once a day. Other markers of the goal would be developed according to the student's needs (see figure 29.1). Like endpoint-only scales, GAS can be used for weekly check-ins on progress toward goals and can be aggregated across different goals to note group progress, even when group members have different goals.

While self-anchored scales are likely less reliable than measures that have been standardized, they may be quite valid. Because the social worker develops these scales to meet the individualized needs of students in the

FIGURE 29.1   Goal Attainment Scale for the Goal of Improving Anger Management

Levels of Progress	Description of Behaviors
1. If the goal were completely met	1. Lose my temper less than once a month
2. If the behavior got a lot better	2. Lose my temper once a week
3. If the behavior got a little bit better	3. Lose my temper three times a week
4. Current behavior on goal	4. Lose my temper once a day
5. If the behavior got worse	5. Lose my temper two or more times a day

group, members are likely to understood them well. In addition, the goals are likely to accurately reflect student needs.

A final quantitative measurement strategy is to use satisfaction reports. Questions about whether members are happy with the group can be very helpful. Member satisfaction, while not necessarily linked to goal attainment, can tell the school social worker if groups are meeting member needs and can provide ideas for making changes in the way group services are provided. The worker can measure satisfaction by using a survey at the end of a group asking students to rate their satisfaction with the group or with a specific session on a scale of 1 to 10 (Rose, 1998).

Qualitative Methods

Although there are a number of quantitative ways to monitor practice, Garrett (2004) found that the school social workers in her study tended to focus on qualitative methods of monitoring their group work practice. In this study group leaders used statements from group members, teachers, and parents regarding improvement in school problems; comments on group process; statements about improved peer relationships; notations about member enjoyment of the group; and improvement in members' ability to cope with difficult situations. Their narrative reports included charming anecdotes of the group and quotes from students, parents, and teachers regarding member progress. These reports, and in particular, direct quotes, added a human dimension in reporting group results that would not have been as apparent through the reporting of numerical improvement alone.

METHODS FOR MONITORING GROUPS

It is essential for school social workers to find efficient ways to monitor their practice outcomes. Three methods seem particularly appropriate for monitoring groups in school settings. The first method is the single-system design (SSD) (Monette et al., 2014; Toseland & Rivas, 2012). After identifying goals and quantitative measurements for the goals, the worker tracks students' ratings for several baseline measurements to determine a baseline from which to measure change. If the goals are stable or getting worse before the group begins, the worker has greater assurance that gains toward goal improvement are a result of the group rather than because of some other intervention (e.g., the student was placed on medication or parents sought outside counseling) that is unrelated to the group. When the group begins, the worker and members continue monitoring measurement of the goals on a regular basis, perhaps by weekly checks on the goals with the member, teachers, or parents. In SSDs, these measurements are carefully tracked, usually by using graphs, so progress (or the lack thereof) can be easily identified and discussed with group members. (Group members often like these graphs and enjoy playing with the software and apps that can be used to track goals.) If members are improving in their goal ratings after the group begins, the worker can assume that the group intervention is the cause of the improvement and continue until the goals are reached (or until the predetermined time for the group to end). Should some or all members not be making progress, however, the worker can consider adjustments to the intervention methods to help members succeed in reaching their goals. SSDs are particularly useful in school-based groups because of their flexibility. They can be used when members have different goals or when everyone has the same goal. They can also simultaneously monitor group dynamics (e.g., cohesion) and group goals (e.g., accomplishing a group task). SSDs can be simple or complicated, depending on the needs of the group members. Members can have several goals simultaneously, can change the criteria for their goals, and can add new goals as they progress. The graphs give the school social worker records of progress that he or she can add to IEP records or use for summary reports for teachers or administration.

Another way of monitoring goals is the preexperimental design (PED) (Monette et al., 2014). Instead of continuous measurement with several baseline measurements, the worker gathers data on goals once before beginning the group, then repeats the same measurements at the end of the group to see if members have made progress on goals. PEDs have the advantage of less record-keeping and, therefore, less work. The disadvantage is that the worker cannot be as certain that the group was the cause of positive change, since students naturally grow and change over time, and they may have improved of their own accord. If the students are not improving, the information may not be available until after the group ends. Like the SSD, PEDs are flexible and can be used for multiple goals as well as for group goals.

A third way of monitoring progress is through keeping good records on progress students are making in the group. This more-qualitative approach can serve as a supplement to other methods. The worker can record attendance, observations of member behavior, teacher and parent feedback, interactions among members, and narratives of group sessions. The worker should summarize these ongoing records regularly, perhaps at report-card time and the end of the school year (Raines, 2002). Ongoing reflection of group and member progress provides a supplement to any quantitative methods the worker is using. The school social worker can use such reflection for supervision and consultation regarding the progress of his or her group interventions.

CONCLUSION

The values of the social work profession and external mandates on school social workers demand that workers demonstrate the effectiveness of their group interventions. This means that they must clearly define goals for all students in those groups, search carefully for research on the most effective ways to meet those goals, evaluate the quality of that research, and make decisions about the use of those interventions. This requires fidelity in monitoring the implementation to document what was done, and how the intervention was similar to or different from manuals of protocols for the interventions. Good record-keeping is essential in identifying group and member goals, how those goals were measured, and outcomes. School social workers need this information as they determine what methods to use in future groups and to evaluate where best to devote their all-too-limited time in schools. School administrators need this information on a regular basis as part of their evaluation of social work services. Parents want to know how their children are progressing toward their goals in school-based counseling groups on a regular basis. And student members need feedback as they grow and change. Monitoring outcomes is a professional imperative for school social workers leading small groups.

References

Achenbach, T. M., & Rescorla, L. A. (2001). *Manual for the ASEBA school-age forms & profiles*. Burlington: University of Vermont, Research Center for Children, Youth, and Families.

Beck, J. S., Beck, A. T., & Jolly, J. B. (2005). *Beck youth inventories* (2nd ed.). Retrieved from http://www.pearsonclinical.com/psychology/products/100000153/beck-youth-inventories-second-edition-byiii.html?Pid=015-8014-197

Cohen, M. B., & Garrett, K. J. (1995). Helping field instructors become more effective group work educators. *Social Work with Groups, 18*(2/3), 135–146.

Connors, C. K. (2008). *Connors comprehensive behavior rating scales*. San Antonio, TX: Pearson.

Dibble, N. (n.d.). *Using data to document the benefit of school social work services*. Retrieved from http://sspw.dpi.wi.gov/files/sspw/pdf/sswpgbenefitdata.pdf

Fischer, K., & Corcoran, K. (2007). *Measures for clinical practice: A sourcebook* (4th ed.). New York: Oxford University Press.

Franklin, C., & Kelly, M. S. (2009). Becoming evidence-informed in the real world of school social work practice. *Children & Schools, 31*(1), 46–56.

Franklin, C., Kim, J. S., & Tripodi, S. J. (2009). A meta-analysis of published school social work practice studies 1980–2007. *Research on Social Work Practice, 19*(6), 667–677. doi:10.1177/1049731508330224

Garrett, K. J. (2004). Practice evaluation and social group work in elementary schools. *Journal of Evidence-Based Social Work, 1*(4), 15–32.

Harris, M., & Franklin, C. G. (2003). Effects of a cognitive-behavioral, school-based, group intervention with Mexican American pregnant and parenting adolescents. *Social Work Research, 27*(2), 71–83.

Hilliard, R. E. (2007). The effects of Orff-based music therapy and social work groups on childhood grief symptoms and behaviors. *Journal of Music Therapy, 44*(2), 123–138.

International Association for Social Work with Groups. (2006). *IASWG practice standards.* Retrieved from http://iaswg.org/Practice_Standards

Kendall, P. C., Gosch, E., Furr, J. M., & Sood, E. (2008). Flexibility within fidelity. *Journal of the American Academy of Child and Adolescent Psychiatry, 47*(9), 987–993. doi:10.1097/CHI.0b013e31817eed2f

Larkin, R., & Thyer, B. A. (1999). Evaluating cognitive–behavioral group counseling to improve elementary school students' self-esteem, self-control, and classroom behavior. *Behavioral Interventions, 14*(3), 147–161.

LeCroy, C. W. (2004). Evaluation of an empowerment program for early adolescent girls. *Adolescence, 39*(155), 427–441.

Mackenzie, K. R. (1990). *Introduction to time-limited group psychotherapy.* Washington, DC: American Psychiatric Press.

Mishna, F., Muskat, B., & Wiener, J. (2010). "I'm not lazy; It's just that I learn differently": Development and implementation of a manualized school-based group for students with learning disabilities. *Social Work with Groups, 33*(2–3), 139–159. doi:10.1080/01609510903366210

Monette, D. R., Sullivan, T. J., & DeJong, C. R. (2014). *Applied social research: A tool for the human services* (9th ed.). Belmont CA: Brooks/Cole Cengage.

National Association of Social Workers (NASW). (2002). *NASW standards for school social work services.* Washington, DC: Author.

National Association of Social Workers (NASW). (2008). *Code of ethics.* Retrieved from https://www.socialworkers.org/pubs/code/code.asp

Newsome, W. (2005). The impact of solution-focused brief therapy with at-risk junior high school students. *Children & Schools, 27*(2), 83–90.

No Child Left Behind Act of 2001, Pub. L. 107-110 (2002).

Northen, H., & Kurland, R. (2001). *Social work with groups* (3rd ed.). New York: Columbia University Press.

Pro Ed (n.d.). *The multidimensional self-concept scale (NSCS).* Retrieved from http://www.proedinc.com/customer/productView.aspx?ID=685

Raines, J. C. (2002). Present levels of performance, goals, and objectives: A best-practice guide. *School Social Work Journal, 27*(1), 58–72.

Raines, J. C. (2003). Rating the rating scales: Ten criteria to use. *School Social Work Journal, 27*(2), 1–17.

Raines, J. C. (2008). *Evidence-based practice in school mental health.* New York: Oxford University Press.

Roberts, A. R., & Yeager, K. (2004). Systematic reviews of evidence-based studies and practice-based research: How to search for, develop, and use them. In A. R. Roberts & K. R. Yeager (Eds.), *Evidence-based practice manual: Research and outcome measures in health and human service* (pp. 3–14). New York: Oxford University Press.

Rose, S. D. (1998). *Group therapy with troubled youth: A cognitive behavioral interactive approach.* Thousand Oaks, CA: Sage.

Rose, S. D., & Edleson, J. L. (1987). *Working with children and adolescents in groups.* San Francisco: Jossey-Bass.

Rose, S. D., & Tolman, R. (1989). Measuring and evaluating individual achievements and group process. In S. D. Rose (Ed.), *Working with adults in groups* (pp. 109–136). San Francisco: Jossey-Bass.

Spencer, M. S., Brown, M., Griffin, S., & Abdullah, S. (2008). Outcome evaluation of the intergroup project. *Small Group Research, 39*(1), 82–103. doi:10.1177/1046496407313416

Toseland, R. W., & Rivas, R. F. (2012). *An introduction to group work practice* (7th ed.). Boston: Allyn & Bacon.

U.S. Department of Education (USDOE). (2015). *Elementary and Secondary Education Act.* Retrieved from http://www.ed.gov/esea

Wayne, J., & Cohen, C. S. (2001). *Group work education in the field.* Alexandria, VA: Council on Social Work Education.

Section VII

Tier 3 Interventions in Schools

For this final section of *School Social Work: Practice, Policy, and Research,* we turn to the most urgent and severe issues for school clients—the tertiary (tier 3) level of intervention. Two new chapters in this section extend our learning about how to reach students who have significant social/emotional/ behavioral issues: chapter 31, "Promoting Social-Emotional Learning for Children with Special Needs" by Aaron M. Thompson and his team at the University of Missouri gives a comprehensive overview of the literature for effective social-emotional learning interventions for students with special needs; while chapter 32, Michael S. Kelly's "Evidence-Informed Mental Health Practice in Schools," updates the information about what school social workers need to know about what works to help students with specific mental health disorders. Two additional chapters, both updated for this edition, address the needs of working with families of at-risk students: chapter 30, "School Social Work Practice with Families of At-Risk Students," by Robert Constable and Herbert J. Walberg, and chapter 33, "School-Based Trauma-Informed Care for Traumatic Events: Clinical and Organizational Practice," by new contributors Diane Mirabito and Jay Callahan. Taken together, these four chapters in this final section put the focus squarely on the most at-risk youths in our schools, and offer a wealth of ideas for how school social workers can best serve these students and their families.

30

School Social Work Practice with Families of At-Risk Students

Robert Constable
Loyola University Chicago

Herbert J. Walberg
Stanford University

- ◆ The School as a Community of Families
- ◆ The Necessary Arrangement of Relations between Family and School
- ◆ Family Conditions, Family Risks, and Resilience
- ◆ The School Social Worker's Role with Families

Families are essential to schools, and schools cannot accomplish their missions without connections with families. Since family is essential to the functioning and socialization of children, at the risk of failure schools cannot forget that their clientele are members of families. Families, including extended families, are the most important of the mediating systems that connect and stand between public and private life. These mediating systems allow each person to cope with the complexity of modern society with its necessary institutions—schools, workplaces, and health-care organizations. Families, in turn, need assistance from their surrounding relational and institutional communities. The modern family often experiences social isolation. Sometimes conflict, loss, family dissolution, even a physical move can cut off generational linkages and place families at risk. Losses can create social pathologies and progressive vulnerabilities in succeeding generations. And all of these have important effects on the child's success or failure in school.

Some of the key functions of social workers in schools are to repair the mismatches between school and family, and, in situations of potential difficulty, to develop real partnership. More than simply working with schools and families as separate units, their relationship is the natural focus. When children have difficulty or special needs in school, the relationship of family to school often needs special attention. The school, as a complex community, so salient to development, can either aggravate a youngster's vulnerabilities or compensate somewhat for personal and/or family vulnerability. It can provide alternative socializing relationships and maturational experiences. But it also can damage delicate relationships and create conflicts in loyalty.

THE SCHOOL AS A COMMUNITY OF FAMILIES

The school is a community of families, teachers, parents, and others working in partnership with one another as socializers of children. The development of this supportive community is even more important when children, families, communities, and schools have special needs, where the connection between home and school is not easily developed, or where there is cultural or linguistic diversity. The social worker could help develop this community (Adolfi-Morse, 1982; Nebo, 1963). The cultural diversity of the contemporary U.S. school is now enormous. Pupil diversity is family diversity. In some diverse areas, such as Chicago, it would not be unusual to find as many as thirty-five linguistic groups in an elementary school with a population of perhaps two hundred pupils. Where there is cultural difference between family and school, families may have ambitions for their children, but they are often fearful of involvement and participation. Schools may not be well connected with some of these diverse communities. Parents need help to participate in education and to build an effective school community (Paik & Walberg, 2007). The relationship between parents and schools was the original basis for school social work practice, as early school social workers served as liaisons between home and school.

Resilience in children is promoted when the resources in the school, family, and community are united and dedicated to the healthy development and educational success of children (Christenson & Sheridan, 2001; Kelleghan, Sloane, Alvarez, & Bloom, 1993; Redding, 2000; Subotnik & Walberg, 2006; Wang, Haertl, & Walberg, 1998). Students whose parents are involved with their education show improved social competence (Elias, 2003; Lybolt & Gottfred, 2003; Webster-Stratton, Reid, & Hammond, 2001; Whitbread, Bruder, Fleming & Park, 2007), and lower rates of adolescent high-risk behavior (Resnick et al., 1997). They show better academic achievement across family background, whether racial, income level, or educational levels (Jeynes, 2005). A constant finding across developmental studies suggests that high parent expectations of their adolescents result in outcomes consonant with these expectations (Doran, Gau, & Lindstrom, 2012). The family is the crucial arena for young children to develop self-determination (Lee, Palmer, Turnbull, & Wehmeyer, 2006). Jeanne Brooks-Gunn (2004–5), summarizing developmental research, suggests parents interact with their children along at least seven dimensions: (1) they nurture them; (2) they manage the home; (3) they provide a climate of language and communication; (4) they set standards, expectations, and discipline; (5) they provide materials that children can use for learning and development; (6) they monitor the child's behavior; and (7) finally, they directly teach skills to survive and flourish in their environment. The climate of language, materials in the home, and direct teaching of skills are aspects of parenting most linked with the child's school success. Reflecting these seven dimensions, she estimates that one-third to one-half of the variation in school outcomes between poor and not-poor children can be accounted for by differences in parenting.

Parents and teachers may have different perspectives on the same child. A survey of parents showed that they were better at understanding their children's internalizing emotions, such as being anxious, sad, lonely, or making physical complaints, real or imagined. Teachers, on the other hand, were better at recognizing externalizing behaviors, such as arguing, teasing, threatening, cheating, and lying (Konold, 2006).

What Do Parents Expect?

Whether schools are ready or not, many parents are clearly asking for partnership. This relationship, particularly necessary when the pupil has special needs, can easily break down at precisely the time when schools need to include parents in their processes. Focus group research done with adult family members of children with and without disabilities resulted in six broad indicators of what parents would expect from collaborative partnership with professionals in schools. Parents expect the following:

1. Positive, understandable, and respectful communication
2. Commitment to the child and family
3. Equality in decision making and service implementation, and equal power to influence outcomes
4. Demonstrated professional skills and competence
5. Trust—confidence in the dependability, ability, strength, and veracity of the school professional
6. Respect, mutual regard, and esteem in actions and communications with the school (Blue-Banning, Summers, Frankland, Nelson, & Beegle, 2004)

This climate of parental expectations crosses national and cultural boundaries. Japanese mothers of children with disabilities came up with a similar list with particular concerns about schools' negative-segregative views of disability. They wanted understanding, empowerment, coordination, and advocacy from school professionals (Kasahara & Turnbull, 2005).

Partnerships between Home and School

At least in their policies, schools are beginning to recognize that families are essential to their mission. Family partnership has become a major school policy objective. There is an explicit and expected link of families to schools in national education goals pertaining to school readiness and parent participation (Goals 2000, 1994). Special education has expected some partnership with parents for at least thirty years since the inception of Education for All Handicapped Children Act (later Individuals with Disabilities Education Act of 1990 [IDEA]) in 1975. General education is moving in the direction of enhanced parental involvement and partnership as a matter of public policy in the No Child Left Behind Act of 2001. Many commentators (Bristol & Gallagher,1982; Carter & CADRE, 2003; Lee et al., 2006; Paik & Walberg, 2007; Walberg,1984; Whitbread et al., 2007) have suggested different ways schools can develop effective partnerships with parents. Programs can be made more flexible, with individualized planning, the establishment of meaningful parent roles, and the involvement of both parents. Programs would focus on goals important to the family and would also expect something of the parents. Parents often need help to see the importance of the often-small gains made. Meetings can be scheduled at times when parents are available. School personnel can be available who speak the native language of the parent, or interpreters can be present. School personnel can get involved with the community. Social workers can make home visits. The school social worker might help the parents develop their own support network of friends and relatives or assist expanding their network. Associations of families of children with disabilities are especially important. Parental involvement can be developed in a meaningful way through sharing power with families. The expectation of parental involvement is not simply a matter of asking parents to carry out an existing school agenda, raise money, or volunteer in the school, although each of these tasks has value. Meaningful parental involvement means shared decision making and shared power in the school–parent relationship. Often schools overtly state a commitment to parental involvement, but want it only on their own terms. A true partnership exists when there is time to listen and respond to all voices. Developing such a partnership takes time, but is well worth the effort.

Parent Participation

In the late 1960s Project Head Start, reflecting a general philosophy governing community action programs, was the first to initiate planned parent participation as an essential dimension of schooling. James Comer (1995), a psychiatrist, developed a model of education in disadvantaged communities, where parents were often initially perceived as unmotivated or hard to reach. Comer's model is built on parent participation as essential to the creation of an effective school community, and thus effective education. Social workers took the lead in activities that, over time, developed a community of parents involved in the schools. Schraft and Comer (1979) envisioned three progressive levels of parent participation: (1) general activity geared to involving the majority of families, such as potluck dinners and fun fairs; (2) parents involved specifically in the daily life of the school, such as classroom assistants, as participants in workshops, or making materials for teachers; and (3) parents able to participate meaningfully in the decision-making process in the school. Parents might move from level to level, but Schraft and Comer (1979) cautioned against expecting involvement in the third level without much development of the first two levels over a relatively long period of time—that is, without a chance to develop a relationship with the school and its functions over a number of years.

Adolfi-Morse (1982) applied these concepts to her work in a school for children with emotional disturbances in Fairfax County, Virginia. One of her social work roles was as an organizer of a far-flung, ethnically diverse parent community of children with severe disabilities. She conceived of the school, which served a wide geographic area with many ethnic differences, as a community of families. Adolfi-Morse (1982) used events such as back-to-school night, potluck dinners, and parent-teacher organization meetings to reinforce this concept. Parents of children with severe disabilities, who may have initially been less involved than others, were often able to find important roles for themselves in making the school-community work. The involvement of these parents resulted in an observed change in their children's estimate of themselves.

On a broader scale, some states, such as Florida, Kentucky, and Tennessee, have developed family resource centers as part of state school reform. Schools in Kentucky sponsor family resource centers if at least 20 percent of pupils qualify for the federal free and reduced-price meals program (which is nine out of every ten schools in that state). These centers provide a range of programs, including family crisis counseling, referrals for health and other social services, and preschool and after-school childcare. Evaluation results have been very positive (Southern Regional Education Board, 2001). These centers are now being developed in many other states. They are a new and potentially very effective service delivery system for children. School social workers have very important and natural roles in these centers as mental health service providers, school-family liaisons, crisis workers, and case managers.

THE NECESSARY ARRANGEMENT OF RELATIONS BETWEEN FAMILY AND SCHOOL

Summaries of research on educational effectiveness (Boethel, 2004; Henderson & Mapp, 2002) suggest a necessary order in the relationship between families of all cultural backgrounds and schools. Families would have difficulty educating their children in a complex modern society without the assistance of schools, and schools cannot readily educate without the cooperation of families (Paik & Walberg, 2007; Subotnik & Walberg, 2006; Walberg, 1984; Walberg & Lai, 1999). Each can prevent the other from accomplishing its proper function. This is particularly true for more-vulnerable children and families.

Families are the first educators of their children through their early developing years. School functions exist to help the family carry out its prior functions in accordance with the needs and standards of society and the rights of members of the family. The community, often represented by the school, is obligated to ensure that families have all the assistance—economic, social, educational, political, and cultural—that they need to face all their responsibilities in a humane way.

The relationship of the family unit to the school and the community can be encapsulated by three principles:

1. The family has primary functions in the care and socialization of its children. It has rights and responsibilities derived from this function that include the economic, social, educational, and cultural provision for the needs of its members. As such, the family is the basic social unit of society.
2. The school's primary functions are helping the family to meet its responsibilities and supplying certain cognitive instruction that the family cannot. The work of the family is always personal. Transactions en famille are expected to be based on affection and respect for the other person. Particular types of learning would be distorted if they excluded this dimension of affection and respect for the person as a person, as worthwhile in his or her own right. In families this personal dimension is experienced and learned in work, worship, gender roles, respect for others in social relations, and respect for one's developing sexuality. When affection and respect break down, the partnership of home and school can be developed through social work services that assist the family in developing or redeveloping the complex interactive relationships necessary for their children's survival and personal development.
3. A secondary function of the school (and in a broader sense, of the community) is to monitor potential abridgment of rights of children as pupils and citizens when external conditions of society or internal conditions within the family make it impossible for the family to accomplish its primary function. This moniotoring must be done without inappropriately abridging the family's exercise of those functions it is able to accomplish.

There is a balance between family and school, an order, and a defined relation between their respective functions. The increased awareness of the importance of effective families, the increasing numbers of vulnerable families, and the increasing school responsibility for the education of vulnerable children inevitably lead to the need for relationships that are better integrated between school and family. Even if many parents spend less time with their children (Elias & Schwab, 2004), schools could not necessarily fill the vacuum. Indeed the development of school services closing the gap between family and school could also pose a threat to family autonomy and effectiveness.

A balance needs to be mediated between the need for collaboration and the need to protect the rights of children to appropriate family nurture and socialization—to support the family in carrying out its responsibility. In the face of the weakness of the family and the complexity of the child's problems, schools may attempt to substitute for family functions. This never works well. This situation is legendary among school social workers: providing consultation to an intensely involved and otherwise effective special education teacher who feels the need to rescue a student from the parents. When services take over family functions, rather than empower families to carry out their tasks, the parents' response may be to become either less adequate or more angry. Defining a relationship of collaboration, so that vulnerable children in vulnerable families are helped to make the most of what school has to offer, demands skill and commitment.

FAMILY CONDITIONS, FAMILY RISKS, AND RESILIENCE

Collaborative relationships are often difficult to manage, particularly with vulnerable families. The stress experienced by families with children with disabilities has a well-established evidence base. Children with disabilities have high needs for caregiving. Their families are often isolated from community support systems. Severe family stresses and losses are ordinary experiences for many children. There may be few actual and continuing supports to buffer risk. Parents' energies may be indentured by demanding work roles or the need to survive. Parents of children under age six may have difficulty balancing the demands of participating in the workforce with childcare responsibilities (Children's Defense Fund, 1994; Hanson & Carta, 1995). Children of younger parents are at risk for cognitive, emotional, and physical difficulties (Smith, 1994).

Research and practice experience with children with special needs point out a heightened need for parental involvement and participation in education. Paradoxically, the greater the child's difficulties, the greater the magnitude of disagreement between schools and parents (Victor, Halvorson, & Wampler, 1988). Thus the greater the difficulties, the greater the need for specialized attention of the school to the relationship with families. Partnership between family and school is particularly important when pupils show problems such as conduct disorders (Webster-Stratton, 1993), attention deficit hyperactivity disorder (ADHD) (August, Anderson, & Bloomquist, 1992), and difficulties in social interaction with others (Sheridan, Kratochwill, & Elliott,

1990). Nevertheless, families of children with disabilities, even after long mandated participation in school decision making, still are predominantly passive in response to this process (Fine, 1993; Harry, Allen, & McLaughlin, 1995). Often the school itself creates estrangement from families.

It is helpful to keep the strengths perspective in mind when working with schools and families of children with disabilities. So much of testing, grading, and assessment focuses on the deficits of the child that this process is likely to create defensiveness, despair, or overprotection in parents. A good deal of work is necessary on both sides. Both research and practice experience suggest that parents of children with disabilities, low-income parents, and people with cultural and other differences can become quite actively involved when their school has an inclusion policy that helps them to feel encouraged, supported, and valued (Adolfi-Morse, 1982; Lewis & Henderson, 1997; Schraft & Comer, 1979).

Poverty is associated with great risks for children. These risks are greater for single-parent families and persons with lower job skills. In addition, the income disparity between rich and poor people is increasing, with children the largest age group caught in poverty. Children born in poverty have their risks compounded: illness, family stress, lack of social support, and health and environmental risks (Hanson & Carta, 1995; Schorr, 1988). Further risks are experienced by children in families where there is substance abuse or violence (Hanson & Carta, 1995). On the other hand, resilient children seem to maintain cognitive skills, curiosity, enthusiasm, goal-setting behavior, and high self-esteem. They appear less vulnerable to some of these adverse environmental factors (Hanson & Carta, 1995). In some instances, family characteristics, such as rule setting, respect for individuality, and parental responsiveness, can inoculate children against adverse environmental factors (Bradley, Whiteside, Mundfrom, Casey, & Pope, 1994). Social support from the larger community or kinship group can also act as a buffer (Keltner, 1990). Adults who successfully survived adverse childhood experiences usually identify some significant adult in their environment who encouraged their positive growth. Such family or extended family arrangements, which can occur naturally and in spite of very difficult circumstances, can also be constructed and encouraged with the assistance of professionals, such as school social workers.

There is an extensive literature on family process, family structure, and family intervention (Constable & Lee, 2004; Fine & Carlson, 1992). Every family must create for itself an environment of safety, belonging, and appropriate communication and socialization. These family relational tasks involve the mutual construction of

- ◆ A safe environment for each of their members, protecting dignity and often fragile and developing identities;
- ◆ A place where members can belong—that is, where they can be treated as unique persons of worth; and

- ◆ Sufficient opportunities and models for effective communication, so that members can learn to communicate, respond to each other, and adapt to changes within the family and in its outside environment.
- ◆ Building on these prerequisites, each family needs to develop an environment where there is appropriate freedom, concern, respect, and care. This environment needs to be capable of enabling members to make appropriate developmental choices, to be concerned about each other, to respect each other, and to be able to care for others appropriately (Constable & Lee, 2004).

These are not simply needs and requirements, but are also interactive family tasks, which uniquely organize family process. These tasks have to be created by families themselves and in their own unique ways. In their absence, the effect on the younger members can be devastating. Since these complex, interactive tasks are related to the socializing mission of education, the school social worker may become involved when this breakdown affects the child's development and academic performance.

The concept of family resilience, developed by Froma Walsh (1999, 2003, 2012), extends the concept of family responsiveness to stressful situations. The resilient family forges transformation and growth from adverse circumstances (Walsh, 2003, 2012). In the midst of difficulty, the family is somehow able to develop its own meanings, interact with its surroundings, adapt creatively to them, and preserve its own values. It manages to carry on as a family. Resilience is not a matter of a particular family structure, but of family process. When families are resilient, their members are able to communicate their needs and solve problems. Paradoxically, the effects of oppressive conditions may act on families in different ways, depending on external conditions and the family's own subjective processing of the situation. These conditions may act either to suppress the qualities that could lead to survival or stimulate them. According to Walsh (2012), the resilient family is able to

- ◆ Approach adversity as a challenge shared by the whole family;
- ◆ Normalize and contextualize distress;
- ◆ Use adversity to gain a sense of its own coherence;
- ◆ Make sense of how things have happened through causal or explanatory attributions;
- ◆ Have a hopeful and optimistic bias;
- ◆ Master the art of the possible;
- ◆ Draw on spiritual resources;
- ◆ Develop flexibility and adaptability;
- ◆ Develop its internal connections;
- ◆ Use social and economic resources appropriately;
- ◆ Communicate clearly and openly with each other; and
- ◆ Solve problems collaboratively.

The recognition of individual and family resilience connects with a large body of literature on family intervention and therapy and provides a conceptual map for a strengths-based approach. An ultimate test of the functional power of families is the way they continue their work even under stress. In spite of extreme stresses—slavery and subsequent discrimination, the Holocaust, deportation to refugee camps—some families have attempted to preserve as many of their human processes and functions as possible. They have learned to be responsive, and to support each other in difficult conditions as islands of humaneness in a hostile sea.

THE SCHOOL SOCIAL WORKER'S ROLE WITH FAMILIES

Working with Pupil, Family, and School

The school is a powerful stage where each student plays out the great developmental issues: separation-individuation, self-esteem, social relationships, language, imagination, emotions, assertiveness, achievement, competition, productive work, justice, and the discovery and use of one's self. The quality of a child's interaction with learning tasks and with others in school is usually a very accurate barometer of his or her broader developmental issues and of the family situation. The normal tasks of adapting to school can absorb the student's developmental energy. The possibility that this energy can be harnassed makes school a logical intervention point. The school social work role demands a systems perspective applied to families and schools and the skills to work with each in a mutually reinforcing relationship. The key to family-school intervention comes from the fact that family tasks and school tasks are intertwined and interdependent. Partnership in these tasks, mediated by family culture and history, is possible. Shared tasks place social workers uniquely on the inside of both, facilitating their complex relationship, without taking over the family's natural exercise of its own, appropriate functioning. This is particularly important where pupil or family vulnerability or school conditions might interfere with the effectiveness of the work of school social workers.

The Family Systems Perspective Applied to Schooling

The current body of couple and family therapy literature establishes both the general efficacy of the field and the effectiveness of certain approaches (Sexton, Weeks, & Robbins, 2003, p. 460). This evidence base gives legitimacy to family intervention and allows its methodology to be adopted across a wide variety of areas. School outcomes—that is, whether family interventions are sufficiently effective to specifically produce a change in school behavior—are infrequently measured in studies of the efficacy of general family intervention (Carlson, 2006). Social workers have worked with families for more than a century. Their intervention integrates a systems perspective with family development theory (Constable & Lee, 2004). They have long transferred research and practice from other parts of their field to the situations of school pupils and their families. In this context two therapeutic programs—one dealing with youth violence and one dealing with criminal behavior—have shown comparatively high effectiveness (National Institutes of Health, 2005), with problems of alcohol and drug abuse, and serious emotional disturbance as well. These therapeutic programs focus on the family and its surrounding systems as well as on the youths. The two chapters "Multisytemic Therapy" (Sheidow, Hengeller, & Shoenwald, 2003) and "Functional Family Therapy" (Sexton & Alexander, 2003), have each in its own way succeeded in systematizing the broad approach social workers have always taken to families and their surrounding institutions with intensity of contact. Full-time, master's-level multisystemic social work therapists carry four to six families at any one time (Sheidow et al., 2003). Functional family therapists work with perhaps twenty-six families over the period of a year (Sexton & Alexander, 2003). Both programs have shown their effectiveness with problems of youth violence through high-quality randomized controlled trials with effects sustained for at least one year postintervention and with at least one external such trial replicating the results (National Institutes of Health, 2005). The similarity of both practice models to what many school social workers have been doing, albeit on short rations and without elaborate research protocols, points out possible applications of this research to school intervention with families. Other models focusing on the family system, such as strategic family therapy (Carlson, 2006; Cody, 2006) and solution-focused family interventions (Franklin, Kim, & Tripoldi, 2013), have a good evidence base and have been applied in schools. An extensive review (Hoagwood et al., 2007) of school interventions for academic and mental health functioning from an original universe of 2,000 articles found fifteen programs effectively targeting prosocial, aggressive, and antisocial behaviors in school. In four programs, intensive family and pupil intervention were crucial to positive mental health outcomes, but there was no clear effect on academic functioning. Eleven programs with intensive interventions that targeted parents and teachers, as well as pupils, had a positive effect on both education and mental health outcomes (Hoagwood et al., 2007). These studies indicate that focusing on the pupil alone would not be effective.

Family systems concepts can enrich the interventive repertoire of the school social worker when the social worker applies them to the processes of education. These concepts are useful for complex, systemic problems. The route toward health goes through the family, the student him- or herself, and the living, surrounding institutions, which assist both family and student in their related life tasks. The family systems perspective applied to schooling means that, to help children cope better with developmental needs and life circumstances, it probably would be ineffective to work with the child without working with the teacher, who can influence the school environment, and without some focused connection with parents, who can influence the home environment. The nature of this involvement depends on the assessment of the total situation. It is important to begin with environmental changes: from a systems perspective these changes may have the most rapid results. When changes in the child's real environments take place, the social worker can assist the child to change correspondingly. Or the child will respond without direct, personal intervention. Even small changes taking place in the classroom environment with the teacher or in the home environment with the parents may be enough to give the child an opportunity to cope more effectively. Children who experience a small shift in the classroom or at home may see themselves differently.

We know from developmental research that children are for the most part responsive and flexible, that the child will inevitably be a part of these changes, and that they often do use well what opportunities they perceive (Fine & Carlson, 1992). On the other hand, to focus on the child alone, in the absence of a focus on school or family, would be to expect heroic changes in the child's patterns of behavior and in the multiple worlds the child inhabits. This focus alone is likely to be ineffective and an exercise in frustration. Small changes in the worlds that children inhabit, and corresponding changes in their relations to each other, create larger changes in the total environment supporting the child's learning to cope differently. When there are changes in classroom and family relations, one-on-one work with the child, when necessary, becomes much less complicated. In addition, the social worker would be less prone to take on a role that teachers and/or parents should play when both are already part of the team.

There are five foundational principles for school social work with families:

1. Understand Family Structure and Process. This principle presupposes an understanding of family assessment and social work with families. Families have unique structures that evolve out of their particular stories and cultures, but they have common processes, as discussed in "Family Processes and Family Resilience" above. School social workers need to be able to identify these structures and processes to understand the context of meanings that family members and individual pupils bring with them, in order to work with them and to develop partnership (Constable & Lee, 2004).

2. Use a Strengths-Based Approach. The diversity of family structures encountered in school social work and the individualistic approach often taken by school personnel could lead to misunderstandings and pathological labeling of families. The point where school social workers can work with families is at the point of their strengths; social workers help families to respond and compensate for parts that are breaking down, and help schools to support this process while it is taking place (Kral, 1992; Constable & Lee, 2004).

3. *Develop a Partnership.* Because parents are the first educators of their children, a workable home-school partnership needs to develop, characterized by communication, respect, general agreement on important issues, and reflexivity (appropriate responsiveness) in relation to the changing needs of the pupil. This is especially necessary when the pupil or the family is having difficulty or is under stress (Christenson & Sheridan, 2001; Fine & Carlson, 1992; Lee et al., 2006; Whitbread et al., 2007).

4. *Use the School as a Holding System for Development While Changes Take Place.* Schools often provide some elements of relational stability, a natural holding system, that pupils experiencing chaos and relational confusion at home are able to use. The school social worker can work with the pupil, the school, and the home to make this arrangement work.

5. *Never Work with a Pupil without Some Connection with the Family.* No matter how limited the connection or how difficult the involvement, parents need to become your allies. Just one contact may be sufficient to establish some collaboration. More contact may be necessary to reinforce and support a working relationship. On the one hand, sometimes a limited but clear contact is better than something more ambitious and implicitly more demanding on the parent. On the other hand, it is sometimes more important to work with the teacher and the parent than to work with the child. The decision regarding the focus of intervention is based on the school social worker's assessment. In any case, working with a student without the parents stimulates parents to work against you. Rarely will they lose this unnecessary competition.

Assessment and Intervention

To construct effective relationships between school and vulnerable families, the school social worker needs to have all the assessment and intervention abilities of a good family therapist. Assessment involves understanding relationships, tasks, and expectations in the classroom and in the home, as well as the child's developmental progression and patterns of coping in the context of the small changes that lead to systemic shifts. Much of school social work intervention works to assist parents and teachers to find different ways of responding to and working with the child's active coping strategies. Working between the worlds of home and school, the school social worker assists teachers and parents to discover their own personal repertoire of ways to assist the child's coping, and often modify their expectations of themselves in relation to the real needs of the child. When intervention with the child is necessary, the social worker can assist the child in relation to changes the child can make in his or her own behavior to help the child cope more effectively. The social worker can also assist parents and teachers to respond to the child's present efforts at coping, and correspondingly support the child's efforts to respond to the changing environment in new ways.

The skill of making a good assessment of the whole system in interaction leads to the skill of assisting parents, teachers, and children to manage that interaction. Social workers have not always understood that such a broad, balanced assessment clarifies the possible intervention between school, home, and pupil. The paradox is that it takes less effort to focus on the whole, and then respectfully intervene where needed, than to exclude someone from the assessment and the joint effort and then attempt to compensate for what the excluded person might have offered. In the assessment process, it is critical to maintain a focus on strengths—what we have to build on in order to reach our mutual goals. Every assessment interview with parents should include questions such as, "What is something that your child does very well?," "What do you do that really works when you are helping your child?," or "What are some of your favorite things about your child?"

Choosing Units of Attention

School social work can take two directions: (1) helping family, school, and community work with one another and with the pupil, and (2) helping the pupil find his or her own resources and make use of what the family, school, and community have to offer. The school social worker must choose units of attention—that is, he or she must discover where to focus and what to do to enable the best match to take place between pupil–family needs and school–community resources. A unit of attention should be a point of most effective change, a point or set of points in the systems where, if change takes place, other positive changes will also become possible. Working with each unit of attention demands its own skills. Choosing the most efficient and effective focus, in the context of the time and resources available, is a complex professional task, and by no means a random process. There is a logical progression to the choice, reflecting the systems framework and commitment to family partnership.

Some Case Examples of School Social Work Practice with Families

School social work services may continue throughout the school experience of a student at different levels of intensity as the education process continues. The focus is on the ongoing educational process—that is, on school tasks in every pupil's life and their individual meanings for the child and the family. This focus on tasks brings in a different type of process with the total network of school relationships, which becomes a natural holding system for this process and these tasks. There is also a different way of approaching time. In an elementary school it would be possible for a school social worker to know and work with a child for up to nine years.

The case of Alan in appendix A is a good example of the school social worker working over a number of years through every part of the student's relational system, through the home and through the school. While the home went through great changes the school became a natural holding system, allowing Alan's development to stabilize as the home stabilized. The school social worker carried out a wide range of functions with different units of attention supporting the holding system, supporting the parents' better functioning, as well as supporting Alan's functioning and his developmental maturation. In the beginning Alan had great difficulty. The world as he knew it was falling apart. He could not deal with major changes in his family, his move from his old neighborhood, his learning disabilities, and the demands of schooling. When the school situation showed responsiveness and support, he began to express his depression and suicidal ideation. The school and the social worker responded. Over seven years Alan was able to use the constancy and support of this system to avert possible deterioration. He showed considerable growth, while working steadily on the same problems.

His family went through profound changes over four years—severe marital upset, separation, divorce, single parenthood with joint custody, and remarriage. While the school social worker's focus remained on Alan, she was also a resource for the changing family system. The social worker brought both parents and the school into communication and support of Alan's best functioning. She helped the parents access outside helping resources for Alan. She worked with the complex family system and with Alan in the context of the remarriage. Working between the worlds of family and school, the social worker helped the teacher, the parents, and Alan in different ways to develop this holding system, to support Alan's strengths, and—as Alan grew and matured—to help him to put things together. Alan's breakdown in school functioning—the massive breakdown of his ability to cope with educational and social tasks, his thoughts of dying, and his chronic sadness—were essentially concerns about himself and his family. And here Alan's developmental thrust to adapt to school became the key to the helping process. The parents were willing to have some relationship with the school. They were open to the school social worker and the school at a time when they would not be open to any other resource, and certainly not to each other.

The social worker, from her position in the school, worked at different levels of intensity throughout Alan's elementary school experience, attempting to bring all the elements of the situation together. The focus on different units of attention varied according to the particular situation. At different times she provided consultation to everyone. She met with Alan according to Alan's current need, whether individually or in groups. She set the conditions for Alan and his family to find some resolution of this complicated situation. As a skilled clinician, she used a variety of modalities in the context of Alan's developmental tasks and the school to orchestrate a larger healing process. The school social worker's time spent with the family from a family systems perspective would have a far greater effect than extended sessions with Alan alone.

The two following cases briefly illustrate practice of clinical social work in the school with families and students. As in Alan's case, the school is used as a holding system for simultaneous work with the student and with the family. Given this basic temporal and organizing framework of school, which both adds a further ingredient and provides limits, we can draw from a variety of different effective models of family therapy, such as the two cited earlier, to assist the social worker's understanding of the intervention process. Both cases below involve fragmented and fragile family systems and students whose reactions to these systems were evidence of their developmental risks. Both cases involved outreach to parents and home visits, an outreach that was geared to what the parent(s) could tolerate and what seemed appropriate in the situation. In both cases there was a remarkable healing process. For parent(s) and student the relationship with school, facilitated through the worker, provided the protection and the time (a holding system) necessary for a natural healing and maturing process to take place. For these early adolescents there is a close connection between the educational goals and developmental goals. The descriptions below contain brief outlines of the process.

> Lynda began seventh grade as a very anxious, educationally and socially limited thirteen-year-old with placement recommended to remedy the abuse she was experiencing. She had a mutually explosive, provocative, and destructive relationship with her mother, who was struggling with mental illness. In a rage the mother had once thrown a hot frying pan at Lynda; explosions were becoming the pattern in their relationship. Father was concerned about the situation but felt helpless and passive in the face of his wife. The family is Jewish, but is isolated from any extended family system. When Lynda was in a self-contained class in her elementary school, the Alliance for Jewish Children had made an extensive evaluation of Lynda and her home. They strongly recommended that Lynda be placed in a foster home, but there was no home available. Lynda was put on a waiting list and went on to junior high school. For any early adolescent it would be a great challenge to move from the relative safety and predictability of self-contained classes in a smaller elementary school to the multidepartmental, subject-oriented junior high school. Lynda would not cope with it as long as safety at home was the prerequisite need. The school social worker worked intensively over a period of two years with Lynda, with her teachers, and with her parents; she also collaborated with the Alliance for Jewish Children. Since the parents were unable to get to school, the social worker made weekly home visits during the father's lunch hour. The structure provided by these weekly visits with both parents provided some safety for the family. The parents gradually became responsive. Father became more appropriately involved with Lynda. Mother backed off from the intensity of some of their relationship, checking in with the worker when she felt prone to violence. Lynda became less anxious and provocative. Building on the safer

relationships the family was constructing, the worker assisted both parents to move to a better connection with Lynda. At the same time she was assisting Lynda to use her school experience and what parents could offer her. Gradually feeling less stressed at home, Lynda responded to weekly meetings with the social worker; over the period of two years she translated them into improved school and peer relations. She showed a good deal of creativity, particularly in art. Her grades, once failing, improved. She eventually came to the point of developing normal friendships with other pupils. At this point the social worker provided consultation to a volunteer group leader at the local YWCA. Lynda's membership in this group was an important developmental experience for her. With her graduation from junior high school Lynda was able to recognize and celebrate with her family the major steps she and they had taken. She had grown in resiliency, and the parents, through their small relational and hierarchical shifts, were supporting her growth.

Ed, a twelve-year-old in a Swedish American family, lived in a world of his own. Although he was not psychotic, his relationships, patterns, and perceptions were decidedly schizoid, and his fantasies often simply took over. He had superior intelligence but never engaged with his sixth-grade teacher or the class. Instead, he spent most of his time in fantasy, drawing spaceships and imagining himself on them. He had no social relationships and actively rejected any attempts on the part of classmates to make relationships. At one point he spent free time mapping and exploring the town sewers. He lived with his grandparents and his mother in an emotionally impoverished environment. His mother had never married and was mainly invested in her work. Father was incarcerated. His mother related to Ed casually as if she were an older sister but otherwise avoided him. The grandparents actively rejected Ed as an unwanted child. The social worker learned quickly in their first home visit that he could not ask much of Ed's mother in relation to Ed. She would not come to the school (she was "too busy") and it was clear that she would reject implicit pressure to get more involved in a parental role with Ed. She did agree to work together with the social worker in twice-yearly home visits with some phone follow-up. In their contacts the worker deliberately went slowly with her in a nondemanding, affirmative, strengths-building experience, always with its focus on her relationship with Ed. With Ed the worker had a relationship of twice weekly, then weekly, and later biweekly contacts over the three-year period. Ed made major gains in involvement with school and his friends. From his initial disconnectedness he developed better connectedness with his surroundings through his wonderful sense of humor and his art. The mother eventually felt comfortable enough to make office contacts. She gradually became more effectively involved with her son. Between Ed's seventh- and eighth-grade years this involvment climaxed with an enjoyable auto trip through the West together. When Ed's father was released from prison the worker had some good sessions with him and with Ed as Ed got to know his father for the first time. The connection with school held everything together until both were able to find a better relationship. Ed's gains assisted his mother to find a connection with her son. Her better connection helped Ed to take major developmental and social steps.

Respecting Relational Structure

In working with parents and children in the present family structure, the social worker needed to respect the necessary power of the parent(s) in relation to their children, the parents' concerns, the educational functions of the parents, and the parents' responsibilities. In Lynda's case the mother-daughter relationship was explosive and unsafe. In Ed's case the mother would have preferred not to take charge or invest much in their relationship and the power was unclear in the family unit. How does the social worker avoid taking over the process and thus displacing the parents? The temptation will be very strong for the social worker to enter a dysfunctional family as an "expert" and then to undercut the already tottering parental power. When the so-called expert takes charge, both parents and child(ren) either move into further dysfunction and invest energy elsewhere, or they fight the agency and social worker in order to remain in control. It may be better for parents to fight with the agency and the worker, since moving into dysfunction is usually self-confirming and relationally circular. It eliminates the possibility of improvement. But such conflict may be unnecessary.

Home Visits

All of these cases involved at least initial home visits with parents. Normally an office interview at the school is preferable. The office interview relates the parent(s) to the school, to their child's experience, and to his or her emerging developmental world. It is also an effective use of the school social worker's time. On the other hand, sometimes parents will not or cannot come to school for an interview, even to a school open house. A home visit becomes the only way to develop a connection and the basic mutual understandings and agreements to work together in the interests of the student (Allen & Tracy, 2004; Wasik & Shaffer, 2013). In Lynda's case her safety demanded a more intensive outreach and the social worker simply decided to use her lunchtime once a week to address the family's particular need. It appeared at the time to be the only effective way for the worker to help the parents to work on Lynda's safety and their relationship with her. Not every school system would give the social worker the amount of time needed for her to do fine work with the family.

In Ed's case the combination of one home visit and some phone contacts maintained a relationship that supported the mother's functioning while she supported Ed's development and began to discover a relationship with him. The mother would not have tolerated an intense relationship with the social worker, but was willing to be in contact. Once a person-to-person contact took place, occasional phone contacts were workable for a while. It did not take much time for either the social worker or the mother. After she took Ed on vacation, she was willing to come in to the school, and this made a big difference.

On the other hand, sometimes the neighborhood or the immediate circumstances preclude home visits. Sometimes the social worker can choose a neutral spot, such as a community center. Social workers should avoid any situation where they are afraid or where they sense danger. Parents for the most part do understand this and will usually go out of their way to facilitate an outreach of the social worker and make sure that everyone is safe.

It is very important to share with the school principal the fact that you are making these contacts in the community (without sharing particular details of these contacts). Such contacts are often new to schools. Schools are generally not accustomed to collaboration with parents other than on open house night or in the Parent-Teacher Association. However, a more extensive involvement is often precisely what is needed in the situations social workers encounter, particularly in special education. Generally principals will support this involvement if you discuss it with them. You are not practicing extramural family therapy: rather you are taking the process of education and the school into the community, developing a partnership with parents over your shared concerns, and helping parents carry out their roles. Time spent with parents often pays enormous dividends, particularly with the overstressed, often single-parent, families of today. As in Ed's case, from a systems perspective, small changes, a strengths-based approach, and a cooperative attitude made other things possible.

School social workers will find an enormous range and variety of family structures in their school communities for which the task-oriented, family strengths, whole-system approach, discussed here, will be equally effective. Alan's (appendix A) family went through a variety of structures—two parents, single parent, both spouses remarried. Ed's family was more complex—his mother and grandparents were in a confused power hierarchy, and his father in prison. The social worker found a different role with each part of the family system as the situation developed.

There are more than half a million children living in out-of-home placements. The majority of children in foster care attend public schools (Altshuler, 2009). Foster children can have many problems with school, reflecting some of their losses, their uncertainty and ambivalence about their foster parents, while they still have contact with birth parents. With these uncertainties, the school remains an important holding system, and the foster parents and child must still carry out relational tasks. The social worker can work with foster parents, develop a collaborative relationship with the child welfare agency, and work with the pupil. The pupil needs to begin to understand the meanings of relational losses and new, but insecure, relationships being formed. In addition, there is always a need for the school social worker to coordinate with the child welfare agency.

Many children in school are raised by kinship caregivers—a network of relatives, including uncles, aunts, and grandparents—who have taken responsibility for the child in the absence of a birthparent. In some cases there is a large family network. In other cases the caregiver may be supported primarily by complex agency wraparound structures. While each member of the network may be more or less available, it is the family network itself that, with the school, becomes the holding system. Here there is some similarity with working with tribal or clan arrangements: for example, in traditional Hmong society the clan system itself provides security and stability, and the leaders of the system and appointed index parent(s) (perhaps an aunt or grandparent) become the key people for the school to work with. It is important for the social worker to assess the system and its cultural under-standings to work out what type of a partnership may be possible.

Social workers often work with parents in groups. Discussed in chapters 27, 28, and 29, the strength of any group of peers is its ability to normalize a situation everyone in the group is experiencing, and to support its mem-bers' confrontation of a problem they would have great difficulty facing alone. There are groups of parents using a variety of programs available for child-rearing issues. There are parents with something in common, whether kindergartners, children with certain disabilities, or early adolescents; newly arrived parents in a school community; and parents undergoing divorce or grieving losses. All these, and more, are among the many parents who can use a group as a vehicle for learning, support, and problem solving. Parent groups and family life education, particularly when the pupil's disability would carry a predictable amount of stress, can be a most effective resource for the school social worker (Constable & Lee, 2004).

In addition groups are very useful in crises as well as in longer-term healing processes when a tragedy has taken place. There is a great deal to learn from the coping of others, particularly if this is the first time one has faced a particular situation. For mobile families the group often becomes a substitute family network where they can discuss concerns. For school social workers it is an effective and productive use of their time in a type of family education cum group therapy. Their needs assessment for the partic-ular school will dictate their approach to the school community and their use of the limited amount of time available.

Difficulties in Developing Parent Involvement

In actuality, over a half century of observing school social work practice in many different venues, the author has observed, both as a practitioner and as a university liaison, that with the further development and involvement of the school social worker in classrooms and in schooling, there has been a gradual compression of the time spent with parents. Eventually in many schools this has become a procedural recognition of parental signoff power without any real home-school partnership ever developing. To the extent that partnership does not develop in the family systems framework discussed above, the predictable results would be an increased amount of time spent with the pupil in weekly sessions, and a decreased effectiveness in relation to the effort expended. There are several systemic reasons that might explain why this is happening. First, as discussed above, schools have always been more accustomed to excluding parents from their domain and activities than including them. Despite policies promoting partnership, there is still not a clear understanding of what partnership is or can be. For working parents, "partnership" means that there needs to be evening avail-ability in a safe place. It means the principal will not look askance when the social worker goes off campus for a home visit or meets with a parent at a mutually safe place in the community, if the parent cannot come to the school. It means the social worker will get credit for parent involvement. Second, not all school social workers are committed to or knowledgeable about family intervention. They correctly perceive that there are systemic obstacles to family intervention in school systems and few rewards for it. They may not be prepared for family work. Schools of social work do not always require a course in family dynamics and intervention in their school social work specializations, nor may a family intervention experience neces-sarily be required as part of the field experience. Finally, parents themselves may also have accurately assessed the obstacles in the school to their involve-ment with their child's education. From their perspective there are costs and few payoffs for involvement. "Why do you want to see me? How much time is it going to take? Couldn't we do it over the phone? Just send it to me. I'll sign. Don't worry. I've got shopping, a meeting and a doctor's appointment today and I'm busy all next week." "I'm on call and I don't have time to come in." Fathers, as important as they are, may be even more difficult to get involved. The actual amount of time expended may not be enormous. A beginning understanding with parents probably should be face to face. Much more than a signoff is involved. From that point the social worker's assessment and the agreement made with the parents would dictate the amount of time needed. Parents usually welcome this involvement with the school social worker when they understand in a concrete way what it is. Fur-thermore, a foundation with the school needs to be developed so that par-ent involvement becomes an important part of the school social work role. School personnel are rarely comfortable or trained to work with parents. Nevertheless, they are usually surprised and gratified that someone would take a skillful and professional interest in parents. The author remembers his first principal, who was quite afraid of parents, saying, "I want you to be in my office for this interview, if you can" whenever the principal felt insecure with a particular parent. However the beginning step may seem as humiliat-ing as asking the principal's permission to make a home visit, and following up the visit with some general discussion of why home visits are important. My principal was always my most important client.

The Child with Disabilities and the Family

All families experience some stress. However, families of children with disabilities face special levels of stress, frequently related to increased and more complex childcare demands. The special needs of a child with a disability levy a heavy physical, financial, and emotional tax on the family. Most obvious are the financial burdens (Moore & McLaughlin, 1988). There are also needs for information, particularly medical and diagnostic information (Bailey, Blasco, & Simeonson, 1992; D'Amato & Yoshida, 1991). Moreover, parents must develop the skill to manage the specialized services needed. Otherwise, these services might seriously intrude on other aspects of the child's development, sense of mastery, self-esteem, as well as the family's ability to function independently. These families can experience increased divorce and suicide rates, a higher incidence of child abuse, increased financial difficulties, and a variety of emotional manifestations, such as depression, anger, guilt, and anxiety. Different types of disabling conditions may create secondary problems. In the National Longitudinal Transition Study of Adolescents-2 with disabilities, parents of adolescents with learning disabilities held higher expectations of their adolescents' educational and occupational achievement than parents of adolescents with intellectual disability, autism, or multiple disabilities (Newman, 2005). These expectations were predictive of the young person's actual employment and educational outcomes regardless of family background, gender, or minority status (Doran et al., 2012). Families of children with difficulty in communication (Frey, Greenberg, & Fewell, 1989), delay in developmental tasks, difficult temperament, need for constant supervision, or repetitive behavior patterns experience increased family stress. Families of children with severe disabilities, such as autism spectrum disorder, experience stress throughout—in their marital subsystems, their parental subsystems, and their sibling subsystems (Meadan, Halle, & Ebata, 2010). As the child develops physically and emotionally, increased age and caregiving demands can exacerbate the situation (Gallagher, Beckman, & Cross, 1983; Hanson & Hanline, 1990; Harris & McHale, 1989; McLindon, 1990). The perceived need for more-complex support and protection may make real self-determination an elusive, although crucial, goal. Special educators are finding that specific collaborative partnerships with parents can assist reaching this goal (Lee et al., 2006). Parents of children with serious, permanent disabilities go through a mourning process that includes all the usual stages of anger, guilt, depression, and grief over loss of the "perfect child who never came." The parents may eventually reach a realistic acceptance of the child. Yet parents often experience chronic sorrow for what some see as a loss in the day-to-day struggle to meet the needs of the child while maintaining personal self-esteem, integrity as a family, and a meaningful place in the community (Bernier, 1990; Bristol & Gallagher, 1982; Lachney, 1982; Olshansky, 1962;

Turnbull & Turnbull, 1978). The initial grieving may return, continue, or intensify when the child is unable to accomplish developmental milestones adequately or at the prescribed times (Davis, 1987).

Some parental attitudes are reflective both of culture and of the nature of the special education system they encounter. Research suggests that U.S. and Japanese parents of children with disabilities report similar difficulties, including difficulties establishing relationships with professionals providing services for their children, but that they have different expectations regarding these relationships. Japanese parents are more likely to emphasize the importance of emotional connections such as empathy with professionals, and to express feelings of stigma. U.S. parents are more likely to assert that their children are entitled to receive appropriate educational resources (Kayama, 2010).

Coping with a Child with Special Needs

Intense and unrelieved involvement in caregiving for a child with special needs can put severe pressure on parents and siblings. Rather than seeing a child for his or her strengths and uniqueness, burned-out parents may construe the child as a constant burden, as was found in a classic study of a British sample of parents of children with disabilities in the early 1970s (Voysey-Paun, 2006). If family members cannot adaptively share the caring role, the result is often rejection of the child or a split in the family into caregivers and noncaregivers, with the child empowered by the disability itself, and thus able to exploit the split. The effect of such increased and unresolved caregiving demands on spousal relations can be dramatic. Increased caregiving demands and perhaps excessive feelings of personal responsibility for a disability may cause parental roles to split into caregiving and noncaregiving specialties. One parent (often the mother) assumes the caregiving role to the (often voluntary) exclusion of the other parent. Without constructing shared responsibility together, the stress becomes overwhelming for the caregiver or can lead to other pathological relationship outcomes. The effect for parents of such overadequate-underadequate role patterns is to seriously split and distort the spousal relationship. The distortion is often carried to the siblings, generating more caregiving and noncaregiving specialists. Such families often need professional help to balance caregiving over the entire family and to use the support of other informal or formal caregiving systems in the community. For various reasons connected with feelings of personal responsibility, families of children with disabilities may have real difficulty accepting help from the outside and often suffer profound isolation at the time they most need workable social relations with friends, kin, and neighbors, as well as with extended community resources. Such informal support can be a source of respite care, advice, information, and material assistance, as well as empathy and emotional support. This support can be a buffer against the stresses of child care (Beckman, 1991; Beckman & Pokorni, 1988), but it still may not be sufficient to prevent parental dysfunction (Seybold, Flitz, & MacPhee, 1991).

Tavormina et al. (1981, as cited in Bristol & Gallagher, 1982) noted four major parental styles of adapting to the realities of raising a child with disabilities:

1. One parent emotionally distances himself or herself from the child, leaving the care of the child entirely up to the other parent, and concentrates entirely on outside activities unrelated to the child, such as job and organizations.
2. The parents draw together in rejecting the child. The child in this type of family is most apt to be institutionalized, regardless of the severity of his or her disability.
3. The parents make the child the center of their universe, subordinating all of their own desires and pleasures to the service of the child.
4. The parents join in mutual support of the child, and of each other, but maintain a sense of their own identities and create a life as close to normal as possible.

The relations of such parents with institutions and organizations, such as schools, may become complicated. Despite an assumed community expectation that families will be assisted in their functions, formal social support (from formal organizations such as schools, social agencies, etc.) does not seem to significantly reduce stress in parents of young children with developmental delays (Beckman, 1991; Beckman & Pokorni, 1988). Indeed, parent–professional relations can be a source of additional stress (Gallagher et al., 1983). These paradoxical findings point out the problems of organizations or professionals that attempt to supplant the parents. These findings challenge school social workers to assist families to construct appropriate relationships with formal resources. Families desperately need to benefit from these relationships without distorting their own internal relationships.

Parenting a child with disabilities is a 24-hour, 7-day-a-week involvement, drawing considerable energy away from other children and other responsibilities. When parents attempted to describe their experiences, they described great pressure from the child:

> Christine stated, "he'll do a lot of things purposely to get my attention, like break something or turn on the TV, turn off the TV or start yelling." Luz stated emphatically that Juan's behavior was about attention, "24 hours he wants my attention. And that's the problem. That's why he breaks things, writes on the walls, and everything. He just wants my attention."
>
> Carmen shared with us, "Everything is difficult. And then when you've got other kids and they've got homework and they've got to be at school in time and everything. It's just hard to put everything together. . . . At that point I was working full time, but I couldn't do it because I had so many appointments

with Arturo, so then I cut my hours to part-time. . . . We didn't know about it. It was a world we were thrust into when Arturo was born." (Fox, Vaughn, Wyatte, & Dunlap, 2002, p. 445)

Research points out that the disability systemically affects all relationships, including family relationships and social networks. There is a need for community and network resources, policy development, and an ecological approach to assessment, going well beyond the simple focus on child-in-school and certainly involving the home (Fox et al., 2002).

A Family with Severe Caregiving Demands

Many families of children with disabilities are at the point of breakdown, when the extreme caregiving demands of the child do not mesh with what family members see themselves as able to do. The school social worker works with both family and pupil to help them to develop a workable environment. A child with severe disabilities, Betty Benson did better at school than at home. The parents wanted Betty placed in residential placement. Placement was unavailable and the family's difficulties left the school in an unwanted position of offering the major consistent, developmentally appropriate relationships that Betty was experiencing.

> Betty Benson is a six-year-old with cerebral palsy who currently ambulates by rolling and crawling. She has a seven-year-old brother doing well in school. She shows autistic-like behavior but seems to have higher ability than her current diagnosis of profound developmental disability. Although her use of language at home is minimal, she follows directions in school and is able to indicate her need to use the toilet. She is expected to get a walker and orthopedic shoes from United Cerebral Palsy by the end of the year. At home her dominant activities are described by the parents as screaming, crying, grabbing, hitting, head banging, pulling her own hair out, and self-stimulating. The mother works in a factory, and the father is a janitorial worker. Mother is gone in the mornings, and the father is gone in the afternoon and evening. Grandmother watches the children sometimes during the day, and the family receives twenty-five hours a month of respite care. Mother is overwhelmed. She believes her only way to handle Betty is to give in to her demands to keep her from screaming and insists that the brother do the same. Father believes Betty's main problem is that she cannot walk, which limits her contact with other children. Neither parent seems to have a clear idea of what can be expected from Betty in the future or how far she could advance in her ability to function normally.
>
> Betty shares a classroom with five other students, a teacher, and an aide. She showed no behavior problems this year. Last year when the teacher used restraining techniques to manage her, she would scream, grab, and hit. This year the teacher is more nurturing. Betty appears happy and follows directions. When observed in class she quietly worked behind a privacy screen, putting paint brushes together. She kept trying, even when it was difficult for her, and managed to have some success. The school would like the parents to use

medication and behavior modification techniques at home, but they refused. Mother did not believe that she could change her own behavior. The parents did put Betty briefly on medications, but discontinued them after a short trial. The school believed they should have waited longer for them to have an effect. Mother and Father are requesting a residential placement. The school administrator believed that Betty is currently placed in the least restrictive environment and is adequately served in their program. In her opinion, the district should not pay for residential treatment simply because there are problems at home. In any case, she believes Betty would get more services from their school than from a residential placement. Both parents were surprised at how well Betty is doing in school this year. Father would like to know specifically how school personnel are handling Betty in school so they could do the same things with her at home. Mother fears that if Betty were doing well, it might endanger the possibility of placement.

Aside from its ultimate, positive effect on Betty, the amount of time spent with Betty's family, if done with skill, would be minuscule compared with the time-and-treasure cost of the coming extended conflict with the family over placement inherent in this case. Because Betty is doing well in school, there is no likelihood of the school (or the state) funding residential placement; everything now depends on the social worker working between family, school, and Betty. There needs to be a channel of ongoing communication with the school. As Father indicates, it may be possible to help Betty generalize her gains made in school, thus relieving some of the pressure on the parents and brother. Mother feels desperate and hopeless and will need additional help. Someone needs to work with the parents at home to explore rebalancing their roles, and the support they might receive and provide each other in this stressful situation. They need to be able to mourn their situation and then to begin to see Betty as a real person with real strengths. Some additional respite help might be possible. There is also the possibility of helping these very isolated parents connect with a group of parents of children with severe disabilities. As the social worker follows the situation over a period of time, the capabilities of the home to care for Betty could become more evident. Betty's resiliency in school could be extended to the home. In the meantime, concrete supports for the parents, the possibility of a walker, orthopedic shoes for Betty, and most of all help and encouragement for the parents in management of Betty are important.

CONCLUSION

The case illustrations of Alan, Lynda, Ed, Betty, and their complex families are emblematic of clinical social work with pupils and families. The school social worker offered a wide range of help in a minimally intrusive way, using the child's and the family's own adaptive efforts to cope with the life tasks and family transitions. The social worker could use the ordinary work of a social institution, the school, the child, and the family to enhance the positive coping skills eventually developed in a healing process.

References

Adolfi-Morse, B. (1982). Implementing parent involvement and participation in the educational process and the school community. In R. T. Constable & J. P. Flynn (Eds.), *School social work: Practice and research perspectives* (pp. 231–234). Homewood, IL: Dorsey Press.

Allen, S. F., & Tracy, E. F. (2004). Revitalizing the role of home visiting by school social workers. *Children & Schools, 26*(4), 197–208.

Altshuler, S. J. (2009). School social work collaboration with the child welfare system. In C. R. Massat, R. Constable, S. McDonald, & J. P. Flynn (Eds.), *School social work: Practice, policy, and research* (7th ed., pp. 674–691). Chicago: Lyceum Books.

August, G. J., Anderson, D., & Bloomquist, M. L. (1992). Competence enhancement training for children: An integrated child, parent and school approach. In S. L. Christenson & J. C. Conoley (Eds.), *Home-school collaboration: Enhancing children's academic and social competence* (pp. 175–192). Silver Spring, MD: National Association of School Psychologists.

Bailey, D., Blasco, P., & Simeonson, R. (1992). Needs expressed by mothers and fathers of young children with disabilities. *American Journal on Mental Retardation, 97*, 1–10.

Beckman, P. (1991). Comparison of mother's and father's perceptions of the effect of young children, with and without disabilities. *American Journal of Mental Retardation, 95*, 585–595.

Beckman, P., & Pokorni, J. (1988). A longitudinal study of families of preterm infants: Changes in stress and support over the first two years. *Journal of Special Education, 22*, 55–65.

Bernier, J. (1990). Parental adjustment to a disabled child: A family system perspective. *Families in Society, 71*, 589–596.

Blue-Banning, M., Summers, J. A., Frankland, H. C., Nelson, L. L., & Beegle, G. (2004). Dimensions of family and professional partnerships: Constructive guidelines for collaboration. *Exceptional Children, 70*(2), 167–184.

Boethel, M. (2004). *Readiness: School, family and community connections.* Austin, TX: National Center for Family and Community Connections with Schools. Southwest Educational Development Laboratory. Available from http://www.sedl.org/connections/resources/readiness-synthesis.pdf; or from Southwest Educational Development, 211 E. 7th St, Austin, TX 78701.

Bradley, R. H., Whiteside, L., Mundfrom, D. J., Casey, P. H., & Pope, S. K. (1994). Early indicators of resilience and their relations to experiences in the home environments of low birthweight, premature children living in poverty. *Child Development, 65*, 346–360.

Bristol, M. M., & Gallagher, J. J. (1982). A family focus for intervention. In C. T. Ramey & P. L. Trohanis (Eds.), *Finding and educating high risk and handicapped infants* (pp. 137–161). Baltimore: University Park Press.

Brooks-Gunn, J. (2004–5, Winter). A conversation with Jeanne Brooks-Gunn. In *Evaluating family involvement programs. The evaluation exchange, 10*(4), Harvard Family Research Project. Retrieved from http://www.hfrp.org/evaluation/the-evaluation-exchange/issue-archive/evaluating-family-involvement-programs/a-conversation-with-jeanne-brooks-gunn

Carlson, C. (2006). Best models of family therapy. In C. Franklin, M. B. Harris, & P. Allen-Meares (Eds.), *The school services sourcebook; A guide for school-based professionals* (pp. 663–670). New York: Oxford University Press.

Carter, S., & CADRE. (2004). *Educating our children together: A sourcebook for effective family-school-community partnerships.* Retrieved from http://www.directionservice .org/CADRE/EducatingOurChildren_01.cfm

Children's Defense Fund. (1994). *The state of America's children.* Washington, DC: Author.

Christenson, S. L., & Sheridan, S. M. (2001). *Schools and families: Creating essential connections for learning.* New York: Guilford Press.

Cody, P. A. (2006). Working with oppositional youths using brief strategic family therapy. In C. Franklin, M. B. Harris, & P. Allen-Meares (Eds.), *The school services sourcebook; A guide for school-based professionals* (pp. 671–680). New York: Oxford University Press,

Comer, J. P. (1995). *School power: Implications of an intervention project.* New York: Free Press.

Constable, R., & Lee, D. (2004). *Social work with families: Content and process.* Chicago: Lyceum Books.

D'Amato, E., & Yoshida, R. (1991). Parental needs: An educational life cycle perspective. *Journal of Early Intervention, 15,* 246–254.

Davis, B. (1987). Disability and grief. *Social Casework, 68,* 352–357.

Doran, B., Gau, J., & Lindstrom, M.(2012). The relationship between parent expectations and post-school outcomes of adolescents with disabilities. *Exceptional Children, 79*(1), 7–23.

Education for All Handicapped Children Act of 1975, Pub. L. 94-142 (1975).

Elias, M. J. (2003). *Academic and socio-emotional learning.* Educational Practices Series 11, Geneva: International Academy of Education, United Nations Educational, Scientific and Cultural Organization. Retrieved from http://www.unicef.org/eapro/ 3A_Academic_SEL.pdf

Elias, M., & Schwab, Y. (2004, October 20). What about parental involvement in parenting? *Education Week, 24*(8), 39, 41.

Fine, M. J. (1993). (Ap)parent involvement: Reflections on parents, power, and urban public schools. *Teachers' College Record, 94,* 682–711.

Fine, M. J., & Carlson, C. (1992). *The handbook of family-school intervention: A systems perspective.* Boston: Allyn & Bacon.

Fox, L., Vaughn, B. J., Wyatte, M. L., & Dunlap, P. G. (2002). "We can't expect other people to understand": Family perspectives on problem behavior. *Exceptional Children, 68*(4), 437–450.

Franklin, C., Kim, J. S., & Tripoldi, S. J. (2013). Solution-focused, brief therapy interventions for students at risk to drop out. In C. Franklin, M. B. Harris, & P. Allen-Meares (Eds.), *The school services sourcebook: A guide for school-based professionals* (pp. 419–432). New York: Oxford University Press.

Frey, K., Greenberg, M., & Fewell, R. (1989). Stress and coping among parents of handicapped children: A multidimensional approach. *American Journal on Mental Retardation, 95,* 240–249.

Gallagher, J. J., Beckman, P., & Cross, A. H. (1983). Families of handicapped children: Sources of stress and its alleviation. *Exceptional Children, 50*(1), 10–18.

Goals 2000. (1994). Educate America Act. Pub. L. 103-227 (1994).

Hanson, M. J., & Carta, J. J. (1995). Addressing the challenges of families with multiple risks. *Exceptional Children, 62*(3), 201–212.

Hanson, M. J., & Hanline, M. (1990). Parenting a child with a disability: A longitudinal study of parental stress and adaptation. *Journal of Early Intervention, 14,* 234–248.

Harris, V., & McHale, S. (1989). Family life problems, daily caregiving activities, and the psychological well-being of mothers of mentally retarded children. *American Journal on Mental Retardation, 94,* 231–239.

Harry, B., Allen, N., & McLaughlin, M. (1995). Communication vs. compliance: African-American parents' involvement in special education. *Exceptional Children, 61*(4), 364–377.

Henderson, A. T., & Mapp, K. L. (2002). *A new wave of evidence: The impact of school-family and community connections on student achievement.* Austin, TX: National Center for Family and Community Connections with Schools. Southwest Educational Development Laboratory. Available from https://www.sedl.org/connections/resources/evidence.pdf; or from Southwest Educational Development Laboratory, 211 E. 7th St, Austin, TX 78701.

Hoagwood, K. H., Olin, S. S., Kerker, B. D., Kratochwill, T. R., Crowe, M., & Saka, N. (2007). Empirically based school interventions targeted at academic and mental health functioning. *Journal of Emotional and Behavioral Disorders, 15*(2), 66–92.

Individuals with Disabilities Education Act of 1990 (IDEA), Pub. L. 105-17, U.S.C. 11401 et seq. (1990).

Jeynes, W. H. (2005). A metaanalysis of the relation of parent involvement to urban elementary school student academic achievement. *Urban Education, 40,* 237–269.

Kasahara, M., & Turnbull, A. P. (2005). Meaning of family-professional partnerships: Japanese mothers' perspectives. *Exceptional Children, 71*(3), 249–265.

Kayama, M. (2010). Parental experiences of children's disabilities and special education in the U.S. and Japan: Implications for school social work. *Social Work, 55*(2), 117–125.

Kelleghan, T., Sloane, K., Alvarez, B., & Bloom, B. S. (1993). *The home environment and school learning.* San Francisco: Jossey-Bass.

Keltner, B. (1990). Family characteristics of preschool social competence among black children in a Head Start program. *Child Psychiatry and Human Development, 21*(2), 95–108.

Konold, T. (2006). *Who knows their children best, teachers or parents?* University of Virginia, Charlottesville. Retrieved from https://news.virginia.edu/content/who-knows-their-children-best-teachers-or-parents-it-depends-says-university-virginia

Kral, R. (1992). Solution-focused brief therapy: Applications in the schools. In M. J. Fine & C. Carlson (Eds.), *The handbook of family-school intervention: A systems perspective* (pp. 330–346). Boston: Allyn & Bacon.

Lachney, M. E. (1982). Understanding families of the handicapped: A critical factor in the parent-school relationship. In R. T. Constable & J. P. Flynn (Eds.), *School social work: Practice and research perspectives* (pp. 234–241). Homewood, IL: Dorsey Press.

Lee, S., Palmer, S. B., Turnbull, A. P., & Wehmeyer, M. L. (2006). A model for parent-teacher collaboration to promote self-determination in young children with disabilities. *Teaching Exceptional Children, 38*(3), 36–41.

Lewis, A. C., & Henderson, A. T. (1997). *Urgent message: Families crucial to school reform.* Washington, DC: Center for Law and Education.

Lybolt, J., & Gottfred, C. (2003). *Promoting pre-school language.* Educational Practices Series 13, Geneva: International Academy of Education, United Nations Educational, Scientific and Cultural Organization. Retrieved from http://www.ibe.unesco.org/publications/EducationalPracticesSeriesPdf/prac13e.pdf

McLindon, S. (1990). Mother's and father's reports of the effects of a young child with special needs on the family. *Journal of Early Intervention, 14,* 249–259.

Meadan, H., Halle, J. W., & Ebata, A. T. (2010). Families of children who have autism spectrum disorders: Stress and support. *Exceptional Children, 77*(1), 7–36.

Moore, J., & McLaughlin, J. (1988). Medical costs associated with children with disabilities or chronic illness. *Topics in Early Childhood Special Education, 8,* 98–105.

National Institutes of Health. (2005, January 18). *Preventing violence and related health-risking social behaviors in adolescents* October 13–15, 2004. State-of-the-Science Conference Statement. Final Statement. Washington, DC: National Institutes of Health. Retrieved from http://www.ncbi.nlm.nih.gov/books/NBK11868/

Nebo, J. (1963). The school social worker as community organizer. *Social Work, 8,* 99–105.

Newman, L. (2005). *Family involvement in the educational development of youth with disabilities.* A special topic report of findings from the National Longitudinal Transition Study-2. Menlo Park, CA: Office of Special Education Programs, U.S. Department of Education by SRI International.

No Child Left Behind Act of 2001, Pub. L. 107-110 (2002).

Olshansky, S. (1962). Chronic sorrow: A response to having mentally defective children. *Social Casework, 43,* 190–192.

Paik, S. J., & Walberg, H. J. (2007). *Narrowing the achievement gap: Strategies for educating Latino, black, and Asian students.* New York: Springer.

Redding, S. (2000). *Parents and learning.* Educational Practices Series 2, Geneva: International Academy of Education, United Nations Educational, Scientific and Cultural Organization. Retrieved from http://www.ibe.unesco.org/publications/Educational PracticesSeriesPdf/prac02e.pdf

Resnick, M. D., Bearman, P. S., Blum, R. W., Bauman, K. E., Harris, K. M., Jones, J., . . . & Udry, J. R. (1997). Protecting adolescents from harm: Findings from the National Longitudinal Study on Adolescent Health. *Journal of the American Medical Association, 278,* 823–832.

Schorr, L. B. (1988). *Within our reach.* New York: Doubleday.

Schraft, C. M., & Comer, J. P. (1979). Parent participation and urban schools. *School Social Work Quarterly, 1*(4), 309–326.

Sexton, T. L., & Alexander J. F. (2003). Functional family therapy: A mature clinical model for working with at-risk adolescents and their families. In T. L. Sexton, G. R. Weeks, & M. S. Robbins (Eds.), *Handbook of family therapy* (pp. 323–350). New York: Brunner-Routledge.

Sexton, T. L., Weeks, G. R., & Robbins, M. S. (2003). *Handbook of family therapy.* New York: Brunner-Routledge.

Seybold, J., Flitz, J., & MacPhee, D. (1991). Relation of social support to the self-perceptions of mothers with delayed children. *Journal of Community Psychology, 19,* 29–36.

Sheidow, A. J., Hengeller, S. W., & Schoenwald, S. K. (2003). Multisystemic therapy. In T. L. Sexton, G. R. Weeks, & M. S. Robbins (Eds.), *Handbook of family therapy* (pp. 303–322). New York: Brunner-Routledge.

Sheridan, S. M., Kratochwill, T. R., & Elliott, S. N. (1990). Behavioral consultation with parents and teachers: Delivering treatment for socially withdrawn children at home and at school. *School Psychology Review, 19,* 33–52.

Smith, T. M. (1994). Adolescent pregnancy. In R. J. Simeonson (Ed.), *Risk, resilience, and prevention: Promoting the wellbeing of all children* (n.p.). Baltimore: Paul H. Brookes.

Southern Regional Education Board (SREB). (2001). *Helping families to help students: Kentucky's family resource and youth services centers.* Atlanta, GA: Author.

Subotnik, R. F., & Walberg, H. J. (Eds.). (2006). *The scientific basis of educational productivity.* Greenwich, CT: Information Age Publishing.

Turnbull, A. P., & Turnbull, H. R. (1978). *Parents speak out: Views from the other side of the two-way mirror.* Columbus, OH: Merrill.

Victor, J. B., Halvorson, C. F. Jr., & Wampler, K. S. (1988). Family-school context: Parent and teacher agreement on temperament. *Journal of Consulting and Clinical Psychology, 56,* 573–577.

Voysey-Paun, M. (2006). *A constant burden: The reconstitution of family life.* Aldershot, UK: Ashgate Classics.

Walberg, H. J. (1984). Improving the productivity of America's schools. *Educational Leadership, 41*(8), 19–27.

Walberg, H. J., & Lai, J. (1999). Meta-analytic effects for policy. In G. J. Cizek (Ed.), *Handbook of educational policy* (pp. 418–454). San Diego, CA: Academic.

Walsh, F. (1999). *Strengthening family resilience.* New York: Guilford Press.

Walsh, F. (2003). Family resilience: A framework for clinical practice. *Family Process, 42*(1), 1–18.

Walsh, F. (2012). Family resilience: Strengths forged through adversity. In F. Walsh (Ed.), *Normal family processes* (4th ed.). New York: Guilford Press.

Wang, M. C., Haertl, G. D., & Walberg, H. J. (1998). *Building educational resilience.* Bloomington, IN: Phi Delta Kappan Educational Foundation.

Wasik, B. H., & Shaffer, G. L. (2013). Home visiting: Essential guidelines for home visits and engaging with families. In C. Franklin, M. B. Harris, & P. Allen-Meares (Eds.), *The school services sourcebook: A guide for school services professionals* (pp. 719–732). New York: Oxford University Press.

Webster-Stratton, C. (1993). Strategies for helping children with oppositional defiant and conduct disorders: The importance of home-school partnerships. *School Psychology Review, 22,* 437–457.

Webster-Stratton, C., Reid, M. J., & Hammond, M. (2001). Preventing conduct problems, promoting social competence: A parent and teacher training partnership in Head Start. *Journal of Clinical Child Psychology, 30,* 283–302.

Whitbread, K. M., Bruder, M. B., Fleming, G., & Park, H. J. (2007). Collaboration in special education: Parent-professional training. *Teaching exceptional children, 39*(4), 6–7.

31

Promoting Social-Emotional Learning for Children with Special Needs

Aaron M. Thompson
Wendy M. Reinke
Keith C. Herman
University of Missouri Columbia

Faced with failing schools and declining test scores, policy makers in the United States implemented reforms such as the No Child Left Behind Act of 2001 and Race to the Top (U.S. Department of Education, 2009). The intent of the reforms was to accelerate academic progress and performance of all students, as measured by mathematics and language arts skills. However, emerging research indicates many other factors are essential to the success of children in school and life. That is, successful students develop both academic skills and personal attributes such as perseverance and grit, self-control, socially conscious decision making, and positive mindsets about learning. The processes by which children—particularly children with special needs—are taught to acquire essential intra- and interpersonal skills is known as social-emotional learning (SEL). A growing body of research underlying SEL requires that we as educators cultivate and foster the SEL context essential for academic learning if we are to nurture successful students who will eventually mature into responsible citizens.

SEL builds on knowledge accrued from research in child development, classroom management, prevention science, and emerging research on the role of neurology and the impact of trauma on social and cognitive development (Zins & Elias, 2007). SEL, similar to social and character development and positive youth development efforts, aims to improve student behaviors. However, SEL extends those prior frameworks by integrating the work of Daniel Goleman (2006), which emphasizes the social and emotional processes that underlie development and are essential for learning. By promoting SEL, educators may buffer the negative experiences that have accumulated across systems and throughout development—but absent effective SEL supports, cumulative risk factors may potentiate a cascade of poor academic and life-course outcomes.

CASCADES MODEL: IMPORTANCE OF PROMOTING SOCIAL-EMOTIONAL LEARNING FOR CHILDREN WITH SPECIAL NEEDS

Though research suggests it is important to promote SEL for all students, it is particularly important for school social workers to promote the development of SEL skills for children with special needs. Highlighted by the developmental cascades model (Masten & Cicchetti, 2010), children with special needs face particular challenges that place them at increased risk for peer and teacher rejection and early academic problems (Dodge & Pettit, 2003; Moffitt, 1993; Patterson, DeBaryshe, & Ramsey, 1989). If parent and child relationship patterns are characterized by coercive interactions, children may develop and solidify maladaptive behavioral patterns that interfere with normal development—challenges that are amplified for children with expressive language or executive functioning delays.

The transition to elementary school represents a key milestone for children (Kellam, Rebok, Ialongo, & Mayer, 1994). If school social workers and early childhood and elementary educators fail to provide consistently effective and supportive environments, the coercive interactions learned at home will likely occur in the classroom (Reinke & Herman, 2002). As such, children exhibiting early aggressive or antisocial behaviors may develop poor relationships with teachers, which will be characterized by negative interactions (Arnold, Griffith, Ortiz, & Stowe, 1998; Campbell & Ewing, 1990; Carr, Taylor, & Robinson, 1991). Subsequently, children with noncompliant behaviors are often rejected by teachers and well-adjusted peers in the early school years. Early rejection results in fewer opportunities for them to develop the prosocial skills necessary for academic and social success (Kellam et al., 1994).

The initial complications may then lead to later and more-serious types of aggressive and antisocial behavioral patterns (Conger, Ge, Elder, Lorenz, & Simons, 1994; Patterson et al., 1989). The cascade described here is intensified for special needs students exhibiting symptoms of learning or behavior problems (Elias, 2004; Nelson, Benner, Lane, & Smith, 2004). Indeed, the rate and severity of challenging behaviors exhibited by special needs students increases as those students enter middle school (Bergquist, Bigbie, Groves, & Richardson, 2004; Mendez, Fantuzzo, & Cicchetti, 2002; Theriot & Dupper, 2010). However, if identified early prevention efforts may reduce the likelihood of later problems and increase the odds of successful outcomes (Kazdin, Esveldt-Dawson, French, & Unis, 1987; Pepler, King, Craig, Byrd, & Bream, 1995; Webster-Stratton & Hammond, 1997).

SOCIAL-EMOTIONAL LEARNING AND TIERED RESPONSE MODELS: A MULTILEVEL AND MULTIDOMAIN APPROACH

Because the targets of SEL interventions occur at multiple levels (i.e., individual, relational [peers and teachers], classroom, and school) and across multiple domains (i.e., social-cognitive, social relational, whole classroom, and school climate), it makes sense for school social workers to promote the use of school-based tiered response models (e.g., response to intervention, multitiered system of supports, positive behavioral interventions and supports [PBIS]) as a framework for providing SEL supports. Below is a summary to inform school social workers of the basic scientifically supported features of tiered response models and SEL supports.

Features of Effective School-Based Tiered Response Models

Tiered response models typically utilize data (i.e., screening and progress monitoring data) to select and deliver primary, secondary, and tertiary supports. Primary supports are prevention efforts applied to all students to address universal risk factors, including both evidence-based SEL programs and school-wide and classroom management practices. Secondary supports are more concentrated and are provided to small groups of students who have elevated levels of SEL need (Cicchetti, 2010; Offord, Kraemer, Kazdin, Jensen, & Harrington, 1998). Tertiary strategies are applied to individual students with early signs and symptoms of a disorder; these strategies are intensive, utilize a multidisciplinary approach, and consist of a package of supports that may include special education services.

Randomized studies suggest tiered response models are associated with improved school safety (ES = 0.23), academic achievement (ES = 0.24–0.38), positive student behaviors (ES = 0.30), improved school climate (ES = 0.29), and increased staff collaboration (ES = 0.26) (Bradshaw, Mitchell, & Leaf, 2010; Horner et al., 2009). (ES refers to an effect size statistic communicating the strength of an association between two variables, or, in this case, between an intervention and a desirable outcome. An ES = 0.2 is considered mild, 0.5 is considered moderate, and 0.8 is considered strong. See Rubin & Babbie [2012].) On balance, studies indicate tiered response models have small but significant effects on important student outcomes, and systematic reviews suggest many effective behavioral programs and practices are available for use within a tiered response model (Bruhn, Lane, & Hirsch, 2013; Durlak, Weissberg, Dymnicki, Taylor, & Schellinger, 2011; Fairbanks, Simonsen, & Sugai, 2008; Mitchell, Stormont, & Gage, 2011; Wilson & Lipsey, 2007). However, research indicates the effectiveness of those programs and practices is enhanced when they include specific features.

Features of Effective Social-Emotional Learning Supports

Effective SEL supports target the following pliable skills:

- ◆ Self-awareness: The capacity to identify emotions and thoughts and their influence on behavior; to accurately appraise one's own strengths and limitations; and to have a well-grounded sense of positive self-assurance
- ◆ Self-management: The capacity to regulate emotions, thoughts, and behaviors; to manage stress and impulses; and to motivate oneself to set and work toward personal and academic goals
- ◆ Social awareness: The capacity to assume the perspective of and empathize with diverse others; to understand social and ethical norms for behavior; and to identify supports
- ◆ Relationship/social competency: The capacity to establish and maintain healthy and diverse relationships; to communicate clearly and listen actively; and to cooperate, resisting inappropriate social pressure, negotiating conflict constructively, and seeking and offering help when needed
- ◆ Responsible decision making: The capacity to make constructive and respectful choices about personal behavior and social interactions based on ethical standards, the well-being of self and others, social norms, and a realistic evaluation of consequences (Zins & Elias, 2007)

SEL supports are most effective when school social workers teach the above skills by direct instructional methods organized around SAFE instructional features (i.e., Sequenced training, Active learning modalities, Focused and sufficient exposure, Explicitly defined behaviors). Programs organized by SAFE features compared to those without SAFE features are associated with mild to moderate improvements in SEL skills (ES = 0.69), attitudes toward school (ES = 0.24), classroom behaviors (ES = 0.26), emotional stability (ES = 0.28), and academic performance (ES = 0.28) (Durlak et al., 2011).

Effective SEL supports also preserve autonomy, which facilitates the development of quality relationships between students and teachers, and between students and their peers (Algozzine, Browder, Karvonen, Test, & Wood, 2001; Field, Martin, Miller, Ward, & Wehmeyer, 1998; Lane, Menzies, Bruhn, & Crnobori, 2010). School social workers who promote choice, directly involve students, and increase student opportunities to use SEL skills engage in autonomy support and foster the contextual ingredients that expedite the acquisition and use of SEL skills in daily life (Wigfield, Eccles, Roeser, & Schiefele, 2008; Wigfield, Eccles, Ulrich, Roeser, & Davis-Kean, 2002). In addition, autonomy support is a necessary ingredient for encouraging quality student–teacher and student–peer relations (Wentzel, 1993, 2002; Wentzel, Filisetti, & Looney, 2007). Quality relations between students with special needs and their teachers and peers diminishes displays of challenging behaviors, alleviates the effects of peer rejection (Leff & Crick, 2010), and makes student discipline for behavioral offenses more effective (Hamre & Pianta, 2003).

Integrating Social-Emotional Learning and Tiered Response Models: Screening and Progress Monitoring

Similar to effective tiered response models, effective SEL supports are informed by data, specifically early screening and progress monitoring data. The purpose of early screening data is to identify school-level SEL domains of concern, to select primary programs to mitigate those concerns, and to pinpoint subgroups of students who may be at higher levels of risk. Students in need of secondary or tertiary supports can be identified within school-based tiered response models through universal screening procedures. An effective universal screening system needs to utilize measures that answer important questions, are technically adequate (i.e., valid and reliable), are efficient to collect and summarize, and demonstrate treatment utility (McIntosh, Reinke, & Herman, 2010).

There are several existing screening instruments useful in determining which students would benefit from additional supports. For instance, the Systematic Screening for Behavior Disorders (Walker & Severson, 1992), Social Skills Improvement System (Gresham & Elliott, 1990), Behavior Assessment System for Children (Kamphaus & Reynolds, 2007), and the Elementary School Success Profile (Bowen, Thompson, & Powers, 2012) are commercially available screening and assessment measurement systems. These systems utilize behavior rating scales to assess multiple domains of social-emotional and behavioral functioning (e.g., internalizing and externalizing problems, social problems) as well as the contextual risk factors intensifying these conditions. With early screening data, school social workers can determine primary support gaps, identify students in need of secondary and tertiary supports, target specific domains of functioning for those students, develop a work plan to deliver proper supports and services, and establish an adequate baseline from which to gauge whether improvement occurs following the allocation of selected primary, secondary, and tertiary interventions.

It should be noted that many schools operating a tiered response model utilize existing data (e.g., office discipline referrals, truancy or attendance, free and reduced-lunch participation, grades, achievement scores, etc.) as screening indicators to identify at-risk students and to drive decisions regarding resource allocation. Clarifying this point, the National Center on RTI presents forty-eight screening tools to measure concurrent academic performance. Similarly, the Technical Assistance Center for PBIS lists office discipline referrals, attendance, and academic performance data as screening metrics (https://www.pbis.org/). Although these data are excellent student- and school-level progress-monitoring indicators—they are absolutely not screening tools. That is, these forms of data provide information about the magnitude (i.e., intensity and frequency) of an existing problem, but they do not screen or assess the early indicators that predict later social, emotional, and behavioral problems. To properly develop a tiered response model, school social workers must use early screening tools to identify individual and contextual risk factors underlying the development of later problems (Bowen et al., 2012).

Following a screening and selection of primary, secondary, and tertiary supports, the forms of ongoing data discussed above are extremely useful progress indicators to assist school social workers in gauging the effect of those supports. Progress monitoring data are important as an ongoing and formative feedback tool to (1) monitor the gap between baseline and expected levels of SEL functioning, (2) inform mid-course SEL strategy corrections, and (3) monitor the overall effectiveness of a package of SEL strategies (Shute, 2008). Data gathered as part of this process can occur through student and teacher reports, direct observation, and use of existing sources of data listed above.

A TIERED SOCIAL-EMOTIONAL LEARNING RESPONSE MODEL FOR STUDENTS WITH SPECIAL NEEDS

Within a tiered response model, the premise is that all students will benefit from primary SEL supports. Although students with special needs will likely require additional services, primary supports provide a base for enhancing the effects of interventions that are more intensive. It is tempting to conceptualize SEL as an instructional strategy only, but it would be a mistake to neglect the broader social context in which these skills are taught. Although explicit instruction is an essential element of SEL, fostering SEL starts with providing a safe, nurturing, and orderly environment. Conceptually, children may only benefit from classroom instruction when they have their basic needs met and if that instruction is offered in a safe and predictable environment. In disorderly classrooms or where instruction is poorly delivered, children feel less safe and have fewer learning opportunities.

The importance of contextual supports for learning was most recently articulated in a theory of contextual nurturing posited by Biglan and colleagues (Biglan, Flay, Embry, & Sandler, 2012; Biglan & Hinds, 2009). In their theory, the authors provided extensive support for their central idea that normal development is preceded by a common set of environmental conditions. These environments (1) minimize toxic events such as maltreatment and physical injury; (2) model, teach, and reinforce prosocial behaviors; (3) provide monitoring and supervision to support positive behaviors and minimize opportunities for misbehavior; and (4) teach and encourage awareness of thoughts, emotions, and values-based decisions. When the conditions for nurturing environments are met, children can and do flourish. Tiered response models provide a framework for integrating SEL supports to create supportive environments.

PRIMARY SOCIAL-EMOTIONAL LEARNING SUPPORTS FOR STUDENTS WITH SPECIAL NEEDS

School-wide primary prevention approaches attempt to facilitate effective and nurturing school environments as the basis for fostering student social and academic success (Sprick, Garrison, & Howard, 2002; Sugai & Horner, 2006). Common elements of effective primary supports include establishing clear adult expectations in all school settings, providing high rates of positive attention for students when they meet the expectations, creating frequent positive adult-student interactions, enforcing consistent consequences, and using data to drive decision making. Many resources are publically available to assist schools in adopting scientifically based primary supports (see www.pbis.org), including strategies and approaches to SEL focused on classroom management, student coaching, and evidence-based curricula.

Social-Emotional Learning Classroom Management

Even with effective school-wide programs in place, many schools struggle to implement SEL practices. For instance, one study with three elementary schools meeting criteria for implementing school-wide PBIS with high fidelity found that only three of thirty-five teachers had higher rates of positive versus negative interactions in their classrooms (Reinke, Herman, Stormont, & Newcomer, 2013). Thus, teachers need additional support in ensuring effective environments are arranged in all school settings.

Fortunately, several universal classroom management training programs have been developed for this purpose. Most notably, the Good Behavior Game (GBG) was developed in 1969 as a strategy to foster effective classroom management skills (Barrish, Saunders, & Wolf, 1969). GBG has been evaluated in more than twenty randomized studies demonstrating its positive proximal and distal effects on youth development (Embry, 2002). Embry argued that the extensive evidence-base for the GBG justified its description as a so-called behavioral vaccine, inoculating youths exposed to it from future adverse outcomes. The GBG has since been rebranded as the PAX GBG and it provides school social workers and educators with an increased focus on contextual SEL supports.

The Incredible Years Teacher Classroom Management (IY TCM) program was developed to promote more effective elementary classroom environments. Although IY TCM shares some of the same conceptual foundations of the PAX GBG, it also includes strategies for promoting SEL through positive teacher–student interactions. In addition, IY TCM is unique in its training format: the training occurs in groups of teachers and is facilitated by video-based modeling where teachers watch videos of real teacher-student interactions. A recent randomized trial found that IY TCM increased student prosocial behaviors and emotional regulation skills (Reinke, Herman, & Dong, 2014).

Similar effects have been found for effective teacher training programs on the secondary level as well. For instance, a recent trial published in the journal *Science* found that a teacher-level consultation model called My Teaching Partner (MTP) increased academic achievement of middle school students, an effect that was mediated by increases in student autonomy (Allen, Pianta, Gregory, Mikami, & Lun, 2011). As with the IY TCM study described above, the intervention did not provide students with explicit academic or autonomy support instruction. Instead, it provided teachers with skills to provide nurturing classroom environments that promoted academic and social competence in students. School social workers can assist teachers to learn these SEL management practices by introducing teachers to, then coaching and training them to use, effective classroom practices. School social workers do not need to be experts in classroom management practices, per se, but they do need to know where to locate effective training models to assist teachers in a school to increase SEL supports.

Social-Emotional Learning Student Coaching

An additional element of IY TCM, social and emotional coaching, bears special mention because of its innovation around supporting student SEL.

Student coaching involves helping children become aware of their feelings and coping responses during naturally occurring social situations. Such coaching can occur throughout the schoolday in brief interactions between students and school personnel. These interactions—when engaged in by school social workers—provide teachable moments involving real-life situations and typical settings that enhance students' learning, retention, and repetition of the skills. The benefit of real-time coaching is that the skills become linked to the situations where students are able to practice adaptive responses. For instance, when a student is frustrated by a peer interaction, the social worker can prompt, "You are feeling sad because Tracey didn't share the glue with you. Use your words to tell Tracey that you are feeling upset and ask her to share the glue." Thus, coached skills are more likely to be generalized and maintained if they are presented in the moment rather than through classroom discussions. School social workers can find details about social and emotional coaching in Stormont, Reinke, Herman, and Lembke (2012).

Social-Emotional Learning Curricula

Scores of SEL curricula have been developed and evaluated for impact on youth development outcomes; but not all SEL programs are equivalent. In their review of more than two hundred SEL programs, the Collaborative for Academic, Social, and Emotional Learning (CASEL, 2003) recommended twenty-two select programs for use in schools. Common elements of these programs included (1) learning environments that are safe, caring, well-managed, and participatory; and (2) social and emotional competency instruction in self-awareness, social awareness, self-management, relationship skills, and responsible decision making. Recommended programs include Promoting Alternative Thinking Strategies (PATHS) program (Greenberg, Kusche, Cook, & Quamma, 1995), Second Step (Grossman et al., 1997), I Can Problem Solve (Shure, 1993, 2001), and Making Choices (Fraser, Thompson, Day, & Macy, 2014).

We describe PATHS in more detail, given its widespread application and because it includes the positive SEL features emphasized in the CASEL review. PATHS is a comprehensive curriculum for grades pre-K to 6 for promoting social and emotional competence and preventing aggression. The skills are designed to be taught by the classroom teacher or a school social worker in training sessions that occur two to three times per week over the academic year. Skills are arranged hierarchically across five domains: self-control, emotional understanding, positive self-esteem, relationships, and interpersonal problem-solving skills. PATHS provides school social workers with well-developed and scripted lessons that include measureable goals and objectives. PATHS has been evaluated over a thirty-year period in various general and special education settings; these evaluations have consistently found that exposure to PATHS improves children's SEL over time, which reduces their risk for negative outcomes. In one study, students in special education were observed to have lower risk for internalizing and externalizing symptoms over a three-year period after use of PATHS (Kam, Greenberg, & Kusche, 2004).

Since the CASEL (2003) review, several other effective SEL programs have emerged (e.g., Positive Action and Strong Kids). We highlight the Strong Kids curriculum here because it is applicable across pre-K to high school settings and is readily available. Strong Kids (Merrell, Carrizales, Feuerborn, Gueldner, & Tran, 2007) is a brief SEL program designed for school social workers to teach social and emotional skills, promote resilience, strengthen assets, and increase coping skills for students. There is a Strong Start for pre-K and for students in grades K to 2. Strong Kids is designed for students in grades 3 to 5. Session topics are designed to be developmentally appropriate and include identifying and understanding emotions, social skills, cognitive reframing, relaxation strategies, and problem-solving strategies (see table 31.1). Several studies have been conducted evaluating the impact of the Strong Kids programs. In general, these studies have produced positive results, showing that exposure to these SEL programs produces significant increases in knowledge of social-emotional

TABLE 31.1   Structure and Lesson Content of the Strong Kids Social-Emotional Learning Curricula

Lesson	Title	Description
1	The Feelings Exercise Group	Introduce students to Strong Start curriculum.
2	Understanding Your Feelings 1	Teach students to name basic feelings/emotions.
3	Understanding Your Feelings 2	Teach students appropriate ways to express feelings.
4	When You're Angry	Teach students about anger and helpful ways to manage it.
5	When You're Happy	Teach students about happiness and basic strategies for using positive thinking.
6	When You're Worried	Teach students to identify and manage worry, fear, and anxiety.
7	Understanding Other People's Feelings	Teach students ways to identify other people's feelings.
8	Being a Good Friend	Teach students basic interpersonal communication and friendship-making skills.
9	Solving People Problems	Teach students ways of managing conflict with other people.
10	Finishing Up!	Review basic concepts and selected activities in Strong Kids curriculum.

SOURCE: Merrell (2010).

concepts and coping skills. In some cases, decreases in problem symptoms have been noted as have increases in social-emotional competence (see Merrell [2010] for a review). Using the preformatted lessons listed in table 31.1, school social workers can work with teachers to coteach whole classrooms of students on the concepts. Alternatively, using screening data, school social workers may use the curriculum to teach students identified as needing secondary supports.

SECONDARY SOCIAL-EMOTIONAL LEARNING SUPPORTS FOR STUDENTS WITH SPECIAL NEEDS

School social workers frequently provide or coordinate secondary supports for students with special needs. Secondary supports are most often group interventions that target students who have been identified as demonstrating at-risk academic and behavior problems. However, prior to considering secondary SEL supports for small groups of students, school social workers should examine the implementation of primary supports to be certain those practices are being implemented as designed. In schools with effective primary supports, it is estimated that approximately 20 percent of students will need secondary supports to be successful. The next section describes specific secondary practices and programs to support SEL skill instruction for students in need of secondary supports.

Function-based Intervention Planning

Although many school social workers provide group-based secondary interventions, those interventions typically do not have data-based decision rules for determining which intervention a student will receive; in addition, these interventions do not define or measure desired outcomes (Campbell & Anderson, 2008). This can be problematic for several reasons. For instance, a student who refuses to participate with peers in academic activities may benefit from a social skills training group, but only if the student lacks the skills taught in the group. If a student has an academic deficit and is acting out to avoid academic tasks, social skills training may not be appropriate, and the student will be nonresponsive to the intervention. Thus, school social workers must consider the function of the student's behavior before implementing a secondary intervention (Reinke, Stormont, Clare, Latimore, & Herman, 2013).

Determining the function or purpose of the behaviors displayed by a student in need of secondary supports does not require an extensive assessment. Instead, school social workers may gather observational data to define what the behavior looks like, what happens just before the behavior (i.e., the antecedent) and what happens after the behavior (i.e., the consequence) to guide the selection of appropriate supports (see Stormont et al.,

2012). Common functions of a behavior include attention seeking (e.g., from adults and/or peers) or escape/avoidance of something (e.g., tasks or social situations). For example, a student who is repeatedly aggressive (behavior) with peers may find these social interactions (antecedent) aversive, and that using aggression ends the contact (consequence and function). The child's behavior could be due to misinterpreting ambiguous social cues as hostile (e.g., believing peers are being aggressive toward them when they are not) or lacking the requisite social skills to regulate anger and express feelings appropriately when the interactions are actually hostile. In either case, this student would likely benefit from a small social skills group intervention targeting problem solving and cognitive coping. Conversely, a student who behaves in a manner to avoid adult interactions may be less likely to respond to an intervention like the Behavior Education Program (BEP) (see "Teacher-Monitoring: The Behavior Education Program" below) or social skills instruction because these interventions rely heavily on the use of adult attention to promote new skills among students.

Self-Management Supports

Students who have been identified as needing secondary supports for SEL may lack the skills necessary to effectively manage their own behaviors. Some efficient strategies for supporting student development in these skill domains include behavioral contracting, self-monitoring with the Self-management Training And Regulation Strategy, and teacher monitoring using the Behavioral Education Program.

Behavioral Contracting with Goal Setting

School social workers may use behavioral contracts (i.e., written agreements defining an expected behavior and outcome if the student meets the terms of the agreement). Use of behavioral contracts has long been shown to be effective for increasing student self-control and productivity (Kelley & Stokes, 1984; White-Blackburn, Semb, & Semb, 1977). The use of behavioral contracting with goal setting can be an effective secondary intervention for students with special needs by supporting them to self-manage their behaviors toward a socially relevant goal.

Behavioral contracting can be effective for students in need of secondary supports when the function of behavior is considered. To increase the likelihood that the intervention will be effective, school social workers should rely on reinforcement that is matched to the function of the student's behavior. For instance, if a student exhibits behaviors that appear to be attention maintained, a socially relevant and reinforcing reward may include lunch with a favorite teacher or free time with a positive peer. Conversely, if a student's behavior is thought to be maintained by task avoidance, utilizing a reward that would allow the student to escape an undesirable activity will be effective (e.g., no homework for that night, stays back from gym class). Contracts are more effective when they include (1) student input to create the contract, (2) goals that are achievable and provide ample opportunities for the student to meet the goals, and (3) direct instruction in the skills needed so that the student can perform the behavior. The contract should be typed up; and signed by the school social worker, teacher, and student. A copy should be provided to everyone involved (see figure 31.1). Once implemented, if the contract does not improve the identified behaviors, the school social worker should revisit the plan to ensure that the student

FIGURE 31.1   Example Behavioral Contract

BEHAVIORAL CONTRACT

TO: PARENT/GUARDIAN AND STUDENT

[Keith Herman] will begin this contract on _1/1/16_____ to help him be successful at school-related tasks.

GOALS FOR STUDENT:

1. *I will keep my hands and feet to myself.*
2.
3.

REWARDS IF GOALS ARE MET:

1. *One lunch with the school social worker and a friend in the student lounge.*
2.
3.
4.

We will review the terms of this contract on this date: __ 1/8/16 _____
By signing this contract all parties agree to the stipulations in the document and will follow accordingly.

Keith Herman _____   _____
(Signature of Student)   Date

Wendy Reinke _____   _____
(Signature of Teacher)   Date

Mrs. Herman _____   _____
(Signed Name of Parent/Guardian)   Date

Mike Kelly _____   _____
(Signature of Principal)   Date

Aaron Thompson _____   _____
(Signature of School Social Worker)   Date

understands the expectations, possesses the requisite skills to engage in the requested behaviors, the terms of the contract are clear, and the reinforcers effectively motivate and reinforce the student.

Self-Monitoring: The Self-management Training and Regulation Strategy (STARS)

STARS is a multistage self-management intervention comprising self-assessment, goal setting, self-monitoring, self-recording, and self-evaluation (Thompson, 2012; Thompson, Ruhr, Maynard, Pelts, & Bowen, 2013). During the self-assessment stage, students identify, define, and set reasonable goals to reduce or increase target behavior(s). During the self-observation stage, students prompt themselves, reflect on their behavior, and discriminate whether the behavior aligned with the goals. The self-recording stage consists of students documenting the observations (usually on a goal sheet with predefined time intervals; see the example in figure 31.2). During the self-evaluation stage, students aggregate the observations and compare the performance with a predetermined goal. The self-evaluation stage may also include graphing observations, comparing current data with prior self or current teacher observations, and using the data to formulate a new performance goal.

Systematic reviews of self-monitoring studies suggest the strategy is related to improvements in both academic and behavioral outcomes with huge effects (ES =2.30–4.11) (Briesch & Chafouleas, 2009; Fantuzzo, Polite, Cook, & Quinn, 1988). To encourage increased autonomy support and direct student involvement, the Self-management Training and Regulation Strategy (STARS) was developed by the first author (Thompson, 2012, 2013, 2014; Thompson & Webber, 2010). STARS is intended to be delivered by a school social worker for students in need of secondary SEL supports. The program lays out the steps and materials necessary to promote student autonomy, provides students with opportunities to practice social accoutrements, and structures opportunities for students to strengthen relationships and discuss social and emotional progress with teachers. Two studies have examined the effect of STARS. The first study, a multiple baseline, single-subject study across ten students suggested STARS was feasible for students and teachers and that social and behavioral responses improved following exposure to STARS (Thompson, 2012; Thompson & Webber, 2010). A follow-up study relied on a cluster randomized design with 108 fourth- and fifth-grade students screened for social and emotional behavioral problems. The results of the randomized study suggested STARS was associated with improvements in teacher-rated disruptive student behaviors (ES = 0.46), authority acceptance (ES = 0.47), social competencies (ES = 0.55), and improved quality of teacher-rated relations with students (ES = 0.39). Statistical improvements were also observed for student-rated perceptions of perceived autonomy and improved relations with their teachers.

FIGURE 31.2 STARS Daily Behavior Goal Card

STARS Daily Behavior Goals

Student: Date:

This student:	Completed his/her work	Kept body parts to self	Was considerate of others	Followed directions	Stayed in assigned area
8:00 - 8:30	Yes - No	Yes - No	Yes - No	Yes – No	Yes - No
8:30 - 9:00	Yes - No	Yes - No	Yes - No	Yes – No	Yes - No
9:00 - 9:30	Yes - No	Yes - No	Yes - No	Yes - No	Yes - No
9:30 - 10:00	Yes - No	Yes - No	Yes - No	Yes - No	Yes - No
10:00 - 10:30	Yes - No	Yes - No	Yes - No	Yes - No	Yes - No
10:30 - 11:00	Yes - No	Yes - No	Yes - No	Yes - No	Yes - No
11:00 - 11:30	Yes - No	Yes - No	Yes - No	Yes - No	Yes - No
11:30 - 12:00	Yes - No	Yes - No	Yes - No	Yes - No	Yes - No
12:00 - 12:30	Yes - No	Yes - No	Yes - No	Yes - No	Yes - No
12:30 - 1:00	Yes - No	Yes - No	Yes - No	Yes - No	Yes - No
1:00 - 1:30	Yes - No	Yes - No	Yes - No	Yes - No	Yes - No
1:30 - 2:00	Yes - No	Yes - No	Yes - No	Yes - No	Yes - No
2:00 - 2:30	Yes - No	Yes - No	Yes - No	Yes - No	Yes - No

Total # yes = 65   70% yes = 46   85% yes = 55   90% yes = 58

Notes & Assignments

_____

_____

_____

_____

_____

Parent signature _____

Teacher-Monitoring: The Behavior Education Program

The Behavior Education Program (BEP) is a secondary support program that provides daily support and teacher monitoring for students with special needs (Crone, Hawken, & Horner, 2010). The BEP is based on the check-in/check-out system (Cheney et al., 2009) that provides students with immediate feedback on behavior, using teacher rating on a daily progress report

(DPR). Expectations for student behaviors are defined and students are provided immediate reinforcement for meeting behavioral expectations. Home-school communication is also emphasized by sending the DPR home each day to be signed and returned. The core components of the BEP may be managed by a school social worker and include (1) clearly defined behavioral expectations, (2) increased positive reinforcement for meeting expectations, (3) contingent consequences for problem behavior, (4) increased positive contact with an adult at school, and (5) increased home-school communication. Research indicates that this intervention is most effective in supporting students with problem behaviors maintained by attention (Mitchell et al., 2011).

Small Group Instructional Supports

Students with special needs often react to problems in ineffective ways. Many of these students will benefit from group-based social skills training to help them learn more-appropriate cognitive and social problem-solving strategies. There are a number of social skills curricula that can be used to support students. We recommend you select a comprehensive social-emotional curriculum with evidence to support its effectiveness to teach students prosocial behaviors. The following is a brief review of evidence-based group interventions for school social workers to consider for students in need of secondary SEL supports.

Coping Power Program

The Coping Power Program (Lochman & Wells, 2002) is a group-based secondary preventive intervention designed for students and the parents of students in the late elementary school years (grades 3 to 5). Social competence, self-regulation, and positive parental involvement are specific targets of Coping Power. The program lasts fifteen to eighteen months in its full form, and incorporates both student and parent groups. Session topics in the student groups include goal setting, anger management, perspective taking, understanding and identifying emotions, relaxation training, social-cognitive problem solving, coping with peer pressure, and using positive peer networks. Parent group sessions are also available for school social workers who work as school outreach personnel to teach positive parenting strategies like giving effective instruction, rewarding and attending to appropriate child behavior, establishing effective rules in the home, and applying effective consequences for negative child behavior. Parents also learn management of child behaviors outside the home, effective communication skills, and strategies to support the skills their children learn in the student groups. Coping Power has been shown to decrease delinquency and substance use as well as behavior problems at home and school (Lochman et al., 2010; Lochman & Wells, 2002).

Incredible Years Small Group Dinosaur School Program

Incredible Years Small Group Dinosaur School Program (Webster-Stratton, Reid, & Hammond, 2004) was developed as a secondary support for students in preschool and early elementary grades. The program is delivered in two-hour weekly small group sessions with approximately six children across twenty-two weeks. The program may be delivered by school social workers to teach students appropriate classroom behaviors, problem-solving strategies, social skills, feelings literacy, and emotional self-regulation skills. Ideally, it is offered in conjunction with the two-hour weekly Incredible Years Parent Group sessions. Research indicates that the program increases student use of prosocial skills, improves social competence, and decreases aggressive behavior (Webster-Stratton et al., 2004).

TERTIARY SOCIAL-EMOTIONAL LEARNING SUPPORTS FOR STUDENTS WITH SPECIAL NEEDS: WRAPAROUND

Tertiary supports require a team-based approach and utilize all relevant ongoing data collected from existing primary and secondary efforts (e.g., office discipline referrals, attendance, grades, functional behavioral assessments, STARS self-monitoring data, BEP teacher-monitoring data). Due to the individualized nature of tertiary strategies, these strategies require student input as well as unwavering guidance from a multidisciplinary team of adults with intimate knowledge of the student. In sum, tertiary supports include a wraparound plan for a child and his or her family. However—as with secondary strategies—school social workers should examine all primary and secondary strategies to be certain those practices are being implemented as designed prior to developing a tertiary support plan.

Wraparound emerged from the system of care philosophy and is endorsed by the Department of Health and Human Services, Substance Abuse and Mental Health Services Administration, the National Institute of Mental Health, and consumer organizations such as the National Federation of Families for Children's Mental Health and the National Alliance on Mental Illness as an evidence-based approach to care. Though wraparound has most often been implemented through community mental health agencies, it has been successfully adopted for use in school by school social workers (Eber, Sugai, Smith, & Scott, 2002). Results from randomized studies suggest wraparound is associated with improvements in child-level outcomes, including fewer foster care, school, and residential placement changes; improved school attendance; behavioral and functional living outcomes; and fewer school suspensions, rearrests, and incidents of aggression (Carney & Buttell, 2003; Clark & Clarke, 1996; Clark, Lee, Prange, & McDonald, 1996). The studies suggest the process improves linkages among schools, families, and community agencies and that the process can improve parent involvement at school—an important mechanism of change that is central to assisting students exhibiting early signs and symptoms of mental health concerns.

School-based wraparound is guided by trained school social workers who facilitate the coordination of school, family, and community resources into a well-defined, strengths-based, and unique child and family plan with a set of targeted goals and measureable outcomes. In addition, school-based wraparound is easily integrated into existing tiered response models. The school-based wraparound process addresses the following key elements (Eber et al., 2002):

- School-based coordinator of school, community, and family supports
- Individualized child-focused plan that is strengths-based and culturally competent
- Families that are full and active partners in the planning
- Team approach that includes relevant community agencies
- Flexible and accessible funding sources
- Unconditional commitment of team members
- Outcomes determined, monitored, and measured by team process

Studies comparing community and school-based wraparound processes are limited. However, increased participation of educators and parents—essential figures for improving child outcomes—has been observed in studies of school-based wraparound programs compared to community-based programs (Nordness, 2005). Studies do suggest that increased attendance of key figures (i.e., parents and teachers) improves, in part, because school-based wraparound programs effectively address community-based barriers to service delivery through increased proximity, accessibility, and reduced stigma for parents (Eber et al., 2002) and increased interagency collaboration (i.e., formal collaboration of professional services, attendance at meetings). These characteristics increase attendance of key figures such as parents and teachers, and these investments are significantly related to achieving treatment goals (Wright, Russell, Anderson, Kooreman, & Wright, 2006).

A wraparound plan should assess strengths and areas of need as well as address problematic behaviors using a behavior intervention plan that is based on existing functional classroom behavioral and academic performance data. If some of the problematic behaviors include aggression, the behavior intervention plan should address emergency procedures for managing such behaviors. To find more tertiary-level supports and documents to guide the wraparound process see the U.S. Department of Education Office of Special Education Programs (2015) or see Eber et al. (2011).

CONCLUSION

School social workers are well positioned to work with teachers, school psychologists, counselors, and community agencies to promote the SEL goals at the primary, secondary, and tertiary levels. The growing literature summarizing the benefits of SEL has coincided with an era in the U.S. education system focused on accountability. Consequently, many schools have adopted data-driven tiered response models to enhance the likelihood of desirable outcomes. However, these outcomes have largely remained focused on mathematics and reading achievement. Ironically, many of the initiatives designed to increase academic outcomes have simultaneously undermined the social and contextual SEL supports required to facilitate true academic success. For instance, by increasing pressure on adults to achieve better outcomes without also attending to the context in which learning takes place, teachers and students report increasing levels of stress and dissatisfaction. Despite more than a decade of policy and intervention aimed at improving academic outcomes, reading and mathematics achievement has not dramatically improved and the achievement gap that characterizes the performance of historically disadvantaged and impoverished subgroups of children persists. In short, academic press will not help children experience success, prepare them to be socially responsible, or encourage them to be contributing members of a community. School social workers, therefore, have an ethical obligation to advocate for effective and evidence-based tools that address primary, secondary, and tertiary SEL programs and practices that, when coordinated, support a nurturing school climate where learning can take place.

Figure 31.3 shows how a school social worker might integrate the content summarized in this chapter into an SEL school-based tiered model of prevention and intervention. The classic public health prevention and intervention triangle represents the whole population of students in a school building. Sources of data are listed on the left of the triangle while the SEL interventions summarized in this chapter are listed on the right for primary, secondary, and tertiary levels of risk. School social workers seeking to develop a seamless school-wide system of interventions should start by conducting universal screening of all students using any one of the suggested systems of data collection. These data can then be used to identify secondary students who are considered at risk (~20% of students) and tertiary students who are considered to be in risk (~5 to 7 percent of students). Adjacent to each level of risk are interventions scientifically proven to mitigate those students' risk. Ongoing performance data sources are also listed (and bolded in the figure for secondary and tertiary levels) from which school social workers may assess the success of the system of strategies to improve student SEL functioning. A brief glance at the figure will reveal that as we implement each level of the system of layered strategies, students who are considered to be in risk and at risk not only have access to more supports, but also those supports are more intensive in terms of implementation and data collection efforts. As such, it is important for school social workers to ensure that each intervention adopted at lower levels is being fully implemented before adopting and layering new strategies over the top of existing efforts. Without ensuring that interventions are being implemented as designed, there is no way of establishing whether a student is a nonresponder to lower-level interventions.

FIGURE 31.3 Connecting Social-Emotional Learning Data and Interventions in a Tiered-Response Model: Data Sources & Prevention & Intervention Strategies

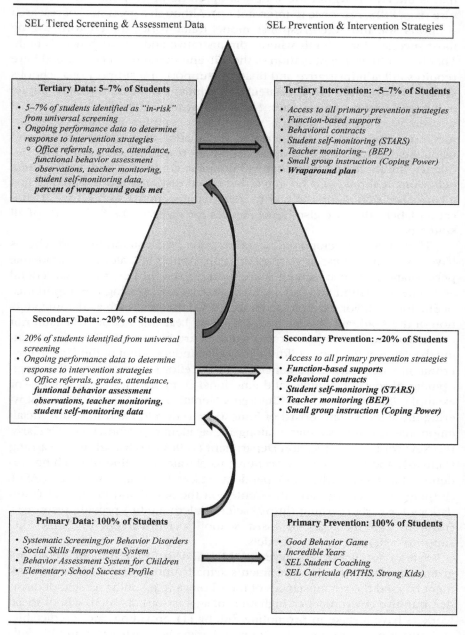

Using data to identify, implement, and evaluate the effects of the interventions listed in figure 31.3 will promote a nurturing SEL environment that is integrated within the widely adopted tiered response model structure (e.g., PBIS, response to intervention). Although a great deal of research supports SEL and tiered response model frameworks, these efforts will be most successful in schools where administrative and faculty buy-in is high. That is, faithful implementation of the SEL and tiered model described here requires full administrative and financial support, full support of a school's staff, and long-term and consistent commitment to achieve proper implementation (five to seven years; Sugai & Horner, 2008). For school social workers working with students who present complex and difficult behaviors, using observations to determine the function of student behaviors and using the data to prioritize students and their respective behaviors (e.g., frequency, duration, and intensity) will untangle competing and confounding behaviors. It should also be noted that tiered response models are not just a barrier or step along the way to identifying students with a special education label—they are also best practices for meeting the SEL needs of all students.

Though SEL development begins at home, the community and schools have a shared interest in purposefully promoting SEL alongside academic performance. As such, school social workers should be aware that federal and state legislation and independent groups are pressing the importance of SEL forward. For example, federal policy initiatives, such as the introduction of the Academic, Social, and Emotional Learning Act of 2011 (still not enacted at the federal level at this writing), are important efforts for elevating the value of teaching children SEL skills. Independent of the federal government, some states have generated policy efforts to encourage the development of social, cognitive, and emotional competencies for students. For example, Illinois passed the Children's Mental Health Act of 2003, empowering the Illinois State Board of Education to develop and measure social-emotional learning standards alongside academic performance. Similarly, the New York State Education Department (2006) also has adopted learning standards and assessment procedures to elevate the value of teaching students SEL skills. Other independent research groups such as CASEL (http://www.casel.org/) and the Center on the Social and Emotional Foundations for Early Learning (http://csefel.vanderbilt.edu/) provide resources, research, and materials to assist school social workers to build SEL-supportive tiered response models.

School social workers have an obligation to foster student well-being given that some school environments actually undermine student development beyond the circumstances of their homes (e.g., bullying, school disorder, punitive environments, high rates of aggression). As such, school social workers have a stake in promoting SEL by (1) providing safe, predictable, and nurturing environments; (2) providing explicit instruction in SEL skills using scientifically supported programs and practices; (3) developing autonomy supportive opportunities for students to practice using SEL skills; and (4) meeting those opportunities with supportive and formative feedback that will cultivate SEL competencies in youths.

References

Academic, Social, and Emotional Learning Act of 2011, H.R. 2437. Not enacted as of this writing. Retrieved from https://www.govtrack.us/congress/bills/112/hr2437

Algozzine, B., Browder, D., Karvonen, M., Test, D. W., & Wood, W. M. (2001). Effects of interventions to promote self-determination for individuals with disabilities. *Review of Educational Research, 71*(2), 219–277.

Allen, J. P., Pianta, R. C., Gregory, A., Mikami, Y., & Lun, J. (2011). An interaction-based approach to enhancing secondary school instruction and student achievement. *Science, 333,* 1034–1037.

Arnold, D. H., Griffith, J. R., Ortiz, C., & Stowe, R. M. (1998). Day care interactions and teacher perceptions as a function of teacher and child ethnic group. *Journal of Research in Childhood Education, 12*(2), 143–154.

Barrish, H. H., Saunders, M., & Wolf, M. M. (1969). Good Behavior Game: Effects of individual contingencies for group consequences on disruptive behavior in a classroom. *Journal of Applied Behavior Analysis, 2*(2), 119–124.

Bergquist, C. C., Bigbie, C. L., Groves, L., & Richardson, G. H. (2004). *Evaluation report for the study of alternatives to suspension.* Tallahassee, FL: Evaluation Systems Design.

Biglan, A., Flay, B. R., Embry, D. D., & Sandler, I. N. (2012). The critical role of nurturing environments for promoting human well-being. *American Psychologist, 67*(4), 257.

Biglan, A., & Hinds, E. (2009). Evolving prosocial and sustainable neighborhoods and communities. *Annual Review of Clinical Psychology, 5,* 169.

Bowen, N. K., Thompson, A. M., & Powers, J. D. (2012). A quasi-experimental test of the elementary-school success profile model of assessment and prevention. *Journal of the Society for Social Work and Research, 3*(3), 178–196.

Bradshaw, C., Mitchell, M., & Leaf, P. (2010). Examining the effects of schoolwide positive behavioral interventions and supports on student outcomes: Results from a randomized controlled effectiveness trial in elementary schools. *Journal of Positive Behavior Interventions, 12,* 133–148. doi:10.1177/1098300709334798

Briesch, A. M., & Chafouleas, S. M. (2009). Review and analysis of literature on self-management interventions to promote appropriate classroom behaviors (1988–2008). *School Psychology Quarterly, 24*(2), 106–118.

Bruhn, A. L., Lane, K. L., & Hirsch, S. E. (2013). A review of tier 2 interventions conducted within multitiered models of behavioral prevention. *Journal of Emotional and Behavioral Disorders, 2*(3), 171–189. doi:10.1177/1063426613476092

Campbell, A., & Anderson, C. M. (2008). Enhancing effects of Check-In/Check-Out with function-based support. *Behavioral Disorders, 33*(4), 233–245.

Campbell, S. B., & Ewing, L. J. (1990). Follow-up of hard-to-manage preschoolers: Adjustment at age 9 and predictors of continuing symptoms. *Journal of Child Psychology and Psychiatry, 31*(6), 871–889.

Carney, M. M., & Buttell, F. (2003). Reducing juvenile recidivism: Evaluating the wraparound services model. *Research on Social Work Practice, 13*(5), 551–568.

Carr, E. G., Taylor, J. C., & Robinson, S. (1991). The effects of severe behavior problems in children on the teaching behavior of adults. *Journal of Applied Behavior Analysis, 24*(3), 523–535.

Cheney, D. A., Stage, S. A., Hawken, L. S., Lynass, L., Mielenz, C., & Waugh, M. (2009). A 2-year outcome study of the check, connect, and expect intervention for students at risk for severe behavior problems. *Journal of Emotional and Behavioral Disorders, 17*(4), 226–243.

Cicchetti, D. (2010). Resilience under conditions of extreme stress: A multilevel perspective. *World Psychiatry, 9*(3), 145–154.

Clark, H. B., & Clarke, R. T. (1996). Research on the wraparound process and individualized services for children with multi-system needs. *Journal of Child and Family Studies, 5*(1), 1–5.

Clark, H. B., Lee, B., Prange, M. E., & McDonald, B. A. (1996). Children lost within the foster care system: Can wraparound service strategies improve placement outcomes? *Journal of Child and Family Studies, 5*(1), 39–54.

Collaborative for Academic, Social, and Emotional Learning (CASEL). (2003). *Safe and sound: An educational leader's guide to evidence-based social and emotional learning programs.* Chicago: Collaborative for Academic, Social, and Emotional Learning.

Conger, R. D., Ge, X., Elder, G. H., Lorenz, F. O., & Simons, R. L. (1994). Economic stress, coercive family process, and developmental problems of adolescents. *Child Development, 65*(2), 541–561.

Crone, D. A., Hawken, L. S., & Horner, R. H. (2010). *Responding to problem behavior in schools: The Behavior Education Program.* New York: Guilford Press.

Dodge, K. A., & Pettit, G. S. (2003). A biopsychosocial model of the development of chronic conduct problems in adolescence. *Developmental Psychology, 39*(2), 349.

Durlak, J. A., Weissberg, R. P., Dymnicki, A. B., Taylor, R. D., & Schellinger, K. B. (2011). The impact of enhancing students' social and emotional learning: A meta-analysis of school-based universal interventions. *Child Development, 82*(1), 405–432.

Eber, L., Hyde, K., Rose, J., Breen, K., McDonald, D., & Lewandowski, H. (2011). Completing the continuum of schoolwide positive behaviors support: Wraparound as a tertiary-level intervention. In W. Sailor, G. Dunlap, G. Sugai, & R. Horner (Eds.), *Handbook of positive behavior supports* (pp. 671–704). New York: Springer.

Eber, L., Sugai, G., Smith, C. R., & Scott, T. M. (2002). Wraparound and positive behavioral interventions and supports in the schools. *Journal of Emotional and Behavioral Disorders, 10*(3), 171–180.

Elias, M. J. (2004). The connection between social-emotional learning and learning disabilities: Implications for intervention. *Learning Disability Quarterly,* 53–63.

Embry, D. D. (2002). The Good Behavior Game: A best practice candidate as a universal behavioral vaccine. *Clinical Child and Family Psychology Review, 5*(4), 273–297.

Fairbanks, S., Simonsen, B., & Sugai, G. (2008). Classwide secondary and tertiary tier practices and systems. *Teaching Exceptional Children, 40*(6), 44–52.

Fantuzzo, J. W., Polite, K., Cook, D. M., & Quinn, G. (1988). An evaluation of the effectiveness of teacher- vs. student-management classroom interventions. *Psychology in the Schools, 25*(2), 154–163.

Field, S., Martin, J., Miller, R., Ward, M., & Wehmeyer, M. (1998). *A practical guide for teaching self-determination.* Reston, VA: Council for Exceptional Children.

Fraser, M. W., Thompson, A. M., Day, S. H., & Macy, R. J. (2014). The Making Choices Program: Impact of social-emotional skills training on the risk status of third graders. *Elementary School Journal, 114*(3), 354–379.

Goleman, D. (2006). *Emotional intelligence: Why it can matter more than IQ.* New York: Bantam.

Greenberg, M. T., Kusche, C. A., Cook, E. T., & Quamma, J. P. (1995). Promoting emotional competence in school-aged children: The effects of the PATHS curriculum. *Developmental Psychopathology, 7,* 117–136.

Gresham, F. M., & Elliott, S. N. (1990). *Social Skills Rating System: Preschool, elementary level.* Circle Pines, MN: American Guidance Service.

Grossman, D. C., Neckerman, H. J., Koepsell, T. D., Liu, P.-Y., Asher, K. N., Beland, K., . . . Rivara, F. P. (1997). Effectiveness of a violence prevention curriculum among children in elementary school. *JAMA: Journal of the American Medical Association, 277*(20), 1605–1611.

Hamre, B. K., & Pianta, R. C. (2003). Early teacher–child relationships and the trajectory of children's school outcomes through eighth grade. *Child Development, 72*(2), 625–638.

Horner, R. H., Sugai, G., Smolkowski, K., Eber, L., Nakasato, J., Todd, A. W., & Esperanza, J. (2009). A randomized, wait-list controlled effectiveness trial assessing school-wide positive behavior support in elementary schools. *Journal of Positive Behavior Interventions, 11*(3), 133–144.

Illinois State Board of Education (ISBE). (2003). *Illinois learning standards: Social/emotional learning (SEL).* Retrieved from http://isbe.net/ils/social_emotional/standards.htm

Kam, C.-M., Greenberg, M. T., & Kusche, C. A. (2004). Sustained effects of the PaTHS curriculum on the social and psychological adjustment of children in special education. *Journal of Emotional and Behavioral Disorders, 12*(2), 66–78.

Kamphaus, R., & Reynolds, C. (2007). *Behavior Assessment System for Children* (2nd ed.). *(BASC-2): Behavioral and Emotional Screening System (BESS).* Bloomington, MN: Pearson.

Kazdin, A. E., Esveldt-Dawson, K., French, N. H., & Unis, A. S. (1987). Effects of parent management training and problem-solving skills training combined in the treatment of antisocial child behavior. *Journal of the American Academy of Child & Adolescent Psychiatry, 26*(3), 416–424.

Kellam, S. G., Rebok, G. W., Ialongo, N., & Mayer, L. S. (1994). The course and malleability of aggressive behavior from early first grade into middle school: Results of a developmental epidemiologically based preventive trial. *Journal of Child Psychology and Psychiatry, 35*(2), 259–281.

Kelley, M. L., & Stokes, T. F. (1984). Student-teacher contracting with goal setting for maintenance. *Behavior Modification, 8*(2), 223–244.

Lane, K. L., Menzies, H. M., Bruhn, A. L., & Crnobori, M. (2010). *Managing challenging behaviors in schools: Research-based strategies that work.* New York: Guilford Press.

Leff, S. S., & Crick, N. R. (2010). Interventions for relational aggression: Innovative programming and next steps in research and practice. *School Psychology Review, 39*(4), 504–507.

Lochman, J. E., Bierman, K. L., Coie, J. D., Dodge, K. A., Greenberg, M. T., McMahon, R. J., & Pinderhughes, E. E. (2010). The difficulty of maintaining positive intervention effects: A look at disruptive behavior, deviant peer relations, and social skills during the middle school years. *Journal of Early Adolescence, 30*(4), 593–624.

Lochman, J. E., & Wells, K. C. (2002). The Coping Power Program at the middle-school transition: Universal and indicated prevention effects. *Psychology of Addictive Behaviors, 16*(4 Suppl), S40–S54.

Masten, A. S., & Cicchetti, D. (2010). Developmental cascades. *Developmental Psychopathology, 22*(03), 491–495.

McIntosh, K., Reinke, W., & Herman, K. C. (2010). School-wide analysis of data for social behavior problems: Assessing outcomes, selecting targets for intervention, and identifying need for support. In G. G. Peacock, R. A. Irvin, E. J. Daly, & K. Merrell (Eds.), *Practical handbook of school psychology: Effective practices for the 21st century* (pp. 135–156). New York: Guilford Press.

Mendez, J. L., Fantuzzo, J., & Cicchetti, D. (2002). Profiles of social competence among low-income African American preschool children. *Child Development, 73*(4), 1085–1100.

Merrell, K. W. (2010). Linking prevention science and social and emotional learning: The Oregon Resiliency Project. *Psychology in the Schools, 47*(1), 55–70.

Merrell, K. W., Carrizales, D., Feuerborn, L., Gueldner, B. A., & Tran, O. K. (2007). *Strong kids—grades 6-8: A social and emotional learning curriculum.* ERIC.

Mitchell, B. S., Stormont, M., & Gage, N. A. (2011). Tier two interventions implemented within the context of a tiered prevention framework. *Behavioral Disorders, 36*(4), 241–261.

Moffitt, T. E. (1993). Adolescence-limited and life-course-persistent antisocial behavior: A developmental taxonomy. *Psychological Review, 100*(4), 674.

Nelson, J. R., Benner, G. J., Lane, K., & Smith, B. W. (2004). Academic achievement of K–12 students with emotional and behavioral disorders. *Exceptional Children, 71*(1), 59–73.

New York State Education Department. (2006). *Social emotional development in learning.* Retrieved from http://www.p12.nysed.gov/sss/sedl/

No Child Left Behind Act of 2001, Pub. L. 107-110 (2002).

Nordness, P. D. (2005). A comparison of school-based and community-based adherence to wraparound during family planning meetings. *Special Education and Communication Disorders Faculty Publications,* Paper 2. Retrieved from http://digital commons.unomaha.edu/spedfacpub/2

Offord, D. R., Kraemer, H. C., Kazdin, A. E., Jensen, P. S., & Harrington, R. (1998). Lowering the burden of suffering from child psychiatric disorder: Trade-offs among clinical, targeted, and universal interventions. *Journal of the American Academy of Child & Adolescent Psychiatry, 37*(7), 686–694.

Patterson, G. R., DeBaryshe, B. D., & Ramsey, E. (1989). A developmental perspective on antisocial behavior. *American Psychologist, 44*(2), 329–335.

Pepler, D. J., King, G., Craig, W., Byrd, B., & Bream, L. (1995). *The development and evaluation of a multisystem social skills group training program for aggressive children. Child and Youth Care Forum, 24,* 297–313.

Reinke, W. M., & Herman, K. C. (2002). Creating school environments that deter antisocial behaviors in youth. *Psychology in the Schools, 39*(5), 549–559.

Reinke, W. M., Herman, K. C., & Dong, N. (2014). *A group randomized evaluation of an elementary school teacher classroom management training program.* Paper presented at the Annual Convention of the Society for Research on Educational Effectiveness, Washington, DC.

Reinke, W. M., Herman, K. C., Stormont, M., & Newcomer, L. (2013). Classroom level positive behavior supports in schools implementing SW-PBIS: Identifying areas for enhancement. *Journal of Positive Behavior Interventions, 15,* 39–50.

Reinke, W. M., Stormont, M., Clare, A., Latimore, T., & Herman, K. C. (2013). Differentiating Tier 2 interventions according to function of behavior. *Journal of Applied School Psychology, 29,* 148–166.

Rubin, A., & Babbie, E. R. (2012). *Essential research methods for social work.* Belmont, CA: Brooks/Cole.

Shure, M. B. (1993). I can problem solve (ICPS): Interpersonal cognitive problem solving for young children. *Early Child Development and Care, 96*(1), 49–64.

Shure, M. B. (2001). I can problem solve (ICPS): An interpersonal cognitive problem solving program for children. *Residential Treatment for Children & Youth, 18*(3), 3–14.

Shute, V. J. (2008). Focus on formative feedback. *Review of Educational Research, 78*(1), 153–189.

Sprick, R., Garrison, M., & Howard, L. (2002). *Foundations: Establishing positive discipline policies, Module I: The process, Module II: Behavior in the common areas, Module III: Safety, discipline and behavior support.* Eugene, OR: Pacific Northwest Publishing.

Stormont, M., Reinke, W., Herman, K. C., & Lembke, E. (2012). *Tier 2 interventions: Academic and behavior supports for students at risk for failure.* New York: Guilford Press.

Sugai, G., & Horner, R. R. (2006). A promising approach for expanding and sustaining school-wide positive behavior support. *School Psychology Review, 35*(2), 245.

Sugai, G., & Horner, R. H. (2008). What we know and need to know about preventing problem behavior in schools. *Exceptionality, 16,* 67–77.

Theriot, M. T., & Dupper, D. R. (2010). Student discipline problems and the transition from elementary to middle school. *Education and Urban Society, 42*(2), 205–222.

Thompson, A. M. (2012). *A randomized trial of the Self-management Training And Regulation Strategy (STARS): A selective intervention for students with disruptive classroom behaviors.* Ann Arbor, MI: Proquest Publishers.

Thompson, A. M. (2013). Improving classroom conflict management through positive behavior supports. In C. Franklin, M. B. Harris, & P. Allen-Meares (Eds.), *The school services sourcebook: A guide for school-based professionals* (2nd ed., pp. 491–506). New York: Oxford University Press.

Thompson, A. M. (2014). A randomized trial of the Self-management Training And Regulation Strategy for disruptive students. *Research on Social Work Practice, 24,* 414–427. doi:10.1177/1049731513509691

Thompson, A. M., Ruhr, L. R., Maynard, B. R., Pelts, M. D., & Bowen, N. K. (2013). *Self-monitoring interventions for reducing challenging behaviors among school-age students: A systematic review.* Retrieved from http://www.campbellcollaboration .org/lib/project/264/

Thompson, A. M., & Webber, K. C. (2010). Realigning student and teacher perceptions of school rules: A behavior management strategy for students with challenging behaviors. *Children & Schools, 32*(2), 71–79.

U.S. Department of Education (USDOE). (2009). *Race to the top* (executive summary). Washington, DC: Author.

U.S. Department of Education Office of Special Education Programs. (2015). *Technical Assistance Center.* Retrieved from http://www.pbis.org/evaluation/evaluation_tools.aspx

Walker, H. M., & Severson, H. H. (1992). Systematic Screening for Behavior Disorders (SSBD). *Remedial and Special Education, 11,* 32–46.

Webster-Stratton, C., & Hammond, M. (1997). Treating children with early-onset conduct problems: A comparison of child and parent training interventions. *Journal of Consulting and Clinical Psychology, 65*(1), 93–109.

Webster-Stratton, C., Reid, M. J., & Hammond, M. (2004). Treating children with early-onset conduct problems: Intervention outcomes for parent, child, and teacher training. *Journal of Clinical Child and Adolescent Psychology, 33*(1), 105–124.

Wentzel, K. R. (1993). Does being good make the grade? Social behavior and academic competence in middle school. *Journal of Educational Psychology, 85*(2), 357–364.

Wentzel, K. R. (2002). Are effective teachers like good parents? Teaching styles and student adjustment in early adolescence. *Child Development, 73*(1), 287–301.

Wentzel, K. R., Filisetti, L., & Looney, L. (2007). Adolescent prosocial behavior: The role of self-processes and contextual cues. *Child Development, 78*(3), 895–910.

White-Blackburn, G., Semb, S., & Semb, G. (1977). The effects of a good-behavior contract on the classroom behaviors of sixth-grade students. *Journal of Applied Behavior Analysis, 10*(2), 312–312.

Wigfield, A., Eccles, J. S., Roeser, R., & Schiefele, U. (2008). Development of achievement motivation. In W. Damon & R. Lerner (Eds.), *Child and adolescent development: An advanced course* (pp. 406–434). Hoboken, NJ: Wiley & Sons.

Wigfield, A., Eccles, J. S., Ulrich, S., Roeser, R. W., & Davis-Kean, P. (2002). Development of achievement motivation. In A. Wigfield & J. S. Eccles (Eds.), *Development of achievement motivation* (pp. 933–1002). San Diego, CA: Academic Press.

Wilson, S. J., & Lipsey, M. W. (2007). School-based interventions for aggressive and disruptive behavior: Update of a meta-analysis. *American Journal of Preventive Medicine, 33*(2), 130–143.

Wright, E. R., Russell, L. A., Anderson, J. A., Kooreman, H. E., & Wright, D. E. (2006). Impact of team structure on achieving treatment goals in a system of care. *Journal of Emotional and Behavioral Disorders, 14*(4), 240–250.

Zins, J. E., & Elias, M. J. (2007). Social and emotional learning: Promoting the development of all students. *Journal of Educational and Psychological Consultation, 17*(2–3), 233–255.

32

Evidence-Informed Mental Health Practice in Schools

Michael S. Kelly
Loyola University Chicago

- ◆ Mental Health Policies and School Social Work
- ◆ The Role of the School Social Worker in Mental Health Services
- ◆ Assessment
- ◆ Use of the *Diagnostic and Statistical Manual of Mental Disorders* (5th ed.)
- ◆ Mental Health Issues Commonly Encountered in Schools
- ◆ The Strengths Perspective in School Social Work Mental Health Practice: The Case of Conduct Disorders

School settings have long been viewed by mental health advocates as important places to assist children and families; what has not been as clear is how school mental health services can best reach students and their families (Kelly, 2008; Mills et al., 2006). Particularly in the absence of community-based mental health resources, children often receive core mental health services in schools. Indeed, many school social workers view their role as primarily that of school-based mental health clinicians and crisis intervention specialists, despite the multiple roles they can also play at the systemic level providing leadership for important school prevention work (Frey & Dupper, 2005; Kelly, Berzin, et al., 2010; O'Brien et al., 2011).

Therefore, every school social worker needs to be familiar with the field of mental health, including relevant federal and state policies, the impact of mental health on academic achievement, and the expanding role of the school social worker in mental health service provision. As this chapter will describe, many school social workers are often the first (and sometimes only) point of contact for youths and families with mental health problems, making it essential that school social workers develop strong mental health assessment, referral, and evidence-informed practice (EIP) skills in this domain. This chapter will provide an overview of mental health issues and mental health services that typically are delivered in the schools. It reviews mental health policy at the federal level, focusing on major changes in the past ten years that are affecting how school social workers deliver mental health interventions in school settings. Additional content in the chapter will cover the ways that school social workers can assess students for specific disorders identified in the *Diagnostic and Statistical Manual of Mental Disorders* (5th ed., or DSM-5; American Psychiatric Association, 2013), as well as possible interventions to address students with those mental health problems. Throughout this chapter as well as the entire book authors pay special attention to an EIP process that can empower school social workers and clients to use the best available evidence to address common children's mental health problems.

School social workers are likely to encounter many children with mental health problems in their schools. According to the first surgeon general's report on children's mental health (Surgeon General's Report on Children's Mental Health, 1999), one in five American children has a mental health disorder, with 5 to 9 percent of all children aged nine to seventeen having a serious emotional disturbance. This finding has been supported by more-recent government studies of youth populations (Pastor, Reuben, & Duran, 2012). More-recent population estimates show that 14 to 20 percent of school-age children face significant emotional and/or behavioral challenges that affect their readiness to learn (Merikangas et al., 2010; Perou et al., 2013). Although there is general consensus in the research and policy arenas that there is a significant prevalence of mental health problems in the school-age population, a number of reviews have found that roughly 80 percent of children with mental health problems do not receive treatment (Merikangas et al., 2010; National Institute of Mental Health [NIMH], 2004).

MENTAL HEALTH POLICIES AND SCHOOL SOCIAL WORK

There is a long history of federal involvement in mental health services. Federal involvement, contemplated from the days of Dorothea Dix, was limited mainly to veterans' services until the passage of the National Mental Health Act of 1946. This act established the National Institute of Mental Health (NIMH) to promote research about mental disease, to encourage training of personnel, and to establish state mental health authorities to develop mental health programs. The first federally administered program that focused specifically on the mental health needs of children was the Comprehensive Children's Mental Health Services Program, administered by the Substance Abuse and Mental Health Services Administration (SAMHSA) through the U.S. Department of Health and Human Services. The program, first authorized in 1992, offers grants to states, territories, Indian tribes, and communities to develop systems of care for children who have mental health needs. Services must involve families, be need driven, collaborative, community based, and culturally responsive.

Federal initiatives to promote safe schools are also related to school mental health issues. The Safe and Drug-Free Schools and Communities Program (SDFSC) is intended to reduce drug, alcohol, and tobacco use and violence through prevention, early intervention, referral, and education in elementary and secondary schools. This program began in 1986 with the Drug-Free Schools and Community Act (1986), which was reauthorized in 1994 as the Safe and Drug-Free Schools Act (1994), and the legislation was most recently reauthorized as part of the No Child Left Behind Act (2001), which imposed new accountability requirements. The work embedded in the Safe and Drug-Free Schools Act has encouraged many schools and school social workers to access programs that meet SAMHSA's evidence-based criteria (New York State Education Department, 2014).

George W. Bush's President's New Freedom Commission on Mental Health (2003) identified a disjointed, fragmented system of provision of mental health care with significant disparities in the availability of treatment. The report found that services vary from state to state and from community to community. The commission's subcommittee on children and families called for better and earlier screening of children for mental disorders and argued that schools are one of the most important areas to focus on improving the nation's mental health infrastructure for children (President's New Freedom Commission on Mental Health, 2003). The commission recommended that the mental health field and schools be partners in the provision of early mental health screening, assessment, and referral to services:

> The mission of public schools is to educate all students. However, children with serious emotional disturbances have the highest rates of school failure. Fifty percent of these students drop out of high school, compared to 30 percent of all students with disabilities. Schools are where children spend most of each day. While schools are primarily concerned with education, mental health is essential to learning as well as to social and emotional development. Because of this important interplay between emotional health and school success, schools must be partners in the mental health care of our children. Schools are in a key position to identify mental health problems early and to provide a link to appropriate services. (President's New Freedom Commission on Mental Health, 2003, p. 58)

This blue-ribbon commission's work informed the work of leading organizations like the Center for School Mental Health at the University of Maryland; that center utilized the commission's findings to advocate for more attention to school mental health services, particularly around the areas of screening for mental health and substance abuse disorders and suicide prevention (Mills et al., 2006).

Several years later, this work affected the Obama administration's efforts to infuse mental health parity legislation further into the Patient Protection and Affordable Care Act (2010). This landmark health-care legislation will expand mental health care to families and children, with estimates of 1.15 million new mental health consumers (adults and children) coming into the system by 2019 (Aggarwal & Rowe, 2013). Despite this progress, recent data indicate that a key feature of expanding mental health services to youths—the development of effective outpatient mental health settings—is not available in many parts of the United States, particularly rural areas: a recent study estimates that just 63 percent of counties in the United States have an outpatient facility that is equipped to provide mental health treatment to children and adolescents, and their families (Cummings, Wen, & Druss, 2013).

THE ROLE OF THE SCHOOL SOCIAL WORKER IN MENTAL HEALTH SERVICES

These data make it even more necessary that school social workers be prepared to act as the first (and possibly only) mental health provider to their student and family clients. Several surveys of school social work practice conducted by this author reveal that school social workers regularly report that the complex, crisis-driven client problems they work with are often not those they can find outside community resources to refer to, making them the de facto mental health facility in their school community (Kelly, 2008; Kelly, Berzin, et al., 2010).

Despite the burden this can cause school social workers, there are some natural strengths that school social workers bring to this situation. Often the school social worker has better access to parents and children than any other community service provider, and parents may feel comfortable talking about their child's mental health needs with someone they see at the school every day (Kelly, 2008).

Based on survey data of the past twenty years, it appears that most school social workers spend most of their time providing services to children who have behavioral or emotional disorders that impede their academic functioning. In some settings, school social workers are responsible for providing extensive therapy in schools (Cawood, 2010; Kelly, 2008; Kelly, Berzin, et al., 2010; Peckover, Vasquez, Van Housen, Saunders, & Allen, 2013). Despite the results survey data consistently show, some school social work scholars advocate that the most critical role of the school social worker should be primarily consultation, teamwork, and short-term support as well as referral and linkage to community services (Dupper, Rocha, Jackson, & Lodato, 2014; Frey & Dupper, 2005; Jonson-Reid, Kontak, Citerman, Essma, & Fezzi, 2004). The recent development of the National School Social Work Practice Model emphasizes school social workers operating at multiple levels of intervention to improve student mental health outcomes (Frey et al., 2012).

Indeed, school social workers are bridges between outside professionals, school administration, and teaching staff. They attend staffings in hospitals when a student has a psychiatric hospitalization. They help to develop transition plans to ease the student's return to school from the hospital, and it is their job to translate medical jargon into functional information for the students, teachers, and allied staff. School social workers help multidisciplinary teams to gain a holistic picture of the student. If community services are unresponsive, however, school social workers find themselves doing much more. Although a few schools offer psychiatric services and medication management (Costello-Wells, McFarland, Reed, & Walton, 2003), most children receive services outside of the school. The school social worker must identify issues of concern, understand effective work with children experiencing mental health disorders, support children's work in school, and assist students who are making a transition from hospitalization (Kelly, 2008; Singer & Slovak, 2011).

School social workers may also partner with community agencies and schools to bring into the school additional social workers, psychiatrists, and other mental health professionals to provide longer-term or more intensive therapeutic services. In this model, the school district contracts with one or more agencies to come into the school to provide services. Grant funding may be used to support services (Anderson-Butcher & Ashton, 2004; Anderson-Butcher, Iachini, & Wade-Mdivanian, 2007). The full-service school offers mental health services to students and community members in the school setting as one of an array of on-site services. Full-service community schools may include vaccination and health clinics, family planning services, drug and alcohol treatment, in addition to mental health services (Benson, Harkavy, Johanek, & Puckett, 2009; Bronstein, Anderson, Terwilliger, & Sager, 2012; Ghuman, Weist, & Sarles, 2013). School social workers are in a great position to draw on the resources around them to establish such community-school partnerships, family-school interventions, and school-wide interventions, as well as individual and group interventions, in caring for the mental health needs of children (Franklin, Harris, & Allen-Meares, 2012; Kelly, 2008).

Both intervention in the school and collaboration with service providers outside of the school are critical in preventing costly outcomes for children with serious emotional disturbances. Therapeutic schools and out-of-state care are costly for the school district and often costly for children: Children placed in residential treatment or therapeutic schools may need such an environment, but there is an emotional cost to the children when they lack normative school socialization. The student may feel isolated from the community and may lose out on critical social support and family contact. If effective services can be provided in the community, those more-restrictive alternatives may be avoided.

ASSESSMENT

State and federal mental health agencies increasingly focus on schools as a primary site for early screening for possible mental disorders (Barrett, Eber, & Weist, 2013; Dowdy, Ritchey, & Kamphaus, 2010; President's New Freedom Commission on Mental Health, 2003). A critical role of a school social worker is assessment, which is often part of a larger process done with the multidisciplinary team and outside professionals. (For more information on assessment of students who are experiencing academic and/or behavioral difficulties, see chapter 14, "School Social Workers and the Prereferral Process: Problem-Solving Teams and Data-Driven Decision Making," chapter 15, "School Social Workers and the Special Education Process: From Assessment to Individualized Education Programs to School Social Work Services," and chapter 16, "The Screening and Assessment of Adaptive Behavior," in this volume.) A mental health concern is one aspect of the pupil-in-school assessment. The school social worker emphasizes student strengths and aspirations; sensitizes the team to the student's cultural, familial, and spiritual needs; and shows how these factors interface with the student's mental health issues and learning requirements.

The school social worker needs to be skilled in making differential decisions as a member of a team. Some students can be well served in the school environment through social skills groups, individual counseling, and crisis intervention. Other students require referral to outside providers for psychiatric evaluation, long-term mental health care, and family counseling. In schools and communities with few resources, school social workers are sometimes the only mental health professional that the student will ever see. School social workers must prioritize and determine which students have the most pressing needs and which interventions will be most efficient and effective. Those students at risk for suicide, child maltreatment, or criminal justice involvement require partnership with outside resources. These partnerships often involve outside professionals with a limited understanding of school social work and with whom it is necessary to develop a common language and a mutual process of learning and sharing. To that end, we share some highlights from the recent new edition of the DSM: the DSM-5 is one of those languages that many outside mental health providers will be speaking in their collaboration with school social workers. We also share more information about the ways that a person-in-environment framework can be used to identify student strengths in working with DSM-5 disorders and other problems of living.

USE OF THE *DIAGNOSTIC AND STATISTICAL MANUAL OF MENTAL DISORDERS* (5TH ED.)

One common language of mental health professionals is the DSM-5 (American Psychiatric Association, 2013), which is the major classification and assessment tool used by the mental health system in the United States. DSM-5 is the first full revision of the DSM since DSM-IV was published in 1994. The DSM-IV featured a multiaxial system consisting of five axes (clinical syndromes, developmental disorders, physical health conditions, psychosocial problems, and global assessment of functioning), but DSM-5 does away with the axes to instead bring the psychiatric diagnostic language closer in line with the *International Classification of Diseases-10*. Major changes to the DSM-5 of particular relevance to school social workers are: the elimination of Asperger's syndrome, subsuming it into autistic spectrum disorder; the cultural formation interview, which will give clinicians more options in how to assess the cultural aspects of a potential DSM-5 diagnosis; and the removal of Axis IV and its emphasis on assessing a patient/client's psychosocial factors to inform a diagnosis (Pomeroy & Anderson, 2013).

MENTAL HEALTH ISSUES COMMONLY ENCOUNTERED IN SCHOOLS

According to the National Mental Health Information Center (2005), schools ranked the following mental health issues as the most common issues encountered in schools: (1) social, interpersonal, or family problems; (2) aggression/disruptive behavior/bullying; (3) behavior problems associated with neurological disorders such as attention deficit hyperactivity disorder, or ADHD; (4) adjustment issues; (5) anxiety/stress/school phobia; and (6) depression/grief reactions. These issues affected boys and girls differently, with boys having more problems with aggression and disruptive behavior problems than girls, and girls exhibiting more difficulty with social, interpersonal or family problems, adjustment issues, anxiety, and depression (National Mental Health Information Center, 2005). A recent review of mental health diagnoses found that parents reported having a child with ADHD (6.8 percent), behavior/conduct problems (3.5 percent), anxiety and depression (3 percent and 2.1 percent, respectively) (Perou et al., 2013). Surveys by the author and his team of school social workers identified these common mental health problems in schools: attention deficit disorder (ADD), anxiety disorders, difficulties with parents' divorce, and social skills deficits (Kelly, Raines, Stone, & Frey, 2010).

Attention Deficit Hyperactivity Disorder

Definitions and Prevalence. ADHD is one of the most commonly identified problems for students in a school setting (Costello-Wells et al., 2003; National Mental Health Information Center, 2005). It can be readily apparent in the school setting and is problematic not only for the student, but also for peers, teachers, and parents, because it is marked by a student's lack of attention, often combined with hyperactive behavior and impulsivity (Kelly, Frey, & Berzin, 2014). To be diagnosed, symptoms must be present before the age of twelve, although the actual diagnosis might not come until an older age. The disorder is more often noted in boys than girls, and can remain an impairment throughout adolescence and adulthood (American Psychiatric Association, 2013). Worldwide estimates put the prevalence of ADHD at 5.29 percent (Polanczyk et al., 2007). ADHD has many co-occurring conditions such as learning disabilities, oppositional defiant disorder, and mood disorders. These co-occurring conditions further complicate a student's ability to learn, and pose significant challenges to social workers and teachers as they attempt to accommodate the student's learning needs (Kelly, Raines, et al., 2010). These co-occurring conditions (often referred to in research literature as comorbidities) also can complicate efforts by school social workers to design effective, school-based interventions for children with ADHD (Teasley, 2012).

Assessment. Examples of screening measures for ADHD and anxiety can be found in table 32.1.

TABLE 32.1   Screening Measures for Attention Deficit Hyperactivity Disorder and Anxiety in Children and Adolescents

Measure	Age (approximate years)	Reading Level (grade)	Spanish Version	Cost	Time to Complete (minutes)	Contact Information for Ordering Scale
Child Behavior Checklist (preschool)	1 1/2–5 (completed by parents)	6	Yes	$150	10–15	http://www.aseba.org/preschool.html
Child Behavior Checklist (school age)	6–18 (completed by parents)	6	Yes	$395	10–15	http://www.fmhi.usf.edu/amh/homicide-suicide/assess_dep.html
Conners' Teacher Rating Scale	3–17 (completed by parents) 12–17 (adolescent self-report)	6–9	Yes	$268	10–15	http://www.mhs.com/product.aspx?gr=cli&id=overview&prod=conners3

NOTE: All of the above three scales have subscales that address anxiety and attention problems.

Evidence-Informed Practice and
Attention Deficit Hyperactivity Disorder

There is a small but growing literature on what interventions can work for students diagnosed with ADHD. The current emphasis in the literature now is on multimodal interventions involving medication for the student, psychoeducation with the student's family, and behavioral coaching with the student and his school context (Kelly, Raines, et al., 2010). In addition to working with the family and coordinating medication, school social workers can also work with teachers to develop effective behavior strategies and classroom management techniques that will allow for optimal student learning. In some cases, students will need specific classroom accommodations. These accommodations might include shortened assignments, breaking tasks into smaller parts, peer tutoring, untimed tests, and taking breaks. Students might need to have their desks placed in the quietest part of the room to avoid overstimulation and distractions (Kelly et al., 2014). School social workers will need to educate students with ADHD about this disorder and how it is affecting their learning, social relationships, and school adjustment. Students may also require social skills interventions. Some students will be best served in a group and others will require individual counseling. Research suggests that multimodal treatment strategies for ADHD present the most promising likelihood of success for most children, combining family therapy, classroom behavior modification, stimulant medication, and individual behavioral therapy (Owens & Fabiano, 2011).

Mood Disorders (Depression and Bipolar Disorder)

The study of depression in children and adolescents is a relatively recent phenomenon. Children and adolescents with depression may experience loss of interest in activities, feelings of helplessness and hopelessness, and disturbances in sleep and appetite. Children and teenagers can and do experience depression, although it may manifest itself differently in young people than it does in adults; this fact has affected how the new DSM-5 views child and adolescent depressive symptoms, with a focus on whether temper tantrums are inconsistent with normal age-appropriate developmental expectations and a need to see the symptoms persist and be observable by multiple people in the students' life such as parents, teachers, and peers (see the new DSM-5 criteria for "Diagnostic Criteria for Disruptive Mood Dysregulation Disorder" in American Psychiatric Association, 2013). Diagnosis of depression in children requires a significant change in mood and functioning that persists over at least a two-week period. The causes of depression are not fully understood, although it is thought to have both biological and psychosocial origins (American Psychiatric Association, 2013).

Students can be referred to the school social worker for obvious symptoms of depression, but are more likely to be referred for abrupt behavioral changes related to their behavior at home or in the classroom. Students with moderate or severe depression often experience disruptions in their ability to learn. Teachers may mistakenly assume that a student's low energy, impaired concentration, or defiance is a result of a behavior disorder when the student may be suffering from an underlying depressive disorder. Some psychosocial or environmental factors that contribute to a student's depression can include family neglect or abuse, or victimization by peers. There is also some evidence that some students may be predisposed to depression because of a family history of depression.

Students who are vulnerable to depression may come to school with inadequate problem-solving and self-regulatory skills and are often overwhelmed by stressors that other children might be able to manage. Major life stressors such as the loss of a parent, pregnancy, moves, divorce, or remarriage can also trigger depressive reactions in children and adolescents (NIMH, 2014).

Bipolar Disorder

Sometimes the first episode of depression for children and adolescents can turn out to be what will later be diagnosed as bipolar disorder. The manic phase of bipolar disorder in children can include periods of crankiness, insomnia, hyperactivity, expansive mood, and racing thoughts. The depressed phase in children with bipolar disorder is not distinguishable from the symptoms of childhood depression discussed above. Some children experience rapid cycling; in the morning they appear depressed, but by afternoon they are displaying a full-blown manic episode with unmanageable behavior (American Psychiatric Association, 2013). Because this is a complicated and somewhat elusive disorder to differentiate in youths from other comorbid conditions like depression (Depression and Bipolar Support Alliance, 2014) and is controversial still to mental health providers and parents alike (Carlson & Klein, 2014), the DSM-5 authors have created new diagnostic criteria for bipolar symptoms that do not rise to the level of severity of Bipolar I disorder but are nonetheless impairing to young people. (American Psychiatric Association, 2013. See box 32.3 for "Other Specified Bipolar and Related Disorder.")

In addition to a clinical interview with a school social worker, some paper-and-pencil assessment tools for depression in childhood and adolescence can be helpful in establishing whether a young person meets the criteria for depression. Some examples of these scales are the Children's Depression Inventory (Kovacs, 2004) and the Center for Epidemiological Studies Depression Scale Modified for Children (Fendrich, Weissman, & Warner, 1990).

Evidence-Informed Practice and Mood Disorders

Practices based on current research for treating students with mood disorders involve a multimodal approach involving counseling, medication, and other psychosocial interventions (Kelly et al., 2014; NIMH, 2014). The primary aim of treatment is to shorten the period of the mood disorder and to decrease negative consequences of episodes of illness. Students need to be encouraged to continue to be active in school and with their studies even when they feel bad. Adding structure to the day will help stabilize the student's mood. Positive reinforcement needs to be implemented to assist students in completing tasks of daily living such as getting ready for and going to school, completing assignments, and staying at school for the whole day (Kelly, Raines, et al., 2010). Studies suggest that a focus on cognitive and behavioral skills is effective in treating students with mood disorders (Johnson, Rasbury, & Siegel, 1997).

Autism Spectrum Disorders

Prevalence and Definitions. With the trend toward inclusion in the last few decades, more and more students with autism spectrum disorders (ASD) are attending local public schools. The Centers for Disease Control and Prevention (CDC) estimates that one in sixty-eight school-age children has ASD (CDC, 2014). This has posed many opportunities and challenges for students, school social workers, and staff. As of the new DSM-5, ASD is being used as the umbrella term that includes a heterogeneous group of conditions, including autism, pervasive developmental disorder, and Asperger's syndrome. Students with autism are characterized by impaired social interactions, communication deficits, and stereotypical behaviors such as rocking, head banging, and echolalia. Students with Asperger's syndrome are different from students with autism because they do possess some communication skills and have average or above-average intellect. The main deficit for students with Asperger's is in the area of social skill development. These students have trouble with nonverbal behaviors such as maintaining eye contact or maintaining appropriate physical boundaries with others (American Psychiatric Association, 2013). Impairments in these areas can be so severe that they require multiple interventions and services to allow these students to participate in school.

Assessment. Numerous standardized scales with good psychometric properties exist to help school social workers assess students for ASD. A few to consider are the Checklist for Autistic Spectrum Disorder (Mayes, 2012) and the Childhood Autism Rating Scale (2nd ed.) (Schopler, Van Bourgondien, Wellman, & Love, 2010). Though it is possible to screen a student in a school setting for ASD and recommend special education services without outside medical professionals weighing in, I recommend that you work with your school parents to explore with them whether they wish to pursue an outside evaluation by medical professionals skilled in diagnosing ASD.

Evidence-Informed Practice and Autism Spectrum Disorders

The role of the school social worker who works with children having ASD begins in early intervention programs before the child starts kindergarten. These students will require early intervention by an interdisciplinary team of school professionals. School social workers can be a bridge between the school, the teacher, and the family, and can be part of a team that would assess eligibility for special education services and identify areas for growth and development (Kelly et al., 2014). When a diagnosis such as ASD is made, many families experience shock, grief, and denial. For many years, parents were blamed for their child's autistic symptoms. As a result, an adversarial relationship could develop between families and the medical or education system on which they depended. It is now well understood that ASDs are neurological conditions, and that parents have not caused the problem but rather are an integral part of the team that will attempt to remediate the student's deficits. In order for parents to function in collaboration with the school, the social worker needs to establish a strong and supportive alliance that acknowledges parents' feelings and aspirations for their child.

In terms of evidence-informed work with the student who has ASD, the school social worker can provide social skills groups and other behavioral interventions as part of the treatment team. They will be responsible for a thorough case-study evaluation and for developing individualized educational program (IEP) goals for social work service. Suggested interventions based on current intervention research would focus on fostering normal development and helping students to compensate for their developmental deficits. Since the social worker's role is in the domain of social and emotional development, the goal of the work will be to increase the pleasure that a child can experience when engaging in social connections with peers and adults. These students will need repetitive training in areas such as greeting skills, personal hygiene, and appropriate classroom behaviors. They may need to be taught how to play with others and to become more aware of social nuance. If students are engaging in self-injurious or aggressive behaviors they will need behavior modification to reduce the frequency of these behaviors (Ballan & Hoban, 2008).

Anxiety Disorders

Definitions and Prevalence. DSM-5 describes eight different types of anxiety disorders in childhood and adolescence. They are (1) selective mutism, (2) separation anxiety, (3) panic disorder, (4) social phobia, (5) specific phobias, (6) generalized anxiety disorder, (7) agoraphobia, and (8) substance/medication-induced anxiety disorder (American Psychiatric Association, 2013). Anxiety disorders are considered internalizing disorders, which means that they are directed toward self, and the symptoms primarily involve excessive inhibition of behavior. Symptoms of anxiety involve avoidant or escape behaviors. The subjective experience often involves a sense of dread, despair, and impending doom. Physical symptoms can include rapid heartbeat, sweating, difficulty breathing, and impaired speech and coordination. Intense anxiety is an aversive experience, and phobic behaviors often result from avoiding the anxiety-producing stimuli. Anxiety problems can be conceptualized as exaggerated fear responses in situations where the fear is no longer functional (NIMH, 2014).

Students with anxiety disorders present many challenges in the school setting. In the early years, it can be difficult for them to get to school and to take risks as part of the learning process. In later years, separation anxiety that is stopping students from attending school can lead to chronic truancy or even to dropping out of high school. Even when these students attend school on a regular basis they are often so anxious and preoccupied with managing their fears that they are unavailable for learning. They may be slow to make friends, unable to establish trusting relationships with teachers or social workers, and unwilling to try new activities. When severely anxious students perceive the outside world as dangerous and when they anticipate impending doom, they may respond with rigidity and inflexibility in dealing with the everyday demands of school. Their reactions may include temper tantrums, aggressive outbursts, and petulant withdrawal. These behaviors are attempts to maintain sameness and predictability in the school (Kelly, Raines, et al., 2010; Sacks, Comer, Pincus, Camacho, & Hunter-Romanelli, 2012)

Suicidality

Suicide is the third-leading cause of death among adolescents and the second-leading cause of death for college age youths (NIMH, 2006). School social workers are frequently the first adults who become aware that a student is experiencing suicidal ideation. This can be one of the most anxiety provoking and troubling issues in school social work practice. Sometimes students reveal these thoughts to the social worker, sometimes a student's friend comes to the social worker, and sometimes a student or teacher passes on a suicide note to the social worker. Many times parents are unaware of their children's suicidal feelings. When they are aware, they can be at a loss about what to do and will frequently turn to the school social worker for support and direction. For more information on how school social workers can be responsive to suicidal behavior with their students, see chapter 25.

Assessment. Examples of screening measures for ADHD and anxiety can be found in table 32.1.

Evidence-Informed Practice and Anxiety Disorders

As recent reviews have shown, a number of effective school-based interventions exist for students with anxiety disorders (Kelly, 2008; Kelly, Raines, et al., 2010; Neil & Christensen, 2009). These include cognitive behavioral one-on-one work or in small groups, classroom-based interventions (mindfulness training and relaxation/meditation), and family-based coaching and psychoeducation. These approaches, combined (when appropriate) with pharmacologic treatment, can improve the anxiety symptoms of many youths in schools (Kelly, Raines, et al., 2010).

THE STRENGTHS PERSPECTIVE IN SCHOOL SOCIAL WORK MENTAL HEALTH PRACTICE: THE CASE OF CONDUCT DISORDERS

Behavior problems are the reason why many children are referred for mental health services (Costello-Wells et al., 2003; Kelly, Raines, et al., 2010; O'Brien et al., 2011). Most children who have a behavior problem do not go on to develop a full-blown conduct disorder, either at the level of oppositional defiant disorder or the more serious conduct disorder, but it is important to recognize the risks in overdiagnosing children rather than treating the behavior issues that are presenting. One of the benefits of the strengths perspective, as practiced in social work, is that it challenges school social workers to look beyond the DSM-5 to see what strengths and capacities a student has, even if he or she is doing poorly in school. The DSM-5 has heightened the importance of the strengths perspective, and has eliminated consideration of psychosocial factors from its primary axes (Pomeroy & Anderson, 2013).

The use of the strengths perspective in social work has its roots in early social work practice, and also in risk and resilience theory (Climie, Mastoras, McCrimmon, & Schwean, 2013; Kelly, Kim, & Franklin, 2008; Whitley, Rawana, Pye, & Brownlee, 2011). Recently, the emphasis in school social work on solution-focused brief therapy (Kelly, Kim, & Franklin, 2008; Kelly & Bluestone-Miller, 2009) and motivational interviewing (Frey, Sims, & Alvarez, 2013) indicates that school social workers realize the need to use more than deficit-based diagnostic language to engage their most at-risk clients. Beyond any moral imperative school social workers may feel to not further pathologize children who likely already view themselves and their school environment negatively, I think that the use of the strengths perspective and its related modalities reveals another important fact about the state of EIP and students with severe behavioral problems. In many ways, as a field we are still figuring out how to best work with this challenging population, and we need to keep our minds open to all the possible ways that we might be able to achieve successful outcomes with these students and their families. While the DSM-5 can and does give us a framework to use to understand a lot of what is happening with these students when they struggle at school, it is not enough to put a label on their difficulties, and the strengths perspective offers further ways to build their capacity.

CONCLUSION

A chapter like this one could take up an entire book, and in fact has several times in the years since our last edition (Clauss-Ehlers, Serpell, & Weist, 2012; Ghuman et al., 2013; Raines, 2008; Raines & Dibble, 2010). This chapter is only a start for school social workers interested in advancing their school mental health practice skills. Other chapters in this book will assist the reader in identifying EIPs across all three tiers of intervention with youths; given the growing interest in an interconnected systems framework (Barrett et al., 2013) of school mental health and positive behavior supports, future editions of this book will further deepen our knowledge about the expanded school mental health models that are emerging.

Please see Internet resources for the following issues:

Attention Deficit Hyperactivity Disorder

LD Online (a site sponsored by the D.C. PBS station): http://www.ld online.org/

Attention Deficit Disorder Association: www.add.org

Mood Disorders

Depression and Bipolar Support Alliance: www.dbsalliance.org

Child and Adolescent Bipolar Foundation/Balanced Mind Parent Network: http://www.thebalancedmind.org

All About Depression: www.allaboutdepression.com

Autism Spectrum Disorders

Autism Research Institute: www.autism.org

Autism Speaks: http://www.autismspeaks.org/

Anxiety Disorders

Anxiety Disorders Association of America: www.adaa.org

Suicide Prevention

American Association of Suicidology: www.suicidology.org

American Foundation for Suicide Prevention: http://www.sprc.org/bpr

Selected Evidence-Based Practice Resources for Designing School-Based Interventions

Campbell Collaboration Systematic Reviews of Social Work and Education Interventions: http://www.campbellcollaboration.org

Cochrane Community (for mental health interventions based on DSM-IV diagnoses): http://www.cochrane.org/

Colorado Blueprints for Violence Prevention: http://www.colorado.edu/cspv/blueprints/

National Registry of Evidence-based Programs and Practices (Substance Abuse and Mental Health Services Administration; SAMHSA): http://www.nrepp.samhsa.gov/

Trip Database www.tripdatabase.com

What Works Clearinghouse (U.S. Department of Education): http://ies.ed.gov/ncee/wwc/

References

Aggarwal, N. K., & Rowe, M. (2013). The individual mandate, mental health parity, and the Obama health plan. *Administration and Policy in Mental Health and Mental Health Services Research*, 1–3.

American Psychiatric Association. (2013). *Diagnostic and statistical manual of mental disorders* (5th ed.) (DSM-5). Washington, DC: Author.

Anderson-Butcher, D., & Ashton, D. (2004). Innovative models of collaboration to serve children, youths, families, and communities. *Children & Schools, 26*(1), 39–53.

Anderson-Butcher, D., Iachini, A., & Wade-Mdivanian, R. (2007). *School linkage protocol technical assistance guide: Expanded school improvement through the enhancement of the learning support continuum.* Columbus, OH: College of Social Work, Ohio State University.

Ballan, M. S., & Hoban, K. S. (2008). Effective interventions for students with autism and Asperger's Syndrome. In C. Franklin, M. B. Harris, & P. Allen-Meares (Eds.), *The school practitioner's concise companion to mental health* (pp. 143–162). New York: Oxford University Press.

Barrett, S., Eber, L., & Weist, M.D. (2013). In *Advancing education effectiveness: Interconnecting school mental health and school-wide positive behavior interventions and supports.* Retrieved from https://www.pbis.org/school/school-mental-health/interconnected-systems

Benson, L., Harkavy, I., Johanek, M. C., & Puckett, J. (2009). The enduring appeal of community schools. *American Educator, 33*(2), 22–47.

Bronstein, L. R., Anderson, E., Terwilliger, S. H., & Sager, K. (2012). Evaluating a model of school-based health and social services: An interdisciplinary community–university collaboration. *Children & Schools, 34*(3), 155–165.

Carlson, G. A., & Klein, D. N. (2014). How to understand divergent views on bipolar disorder in youth. *Annual Review of Clinical Psychology, 10*, 529–551.

Cawood, N. D. (2010). Barriers to the use of evidence-supported programs to address school violence. *Children & Schools, 32*(3), 143–149.

Centers for Disease Control and Prevention (CDC). (2014). *CDC estimates 1 in 68 children has been identified with autism spectrum disorder.* Retrieved from http://www.cdc.gov/media/releases/2014/p0327-autism-spectrum-disorder.html

Clauss-Ehlers, C. S., Serpell, Z. N., & Weist, M. D. (Eds.). (2012). *Handbook of culturally responsive school mental health: Advancing research, training, practice, and policy.* New York: Springer.

Climie, E. A., Mastoras, S. M., McCrimmon, A. W., & Schwean, V. L. (2013). Resilience in childhood disorders. In *Resilience in children, adolescents, and adults* (pp. 113–131). New York: Springer.

Costello-Wells, B., McFarland, Reed, J., & Walton, K. (2003). School-based mental health clinics. *Journal of Child and Adolescent Psychiatric Nursing, 16,* 60–71.

Cummings, J. R., Wen, H., & Druss, B. G. (2013). Improving access to mental health services for youth in the United States. *Journal of the American Medical Association, 309*(6), 553–554.

Depression and Bipolar Support Alliance. (2014). *About pediatric bipolar disorder.* http://www.thebalancedmind.org/learn/library/about-pediatric-bipolar-disorder

Dowdy, E., Ritchey, K., & Kamphaus, R. W. (2010). School-based screening: A population-based approach to inform and monitor children's mental health needs. *School Mental Health, 2*(4), 166–176.

Drug-Free Schools and Community Act (20 U.S.C. 4601) (1986).

Dupper, D. R., Rocha, C., Jackson, R. F., & Lodato, G. A. (2014). Broadly trained but narrowly used? Factors that predict the performance of environmental versus individual tasks by school social workers. *Children & Schools, 36*(2), 71–77.

Fendrich, M., Weissman, M. M., & Warner, V. (1990). Screening for depressive disorder in children and adolescents: Validating the Center for Epidemiologic Studies Depression Scale for Children. *American Journal of Epidemiology, 131*(3), 538–551.

Franklin, C., Harris, M. B., & Allen-Meares, P. (Eds.). (2012). *The school services sourcebook: A guide for school-based professionals.* New York: Oxford University Press.

Frey, A. J., Alvarez, M. E., Sabatino, C. A., Lindsey, B. C., Dupper, D. R., Raines, J. C., . . . & Norris, M. P. (2012). The development of a national school social work practice model. *Children & Schools, 34*(3), 131–134.

Frey, A. J., & Dupper, D. R. (2005). A broader conceptual approach to clinical practice for the 21st century. *Children & Schools, 27*(1), 33–44.

Frey, A. J., Sims, K., & Alvarez, M. E. (2013). The promise of motivational interviewing for securing a niche in the RtI Movement. *Children & Schools, 35*(2), 67–70.

Ghuman, H. S., Weist, M. D., & Sarles, R. M. (Eds.). (2013). *Providing mental health services to youth where they are: School and community based approaches.* Florence, KY: Routledge.

Johnson, J. H., Rasbury, W. C., & Siegel, L. J. (1997). *Approaches to child treatment* (2nd ed.). Needham Heights, MA: Allyn & Bacon.

Jonson-Reid, M., Kontak, D., Citerman, B., Essma, A., & Fezzi, N. (2004). School social work case characteristics, services and dispositions: Year one results. *Children & Schools, 26*(1), 5–22.

Kelly, M. S. (2008). *The domains and demands of school social work practice: A guide to working effectively with students, families, and schools.* New York: Oxford University Press.

Kelly, M. S., Berzin, S. C., Frey, A., Alvarez, M., Shaffer, G., & O'Brien, K. (2010). The state of school social work: Findings from the national school social work survey. *School Mental Health, 2*(3), 132–141.

Kelly, M. S., & Bluestone-Miller, R. (2009). Working On What Works (WOWW): Coaching teachers to do more of what's working. *Children & Schools, 31*(1), 35–38.

Kelly, M. S., Frey, A. J., & Berzin, S. C. (2014). Chronic health conditions in schools. In D. Mostofsky (Ed.), *The handbook of behavioral medicine* (pp. 931–946). Chichester, UK: Wiley.

Kelly, M. S., Kim, J. S., & Franklin, C. (2008). *Solution focused brief therapy in schools: A 360 degree view of research and practice.* New York: Oxford University Press.

Kelly, M. S., Raines, J. C., Stone, S., & Frey, A. (2010). *School social work: An evidence-informed framework for practice.* New York: Oxford University Press.

Kovacs, M. (2004). *Children's depression inventory (CDI).* Toronto: Multi-Health Systems.

Mayes, S. D. (2012). *Checklist for autism spectrum disorder.* Wood Dale, IL: Stoelting.

Merikangas, K. R., He, J. P., Brody, D., Fisher, P. W., Bourdon, K., & Koretz, D. S. (2010). Prevalence and treatment of mental disorders among U.S. children in the 2001–2004 NHANES. *Pediatrics, 125*(1), 75–81.

Mills, C., Stephan, S. H., Moore, E., Weist, M. D., Daly, B. P., & Edwards, M. (2006). The President's New Freedom Commission: Capitalizing on opportunities to advance school-based mental health services. *Clinical Child and Family Psychology Review, 9*(3–4), 149–161.

National Institute of Mental Health (NIMH). (2004). *Treatment of children with mental disorders.* Retrieved from http://www.nimh.nih.gov/health/publications/treatment-of-children-with-mental-illness-fact-sheet/index.shtml

National Institute of Mental Health (NIMH). (2006). *In harm's way: Suicide in America.* Retrieved from https://www.mentalhelp.net/articles/in-harms-way-suicide-in-america/

National Institute of Mental Health (NIMH). (2014). *How do children and teens experience depression?* Retrieved from http://www.nimh.nih.gov/health/publications/depression-in-children-and-adolescents/index.shtml

National Mental Health Act of 1946. *Important events in NIMH history.* Retrieved from http://www.nih.gov/about/almanac/organization/NIMH.htm

National Mental Health Information Center. (2005). *School mental health services in the United States, 2002–2003.* Retrieved from http://files.eric.ed.gov/fulltext/ED499056.pdf/

Neil, A. L., & Christensen, H. (2009). Efficacy and effectiveness of school-based prevention and early intervention programs for anxiety. *Clinical Psychology Review, 29*(3), 208–215.

New York State Education Department. (2014). *Approved science-based SDFSCA programs.* Retrieved from http://www.p12.nysed.gov/sss/ssae/schoolsafety/sdfsca/ScienceBasedProgramslist.html

No Child Left Behind Act of 2001, Pub. L. 107-110 (2002).

O'Brien, K. H. M., Berzin, S. C., Kelly, M. S., Frey, A. J., Alvarez, M. E., & Shaffer, G. L. (2011). School social work with students with mental health problems: Examining different practice approaches. *Children & Schools, 33*(2), 97–105.

Owens, J. S., & Fabiano, G. A. (2011). School mental health programming for youth with ADHD: Addressing needs across the academic career. *School Mental Health, 3*(3), 111–116.

Pastor P. N., Reuben C. A., & Duran C. R. (2012). Identifying emotional and behavioral problems in children aged 4–17 years: United States, 2001–2007. *National Health Statistics Reports; no. 48.* Hyattsville, MD: National Center for Health Statistics.

Patient Protection and Affordable Care Act, 42 U.S.C. § 18001 (2010).

Peckover, C. A., Vasquez, M. L., Van Housen, S. L., Saunders, J. A., & Allen, L. (2013). Preparing school social work for the future: An update of school social workers' tasks in Iowa. *Children & Schools, 35*(1), 9–17.

Perou, R., Bitsko, R. H., Blumberg, S. J., Pastor, P., Ghandour, R. M., Gfroerer, J. C., . . . & Huang, L. N. (2013). Mental health surveillance among children: United States, 2005–2011. *Morbidity and Mortality Weekly Report (Surveillance Summer Supplement), 62*(Suppl 2), 1–35.

Polanczyk, G., de Lima, M. S., Horta, B. L., Biederman, J., & Rohde, L. A.(2007). The worldwide prevalence of ADHD: A systematic review and metaregression analysis. *American Journal of Psychiatry, 164*(6), 942–948.

Pomeroy, E. C., & Anderson, K. (2013). The DSM-V has arrived. *Social Work, 58*(3), 197.

President's New Freedom Commission on Mental Health. (2003). *Achieving the promise: Transforming mental health care in America.* Final report. DHHS Pub. No. SMA-03-3832. Rockville, MD: Author.

Raines, J. C. (2008). *Evidence based practice in school mental health.* New York: Oxford University Press.

Raines, J. C., & Dibble, N. T. (2010). *Ethical decision making in school mental health.* New York: Oxford University Press.

Sacks, H., Comer, J. S., Pincus, D. B., Camacho, M., & Hunter-Romanelli, L. (2012). Effective interventions with students with anxiety disorders. In C. Franklin, M. B. Harris, & P. Allen-Meares (Eds.), *The school services sourcebook: A guide for school-based professionals* (pp. 105–123). New York: Oxford University Press.

Safe and Drug-Free Schools Act (20 U.S.C. 7101) (1994).

Schopler, E., Van Bourgondien, M., Wellman, J., & Love, S. (2010). *Childhood autism rating scale* (2nd ed.). Los Angeles: Western Psychological Services.

Singer, J. B., & Slovak, K. (2011). School social workers' experiences with youth suicidal behavior: An exploratory study. *Children & Schools, 33*(4), 215–228.

Surgeon General's Report on Children's Mental Health. (1999). *Mental health: A report of the Surgeon General.* Retrieved from http://profiles.nlm.nih.gov/ps/retrieve/ResourceMetadata/NNBBHS

Teasley, M. (2012). Effective interventions for students with neurodevelopmental, learning, and physical disorders. In C. Franklin, M. B. Harris, & P. Allen Meares (Eds.), *The school services sourcebook: A guide for school-based professionals* (pp. 191–205). New York: Oxford University Press.

Whitley, J., Rawana, E. P., Pye, M., & Brownlee, K. (2011). Are strengths the solution? An exploration of the relationships among teacher-rated strengths, classroom behaviour, and academic achievement of young students. *McGill Journal of Education/Révue des sciences de l'éducation de McGill, 45*(3).

33

School-Based Trauma-Informed Care for Traumatic Events: Clinical and Organizational Practice

Diane Mirabito
New York University, Silver School of Social Work

Jay Callahan
Loyola University Chicago School of Social Work

- ◆ Crises and Traumatic Events in School Settings
- ◆ Social Work Roles in Response to Crises and Traumatic Events
- ◆ Definitions of Crisis and Key Elements of Crisis Theory
- ◆ The Components of a Crisis
- ◆ Disaster Theory and Phases of Stress Reactions in a Disaster
- ◆ Definitions of Trauma and Common Reactions to Trauma
- ◆ Posttraumatic Stress Disorder
- ◆ Predictors of Distress
- ◆ Microlevel/Clinical Practice: Practice Principles for Crisis Intervention
- ◆ Macrolevel/Organizational Practice: School-wide Crisis Team and Levels of Crisis

- Crisis Team Activation
- Ongoing Consultation with and Support to Teachers and School Staff
- Scope of School Response and Support Services for Students
- Critical Incident Stress Debriefing
- Working with Parents and the Community
- Secondary Traumatic Stress, Vicarious Traumatization, and Self-Care
- Practice Examples of Crisis Intervention in Schools: Natural Disasters
- Violence and Suicide Assessment, Intervention, and Prevention

CRISES AND TRAUMATIC EVENTS IN SCHOOL SETTINGS

Traumatic events take place in schools, on the way to and from schools, and within the homes and communities to which schools belong. Examples of these traumatic events include bomb threats; suicides of students and teachers; school shootings; gang violence and/or death; bullying; hate crimes and attacks on lesbian, gay, bisexual, transgender, and questioning youth; abuse/neglect and domestic/family violence; and sudden death or serious injury of students, teachers, and family members.

Across the country, devastating events have taken place in school communities:

- In Chowchilla, California, children who were buried underground in a school bus kidnapping were missing for twenty-seven hours before escaping from the kidnappers. None of the children received mental health services and five years later all of the children were reported to have symptoms of posttraumatic stress disorder (PTSD) (Knox & Roberts, 2005; Terr, 1983).
- In a small town near Chicago a commuter train plowed into a school bus, killing five high school students and injuring thirty others. Virtually everyone in their high school was traumatized (Washburn & Gibson, 1995).
- In a small town in southeastern Michigan, a ten-year-old boy committed suicide by hanging during the summer. Just after school began in the fall, a twelve-year-old girl from the same neighborhood also committed suicide by hanging. The middle school was thrown into crisis as teachers, parents, and administrators feared that additional suicides would occur (Callahan, 1996).

In 1927 the first and deadliest mass murder in a school in the United States took place in Bath Township, Michigan. In this tragedy, a farmer killed his wife and set off explosions on his farm and at an elementary school, killing himself, six adults, and thirty-eight children, and injuring fifty-eight people.

The consistent increase in violent school shootings within elementary, secondary, and college settings in the past decades has been devastating in its scope and impact:

◆ In December 2012 at an elementary school, in Newtown, Connecticut, Adam Lanza first killed his mother, and then opened fire at an elementary school killing twenty-seven people, twenty of them children.

◆ In April 2007, on the campus of Virginia Polytechnic Institute and State University in Blacksburg, Virginia, a senior student shot and killed thirty-two people, wounded seventeen others, then killed himself in two separate attacks. This was the second-deadliest school shooting incident by a single gunman in U.S. history.

◆ In April 1999, at Columbine High School in Littleton, Colorado, two students, reportedly angry at being bullied and humiliated, brought bombs and guns to school and killed twelve students and one teacher, and wounded twenty-three people before they both committed suicide (Verhovek, 1999).

As indicated in table 33.1, Klein (2012), reports that from 1980 to 2012 there have been 136 fatal school shootings in elementary, secondary, and university/college settings, resulting in 297 deaths. The table includes shootings in which at least one person other than the shooter(s) died. Klein, who was a high school teacher, school social worker, and conflict resolution coordinator, draws links between bullies and school shooters (Cullen, 2012). As indicated in table 33.1, since 1980 the number of incidents and deaths resulting from school shootings has consistently been the highest in high school settings. The largest increase of both incidents and deaths resulting from school shootings have been in university/college settings.

From December 2012 to February 2014 there were forty-four school shootings in twenty-four states, resulting in twenty-eight deaths. Incidents were classified as school shootings when a firearm was used inside a school or campus grounds. Of these forty-four school shootings, 64 percent were in K–12 schools (seventeen in high school, five in junior high school, six in

TABLE 33.1   Violence in School Settings: Elementary, Secondary, University/College

	Incidents: Type of School Setting					Deaths: Type of School Setting				
Years	Total	Elem	JHS	HS	Univ/Coll	Total	Elem	JHS	HS	Univ/Coll
1980–90	25	7	6	7	5	38	15	7	7	9
1991–2001	54	3	9	30	12	100	4	15	61	20
2002–12	57	6	3	25	23	159	39	3	40	77
Total	136	16	18	62	40	297	58	25	108	106

SOURCE: Adapted from Klein (2012).

elementary), and 36 percent were in university/college settings (Everytown for Gun Safety, 2014).

SOCIAL WORK ROLES IN RESPONSE TO CRISES AND TRAUMATIC EVENTS

In response to these traumatic events, many people experience a state of crisis in which they are significantly distressed; as a result, they do not function at their normal levels and are in danger of ongoing dysfunction if they do not receive appropriate help in a timely fashion. In a similar way, a school as a system experiences a state of crisis when many of its members experience tension, anxiety, and depression and the system as a whole does not function at its normal level and capacity. As is the case with the individuals within it, the school system's continued health and ability to function effectively will depend on receiving appropriate help in a timely fashion.

Since the September 11 terrorist attacks, social workers have increasingly been called on to help people who have experienced a wide variety of disasters including hurricanes, school and mass shootings, and other public emergencies (Mirabito, 2012; Patterson, 2009). Indeed, disaster mental health has become an area of expertise for social work practitioners across all fields of practice, including in school settings (Carp, 2010; Mirabito, 2012; Mirabito & Rosenthal, 2002; Pomeroy, 2009; Rosenthal-Gelman & Mirabito, 2005).

School social workers have been central to the interventions that have followed traumatic events. As individual professionals and as members of school crisis teams, school social workers are frequently leaders in providing crisis intervention to the entire school community, including students, school staff, and parents/families. By virtue of their training and education in both clinical and organizational responses to crisis and trauma, school social workers are often better prepared than other school professionals to provide crisis intervention in the aftermath of a traumatic event. In addition to development of these crisis intervention skills, it is also important for school social workers to develop an enlarged vision of practice that focuses on the strengths and resilience of the individuals, organizations, and communities that have experienced chaos (Carp, 2010). As highlighted by Patterson (2009), school social workers need skills in the provision of micro interventions for victims and survivors of disaster and of macro interventions to intervene with complex systems and entire communities.

In this chapter we will provide an overview of theory and practice in the areas of crisis and trauma. We focus on skills, strategies, and practice principles for crisis intervention that can be utilized on a micro, clinical level, with individual students, school staff, and parents as well as on a macro, organizational level, with the whole school system. This includes both clinical assessment and intervention, and leadership within school-based crisis teams. Finally, we provide guidelines for practice in several key areas of crisis in schools—natural disasters, and assessment, prevention, and intervention in situations of violence and suicide.

DEFINITIONS OF CRISIS AND KEY ELEMENTS OF CRISIS THEORY

A crisis is a period of psychological disequilibrium, during which a person's normal coping mechanisms are insufficient to solve a problem or master a situation (Callahan, 1994). Crisis is defined by Hoff (2001) as "an acute emotional upset arising from situational, developmental, or sociocultural sources and resulting in a temporary inability to cope by means of one's usual problem-solving devices" (p. 4). Parad and Parad (1990) expand on this definition by describing a crisis as "an upset in a steady state, a turning point leading to better or worse, a disruption or breakdown in a person's or family's normal or usual pattern of functioning" (pp. 3–4).

Two words that are commonly associated with crisis are "danger" and "opportunity" (Hoff, 2001; Parad & Parad, 1990; Slaikeu, 1990). Danger refers to an individual's inability to cope effectively with the states of disequilibrium, vulnerability, and extreme distress that occur in a crisis or the possibility that the crisis will result in long-term distress and a reduced ability to function. Opportunity refers to the unexpected opportunities for growth and development that can occur when individuals discover previously unknown or underutilized strengths and resources within themselves or their support systems as a result of a crisis (Parad & Parad, 1990). This opportunity for growth comes from openness to considering and trying out alternative coping techniques that individuals exhibit while experiencing a crisis.

THE COMPONENTS OF A CRISIS

According to Golan (1978), the five components of the "crisis situation" (p. 7) are (1) the hazardous event, (2) the vulnerable state, (3) the precipitating factor, (4) the state of active crisis, and (5) the stage of reintegration or crisis resolution (pp. 63–64).

Hazardous Event

The hazardous event is a specific stressful event that occurs to an individual who is in a state of relative stability. This event is a starting point, marking a change in the previous state of stability; this event can also initiate a chain of events to further disrupt the equilibrium. Hazardous events can be anticipated and predictable, such as developmental stages (e.g., adolescence) or unanticipated and unexpected, such as parental divorce, sudden death, a school shooting, or a natural or human-caused disaster (e.g., a hurricane or terrorist attack).

Vulnerable State

The vulnerable state is the idiosyncratic way in which individuals respond to the hazardous event both at the time it occurs and in the future. The vulnerable state can include a wide range of reactions such as anxiety, depression, mourning, shame, guilt, anger, and cognitive or perceptual confusion, as well as feelings of hope, challenge, and excitement.

Precipitating Factor

The precipitating factor is the "straw that breaks the camel's back" (Golan, 1978, p. 66), or the factor in a chain of events that converts the vulnerable state into a state of disequilibrium. In some cases the precipitating factor activates a previous vulnerable state caused by a prior hazardous event; in other cases, a precipitating factor will sometimes be the same as the hazardous event. For example, for some individuals, the September 11, 2001, disaster was the precipitating factor that activated a vulnerable state created by a previous hazardous event, while for others, the September 11 disaster was itself the precipitating factor.

State of Active Crisis

The state of active crisis describes the state of disequilibrium that occurs once an individual's previous coping mechanisms have broken down. The state of active crisis is typically considered to be time-limited, often described as four to six weeks, during which the individual experiences predictable responses including physical, emotional, and cognitive imbalance, as well as preoccupation with the events that led to the crisis. During the state of active crisis, previous defensive and coping mechanisms are ineffective and individuals are typically highly motivated to accept and utilize assistance. A minimal amount of focused assistance can be more useful during this time than more-extensive efforts during times in which individuals are not as accessible to help (Rapoport, 1962).

Stage of Reintegration or Crisis Resolution

During the initial resolution of the state of active crisis, individuals struggle to master a cognitive perception of what has occurred; they also release and accept feelings related to the crisis. In the final stage of reintegration the individual develops new patterns of coping, including improved access to and use of assistance, and identification and utilization of supports in the environment (Golan, 1978).

DISASTER THEORY AND PHASES OF STRESS REACTIONS IN A DISASTER

Golan (1978) defines disaster as "a collective stress situation in which many members of a social system fail to receive expected conditions of life, such as safety of the physical environment, protection from attack, provision of food, shelter, and income, and the guidance and information necessary to carry on normal activities" (p. 125). Three predictable phases after a disaster include (1) impact, (2) recoil and rescue, and (3) recovery (Hoff, 2001; Raphael, 2000):

Impact Phase

During the impact phase victims experience the reality of the disaster and are concerned with the immediate present. Common reactions during the impact phase range from remaining calm and organized, to becoming either shocked and confused, or hysterical and paralyzed with fear (Hoff, 2001). In the aftermath of a disaster, victims often express surprise that they were able to function as well as they did during the impact phase.

Recoil and Rescue Phase

Rescue activities begin during the recoil and rescue phase. There are a wide range of physical and emotional reactions including numbness, denial or shock, flashbacks and nightmares, grief reactions to loss, anger, despair, sadness, and feelings of hopelessness (Raphael, 2000). For those who have survived the disaster, there may be feelings of relief and elation, which may be difficult to accept in the context of the overall destruction and devastation that has occurred, engendering survival guilt (Lifton, 1982).

Recovery Phase

The recovery phase begins in the weeks after the impact phase and continues through the prolonged period in which individuals and the community face the complex task of returning to a new state of normal and attempt to regain a precrisis state of equilibrium. The beginning stage of the recovery phase is often referred to as a honeymoon period in which there is an outpouring of altruism and interpersonal connectedness in response to the disaster. Following this initial stage a period of disillusionment frequently occurs in which realities of the devastation and loss brought about by the disaster must be faced and resolved (Raphael, 2000).

DEFINITIONS OF TRAUMA AND COMMON REACTIONS TO TRAUMA

Traumatic events are extraordinary situations that are likely to evoke significant distress in many people. According to the *Diagnostic and Statistical Manual of Mental Disorders,* fifth edition (DSM-5) (American Psychiatric Association, 2013), such events include "exposure to actual or threatened death, serious injury, or sexual violence" (p. 271) by directly experiencing it, witnessing it, learning it occurred to others, or experiencing repeated exposure to the details of it. Traumatic events include exposure to war, physical assault, childhood physical abuse, threatened or actual sexual violence and abuse, being kidnapped or taken hostage, terrorist attacks, torture, natural or human-made disasters, and severe motor vehicle accidents (American Psychiatric Association, 2013, p. 274).

Even though traumatic events are defined as extraordinary situations that are likely to evoke significant distress in a large proportion of the population, individuals can exhibit a wide range of reactions, from mild to severe. Bonanno (2004) indicates that many people experience highly stressful events and do not develop posttraumatic symptoms. It is evident that many individuals experience only mild, transient responses and symptoms in response to trauma (Bonanno, 2004; Kessler, Sonnega, Bromet, Hughes, & Nelson, 1995). Through our focus on helping people who are harmed, we have overlooked the fact that many individuals are resilient in the face of traumatic events (Bonanno, 2004; Bonanno et al., 2002). In fact, at least in some cases, stress can lead to adaptive and constructive psychological growth. Receiving appropriate support and intervention is frequently crucial in producing these positive outcomes. However, it is also true that many people are able to handle traumatic stress in their own way and with their own natural support systems.

Traumatic stressors, which can take many forms, include both individual events as well as ongoing or chronic circumstances. Other terms that are synonymous with traumatic stressor are psychic trauma, psychological trauma, and emotional trauma. One helpful distinction is between Type I traumas, which are acute, single-blow traumatic events; and Type II traumas, which are multiple or long-standing traumas (Terr, 1991). As described earlier, Type I traumas that affect a school community include suicides, homicides, sudden accidental deaths of students or teachers, and transportation accidents. In addition to these, singular violent events occurring in the school and disasters in the surrounding community, such as tornadoes, hurricanes, earthquakes, and wildfires, are also included as Type 1 traumas. Rare but overwhelming events include school shootings, hostage situations, and sniper attacks on school grounds. National disasters, such as the September 11 terrorist attacks, assassinations, the Newtown, Connecticut (or Sandy Hook) school shootings, and hurricanes such as Hurricane Katrina can also have powerful impacts on school communities.

Type II traumas, also defined as complex traumas, are repetitive and continuous trauma such as ongoing physical or sexual abuse, domestic violence, community violence, war, genocide, experiences of combat or concentration camps, being a prisoner of war, or being the victim of political torture (Courtois & Ford, 2009). Complex traumatic stress reactions are defined by Courtois and Ford as "those that are most associated with histories of multiple traumatic *stressor exposures and experiences*, along with severe disturbances in primary caregiving relationships" (p. 18). Type II trauma is prevalent among children and adolescents; since it is often perpetrated by someone known by or related to the victim, it typically involves betrayal of trust in primary relationships (Courtois & Ford, 2009). Complex trauma can have detrimental effects on a child's physiology; emotions; ability to think, learn, and concentrate; impulse control; self-image; and attachment relationships with others. Complex trauma is associated with a wide range of problems, including addiction, chronic physical conditions, depression and anxiety, self-harming behaviors, and other psychiatric disorders (National Child Traumatic Stress Network, 2014).

The treatment for complex trauma is extensive and goes beyond the scope of the interventions discussed in this chapter. A wide range of trauma-specific service models for children and adolescents are available (Jennings, 2008, pp. 83–84). Trauma-Focused Cognitive Behavioral Therapy is one of several evidence-based treatment approaches for the treatment of complex trauma that addresses both historical trauma, such as physical or sexual abuse, and ongoing and continuous trauma, such as domestic, community, and/or school violence (Cohen, Mannarino, & Murray, 2011; Murray, Cohen, & Mannarino, 2013). Trauma-Focused Cognitive Behavioral Therapy focuses on developing resiliency-based coping skills with children and adolescents and utilizes active parental involvement to support the treatment goals. Components of this intervention include "Psychoeducation, Parenting Skills, Relaxation Skills, Affective Modulation Skills, Cognitive Coping Skills, Trauma Narration and Processing, In vivo Mastery of Trauma Reminders, Conjoint Child-Parent Sessions, Enhancing Safety" (Cohen et al., 2011, p. 638, fig. 1).

POSTTRAUMATIC STRESS DISORDER

PTSD is conceptualized as a syndrome of persistent reactions following a traumatic stressor that can only be diagnosed when a combination of symptoms in four categories have persisted for one month or more, and when the disturbance causes clinically significant distress or impairment in social, occupational, or other important areas of functioning (American Psychiatric Association, 2013). PTSD often coexists with other psychiatric disorders such as anxiety, depression, conduct disorders, and substance abuse. As described by Santucci (2012), "Comorbidity among psychiatric disorders is high, but with PTSD it appears to be the rule rather than the exception" (p. 124). While adolescents' PTSD reactions tend to resemble adult reactions in most ways, the DSM-5 (American Psychiatric Association, 2013) includes a specific set of criteria for symptoms and reactions for children six years and younger. Acute stress disorder has the same symptoms as PTSD, however symptoms are limited to three days to one month following exposure to the traumatic event.

Four Clusters of Posttraumatic Symptoms in the *Diagnostic and Statistical Manual of Mental Disorders* (5th ed.)

The four clusters of posttraumatic symptoms found in the DSM-5 (American Psychiatric Association, 2013) are (1) intrusion symptoms, (2) persistent avoidance, (3) negative alterations in cognitions and mood, and (4) hyperarousal and reactivity.

1. Intrusion Symptoms. Intrusion symptoms include recurrent, involuntary, and intrusive distressing memories of the traumatic event. These can include distressing dreams, intense psychological distress or physiological reactions to internal or external cues (triggers) related to the traumatic event, or dissociative reactions (flashbacks) in which individuals visualize the traumatic event and feel or act as if it were happening again (American Psychiatric Association, 2013). Flashbulb memories are so traumatic that the individual retains the image like a flash photograph. Powerful and painful images of this kind that accompanied the explosion of the Challenger have been described among children of Concord, New Hampshire, who attended the school in which Christa McAuliffe taught (Terr et al., 1996). Dreams and nightmares are common, and children often incorporate trauma themes into their play (Terr, 1991).

Dissociation can serve as a protective mechanism in the aftermath of a traumatic event to shield the individual from the full realization of the horror that has taken place. Dissociation of memory is the common experience of being unable to remember all the details of a traumatic event afterwards, or of having what is called patchy amnesia. Dissociation of emotion is the frequent experience of feeling numb immediately after a trauma. Dissociation of consciousness is the feeling of unreality or disbelief that many individuals have during and after a traumatic event in which the passage of time seems altered (usually slowed down), the world seems unreal, and the event seems to not really be happening. Dissociation of identity is the extreme separation of an individual's personality into several partial personalities (Spiegel & Cardena, 1991). This extreme form sometimes occurs in the aftermath of chronic and severe sexual and physical abuse and is called dissociative identity disorder (American Psychiatric Association, 2013).

2. Persistent Avoidance. The second cluster of symptoms consists of conscious and purposive avoidance of distressing memories, thoughts, or feelings as well as situations, places, and people that are associated with the traumatic event. Children and adolescents are reluctant to return to places where traumas occur, including school or home. For example, significant absenteeism may follow a traumatic event such as a school shooting. Some individuals consciously avoid talking about a traumatic event in an effort not to stir up strong feelings that may be overwhelming. This is a process called affect avoidance, and may be particularly prevalent in children, who often have even more difficulty tolerating strong feelings than adults do.

3. Negative Alterations in Cognitions and Mood. The third cluster of symptoms includes "Inability to remember an important aspect of the traumatic event(s); Persistent and exaggerated negative beliefs or expectations about oneself, others, or the world; Persistent, distorted cognitions about the cause or consequences of the traumatic event(s) that lead the individual to blame himself/herself or others; Persistent negative emotional state (e.g., fear, horror, anger, guilt or shame); Markedly diminished interest or participation in significant activities; Feelings of detachment or estrangement from others; Persistent inability to experience positive emotions" (American Psychiatric Association, 2013, pp. 271–272). Individuals who have been present when others were killed or injured can experience guilt about the fact that they were unable to prevent the loss or that they survived while others died.

4. Hyperarousal and Reactivity. The fourth symptom cluster includes marked alterations in arousal and reactivity associated with the traumatic event. Symptoms include "Irritable behavior and angry outbursts; Reckless or self-destructive behavior; Hypervigilance; Exaggerated startle response; Problems with concentration; Sleep disturbance" (American Psychiatric Association, 2013, p. 272). In the aftermath of a traumatic stressor, people frequently report difficulty sleeping, an increased startle reflex, jumpiness, or a sense of being keyed up, and overall anxiety. One particular aspect of this anxiety is fear that, no matter how rare, the traumatic event could happen again. Similarly, the experience of being exposed to one trauma opens up the possibility of other traumas happening as well.

Trauma vs. Grief

Death or the threat of death has a central role in many of the traumatic events that take place in schools. Almost all deaths of young people, as well as unexpected deaths of adults, involve trauma as well as grief. Many of these deaths are by suicide, homicide, or sudden accidents, and many involve violence; these events evoke trauma responses as well as grief reactions. While we often conceptualize students' and teachers' reactions to death as grief or bereavement, posttraumatic reactions are distinct and involve the range of symptoms and cognitive phenomena that have been described. Research suggests that when grief and posttraumatic symptoms are both present, posttraumatic reactions must be attended to first, before the grieving process can proceed (Nader, 1997).

PREDICTORS OF DISTRESS

The amount of exposure to trauma as well as the meaning of the event to the individual are both important variables in predicting the intensity of posttraumatic reactions (Webb, 1994). According to theories of stress, the concept of appraisal (Lazarus & Folkman, 1984), or the meaning that the individual attaches to the event, is paramount in predicting and understanding one's response. Controlling for the amount of loss of life and property damage, natural disasters are usually less distressing than human-caused accidents, and accidents are less distressing than incidents caused by human malevolence. These distinctions are thought to be due to most people's attributions that conscious human intent to harm others, such as the September 11 terrorist attacks, are considered more preventable and less understandable than a human-caused accident, such as many airplane crashes, which are frequently due to pilot error. Human error is thought to be preventable in theory, but most people realize that it is impossible to prevent 100 percent of accidents. Finally, natural weather disasters are considered inevitable or at least not preventable: they simply happen.

Another aspect of meaning is the possible violation of basic assumptions about life and the world. According to Janoff-Bulman (1985) and other theorists, adolescents and adults from all Western cultures share a small number of common, unstated, but deeply held assumptions. One primary assumption is that the world is predictable, which gives rise to long-standing searches to find an understandable meaning. Survivors of trauma struggle to understand why it happened to them. Many people believe "everything happens for a reason" and a victim "must have done something to have this happen to him," or they ask, "What did I do to deserve this?" Children may draw personal and malignant meanings from an event due to their cognitive immaturity.

Malignant meanings that individuals attach to events lead to higher levels of distress. Individuals who are able to find benevolent or positive meanings in events fare better. Furthermore, there appears to be a natural inclination to try to find some positive meaning in the aftermath of a trauma, and eventually, many people find satisfaction in having survived, and in having done the best they could under the circumstances.

Another important factor that affects outcomes is prior trauma. Research has indicated that multiple or continued trauma is harmful. For example, children and adolescents who have been victims of prior trauma are more likely to be severely affected by current trauma than those who have not. Family discord or a personal history of depression or other emotional problems are also associated with more negative outcomes. Conversely, individuals with stable backgrounds and psychologically healthy families frequently possess the personal qualities of resilience or hardiness, which enables them to withstand very stressful events.

Finally, social support plays an important role in shielding an individual from the most severe impact of traumatic stress. Numerous studies of stress, both normative and traumatic, have demonstrated that people with supportive family and friends cope with trauma better than those without. The initial response of significant others is particularly important. Consequently, in a trauma that affects a school, supportive and positive responses of teachers and staff to traumatized children are crucial aspects of social support that promote resilience.

MICROLEVEL/CLINICAL PRACTICE: PRACTICE PRINCIPLES FOR CRISIS INTERVENTION

Crisis intervention is defined by Parad and Parad (1990) as "a process for actively influencing psychosocial functioning during a period of disequilibrium in order to alleviate the immediate impact of disruptive stressful events and to help mobilize the manifest and latent psychological capabilities and social resources of persons directly affected by the crisis (and often the key persons in the social environment) for coping adaptively with the effects of stress" (p. 4). Accordingly, the goals of crisis intervention are to deal with the immediate crisis and strengthen the individual's coping capabilities for the future.

Consistent with the strengths perspective endemic to social work practice, crisis intervention focuses on the opportunities that a crisis invites for growth-promoting responses.

Specifically, there is an emphasis on mobilizing strengths and capacities in order to help students, teachers and staff, and parents and family members return to the precrisis level of functioning. Ego psychological techniques are useful to assess the individual's level of functioning, coping, and adaptation, and an empowerment perspective is employed to help clients utilize both inner and environmental resources (Mirabito & Rosenthal, 2002).

Several important practice principles that are consistent with strengths and empowerment approaches and ego psychological theory are used when intervening in situations of crisis and disaster. As described by Ell (1996), these practice principles include the following:

- ◆ In the aftermath of a crisis or disaster, help is provided immediately, including outreach to populations who may not otherwise seek assistance.

- Interventions at the time of the crisis or disaster are time-limited and brief.
- The social worker takes an active, often directive, stance in helping efforts. It is often necessary for the practitioner to engage quickly and to explore sensitive and potentially difficult areas.
- The primary goal of intervention is the reduction of symptoms and a return to the earlier state of equilibrium.
- Interventions often include a combination of counseling to handle emotional concerns; the provision of practical information, concrete community resources, and tangible support; and mobilization of environmental support systems.
- The expression of feelings, symptoms, and worries is encouraged.
- Strategies for problem-solving and effective coping are encouraged and supported to help the individual return to a state of equilibrium.

On the clinical level, or microlevel, engagement, assessment, and the implementation of interventions all occur in an expeditious manner so that prompt assistance is provided, which capitalizes on the window of opportunity afforded by the receptivity to helping efforts engendered by the crisis. It is important to conduct a rapid, though thorough and focused assessment, including an assessment of coping styles in previous situations of crisis and preexisting vulnerable states (Rosenthal-Gelman & Mirabito, 2005). In addition, it is essential to directly and thoroughly explore emotionally charged and difficult areas such as suicidality, abuse, violence, or issues related to death and dying. While there is a focus on immediate problems, crises also provide opportunities to address reactivated, unresolved, earlier issues and/or problems (Mirabito & Rosenthal, 2002). In many crises, such as in situations involving abuse/neglect, violence, or self-harming (e.g., suicidality and/or cutting) behaviors, it is necessary to assess safety and to involve other adults, such as parents and teachers, in developing detailed safety plans.

A wide range of clinical skills are utilized in crisis intervention, including rapid engagement and assessment, exploration of risk and harm, provision of practical information such as psychoeducation regarding depression and suicide, helping students and parents develop detailed safety plans, and coordinating referrals to community resources, such as child protective, mental health, and/or psychiatric agencies and organizations. The challenges of crisis intervention require that school social workers develop skills to provide focused, direct, and in-depth assessments; to be effective in taking an active, directive stance in asking difficult questions; to engage in clinical decision making and judgments; to challenge clients who may be at risk to ensure their safety; and to take a confident and proactive stance toward collaboration with interdisciplinary staff.

MACROLEVEL/ORGANIZATIONAL PRACTICE:
SCHOOL-WIDE CRISIS TEAM AND LEVELS OF CRISIS

The school social worker is one of the primary professionals who can offer help when the school as a whole experiences a crisis after a traumatic event. In many schools a school social worker is the director or leader of the school crisis team or has an important role in the development of the school's crisis plan. In fact, a team of professionals, designated as the crisis team, is necessary to offer intervention to a school in crisis. Crisis teams typically include six to eight interdisciplinary members, including the school social worker, school nurse, school psychologist, administrator(s), and teachers. It is helpful to designate specific roles for members, such as coordinators for media and staff notification. Each school and district should have a carefully designed and periodically updated crisis plan. Annual in-service training regarding the crisis plan should be provided to all teachers and school staff (Knox & Roberts, 2005).

Crises are often defined by three levels, corresponding to the scope and impact of the traumatic event:

◆ Level I: A personal tragedy for one individual or a threatening incident primarily affecting a student, teacher, or administrator at one school. Examples are the death of a parent or family member, the serious illness of a student or teacher, a suicide threat in a school, or a student bringing a weapon to school.

◆ Level II: A major personal crisis or threatening incident at a single school, or a major disaster elsewhere that affects students and teachers. Examples include the death of a student or teacher while not in school, an accident with severe injuries, a student abduction, or gang violence.

◆ Level III: A disaster or threatened disaster that directly affects one or more schools. Examples include a tornado or flood; the taking of hostages or sniper fire at a school; an air crash, explosion, or fire at or near the school; cluster suicides; or a death at a school.

A graded series of interventions should be planned, corresponding to the level of crisis. A Level I crisis can often be responded to by one or two school social workers and may not require the active intervention of a larger team. In contrast, a Level II or Level III crisis clearly requires a crisis team, made up of at least six to eight individuals, and may require additional help from other schools or the community (Dallas Public Schools, 1997; Smith, 1997). With Level II and Level III crises, crisis team members need to spend most, if not all, of their time for at least several days responding to the traumatic event. Teachers who are team members will need to be replaced by substitute teachers, and school social workers will rarely be able to carry out many of their regular responsibilities.

While six to eight members on the crisis team is enough to provide the leadership and coverage in a Level II crisis, in a Level III crisis outside help will always be necessary. It is always advisable to include at least one school social worker from another school in the same district, or an outside social worker. In certain crises, in which the members of the crisis team are personally affected, or in which teachers need particular attention, the use of an outside professional consultant eliminates the undesirable situation in which the school social worker needs to provide personal support and intervention to teachers who are his or her peers during regular school days. Such dual relationships should be avoided if at all possible.

CRISIS TEAM ACTIVATION

While many traumatic events take place away from school, at times an event occurs in a place close enough for school personnel, including the school social worker, to become actively involved while it is still unfolding. In rare cases, such as school shootings, students, teachers, and school staff may be involved in the traumatic situation itself.

Consistent with principles of crisis intervention, during the event no psychological interventions should be attempted. The only activities that are appropriate in this kind of situation are keeping order, providing information, and responding to rumors. It is not advised for school social workers to engage parents or students in discussions of their feelings and thoughts at the time of an incident, before it is resolved. Until the safety of everyone concerned is ensured, parents and students are in a psychologically vulnerable state and are primarily experiencing fear, anxiety, and a sense of vulnerability. It is not appropriate to engage them in a discussion of these fears and anxieties when the outcome is unknown. In such situations parents and students have not explicitly or even implicitly agreed to such a discussion. Providing information about support activities that will be scheduled for the near future is appropriate, as are periodic informational updates and rumor control. The only possible exception would be to provide informal support on a one-to-one basis with an individual who is already obviously upset.

In the aftermath of a traumatic event, as soon as knowledge of such an event becomes known to anyone on a school staff, the crisis team and the principal should be notified. As part of team activation, the principal of the school or superintendent of the school district should confirm the details of the event. Most often this entails talking to the police, a hospital, the medical examiner, or the family of the individuals affected by the traumatic event. Although most of the details of these situations may be confidential, authorities usually understand that the event will have a powerful impact on the school and community and accurate information is essential in order to plan an effective response. Confirming the names of the deceased, for example, is often the central issue in a traumatic death.

As a leader or member of the crisis team, it may be the responsibility of the school social worker to coordinate a meeting of the crisis team either later on that same day, if staff is still at school, or early the next morning. Most school crisis teams meet early in the morning prior to school, and before a special teachers' meeting. In the crisis team meeting, the current situation and the crisis plan are reviewed, and a general approach to the current crisis is outlined. If no representative of administration is on the team, close communication with administration must be established and maintained.

Teachers' Meeting

Using a phone fan-out system or other emergency notification system, teachers are notified as soon as possible about the crisis situation and asked to attend a special meeting, which is usually held thirty to forty-five minutes before school begins the next morning. At this meeting, the principal usually briefs the teachers on the nature of the event and then turns the meeting over to the crisis team leader. The team leader describes the range of reactions expected from students, notes interventions and activities to be held over the next few days, and provides an opportunity for teachers to ask questions. If possible, an expert in the specifics of the traumatic event can be brought in to provide more detailed information. However, the range of reactions to almost all traumatic events is similar enough that general knowledge of the nature of traumatic stress is usually sufficient.

It is strongly recommended that information about the event be communicated to students through a prepared statement written by the crisis team and read to first-period classes by each teacher. The written statement is prepared and duplicated by the crisis team in advance and distributed to teachers at the early morning meeting. The written statement should include only information that has been confirmed. Distributing a vague and generic announcement is not useful since by the time school has begun many students will know more details about what happened than most of the teachers, and if the school does not appear knowledgeable, the crisis team and teachers will lose credibility. If the death is a suicide and the family has indicated that they do not want this fact to be announced, the school should gently suggest to the family that little is gained by trying to conceal the manner of death and that the school must abide by the ruling of the medical examiner or coroner. If the medical examiner or coroner does not provide a definitive decision (in some cases, a decision regarding the mode of death is not available for some weeks), the statement should simply indicate that no ruling has been reached.

Notification of Students

Notification of students should take place in a personal manner with teachers reading the statement that has been prepared by the crisis team and administration. Announcements over the public address system are impersonal and inevitably poorly received, while classroom-by-classroom notification by teachers is usually appreciated by students. Inevitably, time for discussion must be provided immediately, and little normal work will be accomplished. In a Level II crisis, there are usually some students and some classes that are not intensely affected by the event, and discussion can be brief. In cases where students knew the victims well, much more time will be needed. If a student or students have died, a member of the crisis team should attend each of the deceased student's classes throughout the day and assist the teacher in structuring the classroom discussion.

ONGOING CONSULTATION WITH AND SUPPORT TO TEACHERS AND SCHOOL STAFF

In many situations teachers are deeply affected and distressed themselves. It is an essential and important aspect of crisis team functioning to hold a meeting, debriefing, or other structured discussion for teachers to talk with the crisis team and each other. Teachers and school staff cannot effectively help students if they are themselves distracted and preoccupied by their own reactions to the tragedy. If possible, meetings with teachers and school staff can be conducted by a school social worker or mental health professional from outside the school so that the teachers are not put in a position of talking about their personal emotional reactions with the school social worker, a person with whom they work on a daily basis.

The school social worker and crisis team can also assist teachers in small ways. For example, teachers may be so distressed that they have difficulty reading the prepared statement to their first-period classes in the aftermath of the traumatic event. A crisis team member should accompany them to class, read the announcement, and cofacilitate the discussion.

SCOPE OF SCHOOL RESPONSE AND SUPPORT SERVICES FOR STUDENTS

Consistent with the crisis intervention principles discussed in this chapter, interventions and services should be "proactive, protective, and pragmatic" (Brymer, Reyes, & Steinberg, 2012, p. 147) and provide activities that promote safety, connections to supports in the family and community, calmness, and hope (Brymer et al., 2012; Hobfoll et al., 2007). Three tiers of responses to crises are described in the literature:

◆ Tier 1 provides outreach, public health information, needs assessments, and psychological first aid.
◆ Tier 2 provides more specialized child and adolescent interventions for those with moderate to severe distress and difficulty functioning.
◆ Tier 3 provides specialized psychiatric services for those who require immediate and/or more intensive intervention, including psychiatric care and/or hospitalization (Brymer et al., 2012).

According to the National Institute of Mental Health (NIMH, 2002), effective early intervention following mass violence can be facilitated by careful screening and needs assessment for individuals and groups. Follow-up should be offered to individuals and groups at high risk of developing adjustment difficulties following exposure to mass violence, including those who (1) have acute stress disorder or other clinically significant symptoms stemming from the trauma; (2) are bereaved (when a death has occurred, the friends and close classmates of the deceased); (3) have a preexisting psychiatric condition; (4) require medical or surgical attention; and/or (5) experienced intense and prolonged exposure to the incident.

Screening for other affected individuals can be done fairly unobtrusively by requesting that teachers observe students for signs of distress and communicate the names of those students to the crisis team. Any student who has frequent absences after the event, or who evidences other indirect indicators of distress, should receive follow-up. In addition, help should be provided to any student who requests it.

Throughout the first few days of a Level II or Level III crisis, a school drop-in center or centers should be established. These centers are easily accessible offices or rooms where students are encouraged to go if they feel the need to talk about the traumatic event or other related concerns. Drop-in centers should be staffed by members of the crisis team, with extra assistance, if needed. While some experts in the field of traumatic stress have recommended that individual sessions be emphasized, the consensus of the field is that group sessions are preferable and more practical, given the limitations of time and staff (Callahan, 2009).

In Level II crises students are typically permitted to leave their regular classes, without an excuse, to go to these drop-in centers for the first two or three days. After two to three days, school should begin to move back toward business as usual. Many students will not be intensely affected and deserve to have their education continue with as few interruptions as possible. In a Level III crisis return to normalcy may take considerably longer. Limiting the availability of the drop-in centers is also appropriate given some students' tendency to become emotionally involved in the trauma in a melodramatic fashion (Callahan, 1996); on the other hand, some students will simply take advantage of the opportunity to miss class.

Support groups are ideal for helping students cope with a traumatic event. A typical group might meet four to eight times on a weekly basis, with a fixed membership. Groups can be formed with naturally occurring groups of students who were strongly affected by the traumatic incident. For example, one group might be made up of the close friends of the student(s) who died, another group might comprise peers from classes, and a third group might be made up of an athletic or extracurricular group of students affected by the traumatic incident. In all cases, participation should be voluntary. Students who request help but are uncomfortable in groups should be seen individually.

The group leader should be a social worker or other school mental health professional who is experienced in group process. Since support groups are not therapy groups, the material discussed is at a conscious level and the leader does not interpret hidden feelings or unconscious motivations. Support groups should be held at a time and place where there will be no interruptions, and the content of the group must be kept confidential (although the usual exceptions apply). Since support groups usually continue for four to eight weeks, there is often a rich opportunity to more fully process the traumatic material. In addition, because support groups normally include the students most affected by the trauma, the social worker can observe how individuals are processing and coping with the incident. The social worker is in a unique position to recommend additional individual help, if necessary.

As the first few days of the crisis unfold, periodic feedback needs to be established so that the crisis team and the social worker can monitor the process and make adaptations as needed. A combined teachers' and crisis team meeting after school on the second or third day is quite helpful; the experience up to that point can be reviewed, and changes can be made if necessary. It may be time to suspend the drop-in centers, for example, or it may be decided to continue them for another day. Specific students who are particularly distressed can be discussed, and in some cases plans can be made for the social worker to speak to those students individually, or to call their parents. If teachers are still distressed themselves, their difficulties can be addressed individually.

CRITICAL INCIDENT STRESS DEBRIEFING

Critical Incident Stress Debriefing (CISD) is a structured group discussion developed by Mitchell and Everly (1995; see also Bell, 1995; Mitchell & Bray, 1990) that incorporates theoretical concepts from both crisis intervention and trauma theories (Miller, 2001). The purpose of debriefing groups is to process the wide range of cognitive, affective, and physical reactions resulting from a traumatic event and to provide mutual aid and support. The format for a debriefing group in response to a traumatic event provides opportunities to (1) review what occurred; (2) process the wide range of reactions experienced; (3) provide psychoeducation about normative responses to trauma and useful coping mechanisms; (4) engage the group in problem solving, support, and mutual aid to help members practice self-care; and (5) provide referrals for individuals who request or require further assistance or services (Kirk & Madden, 2003; Miller, 2003). Miller makes a strong case for the value of social workers utilizing the Critical Incident Stress Management

(CISM) model and the debriefing technique because of the profession's commitment to the strengths and empowerment perspectives, groupwork, and social justice issues.

There has been much debate, disagreement, and controversy regarding the effectiveness of CISD. Although there has been no conclusive evidence that CISD prevents PTSD, anecdotal accounts have reported debriefings to be helpful (Miller, 2001, 2003; Pack, 2012; Pender & Prichard, 2009).

In a small descriptive study of school psychologists and social workers, Morrison (2007a) found that school-based professionals valued the structure, framework, and common language provided by the CISM model. In this study as well as research with teachers and other school staff (2007b), Morrison identified limitations with the CISM model and the CISD technique, including that it did not adequately incorporate developmental issues for children and adolescents or cultural competency for ethnically and racially diverse school populations. While CISD has been shown to have positive aspects, because it has not yet been systematically evaluated in school settings there is a clear need for future empirical study of CISM and CISD models and other crisis intervention strategies in school settings (Miller, 2003; Morrison 2007a, 2007b).

WORKING WITH PARENTS AND THE COMMUNITY

Within a few days of the traumatic incident, a community meeting for parents and relevant community members should be held, led by the principal. Representatives of the crisis team should also attend as they will frequently be called on to explain the details of the school's response to the traumatic event. It is important for staff leading these meetings to be aware that parents and community members can be challenging and demanding at community meetings. If the community turnout is large, as it may be for a Level III crisis, it is helpful to present some information in a large group, and then break into small discussion groups, each led by a crisis team member or teacher who is knowledgeable about traumatic stress and the school's response. If the community includes groups whose native languages are not English, it is helpful to have one or more group facilitators who are fluent in those languages.

Rumor Control Mechanisms

Throughout the period of crisis, numerous rumors will be circulated among students, parents, and the community in general. Frequently these rumors represent people's fears about additional trauma, or their attempts to find a cause. For example, in the aftermath of an adolescent suicide, and especially following two suicides, rumors of additional suicide pacts are extremely common, even though actual suicide pacts are quite rare (Gibbons, Clark, & Fawcett, 1990). Similarly, after an accidental death, whatever the circumstances, rumors may circulate, such as that the driver was drunk, that a student was walking on a certain road because she had been thrown out of her parents' house, or that a student was secretly a gang member.

Various procedures to defuse and debunk these rumors can be useful. Foremost among these is frankly answering questions from students and parents as they arise, and explaining that there is no basis in fact for a particular rumor. Making announcements to large groups or to the media that a particular rumor is untrue is often not effective, but debunking rumors when meeting with small groups of students or parents is usually effective.

Working with the Media

Especially in a Level III crisis, print and electronic media may be present at the school and demand information, access to witnesses, or statements from children. One member of the crisis team, or one member of the administration, should be designated as the media representative, and everyone else should refuse to comment. Students should be informed that they are not obligated to speak to media personnel and that, in fact, the school suggests that they do not. Media representatives can be quite persistent and will often cite the illusory "public's right to know," which has no legal standing at the time of a crisis. The media representative should provide information and answer questions concerning the school's response to the traumatic event. No information about the actual event, such as what happened, who was injured, or who was killed, should be provided; the family or legal authorities should provide this information. The media representative should be straightforward and nondefensive, even in response to what might be perceived as provocative questions. The most effective way to respond to media inquiries is to provide the information that the school wants to provide, regardless of the questions asked.

Community Healing and Memorial Activities

Memorials, rituals, and anniversary ceremonies are often a way to help groups and communities continue to heal in the aftermath of a traumatic event. Especially in the case of major events, these rituals help victims and survivors integrate the event into the context of their lives. Occasions to look back and remember seem to help victims and survivors move on with their lives. The timing and content of memorializations need to be given careful thought and planning, based on the particular type of crisis that has occurred (Knox & Roberts, 2005; Parrish & Tunkle, 2005).

SECONDARY TRAUMATIC STRESS, VICARIOUS TRAUMATIZATION, AND SELF-CARE

Working closely with students, school staff, parents, and families who experience crises and trauma has a significant impact on the health and well-being of practitioners. The terms "secondary traumatic stress," "vicarious traumatization," and "compassion fatigue" refer to the psychological and emotional risks and consequences of providing social work services to traumatized populations (Newell & MacNeil, 2010). These conditions are considered occupational hazards resulting from clinical and organizational practice that focuses on trauma (Bride, Radey, & Figley, 2007). While it is not uncommon for most social workers to develop symptoms of compassion fatigue as normative reactions to working in situations of trauma, at times compassion fatigue can interfere with professional effectiveness and one's own health and well-being (Bride et al., 2007).

Given the ongoing challenges and stress of providing social work services to traumatized populations, it is essential for all social workers in schools to develop and routinely implement strategies for professional effectiveness and self-care. Naturale and Pulido (2012) recommend a range of organizational, professional, and personal interventions that can help to ameliorate the effects of secondary traumatic stress or vicarious trauma, including organizational training and support; regular staff and peer supervision; ongoing training; workload balance; and personal self-care strategies, including getting adequate rest and relaxation and maintaining positive connections with close friends and family.

PRACTICE EXAMPLES OF CRISIS INTERVENTION IN SCHOOLS: NATURAL DISASTERS

Natural disasters include hurricanes and typhoons, earthquakes, tornadoes, floods and tsunamis, wildfires, and landslides. School-age survivors and family members of these disasters often experience a wide range of acute emotional and physical reactions. In addition, families often experience overwhelming property damage, at times necessitating relocation. Reactions of elementary school children include extreme withdrawal, irritability and angry outbursts; disruptive behavior and fighting; school avoidance; somatic complaints; depression, anxiety, and emotional numbing; fear of separation from family; and self-blame. Reactions of secondary school youth include sleep and eating disturbances, poor concentration, flashbacks, agitation, suicidal thoughts, and antisocial behavior (NIMH, 2006).

For example, in 2005 Hurricane Katrina, striking New Orleans and the U.S. Gulf Coast, resulted in 1,800 deaths and $80 billion in damages; it was the most expensive natural disaster in world history and one of the five deadliest hurricanes in U.S. history.

In the aftermath of Hurricane Katrina, 44 percent of parents in the affected areas reported that their children developed mental health symptoms, including depression, anxiety, and difficulty sleeping (Weisler, Barbee, & Townsend, 2006). Moreover, some survivors of disasters experience survivor's guilt if they were unharmed while other family members were injured or killed. For example, Honeycutt, Nasser, Banner, Mapp, and DuPont (2008) indicated that the experience of guilt following Hurricane Katrina, along with fear, anger, and sadness, were predictors of trauma.

In light of rapidly changing climate and expectations that the average number of natural disasters will increase by 320 percent over the next twenty years (Greubel, Ackerman, & Winthrop, 2012), helping youth and families affected by natural disasters will become a key area of practice for school social workers. Assessment should focus on emotional, physical, and concrete needs of students and their parents/families regarding adjustment and frequent relocation. Madrid, Grant, Reilly, and Redlener (2006) recommend that it is important to promote empowerment and normalcy, encourage proactive coping with losses and change, and promote a sense of community among relocated survivors. Research has shown that a key factor for students' adjustment is family support (Baggerly & Exum, 2008). It is most important that school social workers provide emotional and concrete assistance to parents who are struggling with their own challenges so that they can provide guidance and support to their children. It is equally important for school social workers to provide support to teachers who can also be key resources for helping youth manage the aftermath of a natural disaster (Jimerson et al., 2002).

VIOLENCE AND SUICIDE ASSESSMENT, INTERVENTION, AND PREVENTION

Given the frequency and lethal impact of violence in schools, any threat of violence should be taken seriously and appropriate actions should be implemented to ensure safety for all members of the school community. It is imperative to conduct an immediate and detailed assessment of violence potential, similar to a suicide and self-harming assessment (Twemlow, Fonagy, Sacco, & Vernberg, 2008). Dupper (2003) provides a useful set of risk factors for potential violence that school social workers should thoroughly assess, including violent drawings or writings; threats of violence toward others; aggressive history or past violent behaviors; recent relationship break; isolation; being teased or the perception of being teased, harassed, or picked on; animal torturing; substance abuse; familial stressors; low school interest; social withdrawal; inappropriate use or access to firearms; and peers considering someone as being different.

Twemlow (2008) recommends that in addition to individual assessment of the student, clinicians should make a comprehensive assessment of school, family, and community dynamics; the involvement of law enforcement; and a detailed analysis of the student's computer to consider potential cyberbullying activity (Twemlow et al., 2008). Twemlow et al. emphasize that the clinical assessment of potentially violent students is particularly challenging because both experienced clinicians and school staff frequently deny students' potential to harm, which can cause both over- and under-reactions to threats of violence. These authors contend that in ways similar to a high-risk suicidal adolescent, seriously violent youth experience a narrowing of thinking that results in limited response options, loss of perspective, and a sense of urgency to take action against oneself or others. Furthermore, they recommend that "assessments of adolescents with a potential for homicide should include an evaluation of: Previous warning communication of problems; Ambiguous messages containing threats; Availability of guns; Victimization by social groups or individuals; Concern expressed by adults or peers; Mimickry of media figures; Changes in emotions and interests; Families with dismissive attachment patterns" (pp. 140–141).

Mongan, Hatcher, and Maschi (2009), who use a "stages of change" model to understand the potential for school violence, advise school social workers to work closely with both multidisciplinary teams and a student's peers who can be key resources to share information about those students who may be contemplating violence.

Suicide Assessment, Intervention, and Prevention

When the traumatic event is a student suicide, school administrators, teachers, parents, and community members are frequently concerned about the possibility of suicide clusters, the phenomenon of one suicide leading to other copycat suicides. After one suicide, especially of a well-known or popular student, additional suicides are a possibility, although the number of actual suicide clusters in the United States has been fairly small (Davidson, Rosenberg, Mercy, Franklin, & Simmons, 1989; Niedzwiedz, Haw, Hawton, & Platt, 2014; Rezaeian, 2012). In a systematic review of suicide clusters, Niedzwiedz et al. report that suicide clusters occur in specific institutional settings, such as schools. In addition, these authors and Rezaeian indicate that adolescents are more at risk of engaging in cluster suicides than are those in older age groups, and that the use of social media and text messaging is increasingly a part of suicide clusters that needs further study.

While research has shown that after an adolescent suicide grief, depression, and trauma are much more likely to occur than additional suicides (Brent et al., 1992), the prospect of cluster suicides is anxiety-provoking (Centers for Disease Control, 1988). Thus, the goals of a school's crisis intervention program are both to help students process the trauma as well as to prevent additional suicides. The crisis intervention strategies described in this chapter, such as support groups, are useful in reducing suicide risk by providing forums for students to voice their concerns and feelings as well as to give and receive support. In addition, crisis team members and teachers should observe students for signs of unusual distress and provide immediate intervention.

The most important strategy for preventing future suicides is undermining the tendency of students to identify with the deceased suicide victim. Although cluster suicides are not well understood, it appears that the primary mechanism of contagion is identification and imitation in someone already experiencing suicidal impulses. Adolescent suicide is often viewed as a defiant gesture by a heroic individual who was beaten down by powerful but destructive adult forces. The story of Romeo and Juliet exemplifies this concept, and adolescents' tendency to view a suicide as a romantic tragedy (Smith, 1988) could set the stage for a possible cluster suicide.

A key to prevention is to defuse the atmosphere of romantic tragedy. One clear way to do this is to portray the deceased student, in all announcements and especially in small-group and individual discussions, as a troubled, depressed, or substance-dependent isolated young person who made bad decisions. A sensitive, tactful, and sympathetic portrayal will counter students' tendency to idolize and make heroic what is almost always a result, in part, of psychopathology.

A confidential list of students considered to be at risk for suicidal behavior should be prepared and maintained by the crisis team or school social worker. Students considered at risk would include any student with a history of serious depression, previous suicide attempts, or suicide in the family, as well as close friends of the victim and any other students who appear to be strongly affected. All of these students must be interviewed individually by a member of the crisis team or a mental health professional; the interviewer should conduct a detailed and thorough clinical assessment of depression and suicidality and arrange for safety planning, when needed. In any instances in which significant risk exists, parents should be contacted and school staff should meet with them to arrange appropriate community mental health and/or psychiatric treatment, outpatient and/or inpatient.

Although it may appear counterintuitive, the resumption of business as usual in a school is also an antidote to possible suicide contagion (Parrish & Tunkle, 2005). The structure of the school routine is comforting and helpful to most students and teachers. Long-lasting crisis atmospheres, in which usual classes or programming are canceled or altered, can easily contribute to an atmosphere of romantic tragedy and artificially elevated melodrama. A more detailed discussion of reducing suicide contagion is found in the (second) author's case study of a postvention program that inadvertently worsened the situation (Callahan, 1996).

CONCLUSION

As we have discussed and demonstrated in this chapter, in response to crises and traumatic events social workers in schools, individually and as members of crisis teams, provide invaluable assistance to students, school staff, and parents/families through clinical and organizational practice approaches. School social work services provided in times of crisis and trauma enable all members of the school community to work through a crisis and adopt new coping techniques. These could be self-reflection, realizing the value of talking with friends and family about important and personal matters, the ability to tolerate strong feelings, or the adoption of a more adaptive worldview. When a crisis leads an individual or a school system to adopt these or other new coping techniques, the individual and/or the school system becomes stronger, more capable, and more resilient than before the crisis. Many survivors of traumatic events later say, "If I survived that, I can survive anything." This sense of confidence, mastery, and growth that students can build out of tragedy is especially important for children and adolescents, and it is one of the most gratifying processes that a school social worker can experience.

References

American Psychiatric Association. (2013). *Diagnostic and statistical manual of mental disorders* (5th ed.) (DSM-5). Arlington, VA: American Psychiatric Publishing.

Baggerly, J., & Exum, H. A. (2008). Counseling children after natural disasters: Guidance for family therapists. *American Journal of Family Therapy, 36,* 79–93. doi:10.1080/01926180601057598

Bell, J. L. (1995). Traumatic event debriefing: Service delivery designs and the role of social work. *Social Work, 40,* 36–43. doi:10.1093/sw/40.1.36

Bonanno, G. A. (2004). Loss, trauma, and human resilience. Have we underestimated the human capacity to thrive after extremely aversive events? *American Psychologist, 59*(1), 20–28. doi:10.1037/0003-066X.59.1.20

Bonanno, G. A., Wortman, C. B., Lehman, D. R., Tweed, R. G., Haring, M., Sonnega, J., . . . & Nesse, R. M. (2002). Resilience to loss and chronic grief: A prospective study from preloss to 18-months postloss. *Journal of Personality and Social Psychology, 83*(5), 1150–1164. doi:10.1037/0022-3514.83.5.1150

Brent, D. A., Perper, J., Moritz, G., Allman, C., Friend, A., Schweers, J., . . . & Harrington, K. (1992). Psychiatric effects of exposure to suicide among friends and acquaintances of adolescent suicide victims. *Journal of the American Academy of Child and Adolescent Psychiatry, 31,* 629–640.

Bride, B. E., Radey, M., & Figley, C. R. (2007). Measuring compassion fatigue. *Clinical Social Work Journal, 35,* 155–163.

Brymer, M., Reyes, G., & Steinberg, A. (2012). Disaster behavioral health for children and adolescents: Best practices for preparedness, response, and recovery. In J. Framingham & M. Teasley (Eds.), *Behavioral health response to disaster* (pp. 143–158). New York: CRC Press.

Callahan, J. (1994). Defining crisis and emergency. *Crisis, 15,* 164–171.

Callahan, J. (1996). Negative effects of a school suicide postvention program: A case example. *Crisis, 17,* 108–115.

Callahan, J. (2009). School-based crisis intervention for traumatic events. In C. Massat, R. Constable, S. McDonald, & J. Flynn (Eds.), *School social work: Practice, policy, and research* (pp. 638–661). Chicago: Lyceum Books.

Carp, J. (2010). Resiliency: The essence of survival in chaos. *Families in Society, 91*(3), 266–271.

Centers for Disease Control (CDC). (1988). CDC recommendations for a community plan for the prevention and containment of suicide clusters. *Morbidity and Mortality Weekly Report, 37*(Suppl. S-6), 1–12.

Cohen, J., Mannarino, A., & Murray, L. (2011). Trauma-focused CBT for youth who experience ongoing traumas. *Child Abuse & Neglect, 35,* 637–646. doi:10.1016/j.chiabu.2011.05.002

Courtois, C., & Ford, J. (2009). *Treating complex traumatic stress disorders: An evidence-based guide.* New York: Guilford Press.

Cullen, D. (2012, April 29). Mean kids "The Bully Society." *New York Times Sunday Book Review,* p. BR 16.

Dallas Public Schools. (1997). *Crisis management plan: Resource manual.* Dallas, TX: Author.

Davidson, L. E., Rosenberg, M. L., Mercy, J. A., Franklin, J., & Simmons, J. T. (1989). An epidemiologic study of risk factors in two teenage suicide clusters. *Journal of the American Medical Association, 262,* 2687–2692. doi:0.1001/jama.1989.03430190071034

Dupper, D. (2003). *School social work: Skills and interventions for effective practice.* Hoboken, NJ: John Wiley & Sons.

Ell, K. (1996). Crisis theory and social work practice. In F. Turner (Ed.), *Social work treatment: Interlocking theoretical approaches* (4th ed., pp. 168–190). New York: Oxford University Press.

Everytown for Gun Safety. (2014). *School shootings in America since Sandy Hook. Analysis of school shootings: December 15, 2012–February 10, 2014.* Retrieved from everytown.org/article/schoolshootings/

Gibbons, R. D., Clark, D. C., & Fawcett, J. (1990). A statistical method for evaluating suicide clusters and implementing cluster surveillance. *American Journal of Epidemiology 132* (Supp. 1), S183–S191.

Golan, N. (1978). *Treatment in crisis situations.* New York: The Free Press.

Greubel, L., Ackerman, X., & Winthrop, R. (2012). *Prioritizing education in the face of natural disasters.* Washington, DC: Brookings Institute, October.

Hobfoll, S. E., Watson, P., Bell, C. C., Bryant, R. A., Brymer, M. J., Friedman, M. J., . . . & Friedman, M. (2007). Five essential elements of immediate and mid-term mass trauma intervention: Empirical evidence. *Psychiatry: Interpersonal & Biological Processes, 70*(4), Winter, 283–315.

Hoff, L. A. (2001). *People in crisis: Clinical and public health perspective* (5th ed.). San Francisco: Jossey-Bass.

Honeycutt, J. M., Nasser, K. A., Banner, J. M., Mapp, C. M., & DuPont, B. W. (2008). Individual differences in catharsis, emotional valence, trauma anxiety, and social networks among Hurricane Katrina and Rita victims. *Southern Communication Journal, 73,* 229–242. doi:10.1080/10417940802219728

Janoff-Bulman, R. (1985). The aftermath of victimization. Rebuilding shattered assumptions. In C. R. Figley (Ed.), *Trauma and its wake* (Vol. 1, pp. 15–35). New York: Brunner/Mazel.

Jennings, A. (2008). *Models for developing trauma-informed behavioral health systems and trauma-specific services.* Center for Mental Health Services, National Center for Trauma-Informed Care. Washington, DC: U.S. Department of Health and Human Services.

Jimerson, S., Brown, J., Saeki, E., Watanabe, Y., Kobayashi, T., & Hatzichriston, C. (2002). Natural disasters. In S. Brock & S. Jimerson (Eds.), *Best Practices in School Crisis Prevention and Intervention* (2nd ed., chap. 30, pp. 573–596). Bethesda, MD: National Association of School Psychologists.

Kessler, R. C., Sonnega, A., Bromet, E., Hughes, M., & Nelson, C. B. (1995). Post-traumatic stress disorder in the National Comorbidity Survey. *Archives of General Psychiatry, 52,* 1048–1060. doi:10.1001/archpsyc.1995.03950240066012

Kirk, A., & Madden, L. (2003). Trauma related critical incident debriefing for adolescents. *Child and Adolescent Social Work Journal, 20*(2), 123–134.

Klein, J. (2012). *The bully society: School shootings and the crisis of bullying in America's schools.* New York: New York University Press.

Knox, K., & Roberts, A. (2005). Crisis intervention and crisis team models in schools. *Children & Schools, 27*(2), 93–100. doi:10.1093/cs/27.2.93

Lazarus, R., & Folkman, S. (1984). *Stress, appraisal, and coping.* New York: Springer.

Lifton, R. J. (1982). The psychology of the survivor and the death imprint. *Psychiatric Annals, 12,* 1011–1020.

Madrid, P. A., Grant, R., Reilly, M. J., & Redlener, N. B. (2006). Challenges in meeting immediate emotional needs: Short-term impact of a major disaster on children's mental health: Building resiliency in the aftermath of Hurricane Katrina. *Pediatrics, 117,* S448–S453. doi:10.1542/peds.2006-0099U

Miller, J. (2001). The use of debriefings in schools. *Smith College Studies in Social Work, 71*(2), 259–270.

Miller, J. (2003). Critical incident debriefing and social work: Expanding the frame. *Journal of Social Service Research, 30*(2), 7–25.

Mirabito, D. M. (2012). Educating a new generation of social workers: Challenges and skills needed for contemporary agency-based practice. *Clinical Social Work Journal, 40,* 245. doi:10.1007/s10615-011-0378-6

Mirabito, D. M., & Rosenthal, C. (2002). *Generalist practice in the wake of disaster: September 11 and beyond.* Belmont, CA: Wadsworth/Thomson Learning.

Mitchell, J. T., & Bray, G. P. (1990). *Emergency services stress.* Englewood Cliffs, NJ: Prentice-Hall.

Mitchell, J. T., & Everly, G. S. (1995). *Critical incident stress debriefing: An operations manual for the prevention of traumatic stress among emergency services and disaster workers* (2nd ed.). Ellicott City, MD: Chevron.

Mongan, P. S., Hatcher, S., & Maschi, T. (2009). Etiology of school shootings: Utilizing a purposive, non-impulsive model for social work practice. *Journal of Human Behavior in the Social Environment, 19,* 635–645. doi:10.1080/10911350902910583

Morrison, J. Q. (2007a). Social validity of the critical incident stress management model for school-based crisis intervention. *Psychology in the Schools, 44*(8), 765–777. doi:10.1002/pits.20264

Morrison, J. Q. (2007b). Perceptions of teachers and staff regarding the impact of the Critical Incident Stress Management (CISM) Model for school-based crisis intervention. *Journal of School Violence, 6*(1), 101–102. doi:10.1300/J202v06n01_07

Murray, L., Cohen, J., & Mannarino, A. (2013). Trauma-focused cognitive behavioral therapy for youth who experience continuous traumatic exposure. *Peace and Conflict: Journal of Peace Psychology, 19*(2), 180–195. doi:10.1037/a0032533

Nader, K. O. (1997). Childhood traumatic loss: The interaction of trauma and grief. In C. R. Figley, B. E. Bride, & N. Mazza (Eds.), *Death and trauma* (pp. 17–41). Washington, DC: Taylor & Francis.

National Child Traumatic Stress Network. (2014). *Types of traumatic stress, complex trauma.* Retrieved from www.nctsn.org/trauma-types

National Institute of Mental Health (NIMH). (2002). *Mental health and mass violence: Evidence-based early psychological intervention for victims/survivors of mass violence. A workshop to reach consensus on best practices.* NIH Publication No. 02-5138, Washington, DC: U.S. Government Printing Office.

National Institute of Mental Health (NIMH). (2006). *What is post-traumatic stress disorder (PTSD): Treatment after mass trauma.* Retrieved from www.nimh.nih.gov/

Naturale, A., & Pulido, M. (2012). Helping the helpers. Ameliorating secondary traumatic stress in disaster workers. In J. Framingham & M. Teasley (Eds.), *Behavioral health response to disaster* (pp. 189–208). New York: CRC Press.

Newell, J. M., & MacNeil, G. A. (2010). Professional burnout, vicarious trauma, secondary traumatic stress, and compassion fatigue: A review of theoretical terms, risk factors, and preventive methods for clinicians and researchers. *Best Practices in Mental Health, 6*(2), 57–68.

Niedzwiedz, C., Haw, C., Hawton, K., & Platt, S. (2014). The definition and epidemiology of clusters of suicidal behavior: A systematic review. *Suicide and Life-Threatening Behavior, The Official Journal of the American Association of Suicidology,* 1–13. doi:10.1111/sltb.12091

Pack, M. (2012). Critical incident stress management: A review of the literature with implications for social work. *International Social Work, 56*(5), 608–627. doi:10.1177/0020872811435371

Parad, H. J., & Parad, L. G. (Eds.). (1990). *Crisis Intervention book II: The practitioner's sourcebook for brief therapy.* Milwaukee, WI: Family Service of America.

Parrish, M., & Tunkle, J. (2005). Clinical challenges following an adolescent's death by suicide: Bereavement issues faced by family, friends, schools, and clinicians. *Clinical Social Work Journal, 33*(1), 81–102. doi:10.1002/pits.20213

Patterson, G. (2009). An examination of evidenced-based practice interventions for public emergencies. *Journal of Evidence-Based Social Work, 6,* 274–287.

Pender, D., & Prichard, K. (2009). ASGW best practice guidelines as a research tool: A comprehensive examination of the critical incident stress debriefing. *The Journal for Specialists in Group Work, 34*(2), 175–192. doi:10.1080/01933920902807147

Pomeroy, E. C. (2009). The end of a decade: Challenges for a changing world. *Social Work, 54*(4), 293–295.

Raphael, B. (2000). *Disaster mental health response handbook.* New Parramatta, New South Wales, Australia: The New South Wales Institute of Psychiatry.

Rapoport, L. (1962). The state of crisis: Some theoretical considerations. *Social Service Review, 36*(2, June), 211–217.

Rezaeian, M. (2012). Suicide clusters: Introducing a novel type of categorization. *Violence and Victims, 27*(1), 125–132.

Rosenthal-Gelman, C., & Mirabito, D. (2005). Practicing what we teach: Using case studies from 9/11 to teach crisis intervention from a generalist perspective. *Journal of Social Work Education, 41*(3), 479–494.

Santucci, P. (2012). Mental health outcomes of disasters and trauma. In J. Framingham & M. Teasley (Eds.), *Behavioral health response to disaster* (pp. 115–140). New York: CRC Press.

Slaikeu, K. A. (1990). *Crisis intervention: A handbook for practice and research* (2nd ed.). Boston: Allyn & Bacon.

Smith, J. (1997). *School crisis management manual: Guidelines for administrators.* Holmes Beach, FL: Learning Publications.

Smith, K. (1988). *One town's experience with teen suicide.* Presentation at the annual meeting of the Michigan Association of Suicidology, October. Lansing, MI.

Spiegel, D., & Cardena, E. (1991). Disintegrated experience: The dissociative disorders revisited. *Journal of Abnormal Psychology, 100,* 366–378. doi:10.1037/0021-843X.100.3.366

Terr, L. C. (1983). Chowchilla revisited: The effects of a psychic trauma after a school bus kidnapping. *American Journal of Psychiatry, 140,* 1543–1555.

Terr, L. C. (1991). Childhood traumas: An outline and overview. *American Journal of Psychiatry, 148,* 10–20.

Terr, L. C., Block, D. A., Michel, B. A., Shi, H., Reinhardt, J. A., & Metayer, S. (1996). Children's memories in the wake of the Challenger. *American Journal of Psychiatry, 153,* 618–625.

Twemlow, S. (2008). Assessing adolescents who threaten homicide in schools: A recent update. *Clinical Social Work Journal, 36,* 127–129. doi:10.1007/s10615-007-0100-x

Twemlow, S., Fonagy, P., Sacco, F., & Vernberg, E. (2008). Assessing adolescents who threaten homicide in schools. *Clinical Social Work Journal, 36,* 131–142. doi:10.1007/s10615-007-0101-9

Verhovek, S. H. (1999, April 22). Terror in Littleton: The overview: 15 bodies are removed from school in Colorado. *New York Times,* A1.

Washburn, G., & Gibson, R. (1995, October 26). Ride to school ends in tragedy. *Chicago Tribune,* 1.

Webb, N. B. (1994). School-based assessment and crisis intervention with kindergarten children following the New York World Trade Center bombing. *Crisis Interventions, 1,* 47–59.

Weisler, R. H., Barbee, J. G., & Townsend, M. H. (2006). Mental health and recovery in the Gulf Coast after Hurricanes Katrina and Rita. *Journal of the American Medical Association, 296,* 585–588. doi:10.1001/jama.296.5.585

Appendix A
The Practice of School Social Work

Robert Constable
Loyola University Chicago

◆ The Case of Alan
◆ Case Study Assessment Findings
◆ Alan's Family History
◆ Alan's Educational Background and Evaluation
◆ Services Offered Alan, Progress, and Results
◆ Alan's Current Progress
◆ Expert Practitioner Panel's Responses to the Case of Alan

The role of the school social worker, as it has developed over time, involves a complex array of interventions that address issues affecting students.[1] These interventions may focus on the family, the classroom, the individual student, or the community. Multiple interventions at various levels of the environment may occur at the same time. Analyzing practice within schools is often a matter of mapping these interventions in the learning environment and with the pupil as well as the pupil's coping with school in response to them. All of these shifts in focus, together with the responses, can be seen in the following case of a middle school student we call "Alan."

---

1. *Editor's note:* This appendix is an adapatation of a case example from previous editions of this book, a case that originally took place in the 1970s. The case presented here shows the variety of interventions and strategies that can be effectively deployed by an experienced school social worker in the service of one specific student and his family. In addition to presenting the case, this chapter includes commentary by an expert panel of veteran school social work practitioners who reviewed the case, and discusses their ideas about how this case relates to school social work practice in the second decade of the twenty-first century.

THE CASE OF ALAN

The case involves a child, Alan, with whom the social worker (Helen Wolkow) worked over a period of seven years (from second through eighth grade), his parents, his teachers, the school administration, and outside agencies. The case takes place in an elementary school in the southwest suburbs of Chicago. The social worker, who works for a special education cooperative school district, had been assigned to the school for many years. Her teamwork, consultation, and administrative work, as well as her clinical work, reflect some years of development of the school social work program at that school. At the elementary school level, she was able to follow Alan's case professionally for seven consecutive years with the bulk of her work done over three of those years. When Alan moved on to high school, he would stop in from time to time to visit her. The case has been used by the current text since its second edition (Wolkow, 1991) as an illustration of good practice with a situation a social worker would commonly encounter in an elementary school. It has been updated slightly to reflect more-recent developments in education, but it is functionally the same. The work of the school social worker fully reflects school social work expectations outlined by the Illinois State Board of Education (or, by extension, many other states). Since there are differences in emphasis in different areas, the authors asked six practicing social workers from different areas to review and comment on the case. These comments follow the case, and give some idea of similarities and the diversity of school social work in the early twenty-first century.

Background

Alan is a second grader with learning disabilities as well as serious emotional problems. His sadness and confusion at his parents' separation results in his severely dysfunctional response to his situation: suicidal ideation and general inability to cope. He experiences academic dysfunction and notable social skill deficits in his new school. The major social work focus of his highly experienced worker rested on consultation and coordination of the team efforts, working with the parents and working with Alan in individual and group modalities only as needed. The team has been working together for a number of years. In some ways what the social worker does not do, such as seeing Alan weekly apart from his context and apart from the unfolding process, is as important as what she does do.

Questions for Reviewing the Case

There are at least three sets of questions to think of in reviewing this case:

1. What is needed at different phases of the process for Alan to eventually arrive at his developmental potential?

2. What are the risks of not intervening at different stages of the process? What did the teamwork response of the school and the social worker prevent from happening?
3. How does the social worker make use of the capabilities of the school and Alan's educational tasks to assist him to cope with his problems? If this school were on a tier system, what would be the shifts from one tier to another in this case? How does the social worker use and expedite these shifts to assist Alan's coping?

Alan was referred for case study assessment by his second-grade class-room teacher about five weeks after the start of school. He was a transfer student from another school district and was experiencing great difficulty with reading and spelling. He also had difficulty following directions and concentrating on his work; he was easily distracted, and he had poor fine-motor coordination and poor visual perception. Alan often would try to copy from his neighbors or just sit and not attempt to do his work. At times he would sit and suck his fingers. Teachers described him as shy and with-drawn. The teacher presented the situation to the pupil personnel service team, and that team agreed testing should be done. The parents were con-tacted and agreed to the evaluation. As part of this evaluation, the school social worker (Helen Wolkow) completed a full social developmental study. This provided us with some insight into possible causes for his academic, developmental, and social difficulties.

CASE STUDY ASSESSMENT FINDINGS

Alan, a nice-looking, blond, blue-eyed white male, was age seven at the time of our initial interview. When interviewed, he had a very quiet and shy man-ner, and he was almost withdrawn. He spoke very softly, and at times it was difficult to understand what he said. A lot of his emotional energy seemed to be tied up with his parents' divorce process, which had started eighteen months earlier. He found school to be rather difficult, especially reading, but mathematics was okay. He believed his older brother had learned to read as a baby. Later I found out his older brother had been retained, had reading difficulties, and still seemed to be having some academic problems. He said that his parents yelled a lot, both at him and his brother. He talked quite a bit about this, and many of his answers to my questions referred to this yelling. He was able to say that he felt angry when he could not get his way.

ALAN'S FAMILY HISTORY

At the time of the evaluation Alan lived with his mother, his ten-year-old brother, and his three-year-old sister. His mother and father had separated at the end of Alan's kindergarten year. Initially, the mother stayed home with the children during the day but went to her parents' home for the night when the father returned from work. The mother was attending school at a local community college at the time. The father works as an accountant and recently had become a born-again Christian; the mother is Catholic and attends church on a weekly basis. The divorce became final the summer after Alan completed first grade. That summer, mother and children moved to the same mobile home park where her parents resided. This move placed them within our district boundaries. The park had many children in residence and was populated mostly by working-class people. The family fit within the norms of that community. During this time, the father usually would take the children on weekends. He was most consistent in doing so, and both children and father seemed to enjoy the time together very much. Both sets of grandparents were involved with Alan and supportive of the family situation. Alan often would visit a country cottage with the maternal grandparents, and he was quite fond of those visits.

ALAN'S EDUCATIONAL BACKGROUND AND EVALUATION

Alan attended preschool a few days a week at age four and then kindergarten and first grade in a standard educational placement. He came to his present district at the beginning of second grade, and he was evaluated shortly after entry. The assessment pointed out that his support systems were eroding and that his self-concept, along with his academic performance, were rapidly deteriorating. Alan had been wrestling with events in his life with which his cognitive abilities were not yet capable of dealing. Emotionally he had been challenged by events that went right to the core of his worst fears, both in terms of potential abandonment and of his sense of self-competence. Efforts to soothe himself or put events in perspective generally had met with failure. Thus, he was becoming increasingly overwhelmed and anxious, and as a result some regressive behavior was noted (finger sucking, passivity, and disengagement).

As a result of the evaluation, Alan was placed on a learning disabilities watch status, which meant that the learning disabilities specialist consulted with his classroom teacher weekly about possible interventions in the classroom for the perceived problems. In addition, Alan was placed with the reading specialist in a small group to see if this would strengthen his reading skills. The social worker was identified as the interim case manager because it was clear that case management was going to be crucial to Alan's case. As a case manager, the social worker met jointly with the classroom teacher, learning disabilities specialist, and reading specialist to arrange mutual consultation. With regard to direct social work service, Alan needed help with divorce issues, self-esteem, and socialization skills, and with learning appropriate ways to express his needs. The social worker explored with his parents the possibility of outside counseling. They did not agree to this, so the social worker monitored him on a consultative basis until further direct work could be arranged.

SERVICES OFFERED TO ALAN, PROGRESS, AND RESULTS

Alan initially showed minimal response to the planned intervention and continued to regress. The social worker did a classroom observation and a functional behavior assessment (FBA). I found that the teacher's response to Alan's behavior was compounding the problem. Alan's second-grade teacher was highly structured, somewhat inflexible, and unresponsive to the implications of his deteriorating behavior. She was not, initially, very encouraging with him, nor did she recognize the compensation his artistic and creative strengths and his good problem-solving skills offered. She found his slow pace of working, which was part of his perfectionistic need, difficult to relate to. This teacher was not particularly receptive to direct suggestions from me, so the social worker had to develop some alternative strategies to implement through our already established consultation with the reading specialist. In meetings with the reading specialist and the classroom teacher, they discussed what their goals would be in their work with Alan's situation. They discussed some parallel goals that might be implemented by the reading specialist. In this context the classroom teacher was able to discuss her approach. She was able to draw on an approach that she had used with a similar student a few years back. In fact, the earlier situation was close enough to be useful, and she believed she could use the same approach with Alan. By seeing the similarities between students she was able to accept other suggestions.

At the end of February of second grade Alan's classroom teacher went on maternity leave. Alan's new teacher was very warm, caring, and creative. She liked Alan and wanted suggestions on how to help him. The consultation meetings continued. Alan seemed to be having great difficulty and the team suspected that he needed more-intensive support. The social worker did another FBA and shared it with the teacher. The team requested a new individualized educational program conference to amend the findings of the original case conference. In order to arrange this meeting in a timely manner, the school administration had to be consulted about Alan's high-priority status. Given this information, the special education director in particular put in extra effort to reschedule the team along with the parents so the team could all meet within the following week. As a result of the conference, Alan was changed from the learning disabilities watch list to direct learning disabilities services with the learning disabilities teacher in a resource room. The social worker also agreed to work with him thirty to sixty minutes a week in a small group of seven-year-old boys struggling with learning problems.

A week after this meeting and Alan's being placed in the learning disabilities program, his regular education teacher brought to the social worker's attention a picture Alan had drawn of himself with a noose around his neck. When the social worker questioned Alan about it, he said he had just been kidding around but then did admit he had some very sad feelings. The social worker then began another FBA. The team was concerned about his suicidal ideation, an unusual indicator of distress for a seven-year-old. The social worker told him that she wanted to check in with him every day for a while because his being this sad concerned the social worker. She also told him she needed to talk to his mother and father because it was important that they also know about it. When the social worker approached his mother regarding her concerns, Alan's mother said that she believed it really was not serious and that in fact Alan seemed to be doing much better. His father believed it was serious and wanted Alan in outside counseling. The social worker sensed the mother's resistance and that this conversation had ventured into an old area of marital disagreement, giving the social worker the impression that she would not accept a referral at the time. The social worker suggested to both that she continue to work with him until school was out in June and that they should think about an outside therapist then, if not sooner. Both agreed. The social worker sensed that she needed to have another conference with his mother to support her awareness that in many ways Alan was doing much better, but that this new development was still something the team hoped she would take seriously. She listened attentively and asked some very perceptive questions. Although she did not seem as convinced about the seriousness of Alan's situation as the social worker had hoped, her attitude did seem to be much more open and cooperative.

Alan started to do much better after he started seeing the learning disabilities teacher. She continued to consult with the social worker and the classroom teacher until the end of the year, and the classroom teacher began implementing similar strategies in the classroom to support his progress. Likewise, he became more outgoing and started displaying improved social skills, first in his social work group and then in the classroom setting. When it was determined that he was starting to generalize the skills that he was learning in our small group, the social worker met with each of his teachers to request that they encourage his fledgling efforts to become more assertive and outgoing. Most of them were cooperative and actively helped him with this. They regularly reported to the social worker informally. Retention still was considered at the end of the year because his academic progress was not as great as the team had hoped, but the team in collaboration with the parents agreed that they wanted to wait to see how things would progress for him in third grade. The social worker then went to the principal to encourage her to consider placing Alan with the more-flexible and care-giving third-grade teachers. She said she would take the request into consideration when making class assignments.

When the school year was nearly ended and as part of our annual review process, the social worker contacted the mother and father about making arrangements for Alan to see an outside therapist and gave them some names of therapists the social worker could recommend. The social worker asked that when they had made arrangements, they give the therapist permission to call her regarding Alan's case, and that they give her permission to discuss the case with the new therapist. The mother was very uncomfortable about the whole arrangement, stating that Alan would not like talking with a stranger, just as she would not be. Because the social worker believed that her relationship with the mother was fairly strong by this time, she encouraged Alan's mother to at least meet with one of the therapists that had been recommended; then, if she wished, she could call the social worker to talk further about her concerns. She thanked the social worker but did not act on this offer. In two weeks, just at the end of the school year, the social worker received a call from the therapist whose name topped the list. She mentioned that the father had made the arrangements for a meeting, but that only the father came. However, the therapist had called the mother, and she had agreed to cooperate in getting Alan to his appointments.

At the beginning of third grade, the social worker met with Alan and his parents separately after discussing his progress with his outside therapist. The team all agreed that, following a few visits to assist in his adjustment to the new school year, direct social work service would not be indicated at this time. Third grade generally went well for Alan. He made good academic progress. He was seen by the reading specialist and the learning disabilities specialist two times a week, with one other student. The social worker had regular contact with his classroom teacher to make sure he was progressing both academically and socially. Initially, she discussed with the classroom teacher his previous struggles and alerted her to watch for signs of depression. The social worker also helped her to institute a behavior modification plan for the whole class, focused on positive social interaction, as a way of keeping a handle on Alan's real social progress. Alan finished third grade on a positive note and was promoted to fourth grade.

Alan continued doing well in fourth grade. He had a male teacher whom he seemed to enjoy. The teacher noted that Alan improved greatly in his academic, organizational, and social skills in fourth grade, and went up several grade levels in reading, health, and social studies. Grades in other subject areas stayed the same or went up slightly. He became more organized and began writing his assignments down each day; his daily homework assignments were consistently completed. The social worker's ongoing work with his teacher that year was less intense than previously. She consulted with him weekly for the first few weeks of school, giving him essentially the same background information as she had done for the third-grade teacher, though in less detail. This was followed by monthly check-ins, except when specific concerns arose.

The social worker had done an FBA with classroom observation at the beginning of the school year. Alan became more involved in class discussions, although he still was shy about sharing experiences. One thing he did share, slowly, with each of us involved with him, was his mother's remarriage at the end of the summer. He was beginning to enjoy his stepfather., although he believed the stepfather sometimes was not confident when problems arose. As Alan suggested, however, perhaps this was because the stepfather had never had children before. The social worker learned of this aspect of Alan's family by asking Alan if he would like to come to talk with the social worker a few times once she learned from his teacher of this new development. The social worker also asked Alan for permission to contact his mother and stepfather to ask them if they would like to come in to talk about any issues surrounding their relationship with the children, especially with Alan. Surprisingly, they agreed and came in the following week. Together the social worker and parents decided to keep in contact throughout the rest of the year. The social worker also agreed to start seeing Alan again in a small group of boys. He interacted with the other students, but he still needed work on social skills. At times he reacted negatively and physically to others when annoyed; however, he eventually learned to walk away from those situations. The social worker reinforced the importance of therapy for Alan for the summer months, given those latest developments, more to prevent backsliding than because of the former concerns regarding serious depression. Most of the work that year was with the teacher and the parents with some availability to Alan when needed. Alan became more comfortable with his academics and the school setting. He would have liked more friends. He enjoyed being with his stepfather and no longer thought so much about the divorce. He visited with his father every weekend and also became involved with outside activities, such as Boy Scouts. His mother then started to work part-time in the office of one of the district schools.

Alan completed his junior high school years (grades 6 through 8) successfully. He was placed on a consult basis for learning disabilities/reading services the last two years of junior high and continued in the Chapter I reading program through sixth grade. Socially he interacted well with others and was involved in the chess club. He was very involved with the youth group at his father's church.

ALAN'S CURRENT PROGRESS

Alan is now a sophomore in high school and doing well academically. He still visits the social worker occasionally and his mother has called once. He does not seem to have many friends in the mobile home park but does have friends in his father's neighborhood, which he visits regularly. He is still somewhat shy and a loner. He does not quite fit in with the tight groupings in our large high school. Mother states he may move in with his father after his junior year, as did his oldest brother. The move will be prompted by the fact he would be attending a much smaller and more personal high school in a small town setting. Alan continues to maintain the academic, social, and emotional progress he has made.

Units of Attention

The locus of concern for the social worker rested at different times and in different ways on Alan, the regular and special education teachers, the principal, mother, father, and stepfather, and the outside therapist. In the beginning of the case there were at least five areas of serious risk for Alan:

1. He had just moved into the district. He has limited skills to handle the shift in schools, friendships, and living arrangements.
2. He has a learning disability, which makes it difficult for him to perform at an expected second-grade level.
3. His mother and father had just separated, and he was reacting to this.
4. His regular education teacher had difficulty responding appropriately to his slowness, his feeling overwhelmed, and his anxiety.
5. Alan was dealing with an overwhelming situation by withdrawal. He showed depression and later displayed suicidal ideation.

The risks at this point were that further deterioration either of the relationship with the teacher or of the home situation would place Alan in danger. The home and the classroom situation needed to be stabilized in their relation to Alan. An appropriate learning situation needed to be developed. Alan needed much support and relational attention as he worked his way through these threatening contingincies in his life.

One way to organize these complex choices for assessment and for intervention is to think of them as units of attention. A unit of attention is a chosen point of most effective change, a point or set of points in the system where, if change takes place, other positive changes will also become possible. For example, the social worker started by assessing the situation, and then interviewing Alan, the teacher, and the parents. Initially the social worker did an assessment and developed collaboration among Alan's teachers. She suggested an outside therapist to the parents and brought in resources from the school to support Alan's coping with school and to help Alan deal with a possible learning disability. The mother would not accept outside counseling at first. The social worker continued to monitor the situation in the meantime and provided consultation to the classroom teacher and the learning disability and reading specialists. Shifts in the situation brought out different units of attention. After the initial second-grade teacher went on maternity leave, Alan's new second-grade teacher was able to make better use of consultation, but then Alan's drawing changed the nature of the problem and brought out a different focus on everyone's part.

The worker got directly involved with Alan and also worked with him through others. She was eventually successful with convincing the parents to get outside help for Alan. They themselves became individually somewhat more involved with Alan. The principal became a unit of attention in planning Alan's third-grade placement. At different points during the following years the team developed different responses to the changing situation. The social worker's focus depended on her assessment of the needs in the situation, her competence in different areas, the time available, and the extent of development of the social work program in the school. She was responding to the realistic limitations and opportunities of a changing process.

Units of Attention: Teachers and School Administration

The social worker provided a good deal of consultation to Alan's teachers, and was active in the process of class placement. With teachers, administrators, and parents, the social worker is working with Alan through others. Many times, developing a program or consulting with teachers provides enough environmental change for the pupil to accomplish his or her own change. Changes in the classroom thus afford the pupil an opportunity to accomplish learning and social developmental tasks. Sometimes nothing more is needed than consultation. In these cases extending intervention to the parents or pupil would be unnecessary and therefore intrusive. It is a matter of assessment.

Unit of Attention: The Parents and the Therapist

The parents had just separated and Alan was reacting to it. For the parents Alan's issues brought out their old, unresolved issues around parenting. It was not the function of the school social worker to focus, as sort of a family therapist, on the marital process in itself. On the other hand, the social worker could help each parent focus appropriately on how this was affecting Alan, as well as to focus on his needs, which were getting lost in the process. Taking a realistic, strengths-based approach, she encouraged each toward positive involvement with him. This eventually opened the possibility of Alan getting outside help. Both parents would relate to Alan's needs in different ways, since they were connected with different sectors of Alan's life situation. The social worker avoided negative involvement with their old marital issues. She also avoided potential old and negative issues with the stepfather when he appeared on the scene. By that time Alan was able to accommodate relationships with both father and stepfather. This would be a major indicator of some beginning resolution of his more dramatic concerns. The social worker would also collaborate with the outside therapist in the same focused way.

Unit of Attention: The Pupil

The third unit of attention is the pupil. Whatever changes take place in the classroom environment and in what the school is able to offer, the pupil needs to use them and to deal with personal change. Building on the sound base of a connection with home and school, the combination of small changes in home, school, and pupil is often much more powerful than an intensive focus on any single factor.

Alan's developmental needs, his learning process, and the family and school worlds that surround that process have centrality in the case. For Alan the family and school worlds were dysfunctional in relation to his attempts at active coping and learning. A whole environmental world—from parent through school secretary, janitor, school psychologist, social worker, teachers, and principal—waits to see whether and how Alan will cope. The social worker moved among all the parts of this world to help that world work for Alan. She adapted methodology to the particular needs in the situation—to help Alan make sense of his world and discover what he could do. With Alan she used individual and group modalities. She used relational qualities of empathy and good communication to help him cope with himself and his relational world. She would be there for him, even though they might not always need to get together in one-to-one sessions. Alan did the work. From Alan's perspective the learning process in school has to be a central developmental event. But his eroding relationships, his learning disabilities, and his social skills problems made it difficult to carry out these tasks. Educational tasks are so salient to the maturation of many children that even more than clinical interventions, there may be no more powerful way to help Alan grow, particularly if the family can participate in and support the process.

The social worker worked with Alan's surroundings, with Alan when necessary, and then indirectly through others. The daily check-ins were crucial in second grade, when Alan's suicidal ideation was of concern. His second-semester teacher was more attuned to him than the first had been. In third grade the carefully chosen teacher was also attuned to Alan. Alan made more progress and another therapist was involved. There were a few contacts in the beginning of the school year and then availability for more when needed. In fourth grade there was some contact with Alan around accommodating his stepfather. Alan also attended a social skills group led by the social worker.

In actual practice, the social worker works with a variety of units of attention at the same time. The focus on these units will also change over time. In Alan's situation there were various permutations of units of attention over the years as the family situation, the teachers, and Alan himself changed. A paradox is that although the worker actively shifted her role to fit the developing situation, most of the work was done by Alan, his family, and the school, as all of them shifted over time and in relation to each other. Thus a way to understand intervention was that the intervention supported the work that would need to be done by Alan. The worker did not need to be the central focus at any time or to give an exhaustive amount of energy to the situation. With the situation and its dynamics accurately assessed, the principal actors did the work. She could use the energy from their tasks in relation to each other as the main tool for change. The task of the social worker was to work with the principal actors, using a variety of intervention modalities, and to develop situations in which this work could be done most productively. Effectiveness did not come from the use of a single modality, but from matching modalities with the situation, the energies, and the capabilities of its participants. This approach to assessment and intervention is more complex, but undoubtedly more effective. As any team member will recognize, effective interventions are accomplished not by one member alone, possibly the school social worker, but by all the participants in the arena. Ineffective interventions are likewise a product of the participants in interaction.

EXPERT PRACTITIONER PANEL'S RESPONSES TO THE CASE OF ALAN

For this eighth edition, Alan's case was reviewed by an expert practitioner panel of six school social work practitioners, reflecting some of the diversity and realities of present-day school social work. These veteran practitioners all agreed to read the case example and provide written responses to the case of Alan focused on (1) what they would have done with Alan's case if Alan went to a school in their community, and (2) what they thought this case could do to inform the current context of school social work as they saw it in their state and region. The responses were written by the following and are excerpted in the section that follows:

◆ Pat Beauchemin, school social worker in the Barrington, Rhode Island, public schools with twenty-two years of experience;
◆ Ann List, retired coordinator of school social work services and school social worker in schools in Albuquerque, New Mexico;
◆ Erin McManis, school social worker in the Chicago suburbs and a faculty member in Loyola University's Family and School Partnership Program;
◆ Barb Mestling, retired school social worker from Prospect Heights, Illinois, and adjunct faculty at Loyola University Chicago;
◆ Dena Radtke, coordinator of school social work, transition school to work, and community services in the Milwaukee Public Schools; and
◆ Kathleen Usaj, past president of the Ohio School Social Workers Association and a retired school social worker from the Cleveland Municipal School District.

All of the panelists identified what the worker did as what they would want to do in schools. All were impressed with the school social worker's level of skill, moving smoothly from one system to another, developing consultation. At the same time they thought she used highly effective clinical skills without simply being drawn into an exclusive (and, as such, potentially ineffective) clinical relationship with Alan separate from his surroundings. No one questioned that this is the way school social worker practice ought to be. Many were quite comfortable that they could certainly practice this way in a school.

Rhode Island school social worker Beauchemin saw in the case a full development of the roles of the school social worker and noted that she also has the opportunity to work with children and teachers on a longer-term basis, given her district responsibilities spanning preschool through fifth grade. From her perspective the key to the case was the fact that the seasoned school social worker in the case intuitively and systematically knew when and where to intervene, thus creating a perception that her work appeared seamless and that she functioned with a high degree of ease. Conceptualizing the interventions provided by school social workers as units of attention not only provides for a clearer picture, but also an appreciation of the multilevel interventions that occur simultaneously, in most instances. This focus recognizes many of the assumptions found in solution-focused practice, that small change is generative (Walter & Peller, 1992). Such efforts enhance a sense of hope, as school social worker and client system coconstruct various interventions for Alan to realize his potentiality in all aspects of his life. Beauchemin added, "When *IT* all comes together, people in the education environment say we work 'our magic'! However, those of us who perform these daily tasks know the tremendous amount of thoughtful deliberation, clinical judgment and energy behind each and every step of the way."

The case illustrates the work of a professional who operates from a strength-based perspective, and thus generates trust and positive change with all members of the client system at various points of contact. From the onset, the practitioner assumes the researcher role as she conducts a comprehensive social assessment. Having an understanding of the sequence and interplay of challenging events, the school social worker is now in a position to provide an interpretation of Alan's affective state, his psycho/social development, and the strengths and weaknesses operating within his home/school/community environments. The practitioner's synthesis of this critical assessment serves to educate the school personnel and contributes to the direction of Alan's education program. This process continues with the practitioner's performing the FBA at specific times through the course of her contact with Alan. The multiple FBAs further inform her practice and provide guidance to the other members of the team for their respective educational interventions. In her role as coordinator, the practitioner provides important case management services to keep communication open and collaborative between the educators as they work together to assist Alan in his learning. By virtue of the ongoing consultation meetings, the social worker recognizes her enabling and facilitative role in the group. She skillfully provides an opportunity for others to share their successful teaching experiences, thereby influencing a change in the thinking of Alan's second-grade teacher. Throughout this unique long-term working relationship, the school social worker remains in her advocate role, as when she approached administration to discuss Alan's high-priority status and the need to move quickly on meeting with parents and educators. In Alan's case, he was on a special education watch with the various targeted interventions in place registering at a tier 2 level. Clearly, these interventions were not enough to prevent his continuing decline when the school social worker provided critical information through a second FBA that moved him in the direction of a wraparound service model, where more-intensive services are delivered.

The arts of mediating and negotiating, two other important roles endemic to our work, require patience, timing, and fostering trust among all the members of the team. This is evident as the social work practitioner in the case of Alan works over time to assist his mother in her recognition of her son's fragile emotional health and in his mother's ultimate acceptance of the referral for outside counseling. Oftentimes, the other education professionals cannot understand and are quick to judge the reasons why families do not "just get counseling." Based on my own experience in similar situations, I am most certain the practitioner assumed the role of educator with the team, helping team members to understand their own biases and develop an appreciation for the motivation of individuals to determine for themselves their own path to finding solutions to complicated situations.

Beauchemin wrote, "I was pleased to see the school social worker recognize the impact of the family and divorce issues on Alan, as well as her encouragement of the parents to address the 'old conflicts' in outside treatment. It is clear she is cognizant of the limitations of her role within the school environment, and moves to preserve the realistic boundaries of her working relationship with Alan and his parents. I believe this is critical in our educational practice setting. The broker role is a significant intervention in making important connections with families and outside of school therapeutic services. We too often see someone take on a direct service role with the child/student in isolation from the work that needs to be done in the context of the family. Such interventions provide a disservice to the child/student and their family."

In addition to what was done, others suggested some additional things that they might have done with Alan's case:

Barb Mestling, retired school social worker from Prospect Heights, Illinois and adjunct faculty at Loyola University Chicago, would have involved the principal in encouraging the parent to take Alan for further assessment to determine the seriousness of his depression and suicidal ideation. She also would have considered whole school programs for social-emotional learning in terms of coping strategies for dealing with loss and change. Erin McManis, a school social worker in the Chicago suburbs and a faculty member in Loyola University's Family and School Partnership Program, would also consider reaching out to the grandparents since they live in close proximity and are mentioned as supportive of Alan. During a time of emotional turmoil in Alan's immediate family, it may be helpful for the grandparents to realize the role they can play in Alan's overall adjustment to a new family situation and his need to develop lifelong resiliency by being a consistent, positive presence for him. Erin said she probably would also have seen Alan on an individual basis more than the social worker did, if she had time. They could work on feelings, identification, coping skills, and support for him during the divorce process without decreasing her focus and teacher consultation. In looking at the whole school context and other possible areas for units of attention, the social worker could set up a program or club designed to welcome and acclimate new students such as a peer leader or peer ambassador program. Additionally, there may also be a need for ongoing work and/or training for teachers such as Alan's second-grade teacher who struggle with students like Alan.

Additionally, the school social worker has a very important role to play in positive behavioral interventions and supports (PBIS) and response to intervention (RTI)/multitiered system support (MTSS). It was interesting to hear how the expert practitioners viewed the practice of school social work with Alan's case and how it would fit within these emergent programs.

Dena Radtke, coordinator of school social work, transition school to work, and community services in the Milwaukee Public Schools, noted that school social workers in Milwaukee Public Schools are at the center of PBIS. They naturally engage, as the social worker did in Alan's case, at all three tiers of support. However, the PBIS framework brings a greater need for school social workers to monitor progress, review and analyze data, use data to determine appropriate interventions strategies, develop FBAs and behavioral plans with other team members, and identify and utilize evidence/research-based practices. Fewer referrals are now made directly to the school social worker because they come through the PBIS system of early identification. School social workers have taken a more active role in facilitating social-academic groups and the check-in/check-out process at tier 2 as well as leading the tier 3 educational wraparound and Rehabilitation, Empowerment, Natural Supports, Education, Work (RENEW) processes. They have been placed into team facilitation roles that require objectivity and the ability to guide the group and its dynamics. This responsibility has led social workers increasingly to be seen in a leadership role. Their work is more visible, as is their accountability. If services are not seen as meeting the current needs of the educational system, their value is diminished. In the same vein, Barb Mestling notes that the language, even some of the procedures, of Alan's case and the emergent language/procedures of schools using PBIS and RTI/MTSS could be different. This could imply a very different understanding of practice. Such translation of practice into education still needs to take place.

There were several concerns about whether the case reflected the actual practice of school social work in their states and localities, and about this level of skill was present in the literature, or was being taught anywhere. In some states school social work is not well supported by the SEA. Educators need a better understanding of the school social worker role, even to the point of a role description. In some school districts, categorical funding limits the school social worker role to direct individual and group interventions for specific pupils, rather than to a fully developed consultative and team presence.

Kathleen Usaj, past president of the Ohio School Social Workers Association and a retired school social worker from the Cleveland Municipal School District, points out that Ohio has school social work licensure laws, but school social work services are not a mandated school service. As a result few districts employ school social workers. Schools contract with mental health agencies to provide counseling services to children on Medicaid. It is important that cases such as Alan's be used to persuade school boards and state legislators that school social work services be mandated in all states. It is imperative that school social workers utilize their macro skills to advocate for these services.

The point is echoed by Ann B. List, who is a retired school social worker from the Albuquerque, New Mexico, schools. She wondered how Alan's case might translate into a job description for school social workers everywhere. Such a description would help clarify social work roles in schools. It would highlight the fluidity of the strategies school social workers employ in their person-in-environment orientation. Concepts such as units of attention, target of intervention and school, community family and child, and so on very effectively reflect the worldview required of school social workers. She wondered how, in the schools she is familiar with, the social worker could get administrative support to work with such flexibility as a case manager and consultant for this pupil. She wondered how the social worker's position in Alan's case was funded. From her perspective, school social work positions that are funded by Medicaid, and special education privilege individual and small group interventions, over consultation, case management, and family and community activities. Finally, the case signals a gap in professional development. A number of respondents, including Ann List, wondered where the worker would get this level of skill, particularly in consultation and teamwork, when training programs and the literature in these areas are just beginning to develop.

CONCLUSION

Six themes emerge from the practitioner comments on the case.

1. Although differences exist, reflecting local conditions, there is a common core of school social work as it has been practiced for many years. Every expert practitioner panelist recognized this core and was comfortable with it. This core is continually updating itself as the developing mission of education, the mission of social work, and emergent effective methodology come together.
2. The social worker brings the resources of the whole school to bear in relation to the pupil's needs. Consultation and developing teamwork are crucial skills in making this happen.
3. There is power in individualizing these resources in relation to the emergent and developing needs of the pupil. It was the individualization, not simply a specific method, that helped make things effective. The individualization reflected an assessment of Alan's development, the inevitable and predictable crises, as well as the whole of his situation, especially his relations with his family and with the learning tasks he faced.
4. Much of this school social worker's effectiveness in the case of Alan comes not from one intervention, but from the totality of interventions in relation to Alan's development, his tasks, his membership in the school, and his relations with his family. In the same spirit, these interventions were often done through others, using consultation for example, rather than merely from one-to-one contacts with Alan.
5. There is an appropriate power in the family involvement, since schooling itself is an expression of family functions. The school social worker assists family members, fragmented as the family may be, to work with the pupil and to support the pupil's progress. Conversely, it is not a function of school social work to work directly on the marriage.
6. The social worker was in charge of her professional initiatives, rather than being pressured by others, perhaps from the team, perhaps from administration, to less-effective interventions.

References

Walter, J. L., & Peller, J. E. (1992). *Becoming solution-focused in brief therapy.* New York: Brunner-Mazel.

Wolkow, H. S. (1991). The dynamics of systems involvement with children in school: A case perspective. In R. Constable, S. McDonald, & J. P. Flynn (Eds.), *School social work: Practice and research perspectives* (2nd ed.). Chicago: Lyceum Books.

Appendix B
The Wonderland of Social Work in the Schools, or How Alice Learned to Cope

Sally G. Goren
University of Illinois at Chicago

- ◆ Systems Theory
- ◆ Visibility
- ◆ Viability
- ◆ Value

A social worker entering a school for the first time may feel a bit like Alice as she tumbled into the Rabbit Hole and landed in the long corridor, finding it lined with locked doors. Only when she discovered the means by which she could change her size and shape did she begin her adventures in Wonderland. Throughout her experience in the pages of Carroll's book, Alice used her judgment, her feelings, and her integrity to deal with the characters whom she met. This chapter will attempt to offer some guidance to the social worker who finds him- or herself in the Wonderland of a school system. The worker may initially feel that his or her district or building resembles a series of locked doors with bits of the madness of Wonderland emerging through the cracks. To function effectively, it is essential that the social worker named Alice (or Alex) learn to identify within this setting the means by which he or she can achieve that optimal effectiveness that will prove his or her value to the system and meet personal professional standards and personal needs. Therefore, an evaluation of the system will be based on some understanding of systems theory. It is this writer's belief that each social worker in a school constitutes a "miniagency" complete in one person. On such an assumption, I will examine the roles the social worker might play, the various constituencies with whom the social worker interacts, and the question of accountability.

SYSTEMS THEORY

To flesh out this view of school social work, it is important to share some common understanding of systems theory. If we view any system as a complex, adaptive organization that is continually generating, elaborating patterns of actions and interaction, we see that the school, as a system, must be understood as an entity that is greater than the sum of its parts. It has discrete properties that need to be evaluated if we are to identify the points in which social work interventions may be made to ensure the maximum effectiveness mentioned previously. To view the school as an adaptive organization supports the social worker's theoretical underpinnings in which linkage, environmental impact, and enablement of each individual's maximum development are held in high value. The systems' definition also emphasizes the interactive elements that may impede or aid goal achievement. Thus the social worker is led to identify the junctures of interactions that bridge or fragment the discrete elements within the system (Costin, 1975).

Looking further into one's own school system, it is important to estimate its openness. An open system receives input, produces output, and interacts with all the actors within and outside of the system. The interactions may not always be agreeable, but there must be the opportunity for the school, its administrators, teachers, support staff, students, parents, and community to be heard and to hear one another. An important element of a viable system is, in fact, tension. This becomes the impetus for change and growth, for negotiation, for development, and for effective, productive relationships. Another element of the open system is that of feedback (Fordor, 1976). This speaks to a communications system that generates action in response to information that is the basis for constructive change.

As an employee of the school, it is critically important that the social worker define him- or herself within the system. The opportunity to be a significant interactor rests on the social worker's ability to inform the other actors of the social work role, to accept the input from others within and outside the school, and to respond and to produce output that is designed to meet needs that have been identified. A systems' understanding speaks emphatically to the need for the social worker to be visible, viable, and valuable. I will examine next how these qualities may be evidenced within the school.

VISIBILITY

To whom is the social worker important? In what ways is the social worker significant? The answer to these questions is that the school social worker is important and significant to everyone and in every way. The social worker has an impact on any person with whom he or she interacts. To look at the possible breadth of the assignment, I examine several factors defined by Lela Costin (1972) as a guide to visibility. The effective social worker will function as:

1. Provider of direct counseling services to pupils,
2. Advocate for specific pupils or groups of pupils whose needs are underserved or unmet,
3. Consultant to administrators in their task of program development and policy change,
4. Consultant to teachers to enhance their ability to create a productive climate for maximum learning,
5. Link to community services and facilitator between the school and community in obtaining necessary services for pupils and their families,
6. Leader in coordination of interdisciplinary teams providing service to pupils, and
7. Assessor of needs of individual pupils and of the school system as related to program development.

All of these factors demand that the social worker become known to the administrators, the teachers, and pupil services personnel who function within the school or school district. The social worker also needs to create an identity with the pupils in the school and, from these contacts, with the families whose children may be the recipients of social work services. How one fleshes out his or her visibility will vary but may include:

1. Informal meetings with teachers and other school personnel over lunch or coffee, before or after the pupils are in the building;
2. Regularly scheduled conferences with administrators and with teachers with whom the social worker shares responsibility for a child's welfare;
3. Initiation of contact with community agencies to whom the social worker may refer children or families for service;
4. Explanation of services to families via attendance at meetings of the PTA or other parent groups;

5. Responsibility for presentations at in-service meetings for teachers and/or administrators;
6. Assumption of leadership at pupil services personnel team meetings; and
7. Attendance and presentations at school board meetings.

There are many ways that the social worker's visibility may be developed and the particular manner in which this is demonstrated will depend on the social worker's understanding of the politics of the school and the district. As early in one's entry into a district as possible, one must identify the power structure. Determining that will direct the worker toward the creation of relationships that will provide him or her with the support necessary for provision of service. To attempt to work without such support from the person or persons who wield power is an exercise in frustration and a sure diminution of the effectiveness of the efforts. These remarks are not meant to imply that all workers in all settings need to be allied with the power structure, but the worker does need to identify where the power lies in order to understand how his or her work may be enhanced or inhibited. The development of successful working relationships will depend on the clinical assessment skills and the use of relationship building skills that are in the educational and employment experience of all social workers. However, it must be stated that even the most highly skilled workers may be unable to achieve an alignment with the administrative power structure in some instances. Acknowledging that there may be more frustration than gratification in such settings, the social worker may still be able to function as an advocate for children and parents, particularly when the law supports necessary services. The social worker may be a mediator between teachers and administration on behalf of individual children or particular programs. In short, the social worker retains the responsibility to carry out the interventive roles fulfilled by workers in any field of practice (Compton & Gallaway, 1994).

Visibility also implies availability. To be ready to assist a principal or nurse in handling a crisis such as child abuse is an excellent way to cement one's position in the school. To provide linkage to a neighborhood day-care center for a child whose parent has become seriously ill demonstrates the effectiveness of relationship building in the community. To educate parents regarding the symptoms of childhood depression or normal preadolescent behavior presents the social worker in an appropriate and useful educator role. To inform the school board of new legislation affecting the school and to present a plan for meeting the criteria demanded by the law again places the social worker in a position of enormous value to the school community. It is no longer possible to limit one's role to individual or group counseling of children, though only a few years ago studies indicated that many school social workers defined their responsibilities in just such limited terms

(Costin, 1969). Fortunately, there has been a shift in this narrow definition, and social workers in schools are engaging in the variety of tasks that have been mentioned above (Costin, 1969). All of this leads to an examination of the viability of the school social worker.

VIABILITY

Linked to visibility is viability. Not only does the school social worker need to be seen, the social worker needs to be seen in action. Creativity is the catchword, and the ability to use oneself creatively with the interactors in the school system is imperative. No longer remaining in one's office counseling children, the worker must assess special needs of the system and develop programs to meet them. If a classroom appears to be out of control, how can the worker assist the teacher, the students, or their families? What will meet the needs of the greatest number? It might be regular consultation with the teacher or an effective education project with the class, or several small group meetings with a portion of the pupils in the classroom. Perhaps a need for systematic handling of truancy problems exists. The worker may develop a plan to meet this need in coordination with the principal or assistant principal. Families or some members of the school board may be included in the development of the plan. Time spent with community agencies may alter previous adversarial positions or simply establish a modus operandi that had not existed and which can be functional not only for the worker but also for other school personnel who identify children in need of particular services. We again see how assessment skills, organizational skills, and finally treatment skills can be applied to a school system to provide maximum learning opportunities for the pupils served by that system.

Not only might the social worker be creative in relation to direct services to pupils with specific needs; he or she can be equally creative in identifying system needs and developing programs to address them.

A social worker who noted considerable distrust and low morale among teachers in a junior high school established a series of meetings and, assuming the role of facilitator, enabled the teachers to examine some of the system problems and the impact on their work. As concerns were shared and ideas for dealing with them were explored, the suspiciousness of the teachers declined, and fruitful relationships soon developed. They admitted similar anxieties about their classroom performances and, as a unit, were able to prepare criteria for the evaluation of their work and advocate for their adoption by the administration.

In another instance, a social worker worked with a principal and pupil personnel staff to develop an enrichment program for minority first-grade students. The social worker was able to provide some research expertise that aided the program's acceptance by the school board and by the families whose children attended the school.

Since PL 94-142 was passed in 1975 (now reformulated as PL 105-117, Individuals with Disabilities Education Act, IDEA), opportunities to expand social work services in the schools have increased. The law provides funding for districts to provide new services for children with disabilities and therefore has led to the hiring of new staff and the development of creative programs to serve their target groups in ways previously not possible. In many instances, the guidelines of the law have been imaginatively and broadly interpreted in those districts that have seen the mandate as an opportunity rather than a burden. It behooves the school social worker to be in the lead in such program development and to take an active role in the execution of new programs.

Built into the law is the necessity for accountability, an ever-increasing requirement in all fields of educational and social work practice. Without minimizing the additional time this demands, and recognizing that it can be regarded as a burden for an already overworked staff, I want to emphasize that this is also a chance to dramatically detail the breadth, content, and effectiveness of social work services. The law has provided us with the impetus to devise systems that can readily indicate who we serve, how we serve them, and the time allocation the various services require. This brings us to an examination of the final V: the value of the school social worker.

VALUE

Early in this chapter I commented on the total agency concept implicit in each social worker in the schools. It is eminently clear to any reader who is employed in schools that this is true. Is it clear to teachers and administrators? As a professional working within a host setting, the requirement for interpretation of one's function is continual. This is so because the responsibilities are broad and change as needs of the school community change. Because the other professional staff are also continually changing, new staff need to be informed in order to best utilize our services. Implicit in the statement above is the responsibility of the social worker to have control of the definition of his or her role. Although it will always be defined in relation to an accurate assessment of service needs, it is the social worker who has the most intimate knowledge of his or her own skills and training, and this needs to be communicated to staff in a school setting. To expect that teachers, speech therapists, principals, psychologists, and others know what one does is to permit any and all of the staff to dictate what to do, how to do it, and when to do it. Rather than allow the job to be defined by others, it behooves a social worker entering into practice in a school to view him- or herself as that total agency with the intent of meeting the school and community needs. These needs will be addressed within the knowledge, skill, and ethics of the social work profession; therefore, it is incumbent on the social worker to have a comfortable professional identity that can be expressed soundly to delineate the functions the social worker may undertake in the setting.

Just as it is the responsibility of the worker to be visible and viable in the school building, it is even more important that the social worker, from the point of entrance into a school system, share in the control of the evaluation process. Defining one's role and the scope of the job establishes the basis on which an evaluation of the social worker will be made by the responsible administrator. If the social worker regards him- or herself as that total agency, he or she needs to think and act as administrator, supervisor, and line worker.

As an administrator, one partializes time to meet the needs of the organization. This determination of the allocation of one's resources should be cooperatively established with the school district official to whom the social worker is directly responsible. The breadth of function, client contact, and caseload management are all part of this role. In order to have realistic criteria on which one's evaluation will be based, the social worker needs to be a participant in their development. If a district has a standard evaluation form for teachers, it might need to be adapted so that it is appropriate for a social worker or else another one should be developed that will better judge the overall effect of social work services in the building. In the role of administrator, it might be well to establish regular conferences with the building principal, the special education coordinator, and/or any other administrative-level personnel who might have an impact on the worker's position. This will continuously inform them of one's work and, of course, of one's value.

There are a number of situations with which this writer is familiar where administrators avoid contact with the social worker and reluctantly have any interaction. In other districts, the principal or assistant principals are intrusively involved in the case-by-case management of the social worker. In the first-mentioned situation, administrators must be informed via some method of one's overall work. This may be achieved by memos, weekly or monthly statistical and/or case reviews, and extensive written documentation of any cases wherein issues of legal responsibility may be a factor. The reasons for avoidance may be varied, but the worker must maintain professional linkage with administration by whatever means possible. In the case of the overly involved administrator, some methods similar to those employed with the "absent" administrator may serve to satisfy the control needs of that person. If the administrator is convinced that the worker is sharing with him or her the case management issues that the administrator feels necessary to know, the worker may find him- or herself freer to pursue the tasks as they have been assessed.

There are many suggestions for management of the system in this chapter. Each may work in some situations and not in others. Many ideas have not been mentioned. Nonetheless, the message is to experiment with various means of engagement, reporting, and integration of social work services within the educational milieu. Failure of one method does not foretell failure of another, and perseverance will be rewarded in most circumstances.

As one's own supervisor, the social worker must determine individual and group needs of the pupils with whom he or she works. Judging the necessity of a referral, any indication of the need for consultation, and the type of interventive role that will most readily meet the assessed need are assists the line worker receives from a supervisor. In most school districts, the line worker must carry this dual responsibility. Some districts do provide social work supervision or consultation, some have access to psychiatric consultation, but many school social workers have no established avenue to obtain this kind of input. The need for input, feedback, and direction has led some social workers in schools to develop informal consultation groups. Without devaluing the autonomy the school social worker enjoys, the burden of such total responsibility for one's work can be shared with others. However, the significance of the responsibility should be accorded adequate valuation by the district's administration.

There is no need to review the many, varied tasks the social worker, as line worker, undertakes. There is need, however, to account for them. The importance of counting contacts with children, with parents, with teachers, and with community resources cannot be overemphasized. Adding the time to fill out necessary reports and records is imperative. This kind of statistical record will provide the basis for the evaluation of effectiveness of service. Following the time keeping is the need to demonstrate effectiveness of one's action. If the social worker has shared in the development of goals with teachers and administrators, he or she will be able to share in the evaluation of his or her service. The fact that the social worker may not be effective in every instance should not deter him or her from creating an evaluation system that will demonstrate incremental change, diagnostic reassessments, and goal renegotiations. It is important to show that service plans are related to jointly determined goals and to provide some rationale for success or failure of the plans. To reemphasize the importance of one's involvement in this evaluative process, one might consider designing a short form that could be used with any child, group, family, or teacher. The form might include goals, methods for achievement, and time spent in an effort to meet the goals.

This entire section on value may have been better titled evaluation. It is the author's contention that one's value is best understood via evaluation of one's work, and the plea is, therefore, for each school social worker to carry a major responsibility for the negotiation and creation of the criteria on which such an evaluation will be based. This is another way that one informs, educates, and indeed, determines the parameters of one's work. Control is shared, goals are shared, and power is shared. The social workers who can actively demonstrate their value will find that they have a strong advocate in the principal or other administrator, and that kind of advocacy will agitate for more social work services and, hopefully, more social workers.

To be an effective participant in the creation of an atmosphere that will enhance learning opportunities for children, the social worker in the school must use all his or her best clinical and organizational skills. The social worker must first know who and what he or she is professionally. He or she must develop respect for the work of others. Trust will grow as hopes and expectations are shared and common goals are agreed on. The social worker who creates a significant position for him- or herself in a school system will have an accurate knowledge of the system and a clear knowledge of his or her position in it. The social worker will know the loci of power, the system needs, and the style of all the interactors within the system. This assessment will be the basis for the social worker's creation of an appropriate role. The social worker in a school, in essence, is always using professional skills. Whether meeting with a child or a teacher, arranging a contractual agreement with a family service agency, or consulting with a pupil services team, the effective social worker will be actively assessing and treating.

As Alice moved through her adventures in Wonderland and the Looking Glass, she became more assertive and gained control. Alice (or Alex) in the school system will find that active involvement in all aspects of that system will be the foundation for provision of service, acceptance within the system, and professional satisfaction for a job very well done. The social worker will also be very tired at the end of each day, recognizing that he or she has indeed used him- or herself skillfully throughout every contact that he or she has had. The social worker will have been visible, viable, and of value to everyone encountered during the day at school.

References

Compton, B., & Galaway, B. (1994). *Social work processes* (5th ed.). Pacific Grove, CA: Brooks/Cole.

Costin, L. B. (1969). An analysis of the tasks of school social workers. *Social Service Review, 43*, 274–285.

Costin, L. B. (1972). Adaptations on the delivery of school social work services. *Social Casework, 53*, 348–354.

Costin, L. B. (1975). School social work practice: A new model. *Social Work, 20*, 136.

Fordor, A. (1976). Social work and system theory. *British Journal of Social Work, 6*. (Reprinted from *Social work processes* [2nd ed.], pp. 98–101, by B. Compton & B. Galaway, 1979, Homewood, IL: Dorsey.)

Appendix C
Putting It All Together: A Hypothetical Case Study (Devin)

Let us begin by following a simple referral for a case study reevaluation of Devin, with the individualized education program (IEP) process and service sequence through each of the stages of the process. For purposes of our first illustration let us assume that Devin cannot participate in the district-wide general education assessment. Thus he will require annual goals and short-term objectives, as every child has required through the implementation of Individuals with Disabilities Education Improvement Act (IDEIA).

We will break down the steps that should be followed to arrive at those goals and objectives in the school social worker's contribution to the IEP. The steps represent a way of clarifying our own goals and involvement in developing the IEP. The reader should keep in mind that this is a hypothetical case study and that the type and extent of the school social worker's involvement in a particular case will depend on the individual child's needs as determined by the IEP team. We will begin with the presenting problem.

THE PRESENTING CONCERNS

In order to be eligible for funding, the concerns must relate to the categories of disabilities written into the regulations. However, the fact that the child fits into one of the categories—for example, hearing impaired—does not automatically make him a candidate for social work intervention. Inability to deal with stress, potential breakdown of social functioning, or needed improvement of social functioning are general reasons for referral to a social worker. The additional stress of a disability and the need for individualized environmental support systems are reasons that many exceptional children need social work help. The child with a particular disability may have difficulty coping with the educational and social skill demands of the school. He may need help in acquiring such skills and/or in dealing with experiences that are new. One of the best ways to help students through a case study assessment is to use the strengths perspective to help build on things that they already do well (Gleason, 2007).

Devin is a twelve-year-old with multiple physical disabilities who has been receiving special education services for his physical impairments and his educable mentally handicapped service labels since kindergarten. While in elementary school, Devin showed steady progress in being able to function in regular education settings, owing to his generally positive attitude and his own self-described efforts to fit in with his peers. Other strengths noted by Devin's case file and direct contact with Devin and his parents are that he is eager to please adults and respects authority once he knows he is respected; he has a great sense of humor and can be fun for peers to be around when he is calm and focused; and he has parents who are determined to do whatever they can to help him succeed in school. Based on this progress, in starting sixth grade the school recommended that Devin spend the majority of his day in regular education classes with his resource teacher being involved in providing push-in inclusion services. However, he has had some academic and behavioral struggles, and these problems seem to have increased with his transition to junior high. As part of his three-year reevaluation, his resource teacher has expressed concerns that his excessive demands for attention are impeding his learning process in several general education classes, particularly in physical education (gym).

DEVIN'S SITUATION AS A WHOLE

The school social worker's conference with Devin's teacher and parents resulted in a picture of a boy who, while having many personal strengths, has had an uneven performance in school; his ability to function in school has been affected at times by parent-school disagreement on the degree of independence he should be allowed. He is currently enrolled in both special and regular education classes and his teachers report that though he started with his trademark positive attitude, he is now showing poor adjustment to some of these classes, and is often putting lots of demands on adults for attention, and withdrawing from peer contacts. Though the family is close and Devin enjoys close relationships with his parents, for this transition his parents have had difficulty agreeing on the tasks he should be involved in and on his expected level of self-care, even though they are unified in wanting Devin to be in as many regular education classes as possible. Consequently, at this point Devin's participation in the family and in care of himself appears to have regressed, at least with this new school experience. The social worker's assessment draws some connections between Devin's role in the family, his parents' feelings, and the way Devin has played out some of these family-role interactions in school behaviors, particularly with parent-like school figures and teachers. The statement also includes alternative plans for working with the family, Devin, and his teachers. The results of the social worker's assessment, combined with the information gathered by the other team members, will be used by the team in the evaluative conference and later to formulate the statement of present levels of educational functioning in the IEP.

DEVIN'S PRESENTING ISSUES AS THEY ARE EXPERIENCED IN THE CONTEXT OF EDUCATION

The next step is to define Devin's issues as it is being experienced in the classroom and in relation to the goals of education. At the risk of oversimplifying, we may provide several social parameters of the educational problem. One parameter is that of engagement or withdrawal from educational tasks appropriate to the child's capabilities. The child may either engage in the learning process with distracting, attention-getting, inappropriately aggressive behavior, or withdraw from the process, attempting to compensate in other ways for the withdrawal. A second parameter is that of engagement or withdrawal from relationships with other children. Students need to learn social skills appropriate to their own maturational level. The learning of these social skills influences the performance of educational tasks. Thus, there is a direct relation between the learning environment and the child's social maturation.

To follow our example, the school wishes to place Devin in a general education gym class for the first time (he has been previously in an adaptive gym class due to his special education needs). We can predict with some certainty that Devin will place high demands on the gym teacher and the other students. The parents, although accepting of the idea, might endanger the arrangement because of their own anxiety and worries about Devin. Failure in the gym class could generalize to several other classes where he has recently made some adjustment. There is particular concern with the gym class because of dressing, showering, and inherent physical competition. Any one of these factors might place Devin's use of what the school could offer him at risk. What we know about the problem allows us to predict with some degree of accuracy the chances of goal achievement within a behavior setting and some ability to generalize to the overall ecology of the school. This understanding allows us to move to the next stage—definition of the problem in behavioral terms.

The Presenting Behavior

The purpose of this stage is to state the school social worker's formulation of Devin's issues in behavioral terms and to relate it to the educational goals established earlier. Behavioral terms are statements of a person's present functioning, or what Devin is presently doing. These terms establish a baseline for goals and objectives and must be specific. Behavioral objectives risk fragmentation and being meaningless if they do not flow from the process of problem definition discussed earlier. The school social worker may find himself in the position of choosing from a seemingly infinite range of behaviors for any child. Actually, a few well-chosen examples are much better, particularly if they may serve as indicators or milestones of the student's progress.

To go back to our example, Devin appears to show difficulty dealing with a situation that seems competitive and draws attention to his poor functioning. Under stress he has tended to retreat into social relations with adults, from whom he demands high levels of attention. He is particularly uneasy with the dressing and showering aspects of gym. His parents' anxiety adds to the situation and reveals another set of needs. Teachers also can tend to overreact to the situation, increasing the chances of failure. To enumerate specific aspects of Devin's behavior:

1. Devin withdraws from situations involving physical competition. Without intervention, the pattern is expected to continue or increase in gym class.
2. Devin tends not to interact with peers in his general education classes.
3. Social interaction is limited with peers in special education, though Devin does have a great sense of humor and can interact with peers in structured activities.
4. Devin presently has no close friends at school.
5. When stressed, Devin can make excessive demands on adults, especially teachers, but can also calm himself down with some initial assistance.
6. Devin is particularly self-conscious concerning the dressing and showering aspects of gym.

Annual Goals, Objectives, and Resources

Finally, we may define goals and objectives. Annual goals are specific statements of the skills the student should be progressing toward within the framework of the school year. Annual goals evolve out of the assessment of the child's needs and abilities and should be an index of student progress. Although there are different formats that may serve as examples for a particular child's IEP, most would probably contain the following:

1. The direction of change desired—to increase, to decrease, to maintain
2. Deficit or excess—the general area that is identified as needing special attention
3. Present level of performance—what the child now does in deficit or in excess, expressed in measurable terms whenever possible
4. Expected level—where the child realistically could be or what he could gain, with proper resources
5. Resources needed—to accomplish the needed level of performance

Resources could be specialists, materials, situations, or methods required to bring about the desired change.

Measurable terms can be derived in some cases from counting performances, such as attendance, suspensions, grades, homework returned, test scores, extracurricular activities, and referrals to the principal, time-outs, and so on. They can be derived from performance (or nonperformance) of a particular targeted activity. Experienced teachers (natural experts for the normal range for the age group who know the student best) may rate the student on a 1 to 10 scale on some quality in comparison with a normal range for the age group (How does the student get along with his peers, or come prepared to school, or exhibit healthy hygiene?) (Raines, 2002). Data can be gathered by observation of the student's on- and off-task behavior. The measurement should obviously fit the purpose and the meaning of the objective.

In Devin's case, there are three major annual goals. The components are listed in brackets:

> Annual Goal 1: For Devin to increase [direction] positive social relations with peers in general education [deficit] from limited [from] to more informal [to] through interaction experiences in a group with the social worker and regular social work contacts with the parents and teacher [resources].
>
> Annual Goal 2: For Devin to increase [direction] his independence in dressing for gym [deficit] from never dressing for gym to dressing at least two days per week.
>
> Annual Goal 3: For Devin to maintain [direction] his current academic adjustment.

Note that the direction set in the third goal is maintenance of current functioning. Maintenance equates present and expected levels of functioning.

Short-Term Objectives (Benchmarks)

Students who cannot participate in the district-wide general education assessment would need to follow alternative assessments and would need short-term objectives as well as annual goals. For purposes of illustration, let us assume that Devin will not participate in the district-wide assessment. Short-term objectives can be thought of as measurable intermediate steps toward achievement of each annual goal. These steps are benchmarks or major milestones through which progress toward the annual goals can be assessed (see Lignugaris-Kraft, Marchand-Martella, & Martella, 2001). They should specify the conditions under which the behavior is to be exhibited by the student in his class—in unstructured group tasks, the lunchroom, gym, and so on. For the social worker, these can be indicators or changes in behavior and do not have to reflect every single objective that might be defined for that goal. For Devin, our hypothetical case example, some short-term objectives with which the social worker would be involved might be the following:

1. Devin's level of class participation and quality of assignment completion in his regular education classes will be maintained at his current level through January 15.
2. Devin will interact compatibly with general education peers in an unstructured group task by March 15.
3. Devin will interact comfortably and spontaneously with general education peers in an unstructured lunchroom situation by May 15.
4. Devin will form casual friendships with peers in general and special education by June 15.
5. Devin's distractibility and talking out in class will reduce by 50 percent by June 15.
6. Devin will be able to dress for gym without special arrangement by January 15.

The social worker often assists the team by developing the appropriate goals and objectives in their own area of the student's social functioning. These are worked out individually for every student. School social workers have developed lists of areas of learning using various developmental and social skill formulas (see Huxtable, 2004; Micek et al., 1982; Sanders, 2002).

Related Services

The list of services and persons responsible is essentially a resource statement. A list of the specific educational services required must be written into the IEP so that the goals and objectives can be implemented. Parents have a right to request that educational services that are included in the IEP but are not available in the school be purchased by the school district for the child or otherwise provided at no cost to the parents. Such services might include the following:

1. The social worker will see Devin once a week for a thirty-minute period with a group of other children with disabilities who are also dealing with the stress and social skills demands of a general education class. The appropriateness of whether Devin should continue in the group will be reevaluated by mid-year.
2. The social worker will monitor Devin's group progress and act as liaison between the IEP team and the family service agency working with Devin's family and will inform Devin's parents of progress.
3. The teacher will monitor Devin's achievement of these objectives, reinforcing independent and prosocial peer behavior.

In addition to specifying the role that the school social worker and other related service professionals might play to assist Devin, there are more informal unwritten aspects to an effective IEP that might come into play for somebody with Devin's issues. For example, teachers and parents may need help to continue to collaborate in helping Devin make this transition more successful. Specifically, they will need to reach a consensus on what Devin needs to be successful in his gym program, and how they will encourage him to avoid withdrawing from peers.

References

Gleason, E. T. (2007). A strengths-based approach to the social developmental study. *Children & Schools, 29*(1), 51–59.

Huxtable, M. (2004). *Defining measurable behavioral goals and objectives.* SSWAA Bell. January, Northlake, IL: SSWAA.

Individuals with Disabilities Education Improvement Act of 2004 (IDEIA), Pub. L. 108-446, 118 Stat. 2647 (2004).

Lignugaris-Kraft, B., Marchand-Martella, N., & Martella, R. C. (2001). Strategies for writing better goals and short-term objectives or benchmarks. *Teaching Exceptional Children, 34*(1), 52–58.

Micek, D., Barnes, J., Newman, C., Roelofs, M., Rosenbaum, M., & Sices, M. (1982). School social work objectives. In R. Constable & J. Flynn (Eds.), *School social work: Practice and research perspectives* (pp. 251–255). Homewood, IL: Dorsey Press.

Raines, J. C. (2002). Brainstorming hypotheses for functional behavior assessment: The link to effective behavioral intervention plans. *School Social Work Journal, 26*(2), 30–45.

Sanders, D. (2002). Annual goals and short-term objectives for school social workers. In R. Constable, S. McDonald, & J. Flynn (Eds.), *School social work: Practice, policy, and research perspectives* (pp. 279–288). Chicago: Lyceum Books.

Index

About the Authors

Carol Rippey Massat (MSW, PhD, *University of Illinois at Urbana-Champaign*) is professor of social work and director of the social work program at Indiana University South Bend, where she developed a new BSW program that has doubled in size each year since its inception in 2012. She is former editor of *School Social Work Journal* and sat on the board of the Illinois Association of School Social Workers (IASSW) for many years. At the Jane Addams College of Social Work she chaired the school social work concentration and taught school social work practice, policy, and research courses. Professor Massat is the author of numerous social work publications and has been invited to speak about school social work around the world, including Japan and China. She worked as a social worker in Decatur, Illinois, for ten years and in 2013 was given a Lifetime Achievement Award by IASSW and was named Social Worker of the Year by NASW, Region 3, Indiana. In 2014 she was awarded the Gary Shaffer Award from the School Social Work Association of America.

Michael S. Kelly (PhD, LCSW, *University of Illinois at Chicago*) is associate professor of social work and director of the Family and School Partnerships Program at Loyola University Chicago. Prior to that, he was a school social worker, family therapist, and youth minister in the Chicago area for fourteen years. He has authored more than fifty books, journal articles, and book chapters on school social work, evidence-based practice (EBP), and positive youth development. Professor Kelly is also associate editor of *Advances in School Mental Health Promotion Journal* and serves on the editorial boards of *School Mental Health*, *School Social Work Journal*, and *Children and Schools*. He has recently brought his work on school mental health and EBP to researchers and practitioners in Rhode Island, Wyoming, Canada, Chile, and Japan. He is a recipient of the Gary Shaffer Award from the School Social Work Association of America.

Robert Constable (MSW, *Loyola University Chicago*; DSW, *University of Pennsylvania*) is professor emeritus of social work at Loyola University Chicago. He has practiced as a school social worker in Gary, Indiana; Philadelphia, Pennsylvania; Evanston, Illinois; and in Project Head Start. Active in social work education, he has held faculty status at West Chester

State University, the Jane Addams College of Social Work at the University of Illinois at Chicago, Loyola University Chicago, and at several European universities. He organized graduate concentrations in school social work at the University of Illinois at Chicago and at Loyola University Chicago. He was codirector from 1992 through 1997 of the first social work graduate program in Lithuania at Vytautas Magnus University. Former editor of *Social Work in Education*, he is author of more than 100 publications in social work. He currently works as a social worker in private practice.